Cinema as a Worldbuilding Machine in the Digital Era

To Yvain,
our valiant Knight,
roaming with a constant sense of wonder through the world of childhood.

Cinema as a Worldbuilding Machine in the Digital Era

Essay on Multiverse Films and TV Series

Alain Boillat

Translated by Achilleas Papakonstantis

Translation supervised by Ilias Dimopoulos

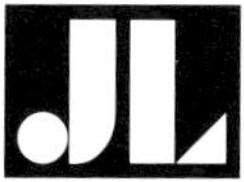

British Library Cataloguing in Publication Data

Cinema as a Worldbuilding Machine in the Digital Era:
Essay on Multiverse Films and TV series

A catalogue entry for this book is available from the British Library

ISBN: 9780 86196 749 0 (Paperback)
ISBN: 9780 86196 981 4 (ebook-EPUB)
ISBN: 9780 86196 982 1 (ebook-EPDF)

Published by
John Libbey Publishing Ltd, 205 Crescent Road, New Barnet, Herts EN4 8SB, United Kingdom e-mail: john.libbey@orange.fr; web site: www.johnlibbey.com

Distributed Worldwide by
Indiana University Press, Herman B Wells Library—350, 1320 E. 10th St., Bloomington, IN 47405, USA. www.iupress.indiana.edu

Printed and bound in the UK by Short Run Press Ltd, Exeter.

Contents

Translator's note: An asterisk (*) appearing after a quotation indicates that the translation given of a text originally written in French is that by the translator of this book.

List of Illustrations

Black & White Illustrations

Fig. 31: Reese Whiterspoon and Tobey Maguire in *Pleasantville* (1998). AF archive / Alamy Stock Photo.

Fig. 32: Production Still from *Je t'aime je t'aime* (1968). Private Collection.

Fig. 33: K. Winslet and J. Carrey in *Eternal Sunshine of the Spotless Mind* (2004). Allstar Picture Library Ltd. / Alamy Stock Photo.

Fig. 34: Jude Law and Jennifer Jason Leigh in *eXistenZ* (1999) (Exis 003 P). Moviestore Collection Ltd / Alamy Stock Photo.

Fig. 35: Kiefer Sutherland in *Dark City* (1998). United Archives GmbH / Alamy Stock Photo.

Fig. 36: Rufus Sewell in *Dark City* (1998). Photo 12 / Alamy Stock Photo.

Fig. 37: William Hurt in *Dark City* (1998). AA Film Archive / Alamy Stock Photo.

Color Illustrations

Color Plate 1: Resident Evil: Retribution (2012). Photo 12 / Alamy Stock Photo.

Color Plate 2: Resident Evil: Extinction (2007). Milla Jovovich © 2007 Screen Gems Photo by Rolf Konow. PictureLux / The Hollywood Archive / Alamy Stock Photo.

Color Plate 3: Giovanni Ribisi in a scene from ©Twentieth Century Fox film *Avatar* (2009). Landmark Media / Alamy Stock Photo.

Color Plate 4: Westworld poster for 1973 MGM film with Yul Brynner. Pictorial Press Ltd / Alamy Stock Photo.

Color Plate 5: Zahn McClarnon in a scene in ©HBO TV Series, *Westworld* (2018) (S2E8). Landmark Media / Alamy Stock Photo.

Color Plate 6: Westworld (2016) HBO TV Series Poster. PictureLux / The Hollywood Archive / Alamy Stock Photo.

Color Plate 7: Brit Marling in *Another Earth* (2011). RGR Collection / Alamy Stock Photo.

Color Plate 8: Avatar (2009). Moviestore Collection Ltd / Alamy Stock Photo.

Color Plate 9: Robin Wright in *The Congress* (2013). AF Archive / Alamy Stock Photo.

Color Plate 10: Jan. 9, 2014 - Hollywood, USA – *The Congress* (2013). Ari Folman (dir). C face to face / Entertainment Pictures / Alamy Stock Photo.

Color Plate 11: The Wizard of Oz (1939). Turner Entertainment / Ronald Grant Archive / Alamy Stock Photo.

Color Plate 12: Oz the Great and Powerful. 2013 Walt Disney Pictures film. Pictorial Press Ltd / Alamy Stock Photo.

Color Plate 13: Film Still from *Pleasantville*. Joan Allen, Tobey Maguire © 1998 New Line Cinema. Photo Credit: Ralph Nelson (Reference # 30996320THA). PictureLux / The Hollywood Archive / Alamy Stock Photo. All rights reserved.

Color Plate 14: The Matrix 1999 Warner Bros sci-fi film. Pictorial Press Ltd / Alamy Stock Photo.

Color Plate 15: The Matrix 1999 Warner film with Keanu Reeves. Pictorial Press Ltd / Alamy Stock Photo.

Color Plate 16: General Scene from *Dark City* (1998). AF archive / Alamy Stock Photo.

Color Plate 17: Dark City (1998) Director Alex Proyas. Photo 12 / Alamy Stock Photo.

Color Plate 18: Scene from *The Thirteenth Floor* (1999). AF archive / Alamy Stock Photo.

Color Plate 19: Scene from *The Thirteenth Floor* (1999). AF archive / Alamy Stock Photo.

Color Plate 20: Tron (1982). AF archive / Alamy Stock Photo

Color Plate 21: Studio Publicity Still from *Tron*. David Warner © 1982 Walt Disney (Reference # 31710008THA). All Rights Reserved. PictureLux / The Hollywood Archive / Alamy Stock Photo.

Color Plate 22: "Light Cycles", *TRON*, 1982. AA Film Archive / Alamy Stock Photo.

Color Plate 23: TRON: Legacy © 2010 Walt Disney. Entertainment Pictures / Alamy Stock Photo.

Acknowledgments

I would like to express my sincere gratitude to the translator of this book, Achilleas Papakonstantis, who managed to survive the constant shifts from one world to another and gracefully found the way out of the maze.

I would also like to thank Larry Blake for his kind permission to reprint the production stills that were part of the promotional material distributed during the original theatrical release of *Kafka* (1991). Finally, my gratitude goes to Frédéric Jaccaud from Maison d'Ailleurs.

The publication of this book was made possible thanks to the subsidies granted by the following institutions:

Fonds des publications UNIL ;

Commission des publications de la Faculté des lettres de l'Université de Lausanne ;

Société Académique Vaudoise.

"What I mean is that to tell a story you must first of all construct a world, furnished as much as possible, down to the slightest details. If I were to construct a river, I would need two banks; and if on the left bank I put a fisherman, and if I were to give this fisherman a wrathful character and a police record, then I could start writing, translating into words everything that would inevitably happen."
Umberto Eco, *Postscript to The Name of the Rose* (2014 [1983]: 549–550)

The objective of this essay is to study the notion of "world", and more specifically that of "multiverse", in movies and TV series, from the standpoint of fiction theory. Emphasis will be placed on the possibilities offered by computer-generated imagery (CGI) and the context of the so-called "virtual" imaginaries. In an effort to confront my theoretical reflection to specific case studies, I shall examine a number of films and TV series whose creative design I qualify as "world-centered". By that, I hold the tendency to privilege space (borders, levels, distance, etc.) over time and the construction of a world (or worlds) over narrative structure. I will focus on the preeminence given to worldbuilding in films where two or more distinct worlds coexist (a multiverse), defined by a variable gap in relation both to the "real" and to each other. Through these case studies, I aim to explore the different modes of representation of audio-visual technologies as "worldbuilding machines" while reflecting on the future of the film medium in the digital age.

In most of the films discussed, actors perform in front of a blue or a green screen, a space that is retroactively "furnished"[1] by digitally inserting a set chosen among the quasi-infinite possibilities offered by computers. Subsequently, the filmmakers and public's awareness to the notion of "world", and therefore to the idea of a plurality of worlds, has considerably increased. The concept of "worldbuilding" has significantly expanded since the publication of the original French edition of this book in 2014, demanding a revised and updated version.[2] Originally broadcast from December 2017 to February 2019 by Starz cable network, the *Counterpart* TV series that illustrates the new cover, highlights the contemporary nature of the issues dealt with in this book.[3] This show offers a *parallel world* that mirrors our current one, a post-pandemic society sadly echoing the global health crisis triggered by COVID-19 less than a year after the release of the series' final episode. Its final scene shows one of the main characters dying in the middle of a park in the "first" world (i.e. "our" world) from a virus that was injected to him by a terrorist coming from the *parallel world*, with a mission to spread an epidemic disease. One might argue that reality took over from (science) fiction by actualizing these possible worlds.

This book opts for a transversal approach on a cultural phenomenon (the primacy of worldbuilding and the rise of multiverse movies), combined with a close study of the narrative, aesthetic, semantic, and ideological aspects of certain films and TV series I regard as exemplary cases of world-centered fiction. By concentrating on individual films (rather than franchises), the choice is to refrain from examining transmedia practices or ancillary products. Nevertheless, my case studies are intimately linked to what Henry Jenkins calls a *convergence culture*. I have discussed elsewhere how the action figures' market participates in strengthening and expanding a fictional world, taking "*Star Wars*"[4] as an example (Boillat 2006a and 2014a). In the case of "*The Matrix*", discussed by Jenkins (2006: 93–130), the tendency to offer a surplus of content is already visible in each of the films in this trilogy, building a multiverse that encourages media branching, particularly in the field of video games (*Enter the Matrix*, 2003; *Matrix Online*, 2005; *CR: Enter the Matrix*, 2009). By focusing on the concept of "world", instead of "story", the present essay emancipates itself from the limits imposed by textual closure and includes a number of TV series, such as *Lost*, *Fringe*, or *Westworld*, in its case studies. However, story and world need to be examined together, so far as the narrative discourse establishes a particular point of view on the fictional worlds, ensures their evolution, and orchestrates (or not) the passages between them.

Chapter 1 opens by outlining the theoretical context and the media landscape out of which the subject matter of this essay emerged. In the following pages, the reader is introduced to the book's central questions through an analysis of *Resident Evil: Retribution* (2012) and its theatrical trailer, as well as a more general discussion of the film series (in itself part of a transmedia franchise) that (provisionally) concluded in 2016 with the release of *Resident Evil: The Final Chapter*. This case study serves as an introduction to a number of themes – immersion, seriality, intermediality, *artificial* and *virtual worlds*, science fiction, and self-reflexivity – developed later in the book. The rest of the chapter looks into the exceptional rise of multiverse movies during the first two decades of the 21st century, by correlating the analysis of the films' technological dimension with a cultural studies approach that focuses on representations. To do so, I examine the ways certain Hollywood productions participate in a wider effort to purge the traumas of the September 11 attacks, by (re)imagining the destruction of a city built out of VFX. Cinema frequently offers "disaster scenarios" whose paradoxical objective means to explore possible *alternatives* to a real-life disaster. This is the case of *Source Code*, a time-loop movie released a few months prior to the tenth anniversary of 9/11 and the inauguration of the National September 11 Memorial & Museum. Furthermore, this type of film reflects a current rise in ostensibly complex plots in mainstream cinema that I observe specifically through Christopher Nolan's body of work.

Chapter 2 investigates the links between film genres and world. When it comes to worldbuilding, the representation of "worldbuilding machines", and issues of immersion, science fiction and fantasy raise particular questions. These are addressed through several case studies (most notably *Total Recall* and its sequel, 1990/2012), followed by a detailed analysis of *Westworld* (1973) and the recent HBO series of the same name. Later in the chapter, I discuss the TV series *Sliders, Lost*, and *Fringe*, considering the ways serial practices may benefit from a multiverse structure in order to maximize the number of possible episodes while keeping viewers curious or in suspense.

Chapter 3 delves into the concept of "diegesis" – central to our study and regularly employed in the field of narratology. In this book, I understand this term following its development in post-war France by the Institute of Filmology, a pioneer in film studies as an academic discipline. After some preliminary remarks on film worlds and their relation to the viewer, I turn to literary theories of "possible worlds". A typology of worlds will be established based on seven categories (*distant*, *artificial*, *supernatural*, *mental*, *alternate, parallel*, and *virtual*). To a certain extent, these types of worlds can be simultaneously or successively present within the same narrative. As my study of the *Westworld* TV series aims to demonstrate, a story can actually derive from the arrangement of different worlds and seriality can be nourished by the plurality, and even coexistence, of different types of worlds.

Whereas Chapters 2 and 3 focus on pragmatic and semantic aspects, Chapter 4 deals with the stylistic implications of worldbuilding in multiverse movies. The structure of this chapter is determined by a set of oppositional couples that prove instrumental in distinguishing between different worlds in films like *The Congress*, *Avalon*, *Je t'aime je t'aime*, or in TV series like *Fringe* and *Counterpart*: live-action vs. animation, black & white vs. color, continuity vs. discontinuity editing, succession vs. alternation. Asking whether a film's colors are diegetic leads to a better understanding of the ways the materiality of the image participates in creating a world. The question remains valid even in the case of some "single-world" films: think of the colorful poster in the prologue of *Carlito's Way* (1993) that comes to life during the film's end credits. Apart from their own visual features, the way individual shots are lined up is also significant in this regard. My analysis of Philip K. Dick's "The Electric Ant" illustrates how (film) *editing* is associated in our collective psyche with worldbuilding. Drawing on several findings from film theory, considered anew from a world-centered perspective, I study those elements within a visual representation that may connote an affiliation to a given world, while exploring the various ways in which the principle of alternation, applied not only to competing (and often convergent) storylines but also to distinct worlds (therefore associated), serves worldbuilding.

When talking about multiverse movies, one invariably encounters the paradigm of cyberculture. Characters questioning the status of reality or finding themselves transferred into a computer-generated universe, are among the most common patterns of cultural productions related to cyberculture. Chapter 5 addresses these issues by comparing *Dark City*'s *artificial world* to *The Matrix*'s *virtual world*, placing this type of dystopian film within a postmodern context that commonly recycles narrative and iconographic motifs from various different genres (in this case, related to film noir). Particular attention is paid to *Simulacron-3*, a novel by Daniel F. Galouye, first adapted in a German TV film in the 1970s (*World on a Wire*), and then in a Hollywood production released the same year as the original *Matrix* (*The Thirteenth Floor*). The final pages of this essay bring the reader closer to the realm of video games, as they focus on *TRON* (1982) and its sequel (2010). For narrative purposes, both films use the opposition between real and *virtual* worlds. Released three decades apart, they constitute a perfect case study for measuring the importance of digital technologies when it comes to the on-screen representation of a multiverse.

The film and TV productions studied in this book offer an overview of the narrative, aesthetic, technological, social, anthropological, and gender-related issues raised by multiverse movies and TV series, particularly during the first two decades of the 21st century, an era radically influenced by the expansion of digital technology at every level of production, distribution, and consumption.

Endnotes

1. I borrow the term "furnish" from Umberto Eco's fiction theory (Eco 1990).
2. While several references from the Anglo-Saxon literature have been added to this new edition, the book also aims to introduce English-speaking readers to some of the research currently carried out in the French-speaking world.
3. I would like to thank Mireille Berton, a researcher at the University of Lausanne, specializing in TV series, for introducing me to *Counterpart*.
4. In this book, I use both quotation marks and italics when referring to a franchise instead of an individual film.

Chapter One

Worldbuilding in the Age of Digital (Trans)Media

> "**Colter Stevens:** What is the Source Code?
>
> Dr. Rutledge: It's quantum mechanics. Parabolic calculus. It's… it's very complicated.
>
> C. Stevens: Try me!
>
> Dr. Rutledge: Fine. When a light bulb is turned off, there's an after-glow, a lingering halo-like effect. [...] The brain is like that. Its electromagnetic field remains charged, just briefly, even after death. Circuits remain open. Now, there's another peculiarity about the brain. It contains a short-term memory track that's approximately eight minutes long. Like a convenience store security camera that only records the last portion of the day's activity on its hard drive. Now, in combining these two phenomena, circuitry that remains viable post-mortem and a memory bank that goes eight minutes, Source Code enables us to capitalize on the overlap. [...] Source Code is not time travel. Rather, Source Code is time reassignment. It gives us access to a parallel reality."
>
> *Source Code* (2011)

The aim of this essay is to study the notion of "world" when confronted to a multiverse. However, this will not entail the discussion of issues of a philosophical nature, like those raised by Nelson Goodman in *Ways of Worldmaking* (1978), related to scientific theories, literature, painting, and music. The process of "worldbuilding" is relevant for all fiction films, indeed even for non-fiction ones, since they all present in a specific manner *the* world as *a* world. But that is an entirely different story (see Boillat 2001). Formalist or aesthetic approaches in film studies have already examined the ways movies create worlds that extend beyond the screen, inviting viewer immersion – see for example Stanley Cavell's *The World Viewed. Reflections on the Ontology of Film* (1979). For my part, I will not deal in this book with similar questions pertaining to cinema as a medium.

Distinguishing from traditional approaches, inherited from structural narratology, that "[reduce] a story to a succession of events", V.F. Perkins proposed to "sketch some of the ways in which it matters for a fictional world to be a world" (Perkins 2005: 22). To this end, he examined "the dependence [of a number of parameters] on the worldhood of the fictional world", such as a film's visual style, its construction of a specific point of view, or the principles presiding the selection between elements kept within the frame and those relegated off-screen (*Ibid.*: 20). Perkins speaks of "worldhood", for lack of a better term ("I would be happy if anyone could suggest a better word than this", he adds in a footnote). He considers this notion valid for all fiction, regardless of the fact that some films may turn out more "world-centered" – a term I will be using in this book – precisely by gestating a multiverse. Consequently, it is not surprising that *The Wizard of Oz* (1939) is given less weight in his analysis than *Citizen Kane* (1941) or *All I Desire* (1953), classic movies that are very different from the "Fantasy Fictions"[1] I will be discussing here. Even though Perkins comments on Fleming's "[film] world of the fantastic" and on the more familiar ways the viewers can comprehend its laws, he never actually mentions the dichotomy established in the film between Dorothy's sepia-toned world and the colorful world of Oz. Studying "the relationship between stylistic gesture and fictional world" (*Ibid.*: 31), his interest lies in capturing the mood of the film, not in discussing how, for example, the selection of a particular color film stock may allude to the ontological status of the represented world (see Chapter 4).

Similarly, James Walters' *Alternative Worlds in Hollywood Cinema* merits from highlighting the structural role played by the laws of the world and by what he calls, in reference to Perkins, "the worldhood", on a film's narrative (Walters 2008: 27). Nevertheless, he remains predicated on an aesthetic model that favors a film's consistency, seeking unity within plurality. In his own words: "Even though the narratives of films can involve alternative worlds, those distinct worlds still exist in one, over-arching, fictional world: the world of the film" (*Ibid.*).

The exact opposite hypothesis interests me here. My goal is to examine the narrative implications of the coexistence of – at least – two distinct worlds within a single film, as well as the ways these worlds: (a) are differentiated on a semantic level, (b) are attached to distinct film genres, and (c) establish the conditions of their mutual accessibility. When Walters introduces a three-term typology of "alternative worlds" (imagined / potential / other worlds), he chooses not to address the issue of reflexivity. Instead, I propose to explore this specific question by considering how worldbuilding technologies are represented inside a film. In many respects, my study crosses paths with the "theory and history of subcreation", referred to in the full title of Mark J.P. Wolf's book *Building Imaginary Worlds* (2012). However, by focusing on cinema and opting for an approach delineated by two specific criteria, namely technology (represented within the films and used in their making) and the plurality of worlds, I break away from the majority of the approximately 1400 imaginary worlds identified by Wolf throughout the history of Western fiction – from

Homer's islands in *The Odyssey* to the country of Narnia invented by Lewis in 1950 and to New Austin County in the video game *Red Dead Redemption* (2010). His inventory includes planets, islands, and cities that have no known reference in the real world, or that are named after a real place while being completely fictional. Film worlds are also part of this list, but Wolf is hardly interested in the mode of their on-screen representation. His study concentrates on their semantic dimension and adopts a transversal perspective that encompasses novels, plays, comic books, films, as well as video games.[2] According to Wolf, *Dark City, The Matrix,* and *Waterworld* offer imaginary worlds classified under the "Future Earth" category,[3] next to the continent Westeros from *Game of Thrones*.[4] In Wolf's essay, the notion of "subcreation" does not indicate the existence of different levels, namely the creation of a world within the world of fiction. Rather, it constitutes a straightforward reference to J.R.R. Tolkien for whom "creation" refers to the act of God and "subcreation" to that of Men (see Chapter 2). Commenting upon the two poles of *narration* and *description*, Wolf considers the latter to be of greater importance in fantasy genres, implying that the world they offer should be considered as more important than their story. From Wolf's standpoint, "world-building" applies exclusively to these genres, which he examines through the special relationship they establish with their public, in reference to the participatory culture favored nowadays by the Internet:

> For works in which world-building occurs, there may be a wealth of details and events (or mere mentions of them) which do not advance the story but which provide background richness and verisimilitude to the imaginary world. Sometimes this material even appears outside of the story itself [...]. Such additional information can change the audience's experience, understanding, and immersion in a story [...] (Wolf 2012: 2).

Wolf examines concisely the case of the multiverse, when different fictions whose story takes place in the same world(s) are brought together thanks to a crossover strategy (qualified as a "retroactive linkage", if the two worlds were "not originally intended to be connected") or through the use of transnarrative characters (*Ibid.*: 216). Nevertheless, he is more interested in the creative process that gestates a non-realist fictional work – cases where invention precedes and in which providing viewers with a sense of *completeness* and *consistency* of the world becomes indispensable.[5]

By the time New Hollywood filmmakers, like George Lucas and Steven Spielberg, turned to family-friendly and teen blockbusters,[6] popular movies dealing with an encounter with *another world* became common currency. Mainstream status then followed when CGI technology allowed for the portrayal of worlds other than our own in an increasingly convincing manner (although the speed of technological advances accelerates too the obsolescence of certain types of representation in the eyes of the public). The screen adaptations of J.K. Rowling's "*Harry Potter*" (2001–2011) and C.S. Lewis' "*Chronicles of Narnia*"

(2005–2010), as well as the "*Jumanji*" series and *Tomorrowland* (2015)[7] are emblematic of this tendency. The fact remains that the current surge in worldbuilding, in the broadest sense of the term and applicable to all fiction, is the result of a cultural and technological context that favors multiverse fictional works, while being reciprocally influenced by their growing popularity. In fact, it seems that storytelling, once indispensable to the proper functioning of the Hollywood industry, is currently being dethroned by worldbuilding. To a large extent, the dream factory has turned into a *factory of worlds*, governed by principles of serialization, franchising, and merchandising.

There is a dialogue scene in *La La Land* (2016), a film regularly interpreted as a critique of modern-day Hollywood, revealing of the ground gained by the notion of "worldbuilding" in recent years. At a pool party, Mia (Emma Stone) is introduced to a writer, named Carlo (Jason Fuchs), who is presented as someone who has "got projects all over town". Carlo immediately brags about his own success: "Yeah. They say I have a knack for world-building. I got a lot of heat right now, people are talking about it".[8] Mia bumps into him again later in the same evening and the writer mentions a preposterous "franchise" project based on a children's tale, *Goldilocks and the Three Bears*.[9] Chazelle's film aims to distinguish itself from this type of family movie through a number of references to jazz and classic cinema.[10] Remarkably, during the casting scene that will prove crucial for Mia's ultimate success, she is praised for her skills as a "storyteller". Still, having a writer like Carlo describe his work through the term of world-building in a movie like *La La Land* is indicative of the renewed conception of the activity of screenwriting.[11] This musical was released the same year as the first season of the *Westworld* TV series, which also features a self-assured screenwriter whose overweening ambition is already evident by his surname: Sizemore. Therefore, it seems only natural that one of the most recent screen-writing manuals, John Truby's *The Anatomy of Story*, is no longer exclusively centered on plot construction and characters, like its predecessors. It also offers recommendations on how to build a "story world" according to certain physical elements (natural settings, man-made spaces, technology, and time) and by virtue of a gradual transformation (which remains however subordinated to the film's character, in turn extending his web to everything around him).[12] The author establishes the following principle: each "key story structure step […] tends to have a story world all its own", its "own unique subworld" (Truby 2007: 191). There is no actual mention in Truby's manual of a world's onto-logical status or a multiverse. The term "subworld" corresponds to a given environment defined by its visual construction,[13] regardless of its affiliation (or the lack of it) to the world of reference. However, the terminology used by Truby, marked by a greater theoretical ambition than the one of his famous predecessors (such as Syd Field in the late 1970s or Robert McKee in the late 1990s), is telling of the current popularity of worldbuilding in discourses devoted to film fiction.

The question of the environment in which a character is immersed at various stages of his journey is certainly not specific to multiverse movies but becomes crucial in their case since it participates in their structuring. For instance, in *Counterpart*, the action is circumscribed within the city of Berlin; at the end of Season 1, the main character buys a train ticket to Marseille, but eventually decides to stay in the German city.[14] The choice of Berlin is meaningful in more ways than one. First of all, it helps *Counterpart* establish a European-like environment: the English-speaking protagonists communicate in German with most of the secondary characters, all of them drive luxurious, black, German sedans, and pass by recognizable historical monuments. In addition, Berlin is a city full of history, separated as it was until 1989 into two distinct "worlds", the East and the West. This referent functions as the starting point for the series' two-world structure: it was in 1987, two years before the fall of the Berlin Wall, that the "Crossing" into a *parallel world* (see my typology in Chapter 3), almost identical to our own, is discovered within the fiction. It also provides certain stereotypes associated with the Cold War era that inform the series' narrative. One finds here a group of fanatical terrorists (also reminiscent of the more contemporary context of a series like *Homeland*),[15] along with a rigidly hierarchical and opaque bureaucracy (as in *Kafka*, 1991), diplomatic disputes, counter-espionage branches, sleeper agents, infiltration/exfiltration companies, military border controls, etc. These components lead to interactions between two ontologically distinct worlds, as in *Fringe*, a series that inspired a specific world-centered stylistic pattern in *Counterpart*: the cross-fade between a shot of the city in the first world and an identically-framed shot of the exact same space in the second world. It should be noted that the city of Berlin, as it appears in the series' first world, does not correspond entirely to "our world". The "Crossing" and the governing bodies of the "Management" (actually disembodied in both worlds) are depicted in a low-tech sci-fi aesthetic echoing the Cold War context. A few characters – mostly women, following a deeply-rooted gender stereotype – show a long-term disconcerting duplicity, navigating between the two "worlds". Nevertheless, characters have their double in the other world that follow the same path but opt for other possible alternatives or suffer setbacks brought on by fate. In this case, a double agent is actually a character's double, actualized in one world and then transiting from one to the other. Obviously then, the existence of an alternate reality not only makes Berlin the "world of the film" (in the common sense of worldbuilding), but also elects this real-life city as a world of reference within the framework of a multiverse.

The digital era of Bill Gates, Steve Jobs or Mark Zuckerberg is one of demiurgic figures. Accordingly, a character acting as a creator of worlds is a recurrent pattern in recent films. *Person of Interest* (2011–2016), already in its opening credits sequence, focuses on Harold Finch (Michael Emerson), the inventor of a powerful surveillance machine capable of anticipating dramatic events. The series' showrunner, Jonathan Nolan, drew from the narrative material offered

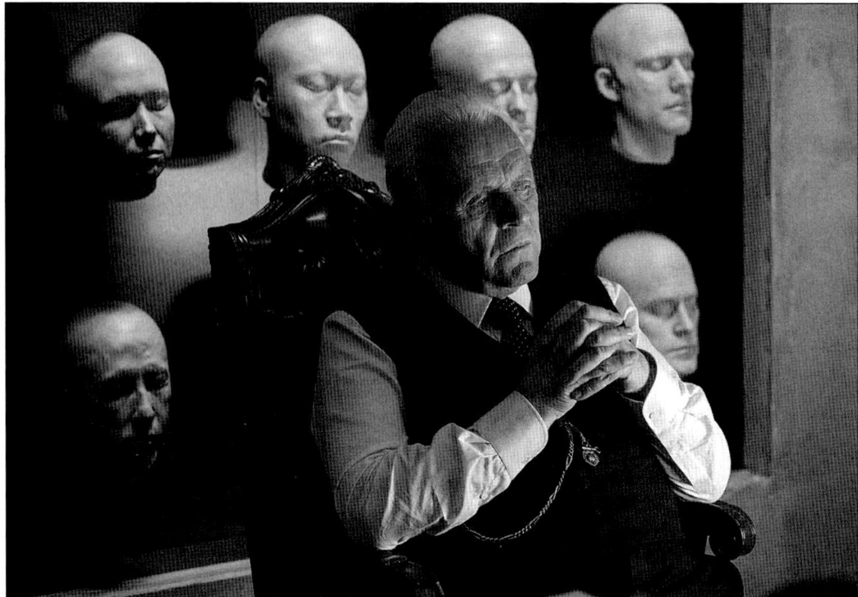

Fig. 1: Dr. Robert Ford (Anthony Hopkins), the "Father" of most artificial beings inhabiting the "small world" he created (*Westworld*, Season 1, 2016).

by *Westworld* (1973) to make a new series of the same name, dealing with issues stemming from contemporary technologies, adding to the teams of white-coated scientists from the original film the character of Dr. Robert Ford, a genius leading the *artificial world* of the theme park (Fig. 1).[16] Played by an actor of Anthony Hopkins' stature, the character exercises absolute power over the worlds he designs, as indicated by the scenes in which all living beings around him freeze as a result of his laconic voice command (a snake in S01E02, a team of farm workers in S01E04, and finally the entire population of a small town in S02E07). A passionate inventor expressing his contempt for the Delos' "money men", he remarks to the company's chief executive: "I told him [Arnold, his partner at the time of the creation of Westworld] that you wouldn't understand what you are paying for. It's not a business venture, not a theme park, but an entire world" (S01E04). His lengthy, philosophical monologues, which continue even after he orchestrates his own death (through flashbacks or in a *virtual world* – see Chapter 3 – in which he has saved a replica of his consciousness), clarify the discourse of the series' authors on issues related to the creation of worlds in the digital age. *Westworld* ruminates on the responsibility bestowed upon a creator of worlds, a brilliant and omnipotent man modeled after Silicon Valley's GAFA founders. The myth of "Frankenstein" becomes relevant once again, but the creature has now taken the size of an entire world. Examples of such fictional scientists include Dr. Schreber (Kiefer Sutherland) in *Dark City* (1998), gifted computer programmer Kevin Flynn (Jeff Bridges) in *TRON: Legacy* (2010), the Merovingian (Lambert Wilson) in *The*

Matrix Revolutions (2003), Walter Bishop (John Noble) and William Bell (Leonard Nimoy) in *Fringe* (2008–2013), or Dr. Rutledge in *Source Code* (2011). The latter is played by Jeffrey Wright, who also appears in the *Westworld* TV series in the role of one of Dr. Ford's creatures (or so we are initially led to believe).

All these fictions offer a multiverse, i.e. a configuration of two or more worlds, sometimes conceived as an extension of Bryce DeWitt's reformulation, in terms of parallel universes, of Hugh Everett's theses on relative states (Barrett 2011). At this point, a clarification must be made: The application of the notion of "possible worlds", as understood in modal logic, to the worlds studied in fiction theory, can only be metaphorical (Eco 1990: 64–65; Doležel 1998: 16–24; Schaeffer 1999: 206–207). These worlds are necessarily incomplete and elaborated within a relatively non-binding framework. In the same way (though for opposite reasons), the implications of quantum physics are miles away from the worlds depicted in fictional films, bequeathed with an ontological status and transformed into representable objects. DeWitt remarks in his discipline that "the chief issues of interpretation are epistemological rather than ontological: The quantum realm must be viewed as *a kind of ghostly world* whose symbols, such as the wave function, represent potentiality rather than reality" (DeWitt 1970, cited in Byrne 2010: 131). Yet, the spectacular live-action[17] films that display a strong "attractional"[18] dimension, immerse viewers into realities asserted as complete worlds, all the more so as these worlds are produced by audio-visual media that maximize the representation's "perceptual richness", as Christian Metz puts it. Now known as VFX, special effects are increasingly used in the digital era for the construction of an environment in which a film's story takes place, as a continuation of the techniques of transparency, occasionally even blurring the boundaries between the characters and the world around them. The famous "warping scene" in *Terminator 2: Judgment Day* (1991), in which the android T-1000 blends with the tiles of a hospital room, thanks to a special effect that elastically deforms the image (in a shift from 2D to 3D), and then is human-like re-formed, plays on the "ontological" pseudo-continuity established between a character and his or her surrounding environment.

One of the three types of special effects identified by RamaVenkatasawmy from the standpoint of their function is the so-called "Filmic 'Fantasy' Construction" (2013: 86–91). As the quotation marks indicate, the author understands this type of effects in a sense that goes far beyond the typically world-centered genre of *heroic fantasy*, this way including all "Fantasy Fictions" (as Anne Besson designates them). In his words: "VFX have indeed more prolifically been used in the creation of imagined, ethereal, bizarre, extraordinary, prehistoric and futuristic worlds" (*Ibid.*: 86). In science fiction, the use of CGI is regularly justified by the presence of audio-visual media within the story that function as the diegetic equivalent of the technology used to produce the film's images. For instance, the first realistic, computer-generated spaceship in the history of cinema appears in *The Last Starfighter* (1984, see Pinteau 2015: 119), associated with a *distant world* with which the film's young hero is brought into contact through an arcade video game. The mediation through a computer has its diegetic counterpart.

Furthermore, recent highly photorealistic 3D polygonal video game environments have paved the way for the exploration of universes, a practice becoming an important commercial issue for this specific industry. This is evidenced by the success of the book series "*The Art of* ...", the sales of downloadable extensions, the gamers' potential to unlock diegetic components (characters, costumes, weapons), the popularity of ancillary products for collectors, and the development of variations through a number of episodes or on different media platforms. A particular type of video games, distributed on a massive scale by the industry, in which users exploit the interactivity of the medium by discovering – along a more or less predetermined path – various environments reminiscent of specific film genres[19], also contributes to the growing popularity of a conception of audio-visual media that I describe as "world-centered". By means of interfaces that become, more or less, part of the diegesis, such video games regularly transmit information on the laws governing their world, parallel to other instructions that concern the rules regulating the gamer's activity, sometimes independently of the evolution of the story. To take one example among many others: the gameplay of Bioware's *Mass Effect* trilogy (2007–2012) is configured in such a way that gamers can access at any time an encyclopedia of the science fiction world in which they find themselves immersed. Upon engaging to a verbal interaction with other characters, they can select a line among different suggestions appearing on screen. The suggested phrases fall into two different categories: performative utterances, that lead to a specific action and advance the story, and lines that transmit additional information about the video game world.[20] The diegesis is then meticulously "furnished" and, consequently, becomes more credible, despite the gap established by the science fiction genre with regard to our world.

The links between cinema and video games became more evident in recent years as video game adaptations of movies gradually moved from the occasional quotation to the complete transcription of film worlds.[21] Cinema is also adapting worlds originally proposed in video games: *Lara Croft: Tomb Raider* (2001), the "*Resident Evil*" series (from 2002 onwards), *Doom* (2005), *Warcraft* (2016), or *Assassin's Creed* (2016), to name a few. A reference to video games is often made explicit in a film by its embedding structure and by its shifting from one world to another. Starting with *The Lawnmower Man* (1992) and *Lawnmower Man 2: Beyond Cyberspace* (1996), a number of films propose a contrast between two worlds through the insertion of ostensibly digital images whose visual style is clearly associated with video games. In cases like these, the video game device acts as a paragon of immersion in another world, whether it appears as a coercive operation, as in *TRON* (1982), or glorified as a means of escape in more recent productions, at a time when avatars have become commonplace (*Ready Player One*, *Free Guy*). Whereas films like *TRON* and its 2010 sequel explicitly refer to video games (see Chapter 5), the screen adaptation of *Assassin's Creed* employs a process of embedding already present in Ubisoft's video game franchise of the same name. Nevertheless, the movie version significantly transforms the "Animus", which gives access to the genetic memory of the "subject", into a device intended to be *spectacular* in various ways. The hero has to fight in order to tame it and gets connected to it through his neck, recalling the technophobic representations of *eXistenZ* or *The Matrix*. A high-tech prosthetic apparatus amplifies the physical performance of the protagonist (played by Michael Fassbender), in a clear reference to the technique of motion capture used during the film's shooting (albeit without the critical dimension developed by a film like *The Congress*, discussed in Chapter 4). This performance becomes a spectacle for the eyes of scientists who seem to have partial access to the images of the Spanish Inquisition era thanks to a holographic projection device. The representation of the past within the present is the result of a desire to maintain the traditional status of the spectator and break away from the interactivity typical of video games.

There is also another medium that has been providing Hollywood with worlds since the turn of the 21st century, especially after Avi Arad's restructuring of Marvel Comics after 1996 and the creation of Marvel West, a branch exclusively dedicated to the promotion of screen adaptations. It is certainly no coincidence that since the dawn of our century and the development of CGI, there is a proliferation of movie versions of superhero comics, especially those published from the 1960s onwards under the pencil of Jack Kirby. In such cases, the movie industry inherits the principle of "reboot", already widespread in the field of publishing.[22] What matters above all is to maintain the public's interest in a set of components affiliated to a given world. In his essay on "transmedia", Henry Jenkins noted some fifteen years ago a tendency to explore worlds beyond the limits of a single work or even a single medium (see Chapter 5). In the case of superhero movies, these worlds are borrowed from the comic book industry, following a recycling strategy integral in creating a mythology. Stories are multiplied and brought together "under the banner" of an emblem (the Hero), that one can also understand in the patriotic sense of the term, as an affirmation of American popular culture and of the values associated with it. These well-known superheroes circulate from one production (or medium) to another, while remaining relatively stable. Their permanence creates a stereotype that guarantees the consumer pleasure of redundancy and reiteration, as Umberto Eco remarked in his study of the reception of the *Superman* comics (Eco 1972). Escaping the comic book pages to reach movie theaters or toy stores, the superhero is defined by a fragment of his world, summoned in a more or less similar way in each story. The ever more frequent use of the term "Universe" to describe the superhero franchises, as well as the hero's assimilation to a world, reached new levels with the release of the self-reflexive, animated movie *Spider-Man: Into the Spider-Verse* (2018). In this film, a portal leading to other dimensions gives access to a great number of variants (also in terms of visual style) of the character whose birth Hollywood has been repeatedly recounting since 2002. Replacing "Man" with "-Verse" is a choice revelatory of the degree to which the character himself constitutes a universe.

Super-heroic patterns offer an opportunity to fully exploit the potential of special effects, insofar as their scenarios – such as those inspired by Stan Lee's stories – are extremely dependent on the physical performance of their protagonists and attached to actions of an almost "cosmic" scope. In fact, the constantly reiterated mission consists in "saving the world", a motto meant to be taken literally. While the narrative structure continues to grant the hero a central role, the latter is no longer dissociated from his environment, since they are both digitally created: "A film character created in *Motion Capture* […] is necessarily implanted inside a chimerical universe modeled from and around him" (Massuet 2011: 291)[*]. In the "*Thor*" series, we deal with several distinct worlds, since the "Marvel Universe" absorbs a part of the Nordic mythology's pantheon of Gods, who are connected to the Earth through a Bifröst, presented in these films more like a "worldbuilding machine" than a magical rainbow.[23] Manuel Hirtz and Harry Morgan insist on one of the implications of the eschatological and cosmogonic dimension in Jack Kirby's work, embodied in the recurring pattern of the "passage between worlds" (Morgan & Hirtz 2009: 67, 141–148)[*]. This type of extravagant representation in movies is only possible thanks to the use of computer graphics that bring cinema closer to comic book drawings. The development of closer ties between these two forms of expression creates a hybrid that some scholars consider as a sign of a powerful comeback of the animation paradigm (Gaudreault & Marion 2015: 152–175).[24] Notably, it leads to a genuine exploration of the spectrum of the various speeds of on-screen movements, going as far as the immobility of the represented bodies (Boillat 2018a), combined with an extremely mobile virtual camera that imitates the multiplication of points of view found in comics, a medium fundamentally more discontinuous than cinema.

The flexibility of the superhero's body is exaggerated through a great number of improbable transformations created by computer graphics (see, for instance, the "*Fantastic Four*" series), but the environment with which the protagonist interacts is equally unstable. Probably, it is in the composition of sets and backgrounds that digital technology proves to be most effective. The development of architectural modeling software has, among other things, brought a significant boost in film production. Cities shaped and staged as worlds are a fundamental element of multiverse movies. Moreover, the megalopolis is the privileged setting for the adventures of superheroes. They are admired by the crowd of citizens that raise their heads to watch Superman lean against a skyscraper, Spider-Man weave his web over the urban network, Iron-Man fly between buildings, or Batman gaze over a tower, as if he were the guardian angel of the city. As post-9/11 films tend to represent the mass destruction of an American city in a cathartic way (see *infra*), superhero stories integrate and revive the conventions of the genre known as "disaster movies". After all, CGI effects are used to visualize destructions with the same ease with which they can depict the act of creation.[25] After adapting comic books centered on the hero's physical characteristics, Hollywood screenwriters have recently focused on characters that master shifting between different worlds, such as Thor, Green Lantern (from 2011 onwards), Ant-Man[26] or Doctor Strange.[27] The latter opens an inter-dimensional portal in the midst of a battle in *Avengers: Infinity War* (2018) and sends one of his enemies to a different world, not before dismembering one of his arms that remains on Earth. *Guardians of the Galaxy Vol. 2* (2017) goes so far as to include a character who looks like the actor Kurt Russell, but actually is a planet-sized living entity, aspiring to absorb the entire universe. According to Rama Venkatasawmy, digital visual effects allow for the expansion of possible stories while building their credibility on a pre-existing and widely popular visual culture (Venkatasawmy 2013: 2, 90–91).[28] This is also true in the case of superhero comics that benefit from an international distribution and are strongly attached to the North American entertainment industry and its values. The variations of scale, the flexibility of bodies capable of transmuting into different materials (sand, liquid metal, fire, etc.), the villains' demiurgic aspirations, and the quasi-instantaneous transportations to the ends of the galaxy, testify to the growing interest of contemporary superhero movies in the concept of world.

This has actually been commonplace to all serial practices, from serial literature emerging in the 1830s and 1840s with the expansion of high-circulation press, to comic book or TV series in the second half of the 20th century. However, it is no longer reduced to second-tier productions, but instead can be found in blockbusters. The phenomenal success of *The Avengers* (2012), which resulted from a large-scale strategy of serial exploitation, confirms the trend. The film follows the so-called "crossover" logic of bringing together in a single story a number of heroes whose adventures are usually published separately, profiting from the interweaving of distinct "worlds".[29] Such a commercial strategy on the part of the film industry induces phenomena of "transfictionality", according to a term coined by Richard Saint-Gelais.[30] These phenomena have been the object of literary theories that examined the modes of intersection between fictional worlds or the transference of diegetic components from one world to another. This approach is indicative of a contemporary world-centered orientation of literary studies that postulates, on a theoretical level, the autonomy – if not the precedence – of the fictional world in relation to the plot.

Seriality concerns the cultural industries of other countries as well. When it comes to science fiction, the case of Japan – to which I will return in the Conclusion of this book – is of a great importance.[31] The "*Godzilla*" franchise, for example, has had its share of sequels, remakes, and reboots over six decades – *Shin Godzilla* (2016) is the twenty-ninth feature film devoted to the mythical monster.[32] This specific franchise is characteristic of the cumulative logic adopted currently by Hollywood in its treatment of superhero crossovers. It derived from the commercial strategy known as franchised merchandising,[33] exemplified in the case of *Destroy All Monsters* (1968), a film which perfectly embodied the "collect them all" motto through a futuristic tale that used the pattern of a gigantic enclosure containing all the great monsters ("Monster(Is)land"), a high-tech landlocked space automatically controlled via an underground command center (as in Michael Crichton's *Westworld* or *Jurassic Park*). After the acquisition of the rights to "Godzilla" by Legendary Entertainment and Warner Bros., as well as the production of a first film in 2014 (*Godzilla* directed by Gareth Edwards),[34] Hollywood developed a movie franchise project, later called "MonsterVerse" (*Godzilla: King of the Monsters*, 2019). The idea is to expand the world by accumulating mythical monsters (Mothra, Rodan, Ghidorah, etc.), leading to the meeting between the famous Saurian Giant and its North American counterpart in *Godzilla vs. Kong* (2021). Though this new exploitation of the Japanese franchise is clearly inspired from the reunion of superheroes in the MCU ("Marvel Cinematic Universe") or the DCEU ("DC Extended Universe"), this strategy is not a new one. By the time the *Star Wars* universe began to expand beyond its on-screen representations of the first film trilogy, Marvel published a series of comic books, between 1977 and 1979, named *Godzilla: King of the Monsters*, in which Godzilla meets the Avengers. Allowing the expansion of a universe at a low cost, the popular medium of comic books, in which science fiction occupies a prominent place, has proven to be a field of experimentations on seriality and worldbuilding. It is therefore not surprising that Hollywood and the comic strip syndicates started working in closer collaboration at the dawn of the CGI era. In the next few pages, I propose to study this transmedia context, supported by the expansion of digital technology, through the emblematic case of the "*Resident Evil*" franchise.

Entering the "Virtual" Era: Alice in the Land of New Technologies

One of the official trailers designed to promote the release of *Resident Evil: Retribution* (2012), in its way of "announcing" the upcoming film, is revealing of a world-centered creative design in moviemaking, which I hold to be prevalent in quite a number of sectors of contemporary mass culture. Moreover, it highlights the importance of new technologies by showcasing the use of interfaces that provide access to visual content, in a context where the circulation of images was about to experience a major paradigm shift, moving from storing and selling physical media to online accessing. The convergence phenomenon stemming from the digital transition has led to the abolition of borders between different media forms, the development of various types of

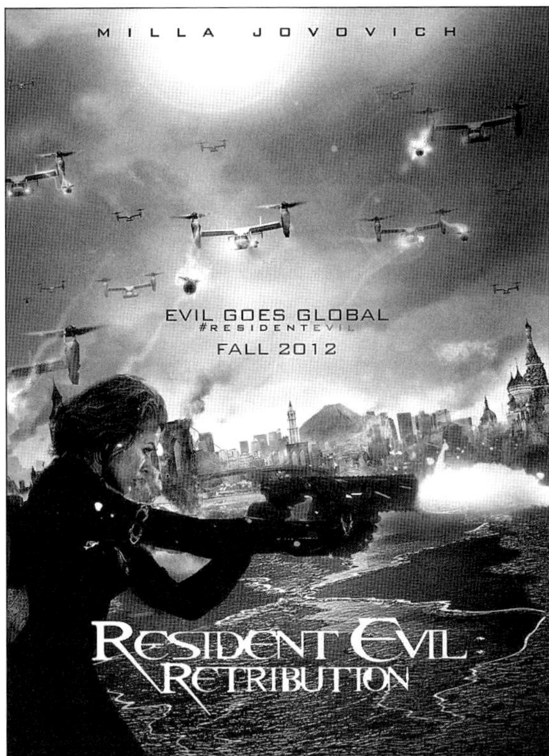

Fig. 2: A post-apocalyptic film in "viral" times: the female cloned hero as the only bulwark against the world's destruction (*Resident Evil: Retribution*, 2012).

private use of images (social networks, film sharing sites, etc.), as well as the expansion of the application area of telecommunications technology[35] from an industrial (multimedia production), commercial (operator services) and institutional (legal framework, standardization processes) standpoint, offering to video content a prominent position within the overall circulation of data (the trailer for *Resident Evil: Retribution* was released via YouTube).

One should not be surprised by the importance attributed to worldbuilding in the advertising campaign of the fifth installment in a film series issued from a Japanese video game license (*Biohazard*, Capcom, since 1996) that currently includes nearly thirty different games, all platforms combined.[36] The marginal position of the franchise in the Hollywood industry (*Resident Evil: Retribution* is a German-Canadian coproduction), its b-movie style, and its process of transmedia transfer are all factors favoring a visual and narrative audacity. What is striking about these sci-fi feature films is that they demonstrate the implications of seriality to the point of absurdity, even though their viewpoint is far less critical and more entertainment-based. They manage to do so through a constant *replay* of the same action loops and navigation of the same locations. The female protagonist and the viewer gradually discover the various traps placed in a high-tech facility by crossing successive airlocks, according to an exploratory logic prevailing also in survival horror video games.[37]

The official trailer for *Resident Evil: Retribution* (Fig. 2) begins with a male voice-over reminiscent of the one usually found in commercials enticing viewers with the promise of an immersion in a fictional world:

> Technology is changing our world, making what was once impossible ... possible. With technology advancing so rapidly today, imagine what our world will look like ... tomorrow.

The world that will host the post-apocalyptic and horrifying tale anticipated by viewers familiar with the series' previous films and video games, is conceived as one of the *possible versions* of our own world: science fiction – a genre that, as Éric Dufour said, is different from others in that it "addresses its world as a world" (Dufour 2011: 200)[*] – is explicitly framed here as a technoscientific extrapolation of our current situation. In the opening seconds of the trailer, science is regarded in a positive light as the voice-over is punctuated by regular interventions from users of telecommunication devices, coming from different regions of the world. All of them express themselves identically with a big smile on their faces that exhibits their too-white teeth. Contrastingly, in the second part of the trailer, technology is presented as a threat. However, before switching to dystopia, the viewer is invited to "*imagine*": a bridge leading to fiction is thus established. Interestingly enough, its anchor point is situated in a factual discourse, namely the one commonly used in commercials for telecommunications operators explicitly parodied by the trailer (see the actors' physical appearance, the tone of their voice, the music, the *mise-en-scene* of each actor's intervention). When we are told that "technology is changing our world", the discourse is deliberately ambiguous since it relates simultaneously to the devices shown inside the trailer (a handheld video game console, a touchpad tablet, a digital camera, a cellular phone), to the scientific experiments conducted by the protagonist's adversaries within the fictional world and, in a subtler and perhaps unconscious manner, to the technology used in the production of the film and its trailer. We might as well think that this opening statement refers to computer graphics, as the environment the viewer is asked to imagine shapes instantly on screen.

However, a continuous zoom out actually reveals something different from the film apparatus itself (Figs. 3–6): ordinary users of new technologies hold a device in their hands, point a finger at the image displayed on its small screen, and invariably repeat the motto "My name is John/Anna/Yumiko/Phong, and this is my world". This self-designation, inherited from video game practices and the film series' previous episodes,[38] is not limited to the speakers' first names (alternating gender and varying nationalities), but applies also to their surroundings, since each of them uses the deictic form "*this* is"[39] and refers to *his/her world*, thus appropriating it by the very act of designation and inscription of this environment to a small screen. A technological mediation seems to be required for the speakers to present themselves, as in social networks where the construction of the Self is composed by a variety of representations. The alleged single continuous shot in the beginning of this trailer[40] – a zoom out that suggests instead of a movement towards immersion a return to the frame story, that is to say the anchor point of the film's principal enunciation (belonging to Alice) – is built around a number of threshold points signified through a continuous succession of interlocked screens: from the second speaker that looks directly at the camera and onwards, all actors, at first shown

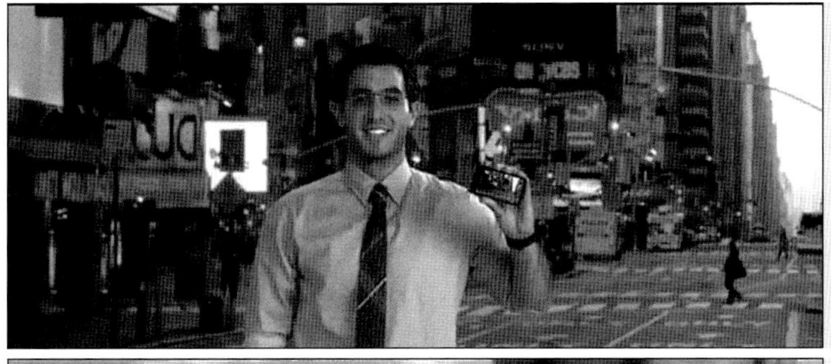

Fig. 3

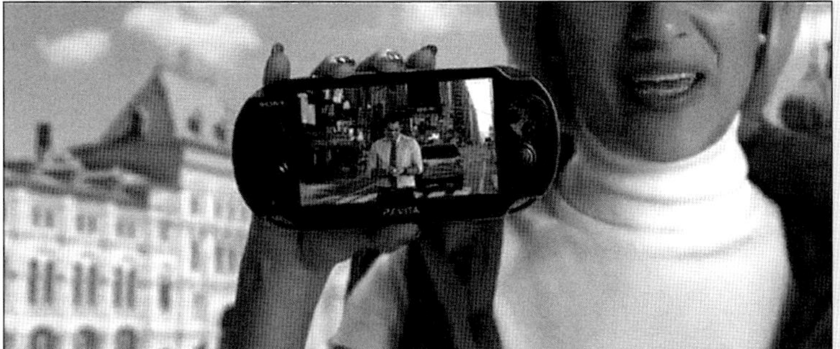

Fig. 4

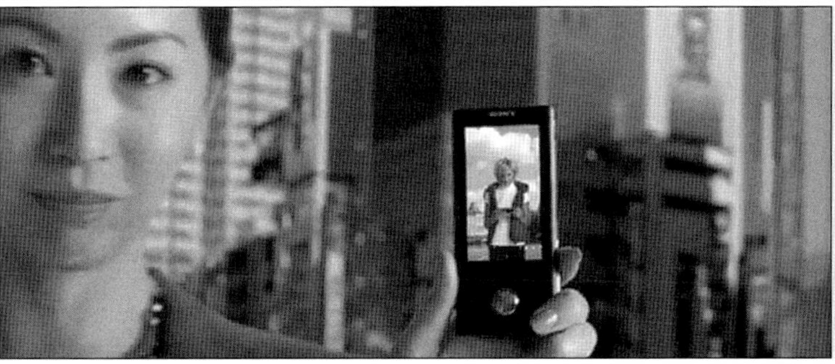

Fig. 5

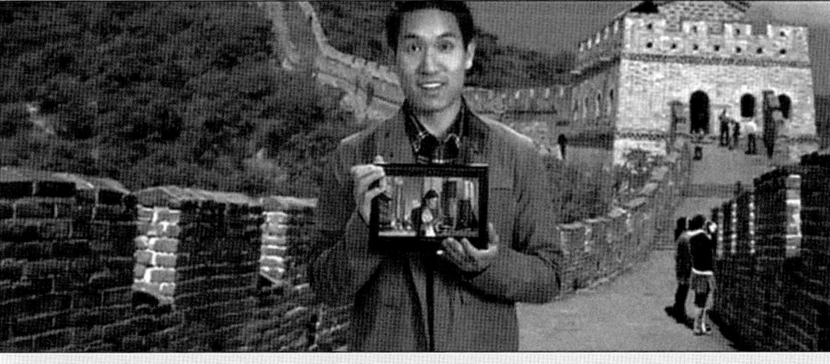

Fig. 6

Figs. 3–6 Hypermediacy: remediating cinema by new media. "Screens within screens" against the backdrop of famous landmarks around the world in the official trailer for *Resident Evil: Retribution* (2012).

in full frame, are then incorporated inside the small screen of the device held by the hand of the next speaker. This Matryoshka doll-like game is indicative of a world-centered logic, all the more so since the embedded representations are limited here to the presentation of a "world" and are therefore completely devoid of narrative logic. The ambivalent relationship with technology that permeates mainstream cinema in the digital era is evident in the trailer. While *Resident Evil*'s story recounts Alice's struggle against the financial and political control exerted by the "Umbrella Corporation",[41] a multinational company specializing in the field of biotechnology, this particular trailer presents itself as a product placement clip for Sony (only few months after Sony Ericsson became Sony Mobile Communications), a Japanese multinational corporation emblematic of the technological convergence phenomenon. However, this principle is subverted when the bright, contrasted image suddenly becomes darker, as we are introduced to a different facet of our planet, flip side of a tourist site or of photographs typically found on Facebook and through which every user offers (or at least thinks he does) "his" vision. Retrospectively, the stereotypical joviality of the first images seems frighteningly naive considering the film's story, focusing on the threat posed to humanity by certain technological advances.

Just like the other "speakers" before her, *Resident Evil*'s protagonist, Alice (Milla Jovovich), pronounces her first name and the phrase "This is my world", followed by some short clips taken from the film. The latter is thus explicitly associated with the concept of "world". Unlike the previous speakers who were occupying the central part of the frame and looking straight at the viewer, Alice, literally placed in the limelight (surrounded by army spotlights) and waiting for the action to begin just like an avatar during the opening moments of a video game, does not hold an electronic device in her hands that would allow her to capture or view images. From now on, *cinema* takes over from this type of device, discarding the lighthearted and watered down representations conveyed by such telecommunication means, in order to impose the uncommon and hostile environment of a sci-fi film series staging the Apocalypse. Remarkably, the shift from the everyday life to the film's world, a metaphor for all fiction, is carried through the use of recent technologies, which are nevertheless inevitably effaced when the time comes to immerse the viewer into the film's universe.

The trailer for *Resident Evil: Retribution* crystallizes various aspects of contemporary, mainstream movies I propose to study in this book: first, the film's assimilation to a world that exceeds the film itself thanks to four previous episodes (released between 2002 and 2010), two animated movies (2008 and 2012) and the franchise's variations through different media (video games, comic books, role-playing games, toys…); second, the display of the technological mediation as means to embed universes and move smoothly from one to the other; third, the reinforcement of the immersion thanks to the public's alleged familiarity with certain contemporary audio-visual technologies. Unlike other action-oriented trailers released for the same film, this one hardly suggests what the story of *Resident Evil: Retribution* is about,[42] intending instead to attach the film to the contemporary technological context while showing how its world differs from everyday life. It seems that we are dealing here with a case of "hypermediacy", in the sense of Bolter and Grusin, insofar as digital imaging paradoxically "seek[s] the real" (or, in our case, the immersion in a world) "by multiplying mediation so as to create a feeling of fullness, a satiety of experience, which can be taken as reality" (Bolter and Grusin 1999: 53). Here, the depiction of users of "worldbuilding machines" naturalizes the digital effects of the trailer and the film's images. When Alice addresses the viewer, the technological mediation exhibited previously persists, though "camouflaged", as an integral part of the fictional pact. Invited to identify with a young woman struggling against the hostility of her environment, we accept the fact that as long as the film's screening lasts, "this is our world".

Furthermore, the world-centered logic displayed in this official trailer foreshadows certain particularities of the 2012 installment. This time, the film's protagonist, bearing the name of Lewis Carroll's famous character, will struggle to survive in Umbrella's high-tech underground facilities (Fig. 7; Color Plate 1). She will not only be confronted with the abominations of genetics but will also have to exit a maze controlled by a computing machine. In the fascinating and "meta-serial" prologue of *Resident Evil: Extinction* (2007) (Color Plate 2), the reiteration of the same sequence of events (actually a repetition of the first episode's opening scene) with a systematically fatal outcome for Alice, finds its explanation inside the diegesis in a genetic factor while relying on the software's ability to multiply one element within a single image.[43] The viewer realizes upon the discovery of a mass grave full of strictly identical bodies that the character he had taken for Alice was actually one of her multiple clones – an offspring of a standardized production, condemned to be recycled – designed to replay *ad libitum*, like a video game avatar, the same stage from a training program.

The development of different narrative alternatives in a single film whose protagonist is trapped in a loop, like the soldier in *Source Code* or the one in *Edge of Tomorrow* (see *infra*), tends to call in question the reality status of the world in which these alternatives are unfolding. In the fantasy/horror film *Triangle* (2009), featuring a cluster of replicated bodies of a female character similar to the one in *Resident Evil: Extinction*, a young woman projects herself repeatedly into an inner world and stands next to the previous versions of herself, in an effort to avoid confronting her own guilt.

Resident Evil: Retribution expands on the idea of assimilating the central hero to a guinea pig doomed to relive the same traumatic episodes, though facticity here affects not just the protagonist's physical identity, but also her environment. Sequestered in the underground laboratories of the Umbrella Corpora-

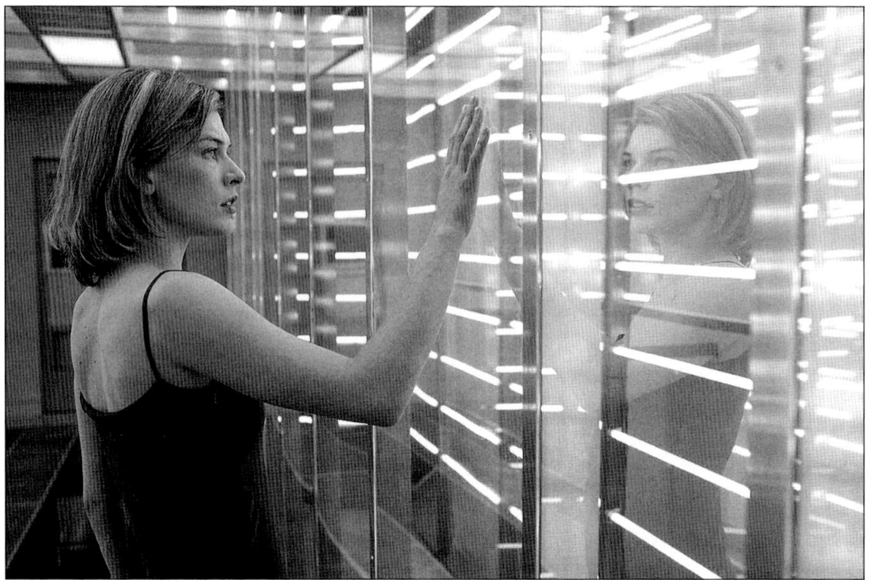

Fig. 7: Survival Horror: The female hero's avatars in a high-tech maze (the "*Resident Evil*" film series).

tion, Alice is subjected to a series of tests, conducted by an artificial intelligence that controls the areas she navigates through as if they were different levels in a video game. The locations are not *virtual* but *factitious*, the product of a simulation that aims to recreate the conditions leading to the contamination of urban centers through the use of a bacteriological weapon (as well as the conditions of using a different weapon, a defensive one: Alice herself). The images depicting the underground base, dematerialized in the form of a 3D computer diagram, are reminiscent of computer graphics and motion capture used in almost every single one of the film's shots, just like the way moving bodies standing out against the white grid walls evoke images obtained once through chronophotography. Also, these images underline the fact that the areas visited are systematically placed under the watchful eye of electronic surveillance. The laboratory, sometimes depicted as a cluster of pixels, is in fact an encompassing space made up of "*small worlds*" (according to Umberto Eco's term, see 1990: 64–82):[44] Tokyo is right next to New York, and the latter is at a stone's throw from Moscow. Consequently, some scenes previously shown in the series are replayed inside this miniature replica. The set's subdivisions take over the role – usually accorded to crosscutting – of transporting us from one city to the other.

Moreover, in order to shift between narrative tracks after the heroes' team has split in two, the film occasionally uses a computer-stylized cartographic representation (reminiscent of a DVD or a video game menu) on which a movement is reported, reminding us that everything we see is the product of a computing machine and a 3D map design. This mode of representation may encourage us to associate images rendered momentarily abstract – under the story's fabric lies the digital image's fabric, as in *The Matrix*'s ending (though the schematic representation is not related here to a single character)[45] – with the "gaze" attributed to the artificial intelligence monitoring every action. However, in at least one particular case, it is the film's "narrator" who guides us elsewhere, interposing a visual interface (inherited from those used in the film's world) between the cinematic representation and the viewer that replaces the traditional optical effects indicating a change of scenes (fade to black, dissolve, etc.). Only a viewer accustomed to the change of levels in video games can receive such an interface without drifting away from the film's story. Space becomes suddenly autonomous while manifested as a construction. Digital visual effects represent an inherently *artificial world*, successively inhabited by identical clones, developed from a limited number of models (in this case, the film's mainactors).

The figure of the clone that in certain narratives applies to the Earth itself (*Another Earth*, 2011; *Upside Down*, 2012, Fig. 8; *Kill Switch*, 2017) entails a deindividuation in terms of the heroes' characterization, which by contrast – and paradoxically – contributes to "de-virtualize" the universe they inhabit. Even if Alice and her little daughter are gripped by fear in *Resident Evil: Retribution*, when they enter the factory where clones are massively produced in their own likeness, these simulacra are perceived by the viewer as human beings made of flesh and blood[46], not as products of digital imagery. This scene echoes several contemporary films where a character mixed with a crowd of identical anthropoid replicas created in his image must *distinguish* himself as a real hero from these mass-produced alter egos (*Alien: Resurrection*, 1997; *Toy Story 2*, 1999; *The 6th Day*, 2000; *Terminator Salvation*, 2009; the sci-fi track in *Cloud Atlas*, 2012; *Oblivion*, 2013). Similar to *Resident Evil: Retribution*, some of these films offer a scene showing humans being confronted with a "storage" space where an army's anonymous units are gathered, be it robots (*Star Wars: Episode I – The Phantom Menace*, 1999; *I, Robot*, 2004; *Total Recall*, 2012) or clones (*Star Wars: Episode II – Attack of the Clones*, 2002; *Moon*, 2009). In such cases, the mechanical concreteness of the industrial production inside the represented world naturalizes the digital artifact on which the representation itself is based. In *The Matrix Reloaded* (2003), the vertiginous proliferation of Agent Smith's doubles echoes directly the conditions of their fabrication insofar as they are, inside the diegesis, the product of a computing machine – in a barely disguised metaphor of a film "projection". Such replicas of a single character, namely one of the major components of the diegetic universe, does not generally involve the establishment of a multiverse. All "avatars" inhabit the same world and are subject to the same laws as their model, even though their capacities, for instance the physical ones, allow them to experience these laws in divergent ways (as in *Surrogates*, 2009). That being said, it also happens that a character's replica signifies a plurality of worlds (*Star Trek*, 2009; *TRON: Legacy*, 2010) or

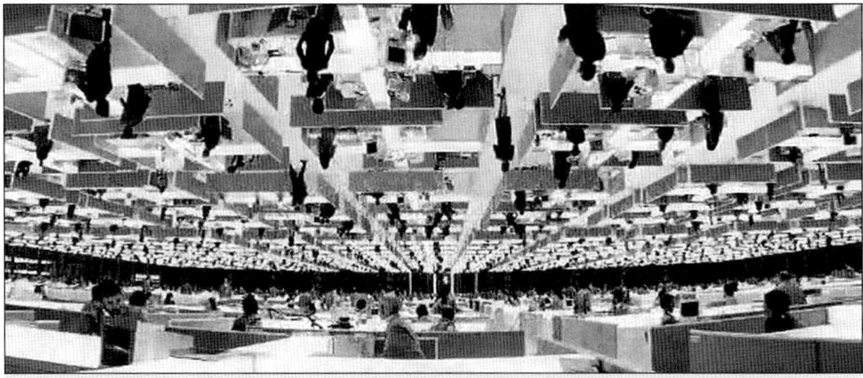

Fig. 8: Two planets mirroring each other: romance across the border (*Upside Down*, 2012).

the transformation of the world's current state (*Next*, 2007). *Resident Evil: Retribution* plays with the possibility of a multiverse while exhibiting the world's artificiality. By having several replicas of the protagonist successively cross a single space-time continuum, the latter tends to become autonomous in its cosmic features that remain stable in spite of the narrative variations. In this regard, the film itself mirrors Umbrella Corporation's underground base, a laboratory for simulation exercises.

The franchise's sixth episode, *Resident Evil: The Final Chapter* (2016), reactivates and develops the post-apocalyptic *Mad Max*-like imaginary found in *Resident Evil: Extinction* (the obelisk stands among Washington's ruins, just like the Statue of Liberty in *Planet of the Apes*). It pushes the narrative aberrations stemming from the massive use of clones inside the diegesis to the limit and exploits (four years before Covid-19) the contemporary fear of destructive pandemics on a planetary scale. It is after all our own blue planet that appears in the first shot of the trailer for *Resident Evil: Retribution*, before turning into a devastated planet, the dark side of (a future version of) the Earth.[47]

Resident Evil: The Final Chapter opens with the image of a plethora of screens within screens depicting fragments of the series' previous episodes that aggregate to form the image of Alice (who, as usual, pronounces her name and presents herself as the unique reference point in a post-apocalyptic world that threatens to become post-human). Above all, her character is constructed as the sum of pre-existing images in a plot in which her identity is constantly threatened. The figure of the clone, favoring all kinds of narrative reboots,[48] becomes central in this story since the protagonist, devoid of memory like an avatar at the beginning of a video game,[49] learns from her enemy and creator (a clone himself) that she is in fact the clone of Alicia, the woman who would have been the daughter of the scientist that fabricated the T-Virus (had she survived). Alicia's voice and physical appearance were recorded with the aim of materializing the artificial intelligence known as The Red Queen. As a character, Alice (aka Alicia's duplicate) is empty, with no past, like so many other cyberculture heroes who come to realize their identity is a simulacrum (see Chapter 5)[50] or like a video game avatar merely conceived to act in a spectacular way.[51] The story thus incorporates certain features of the medium in which *Resident Evil*'s world was originally developed (without Alice, but with Claire Redfield, a character present in the third installment of the film series, before reappearing in its 2021 reboot). The happy ending will precisely consist of rendering Alice "human" (in other words, a unique individual) by downloading into her body Alicia's stored memories.

In *Resident Evil: Retribution*, locations are shown with no regard to the story. Alice discovers them at first as empty and frozen spaces; suddenly, they come alive precisely when the computer's female voice announces "Tokyo sequence initialized" and the merry-go-round launches its new "attraction" – in this case a remake of the opening scene of *Resident Evil: Afterlife* (2010). All of the series' previous episodes are being replayed in a condensed way in this particular installment, as the franchise seems to have reached a standstill, suggesting the vanity of any additional sort of variation in view of the overexploitation of the serial principle. The components that furnish the world precede the narrative dimension. One understands then that the trailer was meant to accentuate the world-centered stakes of *Resident Evil: Retribution*, reminiscent of those in *The Truman Show* (1998), while offering a plurality of environments designed within the context of computer-generated imaging. Whereas Weir's protagonist was confined in a single, neatly circumscribed space, produced by a clever staging intended for television broadcasting (the manipulation was orchestrated live from an editing table of sorts), in *Resident Evil: Retribution* both entities of production and reception of the images are completely "virtualized". Moreover, the trailer affiliates through its music with the corpus of multiverse movies, since it uses the original Daft Punk soundtrack of the recent *TRON: Legacy* – a sequel to *TRON* that set a milestone back in 1982 for its CGI-like representation of the (portrayed by real actors) characters' "projection" inside a video game (see Chapter 5).

As *Resident Evil: Retribution* shows, the popularization of a world-centered creative design in movies owes a great deal to the expansion of digital image processing. Certainly, special effects prior to the digital era, such as rear or front projection, were already raising issues linked to the insertion of characters (foreground) in a set (background) sometimes associated with a specific "world". Nevertheless, the question of the established relationship between an actor's body and the environment in which this body is placed, is nowadays a matter of central concern (see Boillat 2020a), as teams responsible for the creation of computer-generated images attempt to suture the graft in the best possible way in order to immerse the viewer inside different worlds. This would explain why many contemporary films are permeated thoroughly by a world-centered creative design in comparison with films fabricated prior to the commercialization of video games (or, at least, to the dissemination of the imaginary conveyed by/on video games from the '60s–'70s onwards). Moreover, they aim to meet the expectations of an audience whose interest in this type of issue is constantly sharpened both by the recurrence of narrative forms open to the development of possible alternatives (thanks to films like the ones directed by Alain Resnais, Raúl Ruiz, David Lynch, Charlie Kaufman, etc.)[52] *and* by its familiarity with "new" technologies (or discourses and representations related to them), in particular with "sandbox" video games in which the player's avatar navigates for hours through the game's universe. Distributed through various media, "*Resident Evil*" is an example of a product associated more with a world than a story. Furthermore, the same year *Resident Evil: Retribution* was released, magazines and blogs specializing in video game productions unfailingly reacted to a comment made by the producer of the video game *Resident Evil: Revelations* (2012), Masachika Kawata, in an interview published in the online journal *Eurogamer*: "It would almost entail having a slight reboot to get the series into a place where it would work with open-world gameplay".[53] This project, aiming at the franchise's evolution, stems from a desire among designers to renew and develop world-building strategies.[54]

Studying multiverses as a principle of film organization allows us to be at the heart of the current challenges faced by a film industry whose features took shape at the beginning of the previous decade. Nowadays, the film medium is undergoing a drastic reconfiguration in terms of its distribution tactics, finding itself obligated to negotiate its relationship to other mass media products such as video games. How do "multiverse films" work in terms of structure, visual aesthetics, storytelling, editing and viewer-immersion strategies? Are the spatial and temporal relationships negotiated in these films in a specific way? What kind of worldviews do they convey through the shimmer of their *trompe-l'œil* effects? What interpretative tools are relevant in order to study these movies? What are the representational strategies applied in order to portray "worldbuilding machines" inside the fictional universes, and in what way do they testify to the implications linked to the expansion of computer-generated imaging in the mid-1990s? How do these films reflect the cinematic apparatus, itself destined to imminent transformations at a time when video game environments tend to model the relationship of large number of consumers to fiction? These are some of the questions to which I intend to provide several answers by studying the structure and the representations offered by certain emblematic multiverse films. In this way, I will try to relocate certain well-known issues from the field of narratology to a dimension that is more referential and semantic, while also examining the ideology communicated by these particular film discourses.

Post-9/11 Alternate Realities

From the beginning of the 21st century, Hollywood seems to prioritize world-building to an extent never seen before, notably by creating fictions organized as multiverses. Next to the previously discussed wide use of CGI, a sociopolitical factor should be taken into account when discussing the multiverse structure of a number of these films. Certain *parallel worlds* may be interpreted as a fantasy created in response to the trauma of the September 11 attacks to the North American collective consciousness. This cataclysmic event revealed the United States' vulnerability to terrorist attacks on its own soil,[55] by reactivating morbidly a cinematic imaginary, in this case a combination of two successful disaster movies, *Airport* (1970) and *The Towering Inferno* (1974)[56] (Fig. 9).

During these early years of the new millennium, the fear of terrorist attacks constitutes, alongside concerns over climate change, a major source of inspiration for the genre of disaster movies and its sub-genre, the post-apocalyptic film.[57] Images of chaos in a North American metropolis begin to multiply, particularly in superhero movies such as *The Avengers* (2012), sometimes even echoing the World Trade Center attack. For instance, a plane crashes in the background in *Vanishing on 7th Street* (2010), as the hero wakes up in a deserted Detroit. The opening scenes of episodes 1 and 11 from One-Season TV series *Flashforward* (2009), show a world paralyzed by a two-minute blackout while a helicopter crashes on a Los Angeles skyscraper, among other buildings destroyed by fire. Moreover, a flashback in episode 18 focuses on the efforts to prevent a dramatic event that could prove to be much more destructive than the actual September 11 attacks.

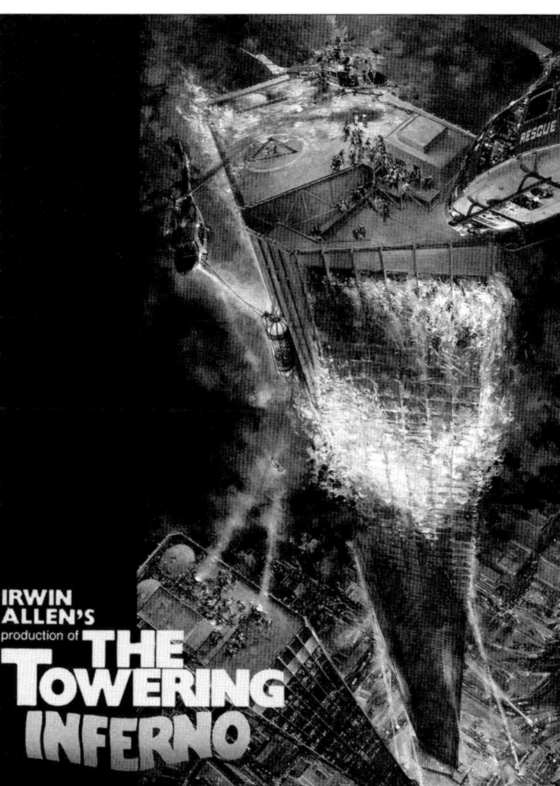

Fig. 9: Pre-9/11 imaginary representation of urban disaster in Hollywood: the high-tech skyscraper of *The Towering Inferno* (1974).

As *Person of Interest* (2011–2016) perfectly illustrates, contemporary American films and TV series frequently resort to the idea of a machine built after 9/11, designed to prevent further threats to national security. In this show, a surveillance AI performs a widespread population tracking, typical of our growing digital society. Although the series' protagonists do not deal with the terrorist acts predicted by this machine, but with less severe cases, each episode replays a last minute rescue that helps avoid a tragic outcome. In Season 3 of *Westworld*, human-like androids are managing personal data, revealing the extent to which TV serial format is well suited to the idea of constantly adapting to the newest social issues. Also present is an advanced AI system, called Rehoboam, created by two brothers, survivors of a nuclear strike, which destroyed the entire city of Paris.

However, there was a "world" that existed before 9/11 too. Since reality has surpassed fiction, an "undamaged" Manhattan urban landscape serves today as a symbolic indicator of a world's otherness. By spotting the Twin Towers the hero of the TV series *Life on Mars* (2008–2009) realizes he has been sent to the past – or rather, as we learn in the final episode (and as suggested by a plot full of incongruities and inconsistencies), into an entirely different world, produced by a worldbuilding machine. At the same time, the crew of a spaceship on an interplanetary flight is connected to this machine, while being trapped in a state of artificial sleep. *Fringe* places an even greater importance on the Twin Towers, as a landmark serving to identify a world. Season 1 finale (S01E20: "There's More Than One of Everything", 2009)[58] relies on the World Trade Center to provide a dramatic demonstration of the existence of a *parallel world*. The series' main character, Olivia Dunham (Anna Torv), takes the elevator inside a Broadway hotel, then gets out in the floor of an entirely different building that a pull-back camera shot reveals to be one of the Twin Towers. The story's temporary suspension at the season's finale occurs with the image of this emblematic monument as a backdrop. This spatial incongruity shall be confirmed later on, after the two worlds superpose each other: a seriously wounded survivor, whose body merged with a different version of himself (a sort of a Siamese twin), claims that in the *alternate (story)world* the World Trade Center was spared the 9/11 terrorist attacks. However, the resurrection of this famous building does not erase the terrorist attack. In fact, the latter becomes more important because it constitutes a point of reference for both of these worlds. When asked by Walter Bishop (John Noble) about the target of the attacks in the *alternate (story)world*, the dying man indicates the White House and the Pentagon (S02E15, "Jacksonville", 2010).

At the beginning of Season 2, Olivia's meeting with William Bell (Leonard Nimoy) at the top of the World Trade Center is put off, as far as the viewer is concerned, until the female hero manages to overcome her amnesia. Prior to this, the images of the Twin Towers emerge in fragments, as if torn away from her subconscious. The recurrence of this referent indicates the degree to which the presence of these buildings is associated with an *alternate (story)world* (see Chapter 2), one of the possible versions of American history. At the beginning of Season 3, when Olivia escapes from the *parallel world* where she was held captive and returns to "her" world (hence, "our" world), the World Trade Center plays a similar role. As she finds herself in what seems to be a gift shop for tourists, she is left wide-eyed and dumbstruck by a view that initially remains off-screen. Suddenly, a postcard draws her attention; as she grabs it, a close-up allows the viewer to identify the image of the Twin Towers, with the following caption on top of the card: "We will never forget". Then, visible through a window, a wide shot reveals New York's "current" skyline, while Olivia's reflection on the glass reminds us her double in another world. The Twin Towers continue to exist only as an image, a visual trace from the past. The series' screenwriters "have not forgotten": there is clearly a before and an after regarding the tragedy. The only way to escape from this fatal turn of events is to exit our space-time frame by imagining a different world where the disaster did not happen, or had a different outcome. Either way, 9/11 serves as the anchor point for a fictional story.

In Alex Proyas' *Knowing* (2009), M.I.T. astrophysics professor John Koestler (Nicolas Cage) deciphers an ominous message addressed by extraterrestrials to a medium, by isolating the digits "09/11/01" from a numerical sequence. The film's eschatological dimension is not concerned with this particular terrorist attack, yet takes it as the starting point for the hero's journey. He is encouraged to act upon realizing that in an alternate reality the September 11 disaster could have been avoided provided the message had been deciphered earlier. In fact, there are several films featuring a worldbuilding machine, that do not directly represent *the* 9/11 attacks, but allude to them by showing that *a* terrorist attack can be avoided by using the appropriate technological means. For instance, *Next* (2007) focuses on an imminent terrorist threat, a plotline that is actually absent from Philip K. Dick's short story ("The Golden Man", 1954) on which this film is loosely based.[59] While FBI's counter-terrorism services try, in vain, to recruit Chris Johnson (Nicolas Cage, again), he decides at the end of the film to help the authorities locate and defuse a nuclear bomb, hidden somewhere in Los Angeles. A small-time magician, Chris has the supernatural power to anticipate his near future and project himself into it, as if he were playing a video game. Every time his avatar is being shot down by one of his enemies, he reappears and repeats his actions based on what he observed during his previous unsuccessful attempts, not unlike Bill Murray's character in *Groundhog Day* (whose scope of learning is nevertheless limited to whatever a single, endlessly repeating day can teach him).[60] It is therefore the hero's body that functions as a machine, allowing him for instance to escape the surveillance cameras of a casino during the film's opening scene. This ability to stay "out of the grid" is common among action heroes in contemporary Hollywood movies, produced in an era of widespread digital surveillance (see Boillat 2014b).

Like in *Edge of Tomorrow* (2014),[61] the narrative structure in *Next* splits into a number of possible alternatives, each one leading to a distinct *alternate (story)world*, and concludes with a variant where the impending disaster is finally avoided. Several scenes flow backwards, favored in that sense by the reversibility of cinematic time whose anthropological importance has been analyzed by Edgar Morin (1958: 52–54). From Lumière brothers' *Demolition of a Wall* (1896), often projected in reverse,[62] to *Vantage Point* (2008) or Youssef Chahine's sketch in *11'09"01 September 11* (2002), where the filmmaker rewinds the tape on his monitor to symbolically undo the collapse of the Twin Towers, and the video clip "Cinnamon Girl" (2004) by Prince, in which the explosion provoked by a young Muslim woman is filmed backwards, the regressive and comforting feeling brought by reversing an act of destruction remains the same. In these cases, temporal inversion aims to prevent in a revisionist manner an otherwise inevitable disaster – this is actually *Tenet*'s central theme, as I will argue below. In *Deja Vu* (2006) and *Source Code* (2011), a machine of this type, producing an audio-visual representation, plays a central role in the films' story and determines their editing. As Garrett Stewart points out, in both of these films "we are plunged again into the post-9/11 crisis of further mass death at the hands of terrorism – before the quantum leap (cinematographically figured) into a happy ending" (Stewart 2015: 207).

Deja Vu begins with the explosion of a ferry in New Orleans. After Hurricane Katrina devastated this region in August 2005, the city is strongly associated with the imaginary representations of disaster, which nonetheless in Tony Scott's film is not attributed to nature. The horrifying sight of bodies in flames, falling from the sky after being thrown to the air by the explosion, is more reminiscent of the 9/11 victims who threw themselves from the burning towers. In *Deja Vu*, the attack could be retrospectively avoided thanks to a machine that allows re-watching "live" events that took place within a given period of time, through a sort of virtual surveillance camera. The notion of panoptic surveillance is pushed to its limit: sitting in front of their computers, a group of experts shift between different viewing-angles,[63] while images scroll on a big screen before them, moving in all possible directions through a delimited space, as if it were a "small world" accessed via their computer system. Gradually, the viewer understands, alongside police officer Doug Carlin (Denzel Washington), that the potential of this fictional technology goes far beyond the viewing of a satellite-recorded stock of images. In fact, this is not pre-recorded material, but a simultaneous, unidirectional contact with a portion of the past, whose representation embraces the "real vs. virtual" oppositional paradigm. Doug wants to believe in the possibility of changing the course of past events, prompting one of the FBI specialists to mention the "branching universe theory", namely the creation of an alternate reality by cracking open a new timeline. The *virtual world* gives access to an *alternate (story)world* that supersedes the actual tragic events. The way the characters in *Deja Vu* discuss the implications of time travel, reflects an era in which cinema is considered above all as a means of establishing worlds that in turn nourish stories told in individual movies. Doug suggests crossing the "bridge" between the past and the present, by entering into the machine, like the guinea pigs in science fiction films.

Source Code (2011) carries even further the fantasy of escaping the inevitability of the code, as well as the prison of the time-loop, by means of a back door. Once again, the goal of the hero is to prevent a terrorist attack. The brain of Captain Colter Stevens, declared clinically dead while serving in Afghanistan, is artificially kept alive. He is mentally projected into a matrix, which repeatedly reconstructs the eight-minute spatiotemporal segment preceding an attack on a train coming from the Chicago suburbs. This recollection, transformed into a world one can roam through, was snatched from the memory of one of the incident's victims who supposedly recorded and stored all the relevant data in his brain. This high-tech fiction preserves the unity of the subject's identity, a notion further guaranteed by the presence of a well-known Hollywood actor like Jake Gyllenhaal. While a prisoner of the "Source Code" program, Stevens constitutes the film's focal character and invites viewers, themselves an integral part of a (cinematic) dispositive,[64] to identify with him. As in *Je t'aime je t'aime* or *Eternal Sunshine of the Spotless Mind* (see Chapter 4), the human factor prevails: in a film like *Source Code*, steeped in American values, the emancipation of the main character who manages to escape from the computer program, signifies the individual victory of an action hero over science and machines. The good soldier takes his revenge for the attack that took his life by preventing a new attack, similar to the ones committed by Al-Qaeda. That said, the completely a-historical and apolitical pattern of the "isolated madman" takes us further away from any explicit reference to 9/11, in a film that was however released in the 10th anniversary commemoration of this real-life disaster.

Time after time, Stevens is immersed in a "sequence" of events that invariably ends with the explosion of the train. The transfer from one world to another is depicted as a form of violence exerted on the hero's body, whether during an abrupt dematerialization (reminiscent of *TRON*) or at the end of the loop, as the victims' bodies burn down, left unrecognizable as a result of the explosion. In between these series of flashes, images of the Cloud Gate in Chicago creep in, a mirror-polished sphere that functions as a metonym for a world that constitutes a distorted reflection of both the city and the human subject – literally a "gate" between worlds. These images announce and at the same time undermine the film's happy ending.[65]

For both the hero and the viewer, this repetition orchestrates the former's romance with Christina (Michelle Monaghan) in a succession of stages, attaching it to the order of the narrative. In every new repetition, Christina sits opposite Stevens on the train and ends up dying next to him in the fire. As in *Edge of Tomorrow*, the male hero's military objective is gradually rivaled by his desire for a female character. In most films of this type, an intimate and emotional dimension, which guarantees the unity of the desiring subject, counterbalances the relative "coldness" of the narrative structure and the potential discomfort felt by the viewer (the *Bandersnatch* episode of Netflix's *Black Mirror* series constitutes an exception in this respect).[66] In *Groundhog Day*, *Dark City*, *The Butterfly Effect*, *The Jacket*, *Eternal Sunshine of the Spotless Mind*, *The Adjustment Bureau* or *Vanishing Waves*, the twists and stammers of a discontinuous plot are ultimately relegated to the background, as the development of a narrative arc – saving the loved one (or at least ensuring her a brighter future) and (re)building a relationship with her – is brought to the forefront. In this respect, and unlike TV series whose format encourages the multiplication of narrative tracks as well as long-term variations in the relations of subordination between them,[67] the films mentioned may very well adopt a complex narrative pattern, but are in fact hardly different from movies of classical Hollywood cinema, as David Bordwell analyzed them:

> The classical film has at least two lines of action, both casually linking the same group of characters. Almost invariably, one of the lines of action involves heterosexual romantic love [...]. Instead of putting many characters through parallel lines of action, the Hollywood film involves few characters in several interdependent actions. (Bordwell, Staiger & Thompson 1985: 16).

All these films focus on a single character around which a network of interactions unfolds. The gap separating the *alternate (story)worlds* is therefore attenuated by an interdependence of parallel lines of actions, sometimes leading to a complete convergence, as when Stevens and Christina contemplate their reflection on the surface of the Cloud Gate Monument, or when John finds Emma on the pier at the end of *Dark City* (the only exception here is *Je t'aime je t'aime*, a film that proves to be far more pessimistic – see Chapter 4). In similar cases, the demiurgic power of the male hero is ultimately celebrated.

The mission of the soldier in *Source Code* is to identify the perpetrator of the attack who is about to commit a (bigger scale) new one in the frame world – this time using a "dirty bomb". Like the hero in *Next*, Colter Stevens develops total control of his environment, anticipating all minor actions that take place within his field of vision. Every time he is outside of this constantly replayed "sequence", he finds himself in a cramped, dark environment that resembles a sort of survival capsule with angular sheet metal walls, a "matrix" strewn with electrical cables (Fig. 10).

Initially, he assumes he is in an army simulator, a hypothesis that turns out to be quite consistent with the experiment in which he is unwittingly participating. Strapped into a chair, he communicates with the program's operators via a screen in front of him (Fig. 11). Later it will be understood that this interface is a hallucination, a mental materialization resulting from the guinea pig's denial of the actual state of his mutilated body, a "disemboweled carcass in a holding tank next door to the computer monitors of his mission controllers, with electrodes wired to his eviscerated torso and brain" (Stewart 2015: 224). Stevens' emotional state modifies the space in which he believes he is being confined: an extremely cold air invades the capsule, sections of the wall start reconfiguring and an opening appears on the ceiling. This liminal space resembles a *mental world* (see Chapter 3), but remains permeable to the frame world where the military experiment is taking place thanks to the monitor

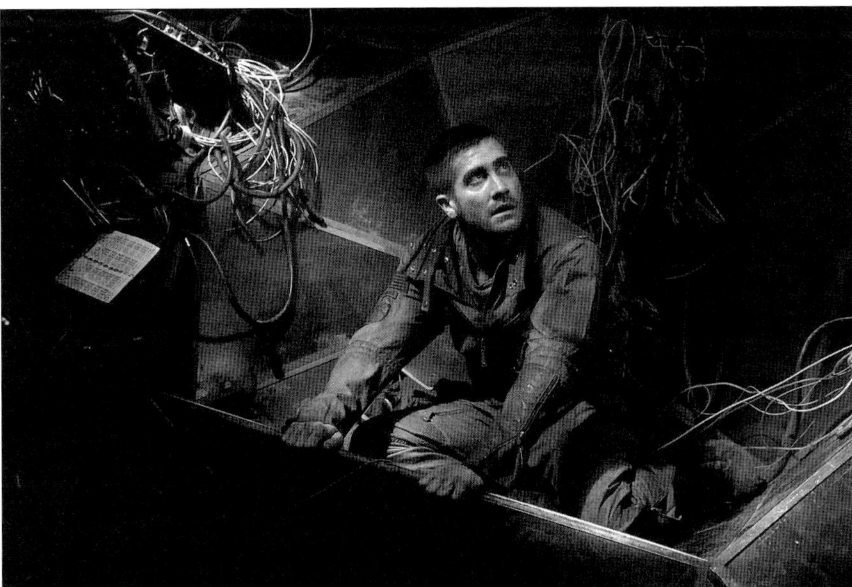

Fig. 10: Metal carcass and electric wires: the claustrophobic representation of the soldier's (Jake Gyllenhaal) mental world in *Source Code* (2011).

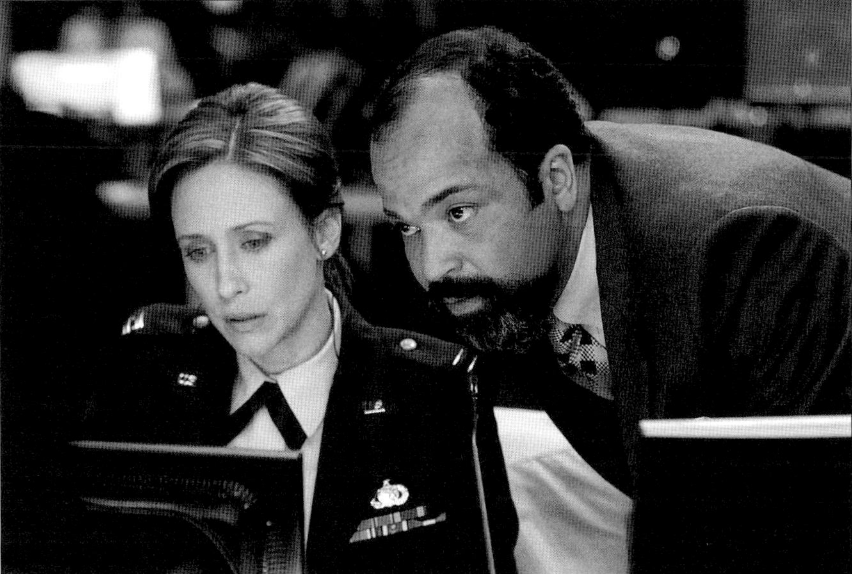

Fig. 11: At the other end of the line, outside the "source code": Colleen Goodwin (Vera Farmiga) and Dr. Rutledge (Jeffrey Wright).

screen. The communication between characters and worlds is carried out by a machine. In its final moments, the film adopts the point of view of Stevens' interlocutor, Air Force captain Colleen Goodwin (Vera Farmiga). The viewer realizes then that every word spoken by Stevens throughout the film had no phonetic reality, but only appeared as text on a computer screen. Nevertheless, *Source Code* ends in a technological utopia, hardly compatible with the soldier's exploitation by the techno-military power that is denounced in the rest of the film.[68] Its finale celebrates the spoken language (and therefore humankind), since the messages Goodwin receives from the other world are read in voice-over by their author, who in that sense regains a hold on the film's narrative. This final scene may be seen as the culmination of the omnipresence of telecommunication technologies in *Source Code*, as they intervene throughout the film in various different ways.

The operating principle of the fictitious machine used in *Source Code* is briefly described by its inventor, Dr. Rutledge (Jeffrey Wright). A hypocritical, self-centered, "bad" father figure, whose impotence is symbolized by his handicapped leg, Dr. Rutledge stands opposite Colter's real (and "good") father. Faced with the resistance of his guinea pig, whom he intends to exploit to the maximum,[69] he is forced to give some explanations. First, as the opening quote to this chapter shows, he describes in an evasive manner the complexity of the theoretical principles underlying the technology used in his machine. Such a reflexive scene conveys the film's ambition to present itself as complex – even though the explication offered by Dr. Rutledge remains implausible and superficial, to say the least. Stevens, supposedly as motivated to understand as the viewers, challenges his interlocutor to initiate him into the mysteries of this fabulous technology ("Try me!"). Then, Dr. Rutledge replies in terms that highlight the world-centered implications of this technology: "Source Code gives us access to a parallel reality". Finally, he informs Colter – who up to that point thought that he had saved Christina by getting her off the train – that the young woman is indeed (or rather "still") among the victims of the attack.

However, the autonomy of the eight-minute time loop – in terms of diegetic duration – will be contradicted by the film's story, in which the fantasy of purging the anguish of a possible terrorist attack takes precedence over the initial logic of a diegetic embedding (transgressed by a metalepsis).[70] Stevens not only succeeds in identifying the criminal, preventing the second explosion planned by the latter in the center of Chicago, but also averts the train attack, making his recruitment by the army within the "Source Code" unnecessary. Dr. Rutledge, who had initially ordered the erasure of Stevens' memory, will eventually become amnesiac due to the *reboot* activated by his own guinea pig. As in *Deja Vu*, the hero manages to establish an *alternate (story)world* and, like Orpheus acting from "the other side of the mirror", brings his lover back to life. The e-mail sent by Colter Stevens at the end of the film, reveals how this reversal is not perceived in a classical way, namely at the level of narrative temporality, but as an act of worldbuilding: "You thought you were creating eight minutes of a past event, but you're not. You've created a whole new world". This type of happy ending concurs with the following view expressed by Jean-Clet Martin: "We are living in the era of the end of the world. But this end is not the apocalypse. Actually, it means that we have begun to accept that our universe is in fact a pluriverse, a world of worlds"[*].[71]

One could argue that a "world-centered" movie such as Christopher Nolan's *Inception* (2010) is also shaped, albeit more subtly, by a post-apocalyptic imaginary typical of the post-9/11 era. The film's promotional posters were conceived as variations of the same pattern, an altered vision of an American megalopolis. Still, precisely at the deepest level of the hero's mind (Cobb, played by Leonardo DiCaprio), this post-apocalyptic imaginary "resurfaces". The intrusion of the disaster motif may seem astonishing at first, insofar as the world in question is supposed to correspond to an idyllic, fusional state of the couple formed by Cobb and his wife, Mal (Marion Cotillard). In fact, this is a *mental world* – since the wife's suicide takes place in what is presumed to be the film's "first" world – on which the threat of disintegration weighs. This world would actually vanish, if Cobb managed to return to "reality".[72] In this deserted town, the skyscrapers along the coast crumble and the cityscape turns into ruins, like the fragments of a memory doomed to dissolve into oblivion (Fig. 12). The actual historical context of the "collapse" of private property, following the subprime mortgage crisis, had certainly something to do with the film's narrative argument and the idea to have its protagonists furnish and populate a deserted city-world. Yet, through the ground zero of a metropolis modeled after the (male) subject's cerebral activity, the fear of losing one's own self in a labyrinth of worlds arises, crossing a point of no return for Cobb (attracted as he is by the voice of a siren) that signals the eventual, permanent loss of Mal.

The embedding of worlds in *Inception* follows a vertical skyscraper-like axis. These worlds are not strictly speaking "*parallel*" (even if the principle of alternation, discussed in Chapter 4, plays a structuring role), but arranged in a vertical hierarchy, a superposition that forms a virtual spatialization. Consequently, the film's story follows the "descent into hell" pattern. The post-apocalyptic urban setting, which is actually the most intimate refuge of the creator of worlds, constitutes the "lowest" level in a film that elevates the motif of the "fall" into an aesthetic and narrative principle. The collapsing buildings correspond to the fall of Mal's body, as she throws herself into the void, as well as to a lapse of rational thinking, deluded as it is by the virtualities at its disposal. Purposely, the characters in *Inception* manage their immersion into a different world through the mastery of a calculated fall (a vehicle plunging from a bridge) and a state of weightlessness.

In contrast to a pre-9/11 movie like *Fight Club* (1999), the convoluted narrative journey of the main characters in *Next*, *Deja Vu*, *Source Code* or *Inception* aims to

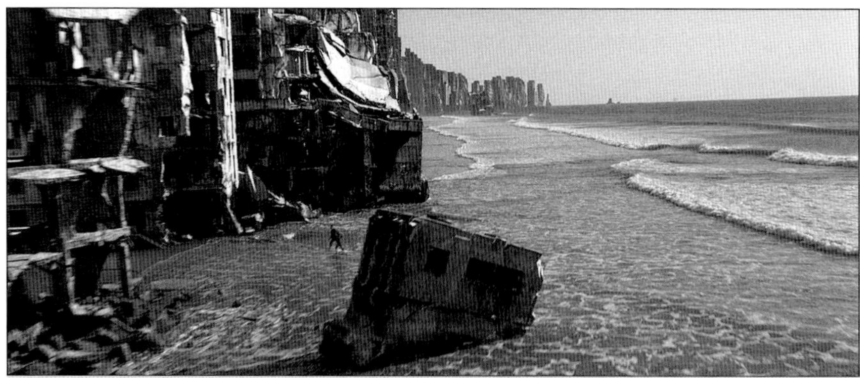

Fig. 12: Out of the ocean and into the Self: the ruins of a world as an inner refuge for Cobb (Leonardo DiCaprio) in *Inception*.

provide the appropriate conditions for the creation of a world in which a terrorist attack can be prevented. This ideology is revisionist, in the most literal sense of the wor(l)d: through some sort of narrative sleight of hand, a disaster is retrospectively averted. It is as if cinema inherited the special power of the fictitious technology found in *Minority Report*, Steven Spielberg's adaptation of a Philip K. Dick sci-fi short story (released a year after the September 11 attacks), which features an interactive visual dispositive similar to some of the most recent video game interfaces. However, unlike Dick's dystopian universe, the relationship to technology in these films is reassuringly positive, encouraging, in the aftermath of 9/11, a process of emotional purging of the collective trauma.

Effects of (Pseudo-)Complex Storytelling on Worldbuilding

Far from the shores of the science fiction genre, the path of a labyrinthine story, requiring an increased audience involvement, has long been explored by arthouse movies, ostensibly against the norms of Hollywood storytelling. To name a few examples of such multiverse films: Alain Resnais' *Last Year at Marienbad* (1961), Jacques Rivette's *Celine and Julie Go Boating* (1974), Raúl Ruiz's *Three Lives and Only One Death* (1996), or David Lynch's *Mulholland Dr.* (2001) and *Inland Empire* (2006).

Assuredly, time travel generated, even in films as mainstream as the "*Back to the Future*" trilogy (1985–1990), certain complications in terms of their world, since the abolition of cause-and-effect links creates a paradox defiant of our casual logic, as *Looper* (2012) or *Predestination* (2014) clearly illustrate. In the original *Back to the Future*, the image of Marty McFly (Michael J. Fox) gradually disappears from a photograph, as he interferes in the relationship between his future progenitors in a way that could lead to his never being born – in other words, a subtractive operation is being carried out in the film's original world (the hero never actually dies; he has simply never existed).[73] In the final scene in the director's cut version of *The Butterfly Effect* (2004), the hero, after having explored a large number of possibilities whose outcome proved systematically harmful to his loved ones, chooses, via his predictive knowledge, to sacrifice himself (like the main character in *Donnie Darko*, 2001) by preventing his own birth. Watching a home movie, Evan projects himself back to the time he was still in his mother's womb and strangles himself with the umbilical cord. Successively, through a combination of *chaos theory* and time travel, *The Butterfly Effect* presents different states of the same world (a case of an *alternate storyworld*, according to my typology). The multiverse exists exclusively for the protagonist and the viewer, since they are the only ones to witness all the consequences of the narrative bifurcations resulting from the time travel. Significantly though, in one particular scene, a doctor mentions the notion of "alternate *worlds*", as he explains why, according to him, an intrusive time travel is impossible. In a book devoted to a group of stories using the time travel leitmotif, David Wittenberg remarks: "Contemporary time travel fiction continues to affirm its link to theoretical physics, especially multiverse models and theories" (Wittenberg 2013: 219). While some time travel movies are obviously more fantasy-based (*Time Bandits*, 1981), most of these films are rooted in scientific theories and depict technologies resembling "worldbuilding machines".[74]

As we have already seen, *Source Code* borrows its narrative argument from quantum physics, pushing this idea to the limit by completely suspending the temporal dimension. Furthermore, Duncan Jones' film repeats the same action loop that circumscribes a specific spatiotemporal segment, repeatedly explored (at a time when digital technology encourages this type of audio-visual content, as in the trend of animated GIFs on the Internet)[75]. The narration often seems to stand still or introduces only slight variations (as in Netflix's *Russian Doll* series, released in 2019), until the hero – a victim of his environment, though still able to accumulate additional knowledge through the reiterations – manages to escape the loop. David Wittenberg calls this type of film "closed loop stories" and specifically mentions *Triangle* (2009) and a subplot from *Lost* (Wittenberg 2013: 81–82). It should be noted however that there are many other examples to be found, coming from different countries[76] or attached to different genres (as for example the horror movie *Happy Death Day 2U*, 2019, or the comedy *Christmas Do-Over*, 2006). Even though these films do not feature a sci-fi machine similar to those of *Deja Vu* or *ARQ* (2016), they do not simply offer different points of view of the same world, but alternative versions of a world seen through the eyes of one character. This may occur exceptionally in only one scene, as in the beginning of *Edge of Tomorrow*, or in the entire film, as in the case of *Arrival* (2016). The notions of *world* and *story* can be considered separately on a theoretical level. However, it is the quest for narrative innovations, explored nowadays also in the field of mainstream cinema,[77] that actually leads the process of worldbuilding to a substantial growth.

For the past twenty years or so, both Hollywood and the so-called "independent" studios have produced movies with extremely complex screenplays. Following the lucrative "*Matrix*" franchise, the plots of these films are sometimes conceived against a backdrop of theoretical bric-a-brac (Marshall McLuhan's reflections on media, Baudrillard's simulacrum, cyberculture, quantum physics, etc.). Justifiably, one can argue that this practice actually exploits, within a certain sector of the public, the surplus value generated by the cultural legitimacy of such references, or simply provides captivating narratives at a time when the narrative *twist* had been imposing itself as an economically viable formula, especially after the success of *Fight Club* (1999) and *The Sixth Sense* (1999). Still, this was also the era of Quentin Tarantino's *Pulp Fiction* (1994), which demonstrated the profitability of films with exploding narratives,[78] *Groundhog Day* (1993), a contributor in the expanding practice of unfolding narrative alternatives, *The Usual Suspects* (1995), which popularized the presence of an unreliable narrator, *The Truman Show* (1998), which plunged viewers into an *artificial world* under surveillance, and *Forrest Gump* (1994) with its design of visual heterogeneity.

In 1998–1999, parallel to the films of David Fincher and M. Night Shyamalan, *Pleasantville*, *Being John Malkovich*, *Arlington Road* and *Virtual Sexuality* hit the theaters, as well as the cyberpunk quartet *Dark City*, *The Thirteenth Floor*, *The Matrix* and *eXistenZ* (see Chapter 5). At the end of a decade that saw the expansion of CGI in cinema and the first days of an ongoing competition between the film and video game industries, stories emanating from a splitting up of worlds were met with enthusiasm. Sometimes, these plots produce a "trompe-l'oeil" effect on the viewer (Ledoux 2012), as one realizes, rather late in the film, that the world in which he has been immersed, does not correspond to what is supposed to be the "reality" within the fiction. Given the keen interest in this type of subject matter, it comes as no surprise that Philip K. Dick's stories, published in the 1960s and the 1970s, passed in the last few decades through the mill of Hollywood's script departments. Eight of his short stories were adapted to the screen between 2002 and 2012, including *A Scanner Darkly* (2006), a movie shot digitally as a live-action film and then transferred into animation using a technique called "interpolated rotoscope". Films like *Paycheck* (2003) or *The Adjustment Bureau* (2011) reactivated the fashionable in the 1970s conspiracy-thriller genre, transposing it into the field of science fiction. As such, they are a part of a group of movies based on the discovery of a hidden world by a hero who manages to escape the illusive power of an alienating representation. Never has the Hollywood *persona* known as many doubles, avatars, or clones as in the era of the pixel. These "end of the century" movies are imbued with schizophrenia and paranoia, while imagining, as *Fight Club* clearly demonstrated, the vanishing of our "world".

Philip K. Dick's pessimistic tales owe their popularity to the ingenuous orchestration of a paranoid confrontation between their main character and a reality constructed from scratch, organized around him (sometimes by his own hand, without him realizing it) and/or implanted into him. In this type of narrative, the line separating the inside from the outside becomes thinner. Examples of this pattern include *Jacob's Ladder* (1990), *Shutter Island* (2010), and more recently, *Joker* (2019) (see Chapter 3, section "*Mental Worlds*"). In all of these films, the main character's inner world is materialized on the screen, but it is not until the final twist that the viewer realizes the true nature of these images. In some cases (*Vanilla Sky*, *The Cell*, *The Jacket*, *Eternal Sunshine of the Spotless Mind*, *The Imaginarium of Doctor Parnassus*, *Repo Men*, to name a few), the subject's introspection is remote-controlled by a technology (or at least a device that gives access to another world), resembling the worldbuilding machines found in *Deja Vu* and *Source Code*. These films explicitly deal with the process of worldbuilding due to plots that are inspired from scientific theories (or perhaps speculations) advanced during the second half of the 20th century, following Einstein's theory of relativity. Fiction thus joins the counterfactuality of quantum physics, which serves as a basis for the paradox illustrated by Schrödinger's cat experiment: contradiction transmutes into superposition, as the cat is simultaneously alive *and* dead, before the box opens and the actual state is externally observed. In his discussion of this experiment, Hugh Everett III postulates the coexistence of different mental states on the part of the observer, following the logic of the quantum theory.

The popularized content of this theoretical research will inspire, explicitly or implicitly, storytelling in cinema and television. For instance, the character played by Dominic Monaghan in *Flashforward* (2009–2010), a series scripted by David S. Goyer (one of *Dark City*'s screenwriters and Jonathan Nolan's occasional collaborator), explains Schrödinger's cat experiment to a young woman he met on the train, in the prologue of episode six (2009). This pre-credits sequence is structured by a crosscutting that builds suspense with regards to the survival of another character. The scientific reference raises the question of narrative alternatives that arises for every character of this one-season TV series. Each of them is asked to choose among the possibilities induced by a brief vision of their future that appears to them during a global blackout, a phenomenon seemingly related to an experiment conducted by physicists. The same holds for the main character in the science fiction film *Repo Men* (2010), played by Jude Law, who also describes Schrödinger's experiment (without mentioning the scientist's name) in a prologue that echoes the final part of the movie, understood retrospectively by the viewer as an immersion in the hero's imagination. The protagonist, unbeknownst to him, is connected to an artificial neural network, manufactured by the biotech company he works for, specialized in organ transplantation.

Bryce DeWitt will later reinterpret Schrödinger's hypothesis in terms of parallel universes, whose number grows indefinitely at each bifurcation performed by any given individual. DeWitt's conception met with a certain degree of success, more in the field of cosmology than in that of physics. This type of scientific theory shares a lot with science fiction plots, except that in DeWitt's case "the various branches of the wave function are globally incapable of interfering with each other and, consequently, the different universes cannot interact" (Lepeltier 2010: 116)[*]. Yet, most science fiction stories are specifically based on this type of "inter-action".

The most characteristic filmography of narrative exploitation of hypotheses formulated by philosophers or physicists is undoubtedly Christopher Nolan's. The theory of relativity seems to have inspired some of the contemporary blockbusters he has directed and (co-)written. These films combine an unprecedented narrative complexity (their story pitch being almost meta-narrative) with spectacular action sequences that succeed one another at a sustained pace. These scenes manage to combine a self-reflexive take on the film medium with a strong viewer immersion into the diegesis.[79] According to Todd McGowan, "the speculative basis of fiction leads directors like Nolan, whether they aim to or not, to wade into philosophical waters" (McGowan 2016). Such implications result from strategic choices made during the composition of a fictional story, which are based on a number of theoretically considered paradoxes, especially those studied by quantum mechanics researchers.

This attitude permeates Nolan's movies even if the filmmaker remains primarily concerned with the consequences such postulates can have on the representation of temporality. The emphasis on worldbuilding – most obvious in the case of *Inception*, where the protagonist hires an architect to build the world of a shared dream in which his team intends to trap the dreamer[80] – generally tends to privilege monstration over action. Some of these films are scripted by the director's brother, Jonathan Nolan (who is also one of *Westworld*'s showrunners, a TV series that, I shall argue, is eminently world-centered). In these movies, temporality becomes an important aspect of the definition of each of the "worlds". Therefore, the exposition of the features attributed to these worlds, and the mutual relation between them, is incorporated into the action. Time appears as relative and, consequently, the world – on a collective and global scale often close to its end – is fluctuating. *Inception* and *Interstellar* alternate narrative tracks where diegetic time does not unfold at the same rhythm. The on-screen actions are not accelerated, but their speed is relative. In other words, viewers perceive it in comparison with the speed in other levels (*Inception*) or spaces (*Interstellar*) with which these actions interact, notably through the use of telecommunication means that frequently guarantee the mutual accessibility between different worlds in multiverse fictions (as the telephone and the walkie-talkies in *Stranger Things*).

These plots often feature characters of scientists (also the case in Denis Villeneuve's *Arrival*) and capitalize on temporal paradoxes observed on a theoretical level in quantum physics or general relativity. The hypotheses on black holes, formulated in *Interstellar*, certainly echo the "Event Horizon Element" telescope (the results of which were not released to the media until April 2019), but they also summon the Penrose-Hawking Singularity Theorems. The characters of *Tenet*, whose world is threatened by a future generation, discuss the "grandfather paradox". The passage from one world to another – or, more accurately, the shift from reality to a world dreamed by a subject to which others are connected through a worldbuilding machine integrated in a strange, silver suitcase with tubes attached to their wrists (*Inception*), the intersection between the two worlds (the library in *Interstellar*), or the meeting of characters and their doubles from the near future within the same space-time continuum (*Tenet*) (Fig. 13) – is justified by the leitmotif of the Time Travel Machine. These movies do not really deal with a multiverse but with the simultaneous co-presence of temporal strata of the same world, encountered in variable states. However, it befalls to the character of Neil (Robert Pattinson) in *Tenet*, the hero's guardian angel, intervening like a *deus ex machina* at key moments,[81] to speak words like these: "In parallel worlds theory, we can't know the relationship between consciousness and multiple realities".

Tenet (2020) echoes more specifically the numerous quantum physicists "who explained the laws of entropy by reference to playing films in reverse" (Canales 2015: 290). Neil, whose only mention of the future is limited to the viewpoint of scientists (a researcher who decided to fragment the algorithm and hide its sections is compared to Oppenheimer at the time of the Manhattan project), indicates that he has a degree in quantum physics, as if this educational background were a prerequisite in order to carry out his mission. *Tenet*'s heroes, with the threat of the end of the world weighing on them by a future society (not unlike *Interstellar* where, as it turns out, a wormhole is created by future humans), must secure that the inversion impacting certain objects inside the world[82] will not extend to the world itself, for that would seal its fate for good. The "world's savior", played by John David Washington, is informed by deputy Wheeler, as she briefly summarizes the rules one has to respect inside the "inverted world": "Gravity will feel normal but appear reverse for the world around you. […] *You* are inverted, the world is not". Having received this skimpy information,[83] the hero enters for the first time into the inverting machine (actually a simple turnstile), which will introduce within the same room, divided by a glass partition,[84] two different versions of himself, each involved in an action vectorized in a different direction.

However, the dissociation between the individual (the subject of a story) and the world, will be blurred later on. As the film's espionage plot gradually unfolds, the Protagonist realizes that the supreme risk is that of a generalized entropy, caused by the activation of "The Algorithm": "Inversion. But not objects or people. The world around us. […] And the algorithm […] can invert the entropy of the world. End of play. Everyone and everything that's ever lived, destroyed. Instantly." In other words, for the action film to exist, the

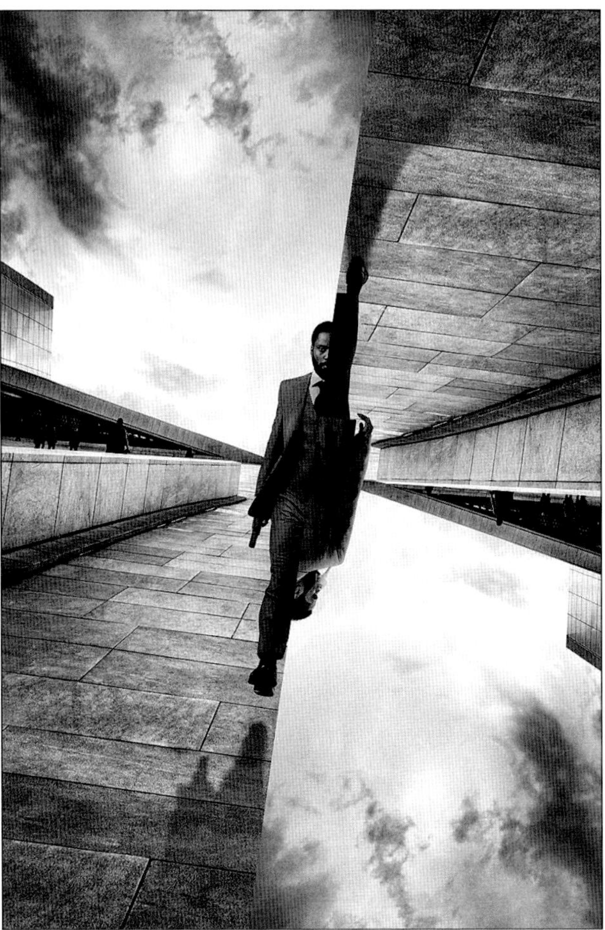

Fig. 13: Christopher Nolan's *Tenet*: the coexistence of two ways to perceive the world on a temporal level.

hero's quest must consist precisely in limiting the narrative principle of the inversion to specific components of the world (the characters or the instruments they use in their actions), and not to the world itself. This limitation allows the viewer to follow a James Bond-like plot (at least until the film's palindrome structure, signified by its enigmatic title, finally asserts itself), as the enemies collect the nine sections of "the Algorithm", a typical Hitchockian "McGuffin". However, this linear path will be later invalidated by the time loop. The protagonists must prevent "the world" from being struck by entropy, in other words a Third World War that would lead to the Apocalypse.

Tenet reactivates a pattern used in "*The Terminator*" series: in the beginning of the second episode, the mechanical arm of the T-800 robot serves as a testimony of a future technology, just like the objects with reverse entropy in *Tenet*, preserved by secret service scientists. Furthermore, the "*Terminator*" franchise offers an *alternate (story)world* to the alternating narrative (the result of a time travel inside the fiction) with its *Terminator Genisys* reboot (2015). Contemporary serial practices play with "time loops", like the one employed in *Tenet*, a film whose story seemingly aims to profit from the public's familiarity with prequels, interquels and reboots appearing within a given franchise.[85]

Through intense physical action and state-of-the-art gadgets that guarantee an impressive spectacle, the hero gains mastery over the laws governing the coexistence between worlds, differentiated by the chronological vectors of their actions and the point from which the inversion is initiated. Following his opponent, Sator (Kenneth Branagh), who at the beginning of the film is the only one to possess this skill, the hero crosses portals arranged in turnstile gates[86] and enters the film's main plot line, only to cruise it in the opposite direction at various instances.[87] As a result, the frequency of the narrative becomes repetitive, according to Gérard Genette's typology: the same action is shown a second time, from a different point of view, attributed to the same character, albeit in a version of him evolving in a different temporal stratum. The crosscutting between the briefings of each of the two teams (the first one progressing in a linear way, the second one moving backwards from the future), just before the attack on the facilities hosting the bomb's hypocenter, implies both a simultaneity and a cognitive gain, as we profit from the things learned by those who move backwards in time. The editing pattern of crosscutting is a recurring figure in multiverse movies, as I shall argue in Chapter 4.

The portal in *Tenet* does not introduce a spatial discontinuity, as in the Sci-Fi Channel miniseries *The Lost Room* (2006), *The Adjustment Bureau* (2011),[88] or in plots including heroes endowed with teleportation powers (*Jumper, Watchmen, Doctor Strange*, etc.). The same places, hosting the exact same actions, are crossed twice, but *differently*. By showing the Protagonist both in the present and in the future, *Tenet* reiterates a recurring leitmotif in Nolan's filmography, namely the duplication of the Self. This pattern is also present in *Interstellar*, linked to the temporal paradox, and in *The Prestige*, where the strange machine invented by Tesla uses electricity to produce a clone, while the hero's enemy conceals the existence of a twin brother. On account of the multiplication of its characters, confronted with their doubles, *Tenet* gives the impression of a multiverse. Nevertheless, seen from the characters' perspective, the film is actually reduced to a two-world universe, since there are only two possible directions: moving forward or backwards (even if a "temporal pincer" may be included in a larger pincer, multiplying thus the possible bifurcations).

The extent to which *Tenet*'s inversion concerns worldbuilding can be understood through a comparison with Nolan's second feature film, *Memento* (2000), which recounts in reverse the story of a character suffering from short-term memory loss. This film reverses the order of scenes that are actually linear. There is one exception, that of the opening sequence which runs backwards and uses a shot showing a bullet exiting its target and returning to the barrel of the gun – a visual motif also present in *Tenet* (and in the opening credits from *Resident Evil: Retribution*). Whereas *Memento* merely plays with the sequential order of the narrative in its segments shot in color,[89] *Tenet* attributes a decisive role to the spatial dimension, in which two different modes of representing the action converge, as well as two opposing definitions of the objects of the world and the physical laws moving them. As such, Nolan's film can be compared to an episode from the *Sliders* series ("As Time Goes By", S02E13),[90] in which a university professor, specialized in ontology, comes to the conclusion that on the alternative planet Earth visited by the heroes, "we are going backwards in a world that is going forwards. Or rather, vice-versa". From this observation, he deduces that, in this *parallel world*, Hawking's singularity theorem proves to be correct. The chronological order is indeed reversed in this planet, unbeknownst to its inhabitants. Only the series' main characters, as they are coming from another world, are able to notice this inversion, jumping back in time and experiencing a discontinuity among scenes that move backwards: the episode starts with a life imprisonment penalty, goes to the trial, and ends with the attempted murder. *Tenet* experiments with the narrative so as to better impose a world-centered logic, while never actually leaving our world or the present, since the enemies from the future that hope to regenerate their world by annihilating ours, are never really shown on the screen. The structuring parallelism is actually confined within this present. Unlike the *Sliders* episode commented above, where the environment surrounding the characters freezes and vacillates every time they jump back in time, or *Memento*, where linear scenes in black & white alternate with sequences filmed in color, *Tenet* deals with a temporal inversion that is completely simultaneous with our standard temporality.

Tenet's spatialization of time, as the present and the future coexist side by side within the same space, as well as its representation of transition points, are in fact commonplace in multiverse movies. Nolan's films add to the plot-character couple the notion of the "world", whose ontology is jeopardized inside the diegesis. Scenes running backwards – an effect that, as I have already shown, dates back to the early days of cinema – generate a sense of unsettling strangeness. This effect, also used in David Lynch's *Twin Peaks* even at the level of speech, establishes an increasing hesitancy as to the degree of reality attributed to the fictional world.

In the near future of *Interstellar*, humanity is nearing extinction after having exhausted most of the Earth's resources. Society is governed by a domination of "soft" human sciences over hard sciences, in a reversal of the power relationship historically established since, at least, the Second World War. In the film's world, space conquest is met with derision, forcing NASA to operate underground. A classroom scene clarifies that, according to the official history accepted by all educated people, the moon landing was actually staged by the government, as in the conspiracy thriller *Capricorn One* (1977). The character serving as the film's main focal point is an astronaut (Matthew McConaughey) who, unjustly victimized by his social environment, goes up against the inaccurate statements of the intellectual class. As *Interstellar* is also inspired by the twin paradox that arises from the theory of special relativity,[91] this reversal advanced by Nolan's science fiction speculation can be related to the "debate that changed our understanding of time" between Albert Einstein and Henri Bergson, initiated in 1922. This phrase is used in the full title of Jimena Canales' book, *The Physicist and the Philosopher*, which rehabilitates, from a history of science standpoint, the impact of the ideas advanced by the French philosopher on many of his contemporaries, at a time when the primacy of hard science over philosophy was by no means as evident as it is today. Nolan's film takes undoubtedly the side of Einstein, even though it does not fail to raise certain ethical and social concerns related to projects kept secret by NASA's top scientist, Prof. Brand (Michael Caine). The case of *Interstellar* is revealing of the way screenwriters currently use the principles of quantum physics in order to nourish and legitimize an undeniable narrative complexity.

Spread more than half a century ago, these scientific theories are today increasingly popular among mainstream fictional films that require significant financial investments. This evolution is undoubtedly related to the fact that screenwriters can rely on a public accustomed to worldbuilding.[92] TV shows,[93] franchises and their reboots, pre- or inter-quels, as well as their transmedia variations, imposing on audiences a sophisticated intellectual exercise, have indeed met with a considerable success in recent years. Transferring a fictional character into a completely different spatiotemporal context is a narrative and financial strategy customary in our era, condoning the consumption of media products (and vice-versa, in particular through what is known as "fandoms"). Thanks to franchises such as "*Star Trek*" or the "*Star Wars*" series,[94] as well as to the "Marvel Cinematic Universe", the science fiction genre has become a privileged venue for such a narrative complexity, reinforced by the leitmotif of characters travelling into Deep Space, in time, or through other "dimensions". This essay will focus on this particular genre for reasons developed and explained in the following chapter.

Endnotes

1. I borrow the term "Fantasy Fiction" from Besson (2021). It refers to an all-encompassing notion designating a set of popular genres, not restricted to the unique case of (heroic) fantasy. It also includes science fiction, horror, as well as the *fantastique*, a well-known genre in French literary and film theory whose distinctive feature is the intrusion of supernatural phenomena into an otherwise realistic narrative. (see infra Chapter 3, "*Supernatural Worlds*")
2. Wolf's understanding of the concept of fiction is determined by his attachment to the field of game studies.
3. In fact, all post-apocalyptic films present a different world, speculated from the real one.
4. From Wolf's standpoint, whether one refers to the novel or to its screen adaptation, the nature of the "world" remains the same.
5. In his glossary, Wolf defines "completeness" as "the degree to which an imaginary world has all the necessary elements needed to be considered feasible, with enough detail present such that the audience can answer questions about the world", while "consistency" refers to "the degree to which world details support each other without contradiction" (Wolf 2012: 376).
6. Teenagers form a particularly receptive audience when it comes to multiverses, as these are regularly present in youth literature and the fantasy genre. Commenting on young adult literary fiction, Laurent Bazin remarked: "There is a reason why popular opinion qualifies adolescence as the age when everything seems possible [...]. A transitional period, adolescence is experienced in a state of cognitive dislocation: on the one hand, the awareness of the impossibility to objectify all potential phenomena by external coordinates (the world

turns without me); on the other hand, the temptation to extend the childhood's *origo* (the world stems from me). One way to overcome this disruptive tension is to perform the shift between these viewpoints by reliving in a projective mode the dialectical interaction between intimacy and otherness. It is therefore no coincidence that this type of literature is obsessed with the theme of traveling between different universes" (Bazin 2019: 62)*.

7. While in the passenger seat of a car, Casey (Britt Robertson) finds herself abruptly and momentarily suspended in the air, over a field, before she touches the magic pin that makes her shift between worlds. This scene from *Tomorrowland* is characteristic of the increasing dissociation in the digital era between figure and background, in other words between a film character and the world he inhabits.
8. While Carlos has actually more lines in the final film than in the original script, the term "world-building" was already present in the latter (see page 16 of the screenplay, available on https://www.story24.film/screenplays/la-la-land.pdf).
9. Notice the intertextual reference of having the character of Carlo played by Jason Fuchs, screenwriter of two family movies, *Ice Age: Continental Drift* (2012) and *Pan* (2015).
10. *La La Land*'s story concentrates on the conflict between the artist's struggle for self-fulfillment and the compromises forced upon him/her by the entertainment industry. Several loans from the genre of the backstage musical and a number of subjective dreamlike song-and-dance scenes grant the film with a world-centered perspective, even if this is clearly not a case of a multiverse. The lyrics from the song "Another Day of Sun", heard during the film's opening sequence, speak of the dreams evoked by the screen as a "Technicolor world made out of music and machine". A few seconds earlier, the "Technicolor" logo switches from black & white to color, and from 1:33 to a scope aspect ratio, plunging us into "another" world, as in certain second worlds discussed later in the book.
11. *La La Land* is co-produced by Gilbert Film, a company responsible for the multiverse TV series *Counterpart*, released in the following year. The main character in this series is played by J.K. Simmons, who has a small role in Chazelle's movie too.
12. "In real life, we are born into a world that already exists, and we must adapt to it. But in good stories, the characters come first, and the writer designs the world to be an infinitely detailed manifestation of those characters." (Truby 2007: 145).
13. The opposition between "words/narration" and "world/images" prevents Truby from discussing the semantic dimension of worldbuilding. In fact, the words themselves, including those used in dialogues, participate in the construction of the film's world(s). For a more nuanced conception of this semiotic question, see our references to Group μ (Chapter 4).
14. A parallel can be drawn between *Counterpart*'s Season 1 finale and the ending of HBO's *Westworld* series. In the latter, the female android Maeve plans to flee the theme park by taking the subway; however, putting her maternal love above everything else, according to the priorities she was programmed for in the first place, she finally returns to the park's facilities.
15. A subtle connection between these two series is also established by the presence of the actress Nazanin Boniadi, playing an undercover agent named Clare (alias "Shadow") in *Counterpart*, as well as the CIA analyst Fara Sherazi in Seasons 3 and 4 of *Homeland* (2013–2014). Clare is torn between the subterfuge resulting from the usurpation of the identity of the original Clare from the first world (whom she murdered) and a sincere maternal affection for her daughter. In this respect, she is very much like the character of Charlotte Elisabeth Hale (Tessa Thompson) in Season 3 of *Westworld*, replaced at the moment of her death by a "host" (i.e. an android created by the same technology used in the Westworld theme park). These similarities are a direct result of the narrative exploitation of a two-world configuration by both of these series.
16. In fact, just like in *Person of Interest*, there was initially a pair of inventors working on new technologies, before a clash ended their collaboration: Ford shall live with the guilt of Arnold's death. In Season 3 of *Westworld*, the same happens with the computer scientist played by Vincent Cassel, who is forced to go separate ways with his brother.
17. Since the films I examine in this essay make ample use of CGI, they are in fact only partially composed of live-action scenes. That said, I have excluded from this study films with no live-action scenes at all, namely animation movies. However, films produced by Pixar or Dreamworks Animation Studios, tend to create multiverses destined for children, as for

example in *Wreck-it Ralph* (2012), *Monsters, Inc.* (2001) or *The Boss Baby* (2017). Significantly, in the last two examples, the other world is represented as a vast, highly organized factory, based on a mechanized, assembly-line production work from which the heroes inside the fiction have to emancipate themselves. Even more than live-action films, animated movies adopt completely different graphic styles in order to distinguish between two worlds. This is the case of the characters living in the young girl's brain in *Inside Out* (2015), where the inside of the human body is transformed into a world, as in *Innerspace* (1987). The realistic depiction of the outside world, which imitates the style of hand-held shots, contrasts the inner world, which appears far more artificial in terms of colors, lights, and 3D rendering. The latter's representation emulates the classic style of the studio era, with its carefully constructed framings and dolly shots. For this film, Pixar went as far as to model virtual camera lenses after real ones, using different types for each of the two worlds that appear alternately on the screen (an interweaving between them occurs, when the Five Emotions from the control center of the inside world view several of the girl's memories). In *Soul* (2020), the real world and the after-life are distinguished thanks to the use of 3D technology for the first world and a very stylized, abstract painting-like 2D image for the second one (a technique already used in *Coraline*, 2009). In the rest of this book, I will only deal with animated scenes only when used to portray a world that is *parallel* to a different one, filmed in live-action scenes, as in *The Congress* (see Chapter 4).

18. The expression "cinema of attractions" was popularized in an article by Tom Gunning on early cinema. The author briefly mentioned the recent resurgence of this regime of film consumption with regards to the "cinema of effects made by the Spielberg-Lucas-Coppola trio" (Gunning 2009: 65). The expression is now commonly used to describe contemporary movies (see for example Strauven 2006).

19. For instance, the video game *L.A. Noire* (2011) plunges its users into a film noir world (without the distancing effect established by a film like *Dark City*).

20. The resulting description of the video game's world is not always exempt of narrative function, as every situation is explained through ancestral tales that nourish the mythological dimension of *Mass Effect*'s universe.

21. The periodization proposed by Alexis Blanchet in *Des Pixels à Hollywood* is based on economic criteria linked to Hollywood's investment strategies in the video game industry. However, it also breaks down historical "sequences" in terms of adaptation practices. Passing from a movie reference encapsulated in the graphic design of a machine at the time of arcade games (1976–1984) to recent video games that inherit a film's diegesis, the distance covered is noteworthy. According to Blanchet, the expansion of computer graphics in film productions from the mid-1990s onwards has boosted the transferring of worlds, since the same software is used by both media during the creative process (Blanchet 2010: 376–377).

22. The term "reboot" designates a practice in serial fiction that aims to restart a specific series, after the release of several episodes, on the basis of similar diegetic data but through the development of new stories. Therefore, it postulates a differentiation between world and story, the latter being in such cases subordinate to the former.

23. *Thor* (2011) brings together the human race and the "gods" inhabiting other worlds (ice giants, the kingdom of Asgard). The abysmal spatial distance separating them from our world tends to imply in the imaginary representations related to Nordic mythology – treated here in a humorous, distant way – an ontological difference. The worlds are connected through a tube of light whose portal is located outside the city, at the end of a suspension bridge over the ocean. The tube dematerializes the traveler in a way similar to *TRON* (though in that case the second world is *virtual*). Therefore, it constitutes a "worldbuilding machine": the supernatural, mythological "Bifröst" (rainbow) is depicted here as a canon. Its activation comes with sound effects that clearly connote an operation of a technical nature (mechanical creaking, electrical crackling). The "*Hellboy*" series (2004, 2008), the "*Thor*" series, and the fictions featuring the character of Dr. Strange, form a group of superhero movies where the world-centered issues, typical of comic books drawn by Jack Kirby, acquire great importance.

24. This hybridity takes a literal form in some of the films studied in Chapter 4, alternating between live-action and animated scenes.

25. See for example *Godzilla* (1998 and 2014), *The Avengers* (2012), "*Transformers*" (2007–2017), *Pacific Rim* (2013 and 2018), or *Rampage* (2018).
26. See for instance the opposition between reality and the Quantum Realm in *Ant-Man and the Wasp* (2018).
27. This world-centered feature has become so common in the superhero movie genre that Mysterio (Jake Gyllenhaal) in *Spider-Man: Far From Home* (2019) tricks Peter Parker (Tom Holland) into believing he comes from a parallel Earth. The young protagonist is all the more easily fooled due to his enthusiasm for quantum physics, viewed as a sign of immaturity. In fact, Mysterio has no superpowers at all. He only uses a technology based on an army of drones to produce an illusionistic holographic representation. The *parallel world* is actually an *artificial* one, produced inside the diegesis by a "worldbuilding machine" that exaggerates the potentials of CGI moviemaking.
28. Despite such visual extravaganzas and their ostensibly "supernatural" character, the principle of credibility persists in Hollywood. This is true even for movies conceived as a pastiche or a parody, such as *Mars Attacks!* (1996) and *Men in Black* (1997), or those that develop a critical vision of society (*Starship Troopers*, 1997), as they also use special effects whose technical perfection guarantees their invisibility.
29. This practice is far from being new. Think of the films recounting the duel between popular horror characters (such as *Dracula vs. Frankenstein*, 1971), especially those from the 1930s horror movies that Universal Pictures recently tried to revive as a single world, called the "Dark Universe". Its development was however cancelled following the commercial failure of *The Mummy* (2017). After a number of productions targeted at fans of genre movies and gamers/film buffs (*Freddy vs. Jason*, 2003; *Alien vs. Predator*, 2004 and 2007), *The Avengers* marks the expansion of the crossover logic into blockbuster production, highlighting the world-centered dimension of these films, by merging several worlds into one and by having its story partly shaped after the "war of the worlds" pattern.
30. Transfictionality is a "machine for travelling through the intertext" (Saint-Gelais 2011: 55)[*], meaning "the case where at least two texts, whether by the same author or not, relate jointly to the same fiction, by using its characters, by extending a previous plot, or by sharing a fictional universe" (*Ibid.*: 7).
31. My comments on the case of Japan owe a great deal to the work of David Javet who wrote a thesis under my co-supervision at the University of Lausanne (along with that of Samuel Guex from the Department of Japanese Studies at the University of Geneva), defended in December 2020, on science fiction in Japanese media productions.
32. This number does not include the various US re-releases and cuts (even if they use a different title). It is based on the official filmography established by Toho regarding the live-action Godzilla movies: https://godzilla.com/filmography/.
33. David Kalat estimates at 150 million dollars the amount of revenue generated by the merchandising of products related to the seven films of the "Godzilla" franchise between 1984 and 1995 (Kalat 2017: 214, quoted in Javet 2020: 184).
34. Roland Emmerich's *Godzilla*, released in 1998 (two years before the success of *X-Men*, which would lead to a surge in the franchise logic of comic books' screen adaptations), was an independent production, conceived as a stand-alone film, and not as a component of a franchise.
35. On the genealogy ties between these "new" technologies and the various uses of telephony, as well as its film representations, see Boillat 2019a.
36. Before directing the first film in the "*Resident Evil*" series in 2002 and then writing the screenplay for the next five episodes, Paul W.S. Anderson made *Mortal Kombat* (1995), another screen adaptation of a very popular video game franchise developed by Midway as a competitor to Capcom's *Street Fighter* series. The battle scenes in *Mortal Kombat* are designed in an environment that underlines the film's world-centered dimension: an island plays the role of an intermediate space and the three heroes are transported in a *parallel world* named the "Outworld". The "*Resident Evil*" series' uniqueness lies in that in all episodes, released over a fourteen-year period, the protagonist that gets to showcase her action skills is a woman.
37. For instance, the opening scene in *Resident Evil: Retribution* is a faithful retake of the previous installment's final scene, shown in reverse and in slow motion.

38. One can quote here *Resident Evil: Afterlife* (2010), a film that begins with the line "My name is Alice …", pronounced in a voice-over. Another example would be the prologue from *Resident Evil: Retribution* in which the same character, appearing in a "screen within a screen" (an inaugural displaying of audio-visual technology reminiscent of the film's trailer), is recounting to *us* the main events of the previous episodes.
39. The phrase "*This is my* world", which postulates the world's ontology and brings it to the present, is in effect composed of a possessive pronoun ("my", an extension of "I") and a demonstrative pronoun belonging to the *discursive* level according to Émile Benveniste's theory, meaning that they inscribe a "subjectivity" (in the linguistic, enunciative sense of the term) in the statement (*énoncé*): "The personal pronouns provide the first step in this bringing out of subjectivity in language. Other classes of pronouns that share the same status depend in their turn upon these pronouns. These other classes are the indicators of *deixis*, the demonstratives, adverbs, and adjectives, which organize the spatial and temporal relationships around the 'subject' taken as a referent: 'this, here, now,' and their numerous correlatives […]"(Benveniste 1971: 226) Here, the *discursive* regime can be explained by the trailer's special status, taking as its object images different from the ones it designates and presents, and from the mirroring effect of the "frame within the frame" process that temporarily establishes the visualized world's subordination to the "diegetic" verbal enunciator. The interpellation regime (see Casetti 1986), associated with a reference to *deixis* (and underlined by the actors' looking straight at the camera), expected more on television than on the big screen, installs an intermediate stage between the parafilmic discourse and the diegetic immersion, making the threshold the latter supposes all the more perceptible.
40. According to Lev Manovich, continuity and fluidity are some of the basic features of the "language of new media": "All these examples – smooth composites, morphing, uninterrupted navigation in games – have one thing in common: where old media relied on montage, new media substitutes the aesthetics of continuity". (Manovich 2001: 135).
41. The corporation's name in "*Resident Evil*" brings to mind the "Umbrella-Rosenblum Films" company that produced Michael Radford's screen adaptation of *1984*, George Orwell's famous dystopian novel (see Chapter 5).
42. Perceiving the film as a world rather than a story suits perfectly the function of a movie trailer consisting, as Vinzenz Hediger has shown, of transmitting information on elements such as "the action and the ambiance" of the film without defiling the story "which represents the [upcoming] product's essence" (Hediger 2001: 24). Conversely, it may be that the industry's craze for multiverse movies or for films primarily conceived as worlds partly results from the experience acquired by filmmakers while working in short movies or commercials (movie trailers, music video clips, etc.).
43. According to Kristen Whissel, films that employ the "crowd" software "all use the digital multitude to spatialize time and to allegorize their protagonist's relationship to sudden, often apocalyptic, historical change" (Whissel 2014: 15). However, one needs to distinguish in "*Resident Evil*" the hero's frozen replicas from the computer-generated hordes of zombies whose production requires the use of motion capture technology.
44. Umberto Eco takes up the concept of "small world" from Jaakko Hintikka (1988). On the opposition between *total* and *small worlds*, see Doležel 2019: 55–56. In the case of cinema, the spatial dimension has a special significance within the process of worldbuilding. Therefore, I will also use the expression "small world" in this essay in a more literal way, with respect to a clearly circumscribed world within the film diegesis, such as an island, an isolated town, or a theme park.
45. Aurélie Ledoux properly explains the incoherence of a specific shot in *The Matrix*, when Neo's messianic hero comes to see, beyond the world produced by the matrix, the lines of code that constitute it: "[…] the moment when the real texture of the matrix's universe is revealed to him is however based on its spatial arrangement and paradoxically, if not 'absurdly' (in its logical sense), the signs and the a-spatial nature of the Matrix mimic the spatial arrangement of visual stimuli" (Ledoux 2012: 73)[*]. What is problematic in this particular shot from *The Matrix* is the intention to reconcile the machine's deindividuation and ubiquity with the point of view of a character with which the viewer identifies himself, unlike the scene in *Resident Evil: Retribution* discussed here, where there is a clear disjunction between the character and the subject of the "visual" perception.

46. In terms of the biological body's design, Paul W.S. Anderson's series constitutes a mainstream variation on Shinya Tsukamoto (the *Tetsuo* trilogy) or David Cronenberg's cyberpunk aesthetics.
47. "*Resident Evil*", originally attached to the zombie genre, is certainly not as "prophetic" in this respect as Soderbergh's *Contagion* (2011). However, Alice's last line in the end of the sixth episode, spoken in a voice-over, is revealing of this contemporary anxiety: "When the T-Virus spread among the Earth, it did so with the speed of the modern world, carried by jetliners across the globe".
48. In this sense, the title of this particular installment (*The Final Chapter*) seems *prima facie* incompatible with the franchise's variation principle.
49. "I can't remember much before all of these started. I can't recall much before that. Sometimes I feel like this has been my whole life. Running. Killing".
50. See Scott Bukatman's book with the evocative title: *Terminal Identity. The Virtual Subject in Postmodern Science Fiction* (1993).
51. This is especially true in this episode as Alice accomplishes a mission entrusted to her by a computing machine while being equipped, like her opponent, with a predictive combat software allowing her to explore the possible outcomes of the various ways she can react in order to defend herself.
52. See Therrien 2006. Aurélie Ledoux made the following remark: "The problematic identity of contemporary fictional characters is thus directly linked to new viewer expectations, more concerned with a character's virtualities than with its 'realistic' consistency" (Ledoux 2012: 120)*. While it is always difficult to assess this type of expectations without putting forth the researcher's own interests (since he is a viewer himself), it is true that certain avant-garde practices in terms of characterization (as in *La Coquille et le Clergyman*, 1928) seem nowadays to be at work in films reaching a wider audience, as in David Lynch's *Mulholland Dr.* (2001), a film discussed by Ledoux, that has met with a relative commercial success, at least in Europe. I have examined the ways this particular film functions precisely from the point of view of the protagonist's characterization and the dislocations/substitutions this characterization generates, in Boillat 2005. As I have also studied elsewhere (Boillat 2009a), a filmmaker like Raúl Ruiz adopts a similar approach – *Three Lives and Only One Death* (1996) provides a perfect example – which he explains himself as follows: "Personally, I sought to work with stories that are quite abstract, I must admit, using what you might call a pentaludic model or, to put it simply, considering my protagonists as 'troops' of dice. The numbers marked in each of the dices' side varies from one troop to the other […]. Inside each dice lies an infinite number of miniature dice […]." (Ruiz 1995: 19–20)*. Since I have chosen to narrow my corpus to science fiction films (mainly made in Hollywood) and to concentrate on questions related to worlds more than stories, I will not study here this type of productions, with the exception of *Je t'aime je t'aime* (1968) examined in Chapter 4.
53. Tom Philipps, "Capcom: There is a possibility of *Resident Evil* series reboot", January 31, 2013, [http://www.eurogamer.net/articles/2013-01-31-capcom-there-is-a-possibility-of-resident-evil-series-reboot]; consulted on August 11, 2013.
54. In the end, it was decided to simply remake the original video game with *Resident Evil 2* (2019) and *Resident Evil 3* (2020).
55. The idea of a successful terrorist attack perpetrated on American soil, with no last-minute rescue, was present in several films from the late 1990s, such as *The Peacemaker* (1997), *The Siege* (1998), or *Swordfish* (2001). However, it was in 2002 that a Hollywood blockbuster, *The Sum of All Fears*, showed for the first time on screen an explosion destroying an entire city (Baltimore) and causing the death of the President of the United States. Based on a Tom Clancy novel published back in 1992, the film was made before but released after the September 11 attacks.
56. This back-and-forth between reality and fiction went on as the Pentagon hired one of the screenwriters of *Die Hard* (1988), Steven de Souza, in an effort to anticipate future plans for terrorist attacks (see Davies 2002: 5).
57. Examples of this sub-genre include *The Day after Tomorrow* (2004), *I Am Legend* (2007), *The Happening* (2008), *The Road* (2009), *2012* (2009), *The Book of Eli* (2010) and *Mad Max: Fury Road* (2015).

58. In this episode, police officer Charlie Francis (Kirk Acevedo), a character that represents rational thinking within this fictional series, ironically refers to *The Wizard of Oz* when he is told that he can open "windows" and connect to different worlds.
59. In fact, the film's screenplay, written by Gary Goldman (who also worked in both versions of *Total Recall* – see Chapter 2), used only one element from Dick's story: the special power bestowed upon the hero. "The Golden Man" describes a future world where a special police force – similar to the "blade runners" – tracks down and annihilates different types of mutants with exceptional powers. This idea was previously developed in A.E. van Vogt's novel *Slan* (1940) and then taken up by Stan Lee in the comic book series *X-Men* that inspired the film franchise of the same name.
60. Janet Murray commented on Harold Ramis' film in the following words: "Because of his simulation structure, *Groundhog Day*, though it has none of the shoot'em-up content in videogames, is as much like a videogame as a linear film can be" (Murray 1997: 36). *Boss Level* (2021) combines the pattern of a hero trapped in a narrative loop and a straightforward reference to shoot'em up video games.
61. *Edge of Tomorrow* transposes in the US army context a Japanese science fiction novel, *All You Need is Kill* by Hiroshi Sakurazaka (2004), illustrated by Yoshitoshi ABe, also adapted into a manga by Ryosuke (script) and Takeshi Obata (drawings). In this *light novel* context, the story becomes similar to the sub-genre of *Isekai*, which will be mentioned in the Conclusion of this book.
62. See for instance the newspaper article, published on January 17th, 1897, and reproduced in Rittaud-Hutinet 1999: 257–258.
63. *Vantage Point* proposes the same thing but through what is known in narratology as multiple internal focalization. According to Gérard Genette, a frequent use of a multiple internal focalization is to be found "in epistolary novels, where the same event may be evoked several times according to the point of view of several letter-writing characters" (Genette 1980: 190).
64. "The notion of dispositive […] includes everything that is laid out in front of the spectator, together with all the elements that allow the representation to be viewed and heard. The dispositive involves both the making and the showing. The term is used when one or other of these aspects is addressed, on condition that it is considered as a network of relations between a spectator, the representation and the 'machinery' that allows the spectator to have access to the representation" (Albera and Tortajada, 2010: 11).
65. On the Kapoor memorial in *Source Code*, see Stewart 2015: 223–224. The couple's meeting in front of the "Bean" can be compared with the final scene in *Total Recall* (1990), discussed in Chapter 2. However, the degree of indeterminacy with respect to the status of reality is higher in Verhoeven's epilogue. This is even more the case in *Inception*'s final image: Christopher Nolan, after having already displayed the codes of the interpretative challenge thrown down to the audience, chooses to cut the shot before the spinning top ends its swirling, a decisive criterion regarding the world's ontological status (in the dream world, the spinning top turns indefinitely).
66. Even though the hero in *Bandersnatch* is haunted by the memory of his deceased mother and feels guilty about her death, his primary objective is to create a video game. The film's self-reflexive ending – Netflix's streaming platform is mentioned – deals with the process of writing a story (in this case, an interactive one).
67. However, TV series often adopt the same (melo-)dramatic patterns. Like the hero in *Source Code*, the character of Peter (Joshua Jackson) in *Fringe* intervenes in a *parallel world* to settle a conflict with his father or to save the woman he fell in love with.
68. In this respect, *Source Code*'s happy ending contrasts with the final twist in Duncan Jones' previous film, *Moon* (2009), which emphasized the alienation of the individual. According to Garrett Stewart: "When the hero of *Source Code* achieves a computerized transcendence of the apparatus itself into an undelimited alternate reality, we learn this […] by a routine mobile transmit from his cell phone within the branching universe. Here is a film whose belated […] suppression of digital phobias – after a plot-long dystopian ordeal centered in fact on the temporal distortions of coercive computer science – arrives with a last-ditch and unconvincing cellular euphoria […]" (Stewart 2015: 213). The presence of telephony encourages the use of crosscutting, an editing pattern that proves to be a capital structuring process for multiverse movies (see Chapter 4).

69. The soldier in this film is more than just a military weapon used by the army: it is expected of him to be so devoted as to accept to die … several times.

70. On the concept of metalepsis, see Chapter 3, section "Principles of Filmology as a Theoretical Framework for a World-Centered Conception of Movies".

71. See the text in the back cover of Martin 2010.

72. In a film released the same year as *Inception*, Martin Scorsese's *Shutter Island*, the character of Teddy Daniels, also played by Leonardo DiCaprio, finds himself in a very similar situation. See Chapter 3 ("*Mental Worlds*").

73. *The Caller* (2011) constitutes an intermediate case in which the diabolical lady with whom the female hero communicates through time via an old wire-line telephone endowed with magical powers, eliminates her boyfriend in the past, so that he only exists as an adult in the memory of one person. *Frequency* (2000) also deals with a similar threat.

74. In *The Butterfly Effect*, "old media", such as writing, photography, or film, are actually good enough to trigger a transfer into the past.

75. See Manovich 2001, section "New Temporality: Loop as a Narrative Engine", pp. 264–269.

76. See for example *Mirror for a Hero* (Russia, 1987), *Naken* (Sweden, 2000, remade in the United States in 2017), *Timecrimes* (Spain, 2007), *Stork Day* (Italy, 2004), *Run Lola Run* (Germany, 1998), *Repeaters* (Canada, 2010), *Haunter* (Canada, 2013), *The Infinite Man* (Australia, 2014), *La Colle* (France, 2017), and *A Day* (South Korea, 2018).

77. Mainstream movies often capitalize on viewers' previous experience as video game players. In the case of *Inception* that I discuss *infra*, Buckland (2015) highlights the role of video game rules in structuring the film's logic, particularly with respect to the so-called "sandbox" mode, based on the exploration of an open-ended simulated world.

78. "The success of *Pulp Fiction* made such a play with story order more acceptable in American filmmaking. […] *Pulp Fiction* and *Go* were independent films, but more mainstream Hollywood movies have also played with the temporal relations of story and plot." (Bordwell and Thompson 2009: 134).

79. Jonathan R. Olson argues that *Inception* and *Prestige* offer "immersive allegories of filmmaking" (2015: 44–61).

80. Lisa K. Perdigao uses the term "dream-*world*" in her analysis of *Inception*, as she focuses on the intertwining of the real and the imaginary: "While inception, that 'subtle art', requires imagination, it is predicated on the manipulation of material objects […]. Yet the dream-world of the inception is a world of ideas as well; as Cobb tells his father-in-law and mentor Miles (Michael Caine), the dream-world's architect has 'the chance to build cathedrals, entire cities, things that never existed, things that couldn't exist in the real world'. However, there are rules to follow […]: 'Building a dream from your memory is the easiest way to lose your grasp on what's real and what is a dream'. With an allusive name signifying her ability to navigate a complex labyrinth, the new architect Ariadne figures out the story of Cobb's traumatic past" (Perdigao 2015: 125).

81. Since the film's narration remains chained to a linear progression, only retrospectively does the viewer realize that Neil has been commissioned by the hero himself in the future to enter into a temporal loop. In this respect, *Tenet* takes up the canvas of the "*Terminator*" series, while being knowingly opaque with regards to the future and to Neil's identity, allowing spectators to interpret it as they wish (they can even see him as Kat's son, returning to save his mother, just like John saves Sarah Connor). The final exchange between Neil and the "Protagonist", during which the former reveals his true mission, draws upon a famous movie reference: to Neil's remark, "for me, I think this is the end of a beautiful friendship", the hero replies "but for me, it's just the beginning". These two inverted points of view correspond to a line from *Casablanca* (1942) where the beginning of a friendship (between an American, Rick, and a French, Louis, in a film released just a few months after the United States' entry into WW2) coincides with the end of the film.

82. To name two examples: a bullet returning from its target to the barrel of a gun that has not fired yet, and the scattered fragments of a wall that violently reassemble before the explosion takes place.

83. The attempt to give credibility to the sci-fi technologies represented on screen is even feebler in *Inception*. The device hidden in a suitcase allowing to project several subjects

inside the same dream and to time its duration, is never evoked by the characters (nor was it ever mentioned in the film's critical reception).

84. The room is filmed with different filters – red and blue – on each side of the glass partition. Color is here used in a "world-centered" perspective, a case discussed in more detail in Chapter 4. This convention is integrated within *Tenet*'s diegesis during the assault on the hypocenter, at the end of the film: each of the two teams, acting in opposite directions in time, wear distinct armbands; the Red Team moves forward, while the Blue Team is inverted.

85. Ryn Vu describes this new spectatorial attitude in the following terms: "The Marvel Cinematic Universe has demonstrated the profitability of ensuring consistency within transmedia worlds. To virtually inhabit these worlds is to think about and discuss their parameters and to make comparisons with other worlds, including the 'real' one, even if the differences between them are assumed to be provisional" (Vu 2017: 289).

86. Turnstile gates are used as a symbol of setbacks brought on by fate since, at least, F.W. Murnau's *The Last Laugh* (1924).

87. Like Neo in *The Matrix*, the hero is advised to rely on his instinct in order to adapt to his own desires the world in which he is immersed. The importance given to the hero's instinct is a common practice in Hollywood movies, ever since Obi-Wan Kenobi gave such an advice from beyond the grave in *Star Wars* (1977). In *Tenet*, it is a scientist, Laura – played by Clémence Poésy, a French actress who had the role of Fleur in the multiverse film series "*Harry Potter*" – that tells the Protagonist to trust his instinct, a recommendation also addressed to the viewer of a film that presents itself as an immersive experience: "Don't try to understand it. Feel it".

88. *The Adjustment Bureau* is freely inspired by Philip K. Dick's short story "Adjustment Team" (1954), while also being very similar to *The Lost Room* TV series. However, *Lost Room* is actually more world-centered than George Nolfi's film. Thanks to a magic key, its protagonist can transfer himself to any given place in *our* world, while invariably transiting through a motel room, disappeared from the real world after an unexplained event in 1961 and now located in a different space-time continuum. The room is constantly reconfigured in order to recover its initial state and sometimes is filled with "Objects" endowed with supernatural powers (like the ones found in the Zone in *Stalker*) that fanatical groups of "Object-seekers" fight over. The character named Karl Keutzfeld (Kevin Pollack) describes these objects in the third and final episode: "They're tools. Tools to reshape reality. The properties that we perceive, they're side effects, tip of the iceberg. The objects allow us to change reality on levels that our brains can't even understand […]. [Arlene] Conroy [one of the members of the Collectors group] opened up a door through reality itself where anything is possible".

89. In this respect, *Memento* is similar to *Irreversible* (2002), although it relies on its identification with a character suffering from anterograde amnesia. Moreover, Gaspar Noé's film systematically uses long sequence shots, reinforcing the continuity within each of the segments edited in reverse order.

90. This episode includes a total of three "slides" and, therefore, four distinct *parallel worlds*. Their succession draws its consistency from the male hero's search for the same woman, whose destiny varies from one world to another. Only two of these worlds, provisionally inhabited by the series' main characters, are developed in their cosmic features. The first one is elaborated at the level of the representation: a dystopia in which San Francisco belongs to the Republic of New Spain and English-speaking population is actually the immigrants, victims of xenophobia on the part of the Spanish-speaking elite. As for the second world, its development occurs at the level of the narration itself, through the principle of reverse chronology. It is worth noting that *Sliders* never resorts to the time-travel pattern. The handheld device called the "timer" imposes a finite amount of time to stay in each world, but all of these worlds are contemporary to the original one in terms of their era. Time travel occurs only in this specific episode, due to the singularity of this particular world.

91. As Jimena Canales explains in detail (2015: 53–51), discussion on what will be later called the "twin paradox" began by a remarkable intervention made by Paul Langevin, during the 4th International Congress of Philosophy in Bologna in 1911. Langevin contributed to the popularization of Einstein's theory by deducing from it that an individual travelling into outer space at a speed close to that of light would return to Earth (like *Interstellar*'s

hero) to find out that time had passed a hundred times more rapidly. Henri Bergson will reformulate this idea, insisting on its paradoxical status, by introducing the story of two twins, Peter and Paul, in which the former travels in a rocket ship, while the latter remains on Earth. When they meet again, Peter would be, according to the principles of physics, younger than his brother, even though time flowed normally for both brothers as far as their biological clock is concerned. Canales' study reveals the decisive role played by Bergson's philosophy (as it was developed in his book *Duration and Simultaneity*) within the controversy developed about this paradox, which produced innumerable interpretations (Bergson argued for the dissymmetry of these two times), as well as within a more general debate on the special theory of relativity. Research on the general relativity continued up until the theories advanced by Stephen Hawking and Roger Penrose. Widely popularized, these theories had a considerable impact on science fiction stories, from Haldeman's novel *The Forever War* to Bajram's comic book *Universal War One*. It is also worth noting that, conversely, Langevin borrows his formulation of the problem from the "conquest of space" leitmotif used in some of the social science fiction of his time. *Interstellar* is inspired from Hawking's theoretical predictions on the effects of crossing through a black hole, the "twin" appearing as the hero's double, as he was prior to his departure into outer space. Therefore, time has not passed more slowly for him; he has in fact entered into a different space-time. I would like to thank Achilleas Papakonstantis for introducing me to Jimena Canales' work, as he supervised the translation and prefaced the Greek edition of her book.

92. This is true not only for cinema, but also for what scholar Jason Mittell called "complex TV", pointing to "a changing landscape of American television, where complex and innovative storytelling can succeed both creatively and economically [see for instance the cases of *Alias* and *24*], while a series with a safe, conventional approach [like *The Agency*] can become a commercial failure" (Mittell 2015: 2). The author located these shifts in the cultural practices of the television industry and its viewership from 2001 onwards, echoing my argument in the previous section of this chapter regarding the uncertainty and the complexity of the world as it is expressed by North American fiction after the September 11 attacks.

93. Mittell frequently uses the example of the ABC series *Lost*, while *Westworld*, a show I will be discussing at length in this book, fits perfectly into the strategy of HBO, a pay television network that defines itself as "Quality TV" and whose slogan used to be "It's not TV, it's HBO".

94. J.J. Abrams participated in both of these franchises, as producer and director, as well as being the showrunner of the espionage series *Alias*, a show that inspired Mittell to coin the expression "complex TV".

Chapter Two

Immersive Sci-Fi Machines: Worlds, Genres, and Seriality

> "In contrast to realistic fiction, SF is a *conjectural* genre in two respects. Its aesthetic goal consists in creating a remote, estranged, and yet intelligible 'world'. The narrative about such a world itself requires a conjectural reading."
> (Angenot 1979: 10)

Science Fiction: A Typical World-Centered Genre

Following the examples of Stanley Kubrick and Andrei Tarkovsky, a number of contemporary arthouse directors like Denis Villeneuve, James Gray, and Claire Denis, have recently ventured in introspective science fiction stories, focusing on the inner rather than the outer space. Yet, the sci-fi genre known for setting up the (urban) landscape as a spectacle in its own right, constitutes a privileged venue for worldbuilding. Its fundamentally speculative dimension concerns primarily a new state of the world, extrapolated from the current state of science and technology, and built on metaphorical or "what if" adjustments. As a result, the future is not so much a temporal affair as it is a different version of our current world.[1] According to Rosalie Moore, science fiction "is based on an exploration or application of any existing or *imaginable* science, or extrapolation from the same" (quoted in Wolfe 1986: 109). What if everyone on the planet lived through surrogate robots, controlled remotely from the safety of home (*Surrogates*, 2009)? What if our life span, "imprinted" on our skin via a digital clock, was strictly limited unless we could afford to extend it by buying time (*In Time*, 2011)?

In the audio commentary provided on *Surrogates*' DVD edition (Touchstone, 2010), director Jonathan Mostow declares, in terms that could equally apply to Season 3 of *Westworld*: "I knew this movie was a metaphor […] People see it as an allegory for living life in this computer age that we're living in, this hyper-connected Internet-Blackberry-Facebook-Twitter age". Elie During highlights the world-centered dimension inherent in the science fiction genre when arguing that these films "produce fictions of world that are less fictional worlds than *conjectures*" whose effect is "to experiment worldviews by testing the consistency of the worlds they induce" (During 2003a: 11)[*]. "Our" world, as it exists on a political, social, cultural, and ethical level, constitutes the starting point for these speculations, which in turn reflect on its possible futures. This would explain the proliferation in sci-fi movies of urban, "supernatural", cosmic, interior, or computer-generated spaces, on the scale of a city, a planet, a galaxy, an artificial intelligence, or the World Wide Web. The audience encounters *another* space, distinct from the realistically depicted daily environment, presenting nonetheless an internal consistency. In the same vein, Eric S. Rabkin suggested the following definition: "A work belongs to the genre of science fiction if its narrative world is at least somewhat different from our own, and if this difference is apparent against the background of an organized body of knowledge" (Rabkin 1976: 119). As a rule, references to a pseudo-hard science are used to give credibility to this world. In addition, a delimited circumscribed space, which the protagonists have to roam through or occupy, often plays a central role, as in the case of the "Zone", described in the Strugatsky brothers' novel *Roadside Picnic* (1972), adapted for the screen by Tarkovsky (*Stalker*, 1979). Borders are crossed, imaginary grounds surveyed, and objects obeying to different physical laws discovered (see for example the entropy affecting the objects coming from the future in *Tenet*).

"*A long time ago*, in a galaxy far, far away …". The prologue from the *"Star Wars"* movies testifies to the precedence given to the world's otherness over an attachment to a given period in the future. Definitions of the science fiction genre traditionally insist on the notion of "imaginary worlds", which must hold a degree of verisimilitude in order to be immersive, especially in terms of environments, language, and technological artifacts.[2] Accordingly, Stephen L. Gillett's screenwriting manual devoted to the genre, *World-Building. A Writer's Guide to Constructing Star Systems and Life-Supporting Planets*, advises, among other things, to rely on Kepler's laws in order to calculate an orbital period, given the masses of the bodies involved (satellites, planets, stars). Novelists like Hal Clement or Poul Anderson actually "use predominantly scientific and conceptual means of making planets: the changing of basic scientific parameters and the logical deduction of what these changes would produce" (Wendland 1985: 69). However, such a "conceptual" approach is more suitable for novels than films. The latter minimize their descriptive/explanatory dimension in order to privilege action. The information concerning the state of humanity and technology in a future world is frequently confined at the very beginning of the film, where almost all of the world's laws are laid down (unless an ambiguity is wittingly maintained, as in the opening scene of *Dark City* – see Chapter 5).[3] This information may be transmitted through brief intertitles, prior to the first diegetic images, as in *Logan's Run* (1976), *Johnny Mnemonic* (1995), and *Ghost in the Shell* (2017). It may also appear as a superimposed text over a set of images only vaguely figurative, as is the case of Asimov's Three Laws of Robotics in *I, Robot* (2004), or descriptive, as in *Akira* (1988), *Total Recall* (2012), *Elysium* (2013), and *Snowpiercer* (2013). Lastly, it may be communicated via a voice-over[4] (*Escape From New York*, 1981; *Escape From L.A.*, 1996; *In Time*, 2011; *Oblivion*, 2013), an explanatory introductory scene (*Soylent Green*, 1973), or fictional radio, TV, and Internet news received by the protagonists (*Total Recall*, 1990; *Strange Days*, 1995; *Children of Men*, 2006) or explicitly addressed to the viewer (*Westworld*, 1973; *Starship Troopers*, 1997; *District 9*, 2009; *Surrogates*, 2009; *What Happened to Monday*, 2017).

At any rate, the laws governing our world serve as a point of reference for understanding those of the *other* world. Marc Angenot considers the presence of an "absent paradigm"[5] from the point of view of semiotics, as a defining criterion for the science fiction genre: "a SF story is by definition void of referent". The author argues that the genre's "aesthetic goal consists in creating a remote, estranged, and yet intelligible 'world'" (see the epigraph at the beginning of this chapter). In terms of style, this goal requires the presence of what Angenot calls "fictive words". In cinema, verbal referents also play an important role, and sometimes even an extensive one, as in Jean-Luc Godard's *Alphaville* (1965). Still, when the object of these referents is visualized, one needs to examine the modes of its representation, as well as the way in which the fictional world is presented to the viewer through the semantic construction of the film and the help of intertextual references.

As fictional universes expand and the authors' concern with the minutia of worldbuilding grows, the audience's "xeno-encyclopedia"[6] is enriched. According to Richard Saint-Gelais, numerous sci-fi novels display a narrative modernity that is quite surprising for such a popular genre. However, this aspect is not detrimental to their referential function, insofar as the formal characteristics are diegetically motivated by the use of "meta-fictional gadgets", such as time machines and other inventions that make it possible to modify the laws of the world and, thereby, those of the fiction (Saint-Gelais 1999: 258–267). In movies, the "self-reflexive movement whereby imagination is, euphorically yet paradoxically, caught up in its own game" (*Ibid.*: 258) consists in combining the mirroring of the cinematic dispositive through the representation of other, similar "worldbuilding machines", with a maximum immersion in the film world. This is especially true in the cases examined in this book, since I focus on films that use such "gadgets" to motivate a passage from one universe to another. These artifices seem like a pure, abstract convention in a verbal representation, but acquire an entirely different dimension in the case of audio-visual media, where the technology represented on screen mirrors the machines that create this representation. In the CGI era, the technological conditions of production of a film's audio-visual representation may be correlated to the features of the world it helps to establish. After all, the vision deployed in a science fiction film is partly shaped (if not constrained) by the technical possibilities available to the special effects (VFX) team.

Regardless of the medium in question, the sci-fi genre is received, appreciated, and evaluated in relation to worldbuilding. In his essay devoted to science fiction literature, *Science, Myth, and Fictional Creation of Alien Worlds* (1985), Albert Wendland examines the work of authors like Hal Clement, Stanisław Lem, Ray Bradbury, and J.G. Ballard, using a typology of worlds: "natural/artificial conceptual worlds", "perceptual worlds of style", and "internal perceptual worlds".[7] As for John J. Pierce, he comments upon Frank Herbert's novel – whose screen adaptation marked the history of sci-fi cinema[8] – in the following terms: "*Dune* is to science fiction what *The Lord of the Rings* is to fantasy: the ultimate created world" (Pierce 1987: 123). The author compares science fiction to fantasy, a genre that exploits even further the so-called "sense of wonder", but without the omnipresence of technology and scientific explanations, establishing instead a "naturalized" supernatural reality. Fantasy offers the audience a pact that postulates the existence of a magical reality, instead of relying on some pseudo-rationality. Nevertheless, Pierce compares the two genres with respect to their propensity to invent worlds. Therefore, it should be no surprise that Mark J. Wolf's list of fictional worlds in *Building Imaginary Worlds. The Theory and History of Subcreation* is mainly composed of fantasy and sci-fi worlds. The book's full title refers to the notion of "subcreation", introduced by J.R.R. Tolkien, the father of modern fantasy and author of *The Lord of the Rings*. Tolkien theorized the "Faërie" genre in his essay *On Fairy-Stories* (1947):

> In such "fantasy", as it is called, new form is made; Faërie begins; Man becomes a sub-creator. An essential power of Faërie is thus the power of making immediately effective by will the visions of "fantasy". [...] This aspect of "mythology" – sub-creation rather than either representation or symbolic interpretations of the beauties and terrors of the world – is, as I think, too little considered (Tolkien 2014: 42).

In his celebration of legendary folk tales, Tolkien subordinates the author of a Faërie (the "sub-creator") to God (the "creator"). His notion of "secondary world" has been regularly employed in literature devoted to popular genres associated with a purported "sense of wonder".[9] As Wolfe points, "in practice, the term has attained a narrower meaning, and is often used to refer exclusively to the environments created by authors of High Fantasy" (1986: 115).[10] Tolkien positions himself as a novelist and a philologist in relation to this generic terminology, promoting a world-centered conception of the "Faërie":

> I said the sense "stories about fairies" was too narrow. It is too narrow, even if we reject the diminutive size, for fairy-stories are not in normal English usage stories *about* fairies or elves, but stories about Fairy, that is *Faërie*, the realm or state in which fairies have their being. *Faërie* contains many things besides elves and fays, and besides dwarfs, witches, trolls, giants, or dragons: it holds the seas, the sun, the moon, the sky; and the earth, and all the things that are in it (2014: 31–32).

Tolkien views the prototypical figures of the supernatural as components of a "realm or state" that includes the environment in its entirety. As the (future) author of the 12-volume *The History of Middle-earth* series, the writer paves the way for a greater appreciation of the process of worldbuilding in discourses on "Fantasy Fiction"[11] and for a topographic conception of fiction (on *The Hobbit*, see Garel-Grislin 2019: 27–29). Digital means of non-sequential representation fit well into this conception, since they are in fact more apt to build a world (or, at least, a space) than organize a narrative. As Ljunberg points out, "the possibilities of mapreading [are] closer to those of interactive computer games and hypertext navigation" (2003: 159). The aerial views over vast landscapes and the immeasurable variations of scale in Peter Jackson's "*The Lord of the Rings*" and "*The Hobbit*" trilogies, as well as the portrayal of a three-dimensional, low-tech, clockwork-like map in the opening credits of *Game of Thrones* (2011–2019),[12] are emblematic of this spatial conception of fiction, affirming the central role given to the creation of a world.

In this book, I will distinguish the "secondary worlds" offered by such single-world productions and defined in contrast to "our" non-fictional world, from the *other worlds* of multiverse narratives. Like *The Lord of the Rings*, Poul Anderson's novel *Three Hearts and Three Lions* (1961) is a fiction set between the world of humans and the Faërie world (the "Middle World"); yet, this fantasy world is presented as a *parallel world* with respect to a first, more realistic one, described in the novel's prologue and epilogue, thus granting Anderson's novel the structure of a multiverse. For some commentators, such as the novelist Walter Jon Williams, the motif of a passage from one world to another is nothing but a crutch that fantasy writers nowadays can do without, since the genre's horizon of expectations is henceforth firmly established:

> The working out of a coherent fantasy world different from our own, however, is a more recent development. This innovation initially seemed to require some literary device to explain the existence of fictional worlds to an audience unused to the concept. Both C.S. Lewis's fantasy world of Narnia and the Zimiamvia of his contemporary E.R. Eddison were reached via some form of gateway from our own world, while works as wildly different in tone as J.R.R. Tolkien's *The Lord of the Rings* and Robert E Howard's stories of Conan the Barbarian were supposed to be set in the dim, mythical past of our own Earth. More recent fantasy writers, with an audience more accustomed to genre tropes, have dispensed with this sort of framing device entirely, and the story takes place in its own world (Williams 2009: 25).

Beyond literary references to Tolkien or Lewis, it is important to consider the legacy of popular practices, such as the role-playing game series "*Dungeons & Dragons*", that have established, via a reference to the fantasy genre, a post-modern relationship to all genres. According to Ryan Vu:

> Fantasy roleplaying games (RPGs) involve the generation of internally consistent "worlds" or narrative plate-form open to audience participation […]. "Tabletop" RPGs are distinguished from most other games (including the countless video games they have influenced) by being noncompetitive; in place of the satisfaction of victory,

> *they offer immersion in genre worlds*, the acting out of fantasies inspired by fiction consumed in other media (Vu 2017: 274; 280; the italics are mine).

In this sense, even though "*Westworld*" is a priori not attached to the (heroic) fantasy genre (except for the medieval part of the original film released in 1973), the promoters of the theme park inside the fiction offer something very similar to what Vu describes above, as the intertextual reference to film genres becomes part of the game.

The notion of a *parallel world* is so attached to fantasy – the worldbuilding genre par excellence – that the "Upside Down"[13] in Netflix's *Stranger Things* is mainly described within the fiction set in 1983 through the childhood imaginary references of the young heroes, who play the fantasy tabletop role-playing game "Dungeons & Dragons" in Mike's basement. The designation of the *other* world as "a dimension that is a dark reflection or echo of our world" (S01E05) is allegedly a quote from the game's rulebook. The monster is called Demogorgon, an allusion to one of the villains in "Dungeons & Dragons", whose origins go back to Boccaccio's mythology. The idea of an "Upside Down" is actualized through a reversal of the game's board, whose back side is completely black. The children's science teacher mentions "Hugh Everett's Many Worlds Interpretation" (S01E05); still, this is actually a two-world fiction in which a realist representation is brought into contact, by means of portals, with a Lovecraftian *supernatural world* whose degree of on-screen actualization remains low. We enter this world for the first time by momentarily adopting Barbara's (Shannon Purser) point of view during the final moments of S01E02, in a scene that owes much to both episodes of the *Silent Hill* film series. However, the dominant viewpoint is the one belonging to the inhabitants of the "real" world, the ones searching Will after his disappearance in Season 1, struggling to close the interworld portal in Season 2, and those fighting against the Soviet enemy determined to reopen the portal in Season 3. *Stranger Things* justifies the existence of another world by crossing various generic references. On the one hand, we deal with imaginary references pertaining to the fantasy genre; on the other, we are confronted with science fictional technologies used by the government in a series of secret experiments (like in the *X-Files* TV series).

Given the importance of the technological factor in this essay, my case studies come mainly from the science fiction genre,[14] that is more inclined to include "worldbuilding machines", like the ones found in *Deja Vu* and *Source Code*, studied in Chapter 1. These machines open up for the – initially rooted in our world – hero the doors of an *elsewhere*, a world not only *distant* but sometimes ontologically different from ours. First and foremost, I am interested in cases where the medium is displayed in its own right, as a *dispositive*, which I conceive as a network of relations between the audio-visual *representation*, the *machinery* that produces it, and the *spectator* (both diegetic and extra-diegetic) that receives it.[15]

That said, the role attributed to worlds in adventure stories in general,[16] and the fantasy and weird tales in particular, is central. For example, the representation of the "afterlife" frequently proceeds from a split between two worlds, as in *Beetle Juice* (1988), *The Frighteners* (1996), *The Sixth Sense* (1999), or *The Others* (2001). Generally speaking, supernatural stories tend to naturalize the shift between worlds. Still, attention may be drawn to the border separating them, as in the characteristic motif of the bridge in *Brigadoon* (1954). Two hunters, lost in the forest, discover beyond this stone edifice a colorful, mischievous and utopian world, where people communicate through songs. Motivating thus the defining conventions of the musical, Minnelli's film proves that this genre could also be examined from a world-centered perspective, since the sing-and-dance scenes present a variable degree of deviation from the "first" world.[17] A film like *Brigadoon*, attached by Rick Altman to the sub-genre of the "Fairy Tale Musical" (Altman 1987: 129–199), reveals how much the fundamentally escapist musical genre ideology favors the creation of another world, either realistically (a show and its backstage), or by resorting to a supernatural tale, and even by attributing the audio-visual representation to the subjectivity of a specific character.[18] *The Wizard of Oz* (1939), *Mary Poppins* (1964) and its recent sequel, *Mary Poppins Returns* (2018), are typical of this last case. Little Dorothy is hardly surprised to see the "good witch" and the dwarfs welcoming her with songs, before she starts recounting her own adventure by gradually switching from speaking to singing. However, audio-visual dispositives used as worldbuilding machines are less frequent in the enchanted worlds of the musical. Mary Poppins needs only to throw herself into the representation drawn on the cobblestones (and, in the sequel, to spin a porcelain vase that sucks in the characters) to reach a different, animated film world.

Yet several examples discussed in this book play on the borders separating worlds and genres. Florent Favard remarked that the central location in *Lost* is an "island that was both fantasy and science fiction" and that "even if the 'generic sliding' clearly plays on fantasy in the last season […], science fiction got in the mix during at least two seasons" (Favard 2016: 8-9). Series like *Lost*, or CBS's quite similar *Under the Dome*, fit "within the new post-1990s televisual landscape of genre-oriented cult television" (SF, fantasy, horror…) (Brown 2017: 270).

Avatar (2009) constitutes the most famous case of generic hybridity linked to worldbuilding and the desire to take advantage of digital tools available to filmmakers. Partly, James Cameron's movie was conceived as a showcase for the efficiency of computer graphics and 3D technology (whose widespread use in recent productions owes greatly to *Avatar*'s success). Its world was presented as a magnificent spectacle demonstrating the potential of current technologies. At the same time, the film had to make its audience forget this technological mediation by gradually substituting, on the basis of a well-known initiatory plot, science fiction by fantasy, and war machines by the sanctuary of "Mother

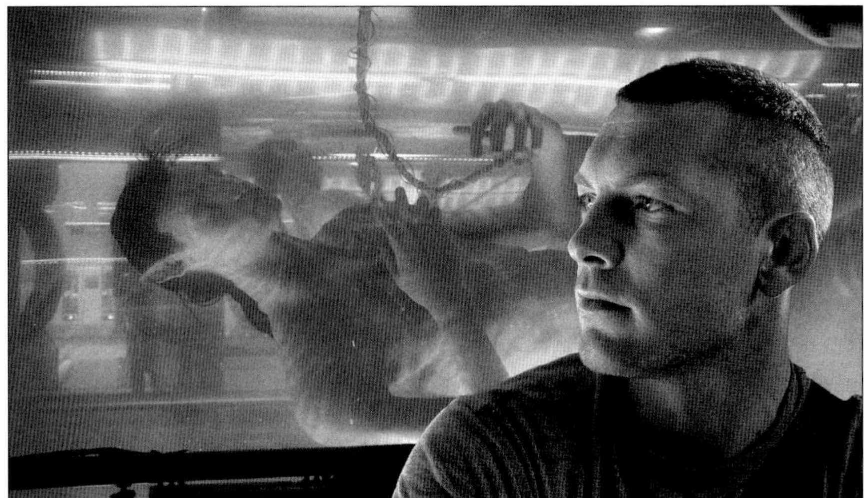

Fig. 14: Two bodies for one character caught between two worlds: the puppeteer and his (computer-generated) alter ego in *Avatar* (2009).

Nature". According to Éric Dufour: "*Avatar* presents itself [...] as a mixture of the science fiction and fantasy genres [...]. Cameron combines two worlds, two types of civilization, as well as two different types of images related to each of these worlds" (Dufour 2011: 10). Indeed, *Avatar*'s ecological dimension proves compatible with a techno-scientific comprehension of the concept of nature: for instance, the mutual relationship between the trees in the Pandora planet is designated as a "global network". **(Color Plate 3)** The analogy reaches its climax in the film's finale, when the technology used to connect human minds with avatars in the form of blue, Na'vi bodies, is replaced by a kind of osmosis with an enchanting plant life.

Jake Sully (Sam Worthington) is connected to his avatar thanks to a machine that looks both like a preservation chamber and a scanner (Fig. 14). However, the device is only briefly shown on screen, while its function is explained in a sketchy way that refrains from technicalities. One could argue that the discrete treatment of this sci-fi component anticipates its symbolic eviction later in the story. Unlike cyberpunk movies, such as *The Matrix* (1999), which cultivate a certain phobia with regard to universes produced by an alienating computing machine, *Avatar* celebrates the disappearance of the human body. As its cleverly chosen title indicates, Cameron's film explicitly refers to virtual realities inhabited by a gamer's double. In video game vocabulary, the term "avatar" acts as a bridge between the world of the gamer and the one represented within the game. Yet its Sanskrit etymology is related to the tale of Vishnu's descent and incarnation on Earth. Therefore, it carries the idea of a shift in the ontological status (God's transformation into a human being), while also being a part of a spiritual isotopy that links the film's title to the states of consciousness achieved through shamanic practices ("out of body", "near death experience", etc.),[19] symbolized in the film by the ties that bind Na'vi to the trees and through Jake's final reincarnation. Appropriately, James Cameron did not fail to publicize his environmental activism and his concern for the fate of living beings populating the Amazon jungle, during the announcement of four sequels to *Avatar* – currently in production.

At the time of the film's release, the use of the term "avatar" in media discourse was linked to a growing concern over the effects of addiction to online games (see Krichane 2011). The protagonist, Jake, no longer showers and even forgets to eat as he spends most of his time wearing his avatar's blue skin. Moreover, he confesses to having a completely skewed view of the time passed since his arrival. As was the case with cinema during its early days, *Avatar*'s diegeticized sci-fi dispositive is part of the paradigm of the prosthetic development of the human body (see Guido 2013), more specifically of a refinement of its motor skills and perceptual capacities, culminating in the advent of cybernetics and genetics. The current vogue for superhero movies, whose characters possess an exaggerated physical strength, is undoubtedly a major expression of the same imaginary, caught between technoscience and mythology, two frames of reference present in *Avatar*. Cameron's film celebrates the dissolution of the body in a world akin to a simulation – in other words a maximum immersion inside the representation, in accordance with the promotional discourse on the technology it became the vehicle of. In this respect, it is revealing that at the time of the release of *Avatar*'s Blu-ray edition, an advertisement for a Panasonic 3D Plasma television showed a spectator leaving his seat and getting sucked into the screen on which Cameron's film is playing.

In *Avatar*, the dive into the world of Pandora is immediate. Right after the opening credit (the 20th Century Fox logo), the hero's voice-over guides the audience through the film's opening tracking shot. A certain intimacy is installed between the protagonist and the viewer, reminiscent of the voice-over narration in Terrence Malick's *The New World* (2005), given also the similarity of the subject matter. This first shot reveals a virgin land covered by wisps of white smoke – instead of the red-orange napalm flames found in *Apocalypse Now* (1979), another famous first-person opening scene that inevitably comes to mind. As the narrator explains, he dreamed of this high-speed aerial view over the brunches while lying in his hospital bed, after having lost both legs in combat. The immediacy established by the character's voice and the immersive camera shot is contradicted by his words: the image actually comes from his past. Nevertheless, it is noteworthy that this fantasized past is directly translated into the immediacy of a vision: we are told that the camera leads us into a dream. Later in the film, a number of close-ups on Jack's eye signify the return to the real body after the use of the avatar, as the hero wakes up from a dreamless artificial sleep. Exiting his "incubator", he is born inside the film as the spectator's double. Short flashbacks come to explain his presence in the orbital base, before introducing to us the *fantasy* world of Pandora (see Chapter 3, "*Distant Worlds*"). Soon we learn that Jack arrived as a replacement of his deceased brother; he is already the ersatz of another, before even projecting himself in his avatar. The proposal uttered by one of the program's directors resounds over the present-day images: "It would be a fresh start, in a new world". This promise sounds like Horace Greeley's "Go West, Young Man, Go West", while also functioning as the concrete expression of a world-centered fiction.

Released the same year as *Avatar*, *Surrogates* is an adaptation of a comic book series. It shares with Cameron's film the idea of a device that "projects" the user's body into a near space. Almost all the inhabitants of our planet – with the exception of those living in the Dread Reservation, a machine-free zone – are homebound, staying in the pilot seat of a mechanical doppelgänger, leading their lives through puppets with superhuman physical powers and supermodel-like plastic beauty.[20] *Surrogates* explicitly offers a sci-fi extrapolation: apart from the technology evoked in the title (remote-controlled androids connected to the organs of their operator), the fictional world is strictly identical to ours, especially since the film concentrates on the everyday life in an urban environment (whereas James Cameron crosses science fiction with the war-action movie, as in *Aliens*). However, Mostow's film is more akin to a technological dystopia. Canter (James Cromwell), wheelchair-bound like Jake in *Avatar*, decides to destroy his own invention, as the film's protagonist, played by Bruce Willis (who also interprets his surrogate with the help of de-aging digital technology) does later on. The sedentary lifestyle, the dissolution of social ties stemming from flesh-and-blood interactions, and the reduction of the individual to an image – namely, the effects of the generalized teleworking and remote interpersonal exchanges during the COVID-19 pandemic – are denounced in *Surrogates* as consequences of the enslavement of humans to technology in the name of comfort and security. Conversely, *Avatar* paradoxically masks the technological mediation in order to celebrate its effects. Cameron's movie embodies "the future of narrative in cyberspace", a motto present in the title of Janet Murray's emblematic study on enthusiastic reactions towards digital technologies:

> A stirring narrative in any medium can be experienced as a virtual reality because our brains are programmed to tune into stories with an intensity that can obliterate the world around us […]. The age-old desire to live fantasy aroused by a fictional world has been intensified by a participatory, immersive medium [the computer] that promises to satisfy it more completely than has ever before been possible (Murray 1997: 98).

Such an "evolutionary" conception of media fiction may be questionable in its quantitative dimension (it is not definite, for instance, that a novel is less "immersive" than a video game), but proves dominant in digital age discourses. It does not only concern the navigable spaces of the Internet discussed by

Murray, but also the massively used CGI during the production of a film like *Avatar*. However, I will return to an early-1990s imaginary by examining *Total Recall* (1990), a film that places at the core of its plot the paradox of a double discourse aiming both to a heightened fictional immersion and a critique of the lured individual's alienation.

Total Recall, Total Immersion

When the worlds within a single film are mutually accessible, the crossing of the threshold separating them may be only slightly – or maybe only in retrospect, if at all – part of the information transmitted to the viewer. In this case, the audience lacks the necessary knowledge to evaluate the configuration of worlds within the fiction, so that we end up being just as deluded as the film's hero. *Total Recall* is one of the most famous Hollywood sci-fi movies resorting to such a plot twist. This "pre-digital" film is highly relevant to my demonstration, since it includes in its diegesis a "worldbuilding machine", it deals with the issue of "immersion", and it is based on a Philip K. Dick sci-fi story (on the author, see also Chapter 4) that was remade thirty years later, in the midst of the digital age.

Loosely based on the short story "We Can Remember It For You Wholesale" (1966), Paul Verhoeven's film rests on an ambiguity that allows for the combination of a dive into the hero's fantasy world with a world-centered embedding structure whose threshold is displayed via a "worldbuilding machine". Everything leads us to believe that the film's plot fully corresponds to the request made by Quaid (Arnold Schwarzenegger) to a company named Rekall Inc., asking for the implantation of false memories that will make him believe he is a secret agent living a heroic adventure on Mars. The fiction-within-a-fiction is initiated as Quaid takes a seat inside a strange machine in the company's premises. This device is actually absent from Dick's story (where the "patient" simply lies on a bed) and the way it functions remains obscure within the film's diegetic logic, as the immersion is in fact provoked by the injection of a hallucinogenic substance.

Therefore, the motivation for the futuristic representation of such a technological artifact must be sought at a different level. The hero takes a seat inside the machine in a way that mirrors the spectator's placement within a movie theater, highlighting the oppressive presence of a technical dispositive that produces subjective visions. The film's frame story recounts a coercive situation, as the represented machine resembles a straitjacket. The same machine, enhanced with a few additional accessories, also appears in the embedded story, where it serves as a torture instrument used against the protagonist, an ex-worker transformed into a top secret agent (Figs. 15–16). This is a visual clue which leads us to interpret the torture scene as part of a *mental world*, where

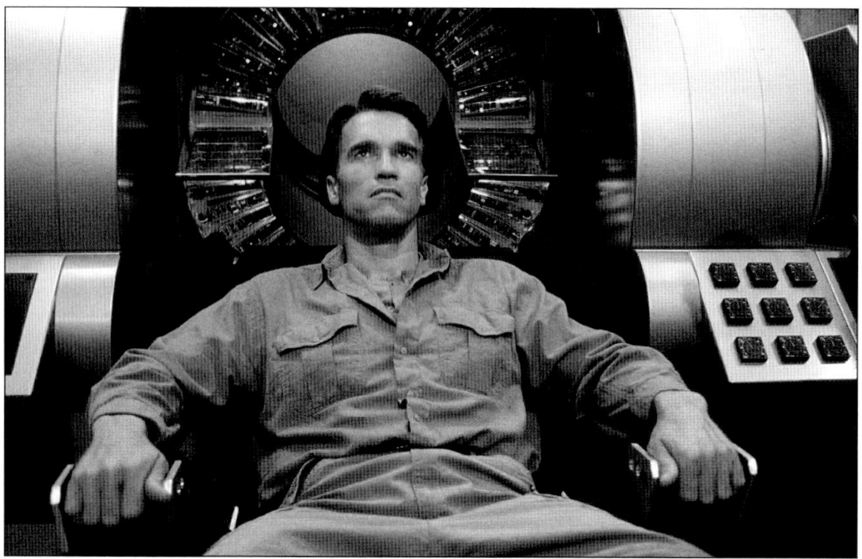

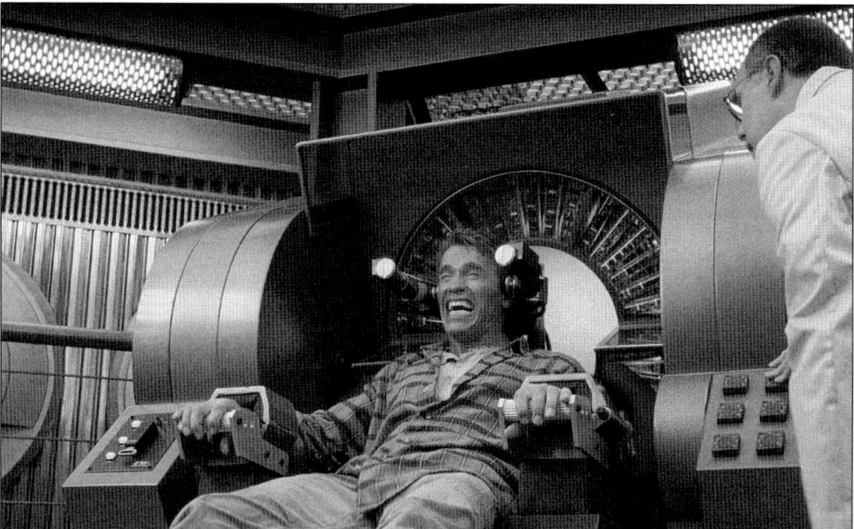

Figs. 15 (upper) and 16 (lower):
Two different ways to use a machine: "reality" and simulation in *Total Recall* (1990).

various elements from the first world reconfigure around the subject, as in a dream.

The embedding of narrative levels is already indicated at the beginning of the film through the multiplication of screens. While at home, Quaid tries to follow the news reporting on the attacks of rebel factions on Mars, when his wife changes the subject, as well as the image on the wall, opting for a soothing landscape visualized in a panoptic format (corresponding to the film's aspect ratio), in order to incite her husband to "keep his feet on the ground". The multiplication of large screens in the domestic space materializes on a visual level the intrusion of another reality into the daily life of the hero. What is shown on the news will reappear later within Doug's "dream", as he relies on the (fictional) real in order to project himself in an alternative version where he can become the hero of the story.

Total Recall does not summon different worlds governed by distinct laws. Unlike the film's viewers, Quaid is not projected into a science fiction world. Rather, he lives right from the outset in a future which constitutes his world of reference. The hero's adventures inside the fiction, whether virtual or not, satisfy our desire for a story filled with spectacular action and romance. The alternative reality offered by Rekall Inc. consists of new attributes conferred on the hero – much like as if he were choosing an avatar – and the creation of a female character that corresponds to his ideal of a woman. At the end of the film, as Mars' glowing landscape spreads out through the depth of field, Quaid, who has saved the oppressed inhabitants of this planet, passionately hugs the "woman of his dreams" against the backdrop of the setting sun, with its rays drawing a halo on the camera lens before plunging the entire frame into a gleaming white screen. *Total Recall*'s happy ending is so stereotypical that leads us to suspect it is only a representation, the subject being in fact still in the premises of Rekall Inc., prey to his delusions and on the verge of being lobotomized. A doctor who manages to enter Quaid's world warns him about this possible outcome and tries to help him escape by offering him a pill, a pattern also found in *The Matrix*, though in a significantly inverted function with respect to the opposition between reality and fiction.[21] Still, unlike *Brazil* (1985), the film does not end with a painful return to reality, since Quaid resigns to the version he has chosen (and upon which his heroic status holds). *Total Recall* adds a number of metafilmic allusions to the representational nature of the spectacle, denouncing the alienating effect of a clichéd but absorbing representation that favors viewer immersion. In this respect, the film is similar to a later Verhoeven film, *Starship Troopers* (1997): as Sylvestre Meininger has shown, this movie fashions distinct target groups by producing "not just one, or even a number of linear discourses, but an abstract and indecipherable intellectual mosaic" (Meininger 2006: 205)[*].

In a way, the proliferation of diegeticized images is part of the same process. For example, when Quaid and Melina (Rachel Ticotin) project their holographic doubles to disorient their adversaries, the viewer also becomes a victim to this illusion. Furthermore, when an armed Quaid walks through a metal detector, he breaks away from the image through the "fourth wall", as he shatters the one-way mirror, freeing himself from the schematic representation of his skeleton – intertextually associated with Schwarzenegger's role in *The Terminator* – and taking form and shape as an *action hero* on the other side of the "mirror". Once a worker, Quaid becomes (or imagines he becomes) a secret agent named Hauser. The intensified egocentrism that typifies a dream leads the protagonist's subjectivity (channeled through Rekall Inc.'s device) to gain complete control on the audio-visual representation. Such a narrative regime, known as fixed internal focalization (Genette 1980: 189), normally limits the audience to whatever is known to the main hero. However, the narration in *Total Recall* is not restricted to this principle. For instance, the use of crosscutting provides us with some information on what is going on within the clan of the hero's enemies. Genette calls this strategy a *paralepsis*, meaning an excess of information with respect to the dominant type of focalization (*Ibid.*: 195–197).[22] Nevertheless, the paralepsis has no effect on our understanding of the world's status, since here the crosscutting exclusively serves the stereotypical formula of action scenes.

Significantly, the very first images of Quaid's transition into his fantasy reality show the office of Rekall Inc. manager, which is adjacent to the "operating room". As he closes his eyes, the hero is staring at Melina's image on a monitor, while synthetic noises and music reminiscent of 1950s sci-fi serials are heard on the soundtrack. The first shot inside the "dream" is a full-frame shot of a screen showing a weightlifter exercising. In the second shot, as the viewers of this TV show are included in the frame, we realize that the male athlete is actually offered as a travel amenity by a salesman to his female customer. The reference to Schwarzenegger's status as one of the emblematic muscular heroes of the Reagan era – designated by Susan Jeffords as the "*Hard Bodies*" (1994) – is obvious. One could argue that Quaid functions as the fantasy projection of another consumer of illusions, the film viewer himself, especially at the dawn of a decade that gradually opened up to different models of virility.[23] Then comes a third shot, revealing at last the entire room, while being fragmented into many different frames: the TV screen, the glass against which the scared secretary persistently knocks, and the videophone monitor showing the operator crying for help after Quaid has suddenly metamorphosed. The proliferation of frames-within-a-frame communicates the feelings of disorientation and disillusionment, in an almost literal representation of the "embedding" structure as a confinement, translating visually the experience of the subject in whom these images have been implanted.

While Dick's short story concentrates on memory manipulation (as in *Dark City*, see Chapter 5), Verhoeven's screen adaptation tends to dismiss this dimension, since everything is delivered with an immediacy typical of Hollywood action movies. In turn, the film insists on the stereotypical and fictitious nature of the character's instinctive participation in the action – in other words, his identification with an action hero. However, as Quaid later says to the doctor, the explanation according to which everything that followed his connection to the machine in Rekall Inc. is the product of pure imagination seems inconsistent. Melina is supposedly living on Mars, but Quaid knew her before he even sought the services of the fictional travel providers. That said, Melina's face appears on the screen only after an injection is given to Quaid, so that this female character may actually be a projection of his subconscious mind.[24]

In Philip K. Dick's original story, there is no doubt that the protagonist's memories did actually take place. They are exhumed through the injection of a false memory that cancels a previous amnesia.[25] Dick's hero, named Douglas Quail, discovers at his house a trace of his Martian adventure, a box filled with specimen of this planet's fauna. Of course, the reader is by that point informed that Rekall Inc. provides such artifacts in order to give credibility to the memories injected to its customers. Still, Quail had never in the past sought the services of this company. In the movie version, a woman with brown hair (Melina), constantly visiting the hero in his dreams, takes the role of this travel souvenir. In this way, a relationship built on desire becomes the driving force of the film's action. Therefore, the *alternate (story)world* may be interpreted as the instrument of a frantic quest for the ideal lover: Quaid rewrites the past he shares with her, just like the male character in *Last Year at Marienbad*. The inversion between a blond and a brunette woman recalls a recurrent trope in noirish movies that frequently feature a protagonist who is a victim of a pathological obsession – *Vertigo* (1958), *Body Double* (1984), *Naked Lunch* (1991), *Lost Highway* (1997), *Femme Fatale* (2002), *Where the Truth Lies* (2005), to name a few examples. This motif is pivotal to *Total Recall*'s plot and constitutes the only element that alleviates the dehumanization experienced by the main character, swept along by a largely pre-programmed story.[26]

The film begins with a nightmare that foreshadows Quaid's final fall on Mars. In this opening scene, a young brunette lovingly holds Quaid's hand while walking next to him on the side of a blood-red mountain (a scene actually proposed by a Rekall Inc. commercial the protagonist watches while in the subway). Later in the film, Quaid recognizes the woman's face, (re)created digitally on the screen in the operating room of Rekall Inc., and then again in a bar on Mars. Consequently, the only clue that could anchor the components of the universe produced by Rekall Inc. in reality is a reference to a …dream. From the very beginning, the film blurs all tracks. Moreover, the red light bands in which the opening credits fade away invite viewers to associate the red planet with the scan line of a computer image. However, unlike *The Lawnmower Man* (1992) or *Johnny Mnemonic* (1995), *Total Recall* does not explicitly refer to the cyberpunk tradition. Several plot elements linked to Quaid's (Hauser's) experience on Mars reinforce the ambiguity of the film's world-centered organization. The deception concerning the world's ontology is coupled with a narrative form that firmly restricts the transmission of information. Quaid is manipulated by Cohaagen (Ronny Cox) whose true intentions he figures out – alongside with the viewer – only at the very end of the film. Like Van Stratten (Robert Arden) in Orson Welles' *Mr. Arkadin* (1955), Quaid unintentionally helps an evil man in his search of individuals he intends to eliminate. The illusion, just like everything that belongs to the Martian story, is a transposition of the

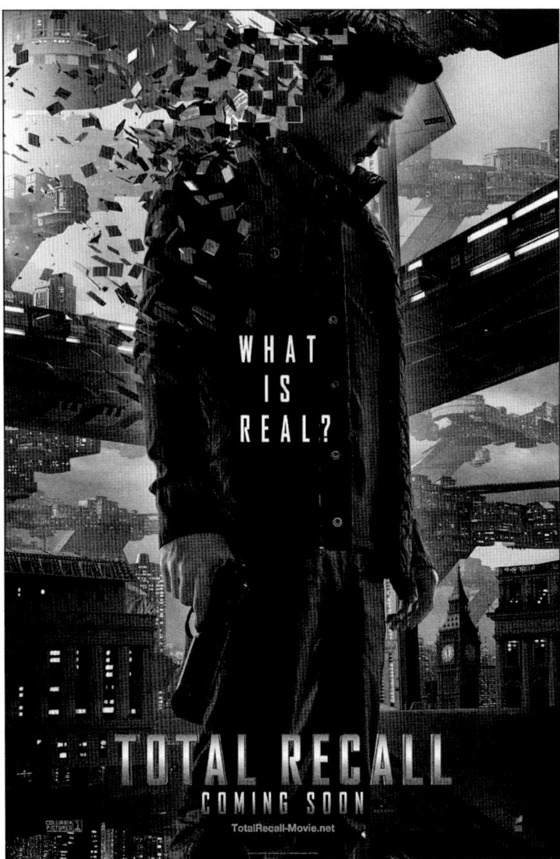

Fig. 17: The fragmented identity of the sci-fi hero (*Total Recall*, 2012): a pixel-by-pixel disintegration of the subject.

preoccupations of the subject of the dream. The unveiling of this illusion supplants in the film the desire to investigate the nature of the simulacrum, which ends up repressed. In this way, *Total Recall* negotiates the relationship between story and diegesis, favoring the former. Certainly, it can appear somewhat surprising that a story fantasized by the film's hero is actually based on a deception organized against him, as if Quaid did not control – at least temporarily – what is nonetheless the product of his own fantasy. To resolve this paradox, the screenwriters resorted to the motif of the double.[27] Quaid is lured by a different version of himself, the one he used to be before he had his memory erased and who now appears only through audio-visual recordings. In this way, the opposition between reality and illusion – or the character and his avatar – is limited to the embedded story. At the beginning of the movie, Quaid confesses to the one who may or may not be his wife (Sharon Stone) that he wants "to be somebody". Then, he chooses the "Ego Trip" option, tempted by the salesman's offer ("Let me suggest that you take a vacation from yourself"), who presents him a selection of alternate identities: "millionaire playboy", "sports hero", "industrial tycoon", and, of course, "secret agent". However to the viewer conscious of the film's frame story, these "echo effects" only increase the confusion caused by the split between the two worlds. Will Quaid find, through the Ego Trip, his real self, now forgotten, lured as he is by his close friends and suffering from amnesia?[28] Or will he finally become "somebody", alas in an imaginary world?

The remake of *Total Recall*, released in 2012 (Fig. 17), gives prominence to chase and action scenes. The narrative idea of a trip to Mars – present in Dick's original story, developed in Verhoeven's film, and explored in 2000 by Brian De Palma in *Mission to Mars* – disappears completely from the new film in order to reinforce the homogeneity of its world: this time, everything happens on Earth. Nevertheless, this unique universe is divided into two large zones linked by a futuristic means of transport. Its passengers, once they reach a certain threshold, enter a state of weightlessness, a notion reminiscent of the fall motif in *Inception*. Consequently, the disjunction between the two sub-spaces of the diegesis is undermined; one can actually go from *elsewhere* to *there*. Furthermore, the gory visual style and the horrifying portrayal of the mutants that inhabit the degraded reverse side of the industrial world in Verhoeven's version are completely abandoned. The limits of the humankind are reduced to the sole technological dimension, accentuated through an army of combat robots coming off the assembly line in the factory where Quaid works (unlike the protagonist in the original film who was a construction worker).

In Len Wiseman's remake, the constant plot twists suggest that the hero fantasizes about this frenzied pursuit so as to avoid confronting the facticity of the world he inhabits. The spectacular action scenes are highly implausible, even within the hyper-fictional pact offered to the audience, whereas the extreme obstinacy of Quaid's "fake" wife (Kate Beckinsale), who chases down the male hero and keeps reappearing in front of him, lends a kind of burlesque structure to the narrative. Actually, the screenwriters merged in this villain two different ones from the original film: Quaid's wife and Cohaagen's henchman (Michael Ironside). In doing so, they underlined the plotline of a married couple "armed clash" – especially since Quaid's fake wife dies by the very end of the movie – that has been frequently used in Hollywood productions ever since *Mr. & Mrs. Smith* (2005). In this 2012 action-oriented remake, the "collusion of desires between the character and the viewer" observed by Aurélie Ledoux in the 1990 movie is maximized (Ledoux 2012: 45)[*]. Still, an ambiguity is created at the end, when Quaid contemplates the effects of his accomplishment and sees among the cityscape stretching behind his lover, Melina (Jessica Biel), a Rekall commercial on a giant screen that troubles him. Are we once again facing an improbable happy ending that is nothing but an illusion? Both versions of *Total Recall* follow the same path, making the comprehension of the arrangement between the worlds the main object of the hero's quest – not to mention that this quest invariably becomes a search for an identity that would go beyond the numerous avatars of the "Self".[29]

The alignment between the plot of the film and the stereotypical adventure story sold by the fake memory-implant company is not as clear in the 2012 movie as in the original. In Verhoeven's film, a Rekall employee described the action content of the implant in terms that would later be actualized in the movie: "I don't want to spoil it for you, Doug. But you rest assured, by the time the trip is over, you get the girl, kill the bad guys, and save the entire planet". In Wiseman's remake, the audience is led to believe that the hero is in fact a secret agent, as is the case in Philip K. Dick's original story. Another difference between the two movies is that Colin Farrell's Quaid does not participate in the elaboration of Melina's computer-generated looks, the female character that will turn out to be his object of desire, despite the fact that this technology by 2012 had become commonplace in movies. This element takes on a particular importance given the way the relationship between Quaid/Hauser and Melina is formed. Even though certain motifs are adapted to modern technology, as for example the use of the cell phone network to track a character's location, there is one narrative element that reintroduces the concreteness and the authentication function of the semiotic category of the *index* in a world governed by simulacra and the virtualization of *iconic* signs. Thanks to Quaid's inaugural dream, the new *Total Recall* also begins *in medias res* with an extremely fast-paced action scene.[30] However, this dream serves as an anchor point for the post-factum inscription on the characters' body of an *indexical mark* from a certain "reality": a burn scar in the palm of Quaid and Melina's hands that functions as the carnal counterpart of the virtual implantation. The couple shares this wound after a laser beam pierced their joined hands – at least, this is the version Melina recounts, even though the opening dream scene does not confirm it. Like the Apostle Thomas, Quaid observes the sign Melina produces as evidence. The first explanation offered for this injury is an accident he supposedly suffered at work, one never depicted on screen but mentioned by Quaid to a young trainee at the factory to whom he shows his scarred hand. However, such a reference to the sufferings of an alienated proletarian will be later rebuffed in favor of a second version – an *alternate (story)world* – that emphasizes romance, deemed more credible within this 2012 remake. Such a "stigma" of the union between two lovers, imagined in a dream before the immersion in Rekall Inc.'s second reality, insinuates a kind of return to the indexical value of the image that is able to thwart the *trompe-l'oeil.* In fact, in the film's final scene, Quaid notices Melina's scarless hand, a reversal that retrospectively grants a great importance to the discovery of the mark.[31]

The loss of physical integrity, associated in Verhoeven's film with the degeneration brought on the inhabitants of Mars, as they are deprived of oxygen due to the schemes of an unscrupulous industrialist, is given a positive value in the remake through the formation of an eternal couple, a reassuring factor of unity that tends to make us oblivious of the illusory nature of the world. Cyberpunk-inspired dystopias tend to be conceived nowadays within the potential alternatives of their flip side: utopia. In the remake of *Total Recall*, this opposition is represented through the splitting of the single-world film universe into two subspaces, as in Fritz Lang's *Metropolis* (1927): the "surface", where the ideal city is built, and the dark "underground", where the members of the proletarian class are confined. The two parts of the globe are linked by an elevator that crosses the Earth's crust, ensuring the possibility of interaction between two opposing sides of the same society. The destruction of this means of transportation will put an end to the oppression of the miserable classes and the militaristic imperialism orchestrated by Cohaagen. The elevator plays a similar role to that of the spaceships in *Elysium* (2013), which dock to the orbital station where luxury, serenity, and pleasure reign. The film's hero, Max, also works in a factory that provides the elite with the necessary technological infrastructure in order to maintain their power. In both *Total Recall*'s remake and *Elysium*, the typical in blockbusters populism is expressed by the overthrow of the dominant social order thanks to the heroic actions of a working-class protagonist. However, Wiseman's film differs in that it casts a doubt on the actual impact of Quaid's achievements: the suppression of the passage between a series of thresholds condemns the audio-visualized world in a constant indeterminacy, exhibiting its status as a representation.

Paradoxically, the notion of *trace* resurfaces in the age of pixel (and even takes on an obsessive character). In order to escape remote tracking, Quaid must get rid of his "telephone" whose dial buttons appear in the palm of his hands, as if retro-projected, by extracting the mechanism from his flesh. This Cronenbergian pattern[32] is associated with a more general theme in *Total Recall*, the reversibility between the interior and the exterior, as the body absorbs drugs that in turn absorb the body inside the subject's hallucinations. The doctor's sweat drop that (erroneously) convinced Quaid in Verhoeven's version of the status of his world as the *real*, is transposed in the remake within the romantic story that dominates the narrative: the tear shed by Melina persuades the hero that the young woman is "real". The indexical sign is significant both at the level of the plot (as in any given police story) and that of the world (as it defines its ontological status).

One last difference between the two versions of *Total Recall*, also linked to the indexical paradigm, needs to be addressed. In Wiseman's remake, Rekall Inc.'s employee uses a seal that draws a tattoo in Quaid's arm in order to detect the exact location of the injection, marking the passage of the interworld threshold on the hero's skin. In the film's theatrical version, released in 2012, the close-up on the drawing of this tattoo may appear rather trivial. Yet in the longer cut, available on the Blu-ray disc released by Sony in the same year, the close-up returns as an insert shot in the end, along with several added shots showing Quaid examining Melina's hand and noticing that the seal has now disappeared from his arm. This detail suggests a denial of reality on the part of Quaid, who has apparently erased from his memory his visit in Rekall Inc., in favor of a total and alienating immersion in the *virtual world*. The film's alternative version elicits an *alternate (story)world* within the fiction.

Such modifications, more "profound" than those affecting the story,[33] arguably reveal a need to ward off the dematerialization of the medium of representation by a story that celebrates the embodiment of the character, at least as far as the theatrical version of the second *Total Recall* is concerned. At the same time, these films insist on the sense of futility that the world's ontological status casts on characters who cling to the few material traces of their existence (like the hero in *Dark City*) when confronted with the dissolution of their identity (due to a shift between worlds). In this regard, the legacy left by the author of the short story on which both *Total Recall* movies are based, proves to be of paramount importance. Katherine Hayles highlighted the degree to which Dick's narratives, especially those he wrote between 1962 and 1966, "extend the scope of inquiry by staging connections between cybernetics and a wide range of concerns, including […] a persistent suspicion that the objects surrounding us –and indeed reality itself – are fakes". She adds that in his body of work, "the ontology of the human and the ontology of the world mutually construct each other" (Hayles 1999: 161). This remark applies perfectly to a more recent TV show, *Westworld*, as well as to the title of Dick's famous novel *Do Androids Dream of Electric Sheep?* (originally titled *The Electric Toad: Do Androids Dream?*), written in 1966 and first published in 1968 (a new edition was released in 1982, following the release of Ridley Scott's *Blade Runner*). The study of "*Westworld*" invites us to further explore the hybridity between science fiction and a number of other genres, and more particularly the ways in which generic features may be used in world- and multiverse-building.

Androids of the Far West: Film Genre as World

Michael Crichton is best known today as the author of the bestseller novel *Jurassic Park*, adapted for the screen by Steven Spielberg in a film that marked the history of digital special effects in cinema (combined in the film with traditional animatronics). The movie spawned a franchise of several sequels – with its fourth installment, a huge success at the global box office in 2015, being titled … *Jurassic World* – as well as a number of video games (see Blanchet 2010: 320). It also served as a reference for the attraction built inside the Universal studios theme park in 1996. As Janet Murray noted, "Jurassic Park is essentially a giant computer-driven machine for telling an immersive story" (1997: 107). Crichton had already worked on a self-reflexive story about the act of creating a "small world", exploited by the mass entertainment industry, in his film *Westworld*, produced by MGM and released in US theaters during the autumn of 1973 (Color Plate 4). Inside its fictional universe, Spielberg's "*Jurassic Park*" naturalizes the massive and innovative use of computer graphics by adding a biotech referent. Thanks to genetics, Hammond, a millionaire "showrunner", uses the DNA of dinosaurs to bring them back to life.

In contrast, *Westworld* is a pre-digital film (apart from a small number of shots to which I will return below) whose story is based on a constant exploitation of the potentials of computer science, used for cybernetic purposes. In this way the artifice is exhibited, since the population inhabiting the park is not composed of flesh-and-blood living beings, but robots modeled after humans. It is worth noting that Crichton, who had just published a novel dealing with the risks of developing man-machine interfaces called *The Terminal Man* (1972), was a computer enthusiast and author of a handbook entitled *Electronic Life*, which intended to introduce the idea of personal computers to a wider public. He specialized in techno-thriller stories that often combined medical experiments, a conspiracy fomented by an unscrupulous company, and a backstage look on the production of a simulacrum.[34] The contextualization proposed by Natalie Neill with respect to Ira Levin's novel *The Stepford Wives*, published a year before the theatrical release of Crichton's film and adapted for the screen in 1975,[35] seems also valid in the case of *Westworld*:

> The fields of robotics and animatronics were advancing rapidly when Levin wrote *The Stepford Wives*. The first factory robots were in operation by the 1960s, and the first life-sized humanoid robots were invented just a decade later. Walt Disney's audio-animatronics technology was showcased at the 1964 New York World's Fair and at various attractions at Disney World in the 1960s. The "Hall of Presidents", which featured life-like replicas of all the US presidents, opened at Magic Kingdom park in 1971 (Neill 2018: 258–259).

The idea of a human-like machine resonates with a number of current ethical, social, and economic issues raised by artificial intelligence, while also presenting some kinship with the transhumanist imaginary popularized most notably by some Japanese films.[36] Following the example of contemporary movies like *Ex Machina* (2014) or *Morgan* (2016), the *Westworld* TV series, produced by Bad Robot and broadcast by HBO, reenacts the human vs. machine face-off present in *Blade Runner* (1982) and inspired by the Turing test, while pushing even further the blurring of borders regarding the definition of what falls in the human/not-human categories, gender identities, and – of particular interest in this essay – the ontology of worlds. As the show progresses, the ambiguity of the distinction between human/real and simulation spreads beyond the status of the individuals inhabiting the theme park world, onto the very status of the fictional world(s) (see Chapter 3). For the time being, I aim to study "*Westworld*" from the angle of the film genre question.

Crichton's *Westworld* borrows from the genre of disaster movies, quite popular in Hollywood in the early 1970s, where the sudden danger threatening a large number of people gathered in the same place, frequently results from the malfunction of a high-tech device, originally designed to guarantee their comfort. The robots in the targeted on a luxury clientele Westworld theme park gradually cease to bend to the visitors' wishes and turn into killing machines, transforming this place of leisure into a death trap, much like the airplane in *Airport* (1970), the cruise ship in *The Poseidon Adventure* (1972), or the building in *The Towering Inferno* (1974).[37] However, the environment is actually less confined: the term "world", used in the diegesis (as well as in the film's title) to describe these facilities, is of great significance within the perspective of this essay. In a way, Crichton anticipates a turning point of the disaster movie genre that will become manifest two years later in *Jaws* (1975).[38] Spielberg's film also tells a story inscribed in the context of the tourist industry,[39] where the disaster results from the negligence of individuals driven by the sole lure of profit.[40]

Twenty years prior to Crichton and Spielberg's collaboration in *Jurassic Park*'s screen adaptation, a parallel between the two may be drawn: just like Crichton, Spielberg uses in *Jaws* a non-human and almost indestructible predator that guarantees the ineluctability of the drama. Even if no "shark" appears in *Westworld*, a threat is spread in a mechanical and cold way, embodied in a robot played by Yul Brynner, an actor associated in the mind of viewers back in 1973 with the role of the cold-blooded gunslinger, always dressed in black, wearing a Stetson and spur boots, in films like *The Magnificent Seven* (1960) or *Adiós, Sabata* (1970). Crichton's film confers a singular profile to the android not by constructing its psychology (clearly non-existent, especially since the film refrains from humanizing the androids in terms of their interiority), but by using a specific visual pattern that Spielberg will also apply to the shark of his own movie: the POV-shot. This first-person shot does not encourage in *Westworld* or in *Jaws* our emotional identification with the "monster" whose gaze we share. On the contrary, the audience is invited to empathize with the victims. Instead, it is meant to underline the fundamental otherness of the perceiving subject, which therefore remains off-screen, endowed with the "presence-absence" state and the mechanistic function of the camera itself.[41] The individualization of the gunslinger brings to the fore one of the three different resorts offered by the theme park, each one defined by a specific era – the city of Pompeii in the decadent Roman Empire ("Romanworld"), 12th century-Europe ("Medieval World"), and the American Frontier of the 1880s ("Westworld"). It is actually this resort that gives the film its title (as will be the case later with the "Jurassic Park"). In an interview given during the shooting of the film, Michael Crichton confessed he had originally planned to explore this topic in a novel, before realizing it was only suitable for movies, so far as it deals with "movie fantasies" the public has known "not from reading history books", but "from looking at films", like those starring John Wayne.[42] Therefore, it is not so much a question of reconstructing the past as it is of referring to different film genres.

The "Westworld" resort – and, consequently, the history of the United States – is largely privileged in Crichton's story compared to the other sub-spaces of this high-class entertainment park. No individual characters or actions situated in the locations inspired by *Quo Vadis* (1951) or *The Last Days of Pompeii* (1959) are given screen time. Moreover, the mini-plot taking place in the medieval setting and leading to a deadly outcome, serves mostly as a preparation for the drama developed in the main narrative track. The latter will end up exceeding the space of the American West during the final chase scene in which the other two worlds are reduced to pure sets through which the killer-robot stalks its prey. Having two cowboys crossing the ruins of the other resorts provokes an anachronistic visual disjunction, akin to an inter-penetration between different worlds. The tireless gunslinger, determined to end the duel by using real bullets, only discerns a strongly pixelated color image from his surrounding environment, as we come to realize by momentarily adopting his gaze (through a POV-shot).[43] As a matter of fact, Crichton's film was released precisely at the time when western video games were multiplying in arcades, alongside games full of sci-fi references, both offering interactivity mainly based on the act of shooting. *Westworld*'s POV-shots associated with the character played by Yul Brynner constitute "the first known use of a digital image – a cinematic image readjusted in a 2D rendition" in the history of mainstream cinema (Hamus-Vallée 2001: 34)*. *Futureworld* (1976), a low-budget sequel to Crichton's film,[44] was also a pioneer in terms of the use of digital imagery in cinema. A year before the briefing sequence preceding the Death Star attack in *Star Wars* (1977), Richard T. Heffron's film includes 3D animated models, referring to a preliminary phase of an android's genesis. These models consist in the insertion of a short animation movie, *Computer Animated Hand* (1972), directed by Edwin Catmull (one of Pixar's co-founders and current President of Disney Animation) and Fred Park, as well as that of a 360-degree animated image of a digital model of the main actor's face, making Peter Fonda probably the first movie star to ever have a digital alter ego.

The prominent use of digital technology in the making of *Westworld*, bringing the audience to share the vision of a robot (whose first appearance is immediately followed by the use of electronic music on the soundtrack), is primarily explained by its inscription to a specific film genre: science fiction. The promotional material used during the film's theatrical release highlighted this generic identity by insisting on the presence of human-like robots.[45] This was also true in the case of its sequel, *Futureworld*, and the one-season TV series *Beyond Westworld* (1980).[46] It is no accident that the motto of the Delos company in charge of the *Westworld* park, hammered during the promotional pseudo-documentary featuring in the pre-credits sequence of Crichton's film, is "the vacation of the future, today".[47] *Westworld*'s story is set in the future, as it becomes clear already from its opening scene depicting a group of visitors arriving in the park aboard an aircraft that looks like a spaceship.

In *Westworld*, the science fiction genre embeds those of the medieval film (or swashbuckler, parodied two years later in *Monty Python and the Holy Grail*), the peplum, and the western, evoked by the three eras represented in the park in a way deemed immersive by the visitors-actors inhabiting a specific setting and interacting with mechanical simulacra of humans. That said, movie genres are never mentioned in any of the characters' lines in *Westworld*. Each reconstruction offers first and foremost a form of time travel, as the one experienced by the hero in "*Back to the Future*" who, in the series' third episode (1990),[48] finds himself in the era of the conquest of the West. However, Marty McFly (Michael J. Fox) is being called "Clint Eastwood" and his DeLorean pierces the screen of an abandoned drive-in as he teleports into the past: both clues highlight the extent to which the 19th century is represented in this film through the filter of

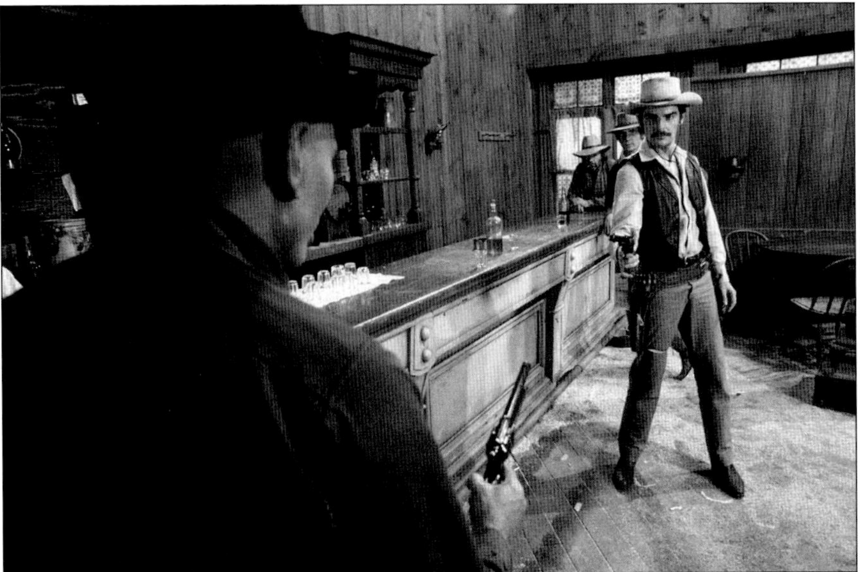

Fig. 18: *Shot* and *reverse shot*: the hero and his opponent draw their guns in the saloon, a constantly replayed cliché of the western genre in *Westworld* (1973).

a cinematic mythology. Although *Westworld* refrains from such self-reflexive allusions, Crichton rounds up a great number of generic stereotypes. As far as the "Westworld" resort is concerned, we get to visit a mean street (with a bank robbery happening off-screen, witnessed only through the sound of gunshots), a saloon (where the film's first duel takes place, Fig. 18),[49] the prison run by a sloppy sheriff, a brothel operated by a notorious madame, as well as the wide open spaces of the Wild West, in which the protagonists ride through the dust that hides the (mechanical) rattlesnakes and the tumbleweeds rolling around in the breeze. The different worlds in *Westworld* are physically co-present on the same territory – the map of the entire park is shown to passengers on the screen of the aircraft – while being *artificial* and *distant* from each other. They remain nonetheless mutually accessible, as is attested by the fact that the hero finds refuge inside Delos' underground facilities (i.e. a science fiction environment), while pursued by the gunslinger, before he finally overcomes the obstacle of the robot-killer – in the manner of Sarah Connor in *The Terminator* (1984).

The technique of alternation, so frequent in multiverse movies (see Chapter 4), is used in *Westworld* to generate analogies and contrasts between the three resorts (although the western scenes largely dominate the film in terms of screen time). To these three spatially adjacent, but semantically distinct worlds the pole of the "machinery" of the park (conceived as a dispositive, see note 15) is added, associated with the sci-fi genre, and mainly consisting of the Delos control center and the Robot Repair Labs. This underground space adjoins the three types of resorts. Interconnections between elements belonging to different worlds take place, most notably when Delos' employees enter discreetly in the middle of the night to recuperate certain androids.[50] A group of technicians in white coats are gathered in a room whose walls are lined with computer mainframes. As the magnetic tapes reel, the technicians remotely monitor the various actions, prepare the reprogramming of robots according to the visitors' choices (the interactivity entails plots emerging within the fiction), and report potential anomalies. The fourth narrative track, dedicated to the park management team, ensures the articulation of the three others with which it alternates. Every time the editing takes us from one world to another without specifically aiming to underline an analogy between two similar situations, shots showing the technicians working on what looks like an editing table – in real time, as in *The Truman Show* – are regularly inserted. In fact, we always shift from one "world" to the other via shots of their monitors, a bunch of remote surveillance screens appearing within the film screen.

The segregation between two different types of space – the technological backstage of the park and the simulated environments – is one of the elements that the HBO TV series best exploits. Its showrunners took up the idea of a Delos underground base, locating the controls carried out on robots in a bluish, cold, and sparsely furnished space, similar to *Ex Machina* (2014), which contrasts with the bright, yellowish light of the scenes taking place on the surface.[51] (Color Plate 6). Furthermore, the two levels are also distinguished in terms of their soundscape: the almost whispered exchanges between technicians sitting next to each other in the laboratory contrast with the loud clamor and the commotion reigning in the streets of Sweetwater. However, these spaces are connected through hidden elevators, similar to the ones found in the prologue of *Resident Evil: Extinction*, as we come to realize in S01E02 by following one of the inventors, Ford, who climbs up to the surface. In addition, the two levels correspond to different film genres. These contrasts underline the importance given to worldbuilding, whose structuring role is reinforced in view of the creation of a multiverse. The western genre predominates in the first two seasons, and then resurfaces rarely during the third one.

The convergence between science fiction and western is endowed with special meaning in Crichton's film. At the beginning of the 1970s, the western is running out of steam. After being part of a popular tradition from the end of the 19th century (in dime novels) and flourishing on the silver screen from the 1920s to the 1950s, the genre is gradually supplanted by laser duels taking place in the interstellar space or on planets inhabited by the pioneers of another "New Frontier". The coexistence of these two genres in a hybrid form can take different forms, in particular the following ones (that I illustrate using exclusively North American productions as examples): (1) a set of sporadic *quotations* of motifs, as the ones found in the "*Star Wars*" franchise,[52] or in certain post-apocalyptic stories, like the horror TV series *The Walking Dead* (2010–) and several episodes from the "*Planet of the Apes*" franchise, such as *Dawn of the*

Planet of the Apes (2014); (2) a *transposition* (from one world to another) from a given film, as in Peter Hyams' sci-fi remake of *High Noon, Outland* (1981), and in James Cameron's *Avatar*,[53] or, more generally, from a number of conventions specific to the genre, as in John Carpenter's *Ghosts of Mars* (2001);[54] (3) a *fusion* of western and SF, as found in Joss Whedon's *Firefly* TV series and its feature film continuation, *Serenity* (2005), or in movies following the steps of *From Dusk Till Dawn 3: The Hangman's Daughter* (1999), like *Undead or Alive: A Zombedy* (2007), *The Burrowers* (2008), *Jonah Hex* (2010), *Abraham Lincoln: Vampire Hunter* (2012), *Gallowwalkers* (2012), and *The Dark Tower* (2017);[55] (4) a cross-genre narrative of a different type, based on a *juxtaposition* (made explicit already in the title of a film like *Cowboys & Aliens*, 2011) or an *embedding*, as in *Back to the Future Part III* (1990) or *Westworld*, where science fiction is the embedding genre that gives access to a subordinate genre. A combination of the above hybrid formulas is possible, as in the standalone expansion pack *Undead Nightmare* to the video game *Red Dead Redemption* (2010), where the world of the western blends with the zombie/horror genre through an embedded story read to a child that "contaminates" the frame story according to the fusion mode and through the addition of horrific elements to the environment and the characters of the game.

Released in 1976 as a sequel to Crichton's film, *Futureworld* offered an inversion of the hierarchy of genres established in *Westworld*. Science fiction is only present in the embedding world, to the point that we are surprised to see the characters using laser pistols during the film's final minutes.[56] In fact, the sci-fi world replaces the "Westworld" resort in the theme park,[57] whose operation has been suspended since the dramatic events recounted in the first film.[58] However, the small, abandoned town of the West hosts one particular scene, as the cold-blooded gunslinger played by Yul Brynner returns for a cameo (a heavy promotional argument used also in the film's posters and lobby cards, presented as a fantasy lover of a female journalist, Tracy Ballard (Blythe Danner), inside her *mental world*, hence outside the western setting. The substitution of the science fiction genre for the western in this sequel is in itself revealing of the kinship between two genres "defined by setting and narrative content" (Grant 2007: 23). In other words, they are defined at a semantic level rather than primarily involving the syntactic levels of enunciation, destination, or function, according to the terms of genre "characterization" introduced by Raphaëlle Moine (2008: 13–17).[59] The author describes the semantic level in the following terms:

> Many genres are distinguished by semantic elements: their themes, their motifs, or their topics. The western is characterized by spaces (mountains ranges, deserts, canyons, etc.), locations (saloons, banks), characters (cowboy, horse, communities of farmers, saloon singer, sheriff, etc.), objects (wagons, coaches, colts and shotguns), situations (confrontation between hero and villain, river crossings, Indian attacks on the wagons, gunfights, etc.), all of which belong to the American West at the end of the nineteenth century (2008: 15–16).

Edward Buscombe, in his pioneering article on the definition of a film genre, takes the western as his starting point and makes a similar enumeration of elements belonging to its world, including sets, weapons, and costumes (a generic feature capitalized upon in *Westworld*'s dressing room scene, then taken up and developed in a sci-fi mode in *TRON: Legacy*). In his words: "To begin with, common sense suggests that it is possible to draw up a list of elements which are found in films that [...] are called Westerns, and to say that any film which includes one or more of these elements is thereby held to be a Western" (Buscombe 1970: 35). Still, as Moine explains later in her book, the western calls for a definition that is both semantic and syntactic. This twofold component can be detected in *Westworld* as long as the syntactic criterion of "an organization of [semantic] elements around a frontier between wilderness and civilization" (Moine 2008: 56) is reworked in view of the generic hybridity and the multiverse structure. Moreover, it is equally present on a thematic level, following Donna Haraway's thesis in *Cyborg Manifesto* on the necessity to go beyond dualisms such as "nature/culture, male/female, civilized/primitive, reality/appearance [...], creator/creature [...], God/man" (Haraway 1991: 177). Therefore, the western lends itself particularly well to a world-centered perspective due to its emphasis on the structural notion of the "frontier". It is possible to draw up an inventory of components furnishing and populating a "western world", associated with a specific historical period (as is often the case in multiverses' secondary worlds).[60] The geographical restriction to the American frontier – "broadly, from the Mississippi river to the west coast" (Grant 2007: 14) – as a defining criterion of the western, makes this genre a perfect candidate for the creation of a "small world" offered in a theme park.

The second example used by Moine, with respect to genres primarily defined by their distinctive semantic elements is the "martial arts film". This is precisely the world that the recent *Westworld* TV series crosses, albeit momentarily, with the western in its theme park. The HBO series abandons the reconstitution of the Roman era and the Middle Ages found in Crichton's film, in favor of worlds that are more directly associated with specific film genres. The seed to this idea is already present in *Futureworld*, with the somewhat incoherent appearance of three hostile samurai during a chase scene, albeit no mention is made of the world they come from.[61] On the contrary, HBO's *Westworld* raises expectations around this unusual encounter between two distinct genres at the end of Season 1, when several deactivated samurai automatons appear in Delos' underground facilities (S01E10).[62] The anticipation is growing when Delos' Head of Narrative, Lee Sizemore (Simon Quarterman), finds a samurai helmet in the snow (S02E03), building suspense exclusively through generic references. The "martial arts" genre is at last actualized in two successive episodes (S02E05 and S02E06). In the first one, whose title is a transliteration from Japanese ("Akane no Mai"), the main narrative track is centered on Maeve (Thandiwe Newton), who has an advantage over the shogun guardians by dictating their actions thanks to a "telepathic" power (Maeve's voice-over is in Japanese), and is entirely set in the world representing the Edo period. The "Shogunworld" plot alternates with the progression of Dolores' troop (Evan Rachel Wood) in "Westworld" and remains subordinated to it. The hierarchy between these worlds is acknowledged by Sizemore, who admits to having plagiarized his own ideas due to lack of time (300 stories to write in only 3 weeks) and populating, in a game of one-upmanship,[63] the Japanese world with duplicates of the characters from "Westworld". Some of the main characters, such as the couple of outlaws, are indeed confronted with their Japanese doubles, made up of the same identity traits and bequeathed with the same narrative roles, despite the difference in their physical appearance (facial features, costumes, weaponry, etc.).

The fleeting representation of this other space, associated with the Jidaigeki genre, does not challenge the centrality of the western (that actually ends up reinforced as a model), especially since the actions taking place there are totally erratic. Sizemore comments upon this when, for example, an army of ninjas implausibly storms the brothels in which the heroes have taken refuge, an intrusion unforeseen by the program. The same goes for the exotic Middle-East environment in the pre-credits scene of S02E03.[64] It does not steal the show from the western insofar as the daughter of the Ed Harris character, pursued by a lion, quickly leaves the resort associated with the sub-genre of the Indian Epic and enters "Westworld" by crossing an electric fence located between the jungle and the desert of the American West. This "Jungleworld" is actually the antechamber to the western world, whereas "Shogunworld" turns out to be only a pale copy of "Westworld". The temporary intrusion of these two genres suggests a potential multiplication of worlds geographically distributed all over Delos' installations but mutually accessible, as Maeve and her acolytes cross into a trap door inside a Japanese temple and come out through a tomb in the Westworld cemetery. This becomes more significant since the series does not provide us with a cartographic view of the installations in their entirety, unlike Crichton's *Westworld* and its sequel, *Futureworld*. Season 1 underlines the gigantic size of the "Westworld" surface through William and Hector's journey, whose duration is also multiplied by the recurrence of narrative loops. However, as William abandons Hector naked on a horse at the border of the park in the final episode, we come to realize that "Westworld" is actually a finite space.

Regarding the series' "meta-generic" dimension, the reference to the Japanese sword fighting movies is in fact part of the history of the post-classical western, developed outside of Hollywood, notably through a number of give-and-takes between Europe and Asia.[65] In *Westworld*, the conception remains US-centric, since Lee Sizemore copies – rather badly – the world of the samurai by taking the western as his primary model. The "*Star Wars*" franchise offers another example of a combination between the martial arts film and science fiction.[66] The co-presence of cowboys and characters in kimono or Japanese armor within the same shot (S02E06), which is actually a reverse shot to an image of Mount Fuji (a Japanese icon that replaces Monument Valley in the credits sequence during Season 2), seals an interpenetration of worlds linked to generic hybridity, transcending the characters and spreading over the series' world.

Back in 1973, Crichton's *Westworld* had already dealt with the kinship between *genre* and *world*, in a reflexive manner. Some of the laws governing the actions represented in this film emanate from its technological dimension and, consequently, from the science fiction genre,[67] while others refer to the western, as for example the fact that an innocent reply to a call from a gunslinger inevitably leads to a duel where the fastest draw wins. The anachronistic ideology that dominates the western played a part in the genre's gradual disappearance during the second half of the 1960s, an era marked by the rise of civil-rights movements (minority-rights protests, feminism, opposition against the Vietnam War). However, Crichton's film does not take sides with respect to these questions and delivers a simplistic and reactionary representation of a small Western town, with the excuse of the stereotypical character of a world openly presented as *artificial*. In the "Westworld" resort, only men have agency, while women are confined to the role of prostitutes or ordered to keep the visitors company.[68] In addition, no Native Americans, and in general no people of color are included in the simulated, factitious humankind populating the park. Both of these issues will be treated in a radically different manner in the recent HBO series of the same name, where the female protagonists, Dolores and Maeve, emancipate themselves from male desire and rebel against their creators.

Both in the "*Westworld*" franchise and *Back to the Future Part III*, the western functions as a fairground attraction. This was also true – in an even more literal way – in some later westerns, such as *Ride the High Country* (1962) and *Buffalo Bill and the Indians* (1976). The genre is presented as a counterfeit collection of clichés, which are meant to open up a playful space – one speaks of a "marvelous playground" in the first episode of *Beyond Westworld*, while the recent HBO series explicitly refers to a video game experience. Following on from Fredric Jameson's theses, Anne Friedberg noted that in postmodern cinema, "the 'old genre' is made the object of representation […] with the possible intention of endorsing, repeating, underlining the earlier form – recapitalizing, in a sense, on a past success" (Friedberg 1993: 174). In the same vein, Jim Collins qualified *Back to the Future Part III* as an "ironic hybridization" (1992). Still, HBO's *Westworld* takes rather seriously its reference to the western, aspiring to bring to the "small screen" the wide spaces that defined the genre's classical era, while at the same time renewing its thematic concerns by bringing the science fiction genre in the mix.

On March 13, 2002, *Variety* announced that Arnold Schwarzenegger, after shooting the third episode of the "*Terminator*" franchise, "has signed on [with Warner Bros.] to star in and produce the remake of Michael Crichton's sci-fi action thriller *Westworld*". In the end, he finally abandoned the project due to his election as Governor of California in 2003. When HBO took up the idea of a return to *Westworld* in 2016, the cable network transformed the project that was originally intended as a blockbuster action movie into a TV series, at a time when the western had already made a comeback on the small screen (the genre's principal venue during the 1950s and the 1960s), notably thanks to the impact of *Deadwood* (2004–2006), also produced by HBO.[69] *Westworld* follows this pattern by meeting a criterion celebrated by promotional discourses, critics, and the public alike, identified by Achilleas Papakonstantis as "an indicator of 'quality'", namely "the reinvention of genres" (2016: 74)[*].

In fact, the series' narrative complexity derives from the properties of the androids supposedly conceived according to principles dictated by cybernetics. In "The General and Logical Theory of Automata" (1951), the computer scientist John von Neumann studied the conditions of self-reproduction. Crichton's *Westworld* tackles the issue when one of the scientists compares the breakdown affecting the park's computers with a viral disease: "In some cases, they [the robots] have been designed by other computers, we don't know exactly how they work".[70] This fictional element from the original film could be considered as the starting point for the HBO series, launched in 2016, at a time when the implications of machine learning and, more generally speaking, of Artificial Intelligence, emerge as an important social issue, as the Swiss produced documentary *The Brain* (2020) clearly showed. However, while the autonomy gained by the androids in Crichton's *Westworld* results from a bug, in the HBO series the same event is presented as a sign of an evolutionary process that ends up questioning the supremacy of Man. One finds here an inversion of the power relations between masters and servants, reminiscent of the plots in the "*Planet of the Apes*" and, of course, the "*Terminator*" franchises. This motif is actually inherited from Karel Čapek's science fiction play *R.U.R.* (1920), in which the term "robot" appeared for the first time – "robota" means "worker" in Slavic languages. The major change the HBO series brought to this tradition, as well as to Crichton's film and its sequels, lies in a radical shift in terms of point of view. We do not enter in the series' world following a group of guests arriving at the park for their holiday vacation, as was the case in the 1973 film. The story begins with Teddy, the "nice cowboy" character played by James Marsden, arriving at Sweetwater by train as a guest, although actually he is a host. The spectator is introduced into the fiction through a group of characters unaware of their status as artificial beings and of the spectacularization of their lives for the pleasure of guests comparable to *The Truman Show*'s TV viewers. The series' audience actually knows from the very first minutes, due to a number of questions addressed in voice-over at Dolores,[71] that these characters are not human and live in an *artificial world*, even if the first two seasons reserve a couple of surprises.

I will discuss in the last part of Chapter 3 the persistence on first-person representations associated with robots in HBO's *Westworld*. It is sufficient to stress that the modes of immersion in the simulated world are ostensibly derived from contemporary video game practices, especially in open-world games such as those produced by Rockstar Games, a publisher responsible for a famous action-adventure game set in a western environment, *Red Dead Redemption* (2010). A sequel to this game was released in 2019, parallel to the broadcast of *Westworld* (see Boillat 2018b). Dolores Abernathy and Maeve Millay are initially caught in action loops, just like an avatar in a video game when operated by a gamer who does not succeed in advancing (see Dolores' five consecutive awakenings/reboots in the first episode alone). They struggle to disentangle from these loops in order to replace the gameplay imposed by Delos with a narrative logic that would allow them to regain control of their own destiny – even if the series' authors demonstrate, not without a certain cynicism, the limits of any pre-programmed universe and, more broadly, those of the submission of the story to the predetermined laws of a fictional world (as in *Tenet*). Their realization is similar to the one of cyberpunk heroes caught up in a situation reminiscent of the allegory of the cave. Moreover, Dolores' father becomes dysfunctional due to a recurrent motif in cyberpunk movies, a photographic trace, leading his daughter to reflect on her own ontological status. A guest takes a selfie outside the park, but instead of the picture, Dolores finds a gun with which she will transgress a structural directive rule dictating that hosts are unable to pull the trigger when aiming at a human (as in Isaak Asimov's *Robot* series).

The entire first season focuses on a constant palimpsest between the science fiction and the western genres, as characters interpret everything that happens from a perspective associated with the latter, while viewers know that all narrative events can be best understood in terms imposed by the former. When Dolores raves about the vast wilderness of the "New World", seeing "a place with unlimited possibilities" (S01E01), she does not only formulate a typical pioneer's dream, but also refers to the possibilities of a tree-like (video game-style) narrative that relies on user interaction. The young woman expresses her regret that her fiancé, now back in town, never considers taking her elsewhere, postponing the prospective trip to uncertain times. In her words: "Sometimes I feel like the world out there is calling me" (S01E03). However, the truth is that this *artificial world*, governed by remote surveillance and geolocation administered from an operations center equipped with a gigantic, real-time holographic map of the park (similar to the one representing Pandora in *Avatar*) (Color Plate 3), has in fact physical borders. Each host is restricted to a path defined by a limited number of possibilities within a pre-programmed narrative. The inhabitants of the small Western town, reminiscent of the one found in films like *High Plains Drifter* (1973),[72] may end up dead in some of Dolores' visions due to the hosts' deactivation. The natives, aka the tribes living outside

Sweetwater, seem to hold a secret stemming from shamanic practices and transmitted via hieroglyphics. Their animism sharpens their sensitivity towards the other world, as evidenced by the statuette modeled after Delos' employees dressed in what seems like chemical suits that a Native-American child drops on the ground in front of Maeve's eyes in S01E04. Hector, an outlaw raised among Indians, will recognize this statuette, scribbled by Maeve, as a representation of "the man who walks between worlds [...] sent from hell to oversee our world". Lastly, the labyrinth drawn inside the scalp (a pattern reminiscent of the spiral in *Dark City*), showing the way to the game's deepest level, combines the initiatory ritual, typical of tales featuring Indians, with computer science's "Easter egg". Dolores and Maeve break free from a violent patriarchy,[73] a gender norm thus exposed, as the cultural industry is represented as an instrument for the satisfaction of male desire.

Westworld's broadcast started in 2016, the year MGM released a remake of one the most famous classic westerns, *The Magnificent Seven* (1960). In the TV series, Ed Harris' "Man in Black" is the evolution of Yul Brynner's character in the original film, simply called "The Gunslinger". Harris is one of the few Hollywood actors in the 21st century associated with the western (alongside Clint Eastwood and Kevin Costner), especially after the release of *Appaloosa* (2008), a movie he directed and co-scripted. The actor-related intertext is crucial:[74] Harris plays one of the main characters in *Sweetwater* (2013), a film that, like *Westworld*, deconstructs the gender stereotypes associated with the western. In fact, one of the main areas in the theme park in HBO's TV series is named after that movie, while its on-screen appearance is specifically associated with one of Ramin Djawadi's music themes. Moreover, Ed Harris' character in *The Truman Show* (1998) also associates the Hollywood actor with a cynical figure that manipulates an *artificial world*. Unlike the gunslinger in Crichton's film, the "Man in Black" is not a host, but a guest who managed to become Delos' major shareholder. Yul Brynner played an empty "shell", a gunfighter deeply rooted in the culture of violence as well as the mythology of the nation's origins and the social construction of heroism in the USA,[75] without keeping any kind of critical distance towards this character (unlike Henry King's *The Gunfighter*, 1950). Contrastingly, Harris' "Man in Black" is a character with an important psychological depth.[76] The disillusionments he experienced during his prolonged stay in the park revealed to him his own taste for power and blood, while his obsessive quest for a deeper meaning, supposedly hidden at the center of the "maze" (i.e. the park), nearly drove him mad. Like a Greek mythology hero, he involuntarily commits an infanticide.

Focusing on the sci-fi production of a western world, the series assimilates worlds and genres, exploiting the affinities between the two notions. In doing so, it becomes a rather obvious case of a meta-serial production,[77] one that is also conscious of its worldbuilding dimension, insofar as the story relies primarily on the relationship between creators and creatures, as expressed through the concepts of paternity and maternity.[78] While the fictional employees of the park working under the direction of Dr. Robert Ford (Anthony Hopkins) advocate total immersion, the audience is barely immersed in the series' world, instead observing its (mal)function. Still, the viewer is also lured, notably with respect to his understanding of diegetic time, distorted by a systematic use of crosscutting, an editing pattern generally associated with the simultaneity between different narrative tracks, and by the insistence on an internal focalization on Dolores, who will only later recognize the "Man in Black" as her lover William.

The most iconic promotional image of Season 1 is a female version of the "Vitruvian Man" (Color Plate 5), standing out from a typical Western landscape, symbolizing the opposition between the rationalism of science and wilderness, between the notion of "Man being at the center of the Universe" and the widescreen expansion of the fictional world he has created. This image is emblematic of the series' generic hybridization and highlights a displacement operated at the level of gender that brings *Westworld* closer to Ira Levin's satire in *The Stepford Wives*, in which "sexually submissive mechanical *hausfraus* [are] designed to replicate and replace the men's real wives" (Neill 2018: 257).[79] Furthermore, the entire credits sequence announces the entanglement of generic affiliations and associates the beginning of each episode with the pattern of the creation of a world.[80] Its first shot suggests, in the absence of any reference points allowing us to measure the scale of the depicted set, that a sun is rising behind a hilly landscape. In fact, we only see the skeleton of a mechanical horse whose ribs are underlined by an artificial lighting and which is being surgically remolded by two robotic arms, in an operation reminiscent of those in the automobile industry's assembly lines. It is certainly no coincidence that the inventor launching Westworld is named Ford, in a clear reference to the era of Taylorism's first applications in the United States. In the age of 3D printing, the manufactured artifact is of a dazzling whiteness, similar to a marble sculpture with its weight, its materiality, and a connotation of harmony that celebrates the act of creation, even if industrially conceived. After all, this is true for all art whose aura has been sacrificed by its reproducibility, as Walter Benjamin showed. At the same time, the creative act also takes on a quasi-marvelous dimension, echoing the acheiropoietic representations of the religious tradition.

The artifact may come into being without the intervention of a human hand ("*sine manu facta*"), but the very hand of the automaton's skeleton that presses the piano keys in sync with the notes of the credits scene's soundtrack, also turns out to be a decoy, after we realize that the piano is a mechanical one: it goes on playing even when the automaton's hands move away from the keys. The player piano reappears in the Sweetwater saloon, associated with Maeve's repetitive scenes and functioning as a symbol of her taking control over her environment. As she stops the scrolling of the player piano's perforated cylinder

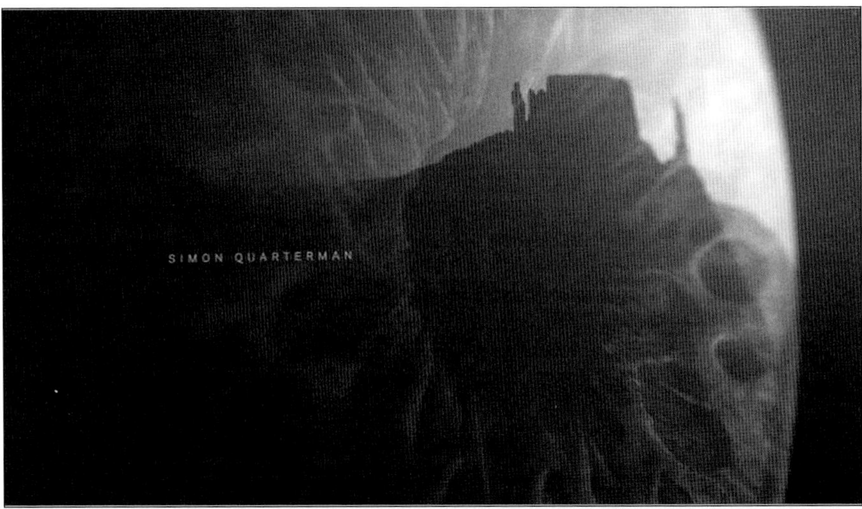

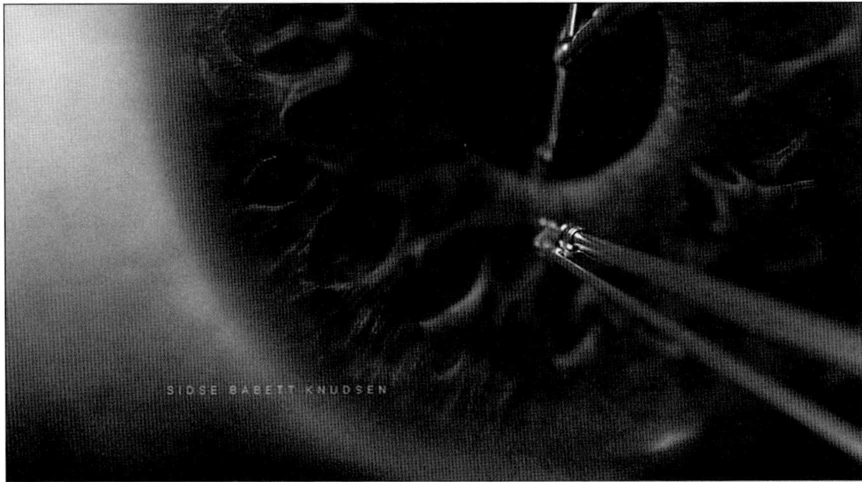

Figs. 19 (upper) and 20 (lower):
Opening credits from the HBO TV series *Westworld*: western landscapes reflected on an artificial eye.

(which is in fact a metonymy for the series' "worldbuilding machine", integrated as it is within the western environment),[81] she passes from a simple character to being the story's narrator (S01E07).

Another of the series' motifs appears next in the credits sequence, showing two opposite sex androids in a posture that evokes mating. We are actually watching machines-making-machines, since the human inventor (Ford) remains off-screen. Soon after, the manufacturing of artificial individuals spreads out, as we witness the creation of the world that will host them. The image of a landscape with a tableland typical of the Wild West – part of the same isotopy as the horse, its female rider, and the barrel of a six-shooter shown in a close-up – appears superimposed on the branches of an optic nerve, as if the perceiving subject were being fabricated at the same time as the object of its perception. The credits scene does not include a direct image of the American West: this environment is but an image reflected on the cornea of an eye under construction (Figs. 19–20). At that moment, the circular membrane of the iris merges with the visual motif of the "Vitruvian Man". This pattern is also integrated inside the diegesis as the logo of the Westworld theme park, in tandem with the motif of the maze featuring a human figure on the inside. The latter may be seen as a metaphor of the consciousness Dolores must access when confronted with a maze of possible alternatives. The faded colors of this evanescent tourist image connote antiquity, as if it were a source found in the archives. Such an image with exaggerated photochemical traits, alongside the player-piano that is part of a tradition of automata (or the strip of tape in a Turing Machine), and the profile shot of the horse whose gallop is filmed in slow motion, evoking the work of Eadweard Muybridge, establishes a framework that is more akin to media archaeology than science fiction. The skein of generic references out of which *Westworld*'s multiverse is interwoven, revolves around the in-between, articulating the past and the future, art and industry, nature and culture. Even in the opening credits of Season 2 that include a brief shot where the reflected on the pupil of an eye tableland is replaced by Mount Fuji from "Shogunworld", the western genre remains dominant through motifs like the buffalo or the Stetson. In the credits scene for Season 3, there is no image representing "Warworld", a world situated in a European city under the yoke of fascism during World War 2, where Maeve and Hector find themselves (a case of a reset). In *Westworld*, the western genre is the matrix of the fictional world inside the fiction.

Season 3, broadcast during the spring of 2020 in the midst of a global health crisis, attempts a complete reorientation in terms of movie genres. In fact, the shift already begins in the previous season, when the objectives of Delos' leaders are unveiled: a massive collection of personal data via the recording of the guests' behavior, as well as a project of transferring one's identity into an artificial body that supposedly leads to immortality (like in *Realive*, 2016). Now that the heroes are out of the park and back in "the" world, the western is only a memory from the first two seasons,[82] supplanted by the science fiction genre that was previously confined to Delos' underground facilities or in Dr. Ford's past. That said, this world is not identical to ours, despite the technological advances introduced by companies like DeepMind. It resembles a version of a near future, extrapolated from 2020, with electric vehicles auto-piloted through complex software straight out of Elon Musk's imagination, drones that can transport passengers inside a limousine cabin, highly advanced methods of tracking and geo-localization, telecommunications producing a confounding holographic visualization, and futuristic architecture.[83] The desert plain is replaced by a crowded urban center, populated by users of "new" technologies on which they are so dependent that Dolores' AI will have no trouble taking control of "their" world.[84] The series goes on dealing with the issue of facticity, in the form of a world superimposed on reality, no longer distinguished from it thanks to generic traits, but denying its own belonging to a specific genre.

Westworld's showrunners, Lisa Joy and Jonathan Nolan, argue that the ultimate stage of the "matrix" consists in the total invisibilisation of technology via its integration into the daily life of users. A seemingly innocent line from a secondary character during a party scene underlines the series' proximity to the cyberculture multiverses I will discuss in Chapter 5: "Just think about this. For one second. How fucking ironic would it be if they had put a simulation within a simulation?" (S01E01). As my analysis will show, the novel Simulacron-3 and its screen adaptations that prefigure "*The Matrix*" franchise, provide the model for such a hypothesis that *Westworld* examines mostly in a metaphorical way rather than in terms of worldbuilding. Dolores takes on the mission of awakening people's conscience so as to "show this world for what it really is" (S03E03), by throwing into chaos a society organized on the basis of a generalized and coercive computer surveillance.[85] In an episode wittingly titled "Genre" (S03E05 – see also Chapter 4), Dolores wreaks havoc by disclosing to everybody the entirety of his or her life stories, as written by the system. While everyone around her discovers, stunned and in tears, the "reality" about themselves and their loved ones through their cell phone screen, Caleb observes the riots in the streets and asks Giggles (Marshawn Lynch), a member of Dolores' armed group: "What genre is this?", to which the latter replies with a laconic phrase that nonetheless touches on the subject of the world's ontological status: "It's reality, man".

Lost in *Fringe* Worlds: Multiverse and Seriality

By definition, a multiverse offers the possibility of multiple developments. It is therefore not surprising that this type of fiction is recurrent in sci-fi plots that put emphasis on worldbuilding and evolve in serial practices, thanks to transmedia storytelling, whether in feature films as those of the "*Resident Evil*" franchise (see Chapter 1), or in TV fiction. The structure of these TV shows has a strong tendency to be serialized. Going from one world to the other (and back) encourages a potential infinite number of narrative extensions (although they can also lead to the dead end of saturation and confusion according to Besson 2015: 156–166).

Sliders (1995–2000) is an indicative case of such a multiverse. In each episode, we discover at least one different version of the planet Earth, as it exists in a parallel dimension. The series' four protagonists visit randomly these parallel dimensions while in search of their world of origin,[86] through an inadequate use of the "Timer", a device controlled by young geek Quinn Mallory (Jerry O'Connell) so as to remotely pilot a machine that creates wormholes connecting universes (a breach qualified as a "portal"). During the opening credits, the hero's voice-over lays down the principle according to which the Earth exists in an infinite number of alternative versions (as do, potentially, the episodes in this TV series), visualized by the spiraled multiplication of the Earth's image (Fig. 21).

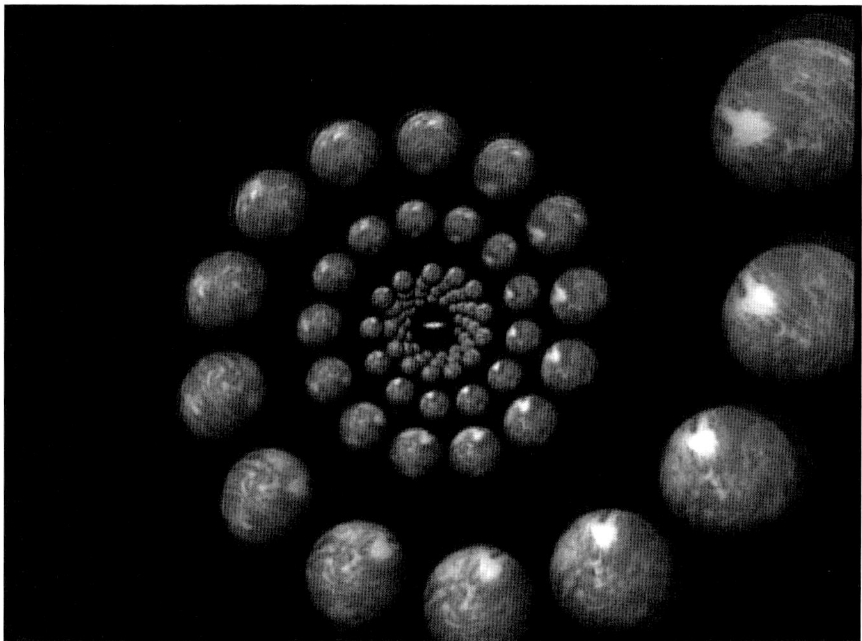

Fig. 21: The vertigo of parallel Earths in the opening credits of the *Sliders* TV series (Season 1, 1995).

This association between the planet Earth and the idea of a *parallel world* is reminiscent of the imagination of the revolutionary Louis-Auguste Blanqui as developed in his book *Eternity by the Stars* (1872 – see Bayard 2014: 21-23).[87] Admittedly, this is a much older model compared to quantum physics to which the series' characters regularly refer – at least the two white male heroes, who embody scientific knowledge, whereas the young woman and the African-American character are presented as the neophytes who need the explanations the series actually seeks to supply its audience. The gadget called "Timer" should not deceive us: as in *Source Code* or *Tenet* (see Chapter 1), the series openly (and proudly) clarifies that this is not a "conventional" time travel. The story deals with successive passages from one *parallel world* to the other, and this is true even when we recognize the past as that of our own world. In S03E04, when Quinn watches himself as a little boy attending his father's funeral in 1984, Professor Arturo (John Rhys-Davies) speaks, rather pompously, of the "Straight Relativistic Time Dilation Theory", supposedly conceived by Van Meer (a fictitious astrophysicist!), according to which there could be a parallel

Earth revolving around the Sun in a rotation speed significantly faster than that of our planet. Such an explanation heavily emphasizes that the series' principal narrative issue is not temporal, but world-centered. Fittingly, the French translation of the title of each episode starts with the words "Un monde …[A world]" or "Le monde selon …[The world according to]".

In the series' pilot, the young inventor of an anti-gravity device goes back and forth between *parallel worlds* before returning to his basement where he keeps his machine. However, *Sliders* refrains from both the embedding and the alternating structures. The worlds are depicted in succession, as the audience never actually leaves the travelers,[88] according to the logic of a tight flow typical of screenwriting in the field of serial fiction. In the pilot, which is in fact divided into two different episodes, Quinn ignores the warnings against the use of the "Timer", confided by one of his doubles who comes from another world and is more advanced in his research than the series' hero. Quinn briefly visits this other world, which differs from his own only in few details (for example, cars have to stop in view of the green light, instead of the red one). In this way, the series establishes a strict respect of the principle of minimal departure that guarantees a certain consistency through the development of the story's possible alternatives and the characters' doubles. Therefore, the creaking sound of the fence door in his mother's house becomes for Quinn a decisive criterion for the identification of the ontology of the world he belongs. Yet, he soon realizes the inadequacy of this criterion when, having entered the house with his friends, confident that he is still in "his" world, he is joined at the table by his father, though his mother has been a widow for many years now (S01E02). Inversely, the door's failure to creak will incite him in the following season to make a deduction that will prove to be erroneous (S02E01): he has been sent to his planet of origin by one of his doubles, who pretends to be a sorcerer in a world governed by the occult. However, as the viewers will later discover in the episode's ironic epilogue thanks to a paralepsis, the gardener oiled the door hinges, right after the four heroes threw themselves into the vortex and towards other worlds, being under the mistaken belief that this one was not theirs. The narrative exploitation of such confusions between different worlds is recurrent in *Sliders* and becomes more complex as seasons go by (see for instance the first episode in Season 5).

Sliders' pilot resembles a time-loop movie, while the following episodes share few elements with time travel stories. In S01E02, Wade discovers a double of herself, who occupies a high rank in a rebel army in an America ruled by a communist dictatorship (represented as a dystopia nourished by Cold War cultural references), just like Sarah Connor learns in *The Terminator* that she will become a leader of the human resistance in a machine-dominated future. The new world offered in each episode is easily accessible from the point of view of the audience's world of reference, constituting in fact both a *repetition* and a *variation*, according to a process essential to seriality. In fact, the diegetic *parallel world* always results from a speculation – mostly a political one – on contemporary (American) reality that operates on the basis of a "what if" adjustment: if penicillin had not been discovered, if the scientific world had not invented the atomic bomb (fearing its consequences), if the American War of Independence had been won by Great Britain and, consequently, North America had become a monarchy, etc.[89] The comparison that presents itself explicitly to the characters (forced to interpret their environment, especially in the case of Maximilian Arturo, a professor of "cosmology and ontology", present until the twentieth episode of Season 3) and implicitly to the viewers, frequently functions as the portrait of a dystopia which celebrates by contrast the real United States of the 1990s, and seldom as an offbeat critique of our world. For instance, in "The Weaker Sex" (S01E08), male characters find themselves in a society exclusively run by women (a female president, mayor, executives, and pope), confronted with prejudices and gender inequalities that prevail in a patriarchal society.

Worth of note is that Fox actually broadcast *Sliders*' episodes defying their intended order. After the second part of the pilot, it was episode number Six that was released – a world where the sixties' "Summer of Love" never really ended – instead of episode Three, "Fever", which depicted a much more dystopian version of planet Earth and was broadcast fifth in order. In this episode, the paranoia, the social inequalities, and the army's intervention due to sanitary reasons are explained by a global pandemic, which, in retrospect, resonates with the upheavals known in our real world due to COVID-19. In a way, "Fever" constitutes a precedent for the *Counterpart* TV series, created by Justin Marks as a premonitory representation of such a possible world. The network's shuffling of the episodes' order testifies to the precedence given in *Sliders* to the multiverse over the chronology of the actual story.

In *Counterpart*, the duplication of each of the main characters with his or her alter ego in the *parallel world* generates a narrative amplification that perfectly applies to the principle of alternating points of view, typical of serialized shows. Although every hero is clearly distinguished from his double on a psychological level,[90] the co-presence of two contradictory versions provides depth to these characters. A double is to his other Self all the latter could have become under different circumstances, provoking that way the viewers' curiosity.

A joint discussion of the possible worlds logic and serial practices allows us to reflect on the ways the same fiction is spread across multiple "movies" (in this case, the episodes of a series' season), within an ensemble identified as unique and generally attached to the same "world-makers", the showrunners. The relationship between serial fiction and cinema, even when it is not as explicit as in cases like *Bates Motel* (2013–2017) or *Gotham* (2014–2019), results from the fact that numerous writers and directors who make world-centered feature films, have cut their teeth in the TV industry. This is the case of Damon

Lindelof, who scripted *Prometheus* (2012) after having co-created the *Lost* series, as well as that of Jeffrey Jacob Abrams, founder of Bad Robot Productions (*Alias*, *Lost*, *Fringe*, *Castle Rock*), who is recognized as one of the major "auteurs" in contemporary Hollywood cinema.[91] He has indeed participated in the conception and production of "high concept" TV series that are essential to any study focusing on worldbuilding, such as *Lost* (2004–2010)[92] and *Fringe* (2008–2013),[93] while he is also the executive producer of *Westworld* (2016–2020). During his TED ("Technology, Entertainment & Design") talk in 2007, often discussed by fans, critics, and academic scholars alike, Abrams, when commenting upon *Lost*, applied the "magic box" model referring to an item also present in films like *Kiss Me Deadly* (1955), the "*Hellraiser*" movie series (1987–2018), *Mulholland Dr.* (2001), *The Lost Room* TV miniseries, and *The Box* (2009).[94] Florent Favard quoted Abrams' remarks on the creative frame of *Lost*'s fictional world:

> Fascinated by "infinite possibility", Abrams values "mystery [as] the catalyst of imagination" and sees stories as mystery boxes, insisting on the fact that there is "what you think you're getting, then what you're really getting" (Favard 2016: 5).

Although Abrams left the *Lost* TV series early in its first season to work on *Mission: Impossible III* (2006), he laid the foundations on which screenwriters Damon Lindelof and Carlton Cruse would depend, in a series which "eventually proved to be one of the most complex pieces of television (and transmedia) storytelling ever devised" (Mittell 2015: 93).[95] A paroxysmal exploitation of the logic of *possible worlds* can be observed in both *Lost* and *Fringe*. Playing on the alternation of different narrative tracks and the implementation, within the filmic universe, of the principle of repetition/variation – a given situation is replayed in another "world" – allows for an almost indefinite expansion of the narrative material and, consequently, for a multiplication of the number of episodes. In order to increase the suspense (or rather, most of all, the curiosity aroused by the enigmatic character of the world offered),[96] Abrams and his collaborators created two series out of inextinguishable matrices of stories and worlds – at the risk of undermining the consistency of these worlds – that only negative ratings seem able to "exhaust". In these series, the borders between real (aka realistic), *mental*, and *parallel worlds* tend to blur, just as in David Lynch's landmark multiverse series *Twin Peaks*.[97]

In *Lost*, the narrative organization is not effaced before the content of the story. Instead, it tends to attract interest in itself. The "dramatic twists" occurring in the final episode in five of the total of six seasons not only bring new narrative elements (even if the emergence of new characters, hitherto hidden on the island, constitutes a springboard for the plot), but also announce a complete reconfiguration in terms of form and/or worlds, just like in *Sliders* (whose episodic dimension is however stronger). The alternation between narrative tracks devoted to actions taking place on the island and the visualization of other space-time continuums, operate according to five distinct modes, introduced in a progressive manner. All of them are subject to the narrative principle of the (internal) variable (or multiple) focalization (Genette 1980: 189–190), appropriate for the development of a network of characters of an increasing complexity, visually inscribed in the opening shots of each episode, showing the wide open eye of one of the protagonists.[98]

During the first two seasons, (1) all insert shots correspond to flashbacks devoted successively to each of the main characters who survived the Oceanic Flight 815 crash (and who also suffer in the present from visions that echo the visualized past). Most of these flashbacks constitute "external analepses", according to Genette's theory (*Ibid.*: 48–50), as they go back to a time before the flight. In this regard, the series' pilot constitutes an exception, since its "flashbacks were just to the airplane prior to it crashing, focused on three characters' different perspective, but that model clearly could not be sustained for long" (Mittell 2015: 64–65). Still, there is room for surprises, as in S02E22 that includes a flashback of only eleven days (while the crash took place more than sixty days earlier), centered on Michael Dawson (Harold Perrineau). The final shot in the second part of the Season 2 finale ("Live Together, Die Alone") shows Penny Widmore (Sonya Walger) at the end of a telephone line.[99] She is Desmond's loved one, absent from the island, whose existence had so far been evoked only in flashbacks focusing on Desmond (Henry Ian Cusick). This shot could suggest that a new mode will be established in the next season, based on the principle of a (never actualized) *simultaneity* between narrative tracks associated with spatially disjointed places (2) by means of characters located outside the confined space of the island. Although the last episodes of Season 3 deal with an attempt to communicate with characters outside the group of the plane crash survivors (and, more specifically, with the alleged "rescue team" of Naomi's boat), it remains overall organized through flashbacks nonetheless extended to the "Others" (the inhabitants of the island, until then off-screen – except for those who have mingled with the survivors by pretending to be part of them). This decentralization in terms of "focal" characters is underlined already in the opening of this season which shows a flashback of the on-flight explosion and the plane crash from the viewpoint of community members settled on the island. At the end of Season 3, in episodes 22 and 23, a new mode is established that will prevail during the entire Season 4. However, once again, the audience will only realize it in the final images of that season, since an ambiguity is maintained up until then (a drunk Jack talks about his father as if he were still alive, whereas the scene is in fact situated well after his death). This mode consists of flash-forwards (3) devoted to the six survivors ("external prolepses" according to Genette 1980: 68–69), who have returned to normal life after the crash, yet some of them are obsessed with the idea of going back on the island.[100] The play on temporality is a priori unexpected, particularly for a series based on suspense, since it involves a form of spoiler (though, on the other hand, it increases the curiosity generated by the enigmatic plot). This process will be placed on a systematic footing, in the specific form of "repeating prolepses" – which "double, however slightly, a narrative section to come" (*Ibid.*: 71) – in *Flashforward*, a series which represented for ABC a (failed) attempt to repeat the success of *Lost*.[101] The show was cancelled after only one season, yet its finale suggests that a variation on the (a–)chronology of the story would have intervened between the two seasons: a new blackout occurs in the final minutes of the last episode ("Future Shock") and the protagonists experience new visions that this time concern a more distant future than the first time. However, in *Lost*, flash-forwards are not consistently related to visions experienced by the characters. In this way, the audience feels especially manipulated by the "grand image-maker".[102] During Season 5, viewers are not alone in time-travelling, (4) as the characters are indeed sent back in the 1970s, at the time of the "Dharma Initiative" project. The mostly psychological experiments conducted under this project are responsible for a series of supernatural phenomena that take place on the island. The discovery of the various Dharma stations, hidden all over the island, marks out John Locke's (Terry O'Quinn) journey – a philosophical one, given the character's name. Lastly, (5) Season 6 presents an *alternate (story)world*, which may be considered in retrospect a *supernatural world*, insofar as the characters meet in a kind of purgatory. The audience gets to see in this world – thanks to what the fans have called "flash-sideways" (a transition consistently marked by a particular sound effect) – what each of the main characters would have become, had the Flight 815 crash not taken place. However, this is not a reboot, since the protagonists gradually come to remember the events of the series' main plotline with which they want to reconnect, just like the female heroes in *Dollhouse* or *Westworld*. The mutual accessibility between worlds is not only guaranteed, but also constitutes the engine of the entire narrative construction. One could argue, by means of a comparison inspired by linguistics, that a shift is taking place in *Lost* from the temporal level (present/past/future) to the modal level (we go from the indicative to the conditional). That said, these categories are constantly intertwined due to the representation's strong subjective dimension, determined by each character's *worldview*.[103]

The exploration of these possible narrative alternatives is constantly carried out alternately with the frame story taking place on the island and identified as the diegetic "present". In Chapter 4, I will discuss the importance of crosscutting in multiverse movies. In *Lost*, a number of connections are established between the different narrative tracks, reinforcing our impression of being confronted with a plurality of worlds and a considerable extension of the series' basic narrative data. Such a world-centered creative design places *Lost* in the category identified by David Lavery as the "Long-Term Television Narrative" (2009). Lavery points out that *Lost*'s screenwriters claim to follow the model of a Dickensian soap opera. We actually find Desmond reading *Our Mutual Friend*, a novel written by the famous English author, in the prologue of the first episode in Season 2 (and once again in a flashback in S02E23), as he steps through the trapdoor, a threshold one has to cross in order to "unblock a level", according to a principle common in video games (Fig. 22).

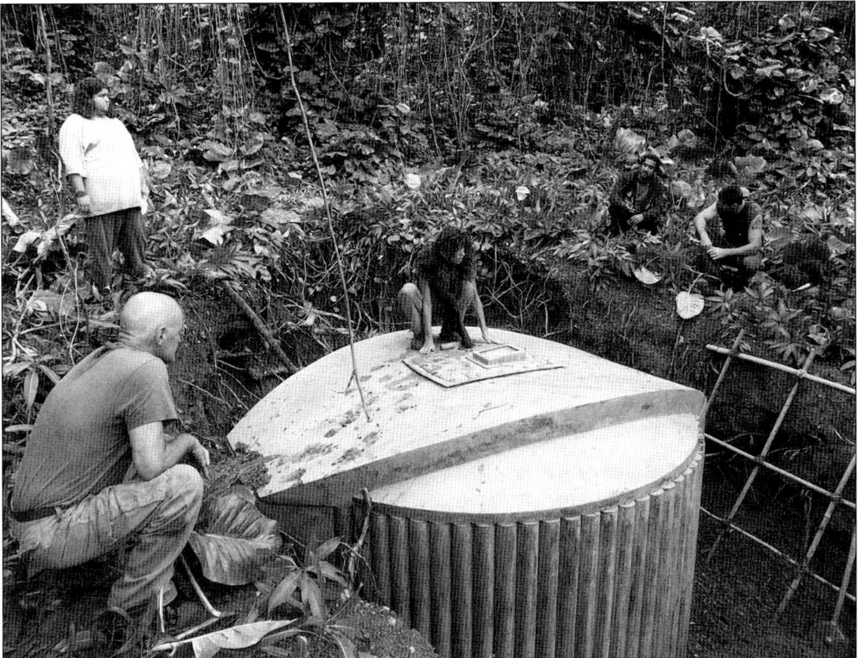

Fig. 22: "Easter egg": one of *Lost*'s "hatches" gives access to the island's underground facilities.

The disruption of temporality beginning in Season 4, impacts not only the way viewers access the story, but also the relationship the characters share with "their" fluctuating world. Therefore, the series' work on temporality has implications openly world-centered. In this respect, S04E05 subverts the existing pattern: Desmond is violently (and involuntarily) tossed back and forth between two temporal strata (the years 1996 and 2004, respectively), ending in complete disorientation. The editing stitches together actions related to the same protagonist while being extremely discontinuous. The episode's title, "The Constant", refers clearly to Desmond's attempt to find the *invariant* between these two worlds, according to the meaning given to this term by Saul Kripke in *Naming and Necessity* (1980), then taken up in literature theory (see Pavel 1986). From a philosophical point of view pertaining to modal logic, it refers to anything that may guarantee the relation of accessibility and, therefore, connection between possible worlds. The screenwriters have integrated into the story the identification of "constant" elements ensuring the consistency of the world by transforming it into the object of the hero's quest. Two names act as invariants: Desmond Hume (again the obvious philosophical reference) and Penny Widmore. Desmond's love for Penny, a character only episodically present in the series, is the narrative element that imposes an *alternate (story)world*.[104] The showrunners also dealt with the question of invariants in a more pragmatic level, as they had to adapt the cast to the new directions taken by the writers. As Mittell has shown, the series' DVD edition introduces a retrospective change in S02E03, comparable to the use of the image of a new Anakin Skywalker (Hayden Christensen, instead of Sebastian Shaw) in the "Special Edition" (1997) of *Star Wars: Episode VI – Return of the Jedi* (1983): "In the post-broadcast versions of 'Orientation', the photograph [of Desmond and Penny] is replaced by an image of Sonia Walger, who was later cast to play Penny" (Mittell 2015: 38).

Emotions, considered an inalienable feature of human individuals, act as reference points allowing the series' characters to orient themselves in the maze of possible alternatives. In the final season's *alternate (story)world*, unleashed by the island's electromagnetic forces (actually a narrative "pretext" that makes it possible to "resuscitate" the protagonists), the world of reference established during the previous seasons gradually becomes attainable, as each of the characters gains access, thanks to a "revelation", to the memory of his alter ego in the other version. From that moment on, the characters "remember" everything they have experienced and felt in a *parallel world*. They recognize their other self during this instantaneous *déjà vu* and decide to enter the *afterlife* together. The religious connotations of this epiphany are reinforced when the characters gather in a church. Jack is the only one reluctant to believe, at least at first, as if he embodied the screenwriters' hesitancy regarding the ultimate convergence of the different versions that would inevitably end a series defined by a supposedly interminable development of possible alternatives.

In an effort to survive[105] on an uncharted island, the protagonists' actions in *Lost* are dictated by their understanding of the components of this *distant world*. In this respect, the show closely follows the pattern envisioned by Jules Verne in *The Mysterious Island* (1875), before leaning towards the storyline found in *The Island of Doctor Moreau* (H.G. Wells, 1896), and then the one in *The Invention of Morel* (Adolfo Bioy Casares, 1940). Its episodes follow the progressive discovery of the "true" identity of the different protagonists present on the atoll, a space divided into the coast inhabited by the Flight 815 passengers – split in two groups, since the plane's tail was detached during the crash – and the interior of the island, populated already by the "Others" whose story remains obscure for a long time. A fundamental aspect of *Lost*'s story is the exploration of this "small world"[106] and its unusual laws. Acquiring information is systematically deferred by radical changes in focus and hindered by numerous lies, conspiracies, abductions, sabotage, and mystifications.

As the characters discover various technological artifacts, the remains of experiments carried out in the seventies and now fallen into disuse, the island turns out to be a laboratory with hidden low-tech machines whose objectives remain cryptic – such as the electromagnetic device that produces "The Light". The main function of such "meta-fictional gadgets" (to borrow, once again, Saint-Gelais' term) with which the survivors of the plane crash improvise, is to exhibit – and therefore naturalize – the complex workings of the series' *narrative mechanism*. As Mittell remarked about series like *Lost*, "often [writers] forgo strict realism in exchange for a formally aware baroque quality in which *we watch the process of narration as a machine* rather than engaging in its diegesis" (2006: 35). For my part, I do not consider that the exhibition of this narrative process functions to the detriment of fictional immersion. Much like in David Cronenberg's horror movies (see Boillat 2002), the metaphorical dimension does not exclude the actual manipulation of such artifacts by the characters inside the diegetic world and their decisive role for the represented actions. Furthermore, the characters, with all their psychological traits, participate in this process of narration within the fiction. As is evidenced by their interactions with fans in social networks, the screenwriters are conscious that "a series like *Lost* asks viewers to believe that the twisty, looping narrative is guided by a master plan exhibiting continuity and consistency" (Mittell 2015: 39). An elusive character like Jacob, who remains unseen for a long time before appearing as a spirit, would also possess a master plan inside the fiction. The viewer's identification with such a hero is not broken insofar as the latter is defined by a meta-narrative quest. Mittell speaks of a double task demanded of viewers by a series "with a heightened degree of self-consciousness in storytelling mechanics": the TV show is "demanding intensified viewer engagement focused on both diegetic pleasures and formal awareness" (*Ibid.*: 53).

During *Lost*'s Season 2, an underground control room filled with monitors and computers is equipped with a countdown timer that determines the exact time the operator must press a button, after a 108-minute cycle. Twenty-four episodes later, Desmond is persuaded by John Locke to disobey this simple ritual: he does not press the button, causing an explosion that will also be that of the series' narrative data. An electronic voice proclaims repeatedly "system failure", an alarm that could also refer to *Lost*'s narrative mechanism. Desmond's turning on the key on the self-destruct device is a gesture that literalizes a kind of hermeneutic *reset* of the show.

The indeterminacy concerning the ontological status of each of the diegeses and their relation to each other, generates a feeling of a profound strangeness that triggered an interpretative fervor among the community of Internet fans of *Lost*, even more vivid and massive than the one aroused by *Mulholland Dr.* (2001).[107] Florent Favard summarized one of the main research topics on TV series studied by scholars like Jason Mittel or Stacey Abbott: "Along with *Lost* and its intricate six seasons plot came another revolution: […] culture became (all the more) participatory thanks to web 2.0, and the collective intelligence of thousands of Mittell's 'forensic fans' allowed the viewers to crack even the most complex alternate reality game" (Favard 2016: 3).

The curiosity provoked and constantly maintained by *Lost* among its numerous fans – at least until an inevitably disappointing finale[108] – is partly due to the esoteric vein exploited by the series' writers, reinforced over the seasons and attached to a mythological account of the world's origins that is only revealed in the 118th episode. In this show, screenwriting is placed under the aegis of Leibnizian Theodicy, as long as the characters are perceived as tiny units in a tightly ordered world, whose rules escape them and tend to limit the field of exercise of their free will. The storyline associated with the character of Hurley (Jorge Garcia) is emblematic in this respect. Hurley heard a patient in a psychiatric institution mumbling a combination of numbers, in a past that constitutes the real side of a *mental world*, which will converge at times with the world of the island. However, the screenwriters will refrain from further exploring the logical and narrative implications of this world, faithful to their habit of casually abandoning a number of possible plotlines successively initiated in the course of the episodes. Thanks to this combination of numbers, Hurley had won the lottery, but he will come across these numbers again on the island, at what seems to be a decisive moment for the series' intrigue. Such enigmatic signs are part of a set of arbitrary patterns that the viewer is nevertheless led to consider as "contingent" (in the Leibnizian sense of the term). We are encouraged to inscribe them in an overarching logic, namely the general architecture of the series (or rather of its world) that is assumed to be coherent and deliver its secrets in dribs and drabs, as if the authors had conceived of everything right from the start – whereas, the reality of the matter is that these patterns are the fruit of an almost constant improvisation practiced by an entire team of screenwriters. One might say, the answer to the mysteries behind these numbers is not to be found in *Lost*, but in paragraph 242 of *Essays of Theodicy on the Goodness of God, the Freedom of Man and the Origin of Evil*, first published in 1710:

> One may propose a succession or *series* of numbers perfectly irregular to all appearance, where the numbers increase and diminish variably without the emergence of any order; and yet he who knows the key to the formula, and who understands the origin and the structure of this succession of numbers, will be able to give a rule which, being properly understood, will show that the *series* is perfectly regular, and that it even has excellent properties. […] That is how we must look upon the irregularities constituted by monstrosities and other so-called defects in the universe. (Leibniz 1985: 280)

One can establish a connection between *Lost* and the philosophical writings of Gottfried Wilhelm Leibniz that goes beyond the pseudo-esotericism of the aforementioned series of numbers. The reflections developed in *Theodicy*, put at the service of a commercial and narrative exploitation, underlie the world-centered design in *Lost*, whose (alleged) consistency is ensured by a mythological "great architect".

Challenging cooperative viewers to grasp a complex film universe, split into several different worlds, as a single, unifying whole, makes it possible to federate the multiplicity of episodes and balance the dissemination inherent in every

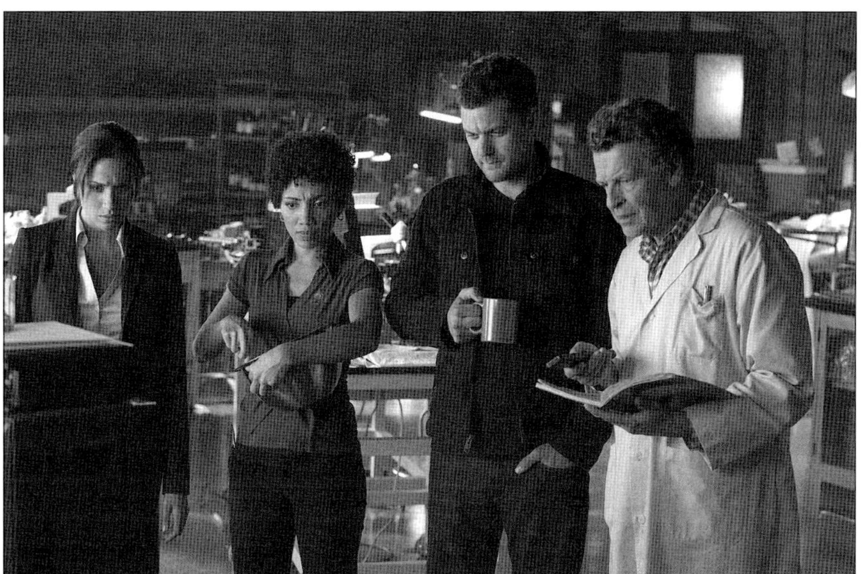

Fig. 23: Walter Bishop's (John Noble) laboratory in the headquarters of FBI's "Fringe Division".

serial practice, while encouraging a discontinuous mode of consumption. That was at least the case for those who followed the series week after week on television, according to a viewing practice currently in decline due to streaming services offering a season in one piece and encouraging users to binge-watch the episodes – even by eliminating credits and recap scenes. The repetition of the Same that establishes the permanence of the diegetic components with which the audience becomes familiar (even though it tends to short-circuit the narration), is counterbalanced by a promise: each episode represents only a piece in a vast puzzle whose retrospective understanding offers meaning to each of the fragments. Still, such a promise is impossible to keep within a similar narrative fragmentation and in view of the proliferation of episodes. In a system where success is established in the immediacy of TV broadcasting, the series' authors capitalize on the limits of the spectator's memory capacities and skillfully channel the latter's recollections by means of recaps that selectively return to previous events, insisting on (or, on the contrary, discarding) specific causal narrative chains.

In *Fringe*, undoubtedly the most characteristic and the most successful of all multiverse TV series[109] (Fig. 23), the world-centered logic is exploited more consciously and conscientiously than in *Lost*, subsuming from the first season onwards the plurality of narrative tracks into a single whole. This approach takes shape and form at the diegetic level in the intention of the investigators of the "Fringe" department to unravel the secret of what they call the "pattern", the common explanation to the various "strange" occurrences they encounter. In this way, the show radicalizes the world-centered implications of a perspective experimented by the showrunner Chris Carter in *The X-Files* series (1993–2002) or in the Season 2 of *MillenniuM* (1997–1998). The will to unify the supernatural phenomena under a single, common explanation is already affirmed in Season 1, when Dr. Walter Bishop (John Noble) reads aloud a German self-published anonymous manuscript called "Destruction by Advancement of Technology". The series' female hero, Olivia Dunham (Anna Torv), suspects this manuscript to be the bible of the terrorist group led by David Robert Jones (Jared Harris) that is about to use a toxic weapon. As Walter starts reading this quasi-esoteric text, his voice turns into a voice-over, as we watch on the screen the journey made by Olivia in search of another of J.J. Abram's "mystery boxes", in this case a box of children's games that will turn out to be some sort of a test. The use of the voice-over confers to Walter's words a certain authority over the diegetic events as well as a programmatic status:

> We think we understand reality. But our universe is only one of many. The unknown truth is that the way to travel between them has already been discovered by beings much like us but whose history is slightly ahead of our own. The negative aspects of such visitations will be irreversible both to our world and to theirs. It will begin with a series of unnatural occurrences difficult to notice at first, but growing, not unlike a cancer until a simple fact becomes undeniable: only one world will survive. And it'll either be us or them. ("Ability", *Fringe*, S01E014).

The creatures of an advanced civilization – an expression that can be equally applied to the *parallel world* of the first few seasons and to the place of origin of the Observers who have invaded the Earth in Season 5 – may be the "great architects" of the universe, but their nature is not divine. In this respect, one could argue that *Fringe* celebrates scientific rationalism[110] and constitutes the atheistic counterpart of *Lost*, a series (perhaps) advocating a cosmogonic archaism. In a way, *Fringe* refers to quantum physics and *Lost* to Leibniz's philosophy. Indeed, there are physicists, like Max Tegmark, who have formulated the hypothesis, actualized in *Fringe*, of the existence of a *parallel world*, simultaneous and almost identical to ours.

Fringe's Season 1 seems to adopt the mode of a series with self-encapsulated episodes, but a serialized storytelling gradually prevails. During the entire season, which will end upon discovering the permeability of the interworld border, the second world is only seen through the interferences it causes within the world of reference. In S01E20, a truck is extracted from the parallel universe through a doorway. From that episode onwards, the interworld threshold is depicted as an invisible, sharp blade that fragments objects and bodies, much like a punitive response to the scientists' Promethean ambition that disrupted the natural cosmogonic order. Each passage from one world to the other leaves a mark on the characters' flesh, as the concretization of the virtual in the biological generates an imagery of the abject, inherited from the cyberpunk tradition (Shinya Tsukamoto, David Cronenberg, Katsuhiro Otomo, the "*Robocop*" franchise, etc.).

From Season 2 onwards, the characters in *Fringe* move from one world to the other and meet their doubles. Consequently, the use of crosscutting is partly motivated by the series' world-centered organization. The temporal criterion only becomes decisive during Season 5,[111] when a leap forward in time takes place and the *war between alternate (story)worlds* gives way to a more traditional *war of the worlds* where the entire population is enslaved by superior beings (actually humans coming from a distant future). Unlike *Sliders*, which juxtaposes the motif of a war against "aliens" to that of *parallel worlds*, *Fringe* has the former succeeding the latter. The expansion of the universe of such TV series through the addition of a *virtual world* represents an effective instrument of narrative amplification since the protagonists, the places, and the stakes are doubled, thus multiplying the number of possible resets. The principle suitable to all serial practices, which lies in introducing occasional variations within the framework of a generalized reiteration, is both literally applied (the *alternate storyworld* is similar, but different) and subverted by the upheavals upon which the show's serialized logic is based.

Fringe's Season 4 is more strongly marked by a sort of rewriting, a "redistribution of the cards" close to the practice of the *reboot*: from now on, the first world is itself transformed into one of its possible versions. Peter Bishop (Joshua Jackson) is obsessed, for a long time, with an obscure, futuristic device. As an intuitive tinkerer, he assembles its parts and realizes that its mechanism activates only at his command. Thanks to this "worldbuilding machine", Peter travels to another world. Upon his return, his entourage[112] *no longer recognizes him*. Or rather, in a version of the world that results from Peter's actions and the demiurgic intervention of the "Observers", they *have never known him*.[113] A new version of the world is presented based on different states of affairs. Tied up in a cross inside this gigantic, mechanical dispositive that comes to life when he takes his place in it, Peter is the expiatory victim (if not a clear-cut Christ figure) whose sacrifice ensures the coexistence of two worlds that threaten to annihilate each other. Saving one world is no longer enough for a fictional hero; he is expected to save *several* worlds. Peter is defined in this show through a sort of ontological aporia. In the episode "The Man From the Other Side" (S02E19), he learns, alongside with the viewer, that he was uprooted from his original world (a motif reminiscent of *Sliders*) by Walter, who had lost his own son in the first world, and therefore raised his double's son as his own, while hiding the truth from him. The theme of a disruption of the ties between two *parallel worlds*, due to the loss of a son and the subsequent attempt of the father to access a *parallel world* where the tragedy has not occurred, is also present in each of the two seasons in *Counterpart*.[114]

During Season 4, *Fringe*'s plot is almost exclusively centered on Peter. Once he understands he is not really in a third – incompatible with his presence – possible world, but in the upper layer of a palimpsest of possible alternatives, he commits to restoring the continuity with the past he experienced in the first world of reference. The hero's diegetic quest is the literal expression of a strategy presumed upon reconnecting with the first three seasons and re-establishing the Same (the core world envisioned in the series' initial concept) within the Other (the development in numerous episodes).

J.J. Abrams followed a similar approach when Paramount, in co-production with his company, Bad Robot, embarked on the project of *Star Trek* (2009), the first film in a trilogy that offers an *alternate (story)world* to all the episodes from the original TV series (1966–1969) as well as to the various film sequels released from 1979 onwards.[115] The filmmaker obviously demonstrates a remarkably systematic attitude with respect to the pre-eminence given to worldbuilding. It was not enough for the Abrams' film to take into account all the previous episodes of the "*Star Trek*" franchise, it also had to be a part of a complex intertextual and multimedia network. Richard Saint-Gelais chose precisely this network as a case study, mapping its productions and discussing certain phenomena of cosmic extension and multiplication of worlds through the proliferation of novels, glosses, online fan comments, etc. (1999: 343).[116] J.J. Abrams and his co-writers in *Fringe*, Roberto Orci and Alex Kurtzman, had to deal with this pre-established universe when making the 2009 feature film, intended as one of the many components of a franchise attached to Gene Roddenberry (creator of the *Star Trek* series) and Paramount. Abrams would later face the same challenge while writing and directing the episodes VII and IX of the "*Star Wars*" franchise, placing himself at the heart of contemporary transfictional practices.

In order to reconnect with the previous narrative material, the authors of *Star Trek* (2009) bring the older double of young Spock (Zachary Quinto) in a *parallel world* that ultimately converges with the aforementioned material. In this way, they address inside the diegesis the issue of transmission between generations that underlies the very project of this prequel. Therefore, transfictional phenomena are manifested within the film via the constitution of a multiverse. Hiding in a cave, Kirk finds himself face to face with a future, aged version of Spock, after having been drawn into an artificial black hole. Spock asks him to restore the hierarchical order in the Starship Enterprise as he has known it and, consequently, to realign the world of the new *Star Trek* movie with the one found in all the previous episodes. The search for consistency in the process of worldbuilding concludes by adopting a reactionary attitude, since the initial value system is reintroduced: the pointy-eared Vulcan, an emblematic figure of otherness, is once again placed under the authority of a white human character.

The character of Uhura (Zoe Saldana) sums up the situation in a concise formula, intended for all the lazy viewers: "An alternate reality". Abrams' film succeeds in its "intertextual mission" by having the actor playing Spock in the old films, the then seventy-seven year old Leonard Nimoy – arguably one of the best known faces in science fiction cinema – play Spock's version coming from the future. In this way, temporal interference is reinforced in the mind of viewers watching the new *Star Trek* by intertextual inferences, especially since the character who first masters shifting from one world to the other in *Fringe*, William Bell, is also played by Nimoy. Although the actor, as an individual, belongs to the realm of the "afilmic" (see *infra*, Chapter 3), his features are also part of the semiotic construction of the "actor figure"[117] and therefore he needs to be taken into account in the study of transfictional processes. The factual world, meaning in this case the world of the spectator's experience *as a spectator*, contributes in the understanding of such world-centered games.

At first, Nimoy's character in *Fringe* is only mentioned verbally, in numerous occasions, and his voice is heard through an old VHS tape. He finally appears in flesh and blood in an episode aired a little more than a month after the theatrical release of *Star Trek*.[118] In a way, this sci-fi icon "brings" back with him on the small screen a part of the teleportation technologies used in many *Star Trek* episodes as well as in the *alternate (story)world* present in J.J. Abrams' feature film. True, the strange, demiurgic character in *Fringe* is not called Spock – otherwise we would have been confronted with a "confirmed" case of transfictional identity. Still, the actor's physical appearance, even with a different make-up, leads the audience to tangentially summon certain components of the diegeses inhabited by other characters Nimoy played in the past. Obviously, this case has no equivalent in literature and there is no doubt that *Fringe* takes advantage of this type of phenomena. By opting for an *alternate (story)world* in *Star Trek*, the filmmakers adopt an approach already employed in the extended universe of this particular franchise, notably in its novels.[119] This multiverse seems to serve as a model for the narrative elaboration of all the original series created by Abrams. With respect to the episode in *Lost* entitled "The Constant" (see *supra*), screenwriters Carlton Cruse and Damon Lindelof admit to having "copied" a number of ideas from the final episode in the series *Star Trek: Next Generation*.[120]

The exploitation of possible alternatives in *Fringe* is not limited to the discovery of a parallel universe by the characters. One could mention the example of the "hallucinated" episode called "Brown Betty" (S02E19, 2010), whose title refers to a type of marijuana consumed by Dr. Walter Bishop as he recounts a story to Olivia's goddaughter. The fable generates an embedding story, with occasional returns to the frame story where the little girl comments upon the storytelling choices made by Walter and even suggests an alternate ending that will also be visualized in this episode. The story told by Walter features several of the series' well-known characters, bearing the same names but living in a world whose visual construction is completely different: as the storyteller clarifies from the outset, we are immersed in the "atmosphere" of a 1940s-1950s film noir mixed with occasional "musical" scenes. The shift to a different genre affects the characterization of the world. In this second story, Olivia does not work for "The Fringe Division". She plays a private detective hired by a client in search of her missing lover. As we will soon discover, this is actually a lie, bringing inevitably to mind the opening scenes from *The Maltese Falcon* (1941) or *Chinatown* (1974). The world is a mixture of generic "film noir" stereotypes and modern-day elements. For instance, everybody drives old cars but uses cell phones. The world is different in that it is seen through the *filter* of various representations recycled playfully.

However, this embedded story is connected with *Fringe*'s main plot in various ways; one could even say that it constitutes an allegorical variant of the principal story. As far as the chronology of the series is concerned, this particular episode is situated right after Peter's disappearance, just as he found out that "his father" had kidnapped him in the other world in an effort to take the place of his deceased double in the "first" world. In the "film noir" story of this episode, the detective is actually looking for Peter, as we learn about his father's misdeeds (he stole a "glass heart" from him, a term that clearly refers to a well-known fairy tale). The episode features a specific type of hybridization between the technological and the organic, omnipresent in the series, yet bestowed here with a supernatural quality, in accordance with the more playful tone of the musical genre. The guilt felt by the visionary scientist, the strange affairs of the Massive Dynamics corporation, the son's disappointment, as well as Olivia's love for Peter, are replayed in a different context, in different settings. Yet the viewer understands that we are still in *Fringe*'s "first" world, temporarily cloaked in a different coat for contextual reasons – namely, a promotional campaign launched by the network that also affected other shows broadcast at the same period, transformed for the time of a single episode into musicals. Therefore, the process of variation, established as a principle with respect to the series' worlds, is also present in terms of style. Even the series' opening credits, one of its major identifiers, is partially affected by the diegetic features of the upcoming episode.[121]

The past is not only that of the series' characters, but corresponds to the very history of popular representations. I have shown in this chapter the extent to which generic references participate in the worldbuilding process, and even in the conception of a multiverse. I will return to this aspect in Chapter 5 through the example of *Dark City*. But first, it seems useful to take stock of the situation by proposing a typology of worlds, preceded by a review of the theories devoted to the notion of "diegesis" that prefigure my approach in this book.

Endnotes

1. For a conception of science fiction as an "art of conjuncture", see Atallah 2016: 32–44.
2. The fantasy genre is equally concerned with the verisimilitude of the first two aspects, namely the creation of believable environments and the language spoken by its characters.
3. However, when a film is part of a series, its introductory scenes function as a reminder, a reprise, and a summary – see for example the "*Resident Evil*" episodes discussed in the previous chapter.

4. The case of *Dune* (1984), in which this type of information is transmitted through a character speaking and looking directly at the camera, constitutes an exception.
5. "Paradigm" should be understood here in the Saussurean sense of the term, as opposed to "syntagm".
6. I borrow the term "xeno-encyclopedia" from Saint-Gelais' book *L'Empire du pseudo* (1999).
7. These categories are conceived with the intention of describing sci-fi worlds. Therefore, the typology I introduce in Chapter 3 follows a different perspective from the one adopted by Wendland. The opposition he establishes between "conceptual" and "perceptual" worlds corresponds to the one between "the impartial scientific data of a postulated world" and "the emotional reactions to the objective data" (i.e. the effects from the establishment of a particular point of view). As for the categories of "natural" and "artificial" worlds, their differentiation is based on whether the elements of a given world are constructed or not: for instance, an alien planet falls into the first category, while an alien city belongs to the second (Wendland 1985: 6). Lastly, the "internal perceptual worlds" correspond to what I will designate in the next chapter as "*mental worlds*".
8. Following Alejandro Jodorowsky's aborted project, David Lynch directed the first screen adaptation of the novel in 1984, while Denis Villeneuve's most recent version was released in 2021. Jodorowsky's partly animated adaptation would have been based on a storyboard prepared by the famous cartoonist Moebius. Some of its pages were filmed and now are included in the documentary feature *Jodorowsky's Dune* (2013).
9. It is worth noting though that the Science Fiction Research Association prefers the term "Secondary Universe".
10. Wolfe gives worldbuilding a central role in his definition of High Fantasy as a "Fantasy set in a fully imagined Secondary World, according to Boyer and Zahorski, as opposed to Low Fantasy which concerns supernatural intrusions into the 'real' world" (1986: 52). Fantasy as a literary genre is marked by a deficit of cultural legitimacy (compared to "realist" stories, or even to science fiction) due to a number of critical presuppositions that Thomas L. Martin deconstructs, most notably through the study of negative reviews that Tolkien's *The Lord of the Rings* received at the time of its publication. See Martin 2019.
11. The terminology used by Lin Carter in his book *Imaginary Worlds* (1973) is symptomatic of this approach. For instance, see the title of its Chapter 9: "Of World-Making: Some Problems of the Invented Milieu".
12. These credits are created by Elastic studio and feature a music theme by Ramin Djawadi, a formula used again in another HBO series, *Westworld.*
13. "Upside Down" is a dark, foggy, rotten place, overgrown with creeping vegetation and populated by hideous creatures. It is a flip side of our own world, a dystopia to our utopia. However, it does not serve as a mirror reflecting our world, unlike what can be seen in the feature film *Upside Down* (2012), where two twin worlds with gravity pulling in opposite directions literally face each other.
14. In doing so, my essay seems to confirm Thomas L. Martin's remark that "fantasy studies have yet to take full advantage of possible worlds theory" (2019: 201). According to the author, "developments in fantasy theory still linger behind those in science fiction studies. Whether that is due to the uncertainty critics feel about the fitness of theory to fantasy, or because science fiction is largely explicable through scientific rules extrapolated from this world, while fantasy's impulses and ultimate meanings remain elusive to the theoretical mind, is unclear. What is clear is that a robust theory of fantasy is needed [...]" (*Ibid.*: 211–212).
15. See Chapter 1, note 64. My aim is to transpose the approach introduced by François Albera and Maria Tortajada to issues more strictly related to the pole of representation, which, by depicting the use of fictitious technologies, echoes a certain way of considering the cinematic dispositive and its future (see Boillat 2006b and 2011a).
16. The rise of the adventure story as a genre is contemporary with the emergence of a consumerist relationship to cultural products. As Matthieu Letourneux has shown with regard to fictional literature, the adventure story is precisely defined through an opposition between realism and imagination, or through a conflict, established within the story, between the everyday life – that the protagonist, alongside with the reader, has to quit before eventually returning to it again – and the improbable but fascinating world of the adventure (Letourneux 2010: 21).

17. This approach could be a useful complement to the notion of "attraction" (see Chapter 1, note 18), frequently employed in the studies of the musical, as it permits to take into account the semantic dimension of the sing-and-dance scenes, beyond the all too schematic concept of the "biplex" narrative, introduced in Altman 1987.
18. This fantasy-like aspect of musicals is exploited extensively by Lars Von Trier in *Dancer in the Dark* (2000), a film located on the margins of the genre.
19. The case of a "near death experience" state is also present in *Lost* (see *infra*, note 98).
20. All shots framing the androids' faces are digitally reworked in order to appear artificially smooth.
21. The pill is a reference to the mind-altering substances whose ingestion underpins the work of the fathers of the cyberculture literature, such as Philip K. Dick or William Burroughs. Their stories are full of secret agents that end up blending in with their own cover.
22. "The two conceivable types of alteration consist either of giving less information than is necessary in principle, or of giving more than is authorized in principle in the code of focalization governing the whole. The first type bears a name in rhetoric [...]: we are dealing with lateral omission or *paralipsis*. The second does not yet bear a name; we will christen it *paralepsis*, since here we are no longer dealing with leaving aside (-lipsis, from *leipo*) information that should be taken up (and given), but on the contrary with taking up (-lepsis, *from lambano*) and giving information that should be left aside" (Genette 1980: 195).
23. According to Jeffords, "[the new man] can transform himself from the hardened, muscle-bound, domineering man of the eighties into the considerate, loving, and self-sacrificing man of the nineties" (Jeffords 1994: 153). The fact that the role of Quaid in the 2012 sequel is given to Colin Farrell is revealing in this respect.
24. The ambiguity is increased even further when a Rekall Inc. employee reveals to the salesman that Quaid was actually anesthetized before the implantation of the Ego Trip. Therefore, both readings remain possible, in keeping with the spirit of Philip K. Dick's work. Quoting Patricia Warrick, Katherine Hayles argued that "Dick's fiction is structured as a series of reversals designed to defeat the reader's expectation that it is possible to discover what the situation 'really' is" (Hayles 1999: 170).
25. This event occurs twice, before a complete reversal of situation whose implausibility and ironical tone is typical of Dick's work.
26. On this specific point, the film differs radically from Dick's "dark-haired girl", i.e. the assimilation between an android and a "schizoid woman" that Hayles examines in her chapter "Turning Reality Inside Out" (1999: 160–191).
27. It is worth noting that Arnold Schwarzenegger has played a number of roles related to questions of technological reproducibility, from the assembly-line production of an endoskeleton modeled after his own body in the "*Terminator*" franchise, up until the topic of cloning in *The 6th Day* (2000).
28. Right after Quaid leaves his apartment at the beginning of the film, the camera lingers in the room in his absence (a case of paralepsis) and does a close up on the face of his wife Lori (Sharon Stone). She suddenly wears a serious, pensive expression, leading us to believe that she was only acting in front of her "husband" and that a process of manipulation is at work in the film's frame story.
29. The identity issues are even more central in the remake thanks to a wider use, inside the diegesis, of a technology allowing the film's characters to cover their face underneath somebody else's "image". In the longer version of the film, released after its theatrical exploitation, Quaid's double, Hauser, is not played by Colin Farrell, but by an equally famous actor, Ethan Hawke, thus underlining the character's *otherness*.
30. In Verhoeven's *Total Recall*, the opening dream scene is more contemplative, ending with an accident, whereas in the 2012 version, the film begins in the middle of a combat scene.
31. This is a similar case to the "Origami Unicorn" scene in *Blade Runner*, discussed by Henry Jenkins. See Chapter 3, note 62.
32. In fact, David Cronenberg started working on the project of the original *Total Recall*, back in the 1980s, before Paul Verhoeven finally took over the helm. See Cronenberg 2000: 81–83.
33. The new storyline involving a scheming "chancellor" who has his government threatened in order to justify the use of a secret army of industrially produced soldiers, is almost

identical to the one found in *Star Wars: Episode II – Attack of the Clones* (2002) and in *Star Wars: Episode III – Revenge of the Sith* (2005).

34. See for example the preservation of bodies fallen into lethargy in *Coma* (1978), or the studio used for shooting "hypnotizing" commercials in *Looker* (1982), two films directed by Michael Crichton.

35. However, Bryan Forbes' *The Stepford Wives* is completely different from *Westworld* in terms of the technology represented within the fictional world. Elyce Rae Helford writes about the screen adaptation of Levin's novel and remarks that it ended up being remembered as "B-grade science fiction (how exactly do the men of Stepford create these near-perfect robot replicas of their wives, and why would they not instead just make enough money from their invention to "buy" themselves nannies and a new young trophy wife every year or two?)" (Helford 2006: 146).

36. It should be no surprise that the Hollywood remake of the animated film *Ghost in the Shell* was released in 2017, while HBO was broadcasting its *Westworld* TV series.

37. Therefore, *Westworld* is in part a continuation of the sci-fi films of the 1950s and 1960s, discussed in Susan Sontag's famous essay "The Imagination of Disaster" (1965).

38. It is worth reminding that visitors of the Universal Park Florida were "attacked" by a robot-shark, reproducing the mechanical special effect used in Spielberg's movie.

39. In this respect, it should be added that visitors to the Westworld theme park are transported by a supersonic plane, which corresponds in the context of the early 1970s to a first step towards the democratization of airline flights to exotic destinations (see Gay 2006: 14).

40. In both films, as in most disaster movies of the time, the carnage appears to be the result of a decision made by the elite in order to maximize its profit. The mayor in *Jaws* is content to see just one shark dead, even though its jaw does not match that of the predator attacking the shores. The scientists' council in *Westworld* decides to keep the park open despite the unexplained malfunction of a mechanical rattlesnake that actually bit a guest – an omen of the bug that will spread among the androids. In the recent *Westworld* TV series, the creator of the park, Charles Ford, dismisses Arnold's remark that the host could possibly develop a consciousness, and opens the park, ignoring his partner's concerns (however, the over-arching plotline in Season 1 focuses on his desire to correct his own mistake).

41. In this respect, see Vernet 1988, as well as our remark on "*mental worlds*" in Chapter 3 (in particular note 30).

42. A CRM/MGM interview quoted in Marc Toullec's documentary *Futureworld: the Future according to Crichton*, available as a bonus feature on *Futureworld*'s DVD edition, released by Sidonis in 2014.

43. This visual effect is also employed in *Sliders* (S03E01, 1996), as the viewer momentarily sees through the eyes of the mechanical dogs. The "park" in this TV series is inhabited by mechanical beings and hosts a deadly game, undoubtedly inspired by *Westworld*, while transposing it not in the future, but in a parallel Earth.

44. *Futureworld* was produced as an independent film. Instead of financing a sequel to *Westworld*, the studio that produced Crichton's film, MGM, chose to invest in another sci-fi movie in 1976, *Logan's Run*. It described a dystopia that shared certain narrative elements with *Soylent Green* (1973). The central idea behind it is the existence of a population confined within a delimited urban space and lured by its leaders (not unlike the ones in *THX 1138*, *Dark City*, or *The Island*). The explanatory intertitle that opens the film testifies to a desire to inscribe the science fictional speculation in a "small world": "Sometime in the 23rd century, the survivors of war, overpopulation and pollution are living in a great domed city, sealed away from the forgotten world outside".

45. This motif, also found in other franchises such as "*Alien*" (from Ash in 1979 to David/Walter in *Alien: Covenant*, 2017) and "*Terminator*" (the machine being the eponymous character), as well as in *Blade Runner* (1982) or in the Japanese video game *Snatchers* (1988), is part of a tradition of automatons and other "projections" (mostly female ones, desired by a diegetic male subject) acting as simulacra of the human that can be traced back to Hoffmann's Olimpia (*Der Sandman*, 1816), Villier de l'Isle-Adam's *Tomorrow's Eve*, published in 1886 (see Boillat 2010a), La Stilla's reincarnation in Jules Verne's *The Castle of the Carpathians* (1892), or the manipulative double of Maria in Fritz Lang's *Metropolis* (1927).

46. I will only briefly discuss *Futureworld* and *Beyond Westworld* in this essay, since in both of them we actually leave the "world" of the park in pursuit of the robots fabricated by Delos, which assume the identity of humans after stealing their appearance (a well-known "they live among us" topic, explored in *Invasion of the Body Snatchers,* 1956/1978). Each of the five episodes in the TV series *Beyond Westworld* (cancelled by CBS due to poor ratings) follows the attempts of a couple of investigators to unmask a hostile robot that has insidiously been introduced in a particular environment – on which is based the series' variation principle – by one of the Delos' designers, Simon Quaid (James Wainwright). The latter utters the promise of a serial repetition in the following terms: "I placed robots all over the world. I have hundreds more". The only episode that partially takes place inside Westworld is the pilot directed by Ted Post (after the western *Hang 'Em High* and the sci-fi sequel *Beneath the Planet of the Apes*), in which Quaid plans to destroy Delos' headquarters by hijacking a nuclear submarine. In this episode, the mechanical inhabitants of Westworld are frozen and deactivated. The other episodes are all set beyond the western genre, apart from the credits sequence that uses a number of images from the 1973 film. Shifting from a population of androids living and animating one of the fictitious worlds of a leisure park, to a single robot that merges into "the" world in each episode, the multiverse disappears in the 1980 TV series.
47. Right after the MGM logo, appearing in a Scope aspect ratio, the movie begins with a promotional TV program in 1:33, featuring interviews with clients returning from their vacation in Westworld, all of whom enthusiastically emphasize the realism of the experience (while at the same time insisting on the pleasure of meeting robots of the opposite sex, an aspect that the recent *Westworld* TV series exploits in a gender studies perspective). The play on the borders between documentary and fiction, typical of this specific period (Peter Watkins' *Punishment Park* was released in 1971), will be transposed into the distinction between different worlds (physical vs. *virtual*) in the 2016 series that will also oppose the classic TV aspect ratio to a wider format.
48. In the final scene of *Time Bandits* (1981), the army gathered by the heroic dwarves, who have brought into their legendary world characters from the various eras visited, includes several cowboys. This encourages a reference to a cliché of the western genre, endowed here with a comic function, that of the cowboys trying to lynch the villain.
49. The outcome of this duel is supposed to be fatal only for the androids. The scene is filmed in slow motion with splashes of bright red blood, reminiscent of Sam Peckinpah's films or the spaghetti westerns of the time. A particular episode from the sci-fi TV series *Battlestar Galactica* ("The Lost Warrior", S01E06, 1978) combines a Manichean storyline reminiscent of a classic film like *Shane* (1953) with a narrative situation similar to the one found in *Westworld.* After a forced landing on an unknown planet, the protagonist discovers a town that seems to come straight out of a western movie and ends up killing the local tyrant's hired gun, a robot called "Red Eye", in a duel.
50. It is quite likely that a nocturnal, silent scene in *Westworld*, introducing the audience to the backstage workings of the park, was the inspiration for a similar scene in *Dark City*, discussed in Chapter 5.
51. There is also a visual contrast in the scenes taking place inside Delos installation, between the high-tech equipment and the nudity of the bodies clustered as commodities – in other words, between the reference to a medical framework and the crudity of a slaughterhouse with its icy cold rooms.
52. A wide variety of examples can be mentioned here, from the Cantina scene in *Star Wars: Episode IV – A New Hope* (1977) and the bounty hunters in *Star Wars: Episode V – The Empire Strikes Back* (1980), to the character of Cad Bane in the TV series *Star Wars: The Clone Wars* (2008), to *Solo: A Star Wars Story* (2018) and, even more explicitly, to Jon Favreau's series for *Disney+, The Mandalorian* (2019–).
53. The discovery of the Pandora planet in *Avatar* refers to a number of stories, from the Discovery of the Americas to *Pocahontas* and the conquest of the West. Jake is part of a long line of white characters that become familiar with the natives and serve as intermediaries during the negotiations between the colonists and the Indians. The people of Pandora, known as the Na'vi, are also threatened with territorial dispossession and genocide. The characters played by John Wayne in *She Wore a Yellow Ribbon* (1949) and James Stewart in *Broken Arrow* (1950) come to mind. Furthermore, *Avatar* makes an obvious allusion to Kevin Costner's hero in *Dances with Wolves* (1990), when the character controlled by Jake

calls out "let's dance!" to the Great Leonopteryx (Toruk) he is trying to tame. The reference to the rehabilitation of the Indians, a process whose various stages marked the history of the western genre, is also evident in the choice to have the Na'vi speak in a credible fictional language.

54. On the use of specific western motifs in John Carpenter's movies, see Boillat 2006c.
55. The open-minded, steampunk way *Jonah Hex* fusions the western, the supernatural, the horror, and the science fiction genres, could be linked to the fact that the movie is a screen adaptation of an Albano DeZuniga DC comic series (in the spirit of the hybrid continuity scripted by Joe Lansdale in the 1990s for Vertigo). The medium of comic books sometimes adopts a less realistic and more anachronistic approach of the hybrid western, for instance by exaggerating the features of the spaghetti western. This practice became popular ever since DC published a comic book anthology called *Weird Western Tales* in the 1970s, at the time of Crichton's *Westworld* and its sequel. For a more recent example inspired by Lucio Fulci's *The Four of the Apocalypse …* (1975), see Jonathan Hickman and Nick Dragotta's *East of West* (Image Comics, 2013–).
56. The shift towards the present is reinforced through a subplot that focuses on a conspiracy unveiled by a couple of reporters, reminiscent of the subject of another film released the same year, *All the President's Men*. The official trailer for *Futureworld* superimposes the film's production era to the diegetic one, placing the first plot in 1973 and the new story in 1976.
57. Some of the scenes taking place inside the park were filmed in NASA's flight simulation facilities in Houston.
58. The resumption of the "Roman World" and the "Medieval World" in *Futureworld* is justified in the plot by the fact that the gunslinger was the first one to be killed and, in view of such dysfunctions, Delos had no choice but to shut down the "Westworld" resort. Nevertheless, this explanation is unfounded, since in Crichton's film, the first non-simulated assassination takes place in the "Medieval world".
59. However, this does not preclude studying these two genres from the standpoint of such levels, as Jim Kitses (1969) showed in his formalist study of the western in terms of syntactic relationships. See Altman 2000: 183–185.
60. For example, the *virtual world* in *The Thirteenth Floor* imitates 1930s style, *Dark City*'s *artificial world* is influenced by the 1940s and 1950s (for both of these films, see Chapter 5), while a collage of early 1960s clichés nourishes the hero's hallucinations in *Vanilla Sky*. The balance may tip either in the direction of historical references (*The Thirteenth Floor*) or towards that of imaginary worlds (*Sucker Punch*).
61. This incongruity (also found in *The Hunger Games*, see Chapter 3) prepares for a cyberpunk interpretation of *Futureworld* that would not be developed until four decades later, during *Westworld*'s season 2.
62. The intertextual references one finds behind-the-scenes at this worldbuilding facilities are multiplied in S03E02 with the cameo appearance of a dragon (in other words, an impossible element in the actual world), known from the fantasy TV series *Game of Thrones*, as if *Westworld* were a multiverse that could potentially aggregate all genres and worlds.
63. This game is specifically targeted at fans of "gore", as the particularly bloody character of the actions taking place in "Shogunworld" will later confirm.
64. "Virtù e Fortuna" (S02E03) is one of the three episodes in Season 2 to feature a pre-credits scene. In other words, such a sequence is not regular in the series and, therefore, does not go unnoticed by the audience. Furthermore, the ten-minute opening scene in this particular episode takes place in a world hitherto absent from the series. The other two episodes featuring a pre-credits scene (S02E01 and S02E07) introduce not a cosmic, but a temporal disjunction thanks to flashbacks focusing on Bernard (Jeffrey Wright).
65. Sergio Leone's *A Fistful of Dollars* (1964) plagiarized Akira Kurosawa's *Yojimbo* (1961), while Takashi Miike mixed the two genres in *Sukiyaki Western Django* (2007).
66. The first drafts of the screenplay for *Star Wars* (1977) used *The Hidden Fortress* (1958) as a clear inspiration (see Jenn 1991: 173–191). The name "Jedi" alone brings to mind the *Jidaigeki* genre. These knights alternate pistol duels and kendo-style sword fights. The recent Disney+ series *The Mandalorian* cleverly mixes bounty hunters and plots centered on Rônin, while one of its episodes ("Sanctuary", S01E04, 2019) refers clearly to the *Seven Samurai* story (1954).

67. Other sci-fi elements in the film include the fact that the hosts operate with a battery of a limited autonomy, that the animals are actually automata (the rattlesnake robot will reappear as a torture instrument in the first episode of the *Beyond Westworld* TV series), that some robots are equipped with infra-red vision, or that the central computer regulates the air-conditioning of the park's control center.
68. There is one exception in the way the film generally deals with gender-related issues. It concerns more specifically the Medieval World: the first robot to suffer from a malfunction is a young female servant, an android designated as a "sex model", who refuses the advances of a guest. The scientists observe the scene from the programming center and declare: "Problem with a girl. Program breakdown".
69. Other recent western TV shows include *Ponderosa* (2001–2002), *Into the West* (2005), *Hell on Wheels* (2011–2016), and the Netflix mini-series *Godless* (2017).
70. During a briefing on the "Westworld" resort in the first episode of the *Beyond Westworld* TV series ("Westworld Destroyed", S01E01, 1980), a similar line is heard: "These aren't ordinary machines. They're complicated pieces of equipment almost as complicated as living organisms. They're so complex that their circuitry has to be worked out by other computers. That's what makes them so incredibly real."
71. The series opens with a voice-over exchange between Bernard and Dolores: "[Bernard]: First, have you ever questioned the nature of your reality? Tell us what you think of your world […]. Do you ever feel *inconsistencies* in your world? Or repetitions?".
72. It is worth noting that Clint Eastwood's first box-office hits in the western genre (following his *Rawhide* TV series) were contemporary with the production of the original *Westworld*, paving the way for Crichton's movie.
73. Dolores is repeatedly raped, while Maeve is regularly offered to Delos' clients.
74. On the importance of the intertext (which could also extend to the star's *persona*) among the multi-layered whole in which a film character is necessarily involved, see Taylor and Tröhler 1998, or Gardies 1999.
75. On this topic, see the brilliant analysis of Richard Slotkin in his book *Gunfighter Nation. The Myth of the Frontier in Twentieth-Century America* (1992).
76. The "Man in Black" is also unique because he is the only major human character who is not duplicated as a robot during the series' first three seasons (the same could be said for Robert Ford, who nevertheless lives only through his digital avatar). This explains the important part of the plot in the first two seasons devoted to the character's past (first inside the park, then outside). *Lost* also features a "Man in Black", embodying the evil forces that reign on the island for centuries and look for a way out.
77. This becomes clear by the exploration of successively updated alternatives and the multiplication resulting from the hosts' reproducible nature. In S01E07, Bernard, noticing that certain hosts deviated from their assigned program, deduces the basic principle of all serial narration: "Out of repetition comes variation. And after countless cycles of repetition, these hosts, they were varying". The hosts' reproducibility is a post-cloning theme that is absent from Crichton's film, where there is only one copy of each of the hosts. In the HBO series, the premises containing numerous replicas of the same artificial person are often shown on screen, addressing the issue of avatars, discussed in Chapter 1 with respect to the "*Resident Evil*" franchise.
78. Maeve becomes aware of her artificial identity by remembering her little girl. She proves to herself that she is not crazy by asking Hector in S01E04 to extract a bullet from her belly, while she screams in pain. At that moment, she gives birth to her new, supposedly free, self – but as we will come to realize later in the series, her free will is also the result of programming. Furthermore, Bernard's fake memories regarding his deceased child evict the mother figure (who is, nevertheless, shown via a video chat), an idea that takes an entirely different meaning as we learn that Bernard is the artificial double of Arnold (the co-creator of the Park). The latter had also experienced a painful loss and is supplanted by Robert Ford, whose desire is to give birth to a whole world.
79. Elyce Rae Helford discusses *The Stepford Wives* (1975) from the perspective of Laura Mulvey's famous piece of feminist film scholarship, "Visual Pleasure and Narrative Cinema" (Helford 2006).

80. The sequence is created by Elastic studio, also responsible for *Game of Thrones'* world-centered credits scene. It will undergo only minor modifications in Season 2.
81. One could relate the motif of the perforated paper with my comments in "Philip K. Dick's World-Editing Process" section in Chapter 4.
82. In S03E07, Dolores and Caleb (Aaron Paul) ride through the real western landscape that inspired the Westworld park. In S03E08, the western set reappears in a scene similar to *Inception*'s shared dreams, in which Maeve and Dolores meet again.
83. The scenes taking place in Delos' headquarters were shot in the City of Arts and Science in Valencia, Spain.
84. This topic becomes explicit in the pre-credits sequence of the first episode in Season 3, when Dolores explains to a company's chief executive: "Bit of a tactical mistake, really. You want to be the dominant species, but you built your world with things more like me".
85. Incite's chief executive (Tommy Flanagan) qualifies the Artificial Intelligence called Rehoboam in terms that constitute a deliberate reference to Westworld: "This is their God. This is how they see the future. How they make the future. In order to do that, they watch everyone. Tell them what to do, where to live, who to love. *Keep them all in a loop*" (S03E05). Humans in the real world are also prisoners of such a "Futureworld", insofar as they have become as predictable as robots to those who have access to their data.
86. The series did not have a narrative closure due to a troubled production that resulted to significant discontinuities, most notably when the show went from Fox Network to Sci Fi Channel for Seasons 4 and 5, a shift that involved important changes in terms of personnel regarding the writing and casting crews. Actually, Wade, an important character played by Sabrina Lloyd, disappears between Seasons 3 and 4, and is replaced by a different female character. The audience learns abruptly in S04E01 that she has been deported by the Kromaggs (advanced humanoid primates coming from a parallel Earth) in a breeding camp. The actor Jerry O'Connell who plays the main hero, Quinn Mallory, is also replaced in the final season, even though his character remains: the script comes up with the idea of a new carnal envelope resulting from a fusion between two sliders at the moment of a transfer in another world. The quest for their world of origin, which initially forms the series' narrative arc, is reconfigured when Quinn learns in the same episode from the one he believed to be his biological mother that his real parents are "sliders". They had entrusted him – as well as a brother whose coordinates in a *parallel world* Quinn will obtain – to their double in "our world" when the Kromaggs took control of their world. Quinn's foster mother extracts from her arm a microchip allowing the young hero to receive a message recorded by his real parents, similar to the one coming from Krypton at the beginning of *Superman* (1978). Quinn's new narrative arc is henceforth determined by the search for a weapon developed by his parents in order to fight the Kromaggs who threaten to enslave "our" Earth. Therefore, our world remains the reference point throughout the series.
87. Pierre Bayard's book was brought to my attention by Mark Cerisuelo (see 2015), who comments quite extensively on the French edition of my book and notes the coincidence of its almost simultaneous publication with Bayard's *Il existe d'autres mondes* that deals with a similar subject matter from a different perspective.
88. The episode called "Summer of Love" (S01E06) constitutes an exception. It shows our world in which the FBI has discovered the disappearance of the four main characters along with Quinn's bizarre machine. Still, this scene is limited to the episode's pre-credits scene.
89. The three alternatives mentioned here correspond respectively to S01E03 ("Fever"), S01E06 ("Last Days") and S01E04 ("Prince of Wails").
90. Howard Silk is an ordinary man, a civil servant who understands nothing about the nature of his own work, whereas Howard Prime is an over-trained, chief secret agent. Peter Quayle is extremely self-confident as the Director of Strategy of the Office of Interchange in the first world and a rather shy and unstable individual in the *parallel world*.
91. See *Cahiers du Cinéma*, June 2013 (n° 690) whose cover features an image of *Star Trek Into Darkness* and the title "J.J. Abrams Galaxy". French film critic Cyril Béghin begins the dossier's introductory article in the following words: "*Cahiers du cinéma* has never been very fond of George Lucas or Captain Kirk [...] world-centered movies, prefabricated box-office hits and viral marketing. Yet, if the name J.J. Abrams is synonymous with all the above, there is much more to it than that [...]" (Béghin 2013: 8)*.

92. Aired on ABC, *Lost* was created by J.J. Abrams, Damon Lindelof, and Jeffrey Lieber. In his previous TV series, *Alias* (2001–2006), Abrams had already used a plotline in which the female protagonist lived in several "worlds" that she had to ensure they were compatible as well as impermeable. However, the spy movie genre and the motif of the "fake secret agent" limited these worlds in a realistic single-world universe rather than a plurality of ontologies.
93. *Fringe* is produced by Fox and created by J.J. Abrams, Alex Kurtzman, and Roberto Orci.
94. Talk available on: https://www.ted.com/talks/j_j_abrams_the_mystery_box/transcript. Consulted on June 25, 2021. The motif of the *box* is recurrent in reflections on the plurality of worlds – see for instance the short story "Sylvan's Box" by philosopher Graham Priest, which illustrates a logically impossible situation (quoted in Alber 2019: 158).
95. It should be noted though that Jason Mittell is not interested in the multiverse aspect of contemporary TV series. His definition of television serial storytelling rests on the fact that it "creates a sustained narrative world" (2015: 10 and 263), that is to say a single world: the world of the fiction.
96. On "curiosity" as one of the modes (along with "suspense" and "surprise") of creating and manipulating narrative interest in fiction, see Sternberg 1978:45–55 and Baroni 2007: 91–120.
97. In the case of *Twin Peaks*, this is especially true for Season 2 (1990–1991) and Season 3, produced and released 26 years later, when multiverse TV series became fashionable, notably thanks to Bad Robot productions. Season 3, whose diegetic temporality corresponds to the actual number of years that separates it from the first two seasons, takes up and develops the spaces from previous episodes located in another dimension (the Red Room in Agent Cooper's dreams, the Black and White Lodges), as well as the motif of Cooper's doppelgänger.
98. As I have shown earlier in this chapter, the eye as a visual motif that signifies the character's awakening inside one of the fictional worlds is also periodically present in *Avatar* (incidentally also set in a vegetated "island"), particularly before and after each subplot. *Lost* presents similar markers: the pilot begins with a close-up of Jack's eye as it opens, while the series' finale, six years and 120 episodes later, includes the exact same shot (as well as its reverse shot) in its final minutes, at the exact moment when Jack recalls the entire story of the series from the point of view of an *alternate (story)world*. He is invited by his deceased father "to remember and let go", alongside with the viewer. The final shot of the whole series shows Jack's closing eye, symbolizing the end of denial, unlike *Avatar*, where the eye opens once again in the end in order to enjoy the imagined world. Jack functions here as the model of all fictional characters who find themselves in a sort of shared vision (typical of the hyper-connected world of the World Wide Web era and the online multiplayer games).
99. This telephone call prepares another one, of great importance, that arrives much later in the series, between Desmond and Penny (S04E05).
100. Episode 7 in Season 4 constitutes an exception insofar as the viewer belatedly realizes he is not watching an alternation between two flash-forward storylines, since one of them is in fact a flashback (see Mittell 2015: 169).
101. In *Flashforward*, the pattern of repetition does not apply to the (very few) characters who succeed in profiting from their knowledge of the future in order to change the course of their lives.
102. This notion has often been used to designate the one who is responsible for the enunciation in a film in all of its manifestations. Sarah Kozloff (1988: 44) borrows it from Christian Metz (1974: 21), who had taken it from Albert Laffay (1947: 1596). On Laffay as a precursor of reflections on filmic enunciation, see Boillat 2007: 322–326.
103. All characters in *Lost* have a very definite identity in terms of their personal beliefs. In the beginning of his article, Florent Favard remarks that "Deus Ex Machina" (*Lost*, S01E19) is "an episode that played on every variation of faith and trust, from Boone following Locke, to Locke's mother claiming he was 'immaculately conceived', Locke trusting his conman father, Sawyer getting played by Jack" (2016: 1). According to Pacôme Thiellement, "the central polarity in *Lost* is that between trust and deception. And it is the corollary of the conflict between, on the one hand, fiction and its rules, and on the other, the real world and its anomie" (2011: 31)*.
104. In S06E11, Desmond acquires the capacity to move from one world to another.

105. Similar to *Battle Royale* (2000) and its sequel, and like *Predators* (2010), or "*The Hunger Games*" quadrilogy (2012–2015), the protagonists in *Lost* are forced to participate in what seems like a role-playing game (in a life-size simulation) or video games that inherit the same formula, and, above all, reality shows following the "Survivor" concept, introduced in the nineties and developed in many different countries. Jason Mittell confirms that "ABC chairman Lloyd Braun came up with a concept in 2003 for a dramatic series modeled on the film *Cast Away* [2000] and the reality program *Survivor*" (2015: 92). However, *Lost*'s plot differs strongly from such individualistic narrative models and ultimately challenges their basic concept, since all the characters on the island are, in fact, *already dead*.

106. Apart from Umberto Eco's theory, the notion may also refer to the small-world experiment conducted by psychologist Stanley Milgram, whose basic argument underlies the flashback plots in *Lost*, as the audience belatedly discovers: the arbitrarily chosen "candidates" are part of the same network and unconsciously linked to each other. Moreover, the experiments organized by Dharma Initiative are in some respects reminiscent of the Milgram Experiment, especially as the observers have as a mission to press a button while they are themselves unknowingly the experiment's subjects.

107. David Lynch, who had already created *Twin Peaks*, had originally intended *Mulholland Dr.* to be the pilot of a new series. In a way, the fragmentation into different episodes was finally integrated into a single feature film.

108. According to Florent Favard, "the complete incompleteness of *Lost*'s fictional world [...] may be partly responsible for the polarizing reception of the finale" (2016: 8).

109. Alberto N. Garcia shares this opinion and also mentions *Awake*, a series that used a chromatic differentiation between two distinct worlds (see Chapter 4, "Are Colors Diegetic?") but, unlike *Fringe*, did not exploit the multiverse structure in the long term: "The limitations of the multiverse for serial narrative also demarcated the narrative path of *Awake* (NBC, 2012). Detective Michael Britten suffered a car accident while traveling with his wife and son. Upon awakening, he sometimes appears in a world where his wife has survived, and other times in one in which his son has. Confused and mourning in two parallel realities, Britten uses his position in the gap between realities to solve crimes on both sides, obtaining information in one that complements the other. If the hairstyles and sets on *Fringe* help distinguish the narrative universes, in this paranormal crime drama the chromatic palette serves as a mooring: the reality in which his wife has survived adopts the hue of a reddish photograph, while the universe of Britten with his son is colored blue. The series was canceled after thirteen episodes, avoiding the greatest difficulty of a product with these characteristics: the survival over time of such a bold premise, which, as we have seen, took its toll on *Fringe*" (Garcia 2016: 14). As one easily understands from this quotation, Garcia emits a critical judgment according to which multiverses are a disadvantage for serial productions because of the confusion inherent in this type of plots (see Besson 2015).

110. This does not exclude Walter's adherence to a perceptual knowledge brought on by the consumption of psychotropic drugs, in a clear reference to the counter-culture of the late sixties and early seventies.

111. Therefore, *Fringe* follows the opposite course from *Lost*, since in the former the disjunction manifests itself first at a cosmic level, then at a temporal one.

112. That includes his girlfriend and his father with whom he forms a trio that constituted, up until then, the main factor of narrative stability in *Fringe*.

113. The same thing happens to the female hero's friend during the second part of *The Caller* (2011).

114. In Season 1, Howard Silk, who had never before met his daughter (she disappeared after his wife's miscarriage), discovers her as a teenager in the *parallel world*, bearing the same name – Anna – he planned to give her (they meet again in S02E08). In Season 2, we learn in a flashback that Yanek (James Cromwell) has lost his son, while his double has been spared such a tragedy. He decides to kill his double and become Mira's surrogate father. As a result, the young woman will be at the heart of the conflict between the two worlds. Played as an adult by Christiane Paul, Mira differs from the other main characters in that we know nothing about her double in the first world (apart from what she briefly recounts to her father's double in S02E09 and from what is briefly shown during the latter's encounter with his daughter that has now become a mother). This choice made by the series' writers defines Mira's objective in Season 2 – to seal the passage between the two worlds – and

testifies, by contrast, to the way the other main characters are built by doubling the storyline via a parallel world.

115. The idea of an *alternate (story)world* was previously explored in an episode from the original TV series, "Mirror, Mirror" (S02E04, 1967), in which an ionic storm occurring during a teleportation causes not only a spatial displacement but also a transfer to an entirely different world. Captain Kirk and two members of his crew find themselves in the place of their alter egos (and vice versa), discovering – for the duration of a single episode – another world (perceived by the characters as a *parallel world*), similar in every way to their own, except that the Federation's democratic and humanist values are replaced by those of an "Empire". The "Mirror Universe" pattern reappears in several episodes from various different series of the franchise, the most recent example being S03E09-10 in *Star Trek: Discovery* (2020).
116. In addition to the media productions mentioned by Saint-Gelais, one could also add the comic book stories published by Marvel since 1967, as well as the entire set of video games based on *Star Trek*'s universe.
117. André Gardies (1999) suggested a stratification of the "actor entity" into four levels, going from the most virtual to the most concrete: the agent, the role, the character, and the actor. One of the defining features of the *motion capture* process is precisely the interaction implicated between these levels.
118. *Star Trek* was released in U.S. theaters on May 8, 2009. The twentieth episode in Season 1 of *Fringe*, in which Nimoy appeared for the first time, is aired in the United States on May 20th of the same year.
119. Saint-Gelais' summary of Della Van Hise's novel *Star Trek: Killing Time* (1985) reveals its close affinities with the film discussed here (Saint-Gelais 1999: 348).
120. Audio commentary for the fifth episode in Season 5 of *Lost*, included as a bonus feature in the DVD released by ABC Studios in 2008.
121. See Chapter 4, especially the note 80. In addition to the world-centered connotations of color, the opening credits in *Fringe* also include variations of a different type. For instance, one finds a pastiche of 1970s TV aesthetics, particularly in terms of typography, in the credits of each episode offering flashbacks that show Walter at this particular era.

Film Diegesis and Multiverse

"The one-world frame [of semantics] is the base of a popular tradition established by Bertrand Russell: 'There is only one world, the 'real world' [...].' The second one-world conception of fictionality is the doctrine of mimesis, which ties fictions to the actual world, explaining them as its imitations or representations. This conception has been dominant in the Western cultural tradition since its emergence in antiquity (Socrates, Plato, Aristotle). [...] The semantics of fictional worlds requires a conception of fiction broad enough to accommodate not only 'realist' fictions but also various types of nonstandard and experimental fictions [...] In contrast to one-world theories of fictionality, the 'Leibnizian conception', based on the idea of the plurality of worlds, enables us to formulate the concept of fictional worlds as possible worlds."
(Doležel 2019: 53–54)

Principles of Filmology as a Theoretical Framework for a World-Centered Conception of Movies

Film theories that adopt a phenomenological perspective have paid particular attention to the notion of "world". Daniel Yacavone's *Film Worlds: A Philosophical Aesthetics of Cinema* (2015) is but one of the most recent examples of this tendency. However, in the present essay, I am less interested in the relationship between a subject and *the* world than in the fictional construction of *a* world (one among many). For this reason, I will refer mostly to the research conducted by the Institute of Filmology in early 1950s France. Prefiguring the development of film semiotics, this research maps the discursive space that forged the notion of "diegesis", which was later met with great success in the field of literary narratology. In their introduction to a devoted to cinema issue of the journal *Studia Phaenomenologica*, Ferencz-Flatz and Julian Hanich note that research studies published in *La Revue internationale de filmologie* "show a certain implicit closeness to the phenomenological method mostly because of their tendency to interpret the phenomenon of the spectator's film experience". They include among these studies "Etienne Souriau's distinction between the diegetical, the spectatorial and the creatorial aspect of film" (2016: 31). In view of the pivotal place given to the notion of "diegesis", in my book, it is essential that I clarify its definition by revisiting its original theoretical framework and by situating my essay in relation to how the term has been used in the past, especially since it has known a widespread circulation in semiotics, narratology, and poetics.[1] Notions forged within the field of film studies and then exported in other domains are actually rare. Therefore, it seems to me that the history, as well as the success, of the notion of "diegesis" testifies to the importance of the world-centered dimension of the film medium.

Specifically understood as the "world" of each work, the concept of "*diégèse*", namely the French term distinct from the Platonic or Aristotelian *diegesis*, was developed by Étienne Souriau and his colleagues in the Institute of Filmology (see Lowry 1985).[2] Their work was an integral part of what is now identified as the first "moment" towards the institutionalization of academic film studies in France – a period set between 1947 and the end of the 1950s – through the development of an internationally established network dedicated to teaching and research with a perspective that was fundamentally multidisciplinary (see Albera and Lefebvre 2009). Since "worldbuilding" is nowadays mostly associated with theories coming from the Anglo-Saxon world, it would seem relevant to trace in this chapter its genealogy within the French-speaking academic domain.

The term "*diégèse*" appeared in 1951 in an article published in *La Revue internationale de filmologie* by Étienne Souriau, a researcher who had already shown a fascination for questions of cosmogony in his book *Les Deux cent mille situations dramatiques* [*The Two Hundred Thousand Dramatic Situations*], published the previous year, where narrative structures were seen as possible constituents of a "world".[3] It was used again in the introduction Souriau wrote for the collective book that carried the significant title *L'Univers filmique* [*The Film Universe*] (1953), in his effort to clarify the main notions deemed useful within the so-called "filmological" perspective. The qualifier that originated from this term – "diegetic" – owes its popularity in French-speaking studies to the structural approach to narrative literature elaborated by Gérard Genette. In his taxonomic endeavor, Genette gives a central place to this concept, thanks to the addition of numerous prefixes (intra-, extra-, homo-, hetero-, auto-, meta-), partly adopted in the English-language film literature by Sarah Kozloff (1988), among others.[4] Genette's classification can prove particularly fruitful in film analysis, provided one does not use this typology in a rigid way, but confronts it against the unique function of any given film.

In the foreword of *L'Univers filmique*, which was signed by Souriau but was the product of collective discussions, the filmologists agree on the necessity of establishing a number of precise terms that would help study the different levels of "reality" present in a given film. They deem this issue as one of the major challenges raised on a theoretical level by this particularly "immersive" medium, as is evidenced by their investigations and reflections on the so-called "impression of reality". To this end, they introduce a well thought out set of *eight notions*, with each one referring to a specific level of reality – the "diegetic" being just one of them.

In his 1951 article, Souriau writes that the diegetic level covers "everything considered as represented by the film", as well as the "kind of reality *postulated* by the film's content" (Souriau 1951: 237)*. He refines this definition in the lexicon proposed in *L'Univers filmique*, as follows: "All that belongs 'in the intelligibility' (in M. Cohen-Séat's use of the term) of the story within the world postulated or suggested by the film's fiction" (Souriau 1953: 7)*. The theoretician painstakingly isolates the phenomena that are proper to the fictional world, particularly those related to time, space, and film characters. Inside this well-organized lexicon, the *diegetic* is also defined by what it *is not*, that is to say in relation to the other levels identified as parts of the "film universe": the *afilmic* ("that exists in the ordinary world" independently of the other levels, which by contrast depend on the existence of a given film), the *creatorial* (relating to a film's genesis and the intentions of those who participate in its creation), the *profilmic* ("everything that was in front of the camera and ended up imprinted on film"), the *filmographic* (the material level of the film stock), the *screenic* (anything visible on the screen), the *filmophanic* (that concerns the screening phase and the film's reception by an audience), and the *spectatorial* ("that subjectively resides in the spectator's mind").

This conceptual network covers the entire spectrum of "levels" extending from a film's production to its distribution and from a reality completely external to cinema (or to a film's screening) to the concrete materiality of film. It also encompasses the viewer's inferences to which David Bordwell and Edward Branigan grant a principal importance. For filmologists, the total of the eight levels listed above constitutes the "film universe". Their successors will sometimes use the concept of "diegesis" as a synonym for "film universe", even though the former was, in the original filmological model, only one of the different levels composing the latter. Distinguishing between them is of particular importance in the present essay, since the films studied here offer *a film universe* composed of *several diegeses*, each of them defined by a specific ontological status and by a distinct set of laws.

In light of the above, it becomes clear that from Souriau's point of view, the defining features of the notion of "diegesis" cannot be grasped separately from its relation to the other levels. Each term is established both *in opposition to* and *in interaction with* all the others. For instance, the "postulated" world of the diegesis calls for a certain spectatorial activity, since what belongs to the diegetic is far from limited to what is visible on the screen; it also includes everything the viewer infers about the world presented in front of him. The spectator makes deductions based largely on his own experience of the real world and imagines what lies beyond the confines of the visual frame.

In order to comparatively illustrate each of the eight levels composing the film universe, let us take the example of *The Cabinet of Dr. Caligari* (1920). In this film, the subjective vision of an alienated character manifests itself mostly through a bizarre environment, improbable in the *afilmic* level, defining the *diegetic* level as a *mental world*. It results from specific *creatorial* intentions (the "expressionist" style most notably inherited from the German theatrical productions of 1910s) expressed simultaneously in the *profilmic* (production design), *screening* (shot composition, especially with respect to the distribution of light and shadows) and *filmographic* levels. Following André Gaudreault (1999), I consider that the filmographic level includes not only features pertaining to the film stock, but also those related to the act of shooting (angle, shot sizes, depth of field, etc.), thus envisaging a *broad filmographic* level. The diegesis' subjective status is understood as such at the *spectatorial* level. Finally, if we were to establish that the distinction between the frame story and the embedded story was actually underlined by a certain musical theme performed live in theaters showing the film, then we would be dealing with the intervention of an element pertaining to the *filmophanic* level.

Therefore, we can distinguish two types of representation of the limits of a given world, as they may appear in a multiverse, when the protagonist realizes that the world he inhabits is not real. In *The Truman Show* (1998), the unwitting hero of a reality show, Truman Burbank (Jim Carrey), decides to quit everything and get as far away possible from the city in which the promoters of a TV network have confined him since his birth. His sailing boat crashes on the *trompe-l'oeil* wall that marks the limit of his "horizon"; the shadow of the "ghost" of an individual he used to be is projected on the surface of that wall. Then, Truman climbs a staircase hitherto hidden from view and leaves the gigantic TV studio that enclosed his whole existence up until that point. In such a case, the boundary between two distinct worlds is located at the profilmic level.

By contrast, in *The Thirteenth Floor* (1999), a programmer named Douglas Hall (Craig Bierko) is also looking to discover the true nature of the world he is living in and speeds ahead at the wheel of his Porsche, leaving his own city behind him. Then, he is confronted with the incompleteness of his world, which fades away in the distance, replaced by a nonfigurative frame (Color Plate 19). In this case, the profilmic gives way to the filmographic in its narrow sense, which is also diegeticized insofar as the hero realizes that his world is actually created by a computer.

The typology introduced by the filmologists seems all the more relevant today as a descriptive tool, since the deliberate confusion of the various levels is both a condition of the effectiveness of certain special effects and a major theme in a number of films. That said, the filmographic level, again conceived in its narrow sense, would no longer be operative in the era of digital cinema, if one were to accept Souriau's definition that considers the "film stock" as its decisive criterion. Nevertheless, it is worth preserving this category in order to refer, more generally, to features pertaining to the representation's material reality, the unit of measure being today the pixel. As Selim Krichane has shown with regards to the notion of "camera" in video games (Krichane 2018 and 2021), cinema remains the prevalent model, despite the emergence of various technologies such as 3D computer graphics and polygonal modeling. The distinction between the profilmic and the filmographic has become blurred, or even meaningless, due to the audience's inability over the last twenty-five years to determine whether the elements visible on the screen actually possess a profilmic existence (meaning that everything framed is materially existent during shooting) or whether they are CGI effects implanted at a later stage (thus inviting us to relate them to the filmographic level in its narrow sense). In any case, *The Truman Show* and *The Thirteenth Floor*, produced during the same year in a quite similar technical context, showcase a number of creatorial choices that establish a specific world-centered design: in the former, we deal with an *artificial world*; in the latter, we enter a *virtual world*.

Moreover, the perceptibility of a special effect is a function of the spectatorial level. It is defined according to what I propose to consider, following Jean-Marie Schaeffer, as the "knowledge of the *arche*".[5] The level postulated by the viewer depends on a knowledge that varies according to his or her familiarity with contemporary films using special effects (each blockbuster setting new standards in this particular area), the potential consultation of parafilmic sources that discuss the making of the film, etc. Unlike the structuralist approach developed in the 1960s and 1970s, Souriau did not limit his theoretical framework to the sole immanence of the filmic text. He insisted on the viewer's cognitive participation, in the context of experiments carried out in the Institute of Filmology and relating to the intellection of films. It is therefore essential to avoid amputating the definition of "diegesis" from its second part (the mention of a "world postulated or proposed" by the film), if one wishes to refrain from reducing this notion to the "story told" by the film, as it was often the case in the past.

Due to the primacy implicitly given to the narrative dimension over the world-centered one, Gérard Genette's understanding of the term "diegetic" did not fully correspond to Souriau's definition, resulting in an ambiguity which left a regrettably lasting mark on studies claiming to follow his approach. In Genette's texts, as well as in those of most of his disciples, the qualifier "diegetic" is a convenient way to refer to elements related to the plot without having to resort to the term "historical", which is liable to create a confusion in French (since "histoire" means both *story* and *history*). To give an example that echoes the idea of "*parallel worlds*" that interests us here, Genette defines a sub-category designated as "heterodiegetic" within his typology of "internal analepses" (flashbacks shorter than the diegetic time supposedly elapsed since the beginning of the discussed work, allowing the rediscovery of a scene previously recounted). In his words, the heterodiegetic analepses are distinguished by the fact that they are "dealing with a story line (and thus with a diegetic content) different from the content (or contents) of the first narrative" (Genette 1980: 50).

Genette specifies what falls under this type of analepses through the example of a "character recently introduced whose 'antecedents' the narrator wants to shed light on, like Flaubert for Emma" (*idem.*). However, unless one opts for a transfictional approach, like Woody Allen in his short story "The Kugelmass Episode" (1977),[6] it seems difficult to imagine how Emma Bovary could find herself in the past in a *different world* than the one inhabited by Charles – not in the sense of a spiritual incompatibility between the two characters, but in that of an ontological difference, as if Charles was physically unable to see the "ghost" of his wife, just like Dr. Crowe's widow in *The Sixth Sense* (1999). In Genette's theory, the "first narrative" and the "different diegetic content" are in no way opposed or external to each other, unlike what happens between the reference world and the *other* world in a two-world universe. He uses the term "first" in a strictly temporal sense, referring to the order of the narrative, while the qualifier "diegetic" becomes a pure equivalent of the adjective "narrative". The term "extradiegetic" is equally problematic, especially in the case of films where the entity designated as such ceases at some point to be an invisible storyteller expressed through voice-over. When the narrator becomes visible, he is immediately attached to a world; this world may very well be different from the primary diegesis but, at any rate, the "exteriority" ceases to be a relevant criterion.

Still, Genette develops a world-centered reflection when discussing what he calls *metalepsis* "with which the narrator pretends to enter (with or without the reader) into the diegetic universe", a trope he deems as "always transgressive" (1980: 101 and 234). Years later, he wrote an entire book devoted to this process (Genette 2004), in which he discussed several cases of reflexivity in movies (not free of certain limitations which I have addressed in Boillat 2012). The plurality of matters of expression in cinema increases the range of possibilities for this type of transgression, in comparison to literature. For example, in *Stranger Than Fiction* (2006), Will Ferrell's antihero suddenly begins to hear a female voice-over narrating his own life, which belongs, as it turns out, to a novelist inhabiting the same world as him. Woody Allen frequently uses metaleptic procedures in his films that formulate as interferences between the afilmic and the film's diegesis (as in *Zelig*, 1983), between the world of a projected film and the world of reference (as in the classic case of *The Purple Rose of Cairo,* 1985), but also in the interactions between the characters and a chorus (*Mighty Aphrodite*, 1995), between diegetic and filmophanic spaces (*Whatever Works*, 2009) or between the afilmic reality (of 1920s historical artistic figures) and a *mental-supernatural world* in the case of *Midnight in Paris* (2011). Such porosity of borders between distinct narrative levels fosters consideration of these films' world-centered dimension.

In fact, Genette suggests considering the places within the "world of the text" where an interaction with the reality of the writer and the reader is postulated: "The most troubling thing about metalepsis indeed lies in the unacceptable and insistent hypothesis, that the extradiegetic is perhaps always diegetic, and that the narrator and his narratees – you and I – belong to some narrative" (1980: 236). By substituting in this statement the term "reality" for the qualifier "extradiegetic" and the notion of "simulacrum" for the term "diegetic", one finds in the functional core of the metalepsis the fundamental theme of the sci-fi cyberculture production (see Chapter 5). By dispensing with the distinction between frame and embedded stories (or worlds), metalepsis paves the way to a world-centered conception of literary production and of any type of representation in general. Therefore, it comes as no surprise that this notion has met with a certain success among theoreticians of fiction, particularly those who have been interested in the semantics of possible worlds (see Lavocat 2010: 37–38).

Furthermore, Marie-Laure Ryan refers to Genette in a chapter of her book *Avatars of Story*, entitled "Metaleptic Machines" (a concept that she never actually defines). Her starting point is that "metalepsis, a rhetorical and narrative figure […], has become one of the favorite conceptual toys of postmodern culture and contemporary critical discourse", presenting "affinities with computers, as well as its multiple manifestations in digital culture" (Ryan 2006: 204).[7] Ryan suggests a distinction between two types of metalepsis: the first one, the rhetorical metalepsis in Genette's sense, concerns a change of narrative voice (a shift from a given storyteller to another); the second one, called "ontological metalepsis", is of particular interest to me as it induces a "change of world": "In this case the reader must recenter herself into a new fictional world and start building its mental image from scratch, rather than viewing this world as an expansion of the world of the preceding level" (*Ibid.*: 205). Ryan discusses a number of procedures within her epistemological reflection on mathematics and computer science that are of the same order as those I study here at the level of film representations, more specifically in the case of "worldbuilding machines"[8] – yet another demonstration of the close links between multiverse and digital age.

Going back to Gérard Genette and to "pre-digital" issues, the narratologist's growing interest in the "diegesis" as we understand it here, testifies to the migration of his preoccupations from the immanence of the text towards phenomena of intertextuality. He becomes aware of his limited grasp of the term when reflecting on a typology of transpositions, referring to cases, for instance, where the story of an older fictional work is recounted in a later one, inside a different spatial or temporal setting. In his book *Palimpsests: Literature in the Second Degree*, Genette revisits the notion of "diegesis" and associates it to a "spatiotemporal world" (Genette 1997: 295). He even refers, for the first time in his writings, to Étienne Souriau, albeit in a parenthesis. Adopting the filmological meaning of the notion, Genette paves the way for a consideration of the back-and-forth between diegesis and story. As Dominique Chateau has shown, the consistency of the diegesis sets the conditions for the development of the story, while the latter in turn allows the constant expansion of data related to the diegesis (Chateau 1983: 128). In some cases, the story unfolds in a way that entails a partial redefinition of the diegesis, retrospectively inscribing it into a particular type of world. For instance, what was perceived as the objective reality may turn out to be part of a *mental* (*Shutter Island*, 2010) or a *virtual world* (*The Matrix*, 1999).

From this standpoint, the diegesis takes the "leading role", setting the laws that delimit the range of possible directions the story may take. My analysis of films in this essay constantly emphasizes the need to distinguish between *diegesis* and *story*, while at the same time examining phenomena of reciprocal determination between these two notions. A flashback scene from Terry Gilliam's *The Imaginarium of Doctor Parnassus* (2009), recounting the first meeting between Mephistopheles (alias Mr. Nick, played by Tom Waits) and the monk Parnassus (Christopher Plummer), perfectly illustrates this issue. Parnassus possesses an extrasensory ability that allows him to project others inside their own imagination, which he then uses in a fairground attraction as a kind of "worldbuilding machine". His confrontation with Mephistopheles symbolizes the clash between two opposite concepts. On the one hand, "Faust" proclaims that the story takes precedence as a factor giving consistency to the world. On the other hand, his opponent takes for granted that the "eternal story" has an optional status in relation to the elements of the world (the "diegesis") whose existence is, according to him, entirely independent of the storytellers' activity. As one would easily imagine, the devil wins the bet. After shutting the mouth of monks who chant the sacred story, by using a power similar to the one possessed by the Agents in *The Matrix*, the ensuing silence induces no change whatsoever in the surrounding world, as Mr. Nick notes with evident satisfaction. It goes to show that there is a Mephistophelian touch in the idea of "de-narrativizing" the world in order to reflect on it as pure phenomenological reality. However, at that moment, a reversal necessary to the reinforcement of the film's narrative structure is paradoxically carried out precisely through this challenge posed to the role of the story. In fact, story and diegesis are two sides of the same coin: one may choose to observe it from one angle, but that does not exempt one from considering the opposite side too.

In movies, the on-screen representation is often crowded with all sorts of elements; yet the diegesis is by no means reduced to the *screenic* level, as it also includes everything that supposedly exists off-screen, beyond the frame of each shot. Moreover, films with a prominent world-centered dimension sometimes opt for a subtractive approach that consists in drastically selecting the number of elements visible within the image in order to exhibit the representation's constructed character. Beyond the array of empty spaces, like the ones in *THX 1138* (1971) where the characters' background is reduced to a luminous white surface, in the case in question the viewer is confronted with a "cosmic" emptiness (and, in a more concrete sense, of a background filled with digital grafts) pointing to the presence of a *virtual world* within the film universe. In *Gamer* (2001), this type of image is used as a stylistic, transitional device (for example, a car appears as the sole figurative element within an otherwise black screen) that echoes the subject of the film whose main protagonist is a video game designer. The scene in *The Matrix* (1999), in which Morpheus (Laurence Fishburne) introduces Neo (Keanu Reeves) to the idea of a virtualized world by placing him inside a bare white environment, furnished solely with an antique television set and two red leather armchairs, has become synonymous of this subtractive approach.

Another illustration of this approach can be found in the TV movie *Virtual Obsession* (1998), adapted from Peter James' novel *Host*, thus confirming the growing popularity at the end of 1990s of the representation of a computer-generated universe as the locus of "emptiness". When the protagonist, an AI specialist, accepts to join his deceased ex-lover, whose spirit has survived by merging with an artificial intelligence (similarly to the hero in *Transcendence*), in what she calls her "Eden", he finds himself in a completely empty set, composed of a white wall and a luminous surface on the floor. In terms of modes of figuration, this non-place embodies the reign of electricity, an irradiation that tends to revoke the representation itself. As a possible world, this virtual space is almost inconceivable, urging us to take literally Marie-Laure Ryan's principle, according to which the reader (or the viewer) "fills *the blanks of the text* by imagining the fictional world as similar as possible to the actual world" (Ryan 2010: 54–55)[*]. In the case of *Virtual Obsession*, given the immeasurable gap between the real and the virtual (albeit through a human-like visual interface), these "blanks" are all that remain, both in a material (the screen becomes a blank page) and a hermeneutical sense (the representation remains extremely elliptical).

Actualized, according to Souriau, "within the intelligibility" of a viewer making a series of assumptions, the diegesis is simultaneously the locus and the actual outcome of what Umberto Eco calls the reader's "interpretative cooperation" (1979: vii). Therefore, in movies, the recipient of the message resorts to his "encyclopedia" in order to mentally complete a universe partially (audio-)visualized. Eco is one of the fundamental advocates of the application in the field of narrative literature of the "possible worlds" concept originating, prior to modal logic, from the Leibnizian philosophy. Souriau referred to both the logicians' "Universe of discourse" (1951: 231–232) and Leibniz's *Theodicy*, inviting his readers to "imagine what the Leibnizian universe (in which every monad is a mirror) would be like if it had been driven by a global purpose that would incite it to produce a privileged monad" (Souriau 1953: 13)*. The way the filmologist phrases his hypothesis proves that he is aware of the twist the metaphysical notion of "possible worlds" has to undergo if one wishes to transpose it into the realm of fiction.[9] A similar displacement is required if one moves from Saul Kripke's modal logic towards theories of fictionality, especially those applied in literary theory. In fact, scholars who studied fictional narratives in terms of "possible worlds" have been only loosely inspired by the methodology established by the semanticists. Whereas the "possible worlds" in modal logic correspond to maximal sets of propositions, a fiction is determined by the criterion of narrative relevance and the principle of minimal departure from the actual world. Therefore, it gives its audience only a limited amount of information about the "state of affairs" composing it; the interpreter does not really need this information in order to understand the story since he "co-constructs" the world of the fiction. Discussing the debate on the applicability of the possible worlds logic to fictional worlds would require a venture into a field too vast for the purposes of this chapter. Suffice to say that the theories Umberto Eco qualifies as "constructivists" (Eco 1979: 222), such as those introduced by Thomas Pavel, Lubomír Doležel, or Françoise Lavocat, testify to the contemporary importance of a world-centered approach to cultural productions.

Departures Between Worlds

Often, to define a given world, theoreticians have recourse to the notion of "gap". Fiction borrows a large amount of elements from the world of reference shared by the author and the reader before introducing a number of modifications in the form of additions, suppressions, or alterations of specific components belonging to the latter. This explains why even science fiction or supernatural tales, which by definition offer speculations out of the existent – the range of possibilities restricted to whatever is *thinkable* at a given time and context – and aspire to comment upon "our" world, differ only narrowly in the end from what is commonly conceived as "real". In order to be comprehensible, a world, however distant from our own spatially or ontologically, must be composed of recognizable elements, a set of *invariants* (Kripke 1980) belonging both to the fictional and the reference world.[10]

Adopting a perspective inspired from the science of logic, Marie-Laure Ryan studied the conditions of identity or compatibility between worlds that would satisfy the "principle of minimal departure" and ensure the accessibility of the "actual world" to the "actual world of the text" (according to her terms). She showed that the relation between these two types of worlds is to be considered within a general framework of reciprocity, since any given fictional work is also received as an intertext: "The frame of reference invoked by the principle of minimal departure is not the sole product of unmediated personal experience, but bears the trace of all the texts that support and transmit a culture" (Ryan 1991: 54). Furthermore, a world's degree of fictionality depends to a large extent on conventions established through our confrontation with other texts. Therefore, we implicitly receive a fictional world through the grid of our knowledge of the actual world, projecting "upon the world of the statement [the world of a fiction and of a counterfactual] everything we know about the real world", making "only those adjustments which we cannot avoid" (Ryan 1980: 406). If it is true that the reader or the viewer mechanically considers as an invariant any element to which the novel or the film pays no particular attention, then it becomes possible to trap him by withholding information about the world one would expect to be made explicit.

Generally speaking, invariants offer some much needed reference points. Richard Saint-Gelais remarks with respect to novelistic alternate histories, which develop other chains of events from fictional alterations of historical sequences (like in Philip K. Dick's famous novel *The Man in the High Castle*, adapted into the four-season TV series of the same name, produced by Amazon Studios from 2015 to 2019): "a lot of them invest a particularly notorious event or period, often (though not exclusively) of a military character, as the site of the bifurcation they operate: the Second World War, the American Civil War, the Napoleonic campaigns …" (Saint-Gelais 1999: 61)[*]. As I demonstrated in Chapter 1, the September 11 attacks (or their metaphorical doubles) play a similar role in a number of contemporary multiverse movies.

Recent films and TV series have devised *althist* (alternate history) worlds through the insertion into historical events of characters that are either fictional (*Zelig*; 1983; *Forrest Gump*, 1994; *Inglourious Basterds*, 2009; *X: First Class*, 2011) or transfictional (*Van Helsing*, 2004; *Sherlock Holmes*, 2009; the *Watchmen* movie and TV series, 2009 and 2019), and props whose technology is, following a *steampunk* tradition, hardly compatible with the main plotline's historical period (*Wild Wild West*, 1999; *The League of Extraordinary Gentlemen*, 2003; the anime *Steamboy*, 2004) or that stand out within an overall low-tech environment (the British TV series *Black Mirror,* 2011- ; Andrew Niccol's *In Time*, 2011; *Counterpart*). These elements accentuate the movie's intertextual dimension as well as its play with the process of worldbuilding. In many cases, "our" world is also that of the characters. It could also be that "our" world lies beyond the limits of their world, as Neo finds out when he finally manages to get out of the matrix. A movie like *Cube* (1997), which establishes from the outset, and with no narrative motivation whatsoever, a significant gap between the *artificial world* it presents and the reference world it excludes from its audio-visual representation, constitutes an exception. The observations made by Ryan and Pavel with respect to all types of fiction are *a fortiori* valid for multiverses in which each of the diegeses is perceived in relation not only to the film's reference world (itself perceived in comparison to the viewers' reference world) but also to other fictional universes, especially when a world's internal organization is based on a specific film genre.

At any rate, the importance of the interworld gap would be inversely proportional to the worlds' mutual accessibility, if the film universe did not include bridges connecting them. Worldbuilding machines play precisely this role by inviting the character and his double (the spectator) to an "immobile journey". They can appear in a minimalist way in the form of a door (*The Wizard of Oz*, *Kafka*, *Monsters Inc.*, *Pan's Labyrinth*, "*The Chronicles of Narnia*"), a bridge (*Brigadoon*, *In the Mouth of Madness*), a trunk (*Vanilla Sky*, *The Jacket*, *Avatar*, *The Thirteenth Floor*, *Vanishing Waves*), the injection of a chemical substance (*Fringe*, *The Congress*), the reading of a text (*The Butterfly Effect*), or, in a more openly self-reflexive way, a screen (*The Purple Rose of Cairo*, *Pleasantville*, *Last Action Hero*), or even a metafilmic device (*Je t'aime je t'aime*, *Total Recall*, *Deja Vu*). These diegetic artifacts guarantee the permeability between the various worlds and, therefore, the importance given to the world-centered dimension (since the confrontation accentuates the contrasts) and the narrative exploitation of the interactions between these worlds. Whereas the *impermeability* between the worlds means that the effects of the parallelism are exclusively meant for the viewer, the interworld bridges allow the characters to experience them as well, thanks to a diegetization that in turn marks the relationship established between the movie and its spectator.

Just the mention of the term "science fiction" is enough to create the expectation of a significant deviation from the world of reference. Yet, this gap is by no means a prerequisite to the genre, as is evidenced by the two-world universe proposed by *Another Earth* (2011), an independent film written and directed by Mike Cahill that addresses the issue in question in a deliberately minimalist approach. The gap separating the world of reference (ours and, hence, that of a realistic fiction) from the one found in another planet that suddenly appears in our sky, is reduced to almost nothing. In a way, the film materializes Hilary Putnam's "Twin Earth thought experiment", or, at least, a version of it that does not deal with questions of language. Putnam's experiments have inspired science fictional arguments in several multiverse movies (see also *infra*, Conclusion). In *Another Earth*, a second globe, mirroring ours, is populated by identical living organisms that have gone through the same experiences as the inhabitants of "our" world, except for a few minor details, as we find out during the TV broadcast of the first contact with what can hardly be called "extraterrestrials". The ontological particularities of the second world are located precisely in these minor differences, which are actually difficult to measure since *Another Earth*'s narrative construction limits its audience to whatever is known to the inhabitants of our planet. The principle on which this two-world universe is based, invites us to consider Cahill's film as a fictional illustration of the astrophysicist Max Tegmark's views on the plurality of worlds, especially since the theoretical positions of different scientists are persistently visualized on the screen. The protagonists formulate a number of hypotheses that corroborate the observation I made in Chapter 1 according to which some of the fictional practices in vogue today are actually rooted in the upheavals provoked by quantum mechanics during the second half of the 20th century. In *Another Earth*, the physical distance separating us from the other planet is evaluated through a series of references to the science of astronomy and to a long line of historical projects of conquering outer space. The film includes a series of shots that draw from the iconic first color photograph, the "Earthrise", taken during the Apollo 8 Mission and offered by NASA to the press on Christmas Eve in 1968 (where the vertical image has been reversed horizontally in order to obtain a landscape format). However, in *Another Earth*, this specific "Earth" is actually contemplated by the earthlings of our world that gaze into the sky (Color Plate 7). The distance between the two planets is considered in terms of possible worlds. A scientist in the movie illustrates his so-called "broken mirror theory" during a TV interview with the following example: "If any small variation arises – they look this way, you look that way – suddenly, maybe, everything changes […]. Well, one might say that you have an exact mirror image that is suddenly shattered and there's a new reality." One could argue that we find here the well-known *Doppelgänger* motif that Cahill's movie extends to a cosmic scale.

The protagonist in *Another Earth* is a vulnerable young woman, named Rhoda (Brit Marling), guilt-ridden after being involved in a car accident which caused the death of a young boy and his mother. While struggling to redeem herself in the eyes of the grieving husband and father, Rhoda dreams of conquering the outer space. The fatal incident happened at the very moment "Earth number two" appeared in the sky and Rhoda turned her eyes away from the road to look at the star. Even though no causal relationship between the two events is postulated, a congruence is established, echoing several other movies whose two-world structure is justified in the diegesis of the frame story by means of a car accident, whether they propose, according to the typology I present in the next few pages, a *virtual* world (*Vanilla Sky*, 2001), a *mental* world (*Stay*, 2005; *Danika*, 2005; *Wrecked*, 2010), an *alternate (story)world* (*Mulholland Dr.*, 2001), or even *alternate (story)worlds* embedded in a *mental world* (*Triangle*, 2009).

In fact, *Another Earth* encourages multiple hypotheses. A four-year ellipsis, corresponding to the time Rhoda spent in prison charged with manslaughter, explains the trivialization of the "extraterrestrial" presence in the sky, discussed thoroughly all over the media. The encounter between the two worlds has led to an asynchrony between the various chains of events, so that it becomes possible for Rhoda to live in a version of the world that is exempt from the accident and its tragic consequences. The sci-fi elements end up acting as a counterpoint to the film's intimist plot, due to their minimal insertion into the daily life of the female hero whose point of view the audience constantly follows.[11] Withdrawal into oneself defines the relationship to the other world: the *elsewhere* corresponds to an objectified *Same*, as is evidenced by the "*tête-à-*

tête" between Rhoda and the second Earth standing out from the sky, beyond the pier and the ocean (Color Plate 7). This type of place is also used as a frontier in Chris Marker's *La Jetée* (1962) and its remake, *Twelve Monkeys* (1995), as well as in *Dark City* and *Requiem for a Dream*. It is as if an emblematic, iconic place is needed in order to anchor events of a cosmic scale.

Another Earth is an art film characterized by an un-spectacular approach. Cahill is obviously sarcastic towards the stereotypical notions of extraterrestrial alterity, most notably when one of the characters in the movie remarks that the new planet is not inhabited by "blue avatars" (an explicit reference to James Cameron's film, released two years earlier). Nevertheless, *Another Earth* turns to worldbuilding too in order to translate spatial remoteness into the emergence of a double and transpose the discovery of an Elsewhere into a process of introspection. The explanation for the appearance of the second Earth varies according to the interpretation – aka the type of world-centered logic – one chooses to adopt. For this reason, it seems useful to create a typology of ontological statuses to which the *other* worlds most likely belong. The definitions that follow will help us specify the nature of the relation of accessibility between the different worlds in a multiverse, as well as the ways in which a film may regulate the relationship between diegesis and story.

Types of Other Worlds

Lubomir Doležel employs the concept of possible worlds in literature through a perspective largely inspired by modal logic. The categories he comes up with in discussing the ways to "shape narrative worlds into orders that have the potential to produce (generate) stories" (1998: 113), are actually derived from the Aristotelian alethic modalities (possibility, impossibility, and necessity). However, they are too broad to be used in a typology of worlds aiming at a more inductive approach and elaborated through specific case studies.

In principle, film universes can include more than two worlds. Still, for the sake of the story's intelligibility and the feasibility of their visual construction, most multiverse movies opt for a two-world arrangement. This structure favors contrasts, for instance through the simultaneous representation of two opposing sides, one "utopian" (often associated with our world, thus celebrated rather than criticized), the other "dystopian" (likely to be thought as an allegory of the current world, thus challenged, albeit indirectly). Doležel also contemplates "dyadic worlds": "the simplest, but very prominent, is a unification in one fictional world of two domains in which contrary modal conditions reign" (*Ibid.*: 128). The need to stick to a two-world arrangement for reasons of simplification persists even when the concept of possible (and theoretically infinite) worlds is openly addressed inside the diegesis, as for example in the TV series *Stranger Things*. The image used in the cover of this book, taken from the opening credits of the TV series *Counterpart*, suggesting a process of infinite multiplication, actually presents a series of encounters between two identical individuals standing on the opposite sides of a partition, mirroring each other within a clustered, gridded, office-like space. The sanitized, geometrical spaces prefigure the coercive dimension of the bureaucratic power in the series.

I have divided the multiverse into seven categories, described in the following pages.[12] Such a classification may seem predictable in a study focusing on "worlds" we are tempted to "map" (Lavocat 2010: 18), but it is in no way intended to be rigid. Its purpose is to set out some benchmarks against which particular cases may be illuminated. A given film may fall – successively or simultaneously (depending on how it is interpreted) – into several of the following categories, as I will show at the end of the chapter through the example of the *Westworld* TV series.

It should be noted that a different typology, concerning a similar kind of films, is proposed by James Walters in *Alternative Worlds in Hollywood Cinema*. The author of that book distinguishes three types of worlds, which he illustrates by systematically comparing two distinct periods of film history, classical Hollywood cinema and more recent productions up to 2004: "imagined worlds" (*The Wizard of Oz*, 1939, and *The Woman in the Window*, 1944 / *Eternal Sunshine of the Spotless Mind*, 2004), "potential worlds" (*It's a Wonderful Life*, 1946 / *Groundhog Day*, 1993), and "other worlds" (*Brigadoon*, 1954 / *Pleasantville*, 1998). My essay expands on the spectrum of worlds imagined by Walters by giving a broader meaning to the notion of "world", by focusing on the different sub-genres of science fiction, and by putting an emphasis on the use of CGI effects in contemporary movies. Walters opts for selection criteria that are more auteur-oriented. Only incidentally does he consider the history of technologies and discourses pertaining to what is known as "virtual realities". Still, his analysis invites us to reassess the alleged novelty of such practices. References and technical processes may change over the years (especially under the impulse of the contemporary intermedial context), but screenwriters occasionally opt for a world-centered perspective even in the so-called "classical" era.

In my typology, presented below but used throughout this book, I identify seven types of worlds ranked in an ascending order according to the impact the collective imagination linked to digital technology has on the process of worldbuilding. Only the last three types seem to have known a significant growth in the age of interactive media and the World Wide Web. Nevertheless, it is important to consider all categories within a broader reflection on cinematic fiction, if only to identify kinship between certain types, or potential shifts from one type to another. Technically, the first two types of worlds cannot be qualified as a "multiverse", but they share common features with the latter and, therefore, require our attention.

Distant Worlds

The worlds I designate as "*distant*" provide a change of scenery typical of adventure stories in which the *elsewhere* temporarily replaces in the eyes of the protagonist-traveler the *here* of the everyday life. Science fiction arguments, such as the presence of machines that are much more sophisticated than the usual means of locomotion, do not suffice to create a truly different world. The hero explores a new physical environment, a distant planet reached in a flash thanks to a teleportation (*Stargate*, 1994; *John Carter*, 2012),[13] a spaceship (*The Last Starfighter*, 1984), a miniaturized submarine injected inside the human body (*Fantastic Voyage*, 1966; *Innerspace*, 1987), or a journey beneath the Earth's crust (*Journey to the Center of the Earth*, 1959; *Pacific Rim*, 2013; *Godzilla vs Kong*, 2021). As Marie-Laure Ryan explains, this type of story does not result in a two-world universe or a multiverse:

> Even sci-fi stories describing the invasion of the Earth by creatures from another planet or recounting interstellar journeys can remain compatible with a classical cosmology, insofar a planet is not a world in the ontological sense of the term, and reality includes a multitude of celestial objects (Ryan 2010: 67)[*].

Ryan's criterion depends on the size attributed to "the" world. There is no other, ontologically different world to be found beyond the limits of the known world (with the exception of *Another Earth*, see *supra*), but simply an extension of "our" world whose existence we previously ignored. The "War of the Worlds" motif, found in the various adaptations of H.G. Wells' novel of the same name (1953/2005), or in movies such as *Mars Attacks!*, *Independence Day*, *Outlander*, *District 9*, *Skyline/Beyond Skyline*, *Cowboys & Aliens*, and *10 Cloverfield Lane*,[14] is precisely based on the abolition of the borders separating the *here* from the *far away*, while retaining the point of view of the Earth's inhabitants (however things are far more complicated in the case of "*Thor*" or "*The Avengers*" movie series).

Most notably marked by the myth of Atlantis, or that of the Austral Lands, and by the maritime exploits of the conquerors of the New World, *distant worlds* often take the shape of an island whose contours delimit a "small world" isolated from everything else. They appear as a playground or the site of an experiment, governed by its own laws (or game rules, as in the screen adaptations of Richard Connell's "The Most Dangerous Game" that the protagonists must discover and master (as in *Lost*). In Wells' *The Island of Doctor Moreau* (1896), adapted for the screen numerous times, the monsters born out of vivisection and subjected to "the Law" of the eponymous doctor, break free. *The Invention of Morel* (1940) by Adolfo Bioy Casares functions more explicitly as an allegory of audio-visual media as it correlates the desert island with a "worldbuilding machine" that reproduces in an immutable and dehumanizing way the same sequences of events. The traveler (as well as the reader) becomes gradually aware of the female character's status as a simulacrum he nonetheless invests with a series of psychological traits, just like a film spectator does in front of

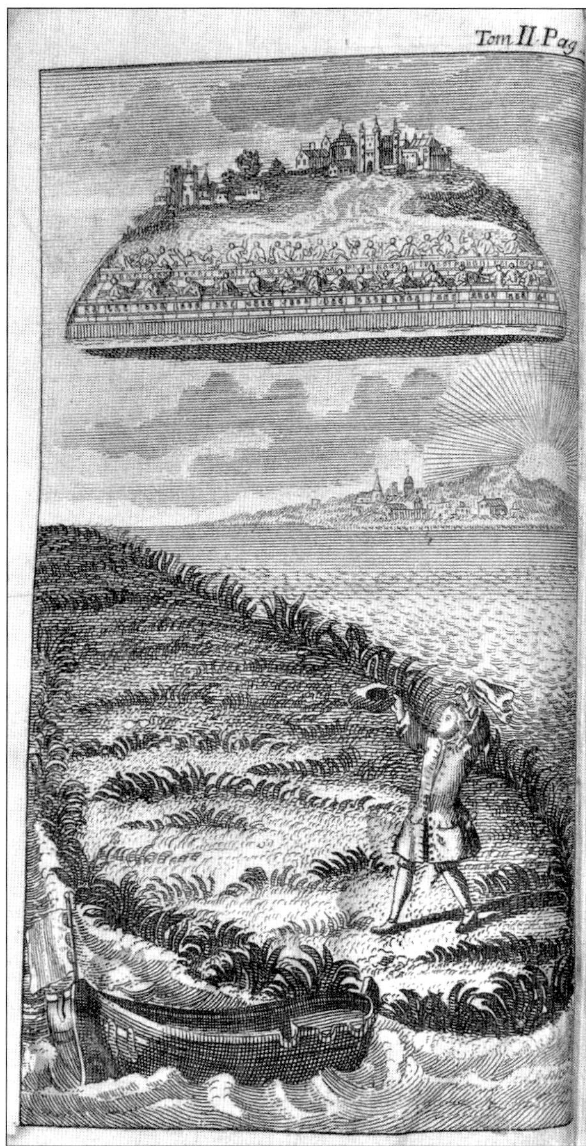

Fig. 24: The Utopia before the eyes of a "distant observer": Jonathan Swift's flying island as illustrated in an engraving from the 1727 edition of *Gulliver's Travels* (1726), a prose satire that inspired Miyazaki's anime movie *Castle in the Sky* (1986).

the two-dimensional image of an actress on the screen. This novel has undoubtedly influenced later fictional works in which a character discovers the backstage of a factitious environment by entering the lair of a machine, like the hero in *Dark City* (see Chapter 5).

Science fiction often employs a maritime iconography, most notably through the depiction of spaceships designed with corridors, hatches, and an engine room.[15] In this genre, planets are sometimes assimilated to floating islands, spatially limited habitable surfaces, as the viewer realizes alongside with the hero in both *Dark City* and *Predators*' finale. Even if these places are anything but hospitable, they are attached to the tradition of the utopian genre by reversing its concept: they constitute a "no-place" ("*u-topos*"), where everything seems possible. The genre's "classical" corpus, constituted from the 16th century onwards in literature and philosophy, is composed of numerous works set on an island, a kind of "ideal" physical materialization of an allegory or a small-scale model of our societies (see Thomas More's island of Utopia, Lesconvel's island of Naudely, Francis Bacon's island of Bensalem, etc.).[16]

According to Jean-Michel Racault, in a literary genre that dates back to the Enlightenment, "utopian locations" present "a common requirement": "a geographical distance from the world of reference of the author and the reader – i.e. Europe, presumably – or at least the spatial materialization of a gap indicating the utopian world's *otherness*" (2016: 503)[*]. Thomas More's island in *Utopia* (1516) constitutes a canonical representation of this genre.

In one of the engravings illustrating the 1727 edition of Jonathan Swift's *Gulliver's Travels,* an atoll levitates on the horizon. The novel is organized around a series of journeys separated from one another by a full-page map of the Seas, indicating the location of each new island visited. This particular engraving depicts Laputa, Gulliver's first stop on his third voyage, a city equipped with an anti-gravity system (Fig. 24). At a time when a number of video games have established the practice of locating their world on a topographical map,[17] a similar wondrous landscape appears in *Avatar*, when the soldiers' helicopter ventures into Pandora's mist. Once the vapors dissipate, the breathtaking spectacle of the "floating mountains" overhanging the luxuriant planet lies before their astonished eyes. In Cameron's film, the spectacular *attraction* results precisely from the fact that these lands defy the laws of *gravity* (Color Plate 8). Beyond the iconographic kinship, the adoption of Swift's utopia motif reveals that *Avatar*, although clearly referring to "virtual realities" (even in its title), also belongs to the great family of imaginary journeys. Nevertheless, one difference should be noted: in Swift's work, the anti-gravity is artificial, produced by the Laputians[18] who worship technology and are constantly distressed due to an excess of scientific knowledge. On the contrary, anti-gravity is a natural phenomenon in *Avatar*, diametrically opposed by the film's discourse to the machines of the colonists and the marines.

In order to avoid associating all travel stories with what Doležel has named the "cross-world journeys" (1998: 131), I shall consider the arrangement of geographical and imagined spaces in *Avatar*, and examine its *limits*, both at the level of the borders around which the imaginary topography is organized and at the level of its capacity to build a plurality of worlds. By some sleight of hand, *Avatar* advocates total viewer immersion while clearly conferring a *different nature* on the world inhabited by the Na'vi. In this way, the film avoids dealing with the question of the passage from one world to the other. A reversal occurs exactly halfway through the film, so that the story's syntactical structure gives the impression of a split between different worlds. In the film's hemistich, Jack, after operating his avatar, opens his eyes in a close-up, and declares via a voice-over: "Everything is backwards now, like out there is the true world and this is the dream." The terms used point to an isotopy of an immersive subjectivity (i.e. a *mental world*) and could lead one to believe that *Avatar*'s divided world is structured around an opposition between the real and the virtual, as in movies featuring video game users (for instance *The Lawnmower Man*). However, this is not true: Pandora is just as "real" as the gigantic war machines or human "harvesters" deployed on its surface. Computer-generated visuals are indiscriminately used to represent the colonists' vehicles and Pandora's fauna and flora.

Therefore, the film seems to draw on the "myth of the frontier" that dates back to the 19th century (see *supra* Chapter 2) rather than exploring the idea, contemporary with its release and referred to both in its title and its promotional campaign, of a frontier separating distinct worlds. The "avatar" as an embodied double does not belong to another realm; it is simply located in a different space nearby that is nonetheless difficult to access. Despite Pandora's utopian character, the audience is not confronted here with a video game-like virtual universe to which the term "avatar" is usually attached in the current media context (unlike what happens in *Gamer* or *Holy Motors*). Still, Cameron's film capitalizes on the concept of a total immersion in *virtual worlds*, focusing on the hero's growing *comprehension*, in the sense of both his rational understanding and his pantheistic integration. To present Pandora's virgin forest, fauna, and people as a different world would mean to accentuate their extraordinary, fairy-like character and to suggest (without exhibiting it) that the splendor in front of which characters and viewers alike become ecstatic, is but the product of computer graphics technology.

Lastly, it should be noted that the motif of insularity, recurrent in movies featuring a second world, can be extended to clearly circumscribed spaces, like the small towns in *Under the Dome* (2013–2015), *Wayward Pines* (2015–2016), or John Carpenter's *In the Mouth of Madness* (1994) and *Village of the Damned* (1995), the mysterious quarantined zone – clearly inspired by Tarkovsky's *Stalker* – named "The Shimmer" in *Annihilation* (2018), the underground spaces in *THX 1138* (1971), *The Island* (2005), and *Us* (2019), or the areas of community gathering, originally conceived as utopias, in *Logan's Run* (1976) and M. Night Shyamalan's *The Village* (2004).

Artificial Worlds

I call "*artificial worlds*" all environments inhabited by the characters that are presented within the diegesis as both *physical* (as opposed to *virtual*) and, as we sometimes realize in retrospect, *fake*. These two defining criteria are valid even if the worlds in question result from the use of CGI effects (meaning that whatever appears to the audience as belonging to the profilmic has, in fact, no material existence) and are components of a fictional work which, in principle, includes the unreality of the represented as one of the terms of its reading pact. Those factors are attached to the creatorial and spectatorial levels, whereas the focus here is rather on the way the film characters perceive their world.[19]

In the "*Resident Evil*" (see Chapter 1) and "*Westworld*" (see *infra*) series, big corporations – Umbrella Corp. and Delos respectively – generate simulated, *artificial worlds* for experimental purposes. The presence of such environments comes inevitably with a certain degree of self-reflexivity. This self-reflexivity may be emphasized in films like *Henry V* (1944) or *Keep an Eye on Amelia* (1949), where characters leave the backstage to enter the representation, in a sort of metalepsis between theatre and cinema. Yet it is most often attenuated by the diegetization of the process of building such an environment as a set, as in the sub-genre of the backstage musical and the "film within a film" plots of movies like *Day for Night* (1973) or *Scream 3* (2000). The same may be argued for films featuring a studio or a television set, as in David Cronenberg's *Videodrome* (1983), the conspiracy movie *Capricorn One* (1977), and Michael Crichton's *Looker* (1981), or those that embed a theatrical representation inside the fiction, as in Ernst Lubitsch's *To Be or Not to Be* (1942), Ingmar Bergman's *Through a Glass Darkly* (1961), and Alain Resnais' *Last Year at Marienbad* (1961).

The perception of such environments as distinct worlds is proportional to the importance given to the "setting". For starters, it depends on the amplitude of their spatial expansion: the impression that we are dealing with a world is weak when the action is limited in a single room, as in *Good Bye Lenin!* (2003), the pre-credits sequence in *Mission: Impossible* (1996), or the final scene in *Captain America: The First Avenger* (2011). It is also proportional to the degree to which the visualized diegetic space is reduced to this factitious environment. The scale is variable from film to film: an elusively large maze in *Cube* (1997), a terrorist's lair in Evey's fake kidnapping experience in *V for Vendetta* (2005), a room (or a house) in which the victim is held captive in *Saw* (2004) or *House of 9* (2005), a forest area located above a huge underground facility in *The Cabin in the Woods* (2011), a playground in *The Hunger Game* series, a small town in *The Truman Show* (1998), an island in *Lost*, a miniaturized parallel society inhabiting in parks made to fit the size of its people in *Downsizing* (2017), or an entire planet in *Dark City* (1998) or *Predators* (2010).

These spaces/worlds, built by men or aliens, are not ontologically different from the "first" world that includes or adjoins them, but they nonetheless raise the issue of worldbuilding inside the fiction. Most of the times, *artificial worlds* are linked to the way the narrative point of view is organized, as illustrated – in a contrasting way – by two scenes previously mentioned. In *Mission: Impossible*, the action is right from the start visualized through the monitors observed by those who pull the strings from a space located just behind the wall of a fake hotel room; the audience thus assumes the position of a TV spectator watching a *Candid Camera*-like show. On the other hand, in *Captain America: The First Avenger*, the viewer shares the point of view of the hero and completely ignores the environment's artificial character.

In David Fincher's *The Game* (1997), the principle of internal focalization organized around the victim of a manipulation is maintained throughout the film. Arrogant businessman Nicholas Van Orton (Michael Douglas) unknowingly accepts the rules of an intriguing "game", offered to him by his brother for his birthday in the form of a voucher to be reclaimed at the headquarters of some mysterious company. After that, his daily life becomes disrupted by a number of increasingly invasive inconveniences and perilous situations. In view of all that, Van Orton – and the viewer with him – becomes convinced that he truly is the victim of a conspiracy. We are immersed in a paranoid, suspenseful atmosphere, as we are led to believe that the masters of the game are actually crooks and murderers who conceal their crimes by passing them off as playful activities, when in fact the opposite is true, as a series of dramatic twists will finally reveal. Just like Schwarzenegger's hero that contacts Rekall Inc. in the beginning of *Total Recall* (see *supra*), Van Orton visits the CRS offices ("Consumer Recreation Services"). He is then immersed into "another world", without even realizing it, since the starting point of the game is undefined (as in dream movies that offer no indication of the exact moment we enter the dream). Van Orton experiences a series of stereotypical actions that correspond to the promises initially made by those who "pull the strings". In the words of a CRS employee describing the service offered to his client: "Think of it as a great vacation, except that you don't go to it, it comes to you."

However, unlike the protagonist in *Total Recall* (of which *The Game* constitutes a kind of realist and moralistic counterpart), Van Orton will ramble in all possible directions, his nocturnal wanderings resembling those of the antihero in Martin Scorsese's *After Hours* (1985). Viewers may momentarily mistake the scene in which the TV host addresses directly Van Orton as a hallucination experienced by the hero,[20] thus activating an interpretation that will eventually prove to be relevant in Fincher's subsequent film, *Fight Club* (1999). At any rate, the audience remains constantly aware that everything in the film takes place within the same world and that all visualized objects share an identical reality status, even when the surrounding environment is unmasked as a pre-fabricated set. As a matter of fact, it is precisely the lack of virtualization of the threats faced by Van Orton that might strike as implausible, insofar as the hero is risking his own life in a game that is only supposed to teach him a valuable life lesson.

Still, *The Game* does allude to a dreamlike or supernatural state, even though it refrains from actually materializing such a reality. As Van Orton tries to trace the CRS bosses, the "masterminds" of a role-playing game in which he unknowingly participates, he cries out: "I'm pulling back the curtain. I want to meet the Wizard". He is, of course, referring to *The Wizard of Oz* and to a particular scene near the end of Victor Fleming's movie that rationalizes, partly at least, its marvelous universe. The places Van Orton passes through are presented as simulation rooms similar to the ones in the laboratory of *Resident Evil: Retribution* (2012). While the hero sits in an ambulance that has just arrived outside the emergency ward of a hospital and is surrounded by dozens of nurses, the lights suddenly go out and the "extras" leave the stage, revealing an almost completely bare room, a set strewn with obstacles. At the end, the alleged traitor pretends that the hero's weapon is actually real and tries to convince him that everything he has experienced has been staged.[21] In her words, this is only "special effects. Squibs, like in the movies". The game inside the fiction is also a fictional game, a "shared playful feint" (Schaeffer 1999: 133–157)[*] between the film and the viewer.

The *artificial world* in *The Game* proves to be immersive precisely because the viewer does not have access, until the film's final scene, to the backstage of this gigantic cover-up. Conversely, in a movie like *The Joneses* (2009), we discover early on that the seemingly perfect family that moves into an upscale suburban neighborhood is not a real family at all: each of its "members" has been hired by a company to promote its products to their unsuspecting neighbors. In this case, the focal characters are not the victims of an illusion, but its creators. That said, the viewer is not directly introduced into the scheme: the characters' performance initially embodies a possible alternative. In this respect, one could argue that the famous "as if" dialogue scene in *Johnny Guitar* (1954) prefigures a number of reiterative simulations in modernist art films (*Last Year at Marienbad*, 1961; *In the Mood for Love*, 2000; *Inland Empire*, 2006; *Certified Copy*, 2010; *Restless*, 2011) or in a Hollywood movie as *Duplicity* (2009) that openly refers to the tradition of self-reflexive acting.

As two-world universes frequently result from a split between reality and appearance, the embodiment of a character by an actor may very well be approached via a world-centered perspective. For instance, it is often difficult to distinguish whether we are dealing with an unreliable, deceitful character *in* the film (in such a case, the actor plays the role of a character who *performs*) or whether the actor of the film simply falls short in his task. In the finale of *Starship Troopers* (1997), we learn that the characters were psychologically manipulated throughout their adventures, although the story knowingly cultivates certain ambiguities (see Meininger 2006). Verhoeven's conscious direction of a cast of TV actors (Casper Van Dien, Dina Meyer and Denise Richards had previously starred in the teen TV series *Beverly Hills, 90210* between 1992 and 1994) whose acting style hardly corresponds to the standards of a Hollywood feature film, contributes to an overall impression of facticity. However, this facticity does not take the form of a distinct (*artificial*) universe, even though one can interpret the protagonists' manipulation as a clear reference to the multiverse in *Total Recall*, an earlier Verhoeven entry. The "facticity" within the fiction is above all a matter of point of view.

Artificial worlds are commonly composed of real human beings, of spaces the characters roam through, and of physical artifacts they get to use. In this respect, *The Hunger Games* (2012) offers an example of what one could designate, by analogy with a narrative figure discussed by Gérard Genette,[22] as a *paralepsis* at the level of worldbuilding: a deviation from a postulated type of world that manifests itself as an overkill. A brief scene in the film acts as a kind of Freudian slip that reveals the contemporary digital context by presenting a certain inconsistency with respect to the previously established diegetic logic and the world proposed in the original novel. A crosscutting establishes a relation of simultaneity between the actions of the players and the deliberations of those who organize the game discussing in front of their screens. The surprised viewer watches as a group of white-coated technicians – half-computer scientists, half-veterinarians and distant relatives of the android repairmen in the 1973 *Westworld* film – digitally create, pixel by pixel, a series of monstrous dogs. Once these artificial beasts obtain the same texture as the rest of the elements in the film, the technicians project them inside the space of the game.

This scene from *Hunger Games*, which has no equivalent in the rest of the film, reveals the influence current digital technologies have on the world-centered creative design of movies. In Suzanne Collins' novel of the same name, the entire story is told in the first person by Katniss Everdeen and the reader has no access to the backstage of the game. Chapter 25 begins with a single-word sentence, actually a neologism: "Muttations". Then, it goes on to describe the appearance of the pack of monstrous dogs. The term used is telling of the different foundations on which the novel's fictional speculation is based compared to its screen adaptation. The narrator will recognize in these monsters certain features belonging to the other participants, affirming that unlike what happens in the film, the principle of denaturation does not involve here the creation of visual effects. In visualizing the materialization of a computer-generated image, the movie version of *The Hunger Games* casts doubt on the embedded "small world" of the game. Should we then infer that the entirety of this spectacular space, and perhaps even the protagonists themselves (whom we have nonetheless seen outside the game, in their daily lives), are simply the product of a machine? The film does not seem to validate such an interpretation. And yet, the screenwriters' choice to include the creation of "virtual" dogs is revealing of the popularity the interaction and the entanglement between the physical world and digital graphics knows nowadays (see for example the case of *Pokémon Go*, an augmented reality game based on the user's spatial location).

As I will show in Chapter 4 with respect to a movie like *The Congress*, contemporary films often insert an actor's performance inside a computer-generated environment, or transform the actor's physical appearance in order to create a wholly different character, sometimes belonging to a fantasy world (one of the most famous examples is of course Gollum, motion captured by Andy Serkis in "*The Lord of the Rings*" trilogy). As the case of *The Hunger Games* shows, the thin line separating *artificial* and *virtual* pleads in favor of a broad typology of worlds that would allow to identify genealogical ties and, consequently, to build a bridge between the digital and the pre-digital eras (especially since the latter may very well allude to a digital imaginary).

Supernatural Worlds

The "super-natural", produced through the alteration of certain laws of our world, mainly appears in films associated with weird and horror stories or belonging to the fantasy genre (unless a two-world structure establishes a set of "*parallel worlds*" instead). The *here* and *there* of our material world coexist with the *beyond*, most often inhabited by ghosts. The connection frequently takes place through a *medium*, be it a human as in *Drag Me to Hell* (2009), or a technology in keeping with the parascientific practice of *channeling*, like the TV set in *Poltergeist* (1982) (see Sconce 2000: 21–28 and Berton 2021). Since the scope of my essay is mostly limited to the science fiction genre, I will not discuss examples of this type of world. However, a distinction should be made between two separate cases falling under this category. In the first case, the entirety of the film representation is attached to the real world, in which *revenants* – who, as their name indicates, *return*, making it unnecessary for the characters in the first world to go elsewhere – manifest themselves periodically as heterogeneous components of the film universe (*Ghostbusters*, 1984; *The Frighteners*, 1996). In the second one, a two-world universe is established, in which the afterlife shapes as a complete, audio-visualized world, like in a number of films made by Tim Burton from *Beetle Juice* (1988) onwards, or in *R.I.P.D.* (2013) where the ghosts play a role similar to that of the aliens in the "*Men in Black*" series (1997–2019).

The Sixth Sense (1999) and *The Others* (2001) prove to be more devious in that they reverse the interworld relations by combining the supernatural hypothesis with a subjective factor: the hero refuses to accept and represses the fact of his or her own death (along with a pervasive feeling of guilt), ending up deluded. As these films stick to a regime of fixed internal focalization and skillfully preserve certain ambiguities, the audience is equally deceived (on *The Sixth Sense*, see Boillat 2001: 207–214). It turns out that the world inhabited by the protagonist during the biggest part of each of these movies is the second world of the supernatural, albeit sufficiently intertwined with the first world so that the viewer is unable to distinguish between the two until the characters themselves are forced to accept the truth (a realization also found in the case of *mental worlds* discussed *infra*).

Therefore, an uncertainty is created between two divergent ways of understanding the world, as Tzvetan Todorov famously discussed with respect to the "fantastic". According to the Bulgarian-French thinker, the "fantastic" refers to an intermediate and evanescent category, located between the uncanny (the rational hypothesis) and the marvelous (the supernatural hypothesis): "The fantastic […] lasts only as long as a certain hesitation: a hesitation common to reader and character, who must decide whether or not what they perceive derives from 'reality' as it exists in the common opinion" (Todorov 1973: 41). It is precisely the attitude shared by the audience and the character that comes into play whenever the film's hero ignores that what he perceives is actually not real. Todorov's principle highlights the dynamic, inferential character of the reception of any given world by the reader or the spectator.

Sometimes, the difference between a *supernatural world* and what I describe below as an "*immersive mental world*" proves to be tenuous, even irrelevant. The latter turns out, "in the end", to be nothing more than a pretext for the representation of the former, allegedly serving an escapist ideology, as in the TV movie *Mazes and Monsters* (1982), or in *Life is a Bed of Roses* (1983), *Big Fish* (2003), *Pan's Labyrinth* (2006), and *Oz the Great and Powerful* (2013). Hollywood's adaptation of *The Wonderful Wizard of Oz* (1900) is revealing of the proximity between these two types of worlds. The actual journey to a *distant/supernatural world*, as described in L. Frank Baum's novel (Dorothy's house is transferred to Oz, a place governed by fairy-tale laws) is transformed into a dream, as we come to realize, in retrospect, when the film returns to the frame story. Dorothy's awakening scene replaces the passage in the novel that recounts the house's return to the first world. As a medium inducing a spectatorial attitude often compared to a dream by adepts of the psychoanalytic theory (see Christian Metz's *The Imaginary Signifier*, 1975), cinema favors this sort of transpositions. This leads me to the next category in my typology, where the duplication of worlds, often imperceptible due to a lack of an obvious threshold between frame and embedded stories (or visions), is motivated by a subjectivation of the representation.

Mental Worlds

The story of Martin Scorsese's *Shutter Island* (2010) takes place in one of the Boston Harbor Islands hosting a complex of buildings that serve both as a mental institution and a maximum-security penitentiary. Therefore, the island mentioned in the title may seem similar to the spaces discussed above under the "*distant worlds*" category. Nevertheless, it differs fundamentally from them on an ontological level. As we watch a boat crossing a thick fog in the film's opening scene, moving towards the shore of the island in order to drop off two US Deputy Marshals, Teddy Daniels (Leonardo DiCaprio) and his partner Chuck Aule (Mark Ruffalo), we are in fact already well inside Daniels' delusion. The character played by DiCaprio has been incarcerated on the island for two years now and imagines an alter ego who allegedly comes from the *outside*. Already in this early scene, several oddities in the editing and the dialogue may strike the viewer. We notice some jump cuts, first as Daniels lights a cigarette, then during an insert shot depicting the two "Marshals" from behind and at a certain distance. Moreover, Daniels seems to be meeting Chuck for the first time on the deck of the boat, even though they are clearly the only passengers on it and the journey is about to end. A second viewing is necessary in order to grasp these elements as discreet hints at the unreality of the representation. Viewers who discover the film for the first time will realize much later, during Daniels' confrontation with the psychiatrist played by Ben Kingsley, that the immersion in the fiction coincided with an immersion in a *mental world*, inhabited by characters and filled with actions stemming from the hero's imagination.

This type of world raises the much more general question of the representation of subjectivity in movies, discussed by Edward Branigan in terms relevant to my approach in this essay:

> Mental process narration, or more loosely, the 'dream sequence', depends principally on the occurrence of undefined temporal markers and the existence of a character's mental condition as the unity, or coherence, of the representation. In addition, the logic which links the character to the framing of the image may be either directly spatial (where the camera assumes the position of the character's spatial perspective, as in a POV shot) or more indirect and rhetorical. In the latter case, a logical network of equivalences is created which acts to substitute, symbolically, a character for the origin of the framing. These rhetorical constructions involve a certain metaphorical transfer and are at the heart of the reflection and projection subjectivities (Branigan 1984: 85).

The rhetorical logic mentioned by Branigan in cases where the framing of the image does not correspond to the gaze of the focal character can be pushed a little further. Everything, or a part of what is included in the frame – belonging to the diegesis as inferred from the screenic – may involve a "metaphorical transfer"[23] and demand to be interpreted as the projection of a given subjectivity. François Jost adds to the narratological model introduced by Gérard Genette the category of "primary internal ocularisation" that he defines as follows: "It is a question of suggesting a regarding look without showing it" (Jost 2007: 75).[24] Like Branigan, Jost refers to the ways the filming apparatus may suggest a subject looking (as in the cases of a slightly shaky camera), but we could shift our interpretation of the framing from the visual to the mental perception of a character and consider the world as represented through the filter of the latter's imagination. The subjective world is then superimposed on (or even substitutes for) what constitutes the "real" world within the fiction.

The cases of interest here feature a representation of a character's inner vision that is not reduced to an easily circumscribed "dream sequence". Subjectivity is insidiously diffused throughout the film so that an important part of the film's world (or even its entirety) is perceived as a "dream", as an alteration of the first world. When the boundary between the inner and the outer world is blurred, subjectivity permeates all of the film's images and sounds. This is precisely what happens in the following productions: *Jacob's Ladder* (1990), *Naked Lunch* (1991), *Lost Highway* (1997), *Fear and Loathing in Las Vegas* (1998), *Fight Club* (1999), *Chasing Sleep* (2000), *Requiem for a Dream* (2000), *Solaris* (2002), *Spider* (2002), *Identity* (2003), *Secret Window* (2004), *The Machinist* (2004), *Stay* (2005), *Danika* (2006), *Triangle* (2009), *Wrecked* (2010), *Black Swan* (2010), *Lost Identity* (2010), *The Ward* (2010), *Shutter Island* (2010), *Mr. Robot* (2015–2019) and *Joker* (2019).

Mental worlds constitute an exaggerated form of attribution of a coefficient of subjectivity to the audio-visual representation. The world of the film is perceived as the subjective variant of another world – in this case, the world of reference for the rest of the characters in the film. Jan-Noël Thon, who incidentally cites the example of *Fight Club*,[25] uses the term "psycho-narration" (2016: 254–255). However, it is important to clarify that the character whose "conscience" produces the world of the film does not necessarily assume the role of the narrator, even if we are clearly dealing here with a process of worldbuilding. This process may be strictly internal or caused by an external agent, for example a chemical substance or the hypnotic power of another character, as in two successive episodes of *X-Files*' Season 2 ("Blood" and "Sleepless", 1994). However, in the case of *Fight Club*, the protagonist actually assumes the role of the narrator: we hear Edward Norton's voice-over speak in the first person. Other films, in which the world is experienced by a character-writer differently from the rest of the characters, like *Naked Lunch* or *Kafka*, implicitly assume that the protagonist imagines the world of the film.[26] Beyond the *narration* itself, this may also turn out to be a matter of *(audio-)vision*: what is shown on the screen corresponds to the way the character sees the world around him. An imaginary alter ego, like Tyler Durden (Brad Pitt) in *Fight Club*, Chuck (Mark Ruffalo) in *Shutter Island*, or the ten protagonists in *Identity*, is a typical example of a component that differentiates a *mental world* from the "real" world. While examining such phenomena of "projection" of a character's mental state onto the diegetic space, Branigan deliberately excludes the "expressionist" representations of a film like *The Cabinet of Dr. Caligari* (Branigan 1984: 123). Yet, it is precisely these modes of representation that interest me the most here. In his discussion of cases of "projection", Branigan refers to Freud's theory, and most notably to the idea of a "defense mechanism based on a throwing out of what one refuses to recognize in oneself or of what one refuses to be" (*Ibid.*: 137). This is exactly the case in films like *Spider, The Machinist*, *Triangle*, or *Shutter Island*, where the representation in its entirety bends to what the character wishes to imagine in order to successfully repress his guilt.

It should be clarified that a series of subjective insert shots that reinforce the audience's identification with a character through the audio-visualization of his memories or fantasies, is not sufficient to establish a "*mental world*" as I define this type of world here. An opposition (even an implicit one) between these insert shots and a distinct regime of reality is also required, so that these images create a space that is sufficiently stable to be inhabited by the character (and the viewer).[27] This space may be limited in size, like those that frequently obsess the heroes in Darren Aronofsky's movies. An example of this is the pier at the end of which Marion (Jennifer Connelly) stands in *Requiem for a Dream*: at first, we see it through a frame-within-a-frame formed by a window, replacing what normally exists opposite the hero's apartment. After a cross-fade, the pier comes to occupy the entire frame in which Harry (Jared Leto) immerses himself in order to meet the red-dressed woman, who is in turn distracted by the sound of a door opening, reminding Harry of his reality as a junky. Drug-induced paranoia on the perceiving subject, whose visions the audience shares, favors the immersion in a different world. Doležel explains this case in terms inspired by fictional semantics: "Dreams, hallucination, madness, drug-induced altered states are physically possible, natural human experiences; at the same time, physically impossible persons, objects, and events appear in these frames" (1998: 117). One can also think of the reiterated moment a narrative bifurcation occurs in *The Fountain*, when Tommy declines Izzy's invitation to come outside and watch the first snow, arguing that he has too much work.[28] In this case too, a seemingly continuous editing alters a classical pattern, traditionally used when two characters co-exist in the same space. One last example taken from Aronofsky's body of work is *Mother!* (2017) where the protagonist's house turns out to be mentally controlled by the character portrayed by Javier Bardem.

In the examples described above, the environment acts as a "screen" onto which a character's thoughts are projected. The development of an inhabitable world is foregrounded in cases of interpenetration between distinct worlds, for instance when an element belonging to the world of reference is transposed into the second world, instigating an incongruity (like the sound made by the door in the scene from *Requiem for a Dream* mentioned above). This is also true when a character invades the subjective vision of another character, like Marla in the ice cave dream sequence in *Fight Club* (1999), or Mako Mori's co-pilot in *Pacific Rim* (2013). In Guillermo del Toro's film, the subject not only relives her own memories, she also shares them with other characters (similarly to the dreams in *Inception*).

Movies can audio-visualize a *mental world* – meaning that the latter can correspond to the entirety of what a film gives to see and hear – in a discontinuous (for example, in *Naked Lunch*, there is a brief moment that temporarily extracts us from the junkie's hallucinations) or a continuous way (see *Spider*, 2002). I speak of an *immersive mental world* when the viewer is introduced in it without knowing it, deliberately left in total ignorance with respect to the status of the world. In such cases, it is actually the "relation of attribution" established between the embedding and the embedded worlds that is momentarily concealed. In fact the latter is subordinated to the former, but the film does not openly reveal the subjection of one of the worlds to the mental or emotional state of a character inhabiting the other world. I borrow the concept of "relation of attribution" from Jean Châteauvert who, building on the theory of possible worlds, formalizes the links between a narrator speaking in voice-over and the audio-visualized narrative that is generated from this voice-over. Châteauvert describes the "relation of attribution" in the following terms:

> As viewers, we are confronted with two worlds, that of the visualized characters and that of the narrator. A vectorialized relation is established between them insofar the verbal narrator assumes the narration of the audio-visualized world in which the characters appear.[*]

According to Châteauvert, the entire film may be considered as a "possible world" when it is enunciated by an entity commonly qualified by film theoreticians as "extradiegetic". The term is ambiguous in the case of a narrator who is visualized as a storyteller while also being a character inside the film. It is indeed difficult, if not impossible, to postulate the absolute exteriority of such a narrator with respect to the diegesis when considering his world-centered status: it makes more sense to attribute this exteriority to *one of the film's worlds*. Châteauvert goes on to describe this relation on the basis of the notion of "propositional attitude", borrowed from Umberto Eco (1979: 219):

> The individuals and the course of events pertaining to a possible world are not actual, but relative to a specific propositional attitude: someone affirms, believes, dreams, desires, etc., the set of events and individuals of a diegesis (Châteauvert 1996: 68)[*].

Therefore, mental universes are always the product of a propositional attitude that the viewer is nonetheless not always allowed to pinpoint right from the outset. The audience may perceive the establishment of a subjective representation without managing to determine if it relates to a memory, a fantasy, a dream, a hallucination, etc., and without being able to decide which precise elements in this world differ from the "real" world. Furthermore, access to *immersive mental worlds* is accompanied by a strategy of concealment that affects not only the propositional attitude, but also the relation of attribution itself. It may be that the latter is revealed only after the fact, as Châteauvert points out (*Ibid.*: 73) through the example of *The Last Temptation of Christ* (1988). The temptation mentioned in the title of Martin Scorsese's film is provisionally *embodied* as an alternative to the biblical story (and therefore it may be interpreted as an *alternate storyworld*). It takes shape in a complete audio-visual representation that seems to have the same reality status as the gospel narrative: while agonizing on the cross, Jesus imagines himself leading a human life as a husband, father, and lover, until he is called back to his messianic destiny as the film returns to the first story (world).[29]

The case of *immersive mental worlds* pushes the subjectivization of the representation to its paroxysm, resolving thus the problems usually identified by film theoreticians when examining the use of the so-called "subjective camera" (or POV-shot) as a factor that is meant to encourage viewer identification with the character. The debate over *Lady in the Lake* (1946), a film that systematically equates the position of the camera with the location of the protagonist's eyes (with the exception of its prologue) is exemplary (for a summary of this debate, see Robert 2010: 110–112). One of the first studies of this type of films was published in July 1948 in the journal *Les Temps modernes*. It was written by Albert Laffay, a theoretician who explained in detail the reasons why the subjective camera ultimately failed in Robert Montgomery's film. In his words, "movies help us understand, above anything else, what one would call in existentialist terms our way of 'being in the world'", so that "an affective polarization […] requires that a character is shown to us from the outside, even if we actually perceive much more than just his body" (Laffay 1948: 156 and 160–161)*. Several decades later, other theoreticians will take up Laffay's analysis, using similar terms (see notably Simon 1983). The main argument is that, contrary to all expectations (particularly that of a correspondence between the subjective camera and first person narration in novels), the fact that we stick to the eyes of the character tends to work against our identification with the latter insofar as this process rejects the actor's performance off-screen, thus discarding a decisive factor in the conveying of emotions.[30]

On the contrary, the representations discussed here present the advantage of maximizing viewer identification by operating on both sides through a process of superimposition between two worlds: the audience sees the world as the character imagines it while the latter is visible and audible on the screen, allowing the actor to build through his performance a personality the viewer is able to identify with. In *Spider* (2002), the representation of most of the present-day scenes results from a projection of the "subject" (most notably when the same actor plays several characters of the same age but at two different periods). Yet all flashback scenes include an unusual invariant, none other than an adult Spider (Ralph Fiennes), observing certain scenes of his past, physically integrated in their margins. This mode of representation, also used in *Joker*, is certainly not new: a similar case can be found in Ingmar Bergman's *Wild Strawberries* (1957).[31] The term often used by critics – and in the case of *Spider* by Cronenberg himself (Kaganski 2002) – to designate this type of projection of the character's thoughts onto his environment is "expressionist". The extension of this notion is arguably variable, while the reference to the "movement" of the same name, attached to German cinema of the late 1910s and the early 1920s, is certainly imprecise and debatable (albeit generally accepted).

One title is commonly considered as exemplary: *The Cabinet of Dr. Caligari* (1920), discussed in a perspective similar to mine by Aurélie Ledoux in her analysis of *Barton Fink* (1991). According to the French scholar, the "Caligari effect", which is actually valid only if one disregards the film's introduction and epilogue, lies in the pathological subjectivization of reality, "the projection of the inner life onto the outer world" (Ledoux 2012: 50-51)*. By dismissing the beginning and the ending of the movie, Ledoux overlooks the observation made by one of the historians and sociologists of German cinema's Weimar period, Siegfried Kracauer, in his famous book *From Caligari to Hitler*. One of the chapters is devoted to Robert Wiene's film and, in particular, to the ideological implications of the "embedding", a narrative device that, according to Kracauer, was in fact absent from Carl Mayer and Hans Janowitz's original screenplay. In his words:

> In their triumph the philistines overlooked one significant fact: even though Caligari stigmatized the oblique chimneys as scary, it never restored the perpendicular ones as the normal. Expressionist ornaments also overrun the film's concluding episode, in

> which, from the philistines' viewpoint, perpendiculars should have been expected to characterize the revival of conventional reality (Kracauer 2004: 70).

Therefore, the contamination of the representation by the main character's subjectivity, as discussed by Ledoux, is perhaps more pervasive in *The Cabinet of Dr. Caligari* than one might think at first sight. Assuredly, the marks established first by the entry into the embedded story, then by the return to the frame story, constitute a rationalizing factor, a way of confining the paranoid imagery to the product of a diegeticized enunciation from which the film's enunciation is thus disassociated. Nevertheless, the persistence of improbable architectural designs in the finale establishes a certain ambiguity, as if the patient in the asylum were in fact responsible for the film's monstration.

Fundamentally, the questions raised by *Caligari*'s ending scene point to the potential world-centered consequences of the film's visual features. Are we supposed to accept a stylized setting (according to norms of which the characters in the film have no awareness whatsoever, and which are therefore explicitly intended for the viewer), or an unanticipated shot angle that is not motivated by the protagonist's gaze, as diegetic? Given the way we defined the notion of diegesis in the beginning of this chapter, the obvious answer would be negative. Yet, as we will see in Chapter 4 with respect to the co-presence of black & white and color scenes, it is not easy to determine such a simple partition. Sometimes, a film's visual construction or its sets (constructed and then filmed) function as an indicator of the status of the world represented. Although these elements constitute a kind of surface varnish that does not affect the referent of the representation, they help nonetheless define not only the diegetic world, but also the way viewers are supposed to perceive it. In *The Cabinet of Dr. Caligari*, Cesare (Conrad Veidt), hypnotized as he may be, is hardly concerned about the impracticality of the path he takes along the edge of a roof depicted in an "expressionist" style, leading almost into the void (FIG) – an incoherent space indicating that *we are in a different world.*

Therefore, such features pertaining to a film's form and style do not impact on the ontological status of the represented diegetic elements. To argue otherwise is to validate the absurd (or, rather, "metaleptic", in the sense of a confusion between the screenic and the profilmic levels) logic underlying a visual gag in *Top Secret!* (1984) that parodies *Mr. Arkadin* (1955) by keeping the eyes of Peter Cushing's character oversized throughout the entire scene ever since a shot showed him looking through a magnifying glass. On the other hand, this magnifying visual effect that acts as a "filter" between the viewer and the represented could be interpreted as a sign of a subjective vision, a *mental world.* At any rate, the lines separating the different types of worlds are thin. The way the world of a given film is perceived is the result of inferences: the diegesis, as Souriau defined it, exists fully only in the spectator's mind.

Alternate (Story)Worlds

We have thus far underlined the importance of distinguishing between *story* (the main focus of narratological studies) and *world* (a concept that has attracted the attention of a number of theoreticians of fiction). However, these two notions often – if not always, especially in the case of movies coming from the dominant system of film production, like the ones examined in this essay – maintain a high degree of interdependence. This is particularly the case in films where the plurality of worlds stems less from ontological variations and more from the development of possible narrative alternatives. It is important to acknowledge a theoretical distinction between cases of narrative bifurcation that produce *alternate (story)worlds*, and multiverses per se, which summon *within the same plot* at least two worlds distinct in their governing laws, the vast majority of living beings inhabiting them, and the furnishing that defines them. However, movies exploring a number of possible narrative alternatives are frequently referred to as "multiverses".

In the ABC TV series *Flashforward*, Dyson Frost (Michael Massee) did not just experience a two-minute glimpse of his life six months into the future, as most of the survivors of a global blackout, but he actually relived this vision hundreds of times.[32] As the FBI agents discover, he was able to draw on a giant board what he calls his "Garden of Forking Paths" – the title of Episode 17. This is a clear reference to a short story of the same name written by Jorge Luis Borges, an exemplary case of joint actualization of narrative bifurcations. Of all the possible alternatives schematically represented by Frost (this way assuming the role of a "scriptwriter"), only one gets to be actualized in the episode, while the other alternatives are simply mentioned or implied.[33] From the point of view of Agent Demetri Noh (John Cho), who manages to escape the tragic future revealed by the other characters' flash-forward, the visualized narrative alternative constitutes an *alternate (story)world.* Yet *Flashforward* refrains from showing two incompatible events (for instance, the agent dying in the flash but surviving in the present). Demetri's death is never visualized on screen, since he does not experience a flash-forward himself and his assassination is only verbally mentioned, without an immersion in the flash-forward experienced by other characters. In this way, the series avoids the inconsistencies that its pitch could potentially lead to and, as is often the case when alternative paths are explored, sees about not to undermine the *unity* and the *uniqueness* of its diegesis.

This type of story is defined by a pattern that has been studied in recent years by a number of theoreticians in the field of literary narratology, especially in English-language publications (see Ryan 1991 and Dannenberg 2004).[34] I will examine it here specifically with regard to the establishement of a multiverse (and therefore of the alternatives actualized by the story, and not just temporarily envisioned by the reader/viewer during the process of narrative comprehension) and the role attributed to film editing. Generally speaking, all worlds in this type of film present an equal degree of fictionality since they are the objects of a realist representation – the fantasy genre is out of place here. As the audience is led to speculate about the divergences between the different variants, it is important that these variants do not postulate too great a deviation from the world the viewers experience in their lives. The narrative alternatives that coexist in the same film (or even in several films, as in the reversible diptych *Smoking/No Smoking*, 1993) are relative to a world whose ontological status remains identical – with the possible exception of a character disappearing (or appearing) in some of the alternatives.

In the interactive film *Bandersnatch* (2018), an episode from Netflix's anthology series *Dark Mirror*, the hero relives in a loop a series of actions initiated on July 9th, 1984. This is the day he submits to a video game editor his project to adapt a novel with multiple narrative bifurcations. The evaluation of causal relations governing each of the game's levels is based on the opinion of a video game critic appearing in a TV show. His assessment is different in each of the variants. Independently of whether the game is a complete failure or a success, the world inhabited by the protagonist remains the same, with the exception of a few modifications in the latter's actions in some of the variants. The plurality of worlds in *Bandersnatch* can only be conceived as the result of variations applied to a primary story. In such cases, the audio-visual narrative can be measured by variations that affect, at a different level, a film's scriptwriting process (sometimes represented inside the film in the form of narrative alternatives, as in *Paris When It Sizzles*, 1964), or those appearing when a different cut of the same film is released, for instance when the story is left without its initial happy ending as is the case with some "director's cut" versions of movies (*They Were Five,* 1936; *Enough Rope*, 1963; *Brazil*, 1985; *The Butterfly Effect*, 2004).[35]

The notion of possible alternatives is consubstantial with the science fiction genre insofar as novels or films attached to it opt for a specific "projection" (among others) of the future of our society.[36] The time travel pattern brings the risk of creating a second universe out of the disruption of the course of events as they have already taken place, leading to a narrative and diegetic bifurcation ("*Back to the Future*", *Terminator 2*, *Looper*, etc.). In these cases, the story is often devoted to the hero's efforts to undo the implications of such interference and to avoid the co-presence of incompatible versions that would challenge his own ontological status as a character. On the other hand, there are films in which the doubling of the universe constitutes a basic, structural fact that is then developed in a series of episodes – think of the comic book series *Valerian*, written by Pierre Christin, or the TV series *Fringe* (2008–2013, see Chapter 2).

Alternate (story)worlds are founded on the following principle: once arriving at a "turning point", the screenwriter juxtaposes several possible outcomes, instead of choosing just one among them. This is what poet and calligrapher Ts'ui Pên does in his book mentioned by Borges in "The Garden with Forking Paths": "In all fiction, when a man is faced with alternatives he chooses one at the expense of the others. In the almost unfathomable Ts'ui Pên, he chooses – simultaneously – all of them. He thus *creates* various futures, various times which start others that will in their turn branch out and bifurcate in other times. This is the cause of the contradictions in the novel." (Borges 1962: 98). The various narrative tracks instituted create, during their development, different versions of the "same" world that are mutually incompatible with the first world – at least at the level of the actions included, since the only components of the world that are modified are those on which the "new" actions have an actual impact. It may also be that none of the components ends up being modified; they are simply rearranged.

The co-presence of possible alternatives within a film can be realized through two different modes.[37] In order to comment and illustrate these modes, I will quit the SF territory for a moment. The first one is that of succession, as in *Groundhog Day* (1993), *Smoking/No Smoking* (1993), or *Run Lola Run* (1998), where each track is thoroughly explored before a new one begins, like in video games that restart at the same level after every "game over", with each new attempt to complete the level supposedly constituting an improvement on the previous ones.[38] The development of different narrative alternatives in a single film whose protagonist is trapped in a loop, like the soldier in *Source Code* or the one in *Edge of Tomorrow*, tends to call in question the reality status of the world in which these alternatives are unfolding. The linearity induced by the mode of succession (even if it appears as a series of loops) leads to favor the narrative rather than the world-centered dimension of the film.

The official trailer for *Groundhog Day* announces that the hero "is discovering the possibilities and [is] living life like there's no tomorrow". However, Phil (Bill Murray) is rather confronted with a version of the world with which he is supposed to comply, if only in order to fulfill the conditions of a heterosexual romance that will guarantee a *happy ending*. Although he wakes up on the same day and in the same bed every morning, his knowledge of the world actually evolves. Like the protagonist in *The Butterfly Effect* (2004) who has the power to rewrite the past by modifying actions that occurred during the amnesia phases he experienced in his teenage years and who vainly struggles to impose the best possible chain of causality, Phil is put at the same level as the viewer. He has witnessed the previous sequences and can benefit from his Sisyphean experience in order to modify certain components of the world. The freedom of the subject is redeemed: the loop only affects his environment, whereas he can improve himself with each new alternative.[39] Therefore, the possible narrative alternatives do not challenge the story's anthropocentric and psychological foundations. As is often the case in movies with *alternate (story)worlds*, there is no "worldbuilding machine" to be found in *Groundhog Day* that would point to the technological dimension of the filmmaking process. The principle of repetition and variation is exhibited in its total arbitrariness, magnifying the power of a narrator that nevertheless keeps the main character in a position of control.

Movies like *Two Distant Strangers* (Academy Award winner for Best Live Action Short Film in 2021), that use the allegorical dimension of the narrative loop to signify the powerlessness of their protagonist (which, in this case, has strong political undertones), are rare.[40] In this particular example, the *ad nauseam* repeated encounter of a young African-American named Carter James with a white police officer inevitably ends with the former being killed by the latter, no matter how hard the hero tries to counter the prejudices that lead his adversary to resort to a totally unmotivated violence. By putting viewers in the shoes of a victim of police violence, the film's story radically differs from many time loop movies whose protagonist is a soldier that comes to prove his heroic abilities, like *Source Code* (see Chapter 1), *Edge of Tomorrow,* or *Boss Level* (2021). Even though the last attempt visualized in the film (whose short length perfectly accommodates the time loop pattern) is once again a failure due to an even crueler behavior on the part of the police officer, Carter does not lose hope. He stares confidently at the camera for a brief moment before returning to the loop that will once again seal his role as a victim. However, his enthusiasm strikes viewers as nonsensical in view of the degree to which the racist stereotypes, exhibited and deconstructed by the film, are rooted in American society. *Two Distant Strangers*' politically sharp message culminates in the end credits that list the names of African-Americans killed by police officers and, for some of them, the ordinary – or, at least, inoffensive – activities they were engaged in just before they got murdered ("changing the lock of her front door", "playing in a park", etc.). The conclusive anchoring in historical reality – akin to that of a contemporary motion capture French short, *Contraindre* (2020), also dealing with the issue of police violence – explains the development of possible alternatives, since Carter successively embodies a number of potential victims. The plurality of stories is related to a single, sadly irreversible situation – police violence against racial minorities – and to one world, ours (particularly that of the United States during the Donald Trump administration).

Ordinarily, time loop movies depict the variants in successive order. However, some films may present them alternately, as in *Sliding Doors* (1998), *Melinda and Melinda* (2004), or *What If …?* (2008). In the latter, a bifurcation occurs when a young woman, Margot (Alice Taglioni), who works as an executive in the same corporate law firm as her husband Victor (Jocelyn Quivrin), imagines what would have happened if she had dressed differently during an interview with her boss. In the "first" version, Victor gets the promotion over Margot; in the "second" one, the outcome is reversed.[41] Thanks to this narrative device and the echoes between the suppositions made in both versions regarding the changes that the different professional outcome would have brought, a sort of gender studies laboratory is humorously established based on two sets of divergent data, commented upon by Margot's feminist sister. The film's finale will eventually branch out into a third variant in which both the male and the female hero refuse the job. Such a conclusion goes beyond a strictly binary solution and obliterates the possibility of interpreting the second narrative track as belonging to a *mental world. What If …,* whose original French title is *Notre univers impitoyable* [*Our Merciless Universe*] ends by giving precedence to the mode of succession that guarantees a unique narrative closure.

In the case of *Sliding Doors*, the film ends with two parallel closures; yet, it becomes clear that the narrative track shown last is in fact identical to its double. In it, Helen (Gwyneth Paltrow), who failed to meet James (John Hannah) when she missed the subway at the beginning of the film, finds herself at the end in an identical situation to that of her "avatar" in the parallel narrative track. In a manner similar to the competing variant, James picks up one of the young woman's lost earrings from the ground. This type of circularity short-circuits the development of possible alternatives and retrospectively linearizes the action, allowing the "true and *unique*" love to prevail, an otherwise typical rom-com ending. At any rate, a strong unity is created between the two versions insofar as they are both possible variations of a single fiction. The following comment by Françoise Lavocat applies suitably: "The solidarity between the different versions is undeniable: each one of them may present its own consistency, yet their importance lies mostly in the way they reference one another" (Lavocat 2010: 37)[*].

In the cases examined above, the bifurcations in the story are arbitrary. In other words, they are not diegetically justified, as they would have been if a sci-fi element (for instance, a "worldbuilding machine") had been part of the story, or in the case of an immersion in a character's *mental world*. Such arbitrariness allows for a radical cohabitation of incompatible possibilities, as the same characters inhabit the various narrative tracks simultaneously, even if the order of the scenes tends to privilege succession against selection. In a way, the last scene to be seen by the viewer abolishes the previous ones, since it is presented as the only one to be really *actualized* (see for example the happy endings in *Groundhog Day* and *Run Lola Run*).[42] The point of view that would have defined a mental universe gives way, in the case of *alternate (story)worlds*, to the exhibition of a "mega-narrator"[43] who is not bothered to manifest a "propositional attitude", but is revealed through a number of technical procedures (the film scrolling in reverse in *Sliding Doors*, the title cards in the style of *bandes dessinées* in *Smoking*, etc.). However, the variations that are strictly speaking *cosmic* remain relatively small insofar as the world must act as an invariant (same locations, same extras, same props, etc.) in order to facilitate the understanding of the *narrative variants*. Sometimes, a specific visual detail will be given this role, such as the female character's hair that are alternately long and short in *Sliding Doors* and *What if* ... The story underlines the consistency and, paradoxically, the stability of the universe, as in the eight-minute loop in *Source Code*, which constitutes nevertheless a different case from the *deus ex machina* examples discussed here (see Chapter 1).

The gaps between worlds are small enough to allow the implications of the alteration of a single event on the chain of subsequent "dominoes" to be contrastingly perceived by the viewer. The stabilization of the diegetic components concerns in the first place the characters' psychological traits. For example, in *Sliding Doors*, Helen I and Helen II are strictly identical in their respective reactions (and the same goes for the two variants of the man in love with her), as if the modifications in the course of events have no impact on the character's personality. To ensure their intelligibility, movies with *alternate (story)worlds* follow the norms advocated by screenwriting manuals regarding the construction of a fictional character, dictating – more or less openly – that the hero's expected evolution has to be merely the manifestation of innate properties, established from the outset. This is a clearly conservative approach according to which individual identity is independent of its social and political context.[44] On a larger scale, each of the worlds turns out to be similar to the others. In the version where Helen barely makes it onto the subway, she catches her companion in bed with another woman; in the alternative version where she arrives home (the exact same place as before) much later, numerous clues suggest that the same thing happened, this time in her absence. The gaps are thus reduced by virtue of the predominance of common denominators. The relationship between the two fictional variants reproduces the principle of "minimal departure" that governs the relationship between the fiction and the real world. In fact, the responsibility to widen the gap between two ontologically identical worlds falls upon the story. Moreover, mutual accessibility is generally proscribed, except for temporary and rather playful inconsistencies, as when Helen is simultaneously present both in the subway train and on the plateform, during a single panoramic shot in *Sliding Doors*.[45]

In *Melinda and Melinda*, the parallelism between two narrative tracks attributed to each of the variants of the eponymous character persists until the end of the film. Woody Allen assumes the gap between two possible but irreconcilable worlds in a radical way, as the film's particularly abrupt ending shows. In this case, the *alternate (story)worlds* are motivated by an embedding structure. The film begins with a discussion between two playwrights – one specialized in comedies, the other in tragedies. Starting from an identical situation, they will each in turn envisage a story of a completely different tone. Therefore, there is no "first" world from which a "second" one would be derived; both of them are "actual" in the imagination of this duo of worldbuilders. Although Melinda is the only character common to both narrative tracks, the film's world-centered dimension is accentuated by the fact that some elements – like an Aladdin's lamp, a nod to the "magic of storytelling" so dear to Allen – pass from one story to the other. The world inhabited by the heterodiegetic narrators is not systematically inserted in between the shifts between the two narrative tracks. As a result, the alternation tends at times to be perceived in the same mode as that in *What If…* or *Run Lola Run*. However, the principle of embedding introduces a significant difference that testifies Woody Allen's attachment to a more classical tradition of audio-visualized stories recounted by diegetic narrators whose on-screen presence somewhat attenuates the exhibition of the "narrative device".

Melinda and Melinda's playwrights are in a similar situation to that of the couple of screenwriters in *Holiday for Henrietta* (1952), who invent "in front of us" the different versions of a story they must rewrite together, visualized in successive order (see Cornette 2006). The world of reference and the world of the "second degree" fiction are hermetic. Conversely, the Hollywood remake of Duvivier's film, *Paris When It Sizzles* (1964), anxious to spice up the frame situation (thereby transforming it into a story) by inventing a romance between two characters (played by movie stars William Holden et Audrey Hepburn), treats the embedding process as an imaginary mirror of the relationship established between the seductive screenwriter and his typist. In this way, Richard Quine's film mixes *alternate (story)worlds* (organized in reference to specific film genres, according to a common practice in the Hollywood industry) and *mental worlds*, eventually united in the film's ending that will celebrate the formation of the romantic couple (as in many musicals where the alternate narrative tracks converge in the finale).

Therefore, an inescapable tension underlies this type of films between a principle of dissemination over a number of possible worlds and a need to refocus on a unitary universe, compatible with a traditional form of storytelling. Still, *alternate (story)worlds* are not a-narrative. On the contrary, they accentuate the power of storytelling by multiplying the places where this power can be exercised. This is why such a development of different worlds reveals, in my opinion, a creative design that is more narrative than world-centered. After all, the use of bifurcations is not without kinship with the system formalized by Claude Bremond in the 1970s, a narratologist who took up Vladimir Propp's approach in his effort to answer the following question, formulated in the foreword of his book *La Logique du récit*: "Is it possible to describe the complete network of options logically offered to a narrator, at any given point of his narrative, that wants to proceed with the story he begun recounting?" (Bremond 1973: 8)[*].

Parallel Worlds

As viewers come to realize, the second world proposed in *Counterpart* was at the time of its discovery a strict mirror of the first world. Only after the outbreak of a pandemic that wreaked havoc and upset the social order, did it start to evolve in a different way.[46] However, this "forking path" does not fall under the "*alternate (story)world*" category in my typology. There are, of course, important similarities between *Counterpart* and the cases examined above, notably due to a bifurcation that originates on an individual scale during a flashback scene in the episode "Twin Cities" (S02E06), where the story unfolds according to a "butterfly effect".[47] However, it would be an oversimplification to examine these two worlds only in relation to each other, as alternatives, instead of considering them on the scale of the fiction in which they are co-present. It is clearly established inside the diegesis that these worlds exist simultaneously, while being mutually accessible and ontologically distinct. None of them is presented as created by a computer (otherwise, I would have called them *virtual worlds*). The characters do not follow different destinies, but they meet their alter egos living in Berlin in the "other side" (and not a version of themselves living in the same world as them). This *other* Berlin constitutes a *parallel world* that can be reached by passing through an intermediate space called the "Crossing". The same is true in *Another Earth* discussed above except that the *parallel world* in that film manifests itself in the guise of a *distant world* (another planet Earth visible in the sky of "our" Earth). Conversely, films such as *Stargate* (1994) or *John Carter* (2012) apply the rhetoric devices normally associated with a *parallel world* (portals, shifts between different genre conventions) to *distant worlds*.

All multiverse movies that present neither a *mental* nor a *virtual world*, offer worlds that I propose to call *parallel*. This type of world is found in many TV series other than *Counterpart* (see Chapter 2), such as *Sliders*, *MillenniuM*, *Fringe*, *Lost*, *Stranger Things*, or *Lovecraft Country*, as well as in two-world fantasy stories, as in "*The Chronicles of Narnia*" film series, *Beetle Juice*, *Oz the Great and the Powerful*, *Alice in Wonderland*, *Tomorrowland*, or *The Dark Tower*. *Parallel worlds* also appear in supernatural stories that summon a world that lies "beyond", as in *The Testament of Orpheus*, *The Others*, *From Beyond*, the *Silent Hill* diptych, *Monster Hunter* or movie franchises like "*A Nightmare on Elm Street*",[48] "*The Never Ending Story*", or "*Hellraiser*".[49] Finally, they may be found in science fiction movies and TV series as in *The One*, *Star Trek* (the J.J. Abrams version of 2009), *Travelers*, *Doctor Strange*, or *Kill Switch*. All the films discussed in this book present varying degrees of kinship with *parallel worlds* in which the characters are confronted with another "dimension". Therefore, this category could have subsumed all the others. However, it seems more useful to construct it as a specific type of world, located rather at the margins of the corpus of films studied in this essay insofar as it does not constitute a convenient place for the representation of "world-building machines" – unlike the last category in my typology, the one most associated with a computer-generated simulation.

Virtual Worlds

Following the success of the "*Matrix*" franchise (commonly attached to the cyberculture tradition), the generalization of all sorts of online activities, and the rise of VR technology, the association between the notions of *virtual* and *digital* gradually became dominant. However, the concept of virtuality does not necessarily go hand in hand with the field of computer science – for instance, *alternate (story)worlds* also actualize (or not) certain virtualities. Moreover, the idea of producing immersive simulations of a world was well explored before the advent of CGI effects; analog cinema was already conceived in view of such a potential (see *infra* the introduction in Chapter 5). According to Anne Friedberg, "it may be important to soften the agnostic claims of a technologically determined digital break" and "challenge accounts that assume that 'virtual' refers only to electronically mediated or digitally produced images and experiences" (2006: 3 and 7).

From the perspective of this essay, it is by no means necessary for a film to be founded on a sci-fi argument for its universe to be qualified as two-world and for its second world to be a "*virtual*" one. It would suffice that its environment is a representation recognized by the film's protagonists as belonging to another realm of reality, perceived as an act that produces a simulacrum. For example, the young Japanese painter in the "Crows" segment of Akira Kurosawa's *Dreams* (1990) contemplates Van Gogh's "Langlois Bridge at Arles" in a museum and, experiencing the Stendhal syndrome, enters the space of the painting, which therefore becomes a world. Magically, the following shot depicts a profilmic set that duplicates the painting even in terms of its colors. Living an immersive experience such as the one suggested by Alain Resnais in *Van Gogh* (1948), the Japanese painter crosses a number of landscapes drawn by the Dutch painter, represented as "tableaux vivants" or painted surfaces in which the actor, filmed in live-action, is inserted. On his way, he meets Van Gogh himself – played by Martin Scorsese, as if to underline that the act of creation is also cinematic – who explains the relationship between subject and world, analyzed in the film: "When that natural beauty is there, I just lose myself in it. And then, as if in a dream, the scene just paints itself for me. Yes, I consume this natural setting, I devour it completely." At the end of this short segment, a zoom out takes us from the painted space back to the museum and we find the visitor in front of another canvas; he has neither used a multimedia device offered by the museum nor entered an Online Museum, but has simply dreamed of projecting himself into the painting. Nevertheless, the film's images were exhibited as the product of a creatorial act, recognizable by the public as it belongs to a widely circulated cultural heritage (Van Gogh's style). Due to the attention paid to the material thickness of the painted surface in close-up shots, whose scale and composition sharply contrast with those showing the character, the *representation* prevails over the dreamer's *inner vision* (*mental world*). At the manufacturing level of the film (produced by Warner Bros.), the image processing by an ILM visual effects unit made it possible to unfold the pictorial work as an inhabitable world.[50]

Yet, digital technologies are not required in order to produce this type of effect. In his final feature film, *Dionysos* (1984), Jean Rouch had his characters enter a

Giorgio de Chirico painting unfolding in the third dimension. A "dystopian" counterpart of such an immersion which appeals to a certain "sense of wonder" may be found in *Vanilla Sky* (2001), at the moment when the Tom Cruise character realizes that his universe is only a fantasy powered by a futuristic machine, which remains off-screen except for a brief memory flashback showing a cryogenic chamber. Everything he thought he experienced is reduced to a series of still images (fashion photographs, the cover of an album, a frame of Jeanne Moreau in Truffaut's *Jules et Jim*) and songs (whose status is therefore no longer entirely "extradiegetic" for the viewer) from which his brain draws in order to compose his illusory idyllic world.

The two films made by Kurosawa and Rouch display a hybridity of the medium of the representation. Our impression of being in front of two distinct worlds results from the fact the painted image stands out from the cinematic image, creating a visual gap that serves the ontological split between the worlds. In *The Lady and the Duke* (2001), the characters move "inside" famous paintings, but they seem to ignore this; since the mode of representation does not affect the referent as it exists for those inside the diegesis, the universe in Éric Rohmer's film is composed of a single world. For a world to be "*virtual*", it needs to be recognized as such by a diegetic character conscious of having crossed a threshold (unless the audience knows that the latter is deluded as to the status of the world he inhabits) and of having established a relation of accessibility to a space of a different nature. The characters in *The Lady and the Duke* enter places that do correspond to the ones represented by painters. However, from their standpoint, they do not enter inside the pictorial representation, unlike the protagonists in the films by Kurosawa and Rouch who express their relationship to this world, either verbally or with their overall attitude. In cases like these, the contrasts resulting from the composite character of the image reinforce the cosmic heterogeneity in a way similar to the opposition between black & white and color (see *infra* Chapter 4).

The *virtual worlds* are located at a different level of reality from that of the reference world represented in the film and shared by the viewer (unless we deal with an entirely "immersive" world that excludes the possibility of a comparison with what is established as the "real" inside the fiction). The distance is not (only) spatial, but proceeds from a fundamental heteromorphy: the world is made out of a different fabric. The material difference between the worlds raises issues linked to the visual construction of the film's representation. This self-reflexivity brings together, on the one hand, the virtualization of the medium, the intervention of the editing, and the fabrication of special effects, and on the other hand, the features belonging to the virtual universes as they are exhibited inside the diegesis and/or perceived by the audience. Contrary to a *mental world* that strictly emanates from a thinking subject, associated, as we saw before, with a certain "propositional attitude", the *virtual world* is produced from the outside. The border separating these two types of worlds may sometimes be tenuous, as in the examples of *Vanilla Sky*, *Je t'aime je t'aime*, and *Eternal Sunshine of the Spotless Mind* (on the last two films, see *infra* Chapter 4), where a technological device provides an (external) stimulation to an (internalized) simulation.

Some "meta-movies" can also be attached to the category of *virtual worlds*, for example when an actor comes out of the screen to join the audience (*The Purple Rose of Cairo*, 1985) or, conversely, when a character from the "first" world enters the world of a "film within a film" (*Gertie the dinosaur*, 1914; *Sherlock Jr.*, 1924; *Shocker*, 1989; *Pleasantville*, 1998), or even when the permeability allows a two-way circulation, as in *Last Action Hero* (1993). These metaleptic games with the levels of representation are similar to those found in the computer-generated worlds inside the diegesis of *TRON* (1982), *eXistenZ* (1999), or *Avalon* (2001). The final chapter of this book will focus on the now "classic" *virtual worlds* of cyberculture.

The seven types of worlds presented here are not mutually exclusive. Often, they combine either at a macrostructural level (for instance, in *Mulholland Dr.*, the *mental world* is not erased but reinforced by the *alternate storyworld*) or during a specifically circumscribed segment (the *virtual world* in *The Matrix Revolutions*' opening scene is later identified as Neo's nightmare, aka a *mental world*). These worlds, just like the diegesis as the filmologists understood the notion, are to be considered within a pragmatic perspective. It is up to the audience to decide on the type of world offered by the film on the basis of the diegetic (or narrative) information transmitted by the latter. Narrative tension is frequently built by the competition between two ways of understanding the world, as the viewer becomes eager to learn which interpretation is supposed to be the "correct" one and what are the laws governing the other world. In films like these, where story and diegesis are intimately intertwined, the revelation or the confirmation of the status of the world constitutes the high point of the plot. *What Lies Beneath*, *The Others*, *Mulholland Dr.*, and *Total Recall*, all draw from the motif of amnesia, which makes the protagonists become in a way "anew in this world". The erasure of the past has the pragmatic advantage of not allowing the viewer to distinguish between what has not been made explicit by convention (according to the principle of minimal departure) and what has actually no existence in the world of reference but belongs to a second world (we will examine in Chapter 5 the extent to which a film like *Dark City* profits from such an ambiguity). In order for the *mental world* to constitute a hypothesis competing with other types of worlds, the character must be in a way a stranger to his own self: he deceives the audience only because he unknowingly engages in self-deception. An exaggerated example of "navigation" between distinct types of worlds (to the point that they become indistinguishable) is the recent HBO TV series *Westworld*. In the final segment of this chapter, I will discuss this show in order to illustrate the need to conceive these types as flexible, while using them as analytical tools.

The *Westworld* Series: An Emblematic Case of Permeability Between Different Types of Worlds

The typology established in this chapter should not be conceived rigidly. Indeed, it would be very reductive and actually unproductive in terms of film analysis to consider the above-identified categories as mutually exclusive. Rather, their interest lies precisely in the prospect of diagnosing cases where various types are combined, as in the example of *Sliders*' S03E01, where the *parallel world* the heroes find themselves in turns out to be an *artificial world* too, hosting a *Hunger Games*-like deadly competition. Analysts should focus on instances of porosity, deliberate ambiguity, gradual shift from one type to another, or potential transformation of the spectator's interpretative framework midway through a film or a TV series. The last case frequently occurs as a result of a change in the point of view from which the story is told, a revelation of the subjective nature of the representation, or the audience's introduction to a hitherto inaccessible world.

Narrative tension in its various forms – suspense, surprise, or curiosity (see Baroni 2007) – may actually stem from this type of transformations. The clarification advanced by Lubomír Doležel when introducing a number of criteria for defining narrative modalities (e.g., a world of physical vs mental events), is equally valid for my typology here: "These types are ideal structures; they combine in many and different ways to create the categorical order of particular fictional narrative worlds" (Doležel 1998: 113).

A permeability of this order is to be found in many of the films studied in the previous chapters. For example, in *Triangle*, the *alternate (story)worlds* that overlap and interact within a single space-time continuum turn out to be the product of a *mental world* forged by a woman traumatized after a serious accident (similarly to the main character in *Stay*) that cost her son his life. My typology provides some reference points that can prove useful while describing the organization principles of a multiverse caught in the entanglement of different categories. In fact, they may turn out to be indispensable if one wishes to give an accurate account of the vacillations skillfully cultivated to arouse the audience's curiosity and ease its immersion inside the represented world(s).

The *Westworld* TV series, studied in Chapter 2 from the standpoint of generic references, is based on a constant transgression of borders between different worlds and different *types of worlds*. Nevertheless, Michael Crichton's film offered, more than forty years earlier, a rather unequivocal starting point. It dealt with an *artificial world*, divided into several sub-worlds, circumscribed within the limits of a theme park, whose illusionary force was based on the fact that robots and humans were indistinguishable in terms of physical appearance. The voice command in the original film, ordering to "Freeze all motor functions", alluded to the mechanical dimension of the automata, but is replaced in the HBO series by the instruction "Bring yourself back online". At a time when interconnected products are multiplying on the market, introducing in the users' daily life a distinction – but also a possible confusion – between hardware and software, the "back online" motto, signifying a serial narrative's never-ending reboot function, refers not to a mechanical dimension, but to an operation requiring the computer technologies of the Web.

As a matter of fact, the mechanical hosts in the HBO show are like browsers connected to a main server. When a human (or a character that thinks is human) gives this order to an android, he or she is not controlling an online avatar, but links a machine to one of Delos servers. However, the border between a pre-programmed *artificial world* where the protagonists aspire to a free will and a *virtual world* in which they find themselves confined, is actually tenuous. This becomes clear by the systematic narrative ellipses intervening when Delos teams replace the robots in the western setting. Once Dolores or Maeve get "back online", we are immediately plunged, alongside with them, inside a simulation and into a continuous series of verbal interactions, as if the access to this embedded level were carried out through the input of a virtual reality dispositive (similar to the one in *The Thirteenth Floor*) rather than a diegetic *mise-en-scène*. Nevertheless, we are actually dealing with such a *mise-en-scène* at Season One's finale (E10), when the cowboy named Teddy (James Marsden) holds an agonizing Dolores in his arms and evokes, with a tear in his eye, "a path to a new world" and "the beginning of a brand new chapter". All of a sudden, the lovers freeze in the middle of their romantic embrace on a beach under a full moon sky. As an echo effect distorts the music, dislodging it from its extra-diegetic status, and as the sources of an artificial lighting appear on the screen, we discover an audience of hitherto invisible guests attending this final scene, as if it were a live show. The intrusion of the illusion during the climax of the couple's narrative arc is exhibited via a shift from a series of empathetic shots/reverse shots to an abrupt distancing from the characters – now joined by the narrator, Ford, a shift that reveals this universe as an *artificial world*. Furthermore, we may very well interpret this world as a meta-filmic one, since the series' actors too deliver a pre-planned text and move within a set built to accommodate their performance.

Beyond this physical yet *artificial world*, similar to the small town in *The Truman Show*, the modes of (non-)representation of the passage from one world to the other during the "back online" shifts, suggest a proximity with the sci-fi pattern of a *virtual world*, which will finally be actualized in Season 2. As I have shown in Chapter 2, several seasons in *Lost* are distinguished by their world-centered treatment of the temporal dimension. *Westworld* proceeds in a similar way each time it adds a different type of world to the previous ones. The entry into a *virtual world*, whose creation is part of the hidden agenda of Delos' delegates, is signaled in Season 2 via a particular stylistic element: a switch to a widescreen format. The two black bars appearing in the upper and lower parts of the frame signal the subplot's embedded status and mark a heightened degree of unreality, alluding to the conditions of a film screening in a movie theater. Therefore, the western genre's vast wilderness is taken up as the object of a virtual simulation offered by the theme park.

While "Shogunworld" in Season 2 involves samurai and ninjas in "(artificial) flesh and blood", the "Warworld" in Season 3 is presented as a pure, computer-generated simulation. Accordingly, all scenes taking place in it are filmed in a Scope aspect ratio. It is as if the park filled with actual robots had only been one step in an evolution towards the reign of the "all virtual". Or maybe it simply represented the material side of algorithmically calculated experiments. This is what actually happens in "The Forge", where thousands of James Delos' replicas are subjected to tests by a machine generating ad infinitum *alternate (story)worlds*, thanks to data generated by millions of guests over a thirty-year period. In fact, only a few fragments of these *alternate (story)worlds* will end up on the screen.

In *Westworld*, introspection is presented as a palimpsest of incompatible narrative bifurcations. One thinks in particular of the variants of the recurrent and enigmatic scenes taking place in a white church in Escalante, which will turn out to be a former beta-testing location used prior to the park's opening (a miniature replica of this church can be seen on Ford's desk). In Dolores' mind, Escalante appears in different forms: as a very lively place, a ghost town whose streets are strewn with corpses, a ruined site covered in sand, or an old resort excavated and rebuilt by Ford's crews. As the bulldozers work in a western-like landscape, building an *artificial world* (that we access from the "backstage"), one is reminded of *The Making of The Searchers*, one of the first "behind-the-scenes" programs produced and broadcast by Warner Bros in 1956, as part of the promotion of John Ford's famous western, shot on location in Monument Valley. The internal focalization on Dolores leads to a clash of incompatible versions of the same world, as some of her erased memories resurface: the animated streets are abruptly replaced by a series of shots showing a city filled with corpses. These seemingly contradictory versions look like *alternate (story)worlds* until Dolores and the audience succeed in untangling the temporal levels. The possible variants have never actually coexisted but succeeded one another during the park's thirty-year existence. In this respect, *Westworld* is part of the Deleuzian Time-Image concept that I will be discussing in Chapter 4 (see "A Derailed Montage: Alain Resnais' Time/World Machine").

The progression of the HBO series relies on the growing complexity of the arrangement between the different worlds, which takes as its starting point the opposition between the interior of the theme park and the outside world (or between the representation of the Old West and a science fiction cybernetic technology). This complexity reaches its climax during the final episode of Season 2 in which, in addition to the various temporal levels,[51] a number of spaces with a variable degree of (un)reality are multiplied by layers. Bernard comments on the room he finds himself into, following his connection to the "projection" dispositive called "The Forge", a kind of cerebral scanner sketchily represented as a semi-circular neon light: "It's just like the one *outside*". Dolores' self-confessed goal is to reach "something *underneath* this. The system itself". As for Maeve, she is actually heading to the opposite "direction", towards an increasing dematerialization. She is part of the caravan led by the Indians, hoping to find "The Valley *Beyond*", a virtual Eden reserved by Dr. Ford to hosts that have reached a certain elevated stage of consciousness ("It's a door to a new world untouched by blood", S02E09).

The final episode in Season 2, "The Passenger", has the traditional length of a feature film. It shows Dolores and Bernard discovering a Borgesian library whose wood shelves are filled with books. Each of them corresponds to a duplicated individual, with its blank pages serving as punched cards that reduce the spirit of a former guest to an algorithm (a variation of the player piano motif found in the opening credits' sequence). This pattern announces the central theme of the entire Season 3, which is no longer approached from the angle of the heroes' quest for immortality, but from that of a society of control. It also echoes the concept of multiple implantations, namely the storage of brain data that become independent from the rest of the body. A number of robotic scientists, such as Hans Moravec or Marvin Minsky, have actually supported this computation principle. In *How We Became Posthuman. Virtual Bodies in Cybernetics, Literature, and Informatics*, Katherine Hayles studied the epistemological bases of such scientific projects, as well as the imaginary ideas they have forged. The principal argument developed in her book could very well apply to the *Westworld* TV series: "a defining characteristic of the present cultural moment is the belief that information can circulate unchanged among different material substrates" (1999: 1).

Still, the library in Season 2 finale addresses not only the issue of the virtualization of all living beings, but also that of the virtualization of the entire world. Moreover, it becomes the site where two embedded levels become visible. The shots showing Dolores and Bernard connected to the server of "The Forge" and visiting the library, are filmed in a Scope aspect ratio. Then, a screen-within-a-screen replaces the library's antique furniture and a chimney's den, revealing a bucolic landscape bathed in light coming from the Valley Beyond – a yet another Americana cliché, next to the Great Plains of the West. At that moment, in the narrative track centered on Maeve, a gap emerges in the midst of the desert through which a number of hosts enter, shedding their (artificial) bodies (Figs. 25–27).

Page facing: Figs. 25 (upper), 26 (centre) and 27 (lower):
The "Valley Beyond" in the *Westworld* TV series: window or portal leading to another (*virtual*) world, at times visualized in a Scope aspect ratio.

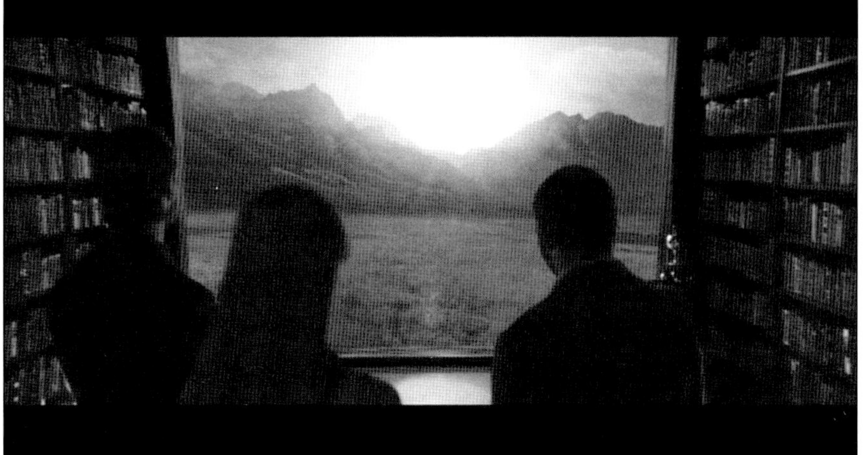

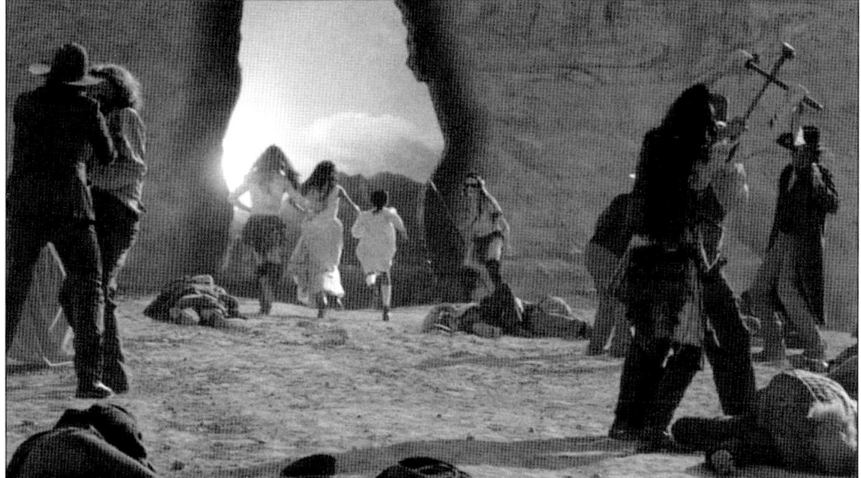

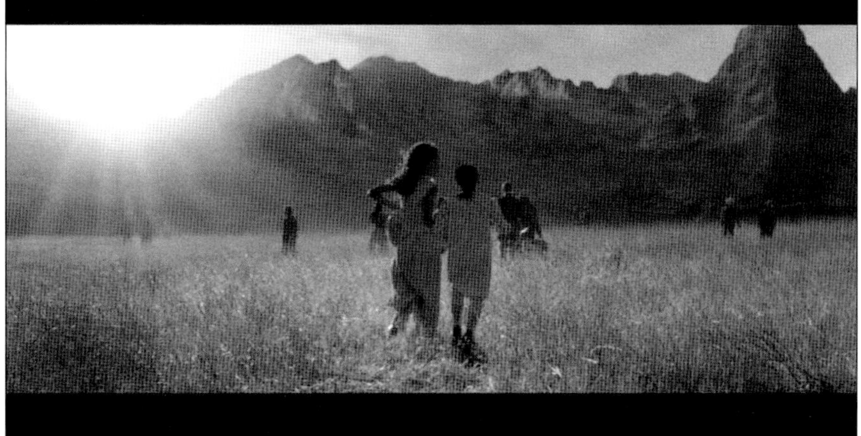

The portal destined for hosts[52] whose artificial intelligence is connected to "The Forge", follows the tradition of thresholds connecting (*supernatural* or *parallel*) worlds. At the same time, it illustrates the interplay between different genres and their visual codes (see Chapter 2). Such a breach towards a dematerialized *elsewhere*, accessible thanks to a sci-fi technology, is literally represented on screen via digital visual effects which inscribe in the materiality of the image the opposition between nature (the represented landscape) and culture (the technical apparatus), ripping through the iconography of the western genre. Through this vagina-like opening, appearing in a scene that openly deals with the issue of maternity (Maeve abandons in the Valley Beyond the little girl she loves as her own daughter – actually the case in a previous storyline), the series introduce a new world. The spectacular representation of the interworld border is reminiscent of manifestations of magic in the fantasy genre. It constitutes the antithesis of the "Crossing" in the *Counterpart* TV series, where a plain underground corridor leads imperceptibly from one world to the other. In *Westworld*, the creator of worlds has adapted his vision to that of the indigenous people to whom he is addressing.

Westworld summons a religious belief in the existence of an afterlife, just like the finale in *Lost*, but not before completing a series of semantic shifts that lead us through the entire spectrum of world types I defined above: (1) the *distant worlds* are composed of a number of distinct zones inside the park,[53] each of them referring to a specific film genre, as discussed in Chapter 2; (2) the "Westworld" and "Shogunworld" resorts are *artificial worlds* (products of physical simulation) when compared to the life outside the park that the series' first two seasons hint at but never visualize in the narrative present;[54] (3) the allusions to American Indian animist beliefs make the world ruled by Delos look like a *supernatural world*; (4) the *alternate (story)worlds* correspond to all the loops accumulated during three decades in the memory of an ancient host like Dolores or Bernard, who tries to assert his free will without being able to completely escape from the God-like figure of Dr. Ford. The attempted conciliation between divine control and a human's contingent futures brings to mind Leibniz's metaphysics, especially since, as Carole Maigné reminds us, the philosopher uses in his *Monadology* the metaphor of automata: "[In Leibniz's work] 'automaton' does not equal 'machine'. The former moves by itself, the latter is moved by something else […]. The soul is defined as a more distinct, memory-laden monad […]. The monad-soul is aware of what has happened, aware of its own perceptions" (Maigné 1998: 23–25)[*]. Whereas the robots in Michael Crichton's original film were Leibnizian machines, the androids in HBO's *Westworld* are "automata". Arnold Weber (Jeffrey Wright), the park's co-founder (along with Dr. Ford), comes to realize that these androids have a conscience. The discovery makes him eager to destroy his own creation before opening the facility, so as to prevent the hosts from suffering. This explains the important role given to memory and perception in the series. We share Dolores and Maeve's subjective visions, whose representation is clearly inspired from the modes of figuration of (5) *mental worlds*. Finally, from Season 2 onwards, *Westworld* includes (6) *virtual worlds* (a computer simulation straight out of *The Matrix*, see Chapter 5), identified at the level of the materiality of the image thanks to the use of a Scope aspect ratio.

The way *Westworld* builds an opposition between the western setting inside the park and the sci-fi world outside (or in the park's underground reprocessing rooms), brings to mind Lubomir Doležel's description of the "mythological world" that constitutes, according to the author, "the prime dyadic structure of the alethic modality" (1998: 128). In this HBO TV series, humans have replaced gods (just like robots have replaced humans)[55] and the "natural domain" is only apparently so, while the rebelling androids attempt to overturn the asymmetry of power defining the hierarchy between the two worlds. However, the following observation made by Doležel with regards to the articulation of a natural and a supernatural domain within a mythological world,[56] applies to the element that nourishes the serial narrative at the level of worldbuilding:

> The two conjoined domains of the mythological world are not only clearly differentiated alethically but also strictly demarcated. The inhabitants of the supernatural domain have access into the natural domain, but for the humans the supernatural domain is, as a rule, off limits. Being physically inaccessible, the supernatural domain is beyond human cognition; it appears as a mysterious, hidden, transcendent "black hole". The minds of the inhabitants of the natural domain are obsessively attracted to this mystery (*Ibid.*: 129).

This type of attraction aroused in Dolores and Maeve is the main driving force in *Westworld*'s plot during Season 1. The two characters may be compared to informers with an exceptional status, "prophet, god-inspired, and so on" (*Idem.*), a category that could include the American Indian sorcerers of the western genre.

According to Doležel, accessibility between the two types of worlds is only possible through "intermediate worlds" that combine physically possible states, like hallucination, with what can be considered, in terms of fictional semantics, as "physically impossible persons, objects, and events" (*Ibid.*: 117). The (eminently subjective) representation of such states is used throughout Season 1 in order to motivate the constant back and forth between different worlds (or between the various domains of a single fictional world, if one were to follow Doležel's perspective). In point of fact, the series' first episodes provide such an immersive entry into the fiction, notwithstanding the perceived facticity of the world(s) they offer, precisely thanks to the prevalence of features pertaining to *mental words*.

However, *mental worlds* tend to take a back seat during Season 2 due to a shift within the series' world-centered logic: the bipartition between the frame world and the embedded world gives way to cases of interpenetration among *distinct embedded worlds*. At first, the artificial nature of the park's world is revealed through the consciousness of hosts who, caught up in the vertigo of a "black hole" (according to Doležel's use of the term that one may associate here to the "black boxes" in computer sciences), gradually remember the previous "games" in which they have participated (beyond the successive reboots) or the traumas experienced in Delos basements, where their bodily integrity was put at risk. Like the protagonist in *Dark City* who, unlike the rest of the inhabitants, does not freeze at midnight when the aliens modify the world, Maeve in S01E07 does not deactivate herself, unlike everybody else around her, when a Delos team arrives in order to evacuate the body of her friend, Clementine (Angela Sarafyan). Against all odds, she wakes up inside the frame world, holding a bird that belongs to the embedded world (S01E05). The series thus progresses through a gradual interpenetration between different worlds. When Maeve or Dolores experience "visions" belonging to men in chemical suits who take possession of them,[57] they actually access the real – that is, a *supernatural world* as far as they are concerned – through a series of flashes in need to be deciphered. Seen from this perspective, it is certainly not surprising that the book Bernard offers to Dolores in S01E03 is *Alice in Wonderland*.

In the original 1973 *Westworld* the artificial nature of the androids can be easily detected via the imperfectly designed palms of their hands. The HBO TV series differs greatly on this point, since the robots are actually more "human" than Delos' men. They are driven by profound aspirations, feel empathy for others, are prey to doubts, etc. A whole arsenal of subjectivizing processes is deployed so that we identify with the androids, despite our cognitive advantage (we already know that "Westworld" is an artificial place). In particular, the humanization of robots is carried out via an analogy between the illusion they are trapped in and certain pathological conditions (paranoia, denial, compulsive disorders, amnesia, hallucinations, schizophrenia…), which end up superimposing on the *artificial world* of the park a layer of enigmatic interior worlds. However, it turns out that these worlds can be objectified: they are the remnants of previously actualized *alternate (story)worlds*. Dolores puts the hesitation between a psychological and a world-centered interpretation into words, when confessing to Bernard that she in the process of discovering herself through her emotions:[58] "I think there may be something wrong with this world, hiding underneath. *Either that, or there's something wrong with me*. I may be losing my mind" (S01E04).[59] Right after this opening scene, Dolores opens her eyes and wakes up under a tree, at William's side. It could be that the world "underneath" was just a dream. Plato's allegory of the cave is not told as a parable by an external narrator, but recounted from the inside, by deluded individuals who are constantly led to speak about themselves (like the patients of a psychoanalyst) so that the Delos technicians can verify if they are conforming to the program. For their part, these individuals aspire to master the story they are partaking in, as Dolores confesses at the end of Season 2, after leaving the park in Charlotte's body.[60]

In *Westworld*, the representation is granted a subjective character most notably through the processes of internal ocularisation and internal auricularisation that produce mental visions shared by the viewers. Actually, these are the moments in which the series ends up being particularly immersive, whereas elsewhere the audience, conscious of the artificial character of the world offered, is invited to adopt a more distanced attitude. In this respect, *Westworld* follows in the footsteps of *Dollhouse* (2009–2010), a series created by Joss Whedon, in which individuals deprived of all free will have their memory regularly erased and are programmed by a genius computer scientist, who works for a powerful company, to correspond in every way to the "character" ordered by a client for a specific mission (each one corresponding to an episode). The fictitious data implanted in their brains contrast with the "real" world outside the underground laboratory in which the subjects are confined. These guinea pigs are not robots, yet they come to realize their state of alienation – maintained for the purpose of satisfying male fantasies – in a way similar to that of the androids in *Westworld*: through a series of memory flashes. The intrusive action of an agent, secretly undermining the system and foreshadowing the threat posed to mankind by a Frankenstein-like science in search of immortality, is another pattern common to both series.

This type of plot is certainly inspired by Philip K. Dick's conspiracy and anxiety-provoking tales that lead readers to doubt the status of reality (within the fiction) or the uniqueness of the world inhabited by the main character, just like in cyberpunk stories.[61] The following words, uttered by Maeve in *Westworld*, could have come out of the mouth of the character named Echo (Eliza Dushku) in *Dollhouse*: "It's a terrible thing realizing your entire life is some hideous fiction" (*Westworld*, S01E09). In *Westworld*, androids do dream – not of electric sheep, but of a world where they would no longer be "sheep", pawns in the service of a destiny "scripted" by others. In stark opposition to many stories from the 1970s and the 1980s that offered the reassuring possibility of grasping the specificities of a human being compared to machines,[62] the androids' aspirations in *Westworld* function in today's world as metaphors for the human condition. Their world could easily become ours. Season 3, set in a future megalopolis outside the Park, shows that the border between reality and the product of an algorithm, permeable during the first two seasons, becomes indistinct as digital technology pervades our daily lives. There is no longer any need for a "matrix" for humans to become slaves, unlike the cyberpunk dystopias discussed in Chapter 5. In the name of the comfort promised by technology, humans submit themselves to machines on their own initiative.

Endnotes

1. A part of this section has been previously published in French in Boillat 2009b. Readers may refer to this article for more details on the various authors who have employed the notion of "diegesis" in their work.
2. On the philosophical systems associated with the notional couple of mimesis/diegesis in the classical tradition (Plato's *Republic* and Aristotle's *Poetics*), see Gaudreault 1999: 55–69. It should be noted that the filmological heritage is more difficult to examine in non-French linguistic areas. In English, there is a frequent confusion between the notion of "*diégèse*" and the Aristotelian "diegesis". Unless noted otherwise, the term "diegesis" is used in this essay in the sense of Souriau's "*diégèse*".
3. For example, Souriau asks readers of *Les Deux cent mille situations dramatiques* to conceive the unity a "situation" represents within a "stellar disposition, including the forces the latter organizes, which must symbolize or communicate with the entire universe thus established" (Souriau 1950: 29)*.
4. English-speaking scholars, such as Edward Branigan (1984) or Claudia Gorbman (1987), have mainly focused on the opposition between the adjectives *diegetic* and *non-diegetic* in relation to film sounds. Branigan refers to Souriau for the origin of the term "*diegetic*" (1984: 68, n. 16). He also employs the adjective "*profilmic*", first introduced by the filmologists. Unlike its use as an adjective, the notion of "diegesis" as a noun refers in a more explicit way to issues of worldbuilding.
5. "Just like with conventional signs, the interpretation of natural signs becomes possible only within the context of a certain understanding. In addition to a knowledge of the world, it is necessary to have the knowledge of the arche: a photograph functions as an indexical image provided that one knows one deals with a photograph, as well as everything that this fact implies" (Schaffer 1987: 41)*. The difference between *analog* and *digital* medium is played out precisely at the level discussed by Schaeffer, namely the way one reads a photograph.
6. "The Kugelmass Episode" tells the story of a literature professor who asks a Brooklyn magician to project him into the world of Flaubert's *Madame Bovary* with the help of a "machine" that looks like a Chinese cabinet (see Saint-Gelais 2011: 105–106).
7. Ryan brings together narratology and the study of digital media by means of a metaphor: "the narrative stack" is compared with stacks maintained by a computer's operating system.
8. In fact, Ryan uses the example of *The Matrix* trilogy when discussing Virtual Reality (2006: 228–229).
9. Lubomír Doležel notes that in the field of metaphysics, the possible worlds "reside in the omniscient divine mind [...], they are *discovered*", whereas in fiction they "are constructed [...], *artifacts* produced by aesthetic activities" (Doležel 1998: 14–15).
10. See *supra* my analysis of the TV series *Lost* (Chapter 2).
11. This strategy is also found in Lars Von Trier's equally contemplative *Melancholia*, a film released in the same year that may be considered as an apocalyptic counterpart to *Another Earth*.
12. The points already discussed in Chapter 1 will be briefly mentioned here. Certain aspects pertaining to *virtual worlds* will be presented extensively in Chapter 5.
13. In this case, the physical distance does not entail a shift into the realm of the supernatural, as in the feature film series "*The Chronicles of Narnia*" (2005–2010).
14. *Outlander* (2008), *Cowboys & Aliens* (2011), and *10 Cloverfield Lane* (2016) employ a generic hybridity at the level of worldbuilding (see supra Chapter 2, "Androids of the Far West: Film Genre as World"). *Outlander* is set in the Viking era (6th century) in which the hero (Jim Caviezel) crash lands on Earth in a spaceship. The *making of* available in the film's Blu-Ray edition (Momentum Pictures, 2009) is significantly titled *Outlander: One Film, Two Worlds*, while the tagline on the cover says "Two Worlds, One Battle".
15. Apart from *Alien* (1979), another famous example is that of the two-volume *bande dessinée Moby Dick*, in which writer Jean-Pierre Pécau transposes Herman Melville's story in a sci-fi universe.
16. A parallel may be drawn between utopia and the so-called "sandbox" games, such as *SimCity* or *The Sims*, which offer a "model of the world" (Triclot 2011: 202–203)*.

17. In an article focusing on RPG game worlds and the "gamification" of genre fiction, Ryan Vu notes: "Paratextuality has been central to modern fantastic fiction from its earliest days. Texts as diverse as Francis Godwin's *The Man in the Moone* (1638), Jonathan Swift's *Gulliver's Travels* (1726), and Horace Walpole's *The Castle of Otranto* (1764), were framed by their author as found documents via prefatory materials, suggesting their place within larger worlds" (Vu 2017: 284).
18. "But, at the same Time, the Reader can hardly conceive my Astonishment, to behold an Island in the Air, inhabited by Men, who were able (as it should seem) to raise, or sink, or put it into a progressive Motion, as they pleased" (Swift 2005: 144).
19. However, the characters may be momentarily lured with respect to their world's reality status. Depending on the case, the facticity exhibited in the film may also go unnoticed by all characters within the diegesis, thus participating in a representational convention that the audience accepts as a component of the fictional pact. This may be true even in cases where the world is only partially furnished, as in Lars Von Trier's *Dogville* (2003) and *Manderlay* (2005).
20. In fact, the hero's memories are objectified in the form of insert shots taken out of a family film, associated with a traumatic event that the game will help to exorcise.
21. The idea of a hero holding the uncomfortable position of a "forced player" is also found in the Spanish film *Nobody Knows Anybody* (1999).
22. Genette discusses two conceivable types of alterations within the category designated as "mood". See Chapter 2, note 22.
23. We know from Paul Ricoeur's *The Rule of Metaphor* that such processes may result into "a possible world". In this book, the philosopher considers the stylistic figure of metaphor as an ability to rewrite reality. Much later, Umberto Eco discusses in *The Limits of Interpretation* the theoretical approach of "recovering the referential treatment of metaphor" by postulating that "the metaphorical expression can be understood literally, provided one projects its content onto a possible world" (Eco 1992: 160)*. [Translator's note: The English version of Eco's book does not feature the passage cited above; it is my translation out of the French version, published in 1992].
24. Genette's "internal focalization" has been erroneously related by some of the author's epigones to the question of subjectivity, which amounts to confusing the two distinct categories of *range* and *depth* introduced by Bordwell, Smith, and Thompson, with respect to information related to the story (2020: 88-90). Actually the notion of "focalization" is strictly a part of an "information-based model" (see the section on "focalization" in Niederhoff's *Living Handbook of Narratology*, 2011/2013) that consists of comparing the amount of knowledge the reader possesses in relation to the character. Avoiding the terms "point of view" or "focalization", which create a certain confusion between seeing, knowing and mentally representing a scene, Jan-Noël Thon proposes "to employ more neutral (and, arguably, more precise) expressions such as *the representation of subjectivity* or, more specifically, *the subjective representation of a character's consciousness or mind*" (Thon 2016: 238).
25. During *Fight Club*'s first minutes, there is a scene in which the furniture illustrating the pages of an IKEA catalog (with the slogan "Use Your Imagination" inscribed on it) is progressively grafted in the hero's apartment following his compulsive tendency to consume. Without doubt, the main function of the scene is to depict the alienating consumer society against which the anarchic side of the schizophrenic character will stand up. Still, it entails in a very literal way a process of "furnishing", in the sense used by Umberto Eco when considering fictional creation. Digital special effects are explicitly used in this case to build a world (that the story will later come to destroy).
26. This refers to the process of metalepsis (see *supra*), i.e. the establishment of permeability between the literary fiction produced by the protagonist *in* the film and the fiction *of* the film.
27. We can draw a parallel between this observation and the following definition of the notion of "textual world", proposed by Marie-Laure Ryan: "I define a world as a space situated in time and serving as a habitat for concrete objects and individuals. These inhabitants evolve, but their evolution presents a certain coherence and a certain continuity that can be explained by the principle of causality. A world has to be a relatively solid and stable totality, not a collection of fluid images like those formed in a dream that constantly transform into entirely different images" (Ryan 2010: 55)*.

28. Later in the film, when Tommy realizes the importance of this fleeting episode, he dreams of a variant in which he actually accepts Izzy's proposition.
29. On the particular mechanism that sets off the embedding process in *The Last Temptation of Christ* and on the way the notion of point of view functions in this film in comparison with Nikos Kazantzakis' novel, see Boillat 2008: 62–71.
30. One could reply to this argument that there are numerous films in which the subjective camera is recurrently and effectively used as a signifier of a character's position, from *Peeping Tom* (1960) and *Halloween* (1978), to *Terminator* (1984) and its sequels, *Predator* (1987), *Pitch Black* (2000), *Ghosts of Mars* (2001) and *Maniac* (2012), not to mention certain shots in the final scenes of *Westworld* (1973) in which momentarily we share the vision of the android played by Yul Brynner, or those in a number of "post-*Jaws*" horror movies where we see through the eyes of a predatory animal, as in *The White Buffalo* (1977), *Cujo* (1983), and *Razorback* (1984). However, in all of these cases, the individual whose gaze we espouse is assimilated to a bloodthirsty monster or a machine of destruction – in other words, a totally de-psychologized being. Consequently, the viewer is not invited to share this character's feelings; rather, he is asked to put himself in the shoes of the victim. The same is true in FPS video games since no emotional connection is established between the player and the avatar (see Triclot 2011: 86). Significantly, when *Doom* was adapted for the screen in 2005, the only "FPS" moment in the film corresponds to a scene in which the hero, after voluntarily injecting himself with a virus in order to increase his strength, actually becomes a stranger to himself.
31. A number of Bergman's movies – *Persona* (1966) being the most well-known among them – inscribe at the heart of their narrative structure issues of troubled identities that prefigure in some respects the question of subjective universes discussed here, while remaining anchored in a sense of realism. The same can be said for some dream sequences in classical Hollywood cinema, strongly marked from the post-war period onwards by popularized versions of Freudian theory (*Spellbound*, 1945; *The Secret Beyond the Door*, 1947; *Suddenly Last Summer*, 1959; *Marnie*, 1964).
32. In the season finale, a second blackout takes place, projecting all the characters twenty years later in a quick flash. However, the story will not further explore this new situation (that is reminiscent of the principle governing *Lost*), since ABC cancelled the show after the end of Season 1.
33. Still, these alternatives are constantly discussed inside the diegesis, and not just by the series' fans outside the fiction as they speculate about the future course of the story. The show is based on a so-called "high concept" that is meant to stimulate this type of interpretative fervor from the audience.
34. I would like to thank Raphaël Baroni for giving me access to his paper "The Garden of Forking Paths: Virtualities and Challenges for Contemporary Narratology" that he presented on March 30, 2013 as part of the 3rd International Conference of the European Narratology Network (ENN), entitled "Emerging Vectors of Narratology: Toward Consolidation or Diversification". In this paper, Baroni gives an enlightening assessment of the reconfigurations induced within the field of narratology by contemporary theories of "alternative possible worlds".
35. On the possible alternatives resulting from the directions successively taken by the creators of a film during its genesis, see Chapter 4, note 5. I have examined such narrative alternatives through the study of the different states of *Love is My Profession*'s screenplay (1958) in Boillat 2020b.
36. See the introduction to Chapter 2. The sci-fi genre is, of course, all but homogeneous in this respect. Considering science fiction and its relationship to our world of reference, Simon Bréan defines three distinct regimes: "The rational regime lets the real world into the fiction; the extraordinary regime turns its back to the real world; the speculative regime produces a world that is somehow orthogonal to the real one" (Bréan 2012: 28)*. It seems indeed appropriate to consider the gap between the (science) fiction world and our world of reference in a gradual way. In the speculative regime, the alternative does not generate a multiverse, since there is only one world represented inside the fiction.
37. I will not discuss here the – theoretically possible but practically difficult to envisage on the scale of a feature film – mode of simultaneity, which can be visualized for instance through the use of a split-screen. Nevertheless, this technique that divides the screen into

two worlds can be found in *Deja Vu* (left-right separation) and in Season 2 of *Counterpart* (top-bottom split, see *infra* note 47).

38. The tree-like structure of Alain Resnais' double film *Smoking/No Smoking* presents an additional complexity in that it presupposes a logic of backtracking whose amplitude varies in a completely systematized way (going back from one to three nodes of the story, in a recurrent order but not without certain occasional elisions of one of the levels), which ends up multiplying the number of possible alternatives.
39. On the contrary, the hero in *The Butterfly Effect* is gradually exhausted since every new reconfiguration of the world requires from him an intense cerebral effort.
40. *Two Distant Strangers* can be seen as a radical yet politically realistic reply to *BlackKklansman* (2018), a comparatively more watered-down and consensual film (see Derfoufi 2018 and Weston 2018/2020). At a time when police crimes targeting African-Americans have emerged as a crucial issue of the anti-racist struggle in the United States, Spike Lee's movie detours the structural and institutional dimension of racism by depicting a "cool", young cop supported by his superiors in the force, so integrated within the police institution that he manages to arrest a white colleague with charges of racism, inevitably narrowing the scope of the film's discourse to an individual case (especially since the latter seems to be the only openly racist cop in town). By multiplying the two opposed characters through *alternate (story)worlds*, Travon Free's short film succeeds in generalizing its message while indicating that a way out seems actually impossible. A more symbolic and satirical representation of the deep-rooted xenophobia and the permanent oppression throughout history is to be found in Jordan Peele's fantasy horror film *Get Out* (2017).
41. Due to the alternation, the order of appearance does not really imply a relation of hierarchy between the two variants, although it is certainly not insignificant that the film begins with the male character's success, a social norm that is alternately deconstructed and reconstructed in the rest of the film.
42. Due to this retroactive cancellation, these movies fall into the "*disnarrated*" category introduced by Gerald Prince, which refers to all the events that have not actually taken place, but are presented by the narrative text in a hypothetical mode (Prince 1988). However, things seem different from a world-centered perspective: some events do take place in one of the worlds of the fiction, but not in the rest of them.
43. Introduced by André Gaudreault (1999), the notion of "mega-narrator" has "demiurgic" connotations that perfectly suit the phenomenon I describe here.
44. See our comment on Robert McKee's *Story* in Boillat 2011b: 34–36.
45. In this specific shot, the doors that close automatically draw a line, impassable from that moment on, between the two possible worlds; the reference to the title of the movie, *Sliding Doors*, is obvious. In the film's promotional material, the two "o's" in the word "Doors" are represented as two circles crossing each other, thus delimiting a zone of intersection materialized in this specific shot.
46. The pattern described implies large-scale consequences typical of *althist* worlds. In general, alternate histories do not establish a multiverse. The reader or the viewer makes a comparison with his own world, which nonetheless is not represented within the fiction. Concerning the motif of the pandemic in alternate histories, one thinks of the comic book series *Hauteville House* by Duval and Gioux (from 2004 onwards). Starting from the last episode of its second cycle (episode 9), a plague, whose origin is the corpse of an octopus belonging to an intelligent species, modifies the outcome of the American Civil War to the benefit of the Southerners, who secretly develop a vaccine following the advice of a race living in the depths of the Earth.
47. In this flashback scene set in the late 1980s, a young Yanek II (Samuel Roukin) decides to distinguish himself from his double by not offering his daughter, Mira, the audio tape of her favorite music band that he bought during a trip to Berlin in "our" world, namely the exact same gift that Yanek I chose when visiting "the other side". The son of Yanek I dies of an epileptic seizure as Mira fails to intervene and save him, absorbed as she is in listening to the tape on her Walkman (such a nostalgic, low-tech component – also present in *Bandersnatch* or *Stranger Things* – is justified by the series' diegetic period). On the contrary, Mira II will save her brother's life, precisely because she did not receive this gift. The two alternative versions are shown thanks to a split-screen that separates the frame first vertically (as in *Deja Vu*), then horizontally, signifying both a temporal simultaneity and a cosmic

disjunction. The music lover motif echoes the sixth episode in Season 1 ("Act Like You've Been Here Before", 2018) in which a customs agent arrests a smuggler who attempts to cross the border between the two worlds with a CD of Prince. As we find out, the singer died in World I (as in ours in 2016) but continues to live in World II.

48. In the "*Nightmare On Elm Street*" series, the world of the dream is less the product of a subjectivity (the *mental world* of the killer's prey) and more a space-time continuum inhabited and controlled by the evil Freddy Krueger who acts from beyond the grave, attacking real people. This procedure borders on the metalepsis in the seventh episode, *Wes Craven's New Nightmare* (1994).

49. In the first installment in this horror movie franchise, the resolution of a puzzle box opens a gateway that puts the victims in contact with a world of demons (the Cenobites). However, it is *Hellbound: Hellraiser II* (1988) that is the most centered on the immersion in a *parallel world*: the characters are thrown for almost half of the film into a labyrinth governed by the god Leviathan that resembles the Piranese's oversized prisons (while looking at times like a ghost train in an amusement park within an overall gory and gruesome movie). *Hellraiser III: Hell on Earth* (1992) is more similar to the *Nightmare on Elm Street* series (whose sixth installment, *Freddy's Dead: The Final Chapter*, is released the year before) in that the main demon, Pinhead, invites himself into the dreams of the female protagonist. The eighth part of the series, released in 2005, presents a meta-narrative component similar to the one found in the *Scream* series; still, the "interface" between the real world and the *parallel world* is provided by the *virtual world* of a MMORPG (which significantly includes the term "world" and gives the film its title, *Hellraiser: Hellworld*). The gamers, who are fans of the series and able to correctly manipulate the puzzle box represented on their computer screen, receive an invitation for a private party (in fact, a party in hell); in other words, the action is not really taking place in "Hellworld".

50. In Lech Majewski's *The Mill and the Cross* (2011), digital compositing is also used for the "live" reproduction of a painting, but with a completely different aim and results.

51. Here, the temporal structure is particularly confusing since the episode intertwines two different periods from Bernard Lowe's life without distinguishing between them, as the character (played by Jeffrey Wright) is temporarily unable to access certain parts of his memory.

52. The subjective character of the images depicting the portal, a kind of augmented reality accessible only to androids, is signaled in S02E10 when two human technicians that accompany Maeve's team express their surprise at hearing talk about such a portal, as an "objective" reverse shot (secondary internal ocularisation on the technicians) shows the western landscape unaltered.

53. Moreover, as viewers belatedly realize, the entire park is built on a distant island, far from everything else.

54. S01E07 has a French term for a title, "Trompe L'Oeil", which refers to an illusionist tradition in art history. Aurélie Ledoux (2012) applied this concept to contemporary Hollywood cinema.

55. "The Bicameral Mind" (S01E10) explicitly addresses this issue. In this episode, Robert Ford shows Dolores Arnold's favorite work of art, Michelangelo's *The Creation of Adam* fresco. It is important to note that Arnold created Dolores but was replicated after his death in a simulacrum that, as we learn in Season 2, was actually fabricated by Dolores. A reproduction of the fresco is found on a wall in the android-repair laboratory. The first shot on this reproduction begins in a blurry image, a sign that we actually see through the eyes of Dolores. As the female character is reconnected, right after an update, the shot comes into focus: the hosts' subjectivity is predominant, even at the level of the image. Ford's *Da Vinci Code*-like speech on Michelangelo's fresco unveils a hidden meaning, following the interpretation advanced by the physicist Frank Meshberger, according to which the figures and shapes portrayed behind and around the figure of God draw a precise image of the human brain. Such a reading would transform the painting into a metaphor on God's evacuation for the benefit of the human.

56. Doležel qualifies as "supernatural" any world presenting components physically (if not logically) impossible according to the laws of the actual world. The term is only partially applicable to *Westworld*'s science fiction universe – that is, unless we stick to the worldview shared by some characters at a given moment during the unfolding of the story (but that

would drive us away from the alethic mode, encouraging us to adopt an axiological one). Therefore, Doležel applies the notion of "supernatural" to all types of multiverse, granting it with a meaning significantly different from the one the term has in my typology. A restricted understanding of the type of stories envisaged by Doležel would have encouraged us to focus our study on adventure films inspired by Greek mythology, similar to those in which a famous special effects pioneer like Ray Harryhausen participated (*Jason and the Argonauts*, 1963; *Clash of the Titans*, 1981).

57. One is reminded of the female protagonist in *Futureworld*, caught in a dream that intertwines fantasies and memories, or of Alice in the laboratories of the Umbrella Corporation in "*Resident Evil*" (see Chapter 1).
58. The way Dolores expresses her emotions remains dependent on a spatial isotopy: "I feel spaces opening up inside of me like a building with rooms I've never explored" (S01E04).
59. In the same episode, Maeve declares: "I'm not crazy after all".
60. Dolores' journey can be summarized in two brief, meta-narrative lines she utters: "I don't wanna be in a story" (S01E07) and "We are the authors of our stories now" (the very last phrase heard in Season 2). The fact that this last line is pronounced in a voice-over connotes Dolores' new authoritative status. While she speaks, we see images of Bernard who, as we have come to realize, is not Dolores' creator; in fact, *he is created by her* instead. The series plays in several ways on the inalienable status of individuality conferred by one's voice, even in the case of cybernetic beings. For example, Charlotte speaks with the voice of the actress who played, up until then, Dolores (Evan Rachel Wood) and Bernard, who had all along believed that he had been guided by Ford's voice in his head, realizes that in fact he was only talking to himself.
61. The scenes showing the subjects under maintenance that are not stored in the "attic" (*Dollhouse*) or in a kind of cold room (*Westworld*), employ a dispositive not unlike the one found in *Total Recall* (1990), a film freely adapted from a Philip K. Dick story (see Chapter 2, "*Total Recall*, Total Immersion").
62. *Blade Runner* (1982) constitutes an obvious exception to this, provided we follow the interpretation suggested by the origami unicorn scene reintroduced in the director's cut. A chapter in Henry Jenkins' book, *Convergence Culture*, is named "Searching for the Origami Unicorn", in reference to a comment made by Neil Young, producer of the video game *The Lord of the Rings: The Return of the King* (2003), concerning this specific scene in Ridley Scott's film. According to Young, the image of this folded paper, representing a mythical creature, signifies a way to "deliver that one piece of information that makes you look at the films differently" (Jenkins 2006: 123). In the director's cut version of *Blade Runner*, the unicorn is first shown in a dream sequence, related to Rick Deckard (Harrison Ford), then represented in an origami shaped by another "blade runner", Gaff (Edward James Olmos). As Deckard kept the contents of his dream to himself, the scene suggests that the motif of the unicorn could belong to a common dream implanted to both Deckard and Gaff (like those created by Dr. Schreber in *Dark City,* see Chapter 5). This would of course mean that both of them may be "replicants" (i.e androids ignoring their own status of artificial beings, like the heroes in the *Westworld* series). On this particular scene in *Blade Runner*, see also Dyer 2017: 214–216.

Chapter Four

Worldbuilding and Film Style

"[Poole] cut a horizontal strip, very narrow, then, after a moment of great concentration, cut the tape itself four hours away from the scanning head. He then rotated the cut strip into a right-angle piece in relation to the scanner, fused it in place with a micro heat element, then reattached the tape reel to its left and right sides. He had, in effect, inserted a dead twenty minutes into the unfolding flow of his reality. It would take effect – according to his calculations – a few minutes after midnight". Philip K. Dick, "The Electric Ant" (1969: 108).

Do the semantic particularities of multiverse movies leave their mark (or conversely do they depend), in one way or another, on the film form or the filmmaking practices, particularly as far as editing is concerned? Considered as processes of assembling multiple universes, *alternation* and *embedding* can also be found in other representational media. In the case of cinema though, their application draws on resources specific to the film medium. These resources have been previously theorized in contexts that are very different from the world-centered perspective developed in this book. Therefore, I propose to revisit some key parameters of the "film language" by considering them through their world-centered implications, with the ultimate aim of studying the links between style (discursive dimension) and world (referential dimension), that some of the films in our corpus openly question. Cinema as a machine and other related audio-visual dispositives (existing or extrapolated) have often been used in various types of discourse in order to metaphorically describe "worlds", whether internal (the functioning of the human psyche)[1] or virtual (the Platonic myth of the cave, see Bubb 2010: 340–342 and 359). In fictional works this metaphor takes sometimes a material form, as is the case in Philip K. Dick's "The Electric Ant". The story's protagonist, Poole, realizes that his perceived reality can be modified through a technical operation resembling *film editing*. This literary reference shows the importance of the cinematographic apparatus as a model when it comes to conceiving, visualizing, or narrating the worldbuilding process.

From Lumière brothers' *Demolition of a Wall* (1895) to contemporary disaster movies it is in the ad libitum assemblage and dismantlement of the world the force of cinema lies. Poole alters his phenomenological relation to the world by tampering with the machinery's circuits in a dispositive that includes him as the receiver of the "representation" thus fabricated. In the case of a mechanical medium like cinema, such endeavors cannot but affect the signifier of the means of expression. In an effort to account for a major paradigm within which the film medium has been conceived since the 1890s, François Albera suggested to return to the expression used by Guillaume Apollinaire in "The New Spirit and the Poets" (1918) inviting to "mechanize poetry as the world has been mechanized",[2] juxtaposing two different meanings of the verb "mechanize" (one rhetorical, the other industrial) inextricably linked in the case of audio-visual productions. Writing about short comedy films of early cinema, Albera explains that these films extend "*to the entire filmed world* the functioning principle of the camera that breaks down movement, then reconstructs it, frame by frame, by segmenting it – jerk, acceleration, reversion, differential speeds, increase or decrease in sizes, flattening and swelling" (Albera 2010: 83, the italics are mine)[*]. In my opinion, this remark also applies to certain contemporary multiverse movies – the most interesting ones in terms of form – in which a "worldbuilding machine" exerts its power on a character, affecting his physical presence, if not the entire world, which then becomes the extension of the subject thanks to this prosthetic machine. In this respect, the films in our corpus frequently resort to the processes analyzed by Albera, which exhibit the "mechanical" origin of the film medium. The diegetization of the machine motivates (within the framework of dominant film production) visual experimentations the avant-garde movements employed as their primary object. A 1968 film like *Je t'aime je t'aime* uses image jerkiness as the structuring principle of a world's genesis. Still, the recent expansion of digital cameras and digital special effects did not alter significantly the paradigm within which cinema is understood, as evidenced by several case studies examined in this book. As we will also see, discontinuity sometimes insinuates itself not only between shots but within a single image. Today, movies and video games "*mechanize*" worlds in a way that viewers can project into them. The presence of a machine in one of the diegeses (or in several of them, acting as a bridge between the different worlds) abolishes the dichotomy between estrangement and immersion, facilitating the viewer's identification with a character that *moves* from one world to another, while often adopting the posture of an immobile spectator connected to a device: the world comes to him and invites him into it.

In *Total Cinema* (1944), writer René Barjavel expressed his enthusiasm for cinema's ability to unfold a world that seems to extend beyond the screen, as *Last Action Hero* (1993) literally illustrated.[3] Barjavel echoes twentieth century's enthusiastic reaction towards the film medium's perceptual richness, which constitutes, prior to the advent of video games and Virtual Reality, one of the main features in the light of which the "seventh art" has been considered by those who have commented on its emergence and its developments. It is therefore not surprising that this specificity of the film medium – at least compared to literature – has led several movies to deal with the immersive power of the representation produced by a "worldbuilding machine" at a diegetic level. As we have already seen, *Avatar* denies the technological mediation in order to better establish the 3D technology it helps to update, whereas *Total Recall* and its remake ruminate instead on the harmful consequences of the erasure of this mediation (see *supra* Chapter 2).

As I have already noted, multiverse movies are often typified by certain stylistic features specifically assigned to each of the film's worlds. I remarked in Chapter 3 that in *The Cabinet of Dr. Caligari*, it is precisely by maintaining a distorted perspective throughout the frame story that the interpretation of the embedded world as a *mental world* becomes complex. The fact is that the co-presence of divergent styles in a film encourages a world-centered reading of its story. In *Holiday for Henrietta* (1952),[4] the frame story shows two screenwriters at work inventing the film's embedded story, keeping some of its elements while discarding others. This type of self-reflexivity prefigures Alain Robbe-Grillet's "meta-screenwriting" film, *Trans-Europ-Express* (1966), which multiplies these metaleptic games by playfully demonstrating the interpenetration between the creators' actual world and the world they create. These films highlight the degree to which the screenwriting process is linked to the question of possible alternatives. After all, Daniel Ferrer, a specialist in the field of textual genetics, inscribes his work in the framework of the literary theory of possible worlds.[5] As in Woody Allen's *Melinda and Melinda* (2004), in which the film's two narrators represent comedy and tragedy respectively, the two writers in *Holiday for Henrietta* do not conceive the film identically – one sees it as a Parisian romance in the style of René Clair's movies, the other as a film noir. Their suggestions, successively represented on the screen, give rise to distinct narrative bifurcations featuring the same main characters. However, the "noir" version comes along with a systematic use of Dutch angles (in a deliberately caricatured reference to Orson Welles' films or *The Third Man*) leading the critic and historian Georges Sadoul to use the expression "writing in italics" with regard to this film (Sadoul 1952)[*]. While these cases concern distinct variations of a single world rather than separate worlds, one gathers the important role played by visual style in connoting an affiliation to a given world. "Italics" are related to typography, not the words' referent; nevertheless, they can have an impact on the way objects belonging to the fictional world are viewed (one is reminded of Alain Damasio, a contemporary French science fiction novelist who frequently plays with variations of fonts in order to create a world situated in the future). In some cases, a film may knowingly maintain an ambiguity in this respect by *not* appointing systematically a particular stylistic element to a world's ontological status, thus blurring the boundaries. For example, Simone Knox has shown that the distinction between the feature film called *The Truman Show* and the diegetic TV show of the same name tends to disappear as far as their filmmaking strategies and style are concerned. The TV show is a "mix of reality TV, sitcom, and soap opera" creating an "*artificial* world-within-a-world" sometimes depicted via "television-shots" and others through "film-shots" (according to a shift that could be considered as a part of a metalepsis, see Knox 2010: 1–2).

In similar cases, a film's visual and aural features, although strictly intended for the viewer and therefore distinct from the diegesis, are related to the world's ontological status. We could compare this type of parameter to what Marie-Laure Ryan calls "stylistic filtering" in her study of the contribution of the possible worlds logic in theories of literary fiction. According to the author, this filtering is a central factor in defining the relationship of accessibility between two worlds insofar as it confers a certain tone, a "color" specific to each of these worlds. Ryan uses the term "color" in a metaphorical sense (for instance, Robbe-Grillet's novel *La Jalousie* selects a landscape of colonial life and *paints it in neutral colors*)[6] but when it comes to visual media this comparison can be taken literally. While we qualify as "diegetic" everything accessible to the film's characters, these features concern the representation itself, not its referent. They tell us something *about* the diegesis that is not perceived by the fictitious beings inhabiting it, just like the voice-over cannot be heard by them.[7]

For instance, in *Speed Racer* (2008), *Gamer* (2009), or *Scott Pilgrim vs. the World* (2010), when the on-screen representation takes the appearance of a video game, with no instance of disjunction motivating this modification in the film's visual texture (so that the hypothesis of a *mental world*, retained in the case of *Mala Noche*, does not hold here), it does not follow that the pilots in each of these films have shifted between worlds like the protagonists in *TRON* (1982) do. In these examples, the representation exhibits its artificiality and takes the representational mode of video games as its referent. This is also the case with screen adaptations of graphic novels in which certain visual features function as a reference to the original medium (*American Splendor*, 2003; *Sin City*, 2005).[8] In these cases the world's otherness is not signified on the level of visual denotation (the referent of the image remains the same and consequently so does the world) but on the one of connotation (a second level is added that relates particularly to the film's style).

For a different universe to actually exist, it is necessary that one of the film's diegeses provides "from the inside" evidence of its own creation, in one form or another. In other words, it is necessary that the film's characters are aware of the formal characteristics of the image in the same manner as the viewer is. Such an affirmation from the protagonists' side is possible so far as movies emphasizing their world-centered dimension tend to transfer to the diegetic level phenomena "logically" external to it, according to a process pertaining to metalepsis. Therefore, certain aspects relating to film language – or, in most cases, a single aspect established as a criterion for distinguishing between worlds

– may be acknowledged by the film's hero who then takes note of this observation, as evidenced in a more or less direct way through his attitudes or words (generally by displacing diegetic referents). Without this acting out from the characters' side or the specific use of color as one of "any number of formal devices [that] function in a perception structure" (Branigan 1984: 94),[9] the viewer has no way of knowing if these characters perceive their world in the same way he perceives the film's representation.

I argue then that stylistic filtering occurs at two distinct levels: the first level relates to the film's visual properties while the second concerns the film's editing. When Daniel Yacavone applied to movies the five processes introduced by Nelson Goodman in *Ways of Worldmaking* (1978), his idea was to "map onto recognizable stylistic features of films, and filmmaking techniques, that contribute to the creation of cinematic worlds" (Yacavone 2015: xxiii). However, in Yacavone's theory (as in general in film critics' discourse)[10] each "world" corresponds to a film in its entirety, but never to a single component of a multiverse, as I suggest here. Through the example of *The Eternal Sunshine of the Spotless Mind* (discussed later in this book), Yacavone notes that the film "move[s] back and forth in virtual time and alter[s] spatial distance in ways that establish a world order based on principles other than the most literal chronology or the most clearly demonstrable cause-and-effect relationships" (2015: 97). Still, he neither suggests that the film offers two different worlds, nor does he clarify the principles according to which these worlds are linked to each other. These are some of the laws of multiverse movies that I propose to explore in this chapter.

On the Materiality of Images: Live-Action and Animation (*The Congress*)

Certain multiverse movies combine and distinguish between animated and "live-action" scenes. In the digital age and in particular the era of *motion capture*, the dividing line between these two film practices has become considerably thinner. André Gaudreault and Philippe Marion introduced the concept of "animage" as a model of apprehension and definition of the film medium that would take animation as its main frame of reference (Gaudreault and Marion 2015: 152–175).

In any case, one easily notices the recurrence of a world-centered use of the hybridity between these two types of images. In his book *The Limits of Interpretation*, Umberto Eco noted the value of the possible worlds theory for approaching a film like *Who Framed Roger Rabbit* (1988).[11] In Robert Zemeckis' film, two ontological types of individuals coexist within the same universe, some of them actual humans, whiles others are animated, coming straight out of a cartoons' "world". This world is presented in an opening scene retrospectively revealed as the shooting of a "film within a film". At that moment the terms of the film's "reading contract" are laid in front of the viewer. These terms postulate that the *toons* have an actual existence beyond the cartoon world (as in "Hollywood metafilms" of the classic era offering behind-the-scenes access to film studios – see Cerisuelo 2000). Once the animated elements in the kitchen are transformed into "real" profilmic elements through a permutation only the viewer notices (we shift levels by going from the metafilmic world to the film's reference world, all props contained inside the refrigerator turning from drawings to "real" three-dimensional objects), the two distinct types of characters are brought together within a single-world universe (whose inhabitants nevertheless present a different "consistency") meticulously furnished with elements belonging to the animated world. Even if the protagonists are aware of the *otherness* of some of the characters with whom they interact, this type of divergence is not that different from Hollywood's regular strategy aiming to distinguish its *stars* (in the case the *toons*) from ordinary people.

Within the hybrid world of *Who Framed Roger Rabbit*, differences related to the characters' ontological status and associated with distinct genres (the burlesque logic of a cartoon movie disrupts the detective film genre) are not without consequences on these characters' interactions with their environment. The *toons'* bodies remain malleable even when integrating the "real" world. These peculiar actors are not subject to the same physical laws or the same behavioral norms as human beings. Moreover, the film's story benefits from this kind of uncertainty prevailing over the "world of *toons*" (or rather the world that hosts the *toons* when extracted from their world of origin), like for instance during a long pursuit scene during which the detective finds himself handcuffed to Roger Rabbit. It actually turns out that the latter is not subject to the handcuffs' metal shackle; he only pretended to be until then and the viewer does not suspect otherwise due to the principle of minimal departure (that being said, it is less plausible that the detective is not aware of these varying physical laws).

Run Lola Run (1998) is a film offering three alternative narrative arcs. All variations of the first obstacle faced by the protagonist during her journey are presented through animated sequences: while Lola is going down the stairs, the neighbor's dog respectively shows its teeth without moving/bites Lola's leg causing her to fall/fails in its attempt to attack Lola who soars high in the sky.[12] This increases the film's visual heterogeneity in the same way as the sequences shot in black & white, the red-filtered scenes, or those filmed in low-resolution video. Although the insertion of animation is motivated by a metalepsis (we are entering the image of a television screen present in the film's diegesis), none of the characters seems to take any notice of this (Lola's mother is busy on the phone and does not even look at the TV screen). Only the viewer is invited to incorporate all different types of images into the fictional pact, starting from the pre-credits sequence which establishes the film's playful character, and especially with the opening credits. The latter foreground the logic of diegetic absorption (different thresholds and openings pass one after another as Lola rushes into them) and, through the use of animated scenes, serve as an explicit reference to video game aesthetics (frantic movements, shots that are seemingly continuous, Mickey Mousing and sound tricks, over the shoulder third-person camera angles, etc.). This reference is also present in the very idea of repeating a series of identical actions – after two "game overs", Lola triumphs. The opening credits illustrate the phenomenon of remediation discussed by Bolter and Grusin (1999), including the hypermediacy level that is expressed here by the multiplication of frames within a frame. The animated, schematic representation of a character, who also happens to be very distinctive in terms of color (red hair and green trousers), makes her resemble a video game avatar, recalling a filiation between comic books, animated cinema, and video games, illustrated by certain transmedia strategies.[13]

Actually, the combination of animation and live-action runs through the history of these two types of practices from Winsor McCay's *Gertie the Dinosaur* (1914) or Bud Fisher's *Mutt and Jeff on Strike* (1920) to *Cool World* (1992) and *Evil Toons* (1992) via *Invitation to the Dance* (1956) or *Mary Poppins* (1964).[14] Such visual hybridity constitutes then one of the procedures available to creators of multiverse films. In an episode from the TV series *Fringe*, whose title "Who Framed Olivia Dunham" (S3E19, 2011, see *infra*) is an obvious reference to the Robert Zemeckis film, one of the protagonists, having reached a threshold (an apartment's door), suddenly asks his interlocutor just as we slip into an animated film during the shot-reverse shot: "Why are you cartooned?". In effect, worldbuilding proves to be a constant topic throughout the series' third season: after being stuck in an *parallel world* (while her evil alter-ego usurped her identity in the original world), Olivia, whose body is occupied by the spirit of William Bell, gets lost in a *mental world*. In search of her, two friends manage to penetrate her world of hallucinations (which then becomes a shared subjective world as in *Inception*) by resorting to the use of LSD. Faced with such a stack of different worlds, animated scenes come to over-signify the world's otherness. Therefore, the series' characters are aware of their body and the environment's conversion into animated images.

The Congress (2013), by Israeli director Ari Folman, whose animated movie *Waltz with Bashir* was highly praised at the 2008 Cannes Film Festival, is a film that employs the live-action/animation hybridity in a productive fashion. It is based on a science fiction novel called *The Futurological Congress* (1971), written by Polish author Stanisław Lem (best known for *Solaris*), in which a professor who attends a congress in a constantly threatened by terrorist attacks future society, finds himself amidst a bomb-wreaked havoc. By drinking contaminated tap water and by inhaling gas bombs thrown by the police forces in their effort to suppress an urban riot, the professor absorbs a "psycho-chemical" substance which causes strong hallucinations and transforms all individuals into obedient subjects, doomed to mirth and benevolence. This is a rather preposterous tale, in which the hero ends up in a cryogenic suspension after his brain has been transferred to somebody else's body. He wakes up forty years later in a world – actually a hallucination from the futuristic story's present time – whose entire population is, as he discovers, completely enslaved through a constant projection into an illusory *parallel world* artfully created by the State.[15] This delirious dive into a perpetual hallucinatory flow – the novel is not chaptered – is transcribed on the screen by Ari Folman, albeit in a very loose adaptation, since the filmmaker reinvents the novel in the context of digital imaging. From an aesthetic point of view however, he distances himself from this context by using traditional 2D animation in order to represent the psychedelic universe of the *parallel world.* In Lem's book there is hardly a reference to visual dispositives other than as an element of comparison, the chemical "cure" being "part of one's own self, much as eyeglasses become in time, which correct defects in vision" (Lem 1976: 69). In the screen version, the story is transposed within the film industry: the protagonist is not an academician going to a congress but a film actress heading to a Hollywood event.

In the live-action scenes the part is played by Robin Wright in a fictionalized version of herself. An animated avatar modeled after her own image replaces the actress immediately after her character passes a border checkpoint. She drives down the road amidst a landscape that turns into a drawing while we watch a shot of her sports car's windshield. The image combines the actress' hands on the steering wheel with the animated character's face visible in the rear view mirror. Nevertheless, the film maintains an ambiguity between the collectively shared subjective world of the hallucination and a certain *virtual world.* In its prologue, we learn that in a near future society, Robin Wright had her face and body fully scanned in a variety of postures and expressions so that her image could be used subsequently in CGI movies freed from any concerns linked to the actress' aging (Color Plate 9). In addition, she is contractually forced to waive all rights of her image to the studio as well as to abandon her acting career. The logic of the dispossession of the Self, inherent in the way the entertainment industry controls the image of its stars, is taken to the extreme. For the most part, the rest of the film takes place in this animated second world (Color Plate 10) before the protagonist returns to the real world by using a capsule (the equivalent of the pill in *Total Recall* and *The Matrix*). The real world is inhabited by a crowd of miserable and emaciated people in rags who wander in dirty streets under the surveillance of Zeppelins – one finds here the same steampunk imaginary as in *Fringe* – staring blankly ahead while imagining themselves living in the luminous world of the hallucination where the borders between the human, the animal, the vegetal, and the technological are blurred thanks primarily to the malleability of the animated image. In the film's epilogue, Robin Wright chooses to plunge back into this illusory world in search of her visually impaired son, Aaron, who has regained his sight in the hallucinatory world by turning into somebody else. She reinvents an alternate ending, represented again in animated scenes (in which we enter via a subtle use of a subjective camera), only to discover that Wright's avatar is modeled after her son's image whereas Aaron has taken on his mother's appearance.

Through the combination of animated and live-action scenes, Folman's film reinforces its two-world character and confronts the notion of hallucination to the infinite possibilities offered by digital technology. Furthermore, this opposition overlaps with another one on which I will focus in the next few pages: in *The Congress*, the bleak images representing the real world, revisited after a 20-year ellipsis, contrast the vividly colored animated scenes. At the same time, live-action scenes inserted into the animated world, depicting the outrageous films Wright imagines her digital clone to be involved with (and whose satirical tone is reminiscent of Kubrick's *Dr. Strangelove*, 1964), are projected on screens or imagined in black & white dreams indicating thus the existence of different world levels.

Are Colors Diegetic?

There are several films that play on the opposition between black & white and color as a heterogeneity factor located within the materiality of the image. With the exception of some examples where this opposition is used to emphasize a film's given moment (as in the Technicolor sequences in *Ben Hur*, 1925, or the depicted in black & white assassination of the governor played by Sean Penn in *All the King's Men*, 2006), a temporal value is generally bestowed upon the co-presence of these two types of images. Given the fact that in the history of the medium black & white is traditionally considered as anterior to the expansion of color (even though movies "in color" are actually contemporaneous with the first black & white film stocks – if not even older provided that we include Émile Reynaud's animated drawings in the history of cinema), there is a clear tendency to relate – through comparison – this type of images to a diegetic past or to associate them with historical archival images (as in *Night and Fog*, 1956).

However, these are nothing more than conventions that may very well be transgressed.[16] For example, *Europa* (1991) constantly plays on connotations associated with monochrome images while creating a world that has less to do with the historical reality in the immediate aftermath of the war and more with fantasies about Nazism. In *Bonjour Tristesse* (1958) the convention is reversed since color is used to represent the past; as James Walters notes, it is not so much the anteriority of the events recounted that is central in Preminger's film, but the expression of a subjectivity, that of the nostalgic character played by Jean Seberg (Walters 2008: 211–212). One could interpret similarly the dream sequences in *Shock Corridor* (1963), shot in 16mm color film in the style of a documentary, or conversely the black & white fantasy sequences in *Jonas Who Will Be 25 in the Year 2000* (1976). A selective use of color within a single black & white image, as in *Sin City* (2005), appears mainly as a stylistic effect, in this case a direct reference to the expressive means of graphic novels. Sometimes the contrast between black & white and color is transposed to that between two distinct types of color film, especially when a filter is used to create a monochromatic image that tinges the representation of the focal character's subjectivity: the red-drenched flashback of the traumatic and bloody scene returning to the surface of the eponymous character's consciousness in *Marnie* (1964), certain POV-shots in *Stir of Echoes* (1999), or the images resulting from the vision of a serial killer hunter with paranormal abilities in *Suspect Zero* (2004). In such cases, we do not actually deal with the creation of a different world within the fictional universe, but with a subjective vision of a single fictional world. However, in this chapter I will focus more specifically on the ways this conventional dichotomy between black & white and color can be used in order to differentiate between worlds.

It is noteworthy that there are cases where the opposition between black & white and color overlaps with the co-presence of animation and live-action scenes already discussed. Jules Feiffer's drawings in *I Want to Go Home* (1989), Betty Boop complaining that black & white actresses have fallen out of fashion in *Who Framed Roger Rabbit* (1988), the duck in *Volere Volare* (1991), or Bugs Bunny in *Looney Tunes: Back in Action* (2003), all stand out as black & white figures in films shot for the most part in live-action and in color. Likewise, a selective use of color is combined with a simultaneous shift from live-action to animation in *Last Action Hero* (1993), during the scene in which the child watching a cartoon on television and imagining his favorite hero as Hamlet suddenly returns to reality.

Therefore, the world-centered coloring of certain types of images needs to be examined. Color seems to be closer to our reference world. After all, this was the reason why a theoretician like Rudolf Arnheim seemed to have a negative view towards the use of color in the early 1930s (with the exception of derealizing saturations and other ostentatious effects) when evaluating, via a Gestalt approach, cinema's artistic character in light of the divergences that distinguish its representations from reality (Arnheim 1957: 161–162). In general, the viewer fills the "blanks" mentally in a film's visual representation: he receives the aesthetic pleasure of black & white images, but at the same time he postulates the existence of colors within the universe presented to him by virtue of the principle of minimal departure established in reference to the world of his own experience. Even if the film itself is in black & white, its world is not, unless there is a clear indication affirming the opposite.

Indeed one wonders to what extent a film's colors, namely a phenomenon pertaining to the *filmographic level*, can be related to the *diegetic* level (see *supra* Chapter 3). In *She Wore a Yellow Ribbon,* Joanne Dru's character is actually wearing a yellow ribbon in her hair. This feature, present in the film's title and announcing a fetishistic attachment to the female character,[17] applies to an element belonging to the diegesis. But is one entitled to claim that the same feature would have been "less diegetic" had the film been shot in black & white with the ribbon's color being specified through dialogue? The obvious answer is no: in that case the color's mode of "presence" would have been different. The verbal referent would have exhibited the conventional character of the monochromatic image. Once viewers accept this convention, it follows that they do not consider black & white as a representation that *lacks* something.

Philipp Schmerheim describes in the following manner the effect produced by the alternate use of black & white and color scenes in *Memento* (2000), each type of image linked to a distinct temporal level (with no world-centered implications, even though the character's impairment in terms of immediate memory muddies the waters by encouraging alternative hypotheses): "The different color schemes support the audience in distinguishing the film's different plot lines, while the presence or absence of color is not an intrinsic element of the diegesis or plot structure. Color does not assume an intra-diegetic narrative function" (2013: 120). Schmerheim rightfully indicates that this lack of diegetic motivation is only one case among many others (and he mentions by way of comparison *Pleasantville* to which I will return below). One conceives of a possible use of metalepsis that would aim to present a world in which the characters would be aware of living inside a black & white film. In a way, they would contemplate their own world from the place assigned to the film's viewer. Still, the degree of explicitness is once again variable. Unless people inside the diegesis talk openly of the way they perceive their own environment,[18] it is difficult to tell for sure if a given reaction from a film's character (his surprise, for example) rests on the chromatic perception of the world he lives in.

In *Kafka* (1991), a black & white film that pays tribute to both German Expressionism and film noir (see Boillat 2017)[19] (Fig. 28), when the eponymous character played by Jeremy Irons enters a castle, looking to unveil all of its secrets, color suddenly appears as he crosses the threshold of a door.[20] At that point the film shifts from a Kafkaesque fantasy to a science fiction movie. This two-world structure is in many ways "faithful" to the writings of the famous Czech author. Kafka is the favorite subject of Lubomír Doležel who studies literature from the perspective of possible worlds semantics. Doležel discusses the ways in which the macrostructural organization of Kafka's work leads to the abolition of borders separating the natural from the supernatural in favor of a "hybrid world" or a "visible/invisible world", depending on the case (see especially Doležel 1983, 1984 and 1998: 187–196). In Soderbergh's film, the hero passes into the Beyond by entering the castle. In this respect, it is revealing that he borrows an underground passage by rushing into one of the tombs in a cemetery near the castle. The Beyond is depicted in color: after a close-up of a door handle in black & white, the following image is a filmed in color, eye level shot of the same door as it opens. In the words of Doležel, colors make visible the invisible world of Franz Kafka's narratives.[21] The protagonist

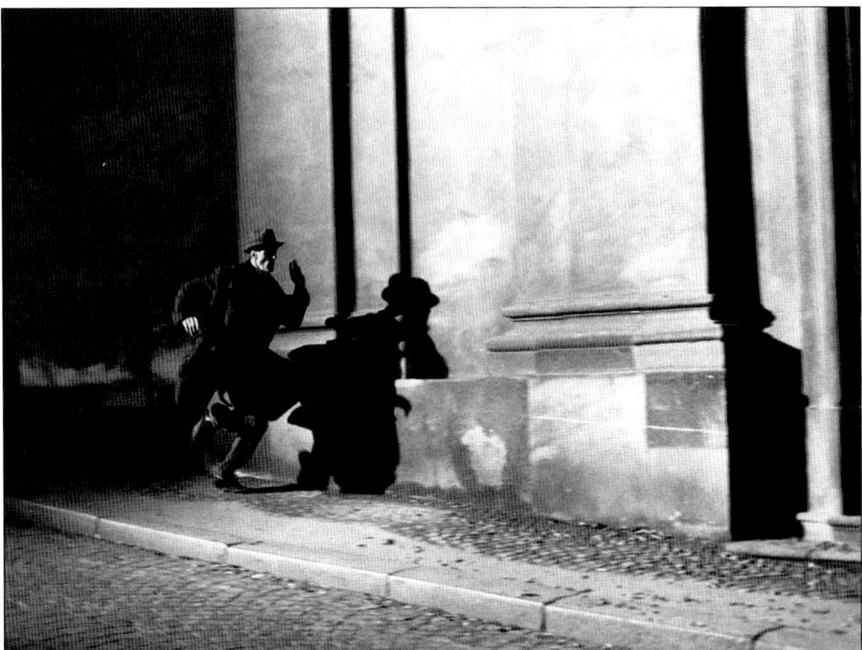

Fig. 28: An image used in the posters of Steven Soderbergh's *Kafka* (1991): a visual style ostensibly inspired by *The Third Man* and its nocturnal Mitteleuropa alleys, in a double homage to German expressionism and film noir.

inscribes his presence in both of these shots exclusively through his shadow, a stereotype associated with the "expressionist" style that spares the character the prerogatives of color representation. The question then arises as to whether these colors are actually perceived by the hero. We change "worlds" during the shot/reverse shot edit but there is no indication in the character's attitude that he is affected by this transformation or that he even notices it. Uncertainty prevails and determining whether the hero actually perceives (or not) any change seems unimportant. There is nothing here like the awareness of the characters in Marc-Antoine Mathieu's *Julius Corentin Acquefaques* (1990–2020), a self-reflexive graphic novel series whose protagonists realize that the comic book representation which hosts them "lacks" several elements, like four-color printing (see Mathieu 1991).[22]

The transgression of the castle's Law by a "hero"[23] who drifts into forbidden territory, passing through a locker in a monumental storage system (an entry/exit door used prior and after the scene in color, Fig. 29), does not only disclose the invisible parts of the worlds imagined by Kafka (as Doležel understands it). It also relates to the metaleptic foundations of a film that projects the Czech author himself, as well as certain elements of his biography (or of a certain mythology surrounding this biography, nourished among other things by his own fictional writings), inside the very world fabricated through-

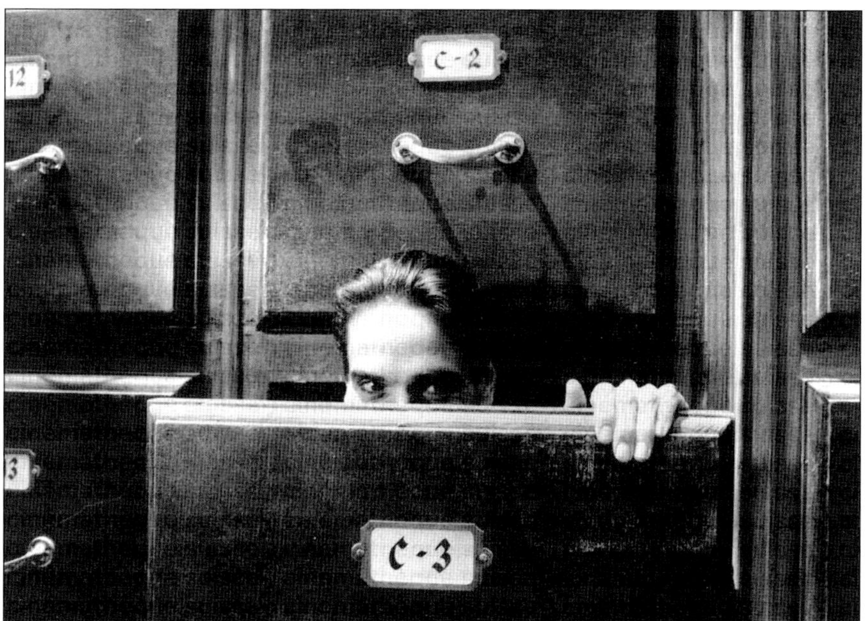

Fig. 29: Promotional photo, *Kafka* (1991). A symbol of an opaque and absurd bureaucracy typical of Kafka's stories, the storage system with its disproportionate dimensions (like the doors in Orson Welles' *The Trial*) absorbs the hero and reduces him to a "file" among others.

out his work.[24] This way, following a transfictional process, the worlds described in several of Kafka's texts are merged into a single world, namely the world of the "author", conceived in a "monolithic" fashion as a monument of international literature. The Kafkaesque imagery now becomes a world, or rather a two-world universe thanks to film style.[25] Staging the Self (the famous "K." in Kafka's short stories and novels) is taken literally. The same goes for the stereotypical imagery associated with the author's absurd tales, as it was established by Orson Welles' *The Trial* (1962) with its black & white photography and its self-reflexive exhibition of the cinematographic apparatus (in the form of the projection in still images of the "Before the Law" allegory), but with no interpenetration of different world levels as in Soderbergh's film. The dialectical relationship between gray and color acts as an interface and a filter between the film's world and the viewer. On the level of connotation, it draws for the audience's sake a cartography of worlds that does not necessarily have a strict diegetic equivalent but nonetheless corresponds to an actual differentiation of worlds on the diegetic level.

The representation of the interworld threshold in *Kafka* seems like a direct reference to *The Wizard of Oz* (1939), an emblematic case of world-centered use of color. In Fleming's movie, the real world is filmed in sepia, literally representative of everyday life as described in the novel, the house being "as dull and gray as everything else", including the characters themselves. Dorothy's aunt is changed by "the sun and wind" that has "taken the red from her cheeks and lips, and they were gray also" (see Baum 2003: 6 and Gunning 1995: 250–251). This fictional "reality" contrasts with the embedded story, represented in color and unfolding in a world governed by its own special laws[26] (Color Plate 11). The Technicolor process is displayed here via a diegetic justification while being at the same time promoted as an element favoring immersion. As such, it plays a similar role to the anamorphic format in *Brainstorm* (1983) and the second season's finale in *Westworld*, or the 3D technology in *Avatar* (2009) and *TRON: Legacy* (2010). The *other* world's splendor is expressed within the film universe through the "magic" of cinematic technology whose attractional character is in such cases far from being incompatible with the demands of narrative integration.[27] Only when she leaves "home" – conceived in opposition to the *Unheimliche* that ultimately proves to be particularly welcoming in this fairy tale – by crossing the threshold of her house whose steps still have the "color" of everyday life,[28] Dorothy discovers – simultaneously with the viewer – the colorful world that lies "Over the Rainbow". The door frame becomes a second screen; a camera movement that follows the young protagonist invites us to enter into this screen. As suggested by the duplication established by the presence of the same actors in both the primary diegesis and the embedded world (albeit in different roles), and as the film's ending affirms, color here "signifies" the dream world.

However, it is difficult to apprehend the semiotic function of this type of use of color by resorting to the two oppositional dualities introduced by Roland Barthes (signifier/signified; denotation/connotation)[29] insofar as what interests us here is more a matter of reference than of meaning. Firstly, it is not a question of isolating one of the colors (or a combination of colors) from the film's image and then interpreting it in relation to culturally predetermined connotations,[30] but to consider coloration in its entirety, as a signifying element within the dichotomy between black & white and color. In addition, the chromatic features of the film stock participate in the denoting signifier (from which the signified is established),[31] but this category does not allow us to determine what the referential implications of the denoting signified are.[32] Furthermore, Martine Joly remarked that Barthes' landmark text on the Panzani advertising image presents certain methodological confusions, in particular due to the fact that the encoded visual message "brings together in a single signifier elements of a different nature, such as objects and colors" (Joly 1993: 63)[*]. Following Joly's suggestion, I will instead refer to a subsequent model introduced by the semioticians of the Group μ who distinguished within visual signs two different and complementary categories: the *iconic signs*, which represent through analogy an element of the world the observer is able to "recognize", and the *plastic signs,* which include the material properties of the image, such as color (Group μ 1992: 113–116). The choice of a discontinuous presence of the plastic sign of color – namely one of the "materials of the cinematic signifier" (in this case a non-specific one) according to Christian Metz[33] – in the examples here examined, falls in the domain of aesthetics and therefore participates in the phenomenon of "stylistic filtering" as envisaged by Marie-Laure Ryan. This is not necessarily a question of viewpoint in the sense of "focalization", as this notion has been theorized by Genettian narratology, since that typology was developed with the film's character as its point of reference, thus excluding any plastic sign not motivated on the diegetic level (Genette 1980). This is more a question of enunciation and we can apply in the case of the film medium what the theoreticians of the Group μ are postulating on narrative discourse in literature:[34]

> Nevertheless, rarely the literary discourse is so transparent as to filter the story only in a naïve way […]. More often than not it opposes its grid, its syntactic play to the imaginary representation of the event. Therefore two universes are taking shape during this development: the story's universe, where beings and objects move according to specific laws, and the linguistic universe, where syntactic norms govern the sentences and impose on these elements an order of their own (Group μ 1970: 175)[*].

Obviously the term "universe" suits my interests: on a level below the diegesis, film language also constitutes a "universe" that grants access to the fiction. I will deal later on with strictly syntactic questions and their world-centered implications. For now, it would seem that the articulation of black & white and color, although not necessarily pertaining to the technical phase of editing (unless we broaden this term so as to include any type of grafting or the underscoring of certain visual elements within a single shot), also falls under the same type of norms. Furthermore, one could view films where the inter-penetration between worlds manifests itself through a targeted insertion of color within a black & white image, as a case of application for creative (rather than analytical) purposes of the approach advocated by the Group μ: an approach which proposes a formalization by looking for discrete elements in intrinsically linear visual facts (Group μ 1992: 41–44). In that case, it is not surprising to see a rise in this type of filmmaking practices in the digital era considering that these semioticians were looking for a mathematical processing of data.

Let us return now to *Oz* after this detour through the "world" of theory. In this 1939 film, color is not strictly speaking "diegetic" since the characters never mention its presence. Nevertheless, the opposition between black & white and colored graphic signs is interpreted in world-centered terms and therefore filters our reading of the film's referents. The viewer then organizes these referents according to the "division" established by the aforementioned opposition. In the film's recent prequel, *Oz the Great and Powerful* (2013), as the magician Oz (James Franco) enters a world of color, his descent is accompanied by a change of ratio (we shift from 4:3 to a Scope aspect ratio) as well as by effects of depth created through the use of 3D technology (Color Plate 12). However, this time the hero is not dreaming: the *supernatural world* described in

Baum's novels comes alive with no explanation that would present it as the result of a dream, as was the case in Victor Fleming's film. Still, *Oz the Great and Powerful* resorts to the differentiation between black & white and color in order to signify the *otherness* of a world, indicating thus, more than seventy years after the first film, the persistence of this parameter. A close-up on Oz's face gradually shifts in color as he contemplates an off-screen landscape from the basket of a hot air balloon. During the same shot, the camera moves away from him to reveal the enchanting scenery. In the course of the camera's circular movement around the balloon, the aspect ratio expands, adding to the spectacular exhibition of both the world represented in the film and the potential of cinematic techniques. Scope, depth, color: we are invited to grasp the image in its "haptic"[35] dimension as the adventures of the film's hero are translated into an extraordinary viewing experience.

In *Kafka*, everything seems to suggest that the "first" world (meaning the world in which we are first immersed) is the direct emanation of the hero's mind, or at least of the mind of the author (Kafka) out of which this character is modeled and whose work is *made into a world* before our eyes. In this sense, the color sequences inside the castle are inviting us behind the scenes, revealing the machine manufactured in order to make this world come about.[36] The film's "mad scientist", the Frankenstein-like Dr. Murnau (Ian Holm) urges the writer, whose visionary work he admires, to enter in his straight out of *Brazil* (1985) laboratory. Kafka crosses the door against his will and finds himself in the room where Dr. Murnau manipulates the minds of his guinea pigs using a giant machine that looks both like a telescope and a torture device (Fig. 30). Then and there, the film switches genres, moving from *weird fiction* to *science fiction*. As he explains to Kafka, his project is to turn the nightmares the novelist describes in his texts into reality, imposing "his" world and transforming individuals into puppets, like Caligari did before him. In this regard, his experiments actually replicate the one the film is conducting by transforming a literary subtext into a world (Murnau is using his "worldbuilding machine" to adapt the environment to his demiurgic aspirations).[37]

It is after all common practice to give a concrete form at a chromatic level to the "grayness" of the world inhabited by a character subjected to the coercion of a dystopian society. In the very first pages of his novel *1984*, published in 1949, George Orwell indicates that in the governed by the totalitarian regime of the Big Brother country of Oceania, "though the sun was shining and the sky a harsh blue, there seemed to be no colour in anything, except the posters that were plastered everywhere" (Orwell 1961: 4). The novel's screen adaptation, directed by Michael Radford, plays on this visual parameter, confronting the de-saturated images of everyday life (as well as the "images within an image" of a "telescreen" broadcasting the Party's voice, filmed in sepia) with the dazzling greenery of the pastures Winston Smith (John Hurt) visits in a dream. Likewise, Ridley Scott, in the commercial he directed in 1984 for the release of

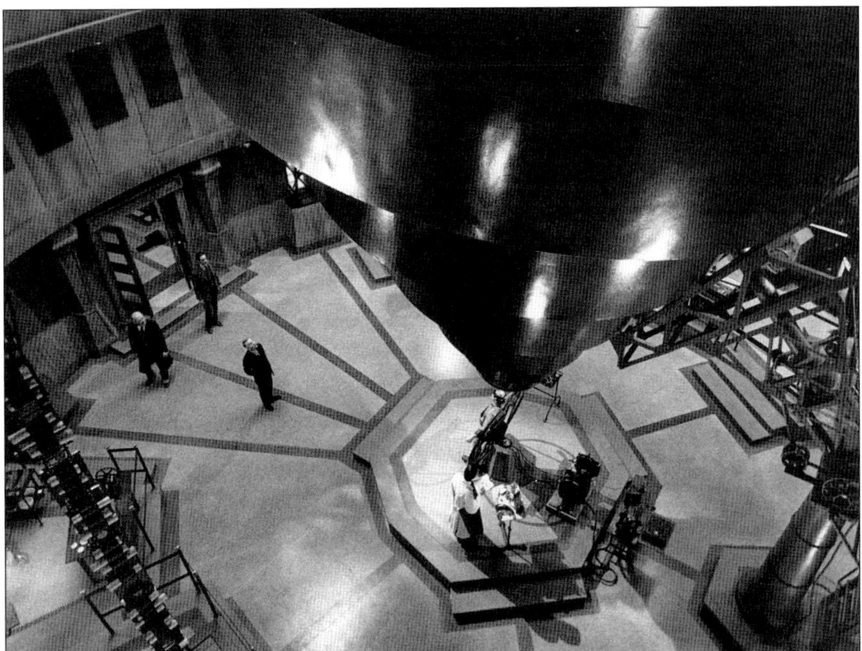

Fig. 30: Black & white promotional image of a scene appearing in color in *Kafka* (1991): a machine that alienates the subject in the backstage of the dystopian regime.

the first personal computer named "Macintosh", in a clear reference to Orwell's work, creates a contrast between the anonymous crowds – the silhouettes of individuals marching in tight ranks like the workers in *Metropolis*, blending with the gray surfaces of the stripped walls – and the athletic female hero dressed in red shorts, embodying the brand whose logo at the time was a rainbow-colored apple. At the end of the clip, this character breaks the screen of IBM's "propaganda" and the ensuing text is detached from the luminous glow thus produced: "On January 24th, Apple Computer will introduce Macintosh. And you will see why 1984 won't be like '1984'". When in 2013 the film *Jobs,* a hagiography of the founder of Apple, quotes this commercial, the rhetoric of the struggle against a powerful rule seems ironic (even though the film does not produce any discourse on this subject) in view of the current status of the firm which benefited in 2012 from one of the largest market capitalizations of all time.

Concerning more broadly the intermingling of values and colors that Barry Salt amply substantiates during his discussion of *Redskin* (1929),[38] I would like to refer to an article by Philippe Dubois studying a corpus of classic films dating from 1930 to 1950. The author begins with the following observation:

> It seems to me that the most important point is that almost all of the films I have been able to track down within this classic period elaborate the dialectic between black &

> white and color around the *question of a passage*. The chromatic relationship is linked inside the story to the circulation between two universes. These two universes, as well as the passage connecting them, can be of an extremely diverse nature and may be materialized in a variety of ways. I chose to focus on two types of diegetic situations: the passage to a dream, the passage to a painting (Dubois 1995: 79)[*].

Simply citing colored paintings, as in Émile Cohl's *The Neo-Impressionist Painter* (1910) or in the 1940s films by Albert Lewin,[39] consists in introducing specific inserts – raising then questions more aesthetic than world-centered – rather than developing the surface of the canvas in a distinct world.[40] However, the second case considered by Dubois participates in the formation of *mental worlds* and, as one learns by reading this article, there were many films prior to the period discussed in this essay that had already used this stratagem so as to motivate the heterogeneity of their signifier. In reality, color is a physical phenomenon strongly linked to questions of subjectivity, since it cannot exist independently of the observer who perceives the luminous range. In a way, this dependence parallels certain paradoxes of quantum physics whose more or less direct influence on the creators of fictional worlds during the second half of the twentieth century is well documented.[41] The role of color as one of the criteria applied to distinguish between different worlds, especially in scenes centered on a character's introspective journey, is unsurprising.

Importantly, Dubois insists on the recurring leitmotif of the passage between two universes. The shift between different types of images introduces a breach in the film's editing flow (as in *Kafka*'s reverse shot) or, when it occurs within a single shot, it breaks up the unity of the image, transforming it into a hybrid representation disposed to the depiction of a two-world universe (as in the occasional and fleeting cases of a "frame within a frame" in *The Wizard of Oz*). The main problem addressed by Dubois is the materialization of a transit point that draws a borderline between two different worlds. *Stalker* (1979) is undoubtedly a science fiction film that articulates most productively all three of the following criteria: spatial organization, multiverse, and variations affecting the chromatic quality of the image. A screen adaptation of a Strugatsky Brothers novel, *Roadside Picnic*, which focuses on the growing fascination of one of its protagonists for a number of curious objects left on Earth by the inhabitants of another world,[42] the film's story leads us into the "Zone", a clearly delimited area littered with industrial and military ruins. The human smuggler, who is in the service of a writer and a professor, describes the "Zone" as a place riddled with traps insofar as it constitutes an ever-changing space, constantly tuning into the psychological state of those who enter it. Crossing its border means transgressing a prohibition. Moving across the railroad track on a small wagon, the protagonists lead us from the reassuring exterior to the sinister interior, but also from a sepia monochromatic image to color – before the hues fade away once again to give way to the characters' subjective gaze. The narration in *Stalker* is organized around the visitors' advance inside the Zone, their destination being the "Room" (said to grant the deepest wishes of a sincere believer). The story focuses almost entirely on a journey punctuated by obstacles mentioned verbally but never really shown on screen. To define the objects of this world is to partake in a mystical belief.

In Andrei Tarkovsky's film, as in the examples mentioned by Dubois, the differentiation between black & white and color is radical, as is the distinction between the opposite sides of a two-world universe. What does appear to be novel in our corpus of contemporary films lies in the discreet and targeted use of color facilitated by the possibilities for a selective desaturation secured by digital technology, thus making it possible to define an entire spectrum of intersections between different worlds. In this way, the first world can be invaded to varying degrees by the second world, while this very process can be correlated to the evolution of the film's story. For instance, the presence of a limited number of elements in color within a black & white (or a monochromatic) shot is rather common in Frank Miller's work (*Sin City,* 2005; *The Spirit,* 2008; *Sin City: A Dame to Kill For*, 2014). As for the little girl's dress in *Schindler's List* (1993), it is not improbable that Steven Spielberg was inspired for this famous scene by the shot of the red-colored flag in *Battleship Potemkin* (1925) that was hand-tinted onto each relevant frame in some of the film's copies. Thanks to its partial (but also biased, subjective) character, this practice – in a way an heir to early cinema's stencil coloring procedures – highlights the artificiality of color as a means of visual representation, not because the film universe is composed of two distinct worlds, but because its referent is not the real, but an already existing representation (for instance Miller's own graphic novels and, in particular, his drawing style).[43]

In the sixth episode ("This Extraordinary Being") of the HBO limited TV series *Watchmen* (2019),[44] the female hero, Angela Bar (Regina King), swallows some "Nostalgia" pills[45] and takes an immersive dive into the memories of her grandfather, a victim of white supremacists. These memories mix color – an episode relating to the Tulsa race massacre of 1921 from which her grandfather managed to survive – and black & white, alternating them from one shot to another or even combining them within a single shot. For instance, during a long sequence shot, a police car drives away and we discover the bodies of two black men attached to the vehicle, depicted in color within a black & white image. This composite image can be seen as a subjective and premonitory vision of a young black police officer intimidated by his colleagues. In the previous episode ("Little Fear of Lightning"), there is mention of a fictitious film allegedly directed by Steven Spielberg, *Pale Horse*, which in this alternate reality is supposed to have triumphed at the 1992 Oscars.[46] As one of the characters describes a shot from this film showing a little girl, the HBO series' viewers will undoubtedly be reminded of the young Holocaust victim in *Schindler's List*[47] (a film that in our world actually won seven Academy Awards in 1993): "There's this one scene with this little girl in a red coat. The movie is black and white, the red really pops, you know". The reference to Spielberg's film allows *Watchmen* to openly pose questions of historical memory: there is a high-tech museum built in the memory of the victims of Tulsa, compared here to the victims of the Holocaust. At the same time, the series transforms the historical trauma into a sci-fi incident: a giant squid suddenly appears in Manhattan and supposedly crosses a teleportation-window that reduces the entire city to ashes and traumatizes its inhabitants (in this case, the fictional "2/11" disaster is reminiscent of 9/11 terrorist attacks).

In *Watchmen*, the co-presence of color and black & white represents an entanglement of temporal strata, pointing to the permanence of racism in a more latent form.[48] The topic of racial struggles was added to the original material – the comic series however deals with the excesses and abuses of vigilantism leading to fascism – and may be linked to the 2018 release of the superhero movie *Black Panther*, while also foreshadowing the impact of the George Floyd protests in 2020. Nevertheless, the representational strategies in the flashback scene from episode 6 have a strong world-centered dimension, since Angela's body is sometimes depicted in the past scenes as her grandfather's, acting like a spectator (the case in *Spider*, *The Awakening*, or *Pacific Rim*) and not a subject. Therefore, it gives the impression that the young black man from the 1940s is being used as an "avatar" by the young woman in 2019. Angela does not listen to someone recounting for her sake the events her grandfather had to undergo; she relives herself these events through him, immersed in the world that was his. Therefore, the question of subjectivity takes on a more complex form here than in *Rumble Fish* (1983). In Coppola's film, where the goldfishes are the only (or almost) element in color in a black & white film, the "vision" of the color-blind "Motorcycle Boy" (Mickey Rourke) contaminates the "world" of his admiring brother, Rusty. Still, the universe in Coppola's film is not stratified into several worlds, whereas *Watchmen*, just like *Westworld*, emphasizes its world-centered dimension. In the episode "Genre" (S03E05) from *Westworld*, a drug is injected into Caleb (Aaron Paul) plunging him into a state that consists in living, as one of his teammates, Giggles (Marshawn Lynch) puts it, a "movie marathon" through different film genres (recognized mostly through the soundtrack). In a series that fundamentally associates worldbuilding with film genres, the subjective perception shared by the viewer and Caleb involves the superimposition of filters on the representation of the sci-fi megalopolis, which in this particular season has replaced the sets of a western. The first of these filters is that of the "film noir" genre, alluded to by the music score and by the insertion of black & white shots in a chase scene filmed in color. This episode is crucial in the story's evolution since the world, whose utopian character was until then guaranteed by an artificial intelligence, is plunged into chaos – none other than "reality" itself created by an android named Dolores (see *supra* Chapter 3). That being said, the black & white images are not connected with the ontology of one of the series' worlds.

This is however the case with *Avalon* (2001). The daily environment of a professional female gamer in retirement, spending her days plugging into a central computer server, is filmed in a monochromatic fashion[49] in contrast with the sepia war video game sequences. Inside this(these) world(s), certain discreet items are represented in color, such as snacks presented as particularly precious (for instance, the "materiality" of a piece of meat is highlighted through a bright red color) or any component related to electricity (like orange markings on computer screens, the computer circuit arrangement bathed in a yellowish light, the yellow-tinted tramway lights, etc.). The selection of specific elements of the environment through color can also be seen as a reference to many other practices in terms of cultural representations. To provide some examples: the traditionally less realistic use of color in early cinema, as studied by Tom Gunning, where color was not "due to indexical photographic processes but was manufactured by various processes of more or less arbitrarily applied color" (Gunning 1995: 249); the shifting between different representational levels as in the bandes dessinées *La Tour* and *Julius Corentin Acquefacques* Vol. 2 (the poster depicted in color in *Avalon* announces the forthcoming concert and participates in a visual self-reflexivity); lastly, the special status of "actionable" objects in "Beat'em Up" video games, most notably meals and snacks (like for example the apples in *Streets of Rage 2*, Sega, 1992). The presence of colored items in *Avalon*, to which the female protagonist does not seem to pay particular attention, underlines the status of the black & white image as an element of discrepancy between representation and "reality". The selective use of touches of color echoes the *subtractive* approach already discussed in regard with multiverse films that aim to signify the virtual nature of one of their worlds (see Chapter 3). It should be mentioned as an anecdotical tip that film technicians use the term "subtractive" in order to qualify the various processes through which color is obtained on screen. These processes, known as "additive or subtractive synthesis", reconstruct color through a filtering of the light captured inside the profilmic space.

At the end of *Avalon*, the restitution of the world is complete. To the protagonist's surprise, we shift to a world filmed entirely in color – an indication that this is the most "furnished" of the film's worlds. Following the principle of inversion at the heart of the story, according to which the deeper one sinks into the levels of the game, the closer she comes to reality's surface (unless we interpret things in the opposite sense and consider this reality to be the ultimate simulacrum), we are invited to think that this colored environment is the "first world" – after all, the message "Welcome to Class Real" appears on the screen. From that moment on, the wastelands filmed in black & white give way to a truly *populated* megalopolis, a world in the common sense of the term. In order to reach this ultimate stage, the protagonist had to eliminate an "end-of-the-level boss", according to a structure typical of video games. However, this particular boss hardly compares with the imposing monsters one is usually forced to deal with in the final stages of a video game. This boss is actually a young girl, the last of the nine enchantresses of the lands of Avalon, coming straight out of the Arthurian legend – thus introducing here a different level of (mythological) fictionality. Represented as a virtual projection in color, she breaks down into strips – namely, lines of code shown as a medium whose facticity is exhibited, like a cracking mirror – as a bullet from the protagonist's revolver hits her body. This virtual character inside a *virtual world* may very well lead one to associate color with the idea of simulacrum (as long as one remains within the confines of a binary conception the film itself invites us to overcome) but other elements plead in favor of a progressive "de-virtualization". Resembling our own world of reference, this "stage" fully imposes its presence upon the viewer at a time when most movies are in color. Moreover, while music was presented as extra-diegetic in relation to the film's previous worlds, it is here reported to a source within the image (the musicians of a Philharmonic in concert), following a process of diegetization that also applies to the chromatic dimension of the image. As the female hero, gun in hand, slowly emerges from an underground passage leaving darkness and entering light, she discovers through a threshold, represented by an iron door, a whole new world: color gradually appears within the close-up shot showing the young woman's surprise at the sight of what still remains out of frame for the viewer. The reverse shot proves to be rather banal, since we see nothing more than an ordinary city (in this case Warsaw) with its trams and crowded streets. However, one might detect here an intertextual reference likely to put into perspective our certainty of being in the presence of the real: the first reverse shot that follows the close-up on the young woman's gaze shows two cable cars crossing each other and the first individuals to appear on the screen are filmed through their reflection in a window. Could we still be in a world of appearances? In composing this shot sequence, Mamoru Oshii was perhaps thinking of a particular shot in *Dodesukaden* (1970), the first film in color by his compatriot Akira Kurosawa. In this shot, a young man who takes himself for a tram driver comes out of the hovel he lives in with his mother, and a cable car (existing only in the boy's mind) is reflected on the dusty windows of the façade, as if it was passing on the other side of the street, when in fact this street is deserted and full of rubble.

Avalon is a multiverse film that uses color as a factor determining the ontological status of diegetic components. These components are isolated through a selective use of color that underlines the constructed character of the world in question, represented as a combination of "monads". At the same time, the film makes explicit reference to video game practices, even if its aesthetics – throughout more Tarkovskian than Wachowskian – are at the antipodes of the representational norms established by the video game industry. Adopting a low-tech aesthetic common in contemporary science fiction films (*Dark City, eXistenZ*, and generally comics and movies referring to the steampunk genre),[50]

Avalon paradoxically combines a virtualization, linked to video game worlds arranged in several stages, with an insistence on the physical and "haptic" presence of the objects in these worlds: the film's soundscape makes the viewer feel the "heaviness" of the old and rusty Soviet armored vehicles of the story, the faded images evoke archival material, etc. The worlds' structure does not possess the smooth clarity of a film like *TRON* (1982) and is further blurred by stylistic choices that summon parasitic or contradictory references, especially on the level of the film's genre.

Filtering through the grid of features commonly associated with distinct film genres plays an important part in a viewer's apprehension of a world. I will end this section and my study of color as an element connoting a world's otherness with the example of *Pleasantville* (1998). The film projects its two young heroes, Jennifer (Reese Witherspoon) and David (Tobey Maguire) (Fig. 31), in the black & white world of a 1950s sitcom while motivating this journey with a playfulness that allows the narrative situation to retain all its incongruity: a TV repairman appears out of nowhere and, noting that David knows inside out all the episodes of a series named "Pleasantville" (as if he already lived inside this fictional world), hands over to the young protagonists a new remote control with magical powers, replacing the one they destroyed during an earlier argument. As the two quarrel again over which show to watch, a button in this futuristic remote control is pressed and suddenly the young protagonists are absorbed into the series' world, at the exact moment they were occupying the same position within the frame as their "alter egos" inside the visible in the background small screen. David and Jennifer are dematerialized and relegated to the status of a representation, their figures woven with stripes, as if the lines of a cathode-ray tube were running through them. After the TV image shifts instantaneously to an anamorphic format, Jennifer and David take the place of their avatars inside "Pleasantville". In what seems like a mild version of Cronenberg's *Videodrome* (1983) – but one could even go back to Méliès and his *La Photographie électrique à distance* (1908) – this transfer takes place in a single "shot" and the continuity reinforces the impact of crossing over the interworld threshold, allowing us to observe for a brief moment the two actors literally framed inside the reference world, prisoners of the black & white small screen. This specific shot attests to the co-presence of two distinct worlds. However, the first world will not appear again until the film's final minutes. *Pleasantville*'s two-world structure is based on the principle of embedding, not of alternation. *WandaVision* (2021), a recent TV mini series based on the "Marvel Cinematic Universe" (that sets some milestones for a forthcoming feature film significantly titled *Doctor Strange and the Multiverse of Madness*), takes up the principle of a parallel world represented in the style of an old sitcom (starring two "Avengers"!). At the same time, it develops this principle following a serial logic, as each episode corresponds to a different decade, signified by its own TV style, going from the 1950s to the early 2000s (black & white is replaced by color only

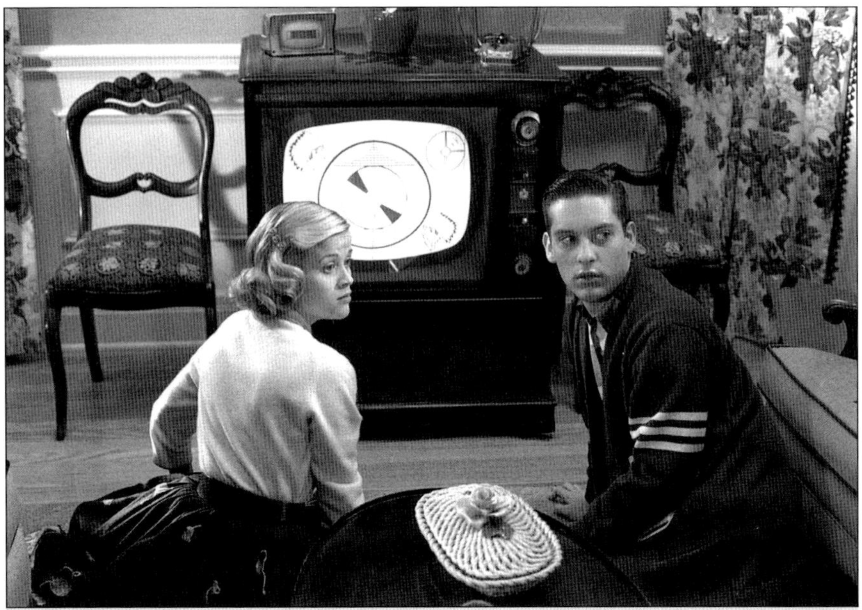

Fig. 31: *Pleasantville* (1998), a film directed by Gary Ross (*The Hunger Games*, 2012): two teenagers (Reese Witherspoon and Tobey Maguire) are thrown into the black & white world of a 1958 sitcom, thanks to the invention of a whimsical TV repairman (a profession destined to disappear in the early 2000s as CRTs are replaced by liquid-crystal displays).

at the end of the second episode). From episode 5 onwards, an alternation is added to the embedding, that between the "fiction-within-the-fiction" and the characters evolving outside the cosmic microwave field they try to fathom.

I will not dwell on the film's narrative construction or the development of its characters since these aspects have already been discussed in detail by James Walters (2008: 191–212). It should be noted though that David's character is defined by a nostalgia for a fantasy vision of the 1950s (rather than the real version of that era), as a sort of pre-Vietnam Eden. According to Fredric Jameson, this nostalgia is recurrent in escapist and reactionary New Hollywood productions of the 1980s – the ones the author classifies as "nostalgia" films (Jameson 1991; see also Jullier 1997: 21–22) – which "construct the adult spectator as a child, or, more precisely, as a childish adult" (Wood 1986: 145).[51] However, *Pleasantville* does not adopt the regressive attitude one finds in *Back to the Future* (1985). Like in *The Truman Show*, released in the same year, where the fantasy representation of the American way of life in a small town reminiscent of the New Urbanism movement is the product of a reality television show,[52] *Pleasantville* addresses this attitude directly and questions it. Instead of striving to abandon the second world altogether and leave it intact, the protagonists enjoy staying there and, at the initiative of Jennifer, undertake the task of transforming it. While *Back to the Future* confused the past with its mythical image, *Pleasantville* concentrates on that image, unfolding it through a world-centered design. Paul Grainge speaks of a "transportation [...] into the *world* of a sitcom" (2003:204), while Walters explains the implications of this strange journey through the history (of TV representations) in these words:

> Yet, David and Jennifer do not move back through time when journeying to Pleasantville. That would involve them moving to a realm spatially, chronologically and dimensionally continuous with the real world they already inhabited. Instead, they transfer into a fictional world, discontinuous with the world they have left (Walters 2008: 194).

The two-world universe of *Pleasantville* is composed of a *virtual world* which, totally disjointed as it is from the space-time of the frame story, cannot give birth to an alternative world, as the protagonists in *Back to the Future* are afraid may happen in their case. Instead of a traditional opening credits sequence, *Pleasantville* proposes a deliberately old-fashioned commercial that already from the beginning grants the film's spectators the position of the viewers *inside* the film, watching the TV series that lends its title to the feature film. The commercial announces a special evening devoted to this sitcom with the broadcast of several of its episodes. In terms of graphic signs, it conforms to the way viewers from the late 1990s would imagine a 1950s TV spot. Therefore, an aesthetic filter conceived in reference to specific representational norms is applied right from the outset. The visual patterns present in this meta-commercial are not insignificant: on a United States map, demarcating the territory within which the values advocated by the series are preeminent, the fictitious locality of Pleasantville appears on numerous occasions as an allusion to the ubiquitous power of TV broadcasting and to the status of the sitcom's world as a model, recognized as such by TV viewers from various different states. This inaugural mapping is also significant to the film and the series' world-centered dimension: the title "Pleasantville" refers to a city, a location on an imaginary map. This incoherent geography – where diversity is reduced to the Same – becomes explicit during the classroom sequence, when Jennifer realizes that for all the inhabitants of Pleasantville, the city is limited to two streets: where the one ends, the other begins. This circularity recalls the motif of insularity, echoes the narrative pattern of the loop (like in *Groundhog Day*), and transforms the representational space into a prison (as in Carpenter's *In the Mouth of Madness* or Shyamalan's TV series *Wayward Pines*),[53] since Pleasantville is described as an outdated utopia, the result of an obtuse moral rigor and patriarchal structure.

At the level of the value system inherent in the dominant representations of the 1950s, the worlds' interpenetration will bring about transformations within the host world. Ignoring the main taboo of the era, Jennifer introduces the characters she meets on her way to sexuality – more precisely to heterosexuality – upsetting the laws of this petty-bourgeois and phallocentric world.[54] Initiated by her "daughter" to solitary pleasures (as she cannot count on her husband whose attitude is shaped by the Hays Code), the mother of the family will literally "set the world on fire": her loud orgasm will ignite an unexplained fire in the garden of this previously prude family, the flames associating the graphic sign of color with the expression of carnal pleasure. From that moment on, the "flame" contaminates other areas of this small town previously condemned to the limitations of platonic love imposed by TV norms of the 1950s. Lovers' lips are red, a student's bubble gum pink, while other teenage couples are depicted in color among their monochrome classmates. Color acts as a metaphor (Color Plate 13). The reaction from the city's male elite to this sudden erotic and social uprising, echoes in a caricatured manner the racial and feminist struggles that rocked America shortly after the period during which the series supposedly takes place. Still, color also transforms the world in a concrete manner that is perceptible to those who inhabit it: a factor of recognition or ostracism, it is visible by all and manifests the intersection of two distinct worlds within the same image. It is therefore not surprising to find the leitmotif of pictorial representation through the character of a bar owner who decides to pursue his artistic aspirations. Color overflows the frame and fills the entire town to which the film's embedded world is reduced.

In conclusion, while being a convention of representation fundamentally extra-diegetic, since it regulates the spectator's relation to the film, color may also be considered "diegetic" in certain multiverse movies. The term "filter" introduced by Marie-Laure Ryan seems even more appropriate here as it is also used concretely to describe a number of technical interventions necessary at various stages of a film's production in order to elaborate the chromatic rendering of the image. This intermediate status of color, related both to diegetic components and the medium of the representation itself, allows metalepsis: in *Avalon* or in *Pleasantville*, color is not only a stylistic element but also a component of a world.

Philip K. Dick's World-Editing Process

In the next few pages, I propose to examine some cases in which the cinematic signifier's discontinuity illustrates the relationship between an individual and an environment caught up in constant fluctuations – provoked actually by the continuous succession of the film's frames – that affect the individual's "being-in-the-world". Famously, this is exemplified in *Sherlock Jr.* (1924) when Buster Keaton's dreamt alter ego straddles the boundaries of the screen. Right before falling into the world of a "film within a film", he suffers the consequences of a series of abrupt transformations in his environment caused by the way the film is edited. Instead of materializing itself through seamless editing, the transition from one world to another occurs through *jump cuts.*

In his short prose poem, "Indifference" (1917), Philippe Soupault transcribes the unique experience of a film viewer whose eyes identify with the angles the camera successively adopts. He describes an environment that undergoes constant retractions, transformations, and/or changes of scale. The immobility of the poem's subject, around which the components of an unstable world revolve, echoes that of the film spectator and, in some movies, that of his diegetic alter ego, as in Resnais' *Je t'aime je t'aime* (1968) where a worldbuilding machine functions the way film projection does in *Sherlock Jr.* One finds in Alain Resnais' filmography (that switches to fiction during the 1960s' "cinematic modernity", while also strongly influenced by the surrealist movement) the patterns advocated by the French avant-garde of the 1920s and translated into literary prose by Soupault around the time of Apollinaire's "New Spirit". Since the transparent, invisible editing constitutes one of the essential principles of Hollywood cinema, I will now turn to another area of world cinema landscape in order to examine this particular issue. First, though, I will take a detour to comment on the short story cited in the beginning of this chapter; as we shall see, the correlation between film editing and worldbuilding is not exclusive to on-screen representations, but also informs the portrayal of technology as imagined by a novelist like Philip K. Dick.

In his short story "The Electric Ant", Dick develops a recurring pattern in his literary work: the implantation of a false memory into the brain of a fictional character consequently deluding himself about his own identity. Once exposed, the past to which this false memory refers to comes to constitute a fiction-within-a-fiction, utterly disjointed from the actual world the hero inhabits. While hospitalized as a result of an accident, the protagonist of this particular short story, Garson Poole, is told by a doctor that he is not human: suddenly, all his life appears to him as an illusion. To assert his free will, he decides to tamper with the mechanism that manufactures his universe: instead of a heart (or the phonograph serving as lungs in the case of the android in Villiers de l'Isle-Adam's *Tomorrow's Eve*), Poole discovers a strip of tape, strewn with holes, that rolls in front of a scanning head. As described by Dick, this mechanism falls midway between the card or the perforated cylinder used since the 18th century for programming the animation of automatons (Poole compares it with a "player piano") and the audio (or the video) tape. Written in 1969, a year after Philips and Sony commercialized the first reel-to-reel video recorders using magnetic tapes, this story reflects the technologies of its time while also engaging to a kind of media archeology. Poole's act of tearing the "reality-supply construct" out of his chest would see its equivalent in the era of magnetic media in *Videodrome* (1983), when pornographic producer Max Renn (James Woods) inserts a videocassette into his womb. The life-saving extraction grants the former the demiurgic control of a world reshaped into an egocentric artifact, while the sexually suggestive penetration leads the latter to a complete alienation from his individuality, his identity dissolving into the cathode ray tube. These patterns are recurrent in cyberculture and will be examined further in Chapter 5. Here, I will focus on the place given to cinema in general, and the editing process in particular, as a model within Philip K. Dick's text.

Poole discovers that by adding or covering a number of "punch-holes" – a term reminiscent of the film perforations or "sprocket holes" used for transporting and steadying the film inside the camera and the movie projector – he can actually alter the universe surrounding him. Thus, this subtractive logic is linked to a worldbuilding process: "He had been right, every punch-hole covered up meant the disappearance of some object in his reality world" (Dick 1969: 107). Then, the protagonist undertakes a different operation, described in this chapter's opening quote, aiming not just to alter the existing world by inserting specific punch-holes, but to create a new world by adding perforations in a random way. This is a decisive moment in the unfolding of the story since Pool shifts from tampering with memories to manufacturing a whole new world. Specifically, this part highlights what Kittler considers, in Lacanian terms, the transition from the Symbolic era typified by the written text (and the musical score) to that of the Real, established by the storage of sound elements thanks to the advent of the phonograph (Kittler 1986). It is no accident that Dick refers to a "player piano" (an element present in the opening credits as well as in numerous scenes in the *Westworld* TV series, as we have seen) since the use for "productive" purposes of such imprints pertaining to the realm of the Real would mainly occur, prior to the "pixel" era, in the field of sound technologies,[55] from Moholy-Nagy's striped drawings (where sound exists unrelated to any prior acoustic phenomenon),[56] studied by Kittler, to *musique concrète* and synthesizer music later on. Poole's actions in "The Electric Ant" should then be analyzed with regards to the operations examined by Kittler at the "encoding" level, associated with phonography, cinematography, and the typewriter. However, what is different in this sci-fi tale is that an entire, immersive and utterly illusionistic world unfolds from the tape.

Poole is a brilliant craftsman, as he proves by plunging his hands into the internal organs of the machine. Substituting the thermal tool with a glue, and the scanning head with the editing table's or the projector's lamp, one quickly realizes, upon reading the detailed description of this particular *operation*, the extent to which cinema serves as a model to the way a relationship between a perceiving subject and a particularly immersive representation is imagined. After reshaping the texture of his world, Poole intervenes on its temporality: the artificial, mechanical construction of a world is envisaged in terms of editing. Reversing the direction the tape scrolls does not seem enough to Poole. In his words: "What would all that prove? A video tape running backward …" (Dick 1969: 112). The aim of the Promethean task he undertakes is closer to a kind of "total cinema" in the way Barjavel conceived it.[57] Reconfigured in a maelstrom of sensory perceptions, the perpetually recreated elements of the world end up illegible, leading Poole to his downfall. The same can be said for the memories reactivated by a "worldbuilding machine" in *Je t'aime je t'aime* (1968), a film based on an original screenplay by science fiction author Jacques Sternberg,[58] released around the same time Philip K. Dick imagined his "Electric Ant". The difference between Dick's short story and Resnais' film lies in the fact that in the latter the act of editing affects the very medium of the representation.

A Derailed Montage: Alain Resnais' Time/World-Machine

Alain Resnais is undeniably familiar with the basic principles of a multiverse movie. The *Smoking/No Smoking* diptych (adapted from the theatrical play *Intimate Exchanges* by British writer Alan Aycbourne), whose story exploits the various possible alternatives from a tree-shaped pattern,[59] is not the only example to be found in his filmography. This is also evidenced by a recurring trope in the director's films, namely the constant transformation of the sets. In *Last Year at Marienbad* (1961), architectural elements are reconfigured into distinct spaces, abolishing the borders between *here* and *elsewhere* (or *outside* and *inside*), in favor of an all-encompassing mental space governed by a voice-over. In *Providence* (1977), a terrace opens onto three different spaces depending on what the character imagines, while stairs appear inside a suddenly expanding apartment (see Liandrat-Guigues and Leutrat 2006: 90–91). In *Life is a Bed of Roses* (1983), the glass paintings, created by comic book author Enki Bilal, interject on the filmed environment the filter of children's imagination, bathed in heroic fantasies; these children take refuge in their own world[60] while an academic conference on children's imagination is taking place (in which the theme of "subcreation" is addressed via the construction of a replica model). One is also reminded of *You Ain't Seen Nothin' Yet* (2012), Resnais' first film ever to use computer-generated images that gradually place the actors-spectators of the "film-within-the-film" in the changing environments mentioned in the text of *Eurydice*, recited by these characters; the film goes as far as juxtaposing the variants of the same set through split-screens that divide the image into two distinct subjective visions.

Resnais' body of work combines in an unprecedented manner literary erudition and pop culture. The latter nourishes the representation of the protagonists' inner world (often depicted as an accumulation of stereotypes), introducing thus a visual and aural heterogeneity. That is for instance the effect produced by the shifts from one genre to another in *Providence* (a film haunted by a Lovecraftian subtext), the inserts of black & white clips in *My Uncle from America*, the embedding of drawn characters in *I Want to Go Home*, or the post-synchronization of excerpts of music hits in *Same Old Song* (see Boillat 2014c and Boillat 2016). In each case, the coexistence of different worlds manifests itself through a shock, not a suture in editing. In Alain Resnais' cinema the representation of a world is exhibited as such, a feature that works against the "suspension of

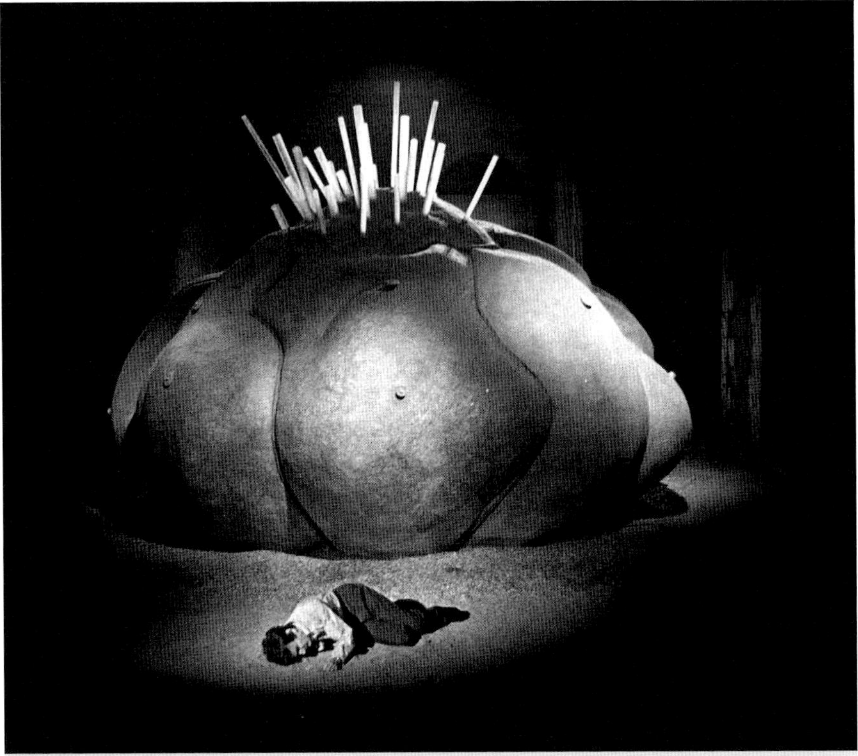

Fig. 32: The body of Claude Ridder (Claude Rich) prostrate before the brain-like machine in a production still from *Je t'aime je t'aime* (1968), an image absent from the film.

disbelief" and the act of immersion in these worlds. This is worldbuilding in action, represented as a process, not as a result.

In *Groundhog Day* (1993), or other similar films in which the hero is trapped in a time loop, the discontinuity established by the numerous repetitions of an identical sequence of events is strongly attenuated by the linear narrative in each of these sequences. By contrast, Alain Resnais shatters this principle of intelligibility: the sci-fi pattern of the time machine in which Claude Ridder is caught (Claude Rich), a survivor of a failed suicide attempt who accepts to be the guinea pig in a scientific experiment, justifies a fragmentation carried out within a single shot, sometimes even within a frame. A device referred to as the "sphere" by the scientists who designed it (Fig. 32), resembling a cocoon, a brain, or a pumpkin (like the one in fairy tales, waiting to be transformed into a modern day carriage) is central to the film's story. The sphere's fetal den, mirroring the film apparatus inside the diegesis, can also be seen as a *mental world*, especially in view of its physical similarity with the organ of the brain. According to Gilles Deleuze, "Resnais has always said that what interested him was the brain, *the brain as world*, as memory, as 'memory of the world'" (Deleuze 1989: 121–122).[61]

The philosopher considers Resnais' cinema as an emblematic case of the "Time-Image" concept he develops in his book, since he implicitly opposes this concept to the Leibnizian notion of incompossibility:[62] the "Movement-Image" is linked to a chronology subjected to the imperatives of an action, the objective, the *actual*, whereas the "Time-Image" concerns the *virtual*, the coexistence of "*undecidable alternatives* between circles of past" (*Ibid*: 105).

In *Je t'aime je t'aime*, the machine, proven operational when applied to laboratory mice, malfunctions when confronted to the complexity of a human subject. The realm of the imaginary contaminates the rationality of science, giving a concrete form to the idea formulated at the beginning of the film by the head of the laboratory: "I always thought that we could benefit from having a team of novelists working for us, paid to put their wild ideas on paper". Claude Ridder is himself a novelist whose behavior is not the one expected by the scientists. For Resnais, who started his career as a film editor, science fiction serves as a pretext for disrupting the arrangement of the film's shots, extending thus some of the filmmaker's earlier experiments. One may be surprised that Resnais, commonly associated by critics with a sort of "cerebral" realism rather than genre cinema, showed an interest in science fiction. Nevertheless, it should be noted that as a great collector of comic books from the golden era and an active member of the *Club des bandes dessinées* (C.B.D.; see Groensteen 2006: 110–117 and Boillat 2010c: 63-65), the director was imbued with this type of culture, as evidenced by the (aborted) project of adapting *Harry Dickson* (Towarnicki 2007). Regarding *Last Year at Marienbad* (1961),[63] Resnais affirmed his influence by *Mandrake* (Thomas 1990: 238–239), a famous series of comics scripted by Lee Falk from 1934 onwards, recounting the tale of a magician whose powers would inspire the most absurd narrative arcs. Likewise, there is a kinship between the fictional "sphere" in *Je t'aime je t'aime* and the bizarre machines found in the multiverse comic strips *Brick Bradford* (William Ritt and Clarence Clay, since 1933).

The presence of a "worldbuilding machine", the references to the sci-fi genre, the entanglement between memory and imagination within a perpetual present, the actual transfer of the dreamer's body whose disappearance we witness in the frame story, as well as the particular aesthetics of montage, attest to the fact that in *Je t'aime je t'aime* memory gives access to a *world of its own*. In Resnais' cinema, the (traumatic) past tends to blend with fiction, as in the case of the French female character in *Hiroshima mon amour* (1959) and her tragic romantic affairs; once in love with a German soldier, she recalls her youth in a scene several commentators compare to a psychoanalytic session (Pingaud 2002: 74). The same could be said of Claude Ridder lying on the sofa during the experiment in *Je t'aime je t'aime*, even though he is actually talking to himself, with the viewer standing in for an absent analyst. Occasionally, the editing's syncopated rhythm suggests that the protagonist is not actually dreaming or remembering, but is simply delusional. Flashback scenes look indeed like a frenzied surge of subliminal images, as Ridder is forced to stay put. The way the film represents the hero's past echoes the way hallucinations have been envisioned in the medical field (Berton 2015: 255–265). The fact remains that Ridder is not subject to "visions": he is actually travelling into the past. Constantly present on screen, he is in truth more of the viewer's double inside the film than a real protagonist performing actions in his own past (we soon come to realize that the character had always been a disillusioned spectator of his own existence). There is one crucial exception to this: at the moment he attempts suicide (a scene replayed repeatedly), the possibility of a different world opens up. In their book on Resnais, Liandrat-Guigues and Leutrat refer to Foucault when examining this particular film. In *Dits et écrits*, the philosopher considers the desire for suicide as "filled with this world in which I would no longer be present only here or there, but everywhere", as a way of seeking to "rediscover the original moment when I make myself a world" (Liandrat-Guigues and Leutrat 2006: 81)[*]. *Je t'aime je t'aime* does not really deal with a journey through time, similar to the one in *La Jetée* (1962), directed by Resnais' close friend, Chris Marker – where, thanks to the use of still images, the element of discontinuity is present in even more radical terms – but with a return to a past governed by the character's subjectivity as conveyed by the film's editing. Paul-Louis Thirard commented on this distinction: "[Ridder] relives these scenes as a spectator. He is not endowed with the power to become alive again, physically speaking, in flesh and blood. When he meets Catrine, the latter does not embody 'the' past, but 'his' past" (Thirard 2002: 209)[*].

Compared to the hero in both Marker's short movie and its remake, *Twelve Monkeys* (1995), Ridder resembles even more a film viewer, passive as he remains in the dark room of his cocoon. As he vanishes from the sphere, he does not reappear anywhere else. He is disembodied into a presence-absence "outside of the film" that corresponds, in the theory of Christian Metz, both to the status of the cinematic "imaginary signifier" (Metz 1975: 28) and to the process of the spectator's "projection" into the film universe which "differs from the primordial mirror in one essential point: although, as in the latter, everything may come to be projected, there is one thing, and one thing only that is never reflected in it: the spectator's own body" (*Ibid*: 48). While the scientists in *Je t'aime je t'aime* see nothing of Ridder's past on their screens,[64] this privilege is nonetheless accorded to the viewer of the film who has access to a visualization of the protagonist's memories.

The recounting of Claude's past takes as its starting point a moment – actually a single minute – of his holiday in the south of France. This short sequence of actions will be tirelessly repeated, diffracted, and rearranged. Most notably, we witness it again in the middle of the film, precisely when Claude realizes that something has gone wrong, as if he could not escape from this moment in which his whole life seems to be enclosed, similarly to the way his body is confined within the "sphere". Martin Bubb, who insists on the role played by the idea of confinement in this film, goes as far as to speak of "Leibnizian monads" (Bubb 2010: 355–356). The repetition does not manifest itself through different versions successively played out by the actors (profilmic variations), as in the loops of *Groundhog Day*,[65] but by reorganizing similar shots within new combinations. The effect produced on the viewer is therefore that of a repetition affecting beyond the actions represented on-screen, *those of the film itself*. Immediately, after the image bounces a few times, while the blue of the sea alternates with the orange of the cocoon's membrane in quick flashes, the machine is set in motion and we discover a "scene" from the past, as Claude finds himself immersed at the bottom of the sea and starts rising to the surface. In this way, Resnais links an element present in the image – the waterline – with the film's editing pattern: when Ridder crosses the line marking the water's surface, the past gives way to the frame story, showing Claude lying on a "couch". On two different occasions, at the exact moment when Claude is about to emerge out of the water, we shift levels and the hero reappears sitting in the machine's armchair while a lyrical chant is audible, granting the scientific experiment a supernatural aura. In fact, one of the scientists compares this device to "a decompression chamber in which divers must be placed before they are brought back in the open air". For a viewer that has been knocked around by the editing's jaggedness and the shattering of all sense of meaning, these punctuations act as an "airlock" and emphasize the feeling of being confronted with two distinct worlds.

This type of two-world structure is reinforced in a more recent film, *Vanishing Waves* (2012), by Lithuanian director Kristina Buozyte, comparable to *Je t'aime je t'aime* in more ways than one. However, in *Vanishing Waves* the immersion works through the fused, sensual relationship between two lovers who meet and embrace in a world shaped by their desire (and more specifically by a female desire absent in Resnais' movie). Buozyte's film also uses the motif of water in order to slip between a shared dream and a scientific experiment. In this experiment, a researcher submerged in a water tank is connected to the brain of a young woman who fell into a coma after attempting to drown herself; he will then save her by gradually extracting her from the sea and from a magma of quasi-abstract images. In *Vanishing Waves*, the story is strongly based on the fact that the subject plugged into the machine deliberately withholds information by keeping the presence of his "virtual" lover secret and by stating that the image appearing in front of him is barely figurative (in stark contrast with the powerful, sensory immersion encouraged by the film itself). He is actually lying during his debriefings to the team of scientists when he allegedly recounts all that he – and the film's viewer alongside with him – observed and experienced during his numerous immersions in the world created by his interconnection with the young woman in a coma. This case constitutes a complete reversal both in terms of gender and of its actual outcome on the topic of suicide as it is presented in *Je t'aime je t'aime*.

In *Je t'aime je t'aime*, the original scene of the couple at the seaside, far more innocuous, is shown from the outside and completely disordered, with lines of dialogue repeated in an identical fashion at short intervals: the mind is already racing. Several autonomous shots follow that are impossible to establish in the chronology of Claude's life. The viewer reconstructs these fragments of dialogue and the various heterogeneous spaces thanks to a few reference points (specific landmarks in the career of the main character and in the evolution of his romantic relationships) and, mostly, thanks to particular diegetic clues (places, furniture, clothes, etc.).[66] Trapped in this kaleidoscopic world, Claude tries in vain to escape, making wild speculations that would probably delight *Lost*'s screenwriters ("the researchers died long ago and I'm stuck *here*, forgotten") as we simultaneously watch the scientists struggle to "bring him back".

Despite this temporal dispersion of clues, a unifying factor exists in *Je t'aime je t'aime*, a specific element around which all of Claude's memories and fantasies revolve: his companion, Catrine. The viewer never finds out for sure if her death was the result of an accident or whether Claude actually murdered her.[67] Catrine is the gravitational center in Ridder's *mental world*, as one of the film's posters graphically illustrates. It is shaped around a contrast between the male hero, depicted at the center of the image (as is the case in almost all of the shots that compose the film's egocentric embedded story), and a number of images of Catrine, as though she were spinning around him.[68] Claude could live "neither with her nor without her", as one of his friends puts it; this would explain the constant trips back and forth through time, regulated by the film's crosscutting, where Catrine is alternatively present or absent from the scenes represented on screen. The film is punctuated by an intentionally abrupt editing, giving access to a *mental world* that resembles a dislocated set of potential alternatives. As the stuttering in the film's title announces, the declaration of love, long repressed and finally uttered by the hero as death approaches, is caught both in a time-loop and the creation of a two-world universe.

Such a declaration could have been delivered by Joel Barish (Jim Carrey) in *Eternal Sunshine of the Spotless Mind* (2004), written by Charlie Kaufman, an author celebrated for his self-reflexive labyrinthine films. Lying on his bed wearing a special helmet, Joel is projected into different versions and various stages of the story of his relationship to Clementine (Kate Winslet). At first, the representation unfolds in a continuous way, in a pre-credits sequence of more than fifteen minutes that ends with the enigmatic appearance inside the embedded story of a character that we will later identify as one of the technicians from the frame story (where an electric short circuit has apparently occurred). However, the film will gradually run loose through jump cuts, accelerations, and various spatiotemporal inconsistencies as soon as a relation of subordination between the two levels is established: namely, a correlation between the gesture of one of the "operators", who tampers with a cable, and the mechanical repetition of the same movement by one of the characters inhabiting the

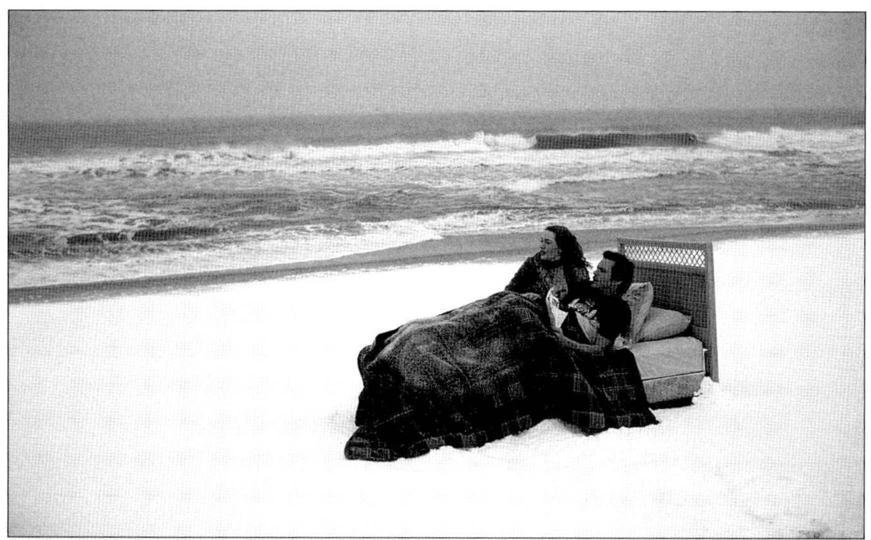

Fig. 33: Like the young hero in Winsor McCay's *Little Nemo in Slumberland*, Joel Barish (Jim Carrey) and Clementine (Kate Winslet) experience some abrupt changes of scenery inside an unstable *mental world* in *Eternal Sunshine of the Spotless Mind* (2004).

"dream". As a matter of fact, the film begins with the hero waking up, an action that in this type of *immersive mental worlds* functions most of the times as a sign of a possible transgression of the borders separating the two worlds (Fig. 33).

Subjected to the inescapable character of such a memory erasure procedure, Barish is trapped in loops that offer no way out, just like Ridder before him. For instance, when he gets out of his car and starts running towards Clementine, he walks, in opposite directions, the same path twice, without ever managing to reach the young woman, caught as he is in a loop from which his loved one is being repeatedly extracted. Michel Gondry breaks here one of the fundamental rules of continuity in cinema, the 180-degree-rule, established so that the characters' respective positions, and therefore the stability of the spatial representation, is maintained (Bordwell and Thompson 2009: 349–352). The resulting instability is not only a stylistic effect (as in *Breathless*, 1960) but also an element defining the represented world. The film's world-centered dimension is thus heightened: the *mental world* in which we find ourselves immersed is actually dissociated from the diegetic subject that creates it, since the latter is alienated from its own self due to a worldbuilding machine constantly re-articulating data extracted from his brain. As is frequently the case in Philip K. Dick's stories, memory gives birth to a series of possible alternatives.

Although seemingly Joel takes the role of a spectator witnessing a sum of repeated or stammered actions, he nevertheless anticipates these actions and even reacts on them, just like the protagonist in *Groundhog Day* (but unlike Ridder). This allows him to take refuge in his most regressive memories, avoiding – albeit temporarily – the Lacuna Inc. staff that seeks to eradicate every possible trace of Clementine from his brain. Jim Carrey's character suffers from the incessant transformations of his environment, witnessing the gradual erasure of some of its components. However, he tries his best to impose his will and keep the memory of his loved one. By comparison, the cynical and dispassionate hero of *Je t'aime je t'aime* is much more akin to the movie viewer, as both are spectators inside a "worldbuilding machine".

Principles of Assembly: Multiverse, Editing and Alternation

In this section, I propose to examine the way a film's editing participates in the alignment of distinct worlds and the passages between them. While examining a film's universe, one tends to extract from its narrative organization data of a semantic value and reorganize them on the basis of all the diegetic information transmitted. However, in order to study the relationship a film establishes with its viewer, it is also important to observe how this transmission takes place throughout the film and at which moment each one of the worlds becomes accessible to the characters and/or the spectator. Therefore, editing constitutes the key vehicle for a film's discursive organization. From the perspective of an analysis that takes as its object a film's diegesis, editing intervenes primarily to single out and organize narrative "tracks" associated with different worlds. I consider three principles to be the basic tools for this type of organization: alternation, embedding and juxtaposition. As in most multiverse movies the last two are combined with (and strongly determined by) the first one, I look at *alternation,* often discussed in film theory, as the single major principle of a multiple-world arrangement.[69]

As already discussed, *Je t'aime je t'aime* goes back and forth between distinct levels. The pattern of alternation is used in Resnais' film in two different ways: traditionally, signifying the simultaneity between two spatially close actions (the interior of the "sphere" and its surroundings), and radically, launching us in spurts into the memories of the experiment's subject. The differentiation between the linearity of the present and the fragmentation of the past is reversed at the very end of the film, once Claude comes full circle by repeating his suicide attempt. Only then the image of his body, lying on the lawn of the property where the experiment is taking place, interweaves with the representation of his past, a materialization that foreshadows the final passage between the worlds, when Ridder starts appearing surreptitiously in several neighboring spaces. The image of Claude lying on the lawn is reminiscent of a shot in *The Time Machine* (1960) in which the protagonist awakes in the distant future. However, there is no such machine at Claude's side, as he does not reappear inside the "sphere" but in the exterior of the building where the latter is to be found. This type of scene depicting an individual escaping the machine echoes, albeit in a more pessimistic fashion, many other multiverse films (i.e. "*The Matrix*"), while raising a question linked to the principle of alternation itself, concerning one essential aspect for the study of the semantic function of multiverse movies: the gap between each of the film's worlds.

The rather exceptional use of crosscutting in *Cloud Atlas* (2012), an adaptation of David Mitchell's novel of the same name, deserves to be addressed here. This film develops in a systematic manner the concept of visual echoes and symbolic resonances between parallel narrative tracks that one also finds in a multiverse film like *The Fountain* (2006).[70] It does so by combining *Run Lola Run*'s variations of possible alternatives with "*The Matrix*'"s world-centered design. *Cloud Atlas* simultaneously develops a number of plots set in six different eras,[71] constantly modifying the sets, the tone, the generic as well as the aesthetic references, but also the characters (even though they are played by the same actors). Whereas in Griffith's *Intolerance* (1916) the stories situated in the past served as allegorical counterparts to the central plot taking place in the present, in the film directed by Tykwer and the Wachowskis the various narrative tracks are organized in a much looser and less hierarchical way, shifting constantly between different eras. In the scale of a feature film, this type of segmentation favors a comparison with the one found in serial productions that are perpetually confronted with the idea of fragmentation and the incessant need to advance the plot. One could certainly argue that in *Cloud Atlas* all represented eras belong to one world ("our" world). Nevertheless, the heterogeneity in terms of representation – especially with respect to the lack of historical references, in a plot set in a post-apocalyptic scenery somewhere in the twenty-second century – as well as the systematic use of crosscutting, reveal a structure that viewers are tempted to consider as that of a multiverse (all the more so as the film's title refers to an imaginary map, if not a cosmogony). The principle of alternation makes one feel the gap between the various narrative tracks. Even if this gap is defined exclusively on a temporal basis, we are inclined to read it in world-centered terms due to the diversity of generic references, sets (a forest, a city, a maritime landscape, etc.), types of characters (from a clone placed in a sanitized environment to an ancient-like anthropophagus from a future conceived from the ruins of our civilization) and visual styles (in terms of dominant colors or certain framing features, such as depth of field).

When a mid-18th century maritime adventure meets a conspiracy plot (typical of '70s post-Watergate Hollywood thrillers) and the undoing of a dystopian society (in the style of *Soylent Green*) set in 2144, and, moreover, when the shift between these eras is periodically repeated, then this time travel offered by the cinematic machine ends up looking like a review of different film genres. It is as if the worldbuilding process is orchestrated by a narrator channel-surfing for the viewer's sake, swapping between images coming from different films. Even though the frequent recourse to continuity editing, based on visual associations, and the constant presence of specific narrative elements establish a certain coherence throughout the film,[72] the alternation itself highlights the act of representation and fractures the unity of "the" world. The similarities with multiverse movies discussed in this book are numerous – for instance the juxtaposition of archetypal sets related to specific film genres by a diegetic mise-en-scène in *Westworld* (1973, see Chapter 2). Still, there are no estrangement tactics to be found in *Cloud Atlas*, whereas in Michael Crichton's film the distanciation effect is based on a specific sci-fi premise. Furthermore, the music in *Cloud Atlas* does not function as the one in *Avalon*, where it oscillates between the diegetic and the extra-diegetic, depending on the world we find ourselves into. Instead, the same melody runs through the various narrative tracks (or levels) like an all-encompassing lyrical breath that federates on a quasi-mystical level the scattering of a multiverse.

The principle of alternation – namely, the minimum configuration of A-B-A-B, which can be repeated *x* times[72] – has been widely discussed within studies focusing on "crosscutting" from the point of view of the evolution of the "film language". Our goal here is to examine these observations in order to identify elements that could prove useful in a theory of worlds (and, conversely, to make a modest contribution in the study of this key figure of film editing by approaching it from a world-centered perspective). The importance given to this editing pattern by scholars who study from a historical-theoretical standpoint the institutionalization of specific narrative practices (exemplified by Griffith's films from 1908 to 1915) is arguably due to the fact that, in Genettian terms, crosscutting allows for the time of the *narrative* to be grasped independently from the time of the *story*. Alternation tends to emancipate the temporality established by the film discourse from the continuum dictated by profilmic actions. Admittedly, this can be said of all types of editing, since this process constitutes the fundamental element on which the distinction between "monstration" and "narration" is founded.[73]

Nevertheless, the ubiquity of a gaze not justified by the presence of any of the film's characters is accentuated in the case of an alternation: by creating two (or more) parallel tracks A and B (C, D, etc.), crosscutting ostensibly emancipates the film universe from its roots in the "real" and introduces it to the order of discourse. When the editing invites (or rather forces) the viewer to switch from track A to track B, the course of actions in track A is no longer "actual", since the spectator does not witness them on the screen but only infers them; one finds here an "open door" inviting the substitution of the actual by the virtual. Therefore, when the film goes back to track A, any temporal signified remains potentially possible, as the example of *Pulp Fiction* (1994) perfectly illustrates, a film that popularized experimentations with narrative temporality in contemporary Hollywood. The editing can resume a previously visualized track *at the precise moment* when we left it, or *at a subsequent time* (thanks to an ellipsis of a variable amplitude), or even *earlier* if the film chooses to show the same action twice.

Following on from Noël Burch's research on the progressive establishment of an "institutional mode of representation" in which "discontinuities in the picture produce narrative meanings" (Burch 1990: 143), Philippe Gauthier studied the recurring use of the principle of alternation in early cinema. He argued that it is necessary to establish certain criteria in order to distinguish between different types of spaces that are diegetically separated but brought together through crosscutting. As he points out, the physical distance separating spaces belonging to two different narrative tracks that appear alternatively on the screen can be understood in various ways:

> Even though it is relatively easy to distinguish between two "different spaces", it will always be possible for someone who wants to play devil's advocate to unify them in one and the same area. Two spaces can just as easily be considered as being part of *one* apartment, *one* block, *one* city or *one* planet (and, of course, *one* universe!) (Gauthier 2008: 39)*.

The maximum extension corresponding to "*one* universe" imagined by Gauthier suggests that if a film analyst with far-fetched ideas applied such a scale, he would immediately invalidate the relevance of all proposed categories. However, from the perspective adopted in this book, assimilating a space to (only) one universe actually proves to be extremely relevant. This does not preclude the division of the space into smaller units, but in such a case one could no longer talk of an *alternation between worlds*. This macro level will not prevent us from using the same "figures" forged to identify "distinct spaces" at a smaller level. The model borrowed by Gauthier from Gaudreault and Jost's *Le Récit cinématographique* (1990), which conceives the distance between diegetic spaces in a progressive manner, can very well be combined, at the level of the film representation, with the semantic definition of interworld gaps. After all, these gaps need to be "materialized" in one way or another. The various categories of "spatial alterity", going from *contiguity* to *disjunction*, may be conceived in a similar way within the framework of a *cosmic alterity*, where the criterion of a character's relocation – namely the accessibility between the world B and a component of the world A – is also a crucial factor. Discussing a concrete, physical space, Gaudreault and Gauthier argue that "the type of *spatial alterity by proximal disjunction* occurs when the camera takes the viewer through two adjacent spaces separated by a wall (spaces that would be contiguous were it not for this wall) without passing through the intermediary of a character leading us from one space to the other" (Gaudreault and Gauthier 2017: 119). For our part, we shall distinguish an alternation among worlds that include some points of intersection from an alternation between worlds that remain impermeable to each other. Therefore, the minimal case of a "visual contiguity" – defined as an "unhindered visual communication (the spaces considered are not separated by a wall)" (Gauthier 2008: 41)* – may present world-centered implications when a reverse shot allows the viewer to discover what lies beyond the threshold, inside another world, as in *Kafka* or *Fringe*'s episode "Who Framed Olivia Dunham" (see *supra*). A "wall" may actually exist between the worlds, visualized on the screen, suggesting the possibility of a mutual accessibility temporarily suspended. This would explain why this wall is often smashed by the film's hero in an emancipating – albeit deceptive – gesture, as in *Dark City*, *In the Mouth of Madness*, *The Cabin in the Woods*, or *Wayward Pines*.

As for the proximal ("there") and distal ("over there") disjunctions mentioned by Gauthier, they each possess a cosmic equivalent. To be sure, only exotic worlds fall under the criterion of spatial distance, the latter being literally "immeasurable" in the cases that interest us here. With that in mind, even in cases in which the physical distance cannot be applied with regard to the relation of one world to another, it provides at least an equivalent of the *gap* between the worlds, measured in light of the differences between laws that respectively govern each of the diegeses. The comparison is enlightening so far as a world's accessibility is very often communicated on screen in the form of a spatial materialization, thus involving the distal criterion – whether at the level of the distance implied during a cut or the distance depicted within a single shot, for instance by arranging actors and objects in order to emphasize the depth of field. Lastly, Gauthier identifies among the narrative programs defining a specific spatiotemporal configuration represented in the mode of alternation, one rather rare in early cinema, namely the "vectorized communication between two non-contiguous spaces" (Gaudreault and Gauthier 2017: 120). As we shall see in the next chapter, telephony constitutes one of the recurring "meta-fictional gadgets" in multiverse movies, from *World on a Wire* (1973) to *The Matrix* (1999).

In many ways, the observations made in the cases of alternation between different narrative tracks considered in their spatiotemporal relationships, also apply to the alternation between different worlds. Due to the requirements of an audio-visual representation, the latter usually occurs under the guise of a physical space, by virtue of a spatialization that may be actual or metaphorical. The ubiquity conferred by the film's editing in cases like these is then over-inflated, transcending the limits of the world.

French theoreticians often distinguish between *crosscutting* (*montage alterné*), that we have discussed so far, and *parallel editing* (*montage parallèle*), namely "a figure alternating two series and connoting some form of *parallelism* between two situations whose *temporal relationship* to each other *is of no relevance*" (Gaudreault and Gauthier, 2011: 27)[*]. One wonders what is actually replacing the suspended temporal signified in such cases. The examples often mentioned are metaphorical shots found mainly in silent movies of the 1920s that provide a counterpoint to the main action. However, this type of practice does not really amount to worldbuilding since it only gives rise to occasional inserts. In *Modern Times* (1936), when Chaplin juxtaposes the subway crowd with a flock of moving sheep, the viewer does not engage in any inferential process with regard to the world inhabited by the cattle. It is rather clear that they are ironically shown on screen to comment on the film's (and the viewer's) reference world.

The difference between the "alternate" and "parallel" categories was also important for the semiotician Christian Metz, who developed in the 1960s the model of the *Grand Syntagmatique*,[75] in an approach guided by the principles of structuralism. This model resulted from a reasoned identification within a film's image of segments likely to function as separate units and whose various combinations were supposed to summarize the ways film language can be used in narrative fiction. In his first effort to create such a practical typology, Metz distinguished between three sub-types of the "alternating syntagma": the "alternative editing" (in French: *montage alternatif*; namely, alternating between different actions as when filming a tennis match), the "alternate editing" (in French: *montage alterné*; known in English as *crosscutting*) in which "the signified of the alternation is diegetic simultaneity", and, lastly, the "parallel editing" (in French: *montage parallèle*) in which "the actions brought together have no relevant relation between them in terms of the temporal denotation and [in which] this defection of the denoted meaning opens the door to all possible 'symbolisms'." (Metz 1966: 121)*.

It is not without significance that this syntagma underwent a multitude of modifications in the final version of the Metzian model: the term of "editing" (*montage*) is replaced in a stricter manner by that of "syntagma", meaning a unit composed of a number of shots just like a phrase is composed of a number of words in verbal language (the heritage of linguistics, a critical and modeling field within structuralism, is obvious). Thus, Metz marks a break from previous literature on editing that approached this process from the perspective of aesthetics. Furthermore, the all-encompassing term "alternating" (*alternant*) is abandoned, as is the first sub-type, the "alternative editing" (Metz 1968: 107)*. Additionally, the semiotician introduced in his book a tree diagram in which eight types of syntagma are drawn, resulting from successive duplications; as a consequence thereof, the "parallel" and "alternate" syntagma occupy distinct and considerably distant spots in this diagram. In Metz's chart, the first element (in turn leading to two distinct branches) is respectively the chronological or the a-chronological character of the syntagma. Adapted to the study of dominant narrative cinema, in which Metz is first and foremost interested, the branch of chronological syntagma is privileged in his theory, since the a-chronological syntagma gives rise to only two sub-categories (distinguished by the presence or the absence of the figure of alternation, even if, incidentally, this criterion does not appear as such in the chart): the "accolade syntagma" and the "parallel syntagma". The latter, presenting "no precise relationship (whether temporal or spatial) between [the alternating] motifs" (*Ibid.*: 127)*, ends up marginalized, since it is ultimately defined in negative terms: to use the three criteria applied to the opposite branch, "parallel syntagma" is neither *chronological*, nor *narrative*, not even *linear*, whereas the "alternate syntagma" meets the first two criteria.

In view of this definition and following Metz's typology, a "parallel syntagma" in a single-world film could be qualified as an "alternate syntagma" in a multiverse movie in which the editing articulates different tracks, each associated to a specific world. In this way, this syntagmatic type becomes a narrative one. Such a shift underlines the importance of the concept of diegesis for the definition of the Metzian categories. In his very precise comments on the *Grand Syntagmatique*, Michel Colin draws attention to the fact that Metz mentions no specific film in the case of the parallel syntagma, but only offers general examples concocted for the occasion. According to Colin, "this does not mean that they are not valid examples but that it is difficult to find a specific example from a film that would exclusively fit the case of a 'parallel syntagma'." (Colin 1989: 20)*. Therefore, the characteristics and functions of this type of segment are diverse, as evidenced by its use in a world-centered perspective. Colin borrows an example from Jean Mitry: in the final scene in Vsevolod Pudovkin's *Mother* (1926), a crowd of workers on strike marching towards a prison, and a river current whose force smashes the blocks of ice floating on it, are depicted alternately. Not only do the workers cross a bridge spanning the same river so that the latter is retrospectively integrated into the diegetic (and even "proximal") space (as Mitry argued), but Colin remarks that an earlier temporal clue links the strikers' action to the images of the melting ice. Even though Metz does not mention it, the key element distinguishing between the parallel and the alternate syntagma is therefore whether the representations of the two series belong to "the" diegesis (or not). Colin devotes several pages of his book on this specific point and even uses the concept of "possible worlds". He envisages the argument of simultaneity made by Mitry as follows: "In order for a relation of simultaneity to be a diegetic relation, the spaces in which simultaneous events take place must be mutually accessible" (*Ibid.*: 21)*. By considering the accessibility between tracks related by the principle of alternation as an essential factor, one could argue that Michel Colin articulates a world-centered theory.

Discussing the effect produced by the use of comparative inserts in Soviet films of the 1920s as a form of alternation between the comparing and the compared,[76] Jean Mitry noted the need to bring the two terms together within the same space (as in the scene from *Mother* mentioned above). He based this normative statement on the following observation:

> On the contrary, in the case of cinema [as opposed to verbal language], the "image" [in the rhetorical sense of the term] does not belong to the same level as the image of the real, since the latter is also an image and, as such, it is objective and concrete just as much as the former. However, this is an image belonging to a different reality, located in a different time and a different place. Those two images cannot coincide. As identical or related they may seem intellectually, there is an antinomy between them from the point of view of the objective reality (Mitry 1963: 371)*.

In this 1963 text, through a perspective far different from the theories on the simulacrum soon to follow, it was precisely the idea that the film universe could actually present the structure of a multiverse that was deemed problematic by Mitry. This structure was considered as incompatible with the undifferentiated ontological status of the film representations, the image constantly anchored in "the" world. Mitry's single-world conception of the film universe led him to rule out the "non-coincidence" type that in our perspective corresponds to the co-presence of incompossible worlds. Unbeknownst to their author, these observations argue in favor of world-centered implications attached to parallel editing. In this book, I argue that in multiverse movies, *parallel* editing associates two or more *impermeable* worlds, whereas *alternate* editing (or *crosscutting*) correlates mutually *accessible* worlds.[77] Both figures can appear in different parts of the same movie and what initially may seem to viewers as parallel editing could be understood in hindsight as crosscutting (the opposite however is not true).

Consequently, the distinction between crosscutting and parallel editing studied by film theoreticians also relates to the dichotomy that interests us in this essay between putting an emphasis either on the story or the world(s). However, this distinction is canceled in the case of multiverse movies where all that belongs to the "extra-diegetic" is not reduced to a symbolic function:[78] being outside of a given diegesis does not exclude belonging to another. Moreover, despite the gap between the worlds – or rather because of it, since the goal is to reduce it – the temporal dimension is rarely abolished (*story* and *world* are mutually defined), as the usual interpretation of the alternation as a signifier of simultaneity allows a potential interworld passage and, hence, the possibility to use the organization of worlds in order to generate a fictional narrative. As Marie-Laure Ryan has shown, the worlds' mutual accessibility constitutes the main condition for the viability of the narrative: "In order for the plural cosmology to produce stories able to sustain the reader's interest, it should allow its parallel universes to communicate with each other while remaining distinct" (Ryan 2010: 71)[*]. No figure can ensure both the conservation of the respective specificities assigned to each world and the establishement of periodic convergences so effectively as the principle of alternation. It comes as no surprise that it constitutes a key organizing factor in multiverse movies, as it combines the priority given to defining each of the film's worlds with a mode of film organization established more than a century ago.

In this regard, the genre of the action movie is not incompatible with a world-centered logic as long as the temporal dimension is sufficiently treated. For instance, in *Inception* (2010), time unfolds at different speeds in each of the interwoven tracks, according to a principle of alternation between worlds (five minutes in the embedding world correspond to an hour inside the dream). Furthermore, due to the omnipresence of the pattern of the chase scene, each of these tracks is organized according to the principle of narrative alternation. In *Eternal Sunshine of the Spotless Mind*, a "chase scene" unfolds not horizontally within a specific course of action, but vertically between the protagonist who tries to avoid being spotted alongside Clementine by the Lacuna Inc. technicians and the latter who are busy in the "first" world trying to restore the process of erasing a part of the audio-visualized memories. In *The Matrix Revolutions* (2003), the discussions between politicians and soldiers in the city of Zion, where the humans (who believe themselves to be) disconnected from the Matrix are gathered, and later on the assault launched by the army of the machines, alternate with the battle between Neo and Agent Smith inside the virtual representation produced by the computer: the sacrificial resolution of the embedded world will retroact in the "real" world.

Although frequently assuming a structuring role in multiverse films, alternation is not always an essential aspect in them. In *Pleasantville*, once the two young heroes leave their world and enter that of a 1950s TV series, the viewer no longer has access to what is happening in the "first" world. The activities of the weird TV repairman in "our" world will not be shown through alternation, but only through the intermediary of a small screen ("alternative editing" in a shot/reverse shot pattern that brings the two worlds closer to each other). In this case, the television device provides the possibility of interaction between the two worlds. Therefore, the absence of alternation is often the result of a choice of focal point in a given film, involving a choice of a specific type of viewer immersion. Sometimes the principle of alternation is present though transposed on two possible worlds distinct from the world of reference. This is the case in *eXistenZ* (1999), in which the gamers in the "first" world are never actually shown, especially as the film's last line suggests the possibility of a multiplication of embedded levels.

When Jean Mitry writes that *comparison* must be held within the same continuous space and *metaphor* within the same shot, he opts for a contraction that corresponds to cases of interpenetration between worlds in certain multiverse films, in which the succession induced by the principle of alternation at the level of the signifier is replaced by a simultaneous co-presence of heterogeneous elements (in terms of "objective reality", in the words of Mitry). This would be the case of the co-presence between humans and toons in *Who Framed Roger Rabbit*, color and black & white in *Avalon*, or characters filmed in live-action and computer generated sets in *TRON* (1982). Moreover, an ontological heterogeneity of visual referents can be produced even without digital special effects – or even editing, for that matter – as certain profilmic elements can be specifically associated, on a semantic level, with a specific world, like the laboratory mouse in *Je t'aime je t'aime*.

In a scene in *eXistenZ*, when the "video game within the film" comes to an end, only a few discrete elements from one world are included in another: in the midst of a battle, the female protagonist is given some accessories never before encountered in the film (the headset and the joystick from the game "tranScendenZ", belonging to the frame story), while several wooden benches appear in the middle of a meadow. This incongruous, seemingly out of place furniture is actually a resurgence of a diegetic component seen at the beginning of the film inside the temple of the video game designer, in a scene the viewer was encouraged to falsely associate with the "first" diegesis. In fact we were already

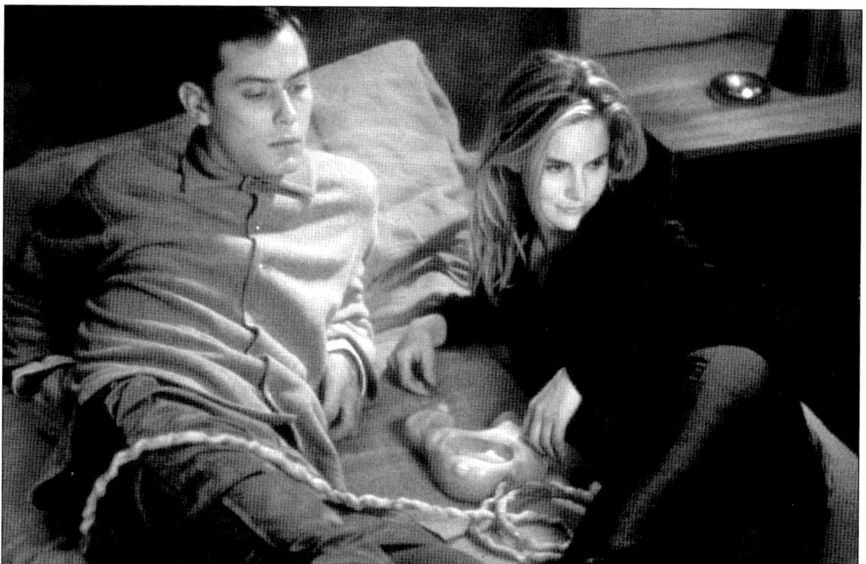

Fig. 34: The organic video game console in *eXistenZ* (1999), connected to the body of the couple of players (Jude Law and Jennifer Jason Leigh) through a sort of umbilical cord, underlines the libidinal dimension of the game as imagined by David Cronenberg.

inside the game and the gender stereotype will be reestablished once we shift levels: "the" world of the game is ultimately attributed to a genius male designer. Nevertheless, as we find out in retrospect, these wooden benches also belong to the "first" diegesis and, consequently, they constitute an invariant, whereas the technological equipment, until now defined by its semi-organic components (Fig. 34), changes in appearance and acquires a different connotation in each world. (The video game constitutes in itself the main theme within the video game worlds of *eXistenZ*, and this self-reflexivity is narratively motivated by the presence of a group of fanatics opposed to virtual realities). Such interpenetrations between worlds require nothing more from the film's production than the presence of a number of props. This representational choice should be attributed to the fact that David Cronenberg is not really interested in the specifics of "virtual" technologies, but – as Ledoux has shown – in renewing the meta-fictional practice of staging a "theater-within-a-theater" (Ledoux 2012: 83–85). The confusion over the levels of embedding in *eXistenZ* results precisely from the director's choice to avoid using the principle of interworld alternation. This in turn would have enabled the viewer to grasp the relations of hierarchy or inclusion between the worlds (or, conversely, the autonomy of each of the worlds).

Even though crosscutting associates two or more worlds, it does not necessarily grant an equal place to each of them. The *degree of actualization* varies insofar as the alternation can be carried out to the advantage of the visualization of world A over world B, for instance in terms of the screen time reserved to each of these tracks. In that event, one of the worlds will be shown in a more partial or allusive way so that it appears to the viewer as less complete due to its opacity (although a higher degree of completeness could actually be inferred). As the artifacts in the Strugatsky brothers' novel, *Roadside Picnic*, show (the garbage left on Earth by Aliens function as trivial and unintelligible traces of the unknown), a world can be inferred while remaining enigmatic. The film then would merely reveal the tip of the iceberg, leaving the invisible part to the imagination of its viewers, unless of course this hidden world is our own world and can be easily completed thanks to our "encyclopedic knowledge". This is the case in *Thor: The Dark World* (2013) where the alternation established during the first three quarters of the film grants only a number of brief scenes to actions taking place on Earth (actions associated after all with the discovery of a portal to another world). At the same time, up to that point, Asgard and the Nine Realms occupy almost all of the screen time. The film's final part is structured at first by a crosscutting serving the story,[79] then by a juxtaposition of abrupt shifts from one world to another, during a titanic duel where the attractional regime prevails (as in the last two installments in "*The Matrix*"'s franchise, or in Dr. Strange scenes in *The Avengers*). The use of crosscutting in the "*Thor*" film series illustrates that this type of practice, considered on a cosmic level, usually places side-by-side entire sequences rather than individual shots (as in chase scenes). Superior and more autonomous as narrative units, these sequences echo each other from one world to another.

Alternation is certainly recurrent in multiverse movies, but in *Fringe* it manifests already during the opening credits through the opposition between blue (actual world) and red (*parallel world*) backgrounds, and is therefore applied among the series' episodes rather than within them (with the exception of "Entrada", S03E08, where the opening credits mix these two colors).[80] That said, it is also important to remark its absence, which can also result from a specific choice (in semiotics the absence of a sign is significant in itself). A film may let its viewers infer the existence of a different world while remaining strictly riveted to the first world. Since the spectator anticipates the alternation, its absence functions as an ostensible (but often provisional, as the narration proceeds with the gradual discovery of the other world) retention of information relating to the building of the secondary world – "secondary" in terms of priority. In the case of cinema, the process of limiting the access to a given world can be accomplished in ways that are all the more diverse as the medium possesses several matters of expression. For instance, the viewer may hear sounds of another world, which is nevertheless not visualized on the screen. This is the case in fantasy films where contact is established with a world from beyond the grave through spirit channeling, as in *White Noise* (2005); the "upside down" parallel universe in *Stranger Things* is initially represented in this mode too, accessible as it is through a telephone. *Another Earth* can also serve as an example: when the researcher specialized in extraterrestrial intelligence makes radio contact with an interlocutor located on a different planet (also small and "blue" as ours), she realizes that she is actually talking to her alter ego in a *parallel world*. In this scene, the principle of alternation is not applied in the visualization of the two worlds, but to a series of shots/reverse shots between a TV screen broadcasting live a conversation with the "extraterrestrials" and the TV viewers, who are actually the protagonist's family.

Furthermore, a different world may be verbally evoked without ever being the object of an audio-visual representation. Worldbuilding may be limited to *word*-building, as evidenced by the frequent use of neologisms – or rather of "fictive words", as Angenot points out – in most sci-fi stories (see *supra*, Chapter 2). Such a world, hardly actualized, does not accommodate the immersion of the viewer (at least not in the film's second world), promoting instead a distanced contemplation with clear implications with respect to the construction of a specific point of view. Nevertheless, this does not mean that the world does not exist within the film's fiction. The "*Jumanji*" film series exemplifies this by making a radical shift in terms of worldbuilding between the first part, released in 1995, and its sequel in 2017. The first film never leaves our world (a small American town) but the characters playing the eponymous board game bring out from the imaginary jungle of "Jumanji" – in which the Robin Williams character has supposedly spent twenty years (totally eluded in the film) – several elements (a rapidly growing vegetation, hordes of monkeys, a lion, a carnivorous plant, etc.) that disrupt their daily life, in a Gremlins-like invasion. On the contrary, *Jumanji: Welcome to the Jungle* delivers the invitation announced in its title: transformed into a video game cartridge (a retro item nowadays) in order to comply with the representation of its user during a prologue supposedly taking place in the year the first film was released, "Jumanji" dematerializes the gamers as in *TRON* and sucks them into a world organized according to video game conventions (life counts, special skills, maps, levels, non-player-characters, game over, etc.). It also grants them body features of various stereotypical adventure game avatars, without any correspondence with the gender or the temperament of the actual players ("gender trouble" is one of the principal resources of comedy in this family movie). Landing into the game world, just like the heroes of *Sliders* in each of the Alternate Earths, the protagonists, as well as the audience, are immersed into an exotic (and *virtual*) world appearing in no terrestrial maps and with a temporality of its own.[81] In the 1995 film, the world of the jungle (and the game) remains almost entirely off-screen, while in its 2017 post-*Lost* sequel it appears as an island (first visualized as a drawn map given to the protagonists and present in the film's closing credits) that the heroes go through, facing various kinds of obstacles. The fauna and flora belong to an imaginary environment reminiscent of "*Indiana Jones*" or "*King Kong*", thus facilitating viewer immersion.

The difference between the two episodes of the "*Jumanji*" series, separated by more than twenty years, is mainly due to a technological factor: the recent film exploits the possibilities created by CGI (the integral creation of universes) while in the 1990s the use of digital effects was limited to occasional superimpositions on the film's image. Worthy of note is that neither of these two films is structured according to the principle of alternation. The first film never leaves the original world, while most of the second uninterruptedly unfolds inside "Jumanji", a world embedded within our own world.[82] *Jumanji: The Next Level* (2019) plays similarly – the shift to the second world arrives at the exact same minute as in its predecessor! – while reassigning differently the avatars to each of the characters. However, this new sequel contains a brief segment that represents what seems like the beginning of a crosscutting[83] motivated by the fact that one of the protagonists was not sucked in time into the world of "Jumanji", before the breaking down of the video console. These movies reveal the degree to which the modes of configuration of film worlds participate in the repetition/variation principle attached to serial productions and, more generally, help distinguishing between different worldbuilding strategies.

The *embedding of worlds*, in its fundamentally chiasmatic form (A-B-B-A, at least when it is not coupled with an alternation), establishes a relation of subordination between an embedding and an embedded diegesis. The latter may derive from the former according to what we designated, following Jean Châteauvert, a "relation of attribution" (see the passage on "*Mental Worlds*" in Chapter 3), or simply because a "worldbuilding machine" justifies the shift in levels. When there is a relation of attribution, the organization of the worlds is based on the establishment of a certain enunciative device: a world actually depends on an authority that cannot be a part of it (since this authority constitutes the world's source; this would explain why it often manifests itself in the form of a voice-over). This does not mean that the same character cannot occupy both positions – that of a narrator (in this case a "homodiegetic" one, in Genettian terms) and that of a character acting within the diegesis produced by the former's narration; however, he cannot be present inside the diegesis *as a narrator* (except in the case of a metalepsis, of course). Defined by the hierarchy it establishes, the embedding constitutes a factor of stability. This explains why certain films that try to cast doubt on the relations between the different worlds tend to undermine this principle. The most common case is that of films beginning *in medias res* and concealing a first level of embedding, as in *eXistenZ*, or mixing-up the worlds' thresholds, as in *Total Recall* (see Chapter 2). In *Je t'aime je t'aime*, one of the many trips back-and-forth between the past and the present precisely stands out due to a reversal of this principle. Everywhere else in the film, the past (B) interweaves with images of Claude inside the "sphere" (A), obeying to a relation that subordinates B to A within the embedding pattern A-B-A. However, in this particular scene, we see Claude and Catrine standing in the corridor of a moving train, crossing through regions where Claude had fought during the Second World War, when a brief moment from within the machine punctuates a conversation taking place continuously and in one place (whereas dialogue scenes in this film are interrupted abruptly) before and after this insert (B-A-B). The hierarchical relationship Resnais subverts is of a temporal, not an enunciative order; in view of the film's general approach, it is unlikely that one would think of Claude during this conversation as someone who is foreseeing his future as a guinea pig in an instantaneous dream.[84] The opposition between the present and the past tends to be canceled out within a perpetual present, actually that of the film's screening to which a disembodied Claude "attends". Therefore, the determining factor in terms of the worlds' organization in *Je t'aime je t'aime* is not the embedding but the alternation.

The *juxtaposition* is a formal type mostly found in films proposing *alternate (story)worlds*, which, as shown in the previous chapter, are subject to a logic that is more narrative and less world-centered. Moreover, by making the different worlds or the variations of the same world follow one another, it could be said that "one universe supersedes the other", thus attenuating to a considerable degree the feeling of being confronted to multiple worlds. While embedding may be combined with alternation, juxtaposition can occur alongside alternation within the same film but not in the same segment (in Metz's theory, alternation and linearity are mutually exclusive criteria).

Sucker Punch (2011) by Zack Snyder, director of *300* and *Watchmen*, and undoubtedly one of the Hollywood filmmakers especially attuned to our contemporary intermedial context, presents a strict juxtaposition of four worlds, strongly differentiated by their respective tributes to distinct genres of mass culture (role-playing games, comics, video games). The only thing these worlds share is that they successively host the characters from the reference world: the female protagonist and her acolytes. The accessibility between worlds is one-sided and defined by a relation of subordination between the embedding world and the embedded ones. Consequently, the latter are impermeable to each other and are only represented in a strictly circumscribed segment of the film. They "exist" only as long as the protagonist's immersion lasts and they are no longer accessible as soon as she completes the "combat sequence". Just like in a video game, defeating an "end-of-the-level-boss" signifies that the objective of the quest is fulfilled. There is however an invariant outside the protagonist and her associates: the "game leader", a recurring figure who functions as a video game tutorial.

Let's see briefly the story of this film before we get to examine what motivates this type of arrangement between the different worlds. Babydoll (Emily Browning), a character reminiscent of both Scheherazade from *One Thousand and One Nights* (an emblematic case of narrative embedding) and Salome, is forced into a mental asylum. An employee is hired to ensure that Babydoll will be lobotomized five days later. In order to be able to escape, the protagonist has to perform a "dance spectacle" to the guards that torture her. These moments of attraction – in the sense given to the term by scholars working on early cinema, designating exhibitionist performances apt to exploit the medium's voyeuristic nature[85] – function narratively as a diversion: while Babydoll dances, another inmate steals one of the objects needed for the escape. It should be added that this psychiatric institution is represented in a totally imaginary way since it also resembles a brothel (with a cabaret-like platform), the young girls' oppression being both physical and mental. The alterations in the "first" world can certainly be attributed to the young girl's imagination but there is no proof to support this hypothesis. It could just as well be a stylistic feature not perceived at the diegetic level: unlike other films in which the hero interned in a mental asylum suffers from hallucinations shared by the viewer without the latter's knowledge (*Spider*, 2002; *Identity*, 2003; *The Ward*, 2010; *Shutter Island*, 2010, etc.), the ending in *Sucker Punch* does not restore any objective version of the world, bringing to mind *The Cabinet of Dr. Caligari* (see Chapter 3).

Snyder's film exists in a timelessness linked to the postmodern recycling of popular culture (following in the footsteps of *Diva*, 1981), where everything – including the "first" world – is already a *representation of a representation*. The reign of the simulacrum is present in the film's first shots, since the few opening credits are shown as diegetic, appearing at first on the curtain of a theater stage that opens to the film's first "act". The camera advances in a forward tracking shot, maintaining a frontal relationship to the profilmic elements, then starts a circular movement around the protagonist: a human subject serves as the center which mediates our access to the entire film universe. The reference world starts unfolding through the elements the camera gradually reveals. The "fourth wall" of the stage vanishes, transformed into a furnished space. The viewer is thus absorbed in an environment that is nonetheless the result of a "mise-en-scène", partially restaged later on in the asylum's "cabaret". The status of the representation shifts constantly in *Sucker Punch*, as the psychodramas replayed by the patients on the theater stage take place not just in front of the therapists (looking like women in charge of a brothel) but also under the lustful gaze of guardians dressed as gangsters from the Al Capone era. It is rather significant that the protagonist's "real" nightmare takes as its starting point the death of the mother: henceforth, young Babydoll will always find herself fighting against male sadism, in a fairy tale-like ambience (the "Big Bad Wolves" lurk, the shameful stepfather being the first among them).

Eroticism is generally banned from this type of super-violent film and video game productions intended for young audiences. *Sucker Punch* takes literally the transposition underlying this specific taboo by replacing the dance sequences with battle scenes. The protagonist, who projects herself mentally inside these worlds (finding thus the courage to endure her humiliations in the present thanks to her achievements as a warrior against extremely virile and dimwit adversaries), achieves a performance that supposedly hypnotizes the men around her, as their reaction testifies once we return to the embedding world. The body-in-action spectacle shifts from one type of performance (dance) to another (combat), highlighting their kinship in terms of cinematic representation. We are actually shifting from one *attraction* to another: striptease, the film's blind spot as far as the viewer is concerned, turns into a *teaser trailer*, as each new embedding world seems to promote a different video game.

Indeed, four "trailers" were released for *Sucker Punch*, all in the form of animated films (in the style of Japanese anime movies). Each of the titles refers to a specific type of universe, in the sense that we deal with different genres determined by the very world they construct: "Feudal Warriors", "Trenches", "Dragon", and "Distant Planet". These "sections" do not refer to historical eras *per se*, as is the case in *Cloud Atlas* or *Westworld* (see Chapter 2). Feudal Japan is here a pretext for a swordfight against gigantic armored monsters. The "Trenches" are not a reproduction of those of the First World War but belong to a world that follows the "retro-futuristic" codes of the steampunk genre (as in *Hellboy*, 2004). In this world, German doctors have found a way to resuscitate corpses thanks to some "clock and steam mechanisms", an automation of the human figure that appears as the dark side of Babydoll, herself a mechanical doll caught in choreographed fights inside a CGI landscape. The role played from the 1970s onwards by certain stereotypical environments, such as regions populated by *heroic fantasy* dragons or sci-fi "distant planets", in the graphic representation of arcade video games (and the correlative contextualization of their worlds) is well documented, especially at a time when these video games were not very figurative.[86] Babydoll's imaginary world is entirely made up of pre-existing representations (also the case in *Vanilla Sky*, 2001): a *mental world* is thus intertwined with a *virtual world*.

The examples discussed in this chapter and throughout the book confirm the importance of studying the modes of arrangement between a film's worlds, linked to certain editing practices. Worldbuilding is not solely about the referent of the representation, but also about film form: in cinema, building a world is inseparable from (not) showing it and from editing its images.

Endnotes

1. Through a detailed analysis of early twentieth century discourses, Mireille Berton has demonstrated how the cinematograph contributed to fashion the way hallucinatory delusions were interpreted in the medical imaginary of the period. These delusions would give rise to a "projection of the patient's internal processes on the environment" (Berton 2015: 255–265)*.
2. "Can poetry be forced to establish itself outside of what surrounds it, to ignore the magnificent exuberance of life which the activities of men are adding to nature and which allow the world to be mechanized in an incredible fashion? The new spirit is of the very time of which we are living, a time rich in surprises. The poets wish […] one day, to mechanize poetry as the world has been mechanized. They want to be the first to provide a totally new lyricism for these new means of expression which are giving impetus to art – the phonograph and the cinema" (Apollinaire 1971: 237).
3. Barjavel published the same year *Future Times Three*, a novel that addresses the world-centered implications of the time-travel paradox. For the 1958 reissue of this book – that is, after the physicist Hugh Everett proposed the many-worlds interpretation in 1957 – the author added an afterword recounting the case of a time traveler who, after having modified the

past, saw his existence become incompatible with the present state of the world. This paradox was popularized thanks to a scene in *Back to the Future* where the protagonist's image (Marty McFly, played by Michael J. Fox) is progressively erased from a photograph in accordance with the evolution of the film's story.

4. Duvivier's film was remade in Hollywood, under the title of *Paris When it Sizzles* (1964). The main change introduced by screenwriter George Axelrod to Henri Jeanson's story is emblematic of the priorities that guide storytelling in Hollywood productions: the frame story's heterodiegetic narrators become homodiegetic as the story they are inventing mirrors the film's frame story, albeit through deformations brought by various generic codifications (western, horror). The representation of the creative duo is an integral part of the story and occupies a central place in a plot driven by the mutual attraction between a screenwriter (William Holden) and a young woman engaged to help him finish his script (Audrey Hepburn). The embedded story's subordination to the frame story (and the romantic affair in it) is manifested not only through the principle of a fantasy projection, but concretely through the screen time granted to each level, since in this remake the total time devoted to the visualization of the two screenwriters exceeds the duration of the sum of the embedded segments.
5. The field of "genetic criticism" (or "textual genetics") was institutionalized thanks to the activities of a Parisian research entity, the Institute for Modern Texts and Manuscripts (ITEM, created in 1982), and the circulation of a journal, *Genesis. Revue internationale de critique génétique*. In his book, Daniel Ferrer, a member of this group, recognizes that "the [Leibnizian] idea of a plurality of possible alternatives represented by juxtaposed universes seems particularly suited to genetic studies" (Ferrer 2011: 143)*. For a study on the possible alternatives in a single film, see Boillat 2020b.
6. In order to distinguish a pastoral romance from a "Nouveau Roman" novel like Robbe-Grillet's *La Jalousie*, Marie-Laure Ryan considers the former as the result of a "thematic focus" combined with an idyllic filter, while the latter "selects a landscape of colonial life and paints it *in neutral colors*" (Ryan 1991: 43, the italics are mine).
7. This convention is not respected in *Stranger than Fiction* (2006) that presents the exact opposite case: through metalepsis, the film's hero is able to hear the female voice-over which recounts the story of his life and is about to announce his death (see Boillat 2012).
8. As I have shown elsewhere with regard to both *300* (2006) and *Watchmen* (2009), whose visual style is affected by a certain conception of comic books' specificities, it is not so much a question of borrowing some of the original work's features than of renewing film practices in the transmedia era. See Boillat (2018a).
9. Commenting on the links between subjective representation and color, Branigan states that the latter may be "metaphorically attributed to [a] character" (1984: 95). The creation of a second world is indeed akin to the process of metaphorizing (as envisaged in particular by Paul Ricoeur in *The Rule of Metaphor*), as illustrated by a number of narrative speculations proposed in the sci-fi genre.
10. Following the precepts of the auteur theory, film critics often use the term "world" in reference to the properties of a single film or those of the entire filmography of a given director. Yacavone adopts this perspective when writing about the "world of *8½*" or "Fellini's world" (2015:7).
11. "It is useful to use the notion of possible world when one refers to a state of affairs, but only if one needs to compare at least two alternative states of affairs. If one says that Donald Duck is an invention by Disney and that we have few chances to meet him on Sunset Boulevard, one certainly says that Donald Duck belongs to a world of fantasy, but no specific Possible Worlds Theory is requested in order to discover or to prove such a triviality. If, on the contrary, one analyzes a very peculiar movie as *Who Framed Roger Rabbit?* in which cartoons interact with allegedly 'real' characters, then problems of mutual accessibility between different worlds can be legitimately debated." (Eco 1990: 69).
12. Each of these actions has a different impact on the temporality of Lola's journey and, consequently, on the entire causality of the film's story.
13. For instance, Nintendo tried to adapt its *Radar Scope* arcades (1980) by integrating the characters from "*Popeye*"'s comic books and cartoon movies (see Blanchet 2010: 159).
14. For a discussion of this type of films as well as of the critical and theoretical discourses surrounding them, see Massuet 2017. The author makes particular mention (*Ibid.*, 340–434)

of our comments on *Who Framed Roger Rabbit* as they appear in the first edition of this book.

15. This topic is in fact closely related to cyberculture's notion of simulacrum that I will examine in detail in the following chapter. In the words of the novel's main hero: "Like a bloodhound hot on the trail my mind sought out all the hollow, empty places in this monumental masquerade, this tinseled cheat that sprawled across the horizon" (Lem 1976: 116).
16. Alain Resnais noted about *Night and Fog*: "Color can be used both in a realistic or an unrealistic way. It seems to me that *a priori* a film is in sound and in color. From that point on, everyone is free to experiment." (quoted in Chardère 1961: 58)[*]. When Resnais himself inserts a number of very brief clips taken out of black & white French films of the classical era in *My Uncle From America*, the idea is to give these visual quotes a subjective aura by attributing them to the imagination of some fictional characters who identify themselves with movie stars.
17. This erotic dimension is magnified in a later western, *The Last Sunset* (1961), written by Dalton Trumbo. His screenplay, filled with an obvious psychoanalytical subtext, highlights the color of a young girl's dress (also yellow) whose presence awakens an irrepressible incestuous desire in the adventurer played by Kirk Douglas.
18. In *Travelers* (2013), a multiverse film directed by Koicihi Sakamoto, the "red world" is simply qualified as such.
19. By associating Hollywood's *film noir* to German Expressionist Cinema, Soderbergh's film perpetuates a common assumption in film history, which Thomas Elsaesser has nonetheless deconstructed: "Precisely because the lineage German Expressionism, German exiles, American *film noir* does not seem to make sense as history of cause and effect, […] it is – or should be – of particular interest to film history. For 'German Expressionism' and '*film noir*' name aspects of cinema which are interesting less as examples of false history, than as a history of the false in cinema: […] the cinema's historical imaginary" (Elsaesser 1996: 129). *Kafka's world(s)* is (are) based on such an imaginary.
20. It is interesting to note that the German title of Kafka's unfinished novel, "*Das Schloss*", means both "castle" and "lock".
21. Doležel qualifies as "domains" the different areas composing the fictional world: "In Kafka's world […], the pattern of control is relatively simple: the visible-domain inhabitants are under permanent threat of an order, a decree, a decision that originates in the invisible domain and deeply affects their existence" (Doležel 1998: 193).
22. Each of the series' albums deals with a different element "missing" from the graphic novel's representation when compared to reality, a mystery that generates curiosity and becomes the hero's main preoccupation. In the first volume the self-reflexivity concerns mainly the narrative organization (correlated with the published medium's materiality) while the next two ones develop a more world-centered topic from which the story – the hero's quest – stems.
23. The term "hero" is far more relevant in Soderbergh's film than in any of Kafka's stories, as the former complies with the standards of dominant narrative cinema.
24. Regarding the modes of representation of the writer himself as well as of the interpenetration between his daily life and the world he imagines, see our comparison of *Kafka* and *Naked Lunch* (another film released in the same year, 1991) in Boillat 2010b: 34–43.
25. As in *Dark City* (see Chapter 5), visual features traditionally associated with film noir are summoned in a self-conscious manner. James Naremore has pointed out that "noir is almost entirely a creation of postmodern culture" (1995–1996: 14).
26. Concerning this world in *The Wizard of Oz*, see Perkins 2005: 27. The author discusses an empirical way of apprehending any film as a world.
27. As opposed to sequences shot in color and intended as a grandiose spectacle, introduced in some prestigious films such as the epics *The Ten Commandments* (1923) and *Ben Hur* (1925). Those scenes seem to adhere to the logic of an autonomous spectacle, placed as they were at the beginning of the film in order to immediately capture the attention of viewers.
28. The variety of metaphorical or symbolic uses of the names of colors favors their inscription in a level of connotation that the image, though it never really escapes from the denotation level, actualizes through a world-centered interpretation.

29. Barthes 1977: 32–51. Commenting on the advertisement for the Panzani pasta brand, Barthes remarks in the introduction of his text: "A second sign is more or less equally evident [than the idea that the half-open bag signifies "a return from the market"]; its signifier is the bringing together of the tomato, the pepper and the tricoloured hues (yellow, green, red) of the poster; its signified is Italy, or rather *Italianicity* [...]." (p. 34). As we can see, Barthes does not examine the signifiers here; he places at the same level the signified of the denotation "tomato" and the signifiers of the denotation composed by the poster's colors (however the color red could be equally linked to the tomato, the pepper and the background of the image).
30. This does not mean that we cannot or should not attempt such an interpretation, especially when a single color is used in a selective manner and independently of others, as in the cases mentioned below. After all, Technicolor's chief supervisor, Natalie Kalmus, connected the choice of specific color palettes in *The Wizard of Oz* with this type of culturally predetermined connotations as well as with their visual interest. See Street 2009: 194–195.
31. It should be clarified that the phenomena mentioned here can also occur at the profilmic level: in *Shadow* (*Ying*, 2018), Zhang Yimou used a color film stock but had all the sets and costumes paint in shades of gray, adopting an aesthetic that references the Chinese tradition of ink paintings. Color, and in particular the red of bloodstains, appears in this film sporadically.
32. "In certain techniques of visual representation, and particularly in cinema, the illusion of realism is such that the presence of signifying forms is hardly felt. We conceive the data of the signified in terms of referents" (Group μ 1970: 175). The instinctive nature of this "projection" is nevertheless hampered by the opposition between black & white and color which makes one feel the presence of these signifying elements.
33. Metz 1975. Christian Metz mentions "colour film/black-and-white film" (43) in his list of the materials of expression, without dwelling on it since he is primarily interested in those materials that are specific in cinema. However, it is precisely this lack of a medium-specific character that allows the creation of worlds by reference to various types of representations, as we have already seen with the example of *Dreams* (1990).
34. However, the semioticians of the Group μ considerably underestimate the range of possibilities for establishing marks of enunciation in a film, given the illusion of analogy between the image and reality.
35. It is at this haptic level that Schmerheim locates the effects of color (Schmerheim 2013: 114–118).
36. I am well aware of developing here a discourse which is the opposite of the one held by Soderbergh at the release of the film. However, in such cases, opposites can meet (to use one of the film's lines, "[it] rather depends on which end of the microscope you're on"). In an interview given to the film journal *Positif*, in which he confirms that the idea of the shift in color came to one of the producers inspired by *The Wizard of Oz*, the filmmaker explains his choice as follows: "According to standard convention nowadays, black & white is used to express a dream, a fantasy, the unreal. I kind of liked the idea that in our film it would be the other way around" (Ciment and Niogret 1992: 41)[*]. Since the scenes taking place outside the castle are the product of a meta-fiction (their referent is not really the city of Prague nor Kafka's biography but the world created by the author's texts), a sense of unreality is produced through intertextual contamination to which one could very well oppose the reality of the cinematographic apparatus. The latter is echoed by the machinery in the castle that "gives shape and form" to Kafka's nightmares (by sacrificing human bodies).
37. The fact that the film's function is compared to experiments associated with the Nazi project of controlling the masses and alienating the individual, leaves nevertheless one wondering about the meaning given by Soderbergh to the concept of immersion inside a given world, a central theme in *Kafka*.
38. Barry Salt notes that a whole series of films have followed *Redskin*'s example in "using the contrast between colour and black and white film to distinguish between sections set in different 'worlds'" (Salt 1992: 181).
39. One can observe a systematic use of this type of practice, in itself rather rare, in the first three films written and directed by Lewin: *The Moon and Sixpence* (1942), *The Picture of Dorian Gray* (1945) and *The Private Affairs of Bel Ami* (1947).

40. For example, in *The Picture of Dorian Gray*, the diegetic painting is filmed in color only on two occasions, at the beginning and at the end of the film. It should be noted that this painting also appears in black & white in other scenes, in particular when it is visible at the farthest end of the set thanks to a wide depth of field. Therefore, color as such does not indicate an ontological distinction between the reference world of the fiction and a representation giving birth to a second world. Rather, it assumes a symbolic function that participates in the discourse produced by the film on the subject of painting. It is about "intensifying the differentiation between the original pure image and the final, putrefied one", between "'the before' and 'the after' of the pictorial act dramatized by the film, in other words the acheiropoietic act which makes the canvas evolve out of itself and submits it to the prerogatives of time, in the manner of a film image" (Robert 2006: 56)[*].

41. See Marie-Laure Ryan's comments on the principle of "complementarity" advanced by the Copenhagen school as an answer (or rather two answers, contradictory but nevertheless both valid) to the following question: "Is light a wave or a beam of particles?" (Ryan 2010: 64)[*].

42. From the very first pages, *Roadside Picnic* puts particular emphasis on the oddity of certain components transferred from the *other* world to the world of reference. It is significant that the very act of denotation is explicitly addressed with regards to an object qualified as "hollow": "No, friends, it's hard to describe this thing if you haven't seen one. It looks much too simple, especially when you finally convince yourself that your eyes aren't playing tricks on you." (Strugatsky 2012: 8).

43. On stylized uses of color in screen adaptations of comics and graphic novels, see Boillat 2010c: 29–33.

44. *Watchmen* is created and co-written by Damon Lindelof (one of *Lost*'s showrunners), as a transmedia extension of the homonymous DC comic series by Moore and Gibbons (1986–1987). In this althist tale, the Seventh Kavalry – a faction of KKK – continues to rage in the midst of the 21st century.

45. In Moore's graphic novel, "Nostalgia" is a line of cosmetic products. They are marketed by a company run by Adrian Veidt, who announces in a memo integrated into the pseudo-documentary material at the end of Volume X that he wants to change the name of the brand so as to stop playing on an iconography evoking a watered-down and imaginary past. The story in the HBO series transposes this idea by having its female protagonist confronting a repressed past.

46. The "real" Steven Spielberg, director of *Amistad* (1997), did indeed make a film named *War Horse* (2011) in which The Cavalry plays a key role but where only the horse is actually black. In the HBO series of *Watchmen*, the title "Pale Horse" refers to a music band that was giving a concert at the time the disaster – orchestrated by Adrian Veidt (Jeremy Irons) – hit Manhattan. This name fits however into a vast web of intertextual references to the eponymous comic book series by Moore and Gibbons (perceived in retrospect as a graphic novel). In its "chapter" X, one finds a vignette juxtaposing a landscape of the metropolis with a huge poster announcing the 2/11 "Pale Rider" concert *and* the interior monologue of Rorschach who is writing his diary ("Oblivion gallops clother, favoring the spur, sparing the rein. I think we will be gone soon"). In the beginning of chapter XII (at the last hour of the doomsday clock), the large vignettes illustrating Madison Square Garden filled with bodies bathed in blood use the same visual motif as the poster promoting the "Pale Horse" concert (alongside the one from the film *The Day the Earth Stood Still*). On the eschatological dimension of *Watchmen*'s story (the end as the *last chapter*), see Boillat 2018c.

47. The girl in red, a visual motif that has sometimes been qualified as a melodramatic individualization of the Holocaust or a film gimmick incompatible with the un-representable character of the genocide, was one of the elements fiercely debated during the critical reception of *Schindler's List* in France, most notably in a virulent article signed by Claude Lanzmann, the director of the documentary film *Shoah*.

48. The opening scene in *Lovecraft Country* (S01E01), another recent HBO TV series that deals with issues of racial segregation in the United States, gradually shifts from black & white (a reference to the war movie genre's realist aesthetics) to color, as we are plunged *in medias res* into the *mental world* of a pulp magazine fan as he reads Edgar Rice Burroughs' sci-fi novel *John Carter of Mars*.

49. However, there are some slight variations within a rather homogeneous hue to be found from one scene to another, bringing to mind the processes of print toning used in movies of the silent era.
50. "The Steampunk genre invites the reader or the viewer to a journey into a phantasmagoric 19th century. Literally meaning 'steam thug', Steampunk was born as a playful distraction before transfiguring itself into a meta-textual fiction drawing on history and imagination to offer a reinterpretation of the past that is both iconoclastic and erudite. An iconography that has since become a trademark was added to all this [...]" (Barillier 2010: 8)*.
51. See also the recent and unpublished (as far as we know) doctoral thesis of Michael D. Dwyer, *Back to the Fifties: Pop Nostalgia in the Reagan Era* (University of Syracuse, 2010).
52. In *Pleasantville* and in *The Truman Show*, access to a secondary world associated with the past is granted by the televisual medium. The difference between these two movies lies in the fact that Weir's film introduces the real-time parameter in its story as well as a demiurgic character, played by Ed Harris (an actor that has a key role in the *Westworld* TV series that also offers a world remotely piloted from a control room). On *The Truman Show*'s world-city, conceived between a 1980s socio-architectural utopia and an amusement park, see Cunningham 2005.
53. *Wayward Pines* expands on the premise found in a previous Shyamalan film, *The Village*. One could argue that the TV series gives a concrete form to the world the characters from the 2004 film believe in, visualizing it as a post-apocalyptic future.
54. On the contrary, the main hero's goal in *Back to the Future* is to maintain the host world as it is, "striving" to rule out the possibility of incest and restore the authority of the future patriarch.
55. In the case of experimental cinema, these sound technologies are sometimes combined with animated film practices, as in the work of Norman McLaren. See Jean 2006: 119–137.
56. Laszlo Moholy-Nagy's radical proposition at the beginning of the 1920s, which consisted in highlighting the mechanical dimension of the means of representation and in "expand[ing] the apparatus (means) which has so far been used solely for purposes of reproduction for productive purposes" (Moholy-Nagy 1969: 30), becomes the watchword of many intellectuals who reflect on the contribution of mechanical reproduction of sound and then discuss, within the same theoretical paradigm, the implications of the expansion of sound cinema.
57. The second title of Mary Shelley's novel *Frankenstein* (1818), whose tale of a mad scientist bringing to life a human-like creature has become the emblem of using techno-scientific means for "productive" purposes, is indeed "The Modern Prometheus". Noël Burch attaches cinema's archeology to the lineage of this Frankensteinian mythology (see Burch 1990, in particular the first chapter: "Charles Baudelaire versus Doctor Frankenstein").
58. Resnais was interested in working with Sternberg on account of the latter's penchant for experimenting with temporality. Sternberg's writing style is akin to surreal, eccentric tales more than science fiction per se, even though the novelist sometimes uses a future world as a pretext (as in *A Working Day*, 1961). As Sternberg noted in a foreword in the published version of the screenplay: "To this core idea [showing flashbacks of seemingly insignificant moments] was attached a sci-fi theme, the most banal of them all, the ABCs of science fiction: time travel. Resnais and I envisaged this theme in the most unspectacular way, as close as possible to the reality of a typical office work" (1969: 10)*. The effect sought by the authors was therefore the exact opposite of the one imagined by Christopher Nolan whose particular way of experimenting with temporality I commented upon in Chapter 1.
59. Tree-shaped diagrams are one of the "paths" examined by Marie-Laure Ryan in a section of her book titled "Poetics of Interactivity" (2001: 248–249).
60. In the legendary world, inspired by the *Prince Valiant* comic strip in *Life is a Bed of Roses*, the characters express themselves only through songs, whereas in the real world everybody speaks in a normal way, an opposition again present in another Resnais movie, *Same Old Song* (1997).
61. Although associated with a "cinema of memory" (especially after his highly regarded documentary *Night and Fog*, 1956), Resnais himself has always rejected the label by maintaining that in fact his interest lies in the realm of the imaginary. As he told Jean-Daniel Roob: "Instead of memory, it is better to talk of the imaginary, since we navigate between what has happened, what will happen, what could happen" (Roob 1986: 131)*.

62. See Hême De Lacotte 2001: 86–88. Quoting also *Difference and Repetition*, the author comments on the Deleuzian distinction between the possible and the virtual (which partly overlaps with the definitions I introduced for the *alternate storyworlds* and the *virtual worlds* respectively).
63. Resnais and his screenwriter, Alain Robbe-Grillet, had divergent interpretations on this particular film. The director saw in its story the coexistence of "different degrees of reality" (Benayoun 1980: 105).
64. We never really learn what the scientists know about Ridder, since the way information is distributed among the characters has no narrative importance in Sternberg and Resnais' film.
65. However, a meticulous analysis (that viewers watching the film in a single sitting may find impossible to carry out) would prove that the repeated shots in *Je t'aime je t'aime* actually come from different takes, as the camera angles and the actors' gestures vary noticeably.
66. The order of shots as published in *L'Avant-scène cinéma*, partly realizes this task of inferring (as also does Jacques Sternberg's screenplay, even more thorough in this regard) by including a specific date (year, day, hour) for each insert related to the hero's past, as well as an introductory description that explicitly formulates a series of hypotheses the viewer might be urged to make with respect to the film's narrative (*L'Avant-Scène Cinéma*, 91, April 1969).
67. However, there is a specific shot in the film that implies Claude's innocence. Sternberg's screenplay insists on this point by providing a meta-textual note informing the reader that Claude is actually leaving the hotel room while the gas heater, eventually fatal for Catrine, functions perfectly (Sternberg 1969: 143).
68. Commenting on this film, Deleuze insists on the importance given to "the eternal nature of Catrine" (Deleuze 1989: 117).
69. Depending on each individual case, embedding or juxtaposition may be regulated by the principle of alternation. For instance, "meta-screenwriting" films that juxtapose the representation of authors-narrators with the world they are imagining (Julien Duvivier's *Holiday for Henrietta*, 1952; Robert Guédiguian's *Charge!*, 2000; Woody Allen's *Melinda and Melinda*, 2004), go back and forth between the frame story and the embedded worlds (or even between alternative albeit contradictory versions of the story of the "film-within-a-film"). *What if?* (2010) alternates between two or three possible variations, even though it is built upon the principle of juxtaposition. In *Interstellar*, the representation of a spatiotemporally distant communication between a father, a cosmonaut sucked into a black hole, and his daughter who remained on Earth, introduces in the film's narrative structure an alternation between two tracks verging on a paradoxical simultaneity within the same two-world space (a library), based on the theories of relativity.
70. In *The Fountain*, the two other worlds consist of: a. a story set in the time of the Spanish Inquisition which turns out to be the visualization of a novel (a fiction-within-a-fiction) written by the female character, Isabel Creo (Rachel Weisz), and ultimately completed by her husband, Tom (or Tommy, or Tomas, depending on the world), b. the *mental world* of the doctor and brain cancer specialist Tom Creo (Hugh Jackman, who also plays a conquistador in the world of the novel) in search of a cure that would save the life of his wife. Practicing a sort of meditation, Tom inhabits a small bubble drifting in space in this *mental world*, a "floating island" containing a "tree of life", inspired by the Mayan mythology (also present in Isabel's novel), as well as a number of components found in the other narrative tracks (a wedding ring, a pen, ink, etc.).
71. Lana and Lilly Wachowski experimented with a similar idea in the TV series *Sense8* (2015–2018) where the resonances between different eras are replaced by simultaneous connections between distant parts in the globe (through mentally connected individuals).
72. Nevertheless, this coherence remains unnoticed by the film's protagonists, since each repetition is based on the principle of the characters' reincarnation.
73. Following Gaudreault and Gauthier, we adopt the distinction between a principle (alternation) and a "figure" (crosscutting): "*alternation* is a discursive configuration that occurs when each term in two series recurs (A-B-A-B). Thus one cannot speak of *alternation* in cases where only one of the terms is repeated (A-B-A); the distinction between *alternation* and *crosscutting* (the latter understood in the strict sense of the expression *montage alterné* in French) is crucial" (Gaudreault and Gauthier 2017: 109).

74. "Focusing on the *here* and *now* of the 'representation' [...], the monstrator is thus unable to open [a] breach in the temporal continuum. It may very well be that what he is showing me has actually taken place before the act of showing, this process of monstration is however a rigorously synchronous 'narration' [...]. It is through editing that the narrator becomes able to control the narrated: [...] editing is the operation that enables him to abstract himself from the present" (Gaudreault 1999: 103–104)*.
75. Translator's note: In this book, we use the expression "Grand Syntagmatique" when referring to the model introduced by Christian Metz in the 1960s, following the translation of the original French expression (la "Grande syntagmatique") in *Christian Metz and the Codes of Cinema. Film Semiology and Beyond* (Tröhler and Kirsten 2018; see, in particular, "Editorial Note", p. 13). The same goes for the translation of the French term "syntagme" as "syntagma".
76. These comparative inserts fall into the type of segment described by Metz as the "non-diegetic insert", meaning an "image of a purely comparative value, presenting an object external to the action" (Metz 1968: 126). In light of what we have explained in Chapter 3, the premise of a total lack of "diegeticity", as well as that of the reduction of the diegetic to the action, are both problematic.
77. It should be noted that this distinction does not entirely correspond to the one between "*parallel worlds*" and "*alternate (story)worlds*" (see *supra* Chapter 3).
78. Unless we consider every second world as a literalization of the metaphorical, a hypothesis that could be considered valid in the case of allegorical tales taking place in *supernatural worlds*, as in *Pan's Labyrinth* or *The Fountain*.
79. This was actually a dominant practice in *Thor* (2011) where the hero is chased down to Earth while his brother wreaks havoc on Asgard.
80. In this regard, *Fringe* provides a very specific answer to the question "are colors diegetic?", the ones considered here (blue or red) appearing in a segment that is only slightly diegetic: numerous intertitles related to the series' themes, quasi-abstract images showing mankind at a cellular level, glyphs in the form of X ray images like a hand with six fingers intended to stimulate the fans' interpretative activity, etc.. Although symbolic (that is to say, resulting from a convention specific to the series), this use of a monochromatic image provides an indication on the status of the film world. In a way, color should be considered in *Fringe* as meta-diegetic.
81. As in the original film, one of the players (present in the game world prior to the arrival of the heroes' team) thinks he has lived there for a couple of months, when in fact he has been absent from the real world for two decades.
82. We leave the first world seventeen minutes into the film and we return to it after an hour and forty-five minutes. Both *Jumanji: Welcome to the Jungle* (2017) and *Jumanji: The Next Level* (2019) offer an explanatory flash-back scene while inside the game world, thanks to a non-player character the film's heroes actually designate as a "cut-scene".
83. In fact, this insert generates a crosscutting A-B-A from which one term, in order to constitute an alternation, is missing (see note 73). Nevertheless, the return to the frame story at the end of the film could be qualified as this missing track B.
84. However, this is the situation Diego (Yves Montand) finds himself in, when he makes up in his mind a (silent) film of what awaits him while riding a train in *The War is Over* (Alain Resnais, 1966).
85. On the notion of "attraction", see Chapter 1, note 18. Regarding the links between dance and cinema during the early years of the film medium, see Guido 2006; on a filiation between the 19th century and contemporary mass culture with respect to the spectators' voyeurism in front of a technologically mediated dance performance, see Guido 2009. In connection with the erotically playful dimension that is at the same time connoted and obscured in *Sucker Punch*, see the "boudoir voyeurism" studied by Noël Burch in connection with a film genre from early cinema he calls "through-the-keyhole" films (Burch 1990: 222). This label is all the more adequate in Snyder's film, which revolves around the idea of putting a key on a hole (the escape carried out thanks to a key being opposed to the satisfaction of the rape fantasy Babydoll arouses in one of the guards).
86. See the example of the *Gun Fight* (1975) arcade game booth, discussed in its generic (western) and intermediate aspects by Blanchet 2010: 103–111.

Chapter Five

Cyberspace: The Simulated World of the "Matrix"

> "No analog mentality can stand up against the knowledge that he's merely a complex of electrical charges in a simulated reality."
> Daniel Galouye, *Simulacron-3* (2011: 54)[1]

In his book *Convergence Culture*, Henri Jenkins dedicates a chapter to "*The Matrix*" franchise, considered to be an emblematic case of "Transmedia Storytelling", meaning a story which "unfolds across multiple media platforms, with each new text making a distinctly and valuable contribution to the whole". In a revealing remark, he adds that "its *world* might be explored through game play or experienced as amusement park attraction" (Jenkins 2006: 97-98) and mentions in particular the collection of animated films *The Animatrix* (2003) as well as the video game *Enter the Matrix* (2003). Jenkins' remark, formulated back in 2006, may seem rather obvious today, in the era of franchises such as "*Star Wars*", "*Star Trek*", "*Planet of the Apes*", "*Alien*", "*Transformers*", or that of film series originating from superhero comics (especially those gathered under the MCU – "Marvel Cinematic Universe" – label). Clearly, the following observation reflects the focus of my essay: "More and more, storytelling has become the art of world building, as artists create compelling environments that cannot be fully explored or exhausted within a single work or even a single medium" (*Ibid*: 116). Beyond the dispersion of its contents, in itself very lucrative following the "variation of the same" principle, a world's unity is imposing here, constituted as it is of recognizable elements (and therefore distinct from our world, hence the privileged role endorsed by the science fiction genre in this context), duly protected by a copyright. The aforementioned commercial strategy, to which most contemporary blockbusters obey, adheres to a serial logic dating back to the 19th century and the vertical (even sometimes horizontal) integration of the Hollywood studio system. Nevertheless, it has known a considerable development in the digital era due to a technological convergence that allows, as Vincent Miller explains, "all forms of media [to be] increasingly stored and transferred on the same format and therefore [to become] completely interchangeable" (Miller 2011: 74).

The Matrix proves to be a particularly interesting case for my study since its world-centered dimension is accentuated not only during promotion, distribution and the potential fan reappropriation of this transmedia production, but also within the story of the film trilogy itself. The narration is organized in line with the evolution of the protagonist's point of view with regard to the *worlds* he is confronted with, passing from one to the other – since the worlds share a relationship of mutual accessibility – at the risk of being eventually lost. Digital technology serves not only as a guarantee for the film's attractional character (thanks to SFX), but it is also incorporated as a technical prerequisite for the worldbuilding process upon which the series' principal narrative stakes are based. The "Matrix city", itself embedded to the level that confronts the City of Zion (humanity's last bulwark) to the City of Machines, has its own "Architect": the "*Matrix*" trilogy is fully a part of this type of contemporary film productions that exhibit the "manufactured" aspect of their fictional universe while at the same time facilitating the viewer's maximal immersion in this world.[2] This chapter, devoted to cyberculture, begins with a study of the famous Wachowskis' trilogy, which I compare right from the outset to *Dark City* (1998). Studying the similarities and the differences between these films proves fruitful in the context of an investigation of the worldbuilding process in films that manifest a pronounced self-reflexive dimension.

However, even though *The Matrix* has turned into an emblem of a certain tradition of contemporary, PC-era science fiction (one the franchise helped to promote to a wide audience), the conception of multiverse narratives does not stem from the growing field of computer science nor from imaginaries related to the cyberspace: its roots are to be found in theoretical reflections on fiction. For instance, the technological dimension is completely absent in some of the short stories by the Argentinian writer Jorges Luis Borges, which offer, in a self-reflexive perspective and through the schematic structure typical of allegorical tales, a theoretical speculation on the consequences of the multiplicity of worlds (or of possible narrative alternatives), rather than stories unfolding within these worlds[3]. In effect, the labyrinth as a recurring motif in Borges' work – namely a metaphor that endows the process of writing with a mythological aura – opens up each story world to its possible alternatives: nothing is impossible to the republic of the immortal men, those capable of allowing themselves a never-ending time limit and, therefore, of performing an infinity of alterations ("The Immortal", 1950), just as all possible variations on every conceivable text are to be found in "The Library of Babel" (1941). At the end of "The Circular Ruins" (1940), the wizard who has created a simulacrum of a son – whose illusory nature seems to be known only to a multifaceted deity known as "Fire" – realizes that his own flesh is invulnerable to flames and, therefore, he too is a but an apparition, an illusion in someone else's dream (see Borges 1998). Such a conclusion that relates to the ontological status of fictional beings – also present in *The Invention of Morel*, a novel written by Borges' compatriot and friend Adolfo Bioy Casares, albeit in a more "mechanical" version – constitutes, as we will see later on, a frequent pattern in cyberpunk narratives whose worlds are governed by the notions of "simulacra and simulation".

John and Neo: Signs of the Times

Born out of a similar science fiction imaginary and the same world-centered design, John Murdoch (Rufus Sewell) in *Dark City* (1998) and Neo (Keanu Reeves[4]) in *The Matrix* (1999) share a lot in common. Under the guidance of an already initiated character, they both become gradually aware of the illusory nature of the world they inhabit. Protesting against the creators of such a simulacrum (manufactured by means of a "worldbuilding machine"), they develop through practice an innate and Promethean aptitude to transform their urban environment by themselves,[5] the former revealing doors and through-wall pathways, the latter avoiding bullets. Detached from the hero, who nevertheless constitutes one of its components, the world is then cast aside in a state of otherness, displaying its *fabricated* character: its status as a representation is made explicit.

The need to escape from their attackers, and then fight against agents sent by "architects" wishing to restore order inside their "small world" (partly dismantled by a "chosen one" representing the human race), urges the white, middle-class, male and heterosexual heroes[6] to use all their powers in action scenes reminiscent of the Jedi or Sith's telekinetic abilities in "*Star Wars*". John masters "tuning" (the ability to manipulate physical reality), while Neo, through mental concentration, manages to penetrate the computer system and break its laws. The training program used by Neo is external to both representations produced by the matrix and the real world:[7] its territory is that of tutorials – indeed, one could hardly be more "didactic" than Neo's mentor, Morpheus (Laurence Fishburne) – typical of video games that serve as a reference to *The Matrix*, even as far as its narrative structure is concerned. As the following pages will attest though, *Dark City*'s cultural references are much different.

Once the masks have fallen and the manipulators' identity revealed (a classic sci-fi pattern, notably present also in *They Live*, 1988),[8] the flexibility of a world subject to the estranging desiderata of a machine (or to those of a society of aliens at the command of such a machine) becomes an asset for the one designated as the savior, serving as a symbol of individuality against the standardized existence of his opponents. The "invaders" in *Dark City*, interconnected as they may be (as are the agents in *The Matrix* with the virtual duplicates of individuals connected to the machine), remain incapable of developing a distinct personality. This inability, likely to prove fatal to their species, motivates the research they conduct in their city-sized laboratory, a research aiming to probe the secrets of the human soul by constantly reshaping the memory of their guinea pigs. At the end of *The Matrix*, Neo exhibits his emancipation from the laws of the computer code by flying in the sky, dominating the urban space and the flow of the crowd underneath, like Superman or like the camera itself in the prologue of *Run Lola Run* (1998), facing from a vantage point of view the various narrative alternatives. At the end of *Dark City*, John instigates the creation of an ocean, a beach and a pier, giving birth to the sun, thus conjuring a setting allowing him, even more so than the hero of *La Jetée* (1962), to bring to life memories until then unknown to him (those, factitious, that were implanted in him without his knowledge) and reiterate his meeting with the woman that in one of the versions "scripted" by the extraterrestrials was his wife. One recognizes here a pattern common to several films of our corpus: the unfolding of variations on the stages of a couple's relationship, caught in a loop.[9] In this type of phallocentric representation, the female character's duplicates twirl around (one is reminded of "la donna è mobile", the stereotypical fear of the "hysterical woman" examined in Bankey 2001) and remain dependent on the male hero's efforts to organize the irrational. This way, *Dark City*'s narrative arc, certainly more conventional than the world that comes up with, advocates the reactionary ideology aiming to restore the norm and resolve the gender identity crisis, as highlighted by Charles-Antoine Courcoux in connection with *The Matrix*'s narrative:

> The reversal of power relations – a white middle-class male found at the bottom of the social ladder, overthrown in terms of gender (Trinity), race (Morpheus), class (Cypher) and strength (Smith) – is correlated with the extended influence of digital technology, the Matrix, which […] undermines the "ontological difference" between the sexes by showing an aptitude for creating the masculine, the agents, from a technology connoted as feminine (Courcoux 2013: 148)*.

In the case of *Dark City* and *The Matrix,* the idea of restoring a certain ontological difference is not exclusively related to questions of gender but also to the distinction between the reference world and the *virtual world*. In fact, both John and Neo are trying to overturn a dystopian universe, transforming it to its double that haunts it as if it were the flip side of the same semiotic construction: utopia. By showing his protagonist transforming the whole planet into an island, as he creates an ocean whose waves flow over the city's circumference,[10] Proyas attaches his film to the (mainly iconographic) tradition of Enlightenment's utopia (see in particular the Map of Utopia engraved by Ambroise Holbein for the 1518 edition of Thomas More's book). Among the various spatial configurations, the utopian genre privileges the "island and its numerous variations that perfectly meet the demands for internal closure and comprehensiveness associated with the representation of a 'different' world" (Racault 2016: 488)*. In an illustration from the original 1728 edition of Jonathan Swift's *Travels into Several Remote Nations of the World*, the island is shown floating in the air, among the clouds, just like the city in Proyas' film floats among the stars (see Chapter 3, Fig. 24).

Writing about this fictional genre, Marc Atallah remarks:

> The systemic invariant of the utopian genre therefore leads to an astonishing conclusion: all utopia is, in essence, a dystopia – and vice versa. This conclusion implies that the utopian perfection is not due to the organization of the represented system: its origin is to be found in the point of view from which one looks at it, since once this point of view is altered, perfection turns into alienation (Atallah 2013: 34)*.

The axiological distinction between utopia and dystopia is not inherent in the world-centered dimension, but results from the narrative organization, since it is imperative that the "focal" character experiences the world through a series of events or discoveries that take place in it. In other words, the utopia of some (the Strangers in *Dark City* who observe their guinea pigs from a distance) is the dystopia of others (the humans who experience this world from the inside). In fact, one wonders what will John have to offer to his fellow citizens outside of a postcard-like sun and an ocean (the maritime landscape of his factitious childhood memories), once he has assumed the powers of a worldbuilder and overthrown the aliens. Driven by the mere satisfaction of his own desires ("You told me I had the power didn't you? I can make these machines do anything I want. Make this world anything I want it to be"), John would in all probability have imposed a totalitarian regime, if only the film's story had taken the risk to go beyond the hero's victory over the Strangers. After all, Emma (who became Anna following the implantation of different memories) is clearly manipulated by him in the film's final images. One finds here the pattern of a male character dominating a woman thanks to a certain cognitive gain (on which the story of a film like *Groundhog Day* is founded). Indeed, while the hero succeeds in finally recreating the unity of his own personality – his last line, pronounced in a very assertive manner, consists simply of speaking out loud his first and last name – the rest of the city's inhabitants remain alienated to themselves. The film's dystopian character rests on a fear that was exacerbated by the standardization induced by mass culture (once denounced by Adorno and Horkheimer), namely the fear of losing one's own identity – a recurring theme in Philip K. Dick's work[11] – favoring this way an interchangeability of subjects. There are many other films (*Total Recall*, "*Resident Evil*", or TV series like *Dollhouse* and *Westworld*) that deal with a similar subject matter, their multiverse dimension often stemming from the ambivalence of the characters that ensure the link between the film's world and its story.

John and Neo's powers are nevertheless limited: Neo only seemingly escapes the matrix, while John discovers, after having torn down at the very end of the film the final wall separating him from the cosmic void, that he lives in a city/planet lost in space[12] operating as a laboratory in which he is one of many guinea pigs (similar to the ones in *Kafka*, a film written by one of *Dark City*'s scriptwriters, Lem Dobbs).[13] Moreover, Dr. Daniel Schreber (Kiefer Sutherland) owns a miniature labyrinth in which he observes the behavior of rats, thus anchoring mechanics to biology and psychiatry[14] (Fig. 35). While John can do

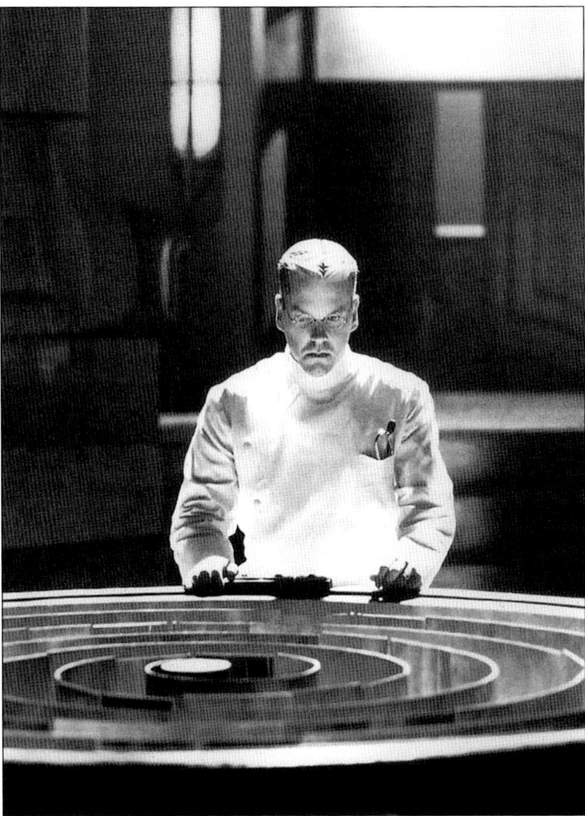

Fig. 35: The activity of the guinea pigs in an *artificial world* is compared to that of mice in a maze, under the gaze of a white-coat "doctor" (Kiefer Sutherland) who collaborates with the aliens. The idea of mastering a claustrophobic place where other characters are held captive is reminiscent of a scene in *The Shining* (1980), when Jack Torrance (Jack Nicholson) contemplates a miniature replica of the Overlook Hotel's labyrinth.

nothing but fight "from the inside" (since anything that goes beyond the city's perimeter is thrown into nothingness), it may seem incoherent that Neo strives to triumph over the matrix's programs on their own ground, instead of destroying them in the "real world". Michaël La Chance aptly recognized that the reason for this pre-eminence accorded to the *virtual world* over the reference world lies at the level of the hero's edification, the notion that "what is at stake here is not so much the possibility of facing a world's reality without illusions but the freedom one achieves within the coercion of appearance" (La Chance 2006: 94)*.

Within this paradigm, *Dark City* and *The Matrix* are perfectly interchangeable. The context of geek culture summoned by *The Matrix*, whose protagonist is a programmer by day and a hacker by night, invites us to transpose this observation into the terrain of reflections on medium specificity, by interpreting it as a celebration of video games' interactivity (the matrix consistently takes into account all types of behavior instilled by the mind of every member of the population enslaved to it), culminating with Neo's gradual control over his environment (similar to the player's "agency" in a videogame). The cinematic representation that hosts this reference to a different medium and illusively models itself on it (by visualizing the world of the matrix as it is perceived by a character who projects its avatar inside this world), appropriates certain iconic features commonly associated with video games, thus reinforcing the immersive nature of the world it proposes. The 'virtual reality' theme serves as a pretext for displaying latest technologies at the service of a blockbuster presented primarily as an action movie, whereas in *Dark City* the action tends to be suspended or aborted by the manipulations made by the "Strangers".

At first glance, while *The Matrix* might appear to echo the dystopian science fiction pattern *Dark City* follows verbatim, it also proceeds from a paradoxical fascination for *virtual worlds* that typifies cyberculture, in order to exploit its attractional potential. Its creators take pleasure in plunging us inside the matrix, visualizing momentarily the immateriality of this non-space[15] (Color Plate 14), gridded by the green lines of code to which Case, the hacker in William Gibson's emblematic cyberpunk novel *Neuromancer* (1984), becomes addicted, living "only for the bodiless exultation of cyberspace", for being lost "into the infinite neuroelectronic void of the matrix", repeatedly seeing "the matrix in his sleep, bright lattices of logic unfolding across that colorless void …" (Gibson 2018: 6, 123 and 4–5). Certainly, Neo does not enjoy evolving in the form of his virtual alter ego in quite the same manner as *Avatar*'s paraplegic hero, Jake Scully, but the film's story compels him to as a result of a certain prophecy. Having gone blind in *The Matrix Revolutions* (2003), he continues to "see" beyond a strictly perceptual standpoint as we do alongside with him (the viewer discerns orange silhouettes that replace the fluorescent green meshes of the embedded level). Instead of a town made of stone, like the one in *Dark City,* schematically illustrated in an aporetic subway map*, The Matrix* confronts us with a cartography of pixels.[16] Movies that temporarily materialize this process of changing worlds, or simply scales, are not rare. In the opening credits of *TRON* (1982) and *TRON: Legacy* (2010), the lights of a city plunged into darkness turn into pixels on a computer screen. During a shot transition in *Hackers* (1995) and in *The Thirteenth Floor* (1999), we surreptitiously shift from the regular distribution of New York buildings and luminous traces of vehicles on the highway, to interconnected transistors assembled on a microchip.[17]

Unlike what happens in "*The Matrix*" trilogy, escaping the machine is inconceivable in the diegesis of a "darker" film like *Dark City*: one can only learn to deal with the machine, with no hope of finding "our" world. Hence, the film does not lend itself to the development of sequels, nourished as they are in the case of *The Matrix* by the principle of alternation between an interior and an exterior. The world's closure in *Dark City*, communicated also through the recurring visual motifs of the circle and the spiral, tends to impose a textual closure as well. Certainly, in the Wachowskis' film, the world at the end of the 20th century (limited to the *model* of a North-American megalopolis) out of which the matrix fashions a *virtual* and interactive world,[18] is superseded in the future (the film's present) by a post-apocalyptic landscape that typifies cyberculture, depicted in an almost monochromatic fashion (red armchairs standing out from the black rock of a desert landscape). Nonetheless, this place remains the possible venue of "revolutions" which, as evidenced by the third part of the series (*The Matrix Revolutions*), do not only refer to the affirmation of the Human against the Machine, but also to the rotational movements of one star around another, suggesting a possible reboot of the matrix. In a scene from *The Matrix Reloaded* (2003), Neo opens a new door and enters in a room bathed in light where he meets the creator of the Matrix, The Architect (Helmut Bakaitis) (Color Plate 15). At that moment, we discover that the Chosen One and the rebellious inhabitants of Zion are the result of an anomaly in the system's "harmony of mathematical precision", which is actually foreseen by the system itself in order to reinforce its own efficiency. The Matrix has already been reset five times following the confrontations with Neo's previous versions. This way, the *virtual world* is combined with *alternate (story)worlds*. From its second episode onwards, "*The Matrix*" trilogy adopts the same kind of skepticism as the one elicited to the viewers of *Total Recall*, whereas *Dark City* presents its finale as a real outcome that celebrates the hero's accomplishment.

Between *Dark City* and *The Matrix*, released a year apart in the twilight of the second millennium, the Wachowskis' film is more in keeping with the contemporary context of "virtual realities", as the computing machine takes the role of a Big Brother, exploiting the energy of the human body. *Dark City*'s *artificial world* belongs to a much older tradition of perceptual illusions. This divergence is manifested even at the manufacturing level of these two productions: the Wachowskis opt for a virtual whole that serves the theme of their film (while effacing itself over this theme), whereas Alex Proyas chooses to have actual sets and models built, displaying the material aspect of the elements populating the urban world (artifacts gathered on an assembly line by the Strangers) (Color Plate 16) so as to better unveil its deceptive nature. The cogwheels set in motion in order to move and reconfigure the city's buildings seem straight out of the iconography of a heavily industrial landscape – as the sound effects emphasize – coming from a period prior to the popularization of discourses on computers and artificial intelligence (discourses that appear after the decline of the "film noir", a genre used in *Dark City* as a "historical" reference). Much like Schuiten and Peeters' comic book *The Great Walls of Samaris* (*Les Murailles de Samaris,* 1983–1984), the first volume in a series precisely named *Dark Cities* (*Les Cités obscures*),[19] Proyas' film refers to the baroque tradition of trompe-l'oeil: the city and the spectacular actions taking place in it are circumscribed by sets that can be changed through the use of stage mechanisms.

The Wachowskis' trilogy features similar characters and locations: the Mega City, the back doors, the intermediate spaces (the Train-Man Station), even the Architect. On the contrary, as numerous commentators have pointed out in promotional and critical discourses, *The Matrix* knowingly builds upon Baudrillard's theories developed in *Simulacra and Simulation*, regarding the world's status in the Computer Age. The philosopher advocates the need to conceptualize the outright liquidation of the notion of the "real". In a film production of *The Matrix*'s scale, anxious to openly deliver its own "user manual" for fear of losing even a tiny part of the targeted mass audience, but also in order to manifest a "cerebral", pseudo-cryptic attitude likely to feed fan discourses, the allusion to Jean Baudrillard's work appears explicitly in the form of a diegetic element: Baudrillard's book is physically present on a shelf in Neo's apartment.[20] We can notice it in the beginning of the film, during the main hero's introduction, as Neo hides the computer data he sells illegally inside a hollowed-out copy of the book, right after the first page of its last section (entitled "On Nihilism"), as if the film itself were to write the final chapter. Nevertheless, by drawing a clear and reassuring dividing line between the *virtual world* of the matrix and the *real* (without quotation marks) where the war against the machines is taking place, the first part of the Wachowskis' trilogy, unlike *eXistenZ* (1999), is far from establishing the prevalence of simulation over representation (in the sense of Baudrillard). In fact, there is no "substituting the signs of the real for the real, that is to say [no] operation of deterring every real process via its operational double" (Baudrillard 1995: 2). As Aurélie Ledoux points out, "to represent a reality behind the simulacrum", as *The Matrix* does, is "to remain inside the simulation while believing in the real" (Ledoux 2012: 72)[*]. In fact, unbeknownst to its own creators, *The Matrix* probably reaffirms the case illustrated by Baudrillard through the example of Disneyland, attached to "the social microcosm, the religious, miniaturized pleasure of real America", aiming at last, vainly and misleadingly, to save "the reality principle" (Baudrillard 1995: 12).

This observation, valid as it may be in the first film of the trilogy, needs to be nuanced in the case of its sequel, *The Matrix Reloaded* (2003). The second installment openly deals with the principle of a strict segregation between the two worlds in order to play on the permeability of borders, materialized in the proliferation of "back doors" normally reserved for programmers, but to which the "Keymaker" (a character straight out of a Coen brothers' movie or *Dark City* itself) can grant access. When Neo opens a door and finds himself entirely displaced, in a castle perched in a mountainous landscape, he is forced to perform the same type of jumps as the main hero in *Sherlock Jr.* (1924) or Desmond in *Lost*, except that here the editing is made invisible by cutting on motion. In this episode, agent Smith assumes the body of a character who is nonetheless to be found outside the matrix, being one of its programs, while Neo, chased by war drones in the surroundings of the city of Zion, manages to stop these machines as if he were faced with a virtual threat.

Unlike *The Matrix*, *Dark City* excludes all possible attachments to a reference world. We never learn what happened to the Earth, since the "Strangers" have induced an irrevocable collective amnesia. This would explain why, even though both films build a typical postmodern world, where all signs contained in the world make sense in relation to other signs, the outcome is different in *Dark City* as far as the ontological interpretation of the world is concerned. As we will encounter further on, in Proyas' film the mechanistic world of the simulacrum is founded on the recycling of a hodgepodge of references.

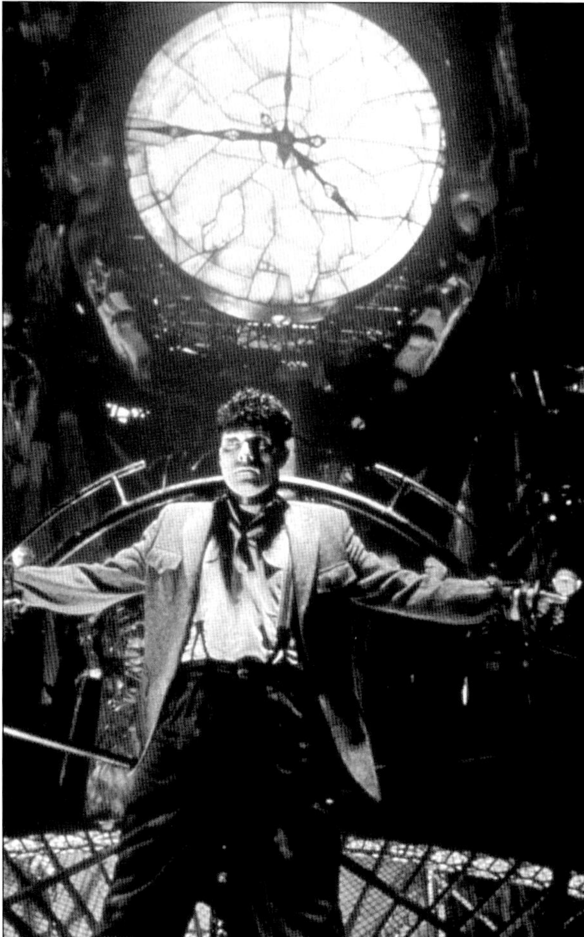

Fig. 36: *Dark City*'s "Messiah" (Rufus Sewell), crucified on the altar of an alien (and alienating) technology, manages to reverse the balance of power by taking control of the "worldbuilding machine".

After a detailed analysis of *Dark City*, which will allow us to articulate the subject of the present chapter with several elements discussed previously (in particular with regard to the connections between style and world), I will turn briefly to a novel by Daniel F. Galouye, *Simulacron-3* (1964), an actual "matrix" of *The Matrix* which has been adapted for the screen twice, first as a TV production (*World on a Wire*, 1973) then as a feature film (*The Thirteenth Floor,* 1999). Including these films – whose particularity is to deny, in a radical manner absent from *Dark City* and *The Matrix,* the very human nature of the main hero – in our corpus will help us tackle the question of representation of *virtual worlds* while going off the beaten track, given that the Wachowskis' blockbuster has been overwhelmingly discussed. There is no doubt, however, that "*The Matrix*" crystallized a tendency to popularize science fiction patterns (especially those attached to the cyberpunk movement) linked to relationships between humans and computing machines; it is therefore symptomatic that this film was released just a few months apart from *Dark City, The Thirteenth Floor*, and *eXistenZ*, in a period that saw a rise in multiverse movies.

From my perspective, one could say that cyberculture, to which the aforementioned films are more or less related, constitutes an atheistic, pessimistic, and paranoid version of Leibniz's Theodicy, already discussed in previous chapters. Indeed, in his effort to reconcile the idea of an absolute divine arrangement with the existence of the human soul, Leibniz explains: "it is easy to believe that the soul is a spiritual automaton still more admirable [than nature's other wonders]" (Leibniz 1985: 369). If the scientistic comparison to "automata" used by the philosopher is considered in a literal sense, as it is possible to do in the cyberculture context, and by replacing the so-called "divine preformation" with a computer program so as to give "gamers" the possibility of a certain *interactivity*, we end up with a typical situation of the dystopian science fiction genre, one that deals with a population alienated by technology. These stories exalt the return of the religious, naturally handed over to human beings, by putting forth messianic, "*Neo*-Christic" figures that assert their free will through their actions, providing viewers with a focal point that fictitiously liberates them from their own motor and psychic enslavement to the "matrix" of the cinematographic apparatus (Fig. 36). Indeed, the viewer meets for the first time John Murdoch, still an "empty" character (naked and amnesiac) but destined to bring the "light" to the city later on, by following the camera as it enters a bathroom through a circular dormer window, inside a building whose facade is almost opaque. This aperture clearly evokes the *oculus* of a *camera obscura*; it is therefore no surprising that religious studies scholar Gerard Loughlin compared *Dark City*'s story to Plato's allegory of the cave in the *Republic* in which "in every way [...] [the] prisoners would recognize as reality nothing but the shadows of [...] artificial objects":[21] "to live in Plato's cave, not as one of the prisoners, but as Socrates or Glaucon, would be to live like John Murdoch in Alex Proyas' *Dark City*. [...] Murdoch answers a certain contemporary nihilism, since unlike Plato, he is disabused of any hope of an outside" (Loughlin 2004: 46 and 48).

The Urban Simulacrum of Postmodern Cinema: *Dark City*

A product of hybridization between science fiction and film noir, *Dark City*, just like *Blade Runner* (1982) before it, had a voice-over imposed on its theatrical version which, according to the producers' rationale, was supposed to reinforce the story's intelligibility. As in the case of Ridley Scott's film, this voice-over was removed from the later release of the "director's cut".[22] This addition raised an extra difficulty in the case of *Dark City*, since the "focal" character, John Murdoch, is amnesiac and therefore has no prior awareness of the world he lives in. Subsequently, as a homodiegetic narrator, it would have been improbable to transmit information right from the outset allowing the viewer's orientation while he himself is lost. Moreover, a retrospective narration would be likely to produce a *spoiler* effect – or else would require a somewhat abusive use of *paralipse*. It is probably for this reason that the voice chosen for this narration is that of Kiefer Sutherland, who plays the part of Dr. Schreber, the only human initiated into the city's mysteries. Nonetheless, the screenwriters had to avoid defiling the film's intriguing character by this narration, which begins as follows:

> First there was darkness. Then came the Strangers. They were a race as old as time itself. They had mastered the ultimate technology: the ability to alter physical reality by will alone. They called this ability "Tuning". But they were dying. Their civilization was in decline, and so they abandoned their world seeking a cure for their own mortality. Their endless journey brought them to a small, blue world in the farthest corner of the galaxy. Our world. Here they thought they had finally found what they had been searching for.

These 'biblical' opening statements, whose first words are pronounced over a completely black screen, fit the 'foundation of a world' concept. Interestingly enough, the "darkness" (a term that is present in its adjective form in the film's title) comes first. Clearly, this is a metaphor that adds a mythological dimension to the narrative. Retrospectively, one can literally deduce that *nothing* actually existed prior to the darkness enshrouding the film's city-world, since this city is fictitious, created for the sole purpose of *experiencing the film*. Through the use of expressions such as "our world" and by deliberately maintaining a temporal ambiguity between the verbal referent (the planet Earth once visited by the Strangers) and the visual referent (the "city" is seen as the voice-over is heard), this narration helps to scale down the otherness of the film's world compared to the viewers' reference world (the possessive adjective "our" including the latter). As a result, it ends up reinforcing the illusion, since the viewer, accustomed to the fact that the voice-over has a decisive role in transmitting information related to the construction of a world (see Boillat 2007: 335–380 and 2009c), is led to exclude the possibility that we might not be on Earth. But then how are we supposed to perceive this world as the "real", "our" world, when all architectural elements, costumes, weapons, and cars pertaining to it come from various historical periods (even if the '50s remain a dominant reference), when it is always dark, the lightning is extremely unnatural, etc.? Here lies *Dark City*'s "coup de force", as it succeeds in temporarily concealing certain features of *the world inside the film* behind *the world of the film*, by playing on the principle of minimal departure. In *The Matrix*, this principle works towards the traditional goal of simplifying the transmission of diegetic information: as Ledoux explains, "the disclosure can occur this early only because the world, whose facticity is revealed, is supposed to be more or less our world; hence, manipulation is redundant [...]; the object of the denunciation elicits an immediate consensus" (Ledoux 2012: 70)*. Things are quite different in the case of *Dark City*, where the world of a post-apocalyptic future, located outside the "matrix", is tightly woven into the "first" world. From the beginning of the film, the viewer has to adapt to the "change of scenery" caused by the retrofuturistic context, before realizing that the illusion lies at the heart of the immersive fiction. More specifically, he is encouraged to interpret a number of *effective aspects of the world* (the illusion of a city build from the memories of an entire population, collected and blended into a moving whole through an industrial exploitation of traces of the past) as *stylistic features* (a regime of timelessness found in other films, such as *Bunker Palace Hotel* or *Avalon*) – in other words, as "alterations" introduced by the "filter" the filmmaker inserted between the viewer and the represented world. This type of inferences rests on an intertextual basis that encompasses not only individual films to which *Dark City* can be compared, like Alex Proyas' previous film, *The Crow* (1994),[23] but also a horizon of expectations determined by a genre, in this case a hybrid. In a way, science fiction is contaminated by film noir (chase scenes in dark alleys or spiral staircases, a serial killer, a female performer in an evening dress singing a languorous song, etc.), following a process that has been studied in the literature devoted to the latter and commented by Anne-Françoise Lesuisse as follows:

> Whereas hybridity in itself is not problematic, the presence of "noir" elements is here considered not only as a cross-generic operation but also as a mutation. The film noir components present a few tangible elements, but also create a specific *aura,* drawing the film from its original genre and transforming it into a film noir in its own right (Lesuisse 2002: 78)[*].

Strictly speaking, the question of the film's generic status is not relevant to my study; it is obvious however that all the elements linked to the detective story in *Dark City* are "false tracks", as the ex-cop character Walenski (Colin Friels) rightly realizes before sinking into "madness".[24] That said, Lesuisse's observation is important for elucidating a fact of reception: while the genre's aura should not normally impact the ontological status of the film's referents, this is precisely what happens in the case of *Dark City*.

The film's pragmatic efficiency results above all from its generic references, associated with a certain era not of plain history, but of history *of film*: the viewer accepts these references as cinematic norms and initially fails to realize their "diegetization". However, he becomes aware of this process when for instance John expresses his surprise at the fact that he has never seen a day dawn in this world. After all, the perpetual darkness could have been the result of ellipses: one does not necessarily wonder what the detectives are up to during daytime hours in certain films precisely qualified as "noir" [black], a term that, as Lesuisse demonstrates, refers simultaneously to their nocturnal diegetic atmosphere and to the use of darkness as a visual element. The principle of assimilating a world to a film genre is similar to the one at work in *Who Framed Roger Rabbit*, as far as the presence of *toons*, or the world-specific use of colors are concerned. Moreover, color plays an important role in *Dark City* in exhibiting the artificiality of the image and in distinguishing between the various diegetic spaces. The city's surface is bathed in a yellowish directional light coming from street lamps, leaving large parts of the image in the shade. At the same time, the city's depths, where the aliens collectively use their minds in order to activate the "worldbuilding machine" overseen by a huge clock that echoes *Metropolis* (1928), vibrate in a more uniform way with an electric blue-green light clearly separating from the dark background the pale, cadaverous faces of the humans inhabited by the aliens.[25] These vampire-like bodies clad in leather costumes seem to come straight out of Murnau or

Herzog's *Nosferatu*, and blend demonism and sadomasochism in a manner reminiscent of the *Hellraiser* film series (1987–2018). The drastic decolorization plays in *Dark City* a similar role to the one in *Avalon*, discussed earlier in this book, except that here nothing is "virtual". The city, reconfigured every day at midnight once the inhabitants are frozen through the suspension of time's unfolding (much like in *Paris qui dort*, 1924), is concretely modified. Buildings rise from the ground and others are transformed, while the hero, chased on rooftops, tries to take advantage of this rapid reshaping of the scenery that proves fatal to some of his pursuers as they are being crushed between two facades colliding in order to create a new building. The "Strangers" visit the quiet, dollhouse-like apartments, injecting false memories with a syringe (sort of modern vampire bites)[26] in the skull of certain inhabitants whose personal environment is then adapted to their new personalities and to the subsequent change in their social status.[27] Alex Proyas' special effects team made an extensive use of the "morph", which, according to Kristen Whissel, is "one of the first digital effects to be recognized by film critics and audiences alike as a computer-generated spectacle that seemed to herald the beginning of a new era in the history of cinematic visual effects" (2014: 131). Whissel considers that this special effect "tends to be featured more spectacularly in films set in imaginary worlds defined by radically closed, even carceral settings [and that] this spatial confinement often has a temporal/historical corollary that subjects a film's protagonists to unavoidable, fated futures over which they have no control." However, in *Dark City*, the hero ends up taking control over "space, time and fate" (*Ibid.*: 17–18), namely over the (*artificial*) world (Color Plate 17).

The instability of the urban landscape in *Dark City* may be viewed as a kind of dystopian version of the experimental work proposed by some architecture theorists attached to the Archigram British movement of the '60s and the '70s, who imagined the creation of mobile and modular cities. It is also the manifestation of a specific North American model, pinned down by Architecture theorist Rem Koolhaas in its proper imaginary dimension (disguised as pragmatism) in his book *Delirious New York*. Not only is the city composite and discontinuous,[28] but, as Koolhaas illustrates through the example of the Waldorf-Astoria Hotel, it undergoes constant modifications: "The Waldorf has instigated a paradoxical *tradition of the last word* […] which, to preserve itself, is forced continuously to self-destruct, eternally to shed its latest incarnation" (Koolhaas 1994: 137). The uninterrupted cycle of the buildings' death and rebirth is accelerated in *Dark City* at a daily pace imposed by the horrifying "demons come out at night" leitmotif, while echoing a very real anguish of individuality crushed under the urban bustle of modernity. The city functions here as a metonymy for the world: the horizon is limited to its size. One is reminded of Leibniz who in his effort to demonstrate in his *Monadology* the compatibility of the idea of an absolute universal order embracing the multiplicity of individual units, resorted to an urban comparison:

> The same town, when looked at from different places, appears quite different and is, as it were, multiplied in *perspectives*. In the same way it happens that, because of the infinite multitude of simple substances, there are just as many different universes, which are nevertheless merely perspectives of a single universe according to the different point of view of each monad (Leibniz 2014: 25).

The city mirrors the world (in which every monad is in turn a mirror itself), even in terms of perspective: the comparison advocated by Leibniz, whose manner of thinking is vastly different from the experience of modernity in the 20th century, calls attention to the kaleidoscopic vision induced by the urban space, in a manner that the city's modularity in *Dark City* (1998) or *Inception* (2010) clearly echoes.

The numerous cinematic references present in *Dark City* – notably to German films of the 1920s and Hollywood productions of the '40s and the '50s – lead to the conclusion that this film, rather than creating a world of "its own", is based on the "world of film history". The representation does not correspond to any referent – after all, the latter is explicitly revoked even inside the diegesis – but to its own semiotic nature, as evidenced by the various occurrences of a publicity message for "Shell Beach", a vacation site by the ocean. Everyone admits its existence and this advertisement is displayed everywhere, like for instance in a gigantic mechanical billboard (a low-tech device if there ever was one) whose faded colors stand nonetheless out from the surrounding greyness (this is the equivalent of the poster announcing the concert located in a different world-level in *Avalon*). Still, none of them remember exactly what they were doing there, or even what route they had taken to arrive. Even the taxi driver suffers from amnesia, despite the fact he has a trinket on his vehicle's dashboard representing this supposedly idyllic place. This is because a differentiation is established between the *here* and the *elsewhere*, or rather a folding: the *elsewhere* is *here*. "Shell Beach" is not a real location, but one that is both purely visual, signifying nothing else than itself, and mental, artificially implanted in the memories of the city's inhabitants. The main hero, a man with no name or past (at least until the very end of the film, when he assumes the last of his many names) has in its possession some relics from the years he allegedly spent in Shell Beach, supposedly his hometown. As a matter of fact, his childhood sketchbook is at first filled with blank pages (that is, before Murdoch materializes on them the images formed in his head). Still, the uncle who adopted him after the fire incident that cost the life of his parents shows slides of him as a child, photographed at Shell Beach, against a maritime postcard-like sunny landscape. The postcard reference is to be taken literally, as it is this type of image that instigates John to find whatever it constitutes the trace of. However, much like one of the versions of *Total Recall*'s final scene (2012), discussed in Chapter 2, John, after approaching the projected image of the postcard (in a way that the image is also projected "on" him), observes an anomaly: the young man in the picture has an indelible burn scar on his arm, whereas John, as he shows to his uncle by rolling up his shirt, has no trace of a similar scar. Everything is but an image, as the child's projected figure on John's shirt seems to imply, occupying the right half of the frame that contrasts to the intact skin located on the left half. The child's gaze, directed towards the camera, an element one can perceive as a pledge of veracity (the absence of any effort to conceal the filming apparatus is a typical trait of family photographs and home movies), is henceforth a sign of otherness. Shell Beach exhibits the illusion while simultaneously concealing it. One must "scratch off" the tourist label in order to find reality's texture, or rather notice its immateriality. In the scene where John and Inspector Bumstead (William Hurt) arrive at the edge of their "small world", they find themselves once again facing an advertising poster for Shell Beach that covers a large part of the wall, the image standing for the real location (since their journey was supposed to lead them to Shell Beach). They tear down a part of this poster and then demolish the brick wall on which it hung, before discovering that the (cosmic) void awaits them on the other side.

There is an added dimension to the artificial objects the "Strangers" use as props in order to give credibility to their staging of the city. John's *mental world* is delivered to us in bits and pieces every time the hero, amnesiac as he is (since the implantation is incomplete), tries to remember who he really is. In this regard, the film is hardly original. Dissolving, anamorphic images are common in movies (nevertheless, its aesthetics will have a clear influence on *Requiem for a Dream*, starring *Dark City*'s Jennifer Connelly, another film that uses the pier-on-a-beach visual motif). However, John's *mental world* is itself the product of a surrounding, *artificial world* that inherits certain representational features: memory flashback images bend, burst, scatter around, surreptitiously give birth to whole new elements, and stretch, like the city's buildings at midnight. Each image emerges within the frame preceding it in a series of rough yet uninterrupted superimpositions. However, the film's final twist reveals the narrative's world-centered roots. Disobeying the aliens, Dr. Schreber changes the syringes and injects an unexpected substance into John's brain, whose visions are now witnessed by the viewer. Instead of a new personality, an earlier version of his past is restored and passes before our eyes. Yet the flashing, oscillating, and blurred visualization of various moments taken out of John's life, regularly elicits the incongruous appearance of a man in the most diverse disguises – specifically that of a teacher standing in front of a blackboard, underlining thus the "didactic" function of this scene – who, filmed in close-ups, addresses him (and us) looking straight at the camera. This *invariant*, itself a manifestation of the worlds' interpenetration, is none other than Dr. Schreber himself, explaining to John, as if in a video game tutorial, who he really is, what his special power (the "tuning") is, and how does the machine he must master in order to free humanity from the yoke of the aliens works. Subsequently, the *artificial world* can be dominated by endowing a *mental-virtual world* since, even if we are into John's mind, his visions are imposed on him from the outside by a – in this case extremely lucid – "mad scientist"! The boundaries between the interior and the exterior, between the human body and the city-world are blurred. In that respect, *Dark City* is indeed the product of a context partly shaped by the cyberculture of the end of the 20th century. The low-tech depiction of machines (including those of the aliens) and the pastiche of different genres establish the film as a product of a postmodern way of thinking, permeated – according to Fredric Jameson – by a nostalgic fascination in which all references to the real are negated in favor of representations that manifest themselves as such (like the Shell Beach pictures) and as the result of a recycling process (the retro style).[29] Jameson detects nonetheless a "new formal inventiveness" in this cinematic postmodernism:

> [I]t being understood that the nostalgia film was never a matter of some old-fashioned "representation" of historical content, but instead approached the "past" through stylistic connotation, conveying "pastness" by the glossy qualities of the image, and […] "1950s-ness" by the attributes of fashion (in that following the prescription of the Barthes of *Mythologies*, who saw connotation as the purveying of imaginary and stereotypical idealities […]). (Jameson 1991: 19)

Dark City corresponds in every respect to this practice described by Jameson who, in order to explain the ahistoricism of this type of film productions, takes the example of *Body Heat* (1981), a film whose aesthetics refer to the film noir. Jameson emphasizes the distinctiveness of the leading actor, William Hurt, in that his construction as a star works in the "death of the subject" mode that "opens up the possibility of a play of historical allusions to much older roles […] so that the very style of the acting can now also serve as a 'connotator' of the past" (*Ibid.*: 20).[30] Interestingly enough, William Hurt plays one of the main characters in *Dark City* too, one who more than anyone else typifies the detective genre in terms of clothing and attitude (Fig. 37).

The film meditates on the evacuation of a past snatched away from the memory of human beings in order to be reproduced in the present – both in terms of diegetic and filmophanic temporalities – in the form of a heterogeneous collage of stereotypes. In this respect, it meets the "perpetual present", identified by Laurent Jullier as one of the main features of postmodern cinema, traces of which can be found in *Je t'aime je t'aime*. In Resnais' film, the pre-emptive value of flashbacks tends to cancel itself out in the very act of viewing these flashbacks, attributed to the character/viewer. Jullier emphasizes the editing between locations "spatiotemporally disjointed" (therefore predisposed to the operation of shifting between different worlds, as examined in Chapter 4 with regard to the principle of alternation) and cites as an example an excerpt from *Un chien andalou* (1929) in which "the female character opens the door of her apartment on the third floor of a bourgeois building in Paris and in the reverse shot, cutting on motion and with matching clothes, we find her at the edge of a beach" (Jullier 1997: 112)[*]. In *Dark City*, the pier appears at the bend of a dark alleyway in the city center and the editing is based on an understanding of the

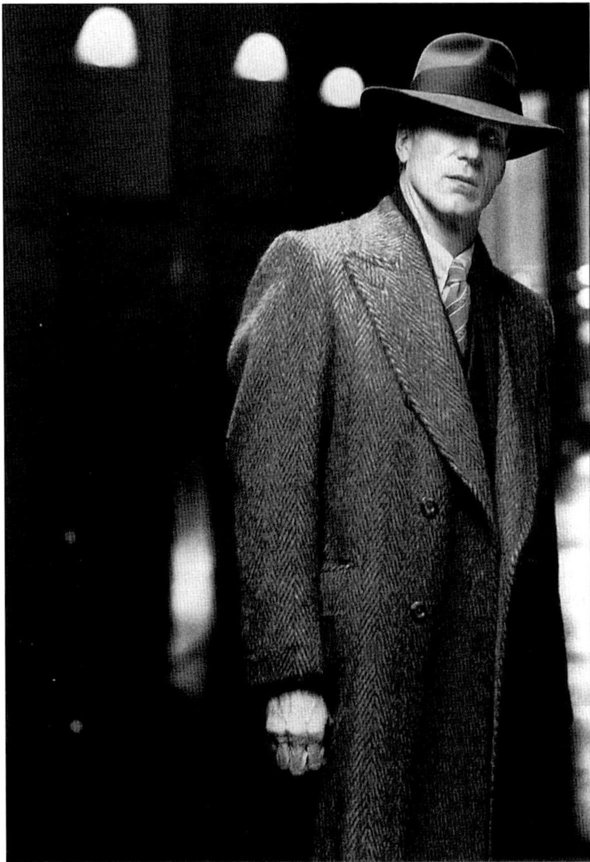

Fig. 37: William Hurt as inspector Frank Bumstead, a neo-noir character in *Dark City* (1998).

changing status of the urban environment itself. Actually, the gigantic clock activated by the aliens (a reference to an apocalyptic motif present in the comic series *Watchmen*) "diegetizes" the film's postmodern endeavor in a properly world-centered fashion. One can argue that the duplication inherent in self-reflexivity (the film "seeing itself" as a representation) is here materialized in splits from the film's universe which, as already pointed out, map the boundaries between the supposedly real reference world, the *artificial world* of the city, and the *mental world*, a combination that establishes, alongside a more general allusion to cyberculture, a connection to contemporary "virtual realities".

Dark City also exploits ahistoricism in terms of the construction of the sci-fi world in it. The latter, much like the one in "*The Matrix*",[31] belongs to the tradition of dystopian imaginaries of which George Orwell's totalitarian society constitutes one of the most famous archetypes. *Dark City* does not only deal with the erasure of an individual memory, but with a constant, daily reorganization of the collective memory of the city's inhabitants who have become victims of a "worldbuilding machine". In this respect, Proyas' film literally illustrates, through the power exerted by the "Strangers", the perpetual reconfiguration of the past transformed into pure fiction, in which the members of the "Ingsoc" ("English Socialism") regime in *1984* are specialized:

> The mutability of the past is the central tenet of Ingsoc. Past events, it is argued, have no objective existence, but survive only in written records and in human memories. The past is whatever the records and the memories agree upon. And since the Party is

> in full control of all records and in equally full control of the minds of its members, it follows that the past is whatever the Party chooses to make it. It also follows that though the past is alterable, it never has been altered in any specific instance. For when it has been recreated in whatever shape is needed at the moment, then this new version IS the past, and no different past can ever have existed (Orwell 1961: 269).

Its attachment to the science fiction genre allows *Dark City*'s story to go as far as the "real" and definitive rejection of all truths undesired by the governing bodies. The question of deleting all traces is therefore just as important here: the images of Shell Beach can be seen as a depoliticized variation on the photograph of the three convicts wrongly accused of treason in *1984*. The ultimate goal of the aliens conducting their experiments on the human soul is similar to that of the Party in Orwell's novel. *1984*'s hero, reflecting on the leaders' indoctrination project, is ascertained in thinking that "with all their cleverness, they had never mastered the secret of finding out what another human being was thinking" (*Ibid.*: 210). Later, under torture, he replies to his hangman that, despite all the humiliations, he did not betray his feelings for the woman he loves, Julia. While *Dark City* concludes with the victory of an inalienable human quality (John and Emma *recognize* each other), *1984* – either in Orwell's novel or in Michael Radford's screen adaptation – ends with the annihilation of all human emotions, as Winston finally rejects his lover in order to escape death. At the end of the film version, O'Brien (Richard Burton), a member of the Inner Party, explains to Winston (John Hurt) a principle that foreshadows the story's tragic ending: "Power is tearing human minds apart and putting them back together in new shapes of your own choosing". This is a particularly dark take on a trend frequent on films that prioritize the establishment of a diegesis, considering the world as a "construction game". The narrative frame, centered on a single character, exists so as to remind us that it is the individual who pays the price. Moreover, most multiverse films focus on the main hero's ever-growing alienation. In Hollywood though, the dystopian character of these films is softened by the inevitable romance that counterpoints the deindividuation produced by the machine, as evidenced by *The Matrix* and *Dark City*'s stories where, thanks to this type of secondary intrigues, the prevalence of the *narrative* over the *diegetic* is ensured. After all, the dominant storytelling norms require that the film's hero ultimately succeeds in changing the world, assuring from an Aristotelian perspective the transformation of the initial state into a different final state, as the ultimate stage of the narrative causal chain.

Simulacron-3: Cyberculture Worlds

At the end of "*The Matrix*"'s last installment, a serious doubt remains as to the effects of Neo's sacrifice: has "the" world really changed, or has it only completed one of its programmed cycles, essential for the proper functioning of the matrix? If the world supposed to be outside the matrix resembles to an underwater world, with its ships and its swarming electric fauna,[32] it could be perhaps signifying that this dystopian world is imaginary itself, subordinated to an alternate level, a more "real" one, located on the "surface" and unknown to the inhabitants of Zion, except Neo. At the end of *The Matrix Revolutions*, when the spacecraft operated by Trinity (Carrie-Anne Moss), looking to escape its pursuers,[33] goes beyond a thick cloud and temporarily reaches the stratosphere before plunging back into the greyness, with sunlight suddenly appearing in the blue of the sky similar to *Dark City*'s ending, it clearly seems as if a new type of borders remains to be crossed. Actually, if a computer program like "agent Smith" (Hugo Weaving) – regardless of the "dysfunction" animating it – is to "possess" the body of one of the crew members of a ship, supposedly outside the matrix, it is essential that everything should be (still) taking place inside the computer-simulated world. Ultimately, "*The Matrix*" trilogy, free of the kind of irony found in *Total Recall*, puts less emphasis on this particular dimension, privileging an ambiguous finale, while also providing a more compatible ending with the one expected of a Hollywood blockbuster. At the same time it manifests, in a rather covert manner, its debt to one of the cornerstones of cyberculture literature: *Simulacron-3*, by Daniel F. Galouye, published in 1964, three years after the author's previous novel, remarkably titled *Dark Universe*.[34]

Adapted to the screen in a German-American production entitled "*The Thirteenth Floor*" (1999), *Simulacron-3* tells the story of a computer scientist, Douglas Hall, assistant to the inventor of a social environment simulator intended to predict consumer behavior. Hall decides to project himself into the simulated world to discover the reasons for the assassination of his boss, Hannon Fuller, who left in the "second" world several clues likely to explain his disappearance. At first, in the "real" world, Hall believes he is suffering from hallucinations. Then he observes some strange reconfigurations of his environment, notably when Morton Lynch, the chief security officer of the company he works for, disappears without a trace: with the exception of Hall (and the reader), no one remembers Lynch. This rewriting – similar to the one at work in *Twin Peaks: Fire Walk With Me* (David Lynch, 1992), though not diegetically motivated there – participates in a worldbuilding process (as in *Dark City*). In *Simulacron-3*, these fluctuations of the real may be initially misinterpreted as the consequence of a large-scale conspiracy, following the model of *The Game* (see Chapter 3), or as a sign of mental disorder. When he notices a "bug" in the landscape, Hall regrets being unable to share his observation with his companion who was at that moment asleep: "Then, by her reaction, I would have known whether half of all creation had blinked out of existence or whether I had merely imagined that effect" (Galouye 2011: 53). At first, Hall opts for the second hypothesis, namely an explanation of a psychic nature, before resigning himself to the fact that his world is merely an illusion. He will finally realize that the dizzy spells result from a faulty coupling with an individual from the frame world.[35] If at first glance the *virtual world* seems like a *mental world*, it is mostly due to a narrative strategy aimed at ensuring the reader's identification with the hero. In fact, the main character's "actual" inexistence would have threatened the interest aroused by the adventures he experiences, all the more so in a first-person narrative. The incongruities perceived by Hall inspire his and the reader's growing distrust, until the moment he realizes he is inside an electronic simulation. Once this truth is unveiled, he fights against the "Manipulator" to prevent him from destroying a world identical to ours as far as we know – just like in *The Matrix*.[36] A world he will finally abandon so as to enter the frame world and join the loved one he had until then only met as a computer avatar.

The story is entirely regulated by a "worldbuilding machine". Not only do scientists project themselves into the simulation by taking over the virtual body of one of the individuals who inhabit it (called "reaction units"), but also a relationship of mutual accessibility is established: "Just as the observer's ego was temporarily planted within the ID's storage unit, so might the latter's sweep up and impress itself upon the brain of the observer in a violent, instant exchange" (*Ibid.*: 43). Foreshadowing a frequent pattern in fantasy and science-fiction movies,[37] a similar kind of alienating possession of one's brain by another (here thanks to technoscientific means)[38] establishes a permeability between the different worlds that guarantees an effective "journey" and thus a series of conflicts between an individual and his host environment. Furthermore, it is Phil Ashton, a simulated character that has seized the body of one of Hall's colleagues, who reveals to the hero that his reality is also a counterfeit. Ashton's goal is to gradually ascend to different world levels, following a common aspiration of heroes in dystopian narratives trying to leave the underground and reach the surface (*THX 1138*, *The Island*). The embedded worlds are conceived in terms of hierarchy (vertical axis) and of quasi-reduplication, as Hall points out when he tries to imagine the place where the computing machines that produce the environment he lives are located:

> What must it be like Up There? How vastly different from the pseudoreality I knew? Then I understood that it *couldn't* be very different at all. The world of Phil Ashton, sustained by the currents in Fuller's simulator, had had to be, in effect, a replica of my own if the predictions we got from that analog creation were to have valid application up here (*Ibid*: 124–125).

The proliferation of levels stems precisely from this mirror effect that reduces the gap between the worlds: the entities living inside the simulation develop themselves a new simulation, paving the way for a potentially infinite multiplication, as the ending of *eXistenZ* (1999) suggests, when gamers project themselves as inventors and users of video games. In *Simulacron-3*, this reproduction is due to the fact that at the diegetic level the simulation's goal is strictly commercial and has little to do with that of entertainment video game products – the story, echoing socio-economic concerns more than contemporary media practices, was written in the first half of the '60s. In each of the dieges es of this multiverse, the simulation offers a mathematical *model* intended to facilitate the development of predictions in the frame world.

Regarding this point, there seems to be a significant difference between Galouye's text and *The Thirteenth Floor*, shot more than thirty years later, even if this screen adaptation remains generally close to the original story. In fact, in this film, the world of the simulation is not identical to the first world since the inventor took pleasure in recreating an American metropolis of the 1930s. Thus, being "projected" into this dematerialized world means traveling through time. The title given to the film for its French release – *Le Passé virtuel* aka Virtual Past – highlights this dimension, whereas the original title places more emphasis on the embedding of different levels. This adjustment corresponds to the visual nature of the cinematographic medium: by presenting itself as a previous state of the upper world *and* as a distinct film genre, the embedded world becomes a spectacle, an object of contemplation. This idea is already present in Galouye's novel, which in a sense anticipates its screen adaptation, or perhaps conceives the illusory world described in it on the model of the viewer's identification with a character from a film. The transfer from one level to another and one body to the next (that in *The Thirteenth Floor* belongs to the same actor, several cast members playing more than one parts) is described in the following terms: "Satisfied with the completeness of the coupling, I (Doug Hall) pulled back from total to perceptive empathy and saw through Thompson's eyes as he glanced at the man in the other seat". Galouye calls attention to the fact that the objective is to obtain the user's *perceptual* identification with the "reaction unit" which here implies the idea of a subjective camera: we are indeed dealing with an immobile traveler who has gained access to an audio-visual representation (*Ibid*: 44).

In addition, the very first scenes in *The Thirteenth Floor* take place in the 1930s and it is only retrospectively that the viewer realizes this is not the first world. As in *Dark City*, the "fiction within a fiction" presents itself as the resurgence of a past with a stereotypical iconography, notably in terms of chromatic features – ochre discolored hues are frequently used to represent this particular era in movies. Hall is clearly aware of this "aesthetic" aspect, which he considers to be a result of the world's programming, specifying to the operator who assists him during his transfers that the rendering is of very good quality, except for the colors that leave, according to him, a lot to be desired. Consequently, the *virtual world* that allows the user to project himself into a different era relates to both the model of the amusement park (one thinks here of the different eras proposed in *Westworld*) and that of the plunging into a film genre (the "film noir" atmosphere in the style of *Chinatown*).[39] It would seem that the world was created here, more than in the novel, for the pleasure of those who explore it. One understands better why its creator, Fuller (Armin Mueller-Stahl), did not fail to go in there himself and mingle with the cabaret dancers, to the chagrin of his avatar, "disconnected" when seized by him (momentarily put "out of play").[40] Thus, the function of this virtual world mirrors the function of the film (a spectacle offered to an audience).

In order to dramatize the shift between worlds, a narrative argument postulates that the immersion cannot be prolonged beyond the traditional feature film duration of a hundred and twenty minutes. When Hall discovers for the first time the *virtual world* created by Fuller, the city is revealed to us with the same playful and nostalgic emphasis as the small 1950s town in *Back to the Future* (1985). After a first shot of the flabbergasted character, a reverse shot reveals a long shot of an urban landscape while a symphonic music and a camera movement – both evocative of Spielberg's mainstream films of the '80s and the '90s – highlight the splendor of the "sets". Unlike other films, like *TRON* or *The Lawnmower Man*, which use the *virtual world* as a pretext for the application of digital special effects (the computer-generated image displayed like a graft), *The Thirteenth Floor* never exhibits this kind of technology. The worldbuilding machine figured in the film is after all quite unspectacular, simply a green laser sizing up the user's body just like a scanner would (Color Plate 18). The "representational" perfection of the diegetic computer's product is conveyed through the use of traditional cinematic visual conventions, implicitly considered at the end of the '90s (a time when cinema imposes itself as *the* referent of computer assisted design, particularly in the domain of video game productions) as the pinnacle of realistic and immersive representation. There is one moment in *The Thirteenth Floor* that constitutes an exception to the general eviction of digital imaging in the film when Hall – just like Jason, his 1930s counterpart – yearns to experience the reality of his world and rushes (behind the wheel of his sports car) to its limits: he then finds himself facing a non-representational space, framed by a computer grid (Color Plate 19). The simultaneous presence of the hero's photographic image and a rudimental digital graft communicates the helplessness of the baffled individual discovering the simulacrum. However, throwing the film's protagonist into nothingness would have been inconsistent with the standards of classical Hollywood storytelling. Hall will eventually quit this incomplete world and reach for the "upper" one.

The presence of images associated with "electronics" is extremely discreet in *The Thirteenth Floor*, but this is all the more true in *World on a Wire*, the first screen adaptation of *Simulacron-3*, directed by Rainer Werner Fassbinder. The film was shot as a TV movie in 16mm and broadcast in two parts for the German television network WDR. The first part was strictly limited to the embedded world, ending with the uncovering of its counterfactual nature. The virtuality of a world located in a near future does not serve here as a pretext to the use of visual effects related to the computer graphics of the era. It is there to portray the strangeness of characters and situations, conjure up a paranoid atmosphere, multiply the incongruities, and shift the point of view depending on the world from which we "look" at a given situation. The science fiction logic is conveyed particularly by the depiction of telecommunication technologies and that of the urban environment (the film was shot in the new districts of Paris). The specification of the world's features is mainly carried out at the level of the mise-en-scène with most special effects pulled off during shooting, thanks to various mirror devices. Talking about *World on a Wire,* Fassbinder remarked: "It was imperative that the film showed World I realistically and endowed with a strong stage presence".[41] In fact, this world seems like one big fake *stage*, designed for the machine's users in the upper world. Space seems to be perpetually (but imperceptibly) vacillating as a result of ample camera movements that trace unexpected diagonal lines, whereas shot composition is fragmented by architectural elements or monitors. Bodies and faces lie frequently next to their double, reflected on mirrored walls or spheres that produce a somewhat altered representation of them. Similar to Jacques Tati's *Playtime* (1967), glass walls and glossy leather coverings give the impression of lingering on the *surface* of things, having no firm grip on the world, which in this case is precisely a *virtual* one. The omnipresence of deep focus foregrounds, which occupy a substantial part of the frame, is meant to be oppressive, implying the assimilation of the camera's point of view into a surveillance apparatus. The gap between the camera and the actors keeps all characters at a distance, as the viewer watches them parading inside huge sets, immersed in the shimmer of immaculate reflective surfaces. The extras seem like puppets introduced inside a static environment "animated" only by tracking camera shots. The human figures that lie around an indoor pool, in a club where everything seems straight out of a spectacle, strike poses like the clients of the thermal spa in *Last Year at Marienbad.* One of the enigmas that the protagonist, Fred Stiller (Klaus Löwitsch), tries to solve is that of a drawing, left for him by a scientist named Vollmer shortly before his death, representing a Greek warrior (Achilles) and a turtle. This drawing refers to one of Zeno's paradoxes that a friend of Stiller (who, precisely, refuses to stand "still") links to the illusory character of all movement, namely the foundation of all film representations.

As the camera roams through the sets, it reveals statues in the rooms' farthest corners, echoing the ritualistic aspect of particular human postures. It also discloses security agents with eyes inexpressive or covered, cut off from any interaction with the rest of the characters, as if they were part of the decoration (which in fact is the case for all "units" in this world, for they are created by the same machine that formed their surrounding environment). The opening shot in the first scene in the club, centered on the performance of a wannabe Dietrich, establishes a principle of dislocation: even though the lateral tracking shot follows the singer's movements, the camera is placed at a significant distance while "furniture" obstructs momentarily the visualization of the scene's main sound source. The wall cut-out and the curtains bring to mind a peep show setting. This sort of arrangement highlights the scene's voyeuristic dimension and hints at the peculiar situation of the characters in the embedded world who watch a representation while *being* themselves watched by those fabricating it. By virtue of this principle of reduplication, the same holds for the relationship between Stiller's "reality" and the *virtual world* produced by the computing machine he is operating. We see him lying down wearing an astronaut's helmet (a canonical motif in science fiction films of that era) connected to several computers, in a transfer room full of *small screens* displaying the various scenes taking place in the embedded world. The operators select among those scenes as if they were choosing from an array of TV channels. This comparison, accentuated by the presence of a remote control, inscribes the historical-technical context of this German TV production inside the film's universe. Just like in Galouye's novel, the first immersion goes wrong, as the machine has been fouled up: the *virtual world* appears only surreptitiously in a single POV-shot, while Stiller's voice-over stands out from the muffled soundscape as if he were scuba diving (an idea present in *Je t'aime je t'aime*), allowing the hero to express in an internal monologue his first impressions of a world that seems to him gray and sparsely populated. This process of internalization brings the viewer closer to Stiller while making the "second" world look even stranger. *World on a Wire* constantly oscillates between actors' performances that underline the materiality of their bodies and an audio-visual representation that exhibits itself as such. Moreover, whereas the operators in "*The Matrix*" infer the events taking place in the *virtual world* through lines of code appearing on their computer screen, the ones in Fassbinder's film can directly access the images shown to the viewer, though in a bluish, low-resolution rendition typical of 1970s analog videos, especially those used in surveillance systems. Smoothly, and in a perfectly continuous way, the camera zooms out from Stiller's conversation with one of the "units" in the *virtual world*, to the experiment's room where the "real" Stiller is plugged into the machine. Simultaneously, his colleagues are watching the entire scene retransmitted on a monitor. The final high angle shot of the embedded world points to the virtual position of a surveillance camera, whereas the mirror unveils the face of Stiller's double, standing out from a background of bronze sculptures. The replicas are assigned to a regime of remote surveillance, "mirrored" in a film destined to television viewers.

In the first of the film's two parts, images of the frame world, in which human bodies are filmed as part of the decoration, are in clear contrast with shots located at the other end of the size spectrum. Among the numerous wide shots in which the film's characters seemed tossed in, the camera violently zooms in and close-up inserts suddenly pop up, in a way that temporarily reinstates the human subject at the center of the "world". Fassbinder's adaptation confers on the *virtual world* a palpable erotic "charge" absent from the novel, let alone from *The Thirteenth Floor*. As in Galouye's original story, Stiller is the victim of a political-financial conspiracy; Fassbinder's film stresses the narrative implications of this conspiracy, yet Stiller is manipulated for the most part by female characters that fit the archetype of the Seductress, sort of lustful androids inherited from an 18th century imaginary of artificial beings created with the aim of satisfying male desire (as in the fantasy tales of E.T.A. Hoffman or Villiers-de-l'Isle Adam). For instance, one thinks here of Gloria (Barbara Valentin), the new secretary "offered" to Stiller by the company's board of directors as a gift for his promotion (alongside with the "car of his dreams"), who constantly spies on him – her glass-walled office is adjacent to Stiller's – and eavesdrops on his telephone conversations. Close-ups on the faces of heavily made-up women (while all male protagonists are soberly dressed in dark suits) seem to imply everything is just a façade: the "*virtual*" nature of the world informs the actors' performance. Almost all of the film's female characters have no equivalent in the novel; their attitude breeds mistrust, but no one really knows if these spies work for the multinational corporation led by corrupt executives, or for the technicians in the frame world (after all, they both operate on the principle of exploiting the lower "classes"). This distribution of men and women to roles according to their gender betrays an exaggerated misogyny that generates disorder, a kind of extravagant, anxiety-provoking artificiality. It is significant that the eradication of the head of security, Günther Lause (Ivan Desny), takes place at the suture of a shot/reverse shot edit in which Gloria emphatically sneaks: Stiller turns his head in an effort to identify the source of a loud noise – just like in *Last Year at Marienbad*, the young woman drops a glass on the floor – and when he turns around to look back at Lause, who was just about to reveal his boss's last words, the chair is empty. This rudimentary trick, based on the fundamental discontinuity of the film medium, serves the ontological fluctuations of a multiverse.

In terms of technologies represented, both screen adaptations of *Simulacron-3* capitalize on different facets of the imaginary related to telephony, just like many other multiverse films do. In the history of film editing, the visualization of remote communication practices has greatly contributed in the emergence of practices of alternation whose implications in terms of worldbuilding are examined in Chapter 4. The young woman's call for help via telegraph in *The Lonedale Operator* (1911) is emblematic not only of this type of diegetic motivation in the use of crosscutting but also, as Tom Gunning has shown in his analysis of D. W. Griffith's film, of a repressive technophobia towards inventions coming from the industrial era (Gunning 1991). In Fassbinder's film, the brightly colored bakelite telephones that connote "modernity" are omnipresent, often acting as the gravitational center of shot compositions. Furthermore, Fred Stiller enters a telephone booth in order for his transfer to take place; as the title of this German TV production suggests, the other world is located on the other end of the wire. *World on a wire* takes up the idea of a transfer ("*projection*") taking place through a "videophone booth", present in Galouye's novel (2011: 59), a sort of a contemporary avatar of the double-bottomed trunk used by magicians that functions as a means of telecommunication associating the interlocutor's voice with his image, as in many scientific and fictional speculations preceding video calling software like Skype (see Boillat 2009d and 2019a). Besides, Fassbinder's film benefits visually from this fictional apparatus since its representation results in "image within an image" inserts, for instance when one of the corporation's bosses transmits an order to his secretary, according to a hierarchical representation of gender relations that runs throughout the film. This type of shot fuels paranoid fantasies against remote surveillance in a rather dystopian take on point-to-point communication and literalizes the principle of embedding between different worlds.

Shot and released in the age of the Internet and mobile telephony,[42] *The Matrix* also refers to the telephone technology developed in the last quarter of the 19th century. Telephone cabins appear as landmarks on the *virtual world*'s map and serve as points of access to the other world. As highlighted by the authors of *Matrix, machine philosophique* in the "Telephone" entry of their glossary, this device is omnipresent in the film and "primarily responds to a tracking problem" (Badiou and al. 2003: 184)[*, 43]. In the first installment of the Wachowskis' trilogy, the outcome of the inaugural action scene is organized around such a cabin. Trinity hastens to pick up the phone while a truck that seems straight out of *Duel* (1971) rushes at full speed, demolishing the cabin right after the young woman successfully shifts between worlds. Alternating between parallel narratives in this "chase scene" – which correlates a mechanical threat with an outcome related to electricity, namely two older types of technology that precede the expansion of computer science – leads to alternating between worlds. In *The Matrix*'s opening credits, when lines of code roll on the screen, the computer's humming noise is supplanted by the sound of a telephone conversation. Exactly when number "6" appears on the screen, in a synchronism that can be perceived only by viewers, a beep sound is linked to the non-representational image composed of an alignment of numbers. Trinity pauses for a moment, then, referring to this particular beep sound, expresses her concern at the possibility her call has been tracked. Telephony functions literally as a "matrix" in the film, given its affiliation to the reticular paradigm that inspired the Wachowskis' simulacrum: for several decades, telephone conversations required the intervention of an operator who was thus controlling a "worldbuilding machine".

An integral part of a retro-futuristic aesthetic, to which *The Matrix* is partly indebted, as well as a sign of analog technology's persistence in the digital era, *fixed* telephony – also in the sense that the telephone is an *invariant* between different worlds – allows for a certain plasticity in the representation of this type of technology thanks to the equipment involved (housing, dial buttons, handset, cord, cabin). The telephone device is a set of furniture, involves issues of ergonomics and requires from its user a series of gestures inscribed in the "script" of everyday life. In a sense, the representation of an "anachronistic" telephone device counterbalances the virtualization of mediums. The "phone call", an essential feature of the stunts performed by the actors each time they rush to lift the phone before being "lifted" and transferred to a different world, constitutes an interworld gateway. Even if no "body" is actually transferred, the visual representation of the shift between worlds adheres to the concept of transition. In *The Matrix Reloaded*, as agent Smith gradually appears behind a member of the Resistance in the process of exiting the matrix, the former appears to be standing in front of a large-scale poster depicting a telephone device. Having seized his body, agent Smith picks up the phone in order to infiltrate into Zion's "reality" and the telephone handset turns into a kind of vortex, sucking the image of the virtual body. Visualizing this kind of chasm undermines from the inside the matrix's grid, forcing it to crack open.

The individual's disembodiment inherent in this type of telecommunication (since a phone user's interlocutor is actually a bodiless voice) is taken literally in *The Matrix*. The film exploits the world-centered implications of the above principle by offering a contact zone between the *here* and the *elsewhere*. As Jeffrey Sconce (2000), among others, has shown, the spiritualist imaginary has been largely nourished by the experience of receiving an electrically transmitted voice and, later on, by that of television viewership (an important reference in the case of a TV production like *World on a Wire*, as already pointed). Within such a paranormal framework, the *elsewhere* truly constitutes, for those who choose to believe in it, a place *beyond* our world. These diverse connotations of a technology associated with Edison's ingenuity and the emergence of the industrial era are summoned in *World on a Wire, The Thirteenth Floor*, and *The Matrix*. Less obviously, these representations are in tune with media archeology discourses that manifest a similar infatuation with practices and imaginaries of the end of the 19th century.

Whether they are consciously or not part of the *steampunk* genre, these films use a *low-tech* aesthetic in their portrayal of "worldbuilding machines" fulfilling a return to the analog era. One is reminded of the fake Olivia in *Fringe*'s Season 2 who, having taken the place of her double inside the reference world, communicates with the *parallel world* not via a computer keyboard, but by using a second-hand IBM typewriter (commercialized in the early '70s), whose design is inspired from the late 19th century George C. Blickensderfer model. Its heavy, steel keyboard, as well as the clatter of keystrokes against paper, is reminiscent of the old days of International Business Machines, way before the brand commercialized its first personal computers. The aforementioned brief sequence showing this particular typewriter is to be found at the very end of Season 2[44] and serves as a revelation for the viewer who only then realizes that the "alternate" Olivia has actually replaced the woman he has been following since the beginning of the series. The latter can be seen languishing in jail somewhere in the *parallel world* in the season's final images. This interworld communication apparatus also includes an oval mirror facing the machine and reflecting the text sent by the other world (which remains off-screen in this particular scene). Despite this "marvelous" component, we are closer here to Friedrich Kittler's ideas (see Kittler 1986) than to the conventional gadgetry of science fiction films. Because of the significant changes it underwent at the beginning of the 21st century, due to the spread of electronic mobile phones, telephony constitutes – alongside typing technologies (following in this particular example the model of the teleprinter, a remote communication tool) – one of the most common objects used in similar representations of anachronism, updating different layers of past imaginaries. Given their obsolescence, these representations acquire a certain weirdness when introduced into a modern context. The use of such devices is frequently found in the films of our corpus.

In order to initiate our discussion on the last film examined in this chapter, it should be noted that the link between *TRON* (1982) and its sequel, *TRON: Legacy* (2010), as well as the one between the computer world in which the character of the father has found himself imprisoned and the "real" world", is established through a signal left on a *beeper*, a device coming from the 1980s. Nevertheless, technology's positive impact – allowing a father to contact his abandoned son after many years of silence – turns out to be a decoy. Those means of telecommunication, entailing *de facto* the interlocutor's disembodiment (taken here to its extreme since the sender is a computer program), was actually used by the computer clone of the protagonist's father in order to lure the son into a trap. This way, the clone hopes to ensure the opening of a portal through which he aims to pass his army in order to invade the designers' world. However, as we will see in the following pages, this "war of the worlds" will not take place.

The Computer System Experienced From the Inside: *TRON* and its "Legacy"

So far, no film has ever taken the idea of projecting a user inside a *virtual world* as literally as *TRON*. In *Ready Player One* (2018), for instance, the avatar remains distinct from the gamer living in the frame world. In *The Lawnmower Man* (1992), a kind of permeability is established between the real world and the cyberspace, but it consists more in transposing the pixelated representation onto reality – as in *Transcendence* (2014) – than in having viewers enter into a world governed by a computing machine. In *TRON*, however, the user's body is transferred from one world to the other, resulting in its disappearance from the first world (in a manner analogous to *Stranger Things*, a two-world TV series more attached though to the tradition of the *fantasy* genre). In 1982, this Disney production popularized on the silver screen a certain type of video game representation. In a special issue published in April 2010 and entitled "The Borders of Cinema", the film journal *Cahiers du cinéma* devoted a double page to an image taken from *TRON* in the opening of "The Digital Era" section. This section examined issues related to the use of digital special effects without ever mentioning though this particular film, considered as emblematic but seldom discussed (probably because its emblematic status is far too obvious).

In *TRON*, there is no skepticism about reality's status: the distinction between the real and a world located inside an arcade game (Color Plate 20), modeled after the typical dystopian societies of the science fiction genre, is clear. The human subject, Kevin Flynn (Jeff Bridges), is coerced by a power-hungry artificial intelligence into the universe of a video game whose programs have, similar to "*The Matrix*", a human form. Forced into the arena like a gladiator in a peplum film, he is compelled to comply with the artificial intelligence's laws. A genius programmer ostracized from the research community, converted into a hacker and owner of a video arcade, Kevin finds himself dematerialized by a computing machine, in the same manner the heroes in the Wachowskis' trilogy are extracted from the matrix by grabbing a telephone handset.[45] Since all online access points into the computer system have been blocked following Kevin's previous hacking attempts, the hero is forced to break into ENCOM's laboratory. He is attempting to penetrate the computer's memory in search of files that could prove he is the designer of a large number of video game programs to which ENCOM owes its prosperity and which were stolen from him by Ed Dillinger (David Warner). Thanks to this usurpation, Dillinger has become the corporation's owner. Clearly, the legitimacy granted by the status of the "worldbuilder" is central in *TRON*'s story. While he is busy working in front of a computer screen, Kevin is struck by a canon's beam directed towards him by an artificial intelligence that acts as Dillinger's digital alter ego. The representation of this fictitious machine that generates the hero's "projection" into the *virtual world* is explicitly modeled after the movie theater apparatus: as he is facing the screen, Kevin is snapped up by a beam of light coming from a "projector" located right behind him. His body freezes in an engraved in a grid image that allows its mathematical apprehension; it is then fragmented and erased piece by piece, transporting both Kevin and *TRON*'s viewers into a *virtual world*.

The hero functions as an *invariant* between the worlds. In fact, all the main characters have their double inside the game where the same actancial model is reproduced. However, Kevin has a different name there – Clu – and appears under the guise of a grey figure whose costume looks like a sports outfit or an armor. Its fluorescent linings copy the integrated circuits of an electronic chip (a synecdoche that reveals a generalized inversion in the film between the interior and the exterior, the macroscopic and the microscopic)[46] and materialize the colored surfaces of pixel clusters perceived by the gamer "on the other side" of the screen. When the characters in the game are in motion, the colored lineaments highlight their movements inside the frame and almost elevate them to a graphic abstraction, underlined as they are by geometric backgrounds and punctuated by synchronous electronic sounds. Therefore, they function almost identically to the sensors placed under the subject's costumes in certain chronophotographic shots, or those used today in motion capture (see Boillat 2018a). While the body benefits from a prosthetic combination, the face remains the core of humanity: in a bleak environment whose volume is perceived through neon rays of light, the occasional close-up on the actor's eyes underscores the insertion of a photorealistic image (Color Plate 21).

In order to represent the world of the electronic simulation, the image features a material heterogeneity that results from the combination of real shots (with actors, sets, and models), drawings, and computer-generated imagery. The backlit human silhouettes, glowing before a dark background, embody this hybridity by blending a black & white image with bright, electric colors. As we have seen in Chapter 4, such contrasts assist the structure of a world. In 1982, color was commonly associated with video games, notably due to the popularity of home consoles during the second half of the 1970s (in particular the 1977 Atari VCS 2600) which, connected to the television set, brought the colorful, interactive, and pixelated representation into the domestic space. It is tempting to contextualize *TRON*'s release in relation to the periodization advanced in the "Game Story" exhibition held at the Grand Palais in Paris between November 2011 and January 2012: among the sequences selected in order to structure the visitors' itinerary, the third one was named "Color (1977–1983)". The lower limit of this periodization corresponds to the VCS 2600's commercial launch and to the expansion of color graphics that *TRON*'s fluorescent surfaces exalted, while its higher limit was defined by the video game market's collapse in the USA (see Donovan 2010: 96–109). *TRON* was released in North America in July 1982, as one of the blockbusters of that summer, and in France in mid-December of the same year, a Disney product ready for the holiday season. Yet, this would prove to be the last time home consoles were largely offered as gifts under the Christmas tree, soon to be replaced by video recorders. Indeed, the film arrived on the market shortly before major changes took place, a historical fact that could partly explain its relative commercial failure[47] and, above all, its limited impact on the modes of film representation of the cyberspace. *TRON* aimed to profit from the video game craze in a year that saw Lucasfilm setting up a subsidiary specifically devoted to video game development (Blanchet 2010: 133). The truth of the matter is that the film referred to a by then already declining form of entertainment. Moreover, it offered comparatively primitive visual representations, soon to be rendered obsolete for the standards of the dominant film production (already at the beginning of the following decade), as far as video game graphics and cinematic special effects were concerned (both indebted to the same type of computer technology). Let us not forget however, that the computer-generated components of *TRON*'s diegesis are more thoroughly representational next to the ones offered by video games at the time, not to mention the insertion of real actors. The lack of interactivity typical of the film medium, as well as the use of analog techniques, allowed to considerably saturate the environment, that is to truly establish it as a *world* experienced from the inside, just like polygonal 3D modeling would allow from the mid-1990s on. By intertwining the moviegoer experience with that of the users of arcade games or home consoles, *TRON* inaugurates the "*mise en abyme*" in blockbuster movies of a computer-like "worldbuilding machine". The following year, targeting a more adult audience, David Cronenberg's *Videodrome* would attempt the same thing for video recording technology in a more horrific style.

In order to define the relationship established between *TRON* and its viewer, it is important to elucidate the film's outset. In the opening sequence, the real world alternates with the computer generated one, but the two sides of the film's universe are not of equal importance. Whereas the real gamer is in no way individuated (his face remains off-screen – only his hand is visible as he introduces a coin that launches the game and, therefore, the film), the "programs" are depicted in close-ups through the window of their racing car, in full speed, as they risk their "lives" during a car chase. This initial action scene aims to immediately give credibility to the *virtual world* at a time when viewers were unaccustomed to digital imagery or the cyberspace. Furthermore, several laws governing the video game universe, in particular those concerning the "rules of the game", are in this way presented to the audience before even the hero makes his entrance, facilitating our immersion as we follow later on the protagonist's adventures. Consequently, the video game universe is immediately established as the *first* world: the film's intrigue will unfold inside it and the viewer will be invited to identify with the programs. The fate of Clu, an exceptional Being not dissimilar to Neo (also a programmer and a hacker), is tied to the liberation of the anthropomorphic computer units from the yoke of the "Master Control Program" ("MCP"). The latter appropriates other programs or destroys them inside the game's arenas after having them "imprisoned" on the grounds of their belief in the existence of "users". The MCP wishes to erase all possible traces of these users, in a clear reference to the persecution of the first Christians that has served as backdrop in numerous peplum films, such as *Ben Hur* (1925/1959). This is a world surrendered to a dictatorship like the one found in Orwell's *1984*, though control over the deindividualized subjects is complete in the case of *TRON*, since these subjects inhabit a space entirely governed by a single ruling authority. It is therefore impossible to escape from the grid on which the "gamers" take their place, as for instance in the motorcycle race scene (the "Light Cycles") (Color Plate 22) where the racing vehicles leave behind them a colored trail that turns into walls and gradually redefines the labyrinth-like space, highlighting the – fundamental in worldbuilding – process of *mapping*.

By presenting a diagrammatic "furnishing" of its *virtual world* and by inscribing the actors' bodies on a strictly geometric background, as if they were undergoing an orthogonal projection on a plane, *TRON* draws upon the *paradigm of the grid*, a major influence on the expansion of digital technologies whose implications on filmmaking are both visual – though as a rule fleetingly present (*TRON*'s systematic use of the grid as a visual component marks an exception) – and narrative. In this respect, the representational style in this Hollywood production resonates with media and practices associated with other fields, mainly photography. Commenting on an article by Rosalind Krauss (1984), an art historian who identifies the grid as a salient feature of modernity linked to the concepts of an autonomous representation and a form of withdrawal from the real (both of them applicable to a *virtual world* like the one proposed by *TRON*), Claus Gunti stressed this notion's relevance in approaching the work of photographers attached to the conceptual art movement (Thomas Ruff, Andreas Gursky, etc.). Gunti suggested the articulation of this particular point with a reflection on the ostensibly pixelated images of some more recent works, themselves part of a genealogy dating back to the end of the 1960s (namely a historical period impregnated by the imaginary of computer technology, like in Galouye's novel), in which the use of the grid stemmed from "an effort to match reality to its representation, the index to its referent" (Gunti 2013)[*]. In cyberculture films, this "matching" process postulates a similar eviction of the "real": in *TRON*, the infographic representation serves no other referent than itself. Surely, tanks, hangars, ships, etc. can be seen on the screen, but only as they would appear in a representation produced by a computing machine similar to the one responsible for the film's special effects. The film's own genesis (the image's indexicality) is therefore exhibited as it merges with the represented world. *TRON* departs from the conventions of cinematic photo-realism, since its attractional aspect is based precisely on the immaterial rendering of an image located halfway between live-action cinema and animated films (see Gaudreault and Marion 2015). The participation of an acclaimed cartoonist such as Jean Giraud (alias Möbius, an emblematic figure in the adult science fiction genre) is telling of the importance accorded to drawings and graphic illustrations in the film's production design.

Due to his being partly human, Clu dispenses with the constraints prevalent inside the system. As a "user", he is endowed with the power to build worlds: when he finds himself in the position of having to repair a scout vehicle in his effort to escape, he rebuilds it from the cockpit by combining elementary shapes and forms, and re-injects energy into the craft while his exhausted teammate remarks: "You shouldn't be able to do that!". Like John in *Dark City* or Neo in "*The Matrix*", two films released more than fifteen years later, the main hero in *TRON* has the demiurgic capacity to adjust the environment to his desires. The *virtual world* serves as a pretext in order to fulfill within the diegesis a fantasy of omnipotence that underlies the production of such blockbusters. From an intermedia perspective, one can also perceive inside this cinematic fiction the staging of a certain type of video game interactivity, particularly present in city-building games (like the *SimCity* series) or in the *Lego Star Wars* video game series, when certain character skills taken from the film franchise (such as telekinesis) allow gamers to build or reassemble the world's objects. It will soon become clear that Clu is a savior figure too: he resuscitates the young Yori, the avatar of a past love, just like Neo does with Trinity. Moreover, in this Manichean world where "individuals" adorned with fluorescent blue-light stripes are enslaved to agents of the ruling authority, distinguished by their red colors, the protagonist will ultimately succeed in imposing his own (blue) color, just like the young heroes in *Pleasantville* bring colors to the fictional 1950s world or John brings out the sunlight in *Dark City*'s finale.[48]

Still, the world, though *virtual*, must be exhibited on the screen. Likewise the activity of the computer scientist, cerebral as it may be, must be translated into a series of actions so as to meet the requirements of a typical Hollywood narrative film as well as the public's expectations. Flynn's dematerialization allows the viewer to install himself inside the game. Fight scenes with laser weapons against some kind of futuristic tanks, popularized in movies thanks to *Star Wars*' first two episodes (1977 and 1980), visualize in *TRON* the system's resistance against the hero who tries to crack its codes. In *WarGames* (1983), although the young protagonist manages to prevent a nuclear war by interacting with an artificial intelligence from an army command post, the real-life consequences are palpable: images of missile ramps set in motion for an imminent launch materialize the ramifications of the assaults schematically represented on screens that serve as an interface to the computing machine. In *TRON*, similar effective consequences are relegated on the second world: just like in *World on a Wire, The Matrix*, and *The Thirteenth Floor*, the virtual character's elimination inside the computer world would lead to the hero's "real" death. The correlation is explicitly formulated in *The Matrix*: when Neo realizes that he's bleeding from the mouth after having been involved in a virtual fight inside the matrix, Morpheus explains that "the body cannot live without the mind" and, consequently, to die inside the simulation means to "really" die. In the case of *TRON*, this cause-and-effect relationship goes without saying since the protagonist is "physically" transferred and recomposed inside the game: the user and the avatar are identified as one. Therefore, the border between the worlds does not abolish the narrative's driving force consisting in the individual's efforts to survive (in the "real" world) and, ultimately, ensure the survival of an entire world (inside the hard drive of a machine). The principle of reduplication – notably that of the film's characters – allows the narrative stakes in the *virtual world* to echo those of the first world. In *TRON*, the frame story's love triangle (Kevin/Lora/Alan), presented to the viewer prior to Kevin's dematerialization, is reproduced inside the game (Clu/Yori/Tron) and is "replayed" to the main hero's advantage.

The story unfolding in *TRON*'s embedded world meets its resolution in a final duel that ends with the machine being deactivated by a human, a pattern that became popular thanks to a scene from *2001: A Space Odyssey* in which Dave (Keir Dullea) disconnects HAL 9000. Just like Neo in the end of *The Matrix*

Revolutions rides back up to the "Source" and shuts down Agent Smith's program, Clu succeeds after the vain attempts of his partner, Tron, in inserting a disk into the MCP's heart that erases the latter's memory and puts an end to the programs' oppression. Light beams come from the "sky", discs transform into halos, and bodies ascend to a higher level. *TRON* is imbued with a mystical dimension that will be further developed several years later in *The Matrix*. Despite the highly unrealistic graphics of the power plant that hosts MCP's protection system, one can easily identify here a dominant mechanical model, mainly thanks to the sound effects. One can also associate the white strip composed of "vignettes" and animated in a rapid circular movement with one of the "pre-cinematic" optical toys: the praxinoscope. In this way, the film's worldbuilding machine, the computer, fits into the genealogy of apparatuses producing the illusion of movement.

Since *TRON*'s release, several video games expanded the "*TRON Universe*" by taking up the model set by the film or by introducing narrative bifurcations.[49] The fact that a sequel to Steven Lisberger's film was finally produced almost three decades after the original 1982 movie is symptomatic of the recent development of a world-centered conception in filmmaking. *TRON: Legacy*'s screenplay was entrusted to Adam Horowitz and Edward Kitsis, two authors who have contributed in more than twenty episodes of *Lost* (a series that, as I have shown in Chapter 2, proposed a contemporary "Theodicy" of sorts) and who were to collaborate later on in a series of animated films (*TRON: Uprising*), created thanks to the sequel's success.

TRON: Legacy is a typical example of a movie whose production is greatly indebted to the industry's desire to capitalize on breakthrough technologies. Following *Avatar*'s release in 2009, a film inspired by video game worlds similar to the ones represented in *TRON* (without fully assuming their virtual dimension, as we saw in Chapter 2), 3D technology became one of the major promotional arguments for Hollywood blockbusters. In this context, Disney launched the production of a *TRON*'s sequel. Its director, Joseph Kosinski, had the idea to reserve stereoscopy only for scenes taking place in the embedded world, thus creating a stylistic contrast between the real and the *virtual* world. This approach is indicative of a contemporary correlation between audio-visual technologies and a world-centered creative design. It was however only partially applied in the film's theatrical version, not only because 3D technology was after all insufficiently exploited, but also because this principle was not rigorously respected (just as variations in the aspect ratio do not follow the shifts between the two worlds).[50] The film begins with a 3D image even though the inaugural scene takes place in the real world. This opening aimed undoubtedly to reassure viewers right from the start that their ticket's additional price was well deserved. There is also an explanatory title right before the opening credits indicating that some scenes were deliberately shot in 2D and requesting viewers to keep their glasses on at all times. However, the film's major technical challenge lies elsewhere. The story follows Kevin Flynn's son, Sam, as he is being projected into the *virtual world*. The main actor, Garrett Hedlund, helps the film reach a younger audience; we first meet his character when he is ten years old, listening to his father's stories and playing with ancillary products from the "*Tron*" franchise.[51] As Sam meets further on a fifty-year-old version of his father *and* Clu (a digital copy created after the 1980s image of his creator), a computer-generated image of the face of a thirty-five year old Jeff Bridges had to be created, while at the same time the actor, then in his sixties, appears himself in the film. This opening flashback scene centers on the last night Sam spent with his father back in 1989. It becomes all the more paradoxical since it shows in the real world (here filmed in 3D) a human character, represented in CGI, supposed to fight inside the diegesis against virtual beings produced by a computing machine. This paradox will be solved in the film's present when the face of a young Kevin will belong exclusively to Clu's program.

Whereas digital technology was exhibited in the original *TRON*, it would seem that the goal in the 2010 sequel, which provides an "update" on the first installment's world, is to efface to the maximum extent possible the means of production behind the representation. This would explain why vehicles and other technical objects represented in the embedded world have a much more palpable form, while their functioning is accompanied by industrial sounds that replace the electronic beep sounds of the original film, suggesting the presence of real machines. The minimization of the gap separating our reference world with the *virtual* one presented in the film becomes noticeable in the similarities between the dilapidated building of the video arcade, in front of which Sam stood when seized by the artificial intelligence, and the spot he finds himself right after his transfer to the *virtual world*, in front of an identical building that is however remodeled in order to match the sparkling futuristic city.[52] Strengthening the credibility of the *virtual world* by reducing its gap with our reference world rests also on a considerably higher degree of anthropomorphism: when Sam finds himself in this world, the armor does not blend with his body (unlike *TRON* in which units were designed in one piece). Some automaton-like "hostesses" get him dressed, performing a ritualized and sensual operation that showcases the young man's bodily presence; in an explanatory flashback, his father will later affirm he has succeeded in "digitizing human anatomy". Furthermore, some of the most ferocious fighters in the *virtual world* let out a beast-like (and not a machine-like) groan. Lastly, the programs are collectively recognized as a genuine population.

During the combat scenes inside the "arenas" (which actually take place inside glass cages), the delirious crowd's cries resound all over the rows surrounding the gigantic stage, bringing to mind the race scene in *Ben Hur* (1959) or the one in *Star Wars: Episode I – The Phantom Menace* (1999). Such clamor transforms completely the ambiance of the games: platforms overflowed by the swarming crowd (or by an army of fanatical soldiers who respond with howls to the orators speaking from the podium) replace the cold and deserted spaces of the original *TRON*.

According to a (meta)diegetic logic, one may wonder on the purpose of having an audience participating in the *virtual world*, when the intended observer should normally be the game's user in the real world. In fact, the referent finds itself relocated following the purported evolution of the units populating this world, now transformed into a "living" city. This is actually the "miracle" Kevin announces to his son in the opening flashback scene, in an enigmatic remark that will find its explanation later in the film. In *TRON: Legacy*, the world of the game is visibly more populated and "furnished" than the one in *TRON* which was schematic almost to abstraction. This would explain why one of the main concerns for the film's creators was to scale up the furnishing of the *virtual world*, if only to correspond to the graphic capacities of contemporary video game productions. Building such a world is far from obvious, as highlighted by a journalist from *Cinefex*, a magazine specializing in the *making of* films that capitalize on special effects:

> Even with the efficient paperless approach, and with the art and visual effects working in proximity, Kosinski – he has a background in architectural design – knew that conceptualizing the film's vast computer world from the ground up would be the single most challenging and labor-intensive aspect of the production. "You can't go anywhere and shoot a scene for TRON in the real world", noted Kosinski. "Everything had to be designed and then built, either physically or on stage, or on a backlot, or digitally in the computer. It was a tremendously laborious movie to make, because we got nothing for free (Duncan 2011: 31).

The significant gap established between the reference and the *virtual world* requires building a new world from scratch, except that it is important to make the latter comply to certain aspects of the one from the 1982 film, renovated according to the 2010 sci-fi standards.

In *TRON: Legacy,* the *virtual world* has become autonomous and reorgani(ci)zed, an argument which tends to obliterate the world's dependence on machines. Therefore, the utopia/dystopia ambivalence is not really established between the exterior and the interior of the computer world,[53] but within the latter (Color Plate 23). Kevin confronts his double, Clu, who might have initially been programmed to ensure the perfection of this computer world (the "Utopia", as the scientist calls it), but has actually seized power and eliminated a new form of spontaneous life only because he deemed it "imperfect". The desire for an admirable society gives often rise to a nightmarish world, as soon as it is experienced *from the inside* – in films like *1984, Equilibrium*, or *Elysium*, the dystopia of some is the utopia of (a very few) others.

Whereas *TRON*'s protagonist was looking to prove he was the video game programs' designer, the sequel's worldbuilding theme is coupled to a typical father-son relationship. By sacrificing himself so as to allow Sam to use the "portal" and quit the *virtual world* in the company of young Quorra (Olivia

Wilde) – a couple arranged by the father figure who agrees to send over his creation, the only survivor of a now extinct species – Kevin redeems himself in the eyes of his son (who felt completely abandoned after having lost his mother) and, in a way, gives him a second birth. Multiverse films are often obsessed with such demiurgic issues that are perfectly suited to dominant cinema's patriarchal ideology (mothers are systematically evicted from this creative process). It falls upon these computer-age Promethean figures to rock their "small world" in order to activate its narrative potential.

Endnotes

1. *Simulacron-3* was first published in 1964. A second edition was released in 1999, the same year *The Matrix* and *The Thirteenth Floor* premiered.
2. Christian Metz examines this paradox from a psychoanalytic perspective in his book *The Imaginary Signifier* (Bloomington, Indiana University Press, 1982 [1977]).
3. For a theoretical reflection on the field of narratology based on Borges' short story "The Garden of Forking Paths" (1941), see Baroni 2017.
4. Keanu Reeves previously played the eponymous character in *Johnny Mnemonic* (1995). Thus, *The Matrix* summons an important intertext through its leading actor since *Johnny Mnemonic*, co-scripted by the emblematic novelist of the cyberpunk movement William Gibson, ranks among the first films (right after *The Lawnmower Man*, 1992) to use CGI special effects that are exhibited as such (in other words, not made to be invisible) in order to represent a character's projection into a *virtual world*, connected to the network via a computing machine. The hero's brain is presented as if it were nothing more but a hard drive, with the exception of memory flashbacks similar to the ones found in *Dark City*.
5. Both *Dark City* and *The Matrix* were filmed at the same studio, the Fox Studios in Sydney, with the Wachowskis having allegedly reused some of the sets created for the film shot earlier by Alex Proyas.
6. In Proyas' film, as in Hollywood's classical film noir, everything is dark but almost no one is actually black: the "vampire-like" physical sheaths adopted by the aliens are pale white. Moreover, while various ages are represented, no feminine presence is to be found in this community, as if the female was restricted to The Machine that created the world (instead of giving life to a dying population).
7. One must distinguish the skyscraper jump scene from the immediate acquisition of skills. The latter results from downloading a software in advance or in the middle of the action (for instance, the helicopter piloting skills activated by Trinity), as in certain role-playing games in which, as the story unfolds, users can at a given point unlock specific abilities. In fact, the software is downloaded from *somewhere else*, underlining the prosthetic dimensions of these additions; dissociated from the character they are grafted, these skills appear as action movie stereotypes. As such they are highly implausible, like movie heroes capable of performing extraordinary feats or the fact that they seem to constantly find themselves in situations inviting them to demonstrate their special skills. In this way, a distancing effect is introduced, similar to the one at work in *Total Recall* where heroic features are shown to be designed from scratch. When a considerable amount of combat skills is downloaded into his body (a close-up on a computer screen visualizes the potential access to these various skills, such as "drunken boxing", jiu-jitsu, etc.), Neo declares to the operator who programs his avatar inside the virtual reality, that he takes pleasure in being "penetrated" this way by all the data (which are transmitted to his brain through an orifice in the back of his neck). This seems like an explicit allusion to the libidinal dimension of being wired up into the machine and immerged in the world it creates. (The operator acts here as Neo's sexual partner: when he asks him if he wants more data, the subtitles in the French version of the movie translate Neo's ecstatic reaction, repeating "Oh yeah!", using the expression "*Envoie la purée!*", literally meaning: "Send the mash!"). In spite of this provisionally established distancing effect, the film delivers on its promise and does not depart from the geeky pleasure of "having fun" in a digitally generated world. A similar but reverse homoerotic situation (focused on suffering, instead of pleasure) can be found in *eXistenZ*,

when the engineer violently installs in the hero's spine the "bio-port" which allows him to connect to the worldbuilding machine.

8. This disclosure occurs relatively early in the case of Neo, for he is a hero of an action movie that hardly relies on the regime of curiosity. In the case of *Dark City* though, the truth will not be revealed to John before the film reaches its final moments.
9. See *supra* our comments on *Je t'aime je t'aime*, *Groundhog Day* and *Eternal Sunshine of the Spotless Mind*, or the example of *Possible Worlds* at the Conclusion of this book.
10. Following one of the laws of its sci-fi world, *Dark City* is setting forth the Strangers' intolerance to water – as well as to light, a pattern more frequent in the representation of vampires – and further develops this narrative idea. At the very beginning of the film, John wakes up in a bathtub and places a fish in his bath water. Heading to his "uncle" Carl's place, he passes by a fairground attraction in the form of a sea monster, the "Neptune Kingdom", highlighting the "Coney Island" aspect of this timeless city. Lastly, Dr. Schreber flees into a swimming pool to avoid being disturbed by his masters, in an atmosphere reminiscent of a famous scene from *Cat People* (1942).
11. In *The Simulacra* (1964), Philip K. Dick presents a dystopia in which a totalitarian regime controls the individual through the powers of illusion.
12. In order to motivate a point of view overlooking the entire city, the film's screenwriters resort to the character of the police inspector throwing himself into the cosmic void. As for John, he remains trapped in the city and could never have an access to this "view".
13. *Dark City*'s second scriptwriter, David S. Goyer, would later work on the "Batman" franchise. This should not be surprising given the obvious similarities between the city (and its underworld) in Proyas' film and Gotham City (a place whose potential in worldbuilding terms becomes explicit in the Alternate Reality Game *Why So Serious?*, designed in 2008 as part of *The Dark Knight*'s promotional campaign – see Bourdaa 2016).
14. The name Daniel Schreber is a clear reference to the German author who was institutionalized after being diagnosed as paranoid and whose memoirs inspired both Freud and Jung. Not only does this reference take us back in the 19th century, but furthermore suggests that John Murdoch's perception of the world could be the result of a pathological condition (an interpretation also implied in one version of *The Great Walls of Samaris*).
15. On this subject, see Aurélie Ledoux's comment, quoted in chapter 1, note 45.
16. There is also a lot of back and forth from the actual city, inhabited by human bodies connected to the computer network, to the *virtual world* created by the latter in Gibson's novel. For instance, in the following passage, the urban space is literally transposed into an electronic signal: "Program a map to display frequency of data exchange, every thousand megabytes a single pixel on a very large screen. Manhattan and Atlanta burn solid white. Then they start to pulse, the rate of traffic threatening to overload your simulation. Your map is about to go nova. Cool it down. Up your scale. Each pixel a million megabytes. At a hundred million megabytes per second, you begin to make out certain blocks in midtown Manhattan […]" (Gibson 2018 [1984]: 47).
17. Such graphic abstractions of urban landscapes are to be found in more "classic" (and single-world) films, as in the opening credits of *North by Northwest* (1959) or those of *Someone's Watching Me!* (1978), in which the glass skyscrapers' surface forms a grid. However, in these cases, a two-dimensional and in a way pre-immersive space is involved, since the diegesis has not, strictly speaking, been constituted yet.
18. This world is shrewdly visualized under the shape of a "small world" on a television screen as Morpheus uses a 1950s remote control that seems straight out of *Pleasantville* (1998).
19. On François Schuiten and Benoît Peeters' series, see Baetens 2020; on *The Great Walls of Samaris*, see Boillat 2019b.
20. The reference to Baudrillard is part and parcel of a diverse set of quotations, "a vast patchwork of references employed as some sort of wink to the audience or a literal exemplification" (During 2003a: 4–5)*. Elie During, who examines the question of the film's eclecticism once more in a subsequent chapter in the same book (During 2003b: 83-86), does not necessarily view this eclecticism in a negative light. Patrice Magnilier also shows that the "plurality of codes" at work in *The Matrix* grants the film its status as a myth in the sense of Lévi-Strauss (Magnilier 2003: 150–151).

21. Plato, *Republic*, translated by F.M. Cornford, quoted in Loughlin 2004: 41. The allegory of the cave is also studied in one of the founding texts of the French apparatus theory (Baudry 1975).
22. Both versions are included in the Blu-ray disc released by Metropolitan Filmexport in 2010.
23. The Gothic-inspired world in *The Crow* not only *seems* to be what it is, but it really *is* – and no one inside the diegesis seems surprised about it or claims the paternity of this world.
24. This type of visionary character is frequent in multiverse films, as for instance when reality blends with literary fiction in *In the Mouth of Madness* or in *The Number 23*.
25. In this respect, *Dark City*, a film whose protagonists are all white (in contrast to "*The Matrix*"'s racial diversity), can be seen as a manifestation of the "whiteness as death" theme analyzed by Richard Dyer, most notably in relation to Romero's zombie movies (Dyer 2017: 210–212).
26. In fact, *Dark City*'s style seems to have influenced some later vampire films, like the "*Underworld*" quadrilogy (2003–2012).
27. However, everything in *Dark City* is represented in such a caricatured manner that the film's political scope ultimately evaporates under the pretext of the world's ontological facticity.
28. In the case of one of the first buildings in Madison Square, the Metropolitan Life Tower, built in 1893, its "structure copies Venice's campanile on San Marco, its shaft activated for business, holes punctured all over to admit daylight" (Koolhaas 1994: 93).
29. See the chapter called "Like Something From a Movie. Film as Object of Representation in Postmodern Popular Film "in Booker 2007: 89–150.
30. See also Friedberg 1993: 174 (though *Dark City* falls into the "pastiche" category, not that of "parody") and Jullier 1997.
31. Actually the Wachowskis' film can be attached to a genealogy leading back to Orwell's Big Brother: "The world described in *The Matrix* evokes – historically and conceptually – the model of totalitarian worlds [...] A world similar to animal societies, like the ones organized around a hive or an anthill, stripped of all freedom. Also Bentham's *Panopticon*, in other words a state of total surveillance [...] which [...] could very well define this world, but above all constitutes the archetype of all totalitarian regimes." (Zarader 2003: 45)*.
32. The representation of the "sentinels", war machines equipped with mandibles that attack in unison the city of Zion, with their sprawling gesticulations and their undulatory trajectories, is undoubtedly modeled on an organic form.
33. Seated at her side, the now blind Neo succeeds in destroying the enemy machines from a distance, while the POV-shot of digits inside the matrix is henceforth replaced by an extrasensory vision in the "real" world. In both cases, POV-shots create a strangeification of perception while revealing an image located beyond appearances.
34. In Galouye's *Dark Universe* (1961), the reader is immersed right from the outset in the daily life of Jared, one of the Survivors living in the "Lower Level" in a deep, completely dark underground world. Jared ends up challenging the obscurantist beliefs held by his people with regard to the "Original World", thanks to a series of discoveries. He eventually succeeds in going beyond the spatial borders separating him from a world that is "unheard of" to his fellow citizens and whose very language makes the ones speaking it unable to conceive of any visual perception. (All of them are physically blind, as the Platonic allegory of the cave is clearly part of the story's subtext). As in *Dark City*, the borders of the "small world", whose inhabitants illusively think of it in its entirety, are defined by the surrounding darkness.
35. "If I were trying to weave your web of fantasy, I would say that the blackouts were the side effects of an upper world simulectronic operator establishing empathic coupling with me. A faulty coupling. You've seen it happen in your own simulator. The ID unit becomes aware *something* is going on." (Galouye 2011: 88).
36. The novel's closing lines, exchanged when Douglas Hall is transferred to the upper level by investing the body of the one who created it in his image, and whose wife fell in love with him, are the following: "'You'll like it up here, Doug, even though it doesn't have quite the quaint atmosphere of your own world. You see, Hall had a flair for the romantic when he programmed the simulator. I thought he showed a lot of imagination in selecting such background prop names as Mediterranean, Riviera, Pacific, Himalayas.' She shrugged, as though apologizing for the comparative drabness of her world of absolute reality. 'You'll

also find that our moon is only a quarter of the size of yours. But I'm sure you'll get used to all the differences."' (*Ibid.*: 169).

37. One can think here of *Scanners'* ending (1981), various episodes from *The X-Files* (like the 15th episode of Season 1, called "Lazarus", 1994), but also "*The Matrix*" (when, for instance, in the third installment, Smith introduces himself into Bane whose carnal envelope admits to hate).
38. This is in fact a world-centered use of a pattern also recurrent in genre movies, when monsters creep into the main heroes' everyday lives by taking on the appearance of their loved ones, as vampires or other werewolves do. From *The Day the Earth Stood Still* (1951, 2008) to *Invasion of the Body Snatchers* (1956, 1978), *The Hidden* (1987) and its sequel (1993), *Species* (1995), *Terminator 3: Rise of the Machines* (2003), *The Invasion* (2007) or several John Carpenter films like *The Thing* (1982) – adapted from Howard Hawks' 1951 film, *The Thing from Another World* – and *They Live* (1988), this motif is extremely popular in science fiction. Some films, like *K-PAX* (2001), *Under the Skin* (2013), or Kiyoshi Kurosawa's diptych *Before We Vanish/Foreboding* (2017), even play on the viewer's expectations regarding this pattern. In the case of *Simulacron-3*, the world is not only distant, as in alien movies, but also *virtual*. Nevertheless, the story follows the same pattern as far as the discovery of a new form of otherness is concerned (in this case, residing inside one's self).
39. Vincent D'Onofrio, who portrays in *The Thirteenth Floor* two of the main characters (one per level), also played one of the four brothers in *The Newton Boys* (1998), released a year earlier, whose plot takes place in the 1920s, associating the actor with this type of period film.
40. The representation of the process of unplugging, accentuated in *The Thirteenth Floor* by the depiction of a disorder induced to the disconnected characters, is undoubtedly nourished by the experience of online games offering "persistent worlds" – in other words, worlds that continue to exist and to develop even when the gamer is not manipulating his avatar. This double temporality (of the daily life and of the videogame, or, in the case of a film, the diegetic and the meta-diegetic ones) causes a confusion of identity that becomes a central theme in *Avatar*.
41. This text is cited in the booklet of the Carlotta DVD edition of the film (page 11).
42. Cellular phones are used inside the film in order to communicate between the two worlds, but they do not serve as exit points from the matrix. When Neo is contacted for the first time by those situated outside the matrix (after receiving an email transmitting him a first command), instructions are given to him on his cell phone so that he flees the agents. During this scene, the interlocutor is omnipotent, anticipating every move and knowing every corner of the room; even though he is himself a human being, he is at this point associated to the machine, at least in relation to Neo whose viewpoint the spectator embraces. One finds similar scenes in *Eagle Eye* (2008) where a computing machine takes control of the city, or in regards to the central hero in *Next* (2007).
43. By immersing themselves completely in the diegetic logic of the film, the authors of this book end up dismissing the communicational paradigm, thus neglecting a substantial part of the imaginary evoked by certain forms of recourse to this particular motif.
44. The scene arrives at the very end of the second part of the 23rd and final episode of Season 2, named "Over There". Its placement is decisive in terms of suspense and therefore telling of the significance of this type of representation.
45. A similar vortex pattern is to be found in *TRON*'s opening credits, converging towards a luminous point that turns into the "O" of the film's title.
46. During the brief opening titles, we switch from electric circuits to a nocturnal vision of an American megalopolis. This change of scale announces its flip side later in the film: when we enter the game, we discover that the programs populate a real city. The urban imaginary studied in the case of *Dark City* leaves its mark also on a film like *TRON* that offers a virtual reality.
47. In 1982, a year marked by the enormous success of *E.T. the Extra-Terrestrial* that brought 360 million dollars to the American box office, *TRON* ranked 22nd among the highest-grossing films in the USA (33 million dollars), five places ahead of *Blade Runner* (27 million dollars). I refer here to the data available on the Box-Office Mojo web site (http://boxofficemojo.com/yearly/chart/?yr=1982). Interestingly enough, this web site includes *TRON* in two different lists, respectively named "Man VS Machine" and "Virtual Reality". In the

latter, *TRON* is placed right behind *The Matrix* and its sequels, *Spy Kids 3: Game Over* (2003), *Vanilla Sky* (2001) and … its own sequel, *TRON: Legacy* (2012), which ranks second, preceded only by *The Matrix*. This highly profitable sequel, discussed in the end of the chapter, managed to reach a wide audience, released as it was during a time of a considerable boom in films with a world-centered creative design, as this book shows.

48. *TRON: Legacy* has a similar ending. Such a "color code" is initially used on an individual level when Tron, having already tried to stop Clu (a "Mr. Hyde" to Dr. Kevin's "Jekyll") and engaged in the heroes' pursuit, suddenly converts into being a defender of the "designers": at that moment, the lights of his suit change from orange to blue.
49. See: http://tron.wikia.com/wiki/TRON_Universe.
50. In the film's DVD version distributed by Disney, an introductory title explains: "To preserve the original IMAX theatrical viewing experience, the picture image will alternate between 2.35 : 1 and 1.78 : 1 aspect ratios. The black matte bars on your screen will adjust accordingly." However, this alternation is not based on a world-centered principle: the wide aspect ratio is used for some particularly spectacular scenes with little dialogue, such as fight scenes taking place inside the arena or the various chase scenes.
51. The miniature replicas of components that will actually appear later on in the film highlight the latter's world-centered dimension as well as the commercial logic behind the principle of franchising. The playful diegetization of this logic functions as a postmodern wink to the viewer-consumer (who, treated as an accomplice, can thus feel more like a viewer and less like a consumer): when Sam faces his first opponent inside the game, he exclaims: "I have a three-inch version of you on my shelf!" The exhibition of ancillary products in the film's first scene constitutes a case of metalepsis not just between the embedded and the embedding worlds, but also between the reference world of the fiction and the reality of the film's production. If we are allowed to imagine that Flynn has commercialized these figurines (modeled after the characters of the 2010 film, not those of the original one, even though the story takes place in 1989), we are nonetheless entitled to wonder why the child would have a large poster in his room identical to the one from the original movie.
52. The idea for these variations between the worlds – namely, the presence of an identifiable *invariant* next to elements that are specific to each of the worlds – is borrowed from films like *Total Recall* or *eXistenZ*, where this principle is systematized. In the case of *TRON: Legacy*, the name "Flynn" is even more important than the connection between the worlds, as the son follows his father's traces, foreshadowing the eventual reconciliation (as well as the celebration of the patriarch).
53. This was not entirely true in the case of the original *TRON* either, since the protagonist in that film would not fail to remark that the computer units' submission was like the one experienced by the employees of multinational corporations like ENCOM.

Conclusion

> "'The cinema', said André Bazin, 'substitutes for our gaze a world more in harmony with our desires'."
> (*Contempt*, 1963)

In this essay, I proposed a methodological framework for studying the currently fashionable notion of "worldbuilding" from the standpoint of a number of academic fields, including narratology, studies of literary fiction inspired by modal logic, (digital) media and cultural studies, as well as theories applied on "traditional" film studies' objects. I explored issues related to film genres (especially in cases of generic hybridity), certain editing practices based on the principle of alternation, character identification, the organization of film spaces, the entry into fiction, the effects of seriality, the role of the voice-over narration, the use of black & white and color, and the audio-visual representation of subjectivity. In particular, I referred to the definitions introduced by the pioneers of the Institute of Filmology in the early 1950s France, not simply by discussing the key notion of "diegesis", but by embracing their entire network of concepts. The relevance of these concepts was not invalidated by the expansion of digital technology, provided one applies them with caution (as they allow us to consider the effects intended by the production team rather than the film's actual genesis), all the more so since the practices of analog cinema continue to function as a model in the digital age. The distinction between the profilmic and the diegetic retains its validity, if only to discuss those cases where the former is (to a varied degree) erased to the benefit of the latter (for instance, according to the way the motion capture technique is actually used in a given film). The filmographic level is often imitated in computer-generated images, whether it is by referring to the camera (as in J.J. Abrams' lens flares) or the film stock (an image similar to the one found at the end of *Two-Lane Blacktop*, 1971, where the film burns on the screen, appears in *Planet Terror*, 2007, with a straightforward reference to the context of the film's projection, defined by the filmologists as the filmophanic level). Moreover, distinguishing between these levels helps differentiating the way the representation is conceived inside the fiction from the techniques actually used during the production of the film's audio-visual representation: an *artificial world* that looks as if it existed at the profilmic level, can be entirely produced through digital technology without nevertheless becoming a *virtual* world on a semantic level.

I proposed to rethink some of the most frequently asked questions in the history of film theory in the light of contemporary productions that establish a multiverse. I did so by showing how these productions present certain particularities while raising theoretical issues that concern all fiction films. Instead of conceiving a theoretical model prior to the analysis of specific movies and TV series, I chose not to reduce my analysis to a strictly illustrative status, but to opt for an inductive approach that gives a central place to the films themselves without any concerns for the degree of cultural legitimacy accorded to the objects studied (in most cases, I dealt with popular culture products). In my analysis, I occasionally adopted a perspective stemming from the field of gender/cultural studies in order to discuss the "ideological" dimension of certain representations. With regard to the list of films examined, one I intended to be vast even if certain titles are mentioned only incidentally (see the index of movies and TV series at the end of the book), this essay aspires more specifically to make a contribution to the study of science fiction and, generally, of all Fantasy Fictions, by approaching them under a new angle. Numerous are the scholars who identify SF as the ideal genre for the process of worldbuilding, but my study on the structuring principles of multiverses led me to pinpoint a number of elements specific to some of the films attached to the genre.

As the examples discussed throughout the book show, the semantic configurations that present at least two worlds highlight what I designate as the "world-centered dimension" in movies. Studying this dimension led me to examine the conditions of an a priori paradoxical conjunction between the immersion of viewers in a fiction conceived (and represented) as maximalist *and* the exhibition of the medium as such. This self-reflexivity may result from the use of metalepsis, from various forms of hypermediacy, or from the mirroring of the cinematic dispositive inside the film through the representation of "worldbuilding machines". A focal aspect of this essay was the discussion of the correlation between the means of representation (digital effects at the service of worldbuilding) and the nature of the represented (the features of the film worlds). Without being totally assimilated to computers on which mainstream movies heavily depended for the last twenty-five years (especially in the case of Fantasy Fictions), the machines represented inside the diegesis reflect nonetheless the technical context of filmmaking in the digital era. This is true even if movies that visualize the infrastructure required for the storage of big data, like *Transcendence* (2014), are actually rare. The image that illustrates the cover of this book is taken from the opening credits of the TV series *Counterpart*, a digital 3D animated shot featuring a highly stylized representation of a world segmented into smaller units (themselves duplicated) that seem to multiply infinitely. The title of the sixth episode in Season 2, "Twin Cities", reveals the filiation between the city of Berlin in a *parallel world*, that the series' characters inhabit or visit, and the 3D online *virtual world* called *Twinity*, developed by a company called Metaversum GmbH.[1] *Twinity* is an immersive simulation inviting users to navigate through a "mirror city", with Berlin being the first one to be made available to the public in 2008.

The notion of "virtuality", whose polysemy guarantees a wide circulation to the imaginary representations associated with it, grants the corpus of films studied in this book with a level of coherence and urges us to regard certain movies and TV series – otherwise stranger to cyberculture – through the lens of the challenges raised by the so-called digital world. At the same time, the definitions introduced in this essay, such as the different types of worlds and their intersections, discussed in Chapter 3, help us avert the danger of a teleological interpretation. In the words of Vincent Miller, "the virtual is real, but not actual" (2011: 33). This is the reality that I have tried to grasp by examining the way movies direct the experience of the viewer and by integrating the question of the representation's materiality, while prioritizing the "ontological" dimension of the fictions studied. Françoise Lavocat recently observed: "The affinity between the imaginary of possible worlds and of cyberculture is so obvious that until recently it has barely attracted scholarly interest" (2019: 272). My goal was to study this "obvious" affinity and several of its implications in a perspective rarely explored thus far, namely through film analysis.

I deliberately chose not to reduce the corpus of films studied to those that are actually "digital" (meaning: shot digitally), by including, for instance, *The Cabinet of Dr. Caligari* (1920), *Sherlock Jr.* (1924), *The Wizard of Oz* (1939), *Je t'aime je t'aime* (1968), *World on a Wire* (1973), or *Total Recall* (1990). Such a limitation would have postulated an epistemological rupture between pre-digital and digital cinema, a hypothesis incompatible with a study that examines history in the long run, focusing on continuities and on imaginary representations that often precede the actual use of a given technology. *TRON* may very well belong to the analog era, released before the development of hyper-immersive video games; yet, Steven Lisberger's film, produced after the success of video games on home consoles and in arcades, is no less part of the history of discourses on machine-produced simulacra and cybernetics. The same goes for Daniel F. Galouye's *Simulacron-3*, or the novels and short stories written by Philip K. Dick, frequently adapted in Hollywood productions (*Total Recall*, *Minority Report*, *Next*, to name a few examples). Furthermore, Dick's work has indirectly influenced many world-centered movies and TV Series (*The Lost Room* is one of the most recent examples). In a conference entitled "How to Build a Universe that Doesn't Fall Apart Two Days Later" (1978),[2] included in the anthology book *The Shifting Realities of Philip K. Dick* (1995), the writer confirms that questioning the ontology of his protagonists and the world that surrounds them has always been a central aspect of his sci-fi tales, structured around an interpenetration of *mental* and *virtual worlds*. Then, he expands on the way he conceives his stories:

> And then I began to think, Maybe each human being lives in a unique world, a private world, a world different from those inhabited and experienced by all other humans. And that led me to wonder, If reality differs from person to person, can we speak of reality singular, or shouldn't we really be talking about plural realities? And if there are plural realities, are some more true (more real) than others? What about the world of a schizophrenic?

When it comes to the science fiction genre, these distinct and multiple private worlds are not simply *mental*, but imposed on the user by a technology conceived as alienating by the novelist: "Because today we live in a society in which spurious realities are manufactured by the media, by governments, by big corporations, by religious groups, political groups – and the electronic hardware exists by which to deliver these pseudo-worlds right into the heads of the reader, the viewer, the listener". In this particular conference, Dick uses television as his main example. Yet, the expression "electronic hardware" effectively points to the success his stories would find in the digital era. According to Dick's paranoid perspective, the world thus created is "more in harmony with our desires" (following Godard's famous quote) only because these desires have been in fact manufactured by the media.

The range of "possibilities" offered by VFX contributes strongly to shaping and modeling representations, as Lev Manovich (2001), Lisa Purse (2013), or Kristen Whissel (2014) have shown.[3] I have already stressed the importance of taking into account the history of digital special effects in movies, from *Westworld* and *Futureworld* to *Jurassic Park* and *Avatar*. However, the objective of this book was not just to study *digital movies* but, more generally, *movies in the digital era*. I chose to focus my study on film representations and, therefore, this essay does not deal with the new modes of distribution and consumption of media products, nor does it discuss – at least not extensively – the transmedia implications at a time of constant exchanges between the film, the comic book, and the video game industries. Nevertheless, similarly to many of the theoretical references summoned here (first and foremost the writings of Marie-Laure Ryan), the reflection carried out in the previous pages is underpinned by the contemporary context in film production, where the exploitation of franchises dominates. The "*Resident Evil*" film series, discussed in Chapter 1, presents a remarkable world-centered creative design, precisely because it constitutes the transmedia extension of a video game series. *Monster Hunter* (2020), also directed and co-written by Paul W.S. Anderson, shows its female hero (played once again by Milla Jovovich) and her troop of soldiers being transported to a *parallel world*;[4] the film is adapted after a video game produced by Japanese publisher Capcom, just like "*Resident Evil*".

Some films, like *Avatar* or *Ready Player One*, produce a discourse in favor of virtual realities (metaphorically in the former, literally in the latter, a film that also promotes, in a politically correct way, the "right" use of VR). However, the majority of movies studied in this book develop a dystopian and rather technophobic vision. As Miller notes: "In the contrast between representation and simulation, the latter is usually viewed in a more negative light. Representation is generally seen as a genuine attempt to portray something 'real' or in a truthful manner. By contrast, simulation is often portrayed as deceptive, something which takes us away from the real or the truth" (Miller 2011: 35). This is also valid for *film representations* of a *computer simulation*: they are predominantly connoted negatively. The alienation of an individual who is a voluntary or unconscious user of a technological device – and especially of "worldbuilding machines" – is a recurrent motif, with *Total Recall* and cyberpunk narratives serving as the most characteristic examples. In these sci-fi extrapolations, each film functions as a philosophical experiment that questions our relationship to the world (mediated, or even created, by digital devices). Commenting upon *Inception*, a film that clearly follows a world-centered logic, Lindenmuth remarks that "all of the characters in the film yearn for reality and are dissatisfied with the prospect of living forever in a dream" (Lindenmuth 2017: 164).[5] Then, he associates Nolan's film with a theoretical idea introduced by the philosopher Robert Nozick in his essay *Anarchy, State, and Utopia* (1974). Here is a passage from the section "The Experience Machine" of this book:

> Suppose there were an experience machine that would give you any experience you desired. Superduper neuropsychologists could stimulate your brain so that you would think you were writing a great novel, or making a friend, or reading an interesting book. All the time you would be floating in a tank, with electrodes attached to your brain. Should you plug into this machine for life, preprogramming your life's experiences? [...] Of course, while in the tank you won't know you're there; you'll think it's all actually happening. Others can also plug in to have the experiences they want, so there's no need to stay unplugged to serve them (Nozick 1974: 42–43).

Nozick aims to disprove the philosophical thesis of hedonism by affirming that humans need to truly experience things – including the effort and the difficulties this entails – in order to derive satisfaction from them. This leads him to discuss a form of human enslavement reminiscent of the false utopia presented in Season 3 of *Westworld*, as well as in a number of other stories discussed above, where the protagonist falls victim to an illusion concerning the ontology of the world he thinks he inhabits. Interestingly enough, Nozick refers to a specific image in his demonstration: "a brain floating in a vat". This metaphor does not entirely correspond to the representation of worldbuilding machines in most multiverse films, with the exception of *Possible Worlds* (2000), an independent movie directed by Canadian-born filmmaker Robert Lepage, which may be considered as a literal adaptation of Nozick's hypothesis.[6] Still, given the recurrence of stories based on the submission of an individual to a computer system, this particular metaphor is kin to a number of films studied in this essay: the female hero in *Fringe* immerses herself in a vat; Neo's physical body is extracted from a container filled with a kind of amniotic fluid in *The Matrix*; Claude Ridder is enclosed in a cocoon that resembles a gigantic brain and is repeatedly transported in an aquatic environment in *Je t'aime je t'aime*; *Dark City*'s hero wakes up in a bathtub; lastly, the immobile bodies of the protagonists in *Eternal Sunshine of the Spotless Mind*, *Source Code*, or *Vanishing Waves* are covered with electrodes connecting them to a machine. All these figures function as the viewer's double inside the film diegesis and are forced to stay put like guinea pigs, at least during the first part of each film, since the story will later ensure the transformation of their initial passive state.

In the first chapter ("Brains in a vat") of his book *Reason, Truth, and History*, the American philosopher Hilary Putnam illustrates his reflections by a set of "science fiction stories" that enable him to discuss the links that exist (or not) between a mental representation and its referent. He encourages the reader to imagine the following situation:

> [I]magine that a human being (you can imagine this to be yourself) has been subjected to an operation by an evil scientist. The person's brain (your brain) has been removed from the body and placed in a vat of nutrients which keeps the brain alive. The nerve endings have been connected to a super-scientific computer which causes the person whose brain it is to have the illusion that everything is perfectly normal. There seem to be people, objects, the sky, etc.; but really all the person (you) is experiencing is the result of electronic impulse traveling from the computer to nerve endings. The computer is so clever that if the person tries to raise his hand, the feedback from the computer will cause him to "see" and "feel" the hand being raised. Moreover, by varying the program, the evil scientist can cause the victim to "experience" (or hallucinate) any situation or environment the evil scientist wishes. He can also obliterate the memory of the brain operation, so that the victim will seem to himself to have always been in this environment. It can even seem to the victim that he is sitting and reading these very words about the amusing but quite absurd supposition that there is an evil scientist who removes people's brains from their bodies and places them in a vat [...]. In this case, we are, in a sense, actually in communication. I am not mistaken about your real existence (only about the existence of your body in the "external world", apart from brains). From a certain point of view, it doesn't matter that "the whole world" is a collective hallucination; for you do, after all, really hear my words when I speak to you. [...] Suppose this whole story were actually true. Could we, if we were brains in a vat in this way, *say* or *think* that we were? (Putnam 1981: 5–7).

The purpose of this long citation is not to discuss the Wittgenstein-inspired reflection on the links between language, thought, and referential process – in fact, Putnam responds negatively to the question of the above quotation. My goal is to underline the numerous similarities between this allegory, qualified by the philosopher as a "possible world" that re-enacts the allegory of the cave at the dawn of information superhighways, and multiverse movies, especially those presenting *artificial* or *virtual worlds*, according to my typology in this book:

- "Evil scientists" are frequent in multiverse films. Their presence, as well as that of their creations, attests the film's inscription to the science fiction genre. Yet, the stereotypical qualifier "evil" does not always apply to multiverse movies whose relativism is opposed to a certain Manichean conception (see Walter and his alter ego in *Fringe*, Dr. Schreber in *Dark City*, Dr. Ford in Season 1 of *Westworld*);

- "Super-computers" are omnipresent in our corpus, from *TRON*'s Master Control Program to Rehoboam in Season 3 of *Westworld*. In the latter, the machine controlled by Serac does not really predict the future; it creates the future by imposing the "possible variations" to the detriment of the free will of the citizens, reduced to simple pawns just like the androids in Delos' theme park;
- Putnam's emphasis on the creation of an "environment" ("people, objects, the sky") is consonant with the "constructivist" approach on fiction promulgated by Umberto Eco that a film like *The Truman Show* showcases. The subject of the experiment is indeed a kind of spectator, since the electric impulses are converted into perceptions;
- Putnam rejects the arguments of the metaphysical realists who advocate a reality conceived independently of the mind. In his proposition to go beyond the dichotomy between objective and subjective, he puts forward a relativist view and describes, from the standpoint of a philosophy of language, a situation that echoes the denial of the subjects of *mental worlds* (*The Machinist*, *Shutter Island*). At the same time, the distinction between a "Brain-in-a-Vat world" (Putnam 1981: 13) and an "external world" is akin to the two-world structure of a film like *Eternal Sunshine of a Spotless Mind*;
- Putnam's fictional story combines a simulation with exceptional illusionist qualities and a "*mise en abyme*" that ultimately benefits the immersion, in keeping with the tradition established by the novel *Simulacron-3* (adapted for the screen twice, by Fassbinder and Rusnak) to which a film like *eXistenZ* is attached;
- In Putnam's "possible world", amnesias are deliberately induced by a manipulative group, like in *Total Recall*, *Dark City*, or the *Westworld* TV series;
- Putnam refers to a "real" communication (or a shared experience), thus highlighting the possibility of a disembodied interaction between individuals subjected to a worldbuilding machine, as in *Inception*, *Source Code*, or *Vanishing Waves*.

In the next section of his book, Putnam explores the notion of "reference" by imagining a kind of Turing test. Released shortly before *Blade Runner* premiered in theaters, *Reason, Truth, and History* deals with imaginary situations conveyed by world-centered sci-fi stories. The "origami unicorn" scene,[7] deleted from the first theatrical release of Ridley Scott's film, would have provided the philosopher with a (counter-)example, all the more relevant since the unicorn is an imaginary animal with no referent in the real world. However, its silhouette is "universally" recognizable – at least in "our" world, as long as we do not presume that "there is a planet somewhere on which human beings have evolved (or been deposited by alien spacemen, or what have you)", and that "these humans, although otherwise like us, have never [...] imagined [a unicorn]" but "one day a picture of [it] is accidentally dropped on their planet by a spaceship" (Putnam 1981: 3). The words used by the philosopher resonate strongly, once again, with the films I have studied in this essay. In *Dark City*, factitious images are omnipresent; the humans have been transferred to another planet by the aliens and have never even seen the sun, but they nevertheless possess a vocabulary that enables them to describe a blue sky or images of seaside vacations from an artificial past. In *Westworld*, a guest has lost a photograph outside the theme park during Season 1, which will be later discovered by Dolores' father; the mere sight of this image provokes a complete dysfunction in him, to the point of doubting his own world.

As these examples indicate, the speculative nature of the science fiction genre does not concern exclusively the "future". In this essay, I tried to show that the temporal dimension traditionally privileged in film studies, due to their emphasis on narrative structures, can be relegated to the background, especially when one examines a multiverse. The world-centered dimension of movies, considered through the ontological implications of possible worlds, may come to the fore. This was my goal when studying the various fictional "laboratories" offered by multiverse films, a place where contemporary technological imaginations and the ways to consider the relationship of man to the world within a digital context, are systematically explored. The predominance of a dystopian vision can be interpreted as a way of denying the technological determinations that underlie this type of film productions and of affirming *in fine* the reassuring domination of a (human) individual over the world(s). However, this type of technophobic representation, one that insists on the theme of alienation within the fiction in order to better reject the notion it could possibly concern the consumers of these movie productions in real life, is actually specific to Western culture. The "*Matrix*" franchise strongly popularized the idea of unveiling the simulacrum inside the fiction. The survival game *No Man's Sky* (2016)[8] further develops this idea by reinforcing the self-reflexive character of its story. *The Matrix* (1999) does not include a "film within a film", whereas the procedurally generated, sci-fi open world in *No Man's Sky* is revealed to be a simulation produced by a super-computer. Despite Hollywood's worldwide impact, the idea of representing a technology harmful to Man needs to be nuanced when one examines the SF productions in other parts of the globe. For instance, Japanese productions – not included in the corpus of this essay – would undoubtedly open the door to other "possible alternatives". In Japanese culture, technology (like robotics or prosthetics) is not necessarily associated with a danger to mankind, nor attached to a strict opposition between nature and culture.

Multiverses are very present in the Japanese media landscape, to the point that a label – "*isekai*" – has met with a widespread success, designating a sub-genre of science fiction and fantasy distinguished by the fact that the protagonists are transported to another world through a technological interface or, in a more supernatural regime, through reincarnation. In both cases, the story involves an "avatar", either in the sense of the user's character in a video game, or in that attached to the Hindu tradition. This trend began with franchises like "*.hack*" (from 2002 onwards), whose story spreads over different media (manga, anime, video games, game cards) and uses a MMORPG simply called "The World".[9] Commenting upon the trend launched by *"Sword Art Online"* (from 2009 onwards), Satomi Sato articulates the transmedia practices of contemporary franchises (amplified in Japan thanks to the so-called *media-mix* strategy)[10] with multiverse fictions that transpose inside their diegesis the economic strategies launched by the entertainment industry: "When such a cross-media development of a story world becomes the norm in media industry, story becomes self-conscious about its own worldmaking and expansion" (Saito 2015: 144). His observation echoes the one I made earlier with respect to the self-consciousness typical of Hollywood productions. Moreover, cases like "*Resident Evil*", *Edge of Tomorrow*, or *Ghost in the Shell* testify to an occasional circulation of fictions between Japan and the United States.

The sub-genre of *isekai* is closely linked to serial fictions (light novels, manga, and animated TV) targeted to young adults, like most fantasy stories all over the world. This is partly explained by the possible alignment between the particularities of teenage life and the theme of *parallel worlds*.[11] Nevertheless, it also represents a tendency towards "world-centered narratives" that can be observed more widely in Japanese productions, including animated feature films made by well-known "auteurs" and, therefore, endowed with a higher degree of cultural legitimacy. Hayao Miyazaki's *Spirited Away* (2001) and Satoshi Kon's *Paprika* (2006) are two of the most famous examples of this tendency. The latter opens with a sequence reminiscent of *Little Nemo in Slumberland*, in which the environment undergoes abrupt transformations,[12] with each new version referring to a distinct film genre, as the protagonists use "a scientific key that allows us to open the door to our dreams". In this way, they obtain from the dreamer's subconscious mind a series of recordings of the journey in the form of video files. Like in *Avalon*, a Japanese-Polish live-action film directed by the famous anime director Mamoru Oshii,[13] discussed in the "Are Colors Diegetic?" section of Chapter 4, the sci-fi animated movie *Summer Wars* (2009) features a realistic frame world and a *virtual world*, each represented in a distinct graphic style. *Summer Wars' virtual world* is named "the World of Oz", in a straightforward reference to the screen adaptation of Baum's novel, and is presented as a massively multiplayer online game that users can access via their cellular phones. This world is depicted in a more stylized way, with its fanciful avatars and other artifacts stored in a gigantic library suspended in the air, standing out on a white background, as if they were part of a world perpetually transformed and waiting to be furnished. The film actually begins with a promotional presentation of this world[14] in which users can purchase various items, an element that clearly inserts the diegetic game within a vast industrial network. As in *Colossus: The Forbidden Project* (1970) or the better-known *War-Games* (1983), whose story focuses on a genius in mathematics young protagonist, the emphasis is placed on the implications of the "in-game" combats on the reality of the users and, therefore, on the – often neglected in our digital age – *material* dimension of the *virtual world*.[15] In order to preserve the remains of the grandmother of the clan, whose members are the central characters in *Summer Wars*, ice blocks are used to cool down an overheated supercomputer. The old matriarch was monitored by sensors that malfunctioned due to a computer crash, resulting in the takeover of the Oz system by an Artificial Intelligence (following a failed experiment by the American Department of Defense, the United States being in this way responsible for the global chaos). This AI progressively absorbs almost all of the users' accounts and causes massive disturbances in the cities by blocking the Internet access to everyone (companies, individuals, and services), hacking their systems, and then threatening to explode nuclear power plants[16] and to cause the crash on Earth of an Asteroid Probe. Mamoru Hosoda's animated feature film capitalizes on the "connection" between the two worlds by integrating the participatory dimension as a new form of solidarity.

Real (2013), directed by one of the leading filmmakers of the J-Horror genre, Kiyoshi Kurosawa, is one of the many Japanese live-action multiverse films released in the 2010s. For this particular movie, Kurosawa borrows several elements from Christopher Nolan's *Inception*.[17] Thanks to a technological interface used by a medical team in order to establish contact between the brains of a subject and a patient in coma, a virtual reality is created in which the two individuals, connected to the device, interact. One is reminded here of the central idea developed in *Vanishing Waves*, but in *Real*, the connected individuals have known each other for a long time and have even lived as a couple. Koichi believes that he is entering the subconscious of his wife, Atsumi, an alleged cartoonist who has fallen into a coma after trying unsuccessfully to kill herself. Like in the *supernatural world* of *The Sixth Sense* and *The Others*, a twist will occur: the male hero realizes, alongside with the viewer, that he is the one to be in a coma; in fact, it is Atsumi who is trying to contact her loved one. It turns out that the frame story of the scientific experiment was initially a part of the *virtual world*, while also having an effective existence in the primary world, as is proven by the shots depicting the young woman connecting herself to the machine. Prior to the establishment of an introspective narrative and a series of flashbacks (a situation reminiscent of the hero's dive into the past in *Je t'aime je t'aime*), each immersion generates the repetition of a discussion between Atsumi and Koichi in an almost identical context, as in certain time-loop movies. The *virtual world* is totally subjugated to the subjectivity of a patient conscious of his inability to wake up (resulting in a very dense fog that envelops the city, restricting the visible space to the couple's building). This world is unstable (a part of the apartment suddenly collapses, then one of the rooms is inexplicably flooded) and populated with strange, blurred-faced individuals (lifeless puppets, sort of "non-player characters" designated by one of the scientists as "philosophical zombies", reminiscent of the ghosts in other supernatural films directed by Kurosawa). While visiting this world, Koichi experiences a series of horrific apparitions that he associates with the manga drawn by his wife; in truth, they are the result of a suppressed feeling of guilt linked to his own childhood (a recurring pattern in *mental worlds*, as I have shown in Chapter 3 through the example of *Shutter Island*).

The contamination between the levels in *Real* does not stop at this metalepsis, typical of the self-reflexive portrayal of the act of creation. In the first part of the film, Koichi is subject to hallucinations in his daily life too, every time he disconnects from the interface (or, rather, when he thinks he does). In a scene reminiscent of *eXistenZ*, Atsumi feels with her hands a drawing of a gun in the *virtual world* and then, in a gesture accompanied by metallic sound that immediately inscribes the representation in a different reality, the weapon is materialized in her hand. As she uses it to shoot her editor and her ghostwriter, the gun abruptly appears in Koichi's hand in the real world, before we realize that it was only a vision and that we were actually in a *mental world*. The circulation of objects and motifs from one world to another[18] and the ever-widening gap between reality and the world that materializes Koichi's subconscious (a world, both *virtual* and *mental*, where most of the film takes place), as for instance when the hero's guilt takes the form of a prehistoric sea monster that attacks the couple in a momentary slip into a different sub-genre of Japanese science-fiction (*kaijū eiga*), highlight the structuring role conferred to the co-presence of two distinct worlds in *Real*, diegetically justified by the use of a worldbuilding machine. As in the *Westworld* TV series, qualified in this essay as "an emblematic case of permeability between different types of worlds", *Real* illustrates the importance of using the typology established in Chapter 3 in accordance with the inferences the viewer is led to make at a given point in a film. The principles presiding over the worldbuilding process in multiverse movies are not necessarily presented right from the outset and, in any case, they are likely to undergo shifts that shape the film's narration.

These few examples, located outside of this essay's main corpus (almost exclusively composed of North American movies and TV series), point to the growing importance conferred over the last fifteen years on worldbuilding and multiverses in Japanese novels and audio-visual productions. Therefore, they testify to the more general scope of my analysis in this book, which can be applied to media other than cinema as well as to other films. The rise of multiverses in cultural productions corresponds to an era in which the notion of "virtual" interferes in all aspects of our daily life, and in particular in the production, distribution, and consumption of moving images.

The notion of "world" may be normally situated at a semantic level, yet I consciously included in my case studies films and TV series whose analysis imperatively calls for the consideration of stylistic aspects. Not only does cinema constitute a singular "worldbuilding machine" (where editing plays a decisive role) but each of the movies examined here actualizes and explicitly confronts this aptitude of the film medium in its own special way. Consequently, I am well aware that the restriction of the corpus not only to dominant North American productions, but also to live-action films (with the exception of a few hybrid movies, such as *The Congress*) narrows, to a certain degree, the scope of the theoretical reflection developed in this book. Even in the pre-digital era, animated movies give the audience the experience of a world ontologically distinct from the phenomenal world, due to its visual construction determined by various animation techniques.[19] Developments in the so-called "3D" animation in the digital era, based on a massive use of motion capture, as in *The Polar Express* (2004) or *The Adventures of Tintin* (2011), have modified the way the camera navigates through the diegetic space and reinforced the feeling of being immersed in a (different) "world". The possibility of varying the degree to which a representation is figurative, as well as the lesser importance given to the referential dimension in this type of movies, favor the structuring of a multiverse. In her book *Digital Imaging in Popular Cinema*, Lisa Purse comments upon *Coraline* (2009), which "takes up this strategy [to use alterations in stereoscopic depth cues to signal a move between worlds] in a highly developed way, to distinguish between the young title character's subjective experience of her real, everyday world, and the 'Other World' she discovers" (Purse 2013: 136). This is a manifestation of world-centered features at the level of the materiality of the image, as discussed in Chapter 4.

Furthermore, some of the franchises I have studied in this essay also include offshoots in the form of animated movies, often conceived simultaneously with a video game, as in the case of the animated TV series *Resident Evil: Infinite Darkness*, launched in 2021 (the same year a new film in the series, *Resident Evil: Welcome to Raccoon City*, is scheduled for release). Another example is the animated TV series *TRON: Uprising* (2012–2013), which extends the story of *TRON: Legacy* (2011), discussed in Chapter 5, while following directly the release of the video game *Tron: Evolution* (2011). *TRON: Uprising* capitalizes on the graphic possibilities of animation in order to represent the "interior" of an arcade game (meaning, the unfolding of a 2D representation into a world) as a constantly reconfigured universe. The TV series opens with a voice-over narration that establishes the world in which the story will take place: "Hidden away inside a computer exists another world. […] A digital utopia filled with infinite possibilities". In the age of "virtual cinema" that combines real actors with 3D animation, as in *Ready Player One*, these "infinite possibilities" offered to the characters inside the fiction are also those available today in a means of expression like cinema that develops in conjunction (and in competition) with a natively digital medium like video games.

Some may claim that *TRON: Uprising* is a TV series mainly intended for children or teenagers, like some of the Fantasy Fictions discussed in this book, and that it would therefore be excessive, or even illegitimate, to pay special attention to it in the context of a theoretical study. However, the selection of case studies in this essay was determined by a criterion of relevance. Additionally, my goal was to give an account of the empirical experience of a viewer of sci-fi movies who has witnessed, from 1980s onwards, the rise of computer-generated images on our screens, used to build the world of fictions that – in cases that explicitly raise issues of worldbuilding – examine current technologies by speculating on what they will become in the future (or what they could have been in the past). A common point to the majority of films and TV series discussed in this book is their explicitly playful dimension: we take pleasure in "pretending", in asking ourselves "what would have happened if…", and we indulge in the demiurgic and regressive pleasure of destroying the sand castle that we have just built (see the example of *Dark City*, where construction and destruction follows one another inside a world with a given set of invariants). This relationship to fiction is in line with the logic of ancillary products that predominates within a given franchise. Lego, a company specialized in constructions toys, manufactures modular objects in the effigy of specific components of the universe shaped by a number of film franchises ("*Star Wars*", "*The Lord of the Rings*", "*Pirates of the Caribbean*", "*Batman*", etc.) or sci-fi movies (*Ghostbusters*, *Wonder Woman 1984*), and then re-injects these products, established as components of an ostensibly *artificial world* of bricks and figurines, inside the audio-visual representations. One thinks in particular of the "*Lego Star Wars*" series of animated films and video games, where a law that governs the fictional world, like the heroes' telekinetic powers, merges with a principle of the game, since the characters (or the gamer's avatars) can dismantle certain elements of the world at will, as a child would do when playing with Lego bricks.

In an effort to shed light on the relationship between diegesis and story, I have used in a previous essay (Boillat 2007: 350–351) the image of a child playing in a sandpit with various figures and vehicles, imagining stories from the toys (i.e., the diegetic components) available in this delimited space, a "small world" that partly determines the horizon of possibilities. This metaphor unintentionally echoed the term "sandbox" used in the field of video games to qualify games whose objectives are mainly chosen by the players themselves (as, for example, in *Minecraft*, 2011) and, more generally, games that offer players a significant margin of freedom, such as "*open world* games where the spatial architecture is offered to exploration to the gamer's avatar but with no predetermined paths" (see Boillat and Krichane 2014)*. Selim Krichane, in a book resulting from his doctoral thesis and published in French in the same collection as the first edition of the present essay, notes that "by observing the trends in the mainstream production of video games since the beginning of the 2000s, one notices that 3D modeling and real-time mathematical calculation of perspective have progressively dominated the video game market" (Krichane 2018: 257)*. The titles published by Rockstar Games are indicative of such a propensity for the exploration of a world: the "*Grand Theft Auto*" series (2001–2003) names each of its episodes after a specific city (fictional, albeit inspired from a real one, like Miami's "Vice City") or state ("San Andreas"). In other words, it resorts to a topographical delineation frequent in world-centered movies (*The Truman Show*, *Pleasantville*, *Dark City*, *The Thirteenth Floor*, or *Silent Hill* – the latter adapted from a video game). The two installments of the video game *Red Dead Redemption* (2010/2018), which represent the Wild West prior to and in parallel with the development of large-scale urban centers, are in a way the model of the theme parks offered by the Delos company to its visitors in HBO's *Westworld* TV series. As I have shown through a detailed analysis in Chapters 2 and 3, this show is indebted to paradigms specific to the digital era, despite its starting point in a "pre-digital" space (the amusement park) and a technology (the automata) imagined as early as the 18th century.

During the 1990s, the notion of a "*spatial turn*" in social sciences and humanities started to spread (especially in the field of history, as an opposition to the linear vision of a "Big History"). Beyond its various extensions and metaphorical uses, this notion may be equally applied to the field of digital humanities (think, for example, of the visualization of the results of a *distant reading*)[20] as well as to the objects – if not the tools – of digital culture studies, particularly in game studies:[21] "Indeed, space is the one category that has come to be accepted as the central issue of game studies, and the one in which all previous categories are integrated – a situation that supports the hypothesis that a paradigm change is taking place" (Günzel 2008: 171). The world-centered perspective adopted in the present essay testifies to the ways film theory may prove useful in studying contemporary audio-visual productions beyond cinema. Certainly, the expansion of "*toy stories*"[22] is part of a movement of infantilization initiated in the 1980s by the movies produced by Steven Spielberg and George Lucas.[23] In this regard, the opening scene in *TRON: Legacy*, discussed in Chapter 5, in which the hero's son plays with figurines from the original film, constitutes the apotheosis of the promotion of ancillary products targeting young audiences. According to a postmodern, consumerist logic, analyzed by Fredric Jameson, "the products sold on the market become the very content of the media image" (1991: 275). This phenomenon is also explained by the growing importance of a world-centered creative design, which, despite the increasing dematerialization of the representational media, takes the concrete material form of a combination of building blocks. The act of creation is visualized in the original *TRON*, when Clu reinvigorates the ship he pilots, as its various dislocated parts agglomerate and interlock according to the desire of a hero who has his creative talents as a game designer transposed inside the *virtual world* in the form of action skills.

Conclusion

The playful dimension, the suspension of the laws of the world and their replacement by those of *another* world controlled by the hero, undoubtedly explains the omnipresence of low-tech motifs and props within the sci-fi logic of contemporary visual productions, even in films openly referring to computer-generated worlds (see, for example, the cities that rise upon the map-world in *Game of Thrones*' opening credits). The demiurgic characters that shape the world they inhabit are for the most part tinkerers, busy repairing some whimsical gear – a common feature from *TRON* and *Jurassic Park* to *The Matrix*, *Inception*, and *Source Code*, following different patterns whose specificities are discussed in the previous chapters. This is also true in *Lost*, as far as the derailments of its narrative device are concerned; a character like the Keymaker in *The Matrix Reloaded*, who gives access to the program's backdoors, would not have been out of place in that series. The film universe is a vast handiwork, malleable to the point of containing several different worlds. It results from a creative approach that welcomes randomness and free associations. The heroes distinguish themselves by using a Frankensteinian power that could be qualified as regressive in that it presupposes a state prior to the separation between the individual and the world, the phase that comes before the mirror stage: this is where *Dark City*'s extraterrestrial pre-(or post-)individuals find themselves in, just like Agent Smith who proliferates through his clones in order to invade the world in "*The Matrix*". In contrast to "virtual realities", the retro-futuristic, steampunk devices or the various anachronistic technologies – the radio in *Hellraiser III: Hell on Earth*, the telephone booths in *The Matrix*, the clockworks in *Dark City*, the typewriter in *Fringe*, the beeper in *TRON: Legacy*, the entire technological arsenal in the *Watchmen* mini-series – become representable in an audio-visual medium like cinema. In the face of the rise of all types of digital imaging, these types of diegetic components, as well as the aesthetics associated with them, reintroduce the tactility of the instrument and the mediation of the body. Furthermore, they highlight the hero's know-how, as the films establish a continuity between the individual and the world, through the representation of a prosthetic tool, attenuating in this way the potential differences in terms of ontological status. In doing so, these objects assume the anthropological function of repressing contemporary issues related to the interaction between Man and (Computing) Machine, by displacing them on far more controllable past technologies.

However, questioning the uniqueness of the world in order to explore its possible alternatives results in an incessant swing between variants falling under two distinct modes, one *utopian*, the other *dystopian*. This is evident in the comparisons I previously made to the "sandpit" (the place of an unfettered development of the imagination) and the "vat" (where all imagination is shaped by the subject's alienating submission to the coercion of a computer program). By comparing *Dark City* to *1984* (the novel *and* its screen adaptation, directed by Michael Radford)[24], I have shown that worldbuilding powers are sometimes placed in the wrong hands, even if the story strives to reverse this ominous situation.

The different variants deployed in world-centered movies confront the audience with the notion of diversity, exploited as a factor of entertainment, especially when considering the spectacular character of a VFX-produced representation. Nevertheless, such multiplicity needs to be organized. This is why crosscutting plays a major structuring role in this type of films. This editing pattern enables associations that recall Lautréamont's phrase (claimed also by André Breton): "As beautiful as the chance encounter of an umbrella and a sewing machine on a dissection table". This is all the more true since "worldbuilding machines" often stem from (pre-)cinematographic inspirations; after all, the mechanism allowing for the perforated film to scroll, patented by the Lumière brothers, was actually inspired by the presser foot system of a …sewing machine. Other times, such collusions may occur within a single image, as my analysis on the use of color in Chapter 4 has shown. The on-screen co-presence of elements belonging to distinct worlds provokes incongruities that defy the logic of the world whose borders are thus transgressed. Such phenomena fall under the category of "metalepsis", a notion conceptualized by theoreticians of literature. Still, in audio-visual representations (and in digital productions, as shown by Marie-Laure Ryan), they produce an effect of strangeness due to the quasi-simultaneity of the perception of divergent information visible on the screen. In *Je t'aime je t'aime*, Claude Ridder recalls his suicide attempt and finds himself dying on a lawn in the present. In *Fight Club*, Marla invades the hero's dream, as she appears in a corner of a frozen penguin cave. In *Possible Worlds*, a number of almost imperceptible transformations in the space-time continuum occur within the same shot by cutting on action or by means of a long sequence shot, a superimposition, or profilmic tricks, as for example when the surface of a stop bath – a "tank" in the embedded level – gradually turns into a glass table where George's character (rather, a different "version" of him) is seated for a job interview. In *eXistenZ*, the same objects circulate under various, more or less organic and low-tech avatars. In the flashbacks that follow John's final injection in *Dark City*, Dr. Schreber appears obsessively in all his memories, in a different disguise on each occasion. The spaces roamed through by the couple in *Vanishing Waves* follow a dreamlike logic filled with discontinuities. Such sudden and brutal short-circuits electrify the viewers with the attractional qualities of these films (or sometimes tire them by resorting to infinite "reboots"). Cinema ostensibly manifests itself as a "worldbuilding machine".

The films and TV series discussed in this essay form a unique body of work. The analysis developed in the previous chapters identified many similarities between these movies. There is a common tendency to privilege a space the characters have to explore – a frequently insular "*small world*" – rather than insisting on temporal data. There is also a tendency to showcase the digital image by capitalizing on its spectacular character, while also raising, through the story, the issue of the *trace*, an inalienable human sign that allows the hero to hold on to something (for example, a romance) in an ever-shifting world dominated by machines. We can add to this list a propensity for organizing the film universe in a way that establishes a hierarchical relationship between its different parts (embedding) and assures their co-presence (alternation). These films often inscribe in the materiality of the image the heterogeneity that prevails at a semantic level to the point that they sometimes undermine the figurative status of this image. They project the film apparatus into fictional "avatars" that testify to both the infatuation and the fears associated with new technologies and their representations, conceived as "total", immersive and, therefore, potentially alienating. They identify editing as a decisive factor in worldbuilding and regulate its rhythm according to that of a diegetized "world-building machine" (that may be a technological artifact, an activity of the brain, or, in most cases, a mixture of both). They refer to specific film genres in order to distinguish between their worlds. Finally, they frequently lure the audience by pretending to assume the artificiality of a postmodern recycling of references, while they actually materialize a paranoid vision, as the protagonists confront a conspiracy organized by a demiurgic figure.

Do all the contemporary movies studied in this essay belong to a specific (super-)genre, that of "multiverse films"? Some of the titles discussed here are grouped together by distributors for promotional purposes (for instance, in the texts included in the DVD covers) or by consumers on websites or blogs (often according to other criteria, such as the context of "virtual realities", or the irruption of a plot twist that urges viewers to reinterpret the whole film). However, the diversity of the cases mentioned in my typology and the variable extension conferred to the notion of "world" resist such labeling. Still, as I have already shown in Chapter 2, it would seem relevant to correlate the notions of *world* and *genre*. Not necessarily as a way to describe existing genres according to the gap established between the world they propose and our world of reference (since in the cases discussed the split between different worlds is internal to the film universe), nor as a step towards the elaboration of a new typology of fictional universes, as Marie-Laure Ryan suggests (1991: 43), but because the coherence of a given world, or simply its identification as an autonomous whole, frequently relies on generic traits (see *supra* the analysis of *Dark City*, the *Westworld* TV series, *Sucker Punch*, or *Cloud Atlas*). The stylistic "filtering" that confers a particular "color" to each world – a "tone" or an "atmosphere" – contributes to defining a certain horizon of expectation often associated with a specific genre. Therefore, the genre can play a role in the interpretation of the ontological status of a given world, even if it is to mislead viewers unable to infer that the iconographic or narrative conventions are actually exhibited as such, rather than truly adopted.

The "worldbuilding machines", whose presence in a film is justified by the latter's attachment to the sci-fi genre, are the repository of an imaginary associated to cinema, proper to an era where the film medium is integrated inside a larger media landscape. This landscape contributes to redefine cinema's functions, including that of building worlds (that one finds to an exaggerated degree in certain video game productions). The principle of "reboot", the multiplicity of worlds, and the expansion of a universe are all part of a strategy of escalation. The viewer has access to several worlds for the price of one (unless he ends ups buying one world for the price of many, as is the case with some franchises). My goal in this book was to provide readers with keys to understanding this type of productions, whose presence has grown over the last twenty years. The ambition was to open the doors to new "possibilities", whose emergence is undoubtedly linked to the expansion of digital imaging and the development of VFX. When a representation is first assembled on a computer screen, everything has to be (re)constructed from the ground up, pixel by pixel. This is also true for film theory. Hopefully, this essay has managed to prove the productivity of revisiting some of the major paradigms of film theory from a world-centered perspective.

Endnotes

1. "Metaverses [like MMOGS, such as *Second Life*] are empty playgrounds that users fill with objects and avatars of their own design" (Lavocat 2019: 275).
2. The title of this conference, as well as its overtly didactic overtones, are disputed by the author over the course of his lecture: "However, I will reveal a secret to you: I like to build universes which do fall apart. I like to see them come unglued, and I like to see how the characters in the novels cope with this problem. I have a secret love of chaos". Later on, Dick discusses "The Electric Ant" (1969, see Chapter 4) and its straightforward references to the film medium.
3. In regard to visual effects, my approach in this essay is similar to the model established by Whissel, which "defines the complex relationship between spectacular effects, story/narrative, and character development" (2014: 6), except that instead of "story/narratives", I focus on types of worlds and worldbuilding.
4. *Monster Hunter* opens with the following intertitle: "It is entirely possible that beyond the perception of our senses, new worlds are hidden of which we are totally unaware". Following the canonical reduction of the notion of a plurality of worlds to a two-world representation (commented upon in Chapter 3), the on-screen text gradually evolves, first by bringing the words "new worlds" to the forefront, then by changing them to "the new world", foreshadowing the film's opening sequence, as we see the female hero snatched away from "our world" during an electromagnetic storm that seems straight out of *The Final Countdown* (1980) – though in Anderson's film the characters do not really travel in time, but in a *parallel world*, crossing through a number of portals.
5. Lindenmuth also mentions *The Truman Show*, albeit incidentally, a film that constitutes a canonical example of an *artificial world*, according to my typology. See Lindenmuth 2017: 162.
6. In *Possible Worlds*, a police investigation of a violent murder (committed by decerebration) alternates with different variants of the encounter between George (Tom McCamus) and Joyce (Tilda Swinton). George imagines being able to live in several worlds at once and control the outcome of the chains of causality that develop in them, like many demiurgic figures found in our case studies. The encounter is replayed on different locations (as in time-loop movies) between two "avatars" associated with distinct life paths. One of the individuals interrogated by the detective is a mad scientist, similar to the one mentioned

by Putnam (see *infra*). The detective brings back from his first visit to the scientist's house a trinket that is actually a kind of "matrix": it contains the brain of a rat connected to a machine via electric wires (one is of course reminded of the rat in *Je t'aime je t'aime*). At the end of the film, we realize that the world in which the investigation takes place embeds all the other fragments, while George's brain is kept "alive" inside a jar.

7. See Chapter 3, note 62.
8. The "Atlas Rises" update, released in 2017, presents a narrative amplification that motivates the creation of a simulation. An argument similar to the one found in *Dark City* is added to the confrontation between the hero and the *TRON*-like super-computer: like the aliens in Proyas' film, the super-computer experiments on guinea pigs, looking for a way to ensure its survival.
9. An article by Eric Margolis, published on August 1, 2020 in *Japan Times*, bore the following title: "Step into another world with isekai, the fantasy subgenre ruling the manga marker". See https://www.japantimes.co.jp/culture/2020/08/01/books/isekai-fantasy-manga/. Consulted on June 16, 2021.
10. Marc Steinberg, who introduced the notion of "*media-mix*" among scholars, notes that the animation industry in Japan favors the development of "a desire not for the character or narrative alone but for the prosumer's participation in the character's world" (Steinberg 2012: 200). In this respect, multiverses make it possible to represent the viewer's real world inside the fiction while also multiplying the worlds presented to the audience.
11. See Laurent Bazin's quote in Chapter 1, note 6.
12. In this respect, the film is similar to Buster Keaton's *Sherlock Jr.* (1924), briefly discussed in the "Philip K. Dick's World-Editing Process" section of Chapter 4.
13. Oshii is the director of the animated series *Ghost in the Shell* (1995/2004/2008) whose first installment is widely considered as a masterpiece of the cyberpunk genre. He will attach another one of his movies, *Assault Girls* (2009), to the same universe as *Avalon*, in a perspective that combines the creation of a multiverse with the expansion beyond the limits of a single film.
14. *Ready Player One* (2018) includes a similar scene that introduces the secondary world within the film. We are immersed in this world through the protagonist who is first shown in the frame world: he describes the *virtual world* in voice-over. Then, we follow his avatar as he roams through the secondary world. This choice is indicative of the way the young hero will ultimately master the *virtual world* and reveals the film's technophile attitude with regards to virtual reality devices. On the other hand, *Summer Wars* begins with an introductory scene explicitly addressed to the film's viewer, as if it were a non-fictional commercial produced by a real-life company. The game's industrial dimension, namely the subject of the critical discourse developed by the film, is highlighted right from the start.
15. Another sci-fi film, *Ender's Game*, deals with this question by recounting the story of a group of young gamers who unknowingly cause the genocide of an extraterrestrial population.
16. Ever since the "*Godzilla*" film series, the importance of the threat posed by US atomic experiments in Japanese SF is well-known.
17. A particular shot from *Real* echoes my commentary on *Inception* in the "Post-9/11 Alternate Realities" segment of Chapter 1. A static shot filmed from the balcony of the couple's apartment shows the Tokyo cityscape disintegrating through a process of liquefaction. Long before the subprime crisis exploded in the United States, Japan was hit hard by a recession resulting from the bursting of a speculative bubble from the mid-1980s to the early 1990s.
18. One finds in *Real* the motif of the sign carved on the hero's body that functions as the "index" of a given world, like those in *Total Recall* (2012) and *Dark City*, discussed in Chapters 2 and 5. In the virtual world, Atsumi draws a circle on Koichi's hand with a felt-tip pen. The male hero will see this sign reappear in the "real" world. However, this trace only reveals that Koichi never "really" left the world produced by the interface.
19. See for example Suzanne Buchan's reflection on the Quay Brothers' puppet animation films. Commenting upon the lack of studies on animation spectatorship, she adds that viewers are confronted with a particular type of representation whose main strategy "ranges from subversion of natural laws that govern representations of live-action films to the

appropriation of cultural codes and imagery that partially informs the 'worlds' and figures it can allow us to experience" (Buchan 2006: 27). The quotation marks the author systematically puts on the term "world" – placed at the heart of her study (as well as in the title of the collective book she edited) – are revealing of a specificity of animated cinema that is both obvious and difficult to grasp.

20. Franco Moretti examines, among other things, the distribution of a part of Hollywood cinema in the "Planet Hollywood" chapter of his book *Distant Reading*. His analysis, hardly convincing, allegedly confirms that "plot and style [are] becoming manifestly de-coupled as a result of their movement (or not) in space" (Moretti 2013: 92).
21. Let us note, among the pioneering studies on this issue, the article by Espen Aarseth, "Allegories of Space" (2000), that examines video games through the lens of their spatial representation (perspectives on the game world) and in terms of representational spaces, as well as Jenkins 2004, in which the author argues that video games are primarily defined by their spatial configuration. On the navigation within a game world, see the chapter "Gamescapes" in King & Krzywinska (2006: 76–123).
22. *Toy Story*, directed by John Lasseter, showcases in 1995 the achievements of computer graphics technology. This film is emblematic of the phenomenon described here in that it features characters corresponding to typical toys, themselves associated with specific film genres (the western's cowboy dreads being eventually supplanted by the science fiction's astronaut). The sequels to this movie, released at different moments within the evolution of computer graphics (1999, 2010, and 2019), are telling of an unceasing fascination with these child-like imaginary worlds.
23. See in particular Wood 1986 and Kellner & Ryan 1990. In the *Star Wars* prequel trilogy, the problems faced by the main hero, Anakin (Hayden Christensen), and the motive for his subservience to the Evil genius lie precisely in the fact that certain adult preoccupations (the death of his mother, the premonition of the tragedy awaiting his companion upon childbirth) can no longer be resolved as easily as when he repaired his racing car toy as a kid (as Anakin himself remarks in *Star Wars: Episode II - Attack of the Clones*, 2002). The fantasy of controlling the world is constantly actualized through the hero of *TRON: Uprising*, a technician capable of accessing the lair of various forms of machinery digitally produced inside "the Grid".
24. Like the other films previously mentioned, *1984* (1984) represents a "futuristic" technology through a retro sci-fi iconography of the post-War era.

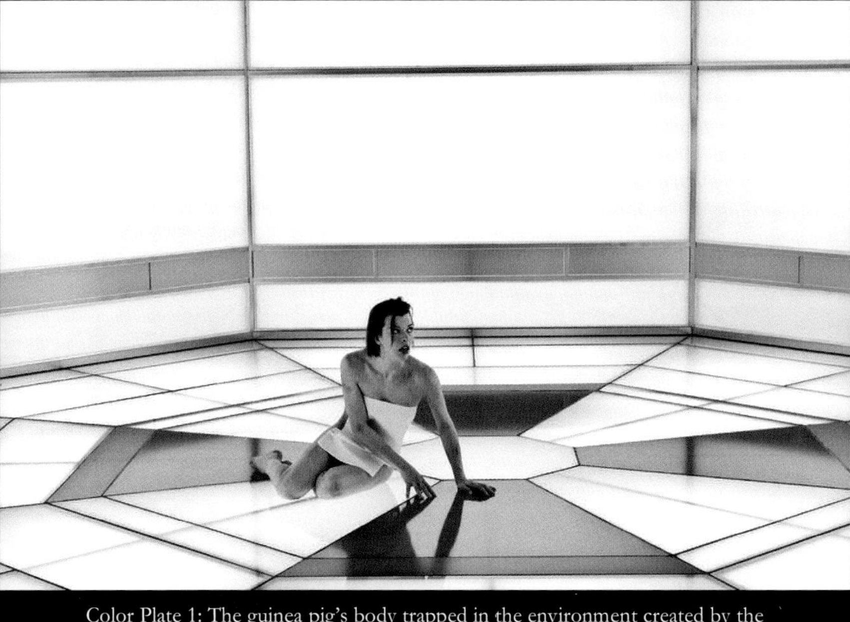

Color Plate 1: The guinea pig's body trapped in the environment created by the Umbrella Corporation (*Resident Evil: Retribution*, 2012).

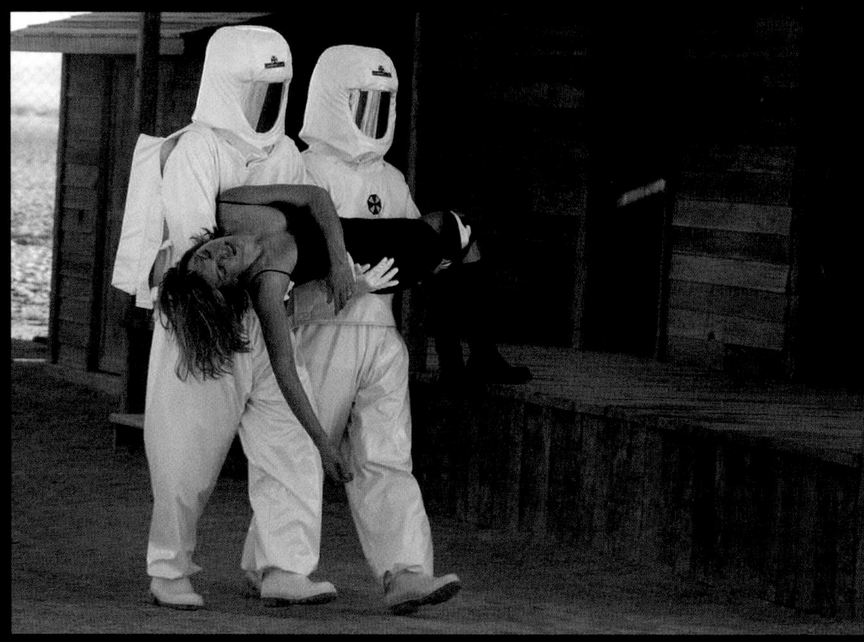

Color Plate 2: In the backstage, after the "game over", Alice's corpse is transported to a mass grave filled with identical clones (*Resident Evil: Extinction*, 2007).

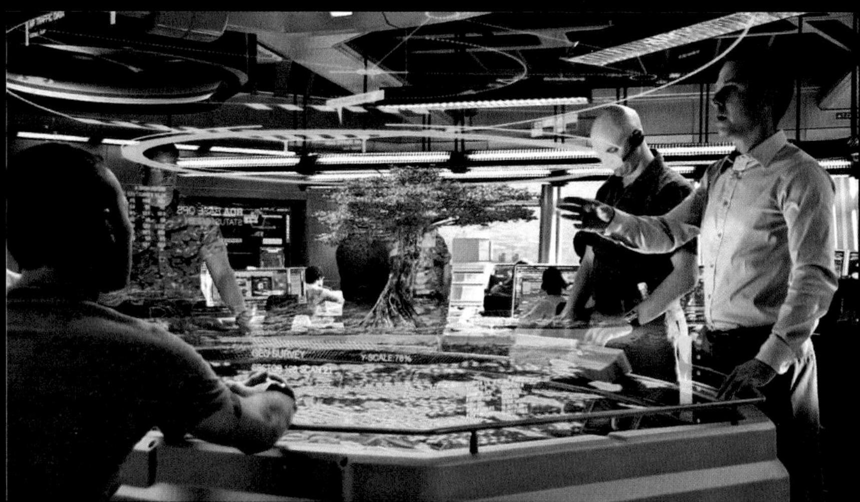

Color Plate 3: 3D holographic mapping as a colonizers' tool in *Avatar* (2009): Pandora's "Tree of Life".

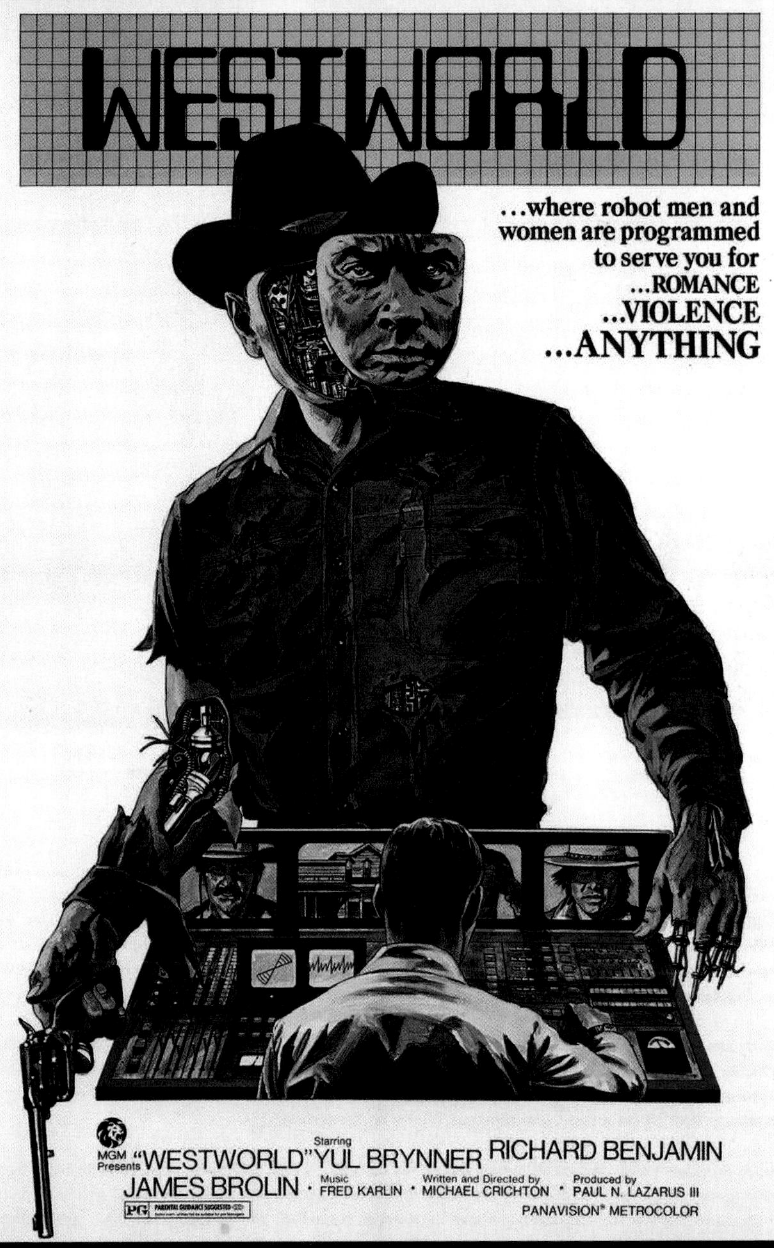

Color Plate 4: The film title on a cross-ruled background evokes the scanning pattern of (cathode) computer screens: the actions of the cowboy-like android are manipulated from the theme park's control room in the poster of *Westworld* (1973).

FROM EXECUTIVE PRODUCERS

J.J. ABRAMS   JONATHAN NOLAN   LISA JOY

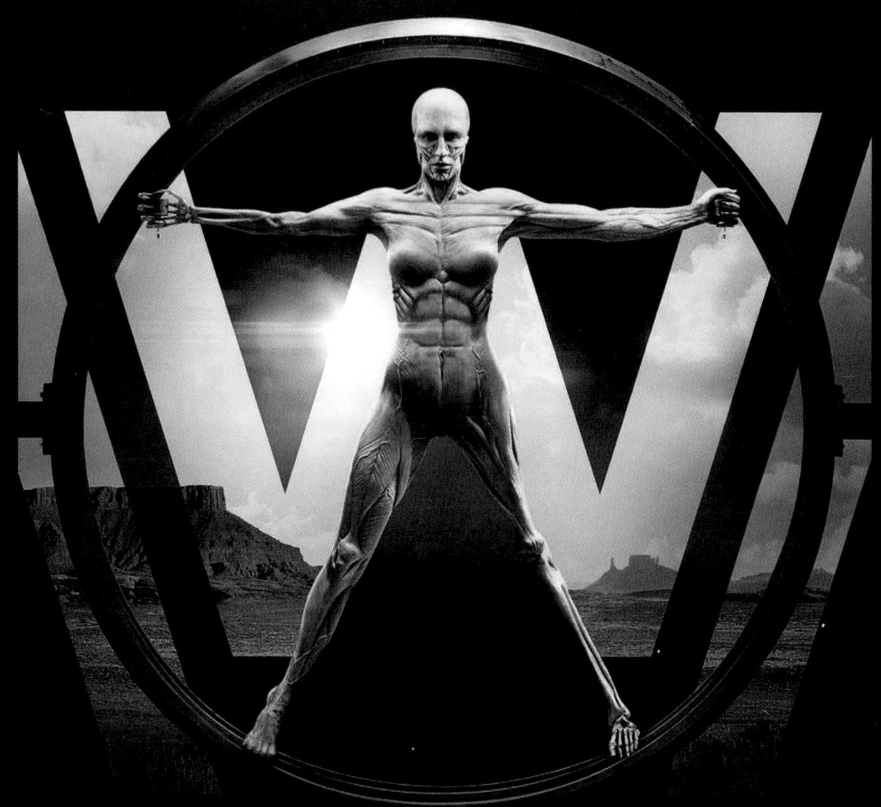

EVERY HERO HAS A CODE

WESTWORLD

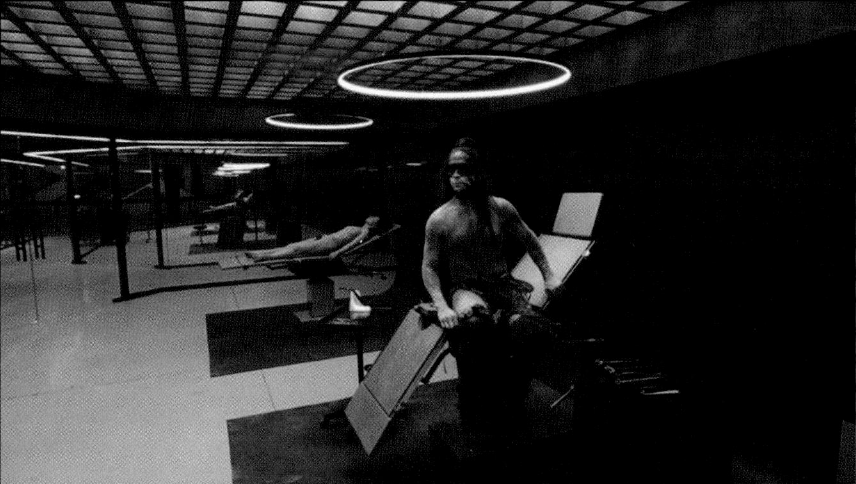

Color Plate 6: Bodies of typical western characters on a science fiction set. Akecheta (Zahn McClarnon), a peaceful Native American reprogrammed as the leader of a bloodthirsty tribe, explains how he accessed "the other side of death", waking up in the artificial light of the theme park's underground base, as the Delos technicians realize that he has not been updated in a decade, "Kiksuya", *Westworld* S02E08).

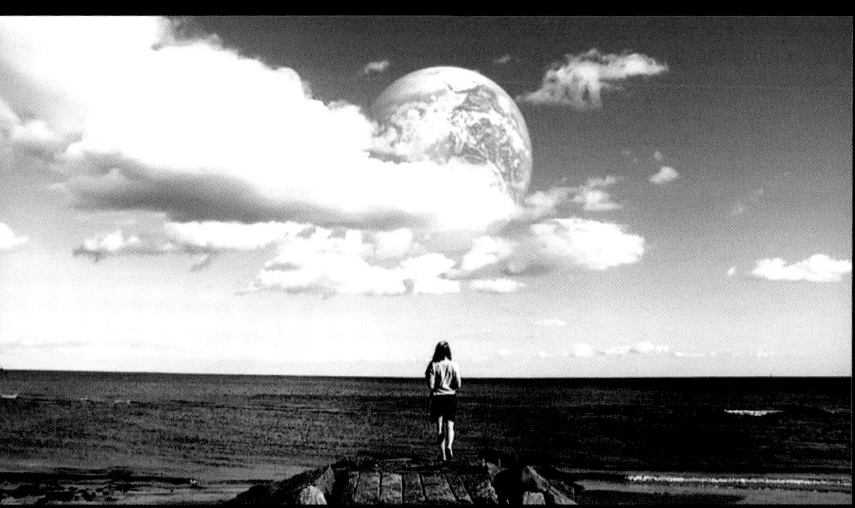

Color Plate 7: *Another Earth* (2011): the female hero standing on the pier and facing a mirror image of the planet Earth, as the ocean marks a horizon of possibilities.

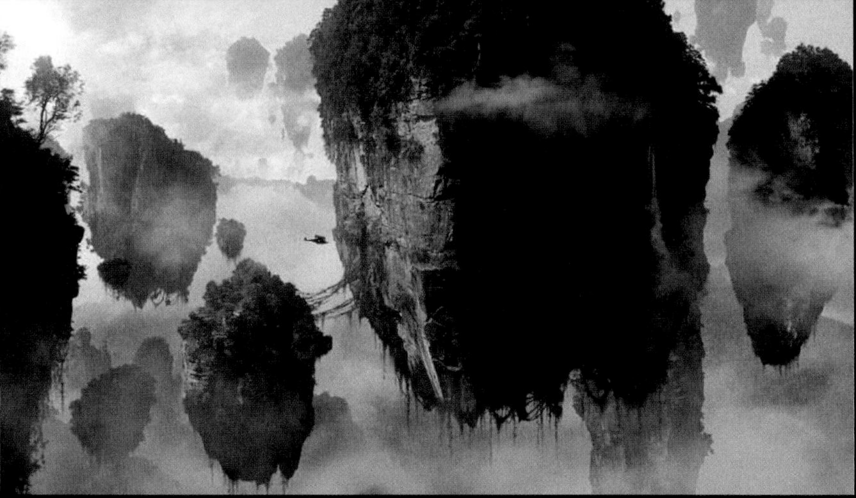

Color Plate 8: James Cameron's flying forest island of Pandora (*Avatar*, 2009).

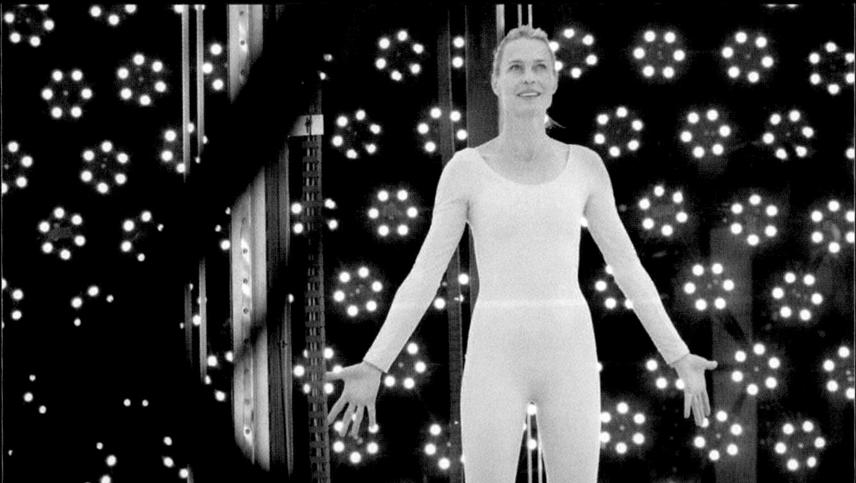

Color Plate 9: Robin Wright as a has-been movie star named Robin Wright during a motion capture session in *The Congress* (2013).

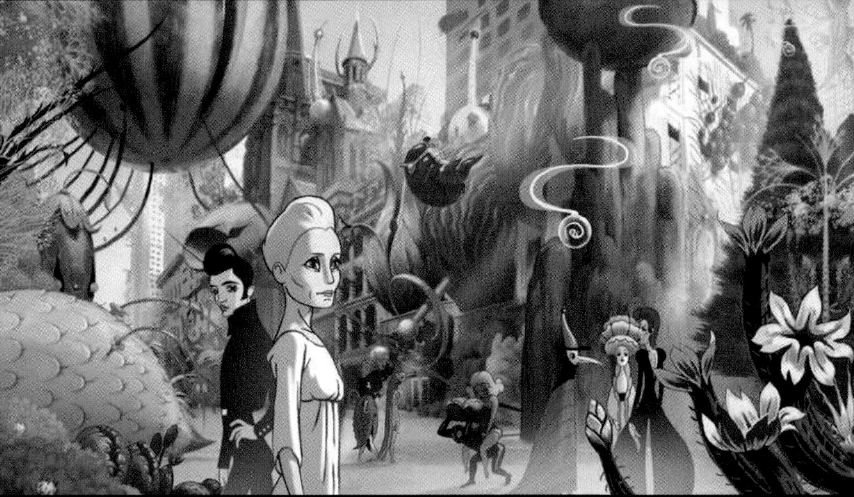

Color Plate 10: Robin Wright's animated avatar inside an image saturated with marvelous/supernatural elements.

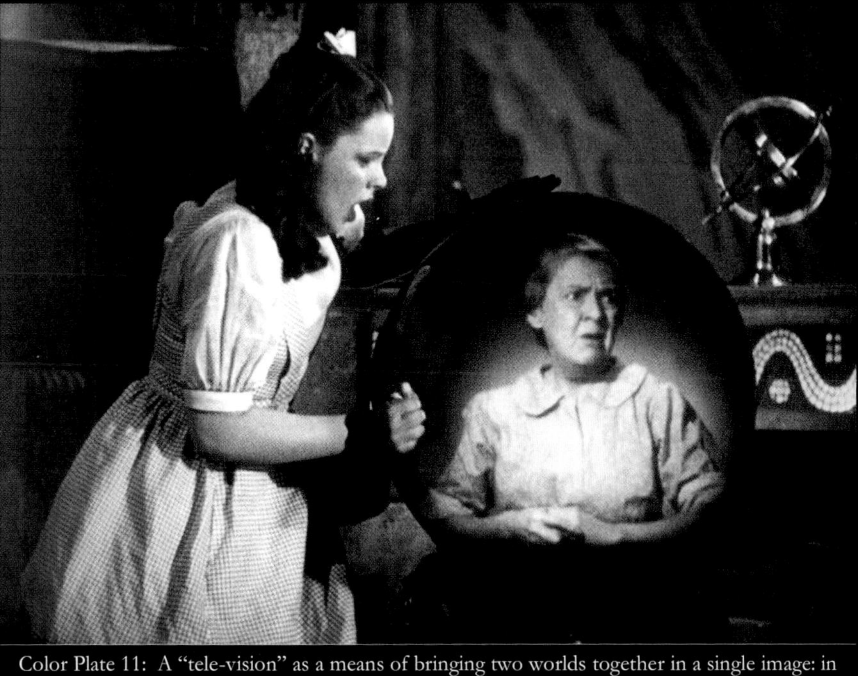

Color Plate 11: A "tele-vision" as a means of bringing two worlds together in a single image: in the MGM musical *The Wizard of Oz* (1939), Dorothy (Judy Garland), held captive inside the witch's castle, sees for a brief moment her aunt Em appear in a crystal ball, as the young protagonist calls for help. The small screen within the big screen brings back the sepia-toned image from the film's opening scenes, anchored in the real word, in contrast with the grandiose Technicolor associated with a *parallel* (and *supernatural*) fairy tale world that the presence of the same actors in different roles incites us to interpret as a *mental* world (like *mutatis mutandis* in David Cronenberg's *Spider*, 2002).

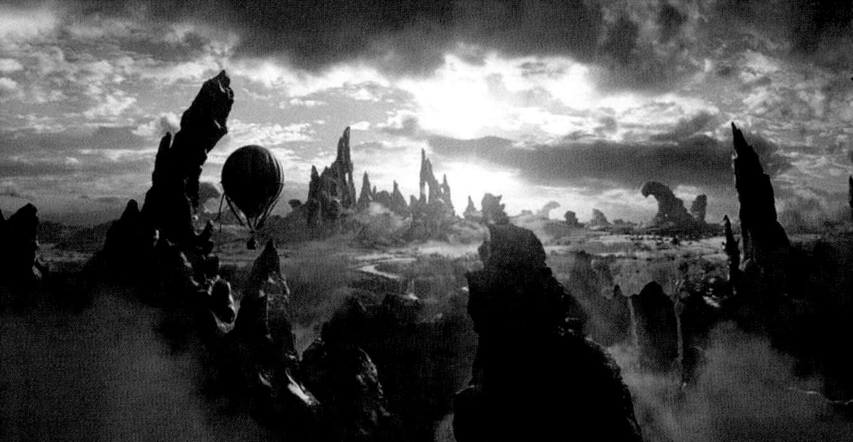

Color Plate 12: A prequel to *The Wizard of Oz*, shot almost three quarters of a century after the original film, at a time when Hollywood is in search of subject matters suited to the development of digital special effects and 3D technology, *Oz the Great and Powerful* (2013) recounts the discovery of another world by means of a hot air balloon. This Jules Verne-like "extraordinary journey" (implying the existence of a *distant world*) borders on the multiverse and offers a retrospective interpretation of Victor Fleming's film that excludes the idea that we were inside Dorothy's *mental world*.

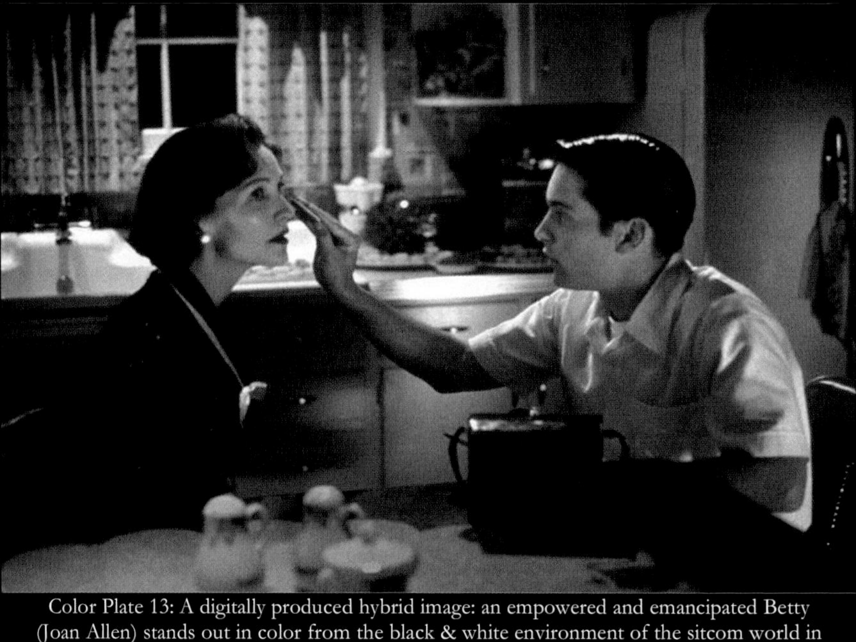

Color Plate 13: A digitally produced hybrid image: an empowered and emancipated Betty (Joan Allen) stands out in color from the black & white environment of the sitcom world in *Pleasantville* (1998). Her son tries to make her up in "black & white" in an effort to conceal the transgression of the patriarchal norms.

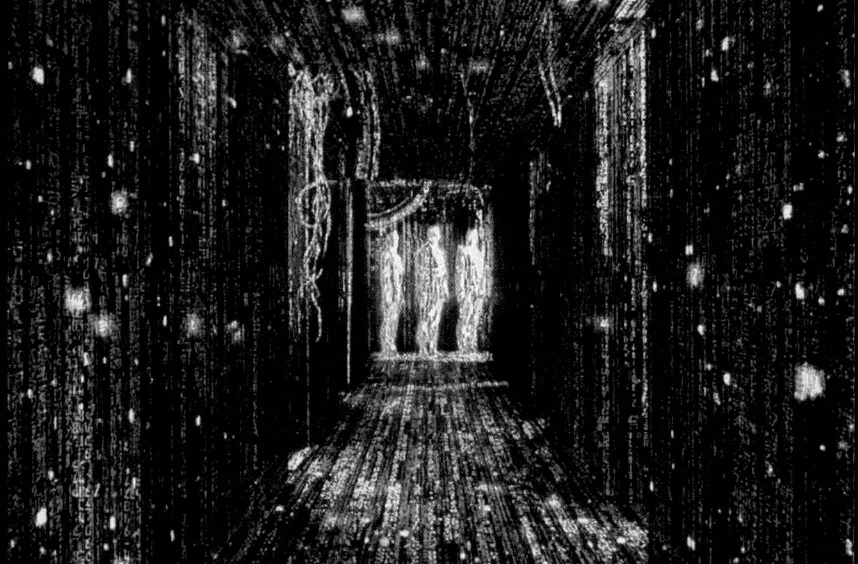

Color Plate 14: Seeing beyond the surface and inside the algorithm's "black box": the figurative image revealed as an accumulation of lines of code in *The Matrix* (1999).

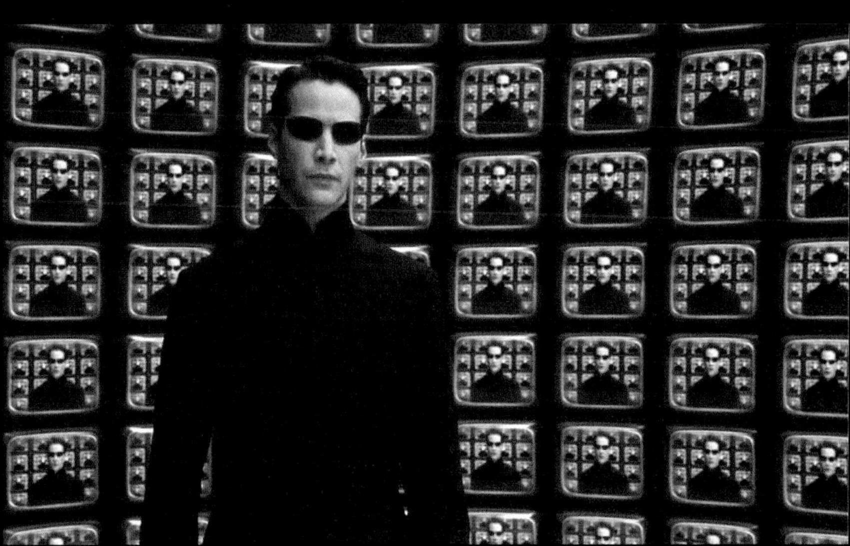

Color Plate 15: Neo (Keanu Reeves) confronts The Architect in front of a wall filled with TV monitors, at the crossroads of 1980s contemporary art (the installations of the Korean video artist Nam June Paik) and a paranoid critique of the surveillance society: the multiplication of his own self that endangers his individuality is in fact the result of system reboots orchestrated by The Architect in order to guarantee the perfection of his world.

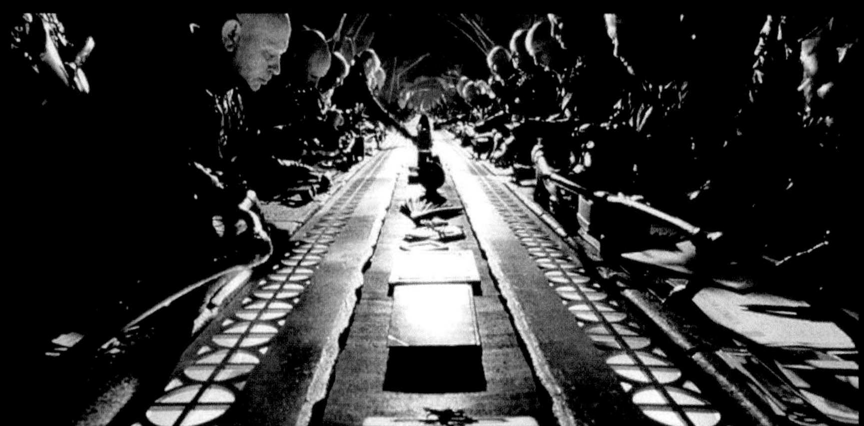

Color Plate 16: The illusion factory: a conveyor belt on which an army of vampire-like aliens works, selecting artifacts from "our" world and integrating them in the dollhouses of their *artificial world* (*Dark City*, 1998).

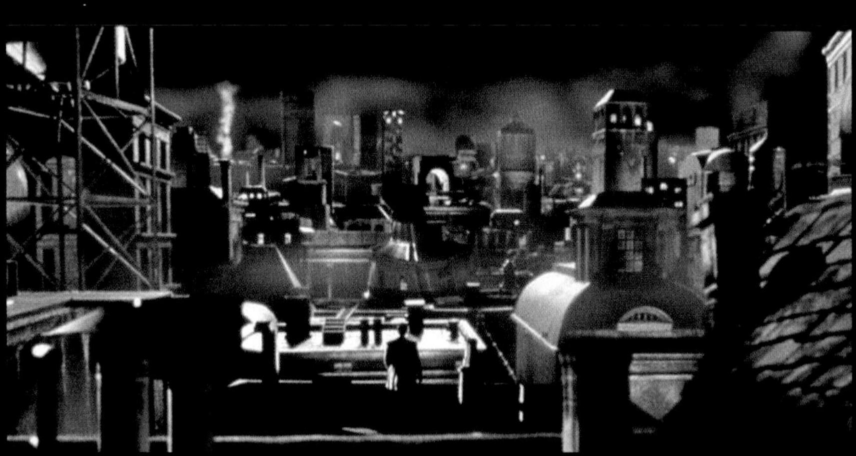

Color Plate 17: A city constantly rearranged whose buildings rise or fall during a single night: a world-centered use of "morphing" in *Dark City* (1998).

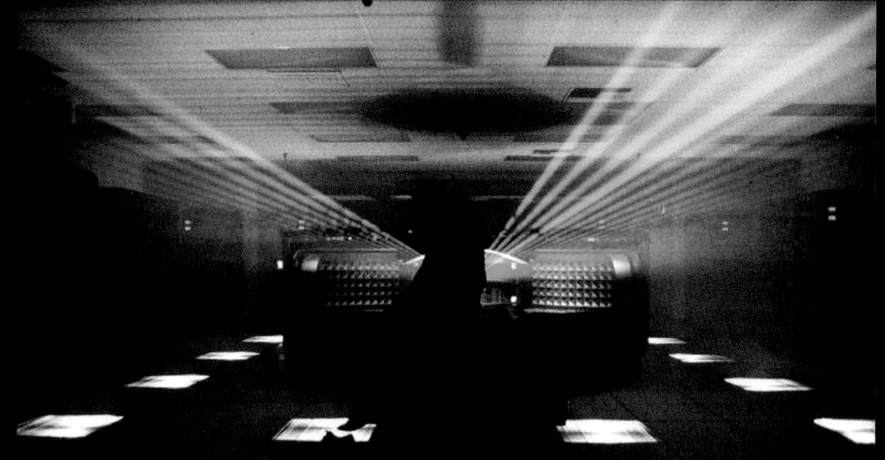

Color Plate 18: The interface for the connection to a VR simulation of 1930s Los Angeles in *The Thirteenth Floor* (1999): a green laser beam scanner sizes up the user's body.

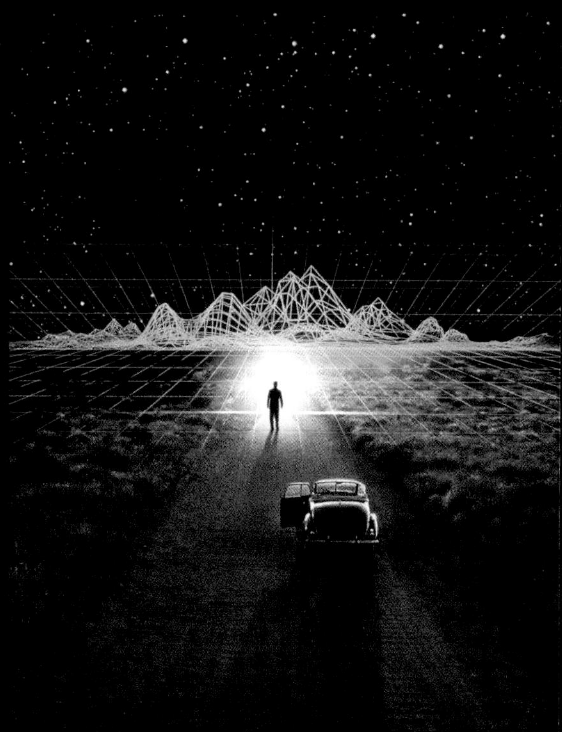

Color Plate 19: End of the road, end of the virtual world: the simulacrum is unmasked by the hero in *The Thirteenth Floor*, as the natural landscape dissolves into green wireframes.

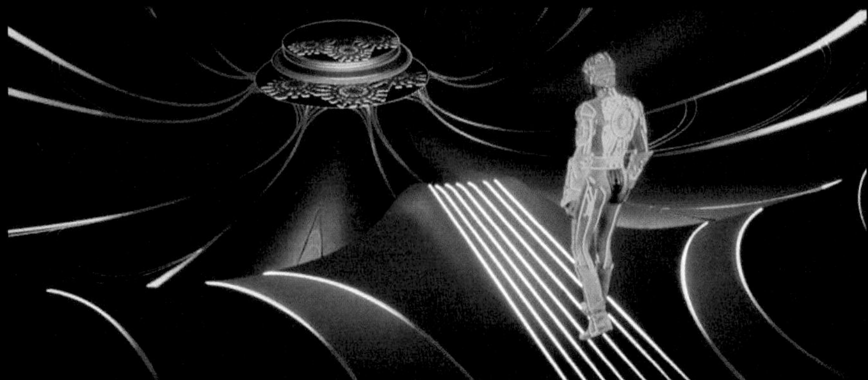

Color Plate 20: After freeing Yori from prison and escaping with her into a maze guarded by faceless soldiers (in a scene reminiscent of the Death Star escape in *Star Wars: Episode IV – A New Hope*), Tron (Bruce Boxleitner), who exists only in the arcade game world, goes to the tower in order to communicate with his user. In a landscape drawn by luminous lines, the hero climbs up an inclined plane as unrealistic as the slope of the roof walked on by Cesare in the expressionist sets of *The Cabinet of Dr. Caligari's mental world.*

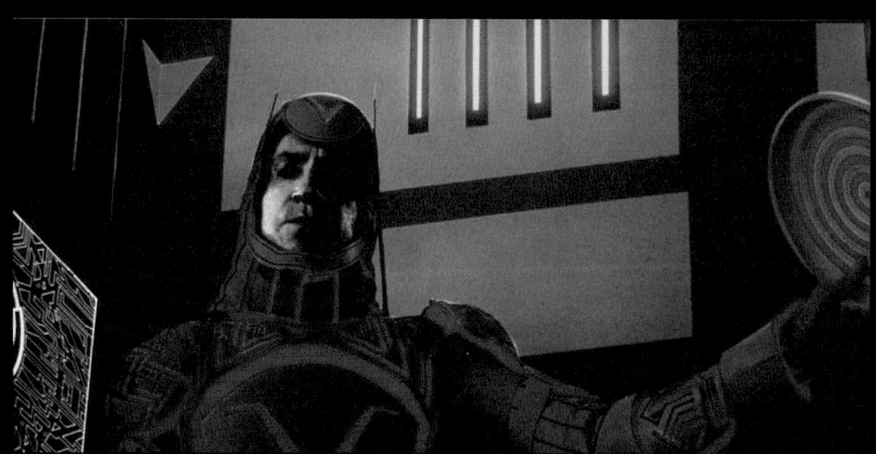

Color Plate 21: A fusion between the user and his avatar (Sark played by David Warner): an "analog" face (filmed in black & white) in a computer-generated world in *TRON* (1982).

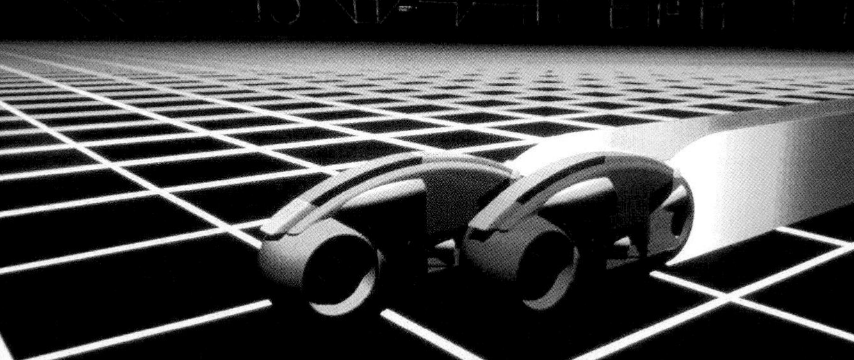

Color Plate 22: A motorcycle race in *TRON*: phosphorescent traces of movement against the black background of "the grid".

Color Plate 23: Utopia and dystopia facing each other: the two versions of Clu (Jeff Bridges) against the landscape of a virtual city (*TRON: Legacy*, 2010).

Bibliography

Aarseth, E. (2000) "Allegories of Space. The Question of Spatiality in Video Games". In Eskelinen, M. and Koskimaa, R. (eds.), *Cybertext Yearbook 2000*. Jyväskylän: University of Jyväskylän, 152–171.

Adorno, T. W. and Horkheimer, M. (2002 [1947]) *Dialectic of Enlightenment: Philosophical Fragments*. Palo Alto: Stanford University Press.

Alber, J. (2019) "Logical Contradictions, Possible Worlds Theory, and the Embodied Mind". In Bell, A. and Ryan, M.-L. (eds.), *Possible Worlds Theory and Contemporary Narratology*. Lincoln/London: University of Nebraska Press, 157–176.

Albera, F. (2010) "'L'école comique française', une avant-garde posthume?". 1895, 61: 77–98.

Albera, F. and Lefebvre, M. (2009) (eds.), *Cinémas*, 19 (1–3).

Albera, F. and Tortajada, M. (2010) "Introduction to an Epistemology of Viewing and Listening Dispositives". In Albera, F. and Tortajada, M. (eds.), *Cinema Beyond Film. Media Epistemology in the Modern Era*. Amsterdam: Amsterdam University Press, 9–22.

Allen, W. (1977) *"The Kugelmass Episode". New Yorker,* May 2, 1977: 34–35.

Altman, R. (1987) *The American Film Musical*. Bloomington: Indiana University Press.

Altman, R. (2000) "A Semantic/Syntactic Approach of Film Genre". In Stam, R. and Miller, T. (eds.), *Film and Theory. An Anthology*. Nalden Mass./Oxford: Blackwell Publisher.

Anderson, P. (1961) *Three Hearts and Three Lions*. New York: Doubleday.

Angenot, M. (1979) "The Absent Paradigm: An Introduction to the Semiotics of Science Fiction". *Science Fiction Studies*, 6 (17): 9–19.

Apollinaire, G. (1971 [1918]) "The New Spirit and the Poets". In *Selected Writings of Guillaume Apollinaire*. New York: New Directions Books, 227–237.

Arnheim, R. (1957 [1933]) *Film as Art*. Berkeley: University of California Press.

Atallah, M. (2013) "Les Utopies, ces miroirs distanciés de la Modernité". In Atallah, M., Jaccaud, F. and Valéry, F. (eds.), *Souvenirs du futur*. Lausanne/Yverdon-les-Bains: Presses polytechniques et universitaires romandes/Maison d'Ailleurs, 21–36.

Atallah, M. (2016) *L'Art de la science-fiction*. Paris/Yverdon-les-Bains: ActuSF/Maison d'Ailleurs.

Badiou, A., Benatouil, T., During E. *et al.* (eds.) (2003) *Matrix, machine philosophique*. Paris: Ellipses.

Baetens, J. (2020) *Rebuilding Story Worlds. The Obscure Cities by Schuiten and Peeters*. New Brunswick: Rutgers University Press.

Bankey, R. (2001) "La Donna è Mobile: Constructing the Irrational Woman". *Gender, Place and Culture: a Journal of Feminist Geography*, 8(1): 37–54.

Barillier, E. (2010) *Steampunk ! L'Esthétique rétro-futur*. Lyon: Les Moutons électriques.

Barjavel, R. (1944) *Cinéma total. Essai sur les formes futures du cinéma*. Paris: Denoël.

Barjavel, R. (1958 [1944]) *Future Times Three*. New York: Award Books.

Baroni, R. (2007) *La Tension narrative: suspense, curiosité et surprise*. Paris: Seuil.

Baroni, R. (2017) *Les Rouages de l'intrigue*. Geneva: Slatkine.

Barrett, J. A. (2011) "Everett's Pure Wave Mechanics and the Notion of Worlds". *European Journal of Philosophy and Science*, 1: 277–302.

Barthes, R. (1977 [1964]) "Rhetoric of the Image". In *Image, Music, Text.* Essays selected and translated by Stephen Heath. London: Fontana Press.

Baudrillard, J. (1995 [1981]) *Simulacra and Simulation*. Translated by Sheila Faria Glaser. Ann Arbor: University of Michigan Press.

Baudry, J.-L. (1978 [1975]) "Le dispositif: approche métapsychologique de l'impression de réalité". In *L'Effet-cinéma*. Paris: Albatros, 27–49.

Baum, L.F. (2003 [1900]) *The Wonderful Wizard of Oz*. Oxford/New York: Oxford University Press.

Bayard, P. (2014) *Il existe d'autres mondes*, Paris: Minuit.

Bazin, L. (2019) "L'âge de tous les possibles? Adolescences et fictions de mondes". In Besson, A. and Manfrin, F. (eds.), "Worldbuilding. Création de mondes et imaginaires contemporains", *Revue de la Bibliothèque nationale de France*, 59, 56–65.

Béghin, C. (2013), "1.1. ∞ Abrams". *Cahiers du cinéma*, 690: 8–12.

Benayoun, R. (1980) *Alain Resnais, arpenteur de l'imaginaire*, Paris: Stock.

Benveniste, É. (1971 [1966]), *Problems in General Linguistics*. Translated by Mary E. Meek. Coral Gables: University of Miami Press.

Berton, M. (2015) *Le Corps nerveux des spectateurs. Cinéma et sciences du psychisme de 1900*. Lausanne: L'Âge d'Homme.

Berton, M. (2021) *Le Médium (au) cinéma*. Geneva: Georg.

Besson A. (2015) *Constellations. Des mondes fictionnels dans l'imaginaire contemporain*, Paris: CNRS Editions.

Besson, A. (forthcoming 2021) "Engagement and Enchantment: Political and Ethical Uses of Fantasy Fictions", in Lavocat, F. and James, A. (eds.) *Does Fiction Change the World?* Leiden: Brill.

Blanchet, A. (2010) *Des pixels à Hollywood. Cinéma et jeux vidéo, une histoire économique et culturelle.* Paris: Pix'n love Éditions.

Boillat, A. (2001) *La Fiction au cinéma.* Paris: L'Harmattan.

Boillat, A. (2002) "La métaphore vivante, pierre angulaire de la création chez Cronenberg". *Hors-Champ*, 8: 25–31.

Boillat, A. (2005) "L'éclatement du personnage chez Lynch. Les "mondes possibles" dans *Lost Highway* et *Mulholland Drive*". *Décadrages*, 4–5: 48–61.

Boillat, A. (2006a) "Du personnage à la figurine: les produits dérivés de *Star Wars*". *Décadrages*, 8–9:106–136.

Boillat, A. (2006b) "*L'Ève future* et la série culturelle des "machines parlantes". Le statut singulier de la voix humaine au sein d'un dispositif audiovisuel". *Cinémas*, 17 (1): 10–34.

Boillat, A. (2006c) "*Les fantômes de l'Amérique. Le spectre de l'Indien chez John Carpenter et dans le cinéma d'épouvante de la fin des années 70*". In Guido, L. (ed.), *Les Peurs de Hollywood*. Lausanne: Antipode, 165–183.

Boillat, A. (2007) *Du Bonimenteur à la voix-over. Voix-attraction et voix-narration au cinéma*. Lausanne: Antipodes.

Boillat, A. (2008) "Jésus par Scorsese. *La Dernière tentation du Christ*: du romanesque au filmique". In Boillat, A., Kaempfer, J., and Kaenel, P. (eds.), *Points de vue sur Jésus au xxe siècle*, *Études de Lettres*, 2: 53–71.

Boillat, A. (2009a) "Trois vies et un seul cinéaste (Raoul Ruiz). Des récits singuliers qui se conjuguent au pluriel". *Décadrages*, 15: 8–25.

Bibliography

Boillat, A. (2009b) "La 'diégèse' dans son acception filmologique. Origine, postérité et productivité d'un concept". *Cinémas*, 19(2–3): 217–245.

Boillat, A. (2009c) "La perpétuation de l'oralité du muet dans quelques incipit filmiques des premières années du parlant". *Cinémas*, 20(1): 113–134.

Boillat, A. (2009d) "Faire pour la vue ce que le téléphone fait pour l'ouïe. Rencontres entre l'image et la voix dans quelques anticipations de la télévision". In Berton, M. and Weber, A.-K. (eds.), *La Télévision du téléphonoscope à Youtube*. Lausanne: Antipodes, 77–97.

Boillat, A. (2010a) "On the Singular Status of the Human Voice. *Tomorrow's Eve* and the Cultural Series of Talking Machines". In Albera, F. and Tortajada, M. (eds.), *Cinema Beyond Film. Media Epistemology in the Modern Era*. Amsterdam: Amsterdam University Press, 233–252.

Boillat, A. (2010b) "Le déni de l'écrit à l'écran. L'écrivain, son œuvre et l'univers filmique". *Décadrages*, 16–17: 9–46.

Boillat, A. (2010c) "Prolégomènes à une réflexion sur les formes et les enjeux d'un dialogue intermédial. Essai sur quelques rencontres entre la bande dessinée et le cinéma". In Boillat, A. (ed.), *Les Cases à l'écran. Bande dessinée et cinéma en dialogue*. Genève, Georg, 25–121.

Boillat, A. (2011a) "L'imaginaire social de la téléphonie. Les dispositifs fictifs du *Vingtième siècle* d'Albert Robida et l'archéologie du cinéma parlant". In Albera, F. and Tortajada, M. (eds.), *Ciné-dispositifs. Spectacles, cinéma, télévision, littérature*. Lausanne: L'Âge d'Homme, 229–259.

Boillat, A. (2011b) "À la recherche du scénario. Le scénario comme objet (d'étude) et pratique (d'écriture)". *Archipel*, 34: 13–59.

Boillat, A. (2012) "*Stranger than Fiction: Métalepse* de Genette et quelques univers fictifs contemporains". *Cinéma et Cie*, 18: 21–31.

Boillat, A. (2014a) *Star Wars, un monde en expansion*. Yverdon-les-Bains: Maison d'Ailleurs.

Boillat, A. (2014b) "Le héros hollywoodien dans les mailles de la télésurveillance et dans la ligne de mire du drone". *Décadrages*, 26–27: 14–47.

Boillat, A. (2014c) "'On connaît la chanson ...', et pourtant! Voix enregistrée et déliaison chez Alain Resnais". In Frangne, P.-H. and Lacombe, H. (eds.), *Musique et enregistrement*. Rennes: Presses Universitaires de Rennes.

Boillat, A. (2016) "I Want to Go Home: l'auteur de *comics* sur sol français. Les (im)possibilités d'un dialogue". In Atallah M. and Boillat, A. (eds.), *BD-US: les comics vus par l'Europe*, Gollion: Infolio, 99–128.

Boillat, A. (2017) "Kafka et le 'kafkaïsme': la référence à l'expressionnisme comme procédé de figuration de l'écrivain à l'écran (*Kafka*, Steven Soderbergh, 1991)". *Captures. Figures, théories et pratiques de l'imaginaire*, 2(1). URL: http://revuecaptures.org/node/739

Boillat, A. (2018a [2015]) "The Comic Book Effect in the Age of CGI: When Film Adaptations of Comic Book Evoke the Fixity of Their Model". In Mitaine, B., Roche, D., and Schmitt-Pitiot, I. (eds.), *Comics and Adaptation*. Jackson: University of Mississippi Press, 135–158.

Boillat, A. (2018b) "Les codes du western à l'ère du codage informatique: le jeu vidéo sur la piste du cinéma (*Red Dead Redemption*)". *Décadrages*, 39: 62–92.

Boillat, A. (2018c) "Douze minutes avant minuit: l'effet 'graphic novel' du chapitrage dans *Watchmen*". *Cahiers de narratologie*, 34. URL : https://journals.openedition.org/narratologie/8757.

Boillat, A. (2019a) "Cinéma et paradigme téléphonique: l'ambivalence de la représentation des télécommunications à l'ère (des imaginaires) du numérique". In Boillat, A. and Guido, L. (eds.), *Loin des yeux ... le cinéma. De la téléphonie à Internet: imaginaires médiatiques des télécommunications et de la surveillance*. Lausanne: L'Âge d'Homme, 25–97.

Boillat, A. (2019b) "Reflets des cités: les mondes en miroir (sans tain) de Schuiten et Peeters ". *Recherches sémiotiques/Semiotic Inquiry*, 37(3): 141–162.

Boillat, A. (2020a) En cas de malheur, *de Simenon à Autant-Lara. Essai de génétique scénaristique*, Geneva: Droz.

Boillat, A. (2020b) "Corps et mondes de synthèse au cinéma". In Baroni, R. and Gunti, C. (eds.), *Introduction à l'étude des cultures numériques. La transition numérique des médias*. Paris: Armand Colin, 271–295.

Boillat, A. and Krichane, S. (2014) "Les arpenteurs de mondes filmiques et vidéoludiques. Seuils et parcours dans la série *The Elder Scrolls*". In Atallah, M., Nova, N. et al. (eds.), *Pouvoirs des jeux vidéos*. Gollion: Infolio.

Bolter, J. D. and Grusin, R. (1999) *Remediation. Understanding New Media*, Cambridge: MIT Press.

Booker, M. K. (2007) *Postmodern Hollywood. What's New* in *Film and Why It Makes Us Feel So Strange*. Westport: Praeger.

Bordwell, D., Staiger, J. and Thompson, K. (1985) *The Classical Hollywood Cinema. Film Style & Mode of Production to 1960*. London/New York: Routledge.

Bordwell, D. and Thompson, K. (2009) *Film Art. An Introduction*. New York: McGraw-Hill [9th ed.].

Bordwell, D., Thompson, K. and Smith, K. (2020) *Film Art. An Introduction*. New York: McGraw-Hill [12th ed.].

Borges, J.-L. (1962 [1944]) "The Garden of Forking Paths", translated by Helen Temple and Ruthven Todd. In *Fictions*, New York: Grove Press, 89–101.

Borges, J.-L. (1998) *Collected Fictions*. London/New York: Penguin.

Bourdaa, M. (2016) "Au-delà du réel… et de la fiction: le cas du jeu en réalité alternée *Why So Serious?*". In Besson, A., Prince, N. and Bazin, L. (eds.), *Mondes fictionnels, mondes numériques, mondes possibles*. Rennes: PUR, 75–85.

Branigan, E. (1984) *Point of View in the Cinema. A Theory of Narration and Subjectivity in Classical Film*. Berlin: De Gruyter Mouton.

Bréan, S. (2012) *La Science-fiction en France: théorie et histoire d'une littérature*. Paris: Presses de l'Université Paris-Sorbonne.

Bremond, C. (1973) *La Logique du récit*. Paris: Seuil.

Brown, S. (2017) "'Alternate Version of the Same Reality': Adapting *Under the Dome* as an SF Television Series". *Science Fiction Film and Television*, 10(2), 267–283.

Bubb, M. (2010) *La Camera obscura. Philosophie d'un appareil*. Paris: L'Harmattan.

Buchan, S. (2016) "The Animated Spectator: Watching the Quay Brothers' 'Worlds'". In Buchan, S. (ed.), *Animated "Worlds"*. Eastleigh: John Libbey Publishing, 15–38.

Buckland, W. (2015) "*Inception*'s Video Game Logic". In Furby, J. and Joy, S. (eds.), *The Cinema of Christopher Nolan. Imagining the Impossible*. London & New York: Wallflower Press, 189–200.

Bukatman, S. (1993) *Terminal Identity. The Virtual Subject in Postmodern Science Fiction*. Durham: Duke University Press.

Burch, N. (1990) *Life to Those Shadows*. Translated and edited by Ben Brewster. Berkeley/Los Angeles: University of California Press.

Buscombe, E. (1970) "The Idea of Genre in the American Cinema". *Screen*, 11 (2): 33–45.

Byrne, P. (2010) *The Many Worlds of Hugh Everett III. Multiple Universes, Mutual Assured Destruction, and the Meltdown of a Nuclear Family*. New York: Oxford University Press.

Canales, J. (2015) *The Physicist & the Philosopher. Einstein, Bergson, and the Debate That Changed our Understanding of Time*. Princeton/Oxford: Princeton University Press.

Čapek, K. (2004 [1920]) *R.U.R.* Translated by Claudia-Novack-Jones. London: Penguin Classics.

Carter, L. (1973) *Imaginary Worlds: The Art of Fantasy*. New York: Ballantine Books.

Casares, A.B. (2003 [1940]) *The Invention of Morel*. New York: NYRB Classics.

Casetti, F. (1986) *Dentro lo Sguardo. Il Film e il suo Spettatore*. Milan: Bompiani.

Cavell, S. (1979) *The Word Viewed. Reflections on the Ontology of Film.* Cambridge, MA: Harvard University Press.

Cerisuelo, M. (2000) *Hollywood à l'écran. Les Métafilms américains.* Paris: Presse de la Sorbonne Nouvelle.

Cerisuelo, M. (2015) "*Remake* secret et univers multiples". *Cinémas*, 25(2–3): 119–137.

Chardère, B. (ed.) (1961) "Alain Resnais". *Premier plan*, 18.

Chateau, D. (1983) "Diégèse et énonciation", *Communications*, 38: 121–154.

Châteauvert, J. (1996) *Des mots à l'image : la voix "over" au cinéma.* Paris: Méridiens Klincksieck.

Ciment, M. and Niogret, H. (1992) "Une exploration du mot Kafka. Entretien avec Steven Soderbergh". *Positif*, 374: 39–43.

Colin, M. (1989) *La Grande Syntagmatique revisitée.* Limoges: Université de Limoges.

Collins, J. (1992) "Genericity in the Nineties: Electic Irony and the New Sincerity". In Collins, J., Radner, H, Preacher Collins, A. (eds.), *Film Theory Goes to the Movies*, New York/London: Routledge: 242–263.

Collins, S. (2008) *The Hunger Games.* New York, Scholastic Press.

Connell, R. (1924) "The Most Dangerous Game". *Collier's*, January 19, 1924.

Cornette, M. (2006) "*La Fête à Henriette*, un film à pile ou face". In Monnier, R. and Roche, A. (eds.), *Territoires du scénario.* Dijon: Centre Gaston-Bachelard, 131–144.

Courcoux, C.-A. (2013) "Neo ou la matrice d'intelligibilité d'un nouveau rapport de l'homme à la technologie". *Alliage (culture-science-technique)*, 71: 146–158.

Crichton, M. (1972) *The Terminal Man.* New York: Alfred A. Knopf.

Crichton, M. (1983) *Electronic Life. How to Think About Computers.* New York: Alfred A. Knopf.

Crichton, M. (1990) *Jurassic Park.* New York: Alfred A. Knopf.

Cronenberg, D. (2000) *Entretiens avec Serge Grünberg.* Paris: Cahiers du cinéma.

Cunningham, D. (2005) "A Theme Park Built for One: The New Urbanism vs. Disney Design in The Truman Show". *Critical Survey*, 17(1): 109–130.

Dannenberg, H. (2004) "Ontological Plotting: Narrative as a Multiplicity of Temporal Dimensions". In Pier, J. (ed.), *The Dynamics of Narrative Form. Studies* in *Anglo-American Narratology*, Berlin/New York: Walter de Gruyter, 159–189.

Davies, M. (2002) *Dead Cities, and Other Tales.* New York: The New Press.

Deleuze, G. (1989 [1985]) *Cinema 2. The Time-Image.* Translated by Hugh Thompson and Robert Galeta. Minneapolis: University of Minnesota Press.

Derfoufi, M. (2018) "*The BlackKklansman*". *Le Genre & l'écran.* URL: https://www.genreecran.net/?The-BlackKklansman

Dick, P. K. (1962) *The Man in the High Castle.* New York: G.P. Putnam's Sons.

Dick, P. K. (1966) "We Can Remember It For You Wholesale". *The Magazine of Fantasy and Science Fiction*, 30 (4): 4–22.

Dick, P. K. (1969) "The Electric Ant". *The Magazine of Fantasy and Science Fiction*, 37 (4): 100–128.

Dick, P. K. (1980) *The Golden Man.* New York: Berkley Books.

Dick, P. K. (1995) *The Shifting Realities of Philip K. Dick. Selected Literary and Philosophical Writings.* New York: Vintage Books.

Dick, P. K. (2002 [1964]) *The Simulacra.* London: Random House Penguin.

Doležel, L. (1983) "Intensional Function, Invisible Worlds, and Franz Kafka". *Style*, 17: 120–141.

Doležel, L. (1984) "Kafka's Fictional Worlds", *Revue canadienne de littérature comparée*, 1(1): 61–83.

Doležel, L. (1998) *Heterocosmica. Fiction and Possible Worlds.* Baltimore: The John Hopkins University Press.

Doležel, L. (2019) "Porfyry's Tree for the Concept of Fictional Worlds". In Bell, A. and Ryan, M.-L. (eds.), *Possible Worlds Theory and Contemporary Narratology*. Lincoln/London: University of Nebraska Press, 47–61.

Donovan, T. (2010) *Replay. The History of Video Games*. Lewes: Yellow Ant.

Dubois, P. (1995) "Hybridations et métissages. Les mélanges du noir-et-blanc et de la couleur". In Aumont, J. (ed.), *La Couleur en image*. Milan/Paris: Mazzotta/Cinémathèque française/Musée du cinéma, 74–92.

Dufour E. (2011) *Le Cinéma de science-fiction*. Paris: Armand Colin.

Duncan, J. (2011) "Legacy System". *Cinefex*, 124: 29–57.

During, E. (2003a) "Introduction. La matrice à philosophies". In Badiou, A. et al. (eds.), *Matrix, machine philosophique*. Paris: Ellipses, 3–18.

During, E. (2003b) "Les Dieux sont dans la matrice". In Badiou, A. *et al.* (eds), *Matrix, machine philosophique*. Paris: Ellipses, 81–97.

Dwyer, M.D. (2010) *Back to the Fifties: Pop Nostalgia in the Reagan Era*. (Unpublished doctoral dissertation) University of Syracuse, USA.

Dyer, R. (2017) *White*. London/New York: Routledge.

Eco, U. (1972) *"The Myth of Superman". Diacritics*, 2(1), 14–22.

Eco, U. (1979) *The Role of the Reader. Explorations in the Semiotics of Texts*. Bloomington: Indiana University Press.

Eco, U. (1990) *The Limits of Interpretation*. Bloomington: Indiana University Press.

Eco, U. (1992) *Les Limites de l'interprétation*. Paris: Grasset & Fasquelle.

Eco, U. (2014 [1980]) *The Name of the Rose*. Translated by William Weaver. New York: Mariner Books.

Elsaesser, T. (1996) "A German Ancestry to Film Noir? Film History and its Imaginary". *Iris*, 21: 129–145.

Favard, F. (2016) "'You Can('t) Let Go Now': Mystery Boxes, Quantum Readings, and Very Bright Lights in Lost". *TV/Series* [online], Special Issue 1, URL : http://tvseries.revues.org/1738.

Ferencz-Flatz, C. and Hanich, J. (2016) "What is Film Phenomenology?". *Studia Phaenomenologica*. 16: 11–61.

Ferrer, D. (2011) *Logiques du brouillon: modèles pour une critique génétique*. Paris: Seuil.

Friedberg, A. (1993) *Window Shopping: Cinema and the Postmodern*. Berkeley: University of California Press.

Friedberg, A. (2006) *The Virtual Window. From Alberti to Microsoft*. Cambridge: MIT Press.

Galouye, D. (1976 [1961]) *Dark Universe*. New York: Gregg.

Galouye, D. (2011 [1964]) *Simulacron-3*. Rockville: Phoenix Pick.

García, A. N. (2016) "A Storytelling Machine: The Complexity and Revolution of Narrative Television". In Bernardelli, A., Federici, E. and Rossini, G. (eds.) "Forms, Strategies and Mutations of Serial Narratives", *Between*, V. 11 (2016). URL: http://www.betweenjournal.it

Gardies, A. (1999 [1981]) "Esquisse pour un portrait sémiologique de l'acteur". In *Le Conteur de l'ombre. Essais sur la narration filmique*. Lyon: Aléas, 35–58.

Garel-Grislin, J. (2019) "Les coordonnées de la fiction: ce que la carte fait au récit". In Besson, A. and Manfrin, F. (eds.), "Worldbuilding. Création de mondes et imaginaires contemporains", *Revue de la Bibliothèque nationale de France*, 59, 22–30.

Garrett, S. (2015) *Closes Circuits. Screening Narrative Surveillance*. Chicago/London: University of Chicago Press.

Gaudreault, A. (1999 [1988]) *Du littéraire au filmique. Système du récit*. Paris/Québec: Armand Colin/Nota bene.

Gaudreault, A. and Gauthier, P. (2011) "Le montage alterné, un langage programmé". *1895*, 63: 25–47.

Gaudreault, A. and Gauthier, P. (2017) "D.W. Griffith and the Emergence of Crosscutting". In Keil, C. (ed.), *A Companion to D.W. Griffith*. New Jersey: Wiley Blackwell, 107–136.

Gaudreault, A. and Jost, F. (1990) *Le Récit cinématographique*. Paris: L'Harmattan.

Gaudreault, A., and Marion, P. (2015 [2013]) *The End of Cinema? A Medium in Crisis in the Digital Age*. Translated by Timothy Barnard. New York: Columbia University Press.

Gauthier, P. (2008) *Le Montage alterné avant Griffith: le cas Pathé*. Paris: Nathan.

Gay, J.-C. (2006) "Transport et mise en tourisme du monde". *Cahiers de géographie*, 4: 11–22, URL: http://www.mgm.fr/ARECLUS/page_auteurs/Gay37.pdf

Genette, G. (1980 [1972]) *Narrative Discourse. An Essay in Method*. Translated by Jane E. Lewin. Ithaca: Cornell University Press.

Genette, G. (1997 [1982]) *Palimpsests. Literature in the Second Degree*. Translated by Channa Newman and Claude Doubinsky. Lincoln/London: University of Nebraska Press.

Genette, G. (2004) *Métalepse. De la figure à la fiction*. Paris: Seuil.

Gibson, W. (2018 [1984]) *Neuromancer*. New York : Ace.

Gillett, S. L. (1996) *World-Building. A Writer's Guide to Constructing Star Systems and Life-Supporting Planets*. Cincinnati: Writer's Digest Books.

Goodman, N. (1978) *Ways of Worldmaking*. Indianapolis: Hackett.

Gorbman, C. (1987) *Unheard Melodies: Narrative Film Music*. London: BFI.

Grainge, P. (2003) *Memory and Popular Film*. Manchester: Manchester University Press.

Grant, B. K. (2007) *Film Genre: From Iconography to Ideology*. London: Wallflower Press.

Groensteen, T. (2006) *Un objet culturel non identifié*. Angoulême: Éditions de l'An 2.

Groupe μ (1970) *Rhétorique générale*. Paris: Larousse.

Groupe μ (1992) *Traité du signe visuel. Pour une rhétorique de l'image*. Paris: Seuil.

Guido, L. (2006) "Rhythmic Bodies/Movies. Dance as Attraction in Early Film Culture". In Strauwen, W. (ed.), *The Cinema of Attractions Reloaded*. Amsterdam: University of Amsterdam Press, 157–178.

Guido, L. (2009) "Le regard et la danseuse. Sur quelques figures télé-visuelles, de la lorgnette romantique à l'écran interactif". In Berton, M. and Weber, A.-K. (ed.), *La Télévision du téléphonoscope à Youtube*. Lausanne: Antipodes, 349–374.

Guido, L. (2013) "Images du corps technologique dans le cinéma de science-fiction". In Atallah, M., Jaccaud, F., and Valéry, F. (eds.), *Souvenirs du futur*. Lausanne/Yverdon: Presses polytechniques et universitaires romandes/Maison d'Ailleurs, 165–180.

Gunning, T. (1991) *D.W. Griffith and the Origins of American Narrative Film: The Early Years at Biograph*, Urbana/Chicago: University of Illinois Press.

Gunning, T. (1995) "Colorful Metaphors: the Attraction of Color in Early Silent Cinema". *Fotogenia*, 1: 249–255.

Gunti, C. (2013) "Grilles, séries, pixels: le protocole Becher comme mécanisme proto-numérique chez Jörg Sasse, Thomas Ruff et Andreas Gursky". In Méaux, D. (ed.), *Protocole et photographie contemporaine*. Saint-Étienne: Presses universitaires de Saint-Étienne, 333–344.

Günzel, S. (2008) "The Space-Image. Interactivity and Spatiality of Computer Games". In Günzel, S., Liebe, M., and Mersch, D. (eds.), *Conference Proceedings of the Philosophy of Computer Games*. Potsdam: University Press, 170–189. URL: https://publishup.uni-potsdam.de/frontdoor/index/index/docId/2555.

Hamus-Vallée, R. (2001) "Histoire des effets spéciaux: de Méliès à *Jurassic Park* en passant par *King Kong, L'Homme invisible, Star Wars* et *2001, L'Odyssée de l'espace*". *CinémAction*, 102: 14–37.

Haraway, D. (1991) *Simians, Cyborgs, and Women. The Reinvention of Nature*. New York: Routledge.

Hayles, N. K. (1999) *How We Became Posthuman: Virtual Bodies in Cybernetics, Literature, and Informatics.* Chicago: The University of Chicago Press.

Hediger, V. (2001) *Verführung zum Film. Der amerikanische Kinotrailer seit 1912.* Marburg: Schüren.

Helford, E. R. (2006) "*The Stepford Wives* and the Gaze. Envisioning Feminism in 1975", *Feminist Media Studies*, 6 (2): 145–156.

Hême de Lacotte, S. (2001) *Deleuze: philosophie et cinéma.* Paris: L'Harmattan.

Hintikka, J. (1988) "Exploring Possible Worlds". In Sture, A. (ed.), *Possible Worlds in Humanities, Arts and Science: Proceedings of Nobel Symposium 65.* Berlin: de Gruyter, 52–73.

Hoffmann, E.T.A. (2003 [1816]) *Der Sandmann.* Stuttgart: Stuttgart Reclam.

Jameson, F. (1991) *Postmodernism, or, The Cultural Logic of Late Capitalism.* London/New York: Verso.

Javet, D. (2020) *La Science-fiction dans les productions médiatiques japonaises à l'ère de la techno-utopie: imaginaires du désastre et réappropriations politiques* (unpublished doctoral dissertation). University of Lausanne, Switzerland.

Jean, M. (2006) *Le Langage des lignes et autres essais sur le cinéma d'animation.* Montréal: Les 400 coups.

Jeffords, S. (1994) *Hard Bodies: Hollywood Masculinity in the Reagan Era.* New Brunswick: Rutgers University Press.

Jenkins, H. (2004) "Game Design as Narrative Architecture". In Wardrip-Fruin, N. and Harrigan, P. (eds.), *First Person. New Media as Story, Performance, and Game.* Cambridge/London : MIT, 118–130.

Jenkins, H. (2006) *Convergence Culture. Where Old and New Media Collide.* New York/London : New York University Press.

Jenn, P. (1991) *Techniques du scénario.* Paris: FEMIS.

Joly, M. (1993) *Introduction à l'analyse de l'image.* Paris: Nathan.

Jost, F. (2007) "The Look: From Film to Novel". In Stam, R. and Raengo, A. (eds.), *A Companion to Literature and Film.* Oxford: Blackwell Publishing, 71–79.

Jullier, L. (1997) *L'Écran post-moderne. Un cinéma de l'allusion et du feu d'artifice.* Paris: L'Harmattan.

Kaganski, S. (2002) "Entretien David Cronenberg – *Spider*", *Les Inrockuptibles*, URL: https://www.lesinrocks.com/cinema/entretien-david-cronenberg-spider-1102-84493-13-11-2002/.

Kellner, D. and Ryan, M. (1990 [1988]) *Camera Politica: The Politics and Ideology of Contemporary Hollywood Film.* Bloomington: Indiana University Press.

King, G. and Krzywinska, T. (2006) *Tomb Raiders and Space Invaders: Videogame Forms and Contexts.* London/New York: I.B. Tauris.

Kitses, J. (2007 [1969]) *Horizons West: Directing the Western from John Ford to Clint Eastwood.* London: BFI.

Kittler, F. (1986) *Grammophon, Film, Typewriter.* Berlin: Brinkmann & Bose.

Knox, S. (2010) "Reading *The Truman Show* Inside Out". *Film Criticism*, 35: 1–23.

Koolhaas, R. (1994 [1978]) *Delirious New York.* New York: The Monacelli Press.

Kozloff, S. (1988) *Invisible Storytellers: Voice-over Narration in American Fiction Film.* Berkeley: University of California Press.

Kracauer, S. (2004 [1947]) *From Caligari to Hitler. A Psychological History of the German Film.* Princeton/Oxford: Princeton University Press.

Krauss, R. (1984 [1979]) "Grilles". *Communications*, 34: 167–176.

Krichane, S. (2011) "*Elephant* ou les jeux vidéo en trompe-l'œil". *Décadrages*, 19: 70–84.

Krichane, S. (2018) *La Caméra imaginaire.* Geneva: Georg.

Krichane, S. (2021) "When Seeing is Playing: The History of the Videogame 'Camera'". *Game Studies. The International Journal of Computer Game Research*, (21)2. URL: http://gamestudies.org/2102/articles/krichane.

Kripke, S. (1980) *Naming and Necessity*. Oxford: B. Blackwell.

La Chance, M. (2006) *Capture totale. Matrix, mythologie de la cyberculture*. Laval: Presses universitaires de Laval.

Laffay, A. (1947) "Le récit, le monde et le cinéma (II)". *Les Temps modernes*, 21: 1579–1600.

Laffay, A. (1948) "Le cinéma 'subjectif' (À propos de *La Dame du lac*)". *Les Temps modernes*, 34: 156–162.

Lavery, D. (2009) "Lost and Long-Term Television Narrative". In Harrigan, P. and Wardrip-Fruin, N. (eds.), *Third Person. Authoring and Exploring Vast Narratives*. Cambridge/London: MIT Press, 313–322.

Lavocat, F. (2010) "Les genres de la fiction. État des lieux et propositions". In Lavocat, F. (ed.), *La Théorie littéraire des mondes possibles*, Paris: CNRS, 15–51.

Lavocat, F. (2019) "Possible Worlds, Virtual Worlds". In Bell, A. and Ryan, M.-L. (eds.), *Possible Worlds, Theory, and Contemporary Narratology*. Lincoln/London: University of Nebraska Press, 272–295.

Ledoux, A. (2012) *L'Ombre d'un doute. Le Cinéma américain contemporain et ses trompe-l'œil*. Rennes: Presses universitaires de Rennes.

Leibniz, G. W. (1985 [1710]) *Theodicy. Essays on the Goodness of God, the Freedom of Man and the Origin of Evil*. Translated by E.M. Huggard. Chicago: Open Court Publishing.

Leibniz, G. W. (2014 [1714]) *Monadology*. Translated by Lloyd Strickland. Edinburgh: Edinburgh University Press.

Lem, S. (1976 [1971]) *The Futurological Congress*. New York: Avon.

Lem, S. (1987 [1961]) *Solaris*. San Diego: Harcourt Brace Jovanovich.

Lepeltier, T. (2010) *Univers parallèles*. Paris: Seuil.

Lesuisse, A.-F. (2002) *Du film noir au "noir": traces figurales dans le cinéma classique hollywoodien*. Bruxelles: De Boeck Université.

Letourneux, M. (2010) *Le Roman d'aventures (1870–1930)*. Limoges: Presses universitaires de Limoges.

Levin, I. (1972) *The Stepford Wives. New* York: Random House.

Liandrat-Guigues, S. and Leutrat, J.-L. (2006) *Alain Resnais. Liaisons secrètes, accords vagabonds*. Paris: Cahiers du cinéma.

Lindenmuth, W. A. (2017) "Spinning Tops and Brains in Vats: Nolan's *Inception* and Nozick's 'Experience Machine'". In Eberl, J. T. and Dunn, G. A. (eds.), *The Philosophy of Christopher Nolan*. Lanham: Lexington Books, 153–164.

Ljungberg, C. (2003) "Constructing New 'Realities': the Performative Function of Maps in Contemporary Fiction". *Swiss Papers in English Language and Literature*, Vol. 16, p. 159.

Loughlin, G. (2004) *Alien Sex: The Body and Desire in Cinema and Theology*. Malden MA: Blackwell Publishing.

Lowry, E. (1985) *The Filmology Movement and Film Study in France*. Ann Arbor: UMI Research Press.

Magnilier. P. (2003) "*Matrix*, machine mythologique". In Badiou, A. et al., *Matrix, machine philosophique*. Paris: Ellipses, 147–156.

Maigne, C. (1998) *Premières leçons sur la Monadologie de Leibniz*. Paris: PUF.

Manovich, L. (2001) *The Language of New Media,* Cambridge: The MIT Press.

Margolis, E. (2020) "Step Into Another World with Isekai, the Fantasy Subgenre Ruling the Manga Marker", *Japan Times*. URL: https://www.japantimes.co.jp/culture/2020/08/01/books/isekai-fantasy-manga/.

Martin, J.-C. (2010) *Plurivers: essai sur la fin du monde*. Paris: PUF.

Martin, T. L. (2019) " 'As Many Worlds as Original Artists'. Possible Worlds Theory and the Literature of Fantasy". In Bell, A. and Ryan, M.-L. (eds), *Possible Worlds Theory and Contemporary Narratology*, Lincoln/London: University of Nebraska Press, 201–224.

Massuet, J.-B. (2011) "La Performance Capture ou la redefinition de l'acteur". In Louget, P. and Maheu, F. (eds.), *Cinéma(s) et nouvelles technologies,* Paris: L'Harmattan, 283–297.

Massuet, J.-B. (2017) *Le Dessin animé au pays du film.* Rennes: PUR.

McGowan, T. (2016) "Antigravity: *Interstellar* and the fictional betrayal of place". *Jump Cut: A Review of Contemporary Media*, 57. Url: https://www.ejumpcut.org/archive/jc57.2016/-McGowanInterstellar/index.html.

Meininger, S. (2006) "*Starship Troopers*, fin de l'histoire ou fin des idéologies?". In Guido, L. (ed.), *Les Peurs de Hollywood.* Lausanne: Antipodes, 203–228.

Metz , C. (1966) "La grande syntagmatique du film narratif". *Communications*, 8: 120–124.

Metz, C. (1968) *Essais sur la signification au cinéma.* Paris: Klincksieck.

Metz , C. (1974) *Film Language.* New York : Oxford University Press.

Metz , C. (1975) "The Imaginary Signifier". *Screen*, 16 (2): 14–76.

Metz , C. (1982 [1977]) *The Imaginary Signifier.* Bloomington: Indiana University Press.

Miller , V. (2011) *Understanding Digital Culture.* London: SAG.

Mitry, J. (1963) *Esthétique et psychologie du cinéma, t. 1.* Paris: Éditions Universitaires.

Mittell, J. (2006) "Narrative Complexity in Contemporary American Television". *Velvet Light Trap*, 58: 29–40.

Mittell, J. (2009) "Lost in a Great Story: Evaluation in Narrative Television (and Television Studies)". In Pearson, R. (ed.), *Reading Lost: Perspectives on a Hit Television Show.* London: I.B. Tauris, 120–138.

Mittell, J. (2015) *Complex TV. The Poetics of Contemporary Television Storytelling.* New York: New York University Press.

Moholy-Nagy, L. (1969 [1967]) *Painting Photography Film.* London: Lund Humphries.

Moine, R. (2008 [2002]) *Cinema Genre.* Translated by Alistair Fox and Hilary Radner. Malden: Blackwell Publishing.

More, T. (1965 [1516]) *Utopia.* New Haven: Yale University Press.

Moretti, F. (2013) *Distant Reading.* London/New York: Verso.

Morgan, H. and Hirtz, M. (2009) *Les Apocalypses de Jack Kirby.* Lyon: Les Moutons électriques.

Morin, E. (1958) *Le Cinéma ou l'homme imaginaire: essai d'anthropologie.* Paris: Minuit.

Murray, J.H. (1997) *Hamlet on the Holodeck. The Future of Narrative in Cyberspace.* Cambridge: MIT Press.

Naremore, J. (1995–96) "American Film Noir. The History of an Idea". *Film Quarterly*, 49 (2): 12–27.

Neill, N. (2018) "The Stepford Frankensteins: Feminism, *Frankenstein* and the *Stepford Wives*". *The Journal of American Culture*, 41 (3): 257–266.

Niederhoff, B. (2011/2013) "Focalization". *The Living Handbook of Narratology*, URL: http://www.lhn.uni-hamburg.de

Nozick, R. (1974) *Anarchy, State, and Utopia.* New York: Basic Books.

Olson, J. R. (2015) "Nolan's Immersive Allegories of Filmmaking in *Inception* and *The Prestige*". In Furby, J. and Joy, S. (eds.), *The Cinema of Christopher Nolan. Imagining the Impossible.* London & New York: Wallflower Press, 44–61.

Orwell, G. (1961 [1949]) *1984.* New York: Penguin.

Papakonstantis, A. (2016) "*How the West Was Won Again.* Les genres aux croisements du cinéma et des séries télé: l'exemple de *Deadwood*". *Décadrages,* 32–33: 73–90.

Pavel, T. G. (1986) *Fictional Worlds.* Cambridge/London: Harvard University Press.

Perdigao, L. K. (2015) "'The Dream has become their reality': Infinite Regression in Christopher Nolan's *Memento* and *Inception*". In Furby, J. and Joy, S. (eds.), *The Cinema of Christopher Nolan. Imagining the Impossible.* London & New York: Wallflower Press, 120–132.

Perkins, V. F. (2005) "Where is the World? The Horizon of Events in Movie Fiction". In Gibbs, J. and Pye, D. (eds.), *Style and Meaning. Studies in the Detailed Analysis of Film*. Manchester and New York: Manchester University Press, 16–42.

Pierce, J. J. (1987) *Foundations of Science Fiction: A Study in Imagination and Evolution*. Westport, CT: Greenwood.

Pingaud, B. (2002) "À propos d'*Hiroshima mon amour*", *Positif*, 35, 1960. In Goudet, S. (ed.), *Positif, revue de cinéma. Alain Resnais*. Paris: Gallimard, 66–87.

Pinteau, P. (2015) *Effets spéciaux: Deux siècles d'histoire*. Paris: Bragelonne.

Prince, G. (1988) "The Disnarrated". *Style*, 22: 1–8.

Purse, L. (2013) *Digital Imaging in Popular Cinema*. Edinburgh: Edinburgh University Press.

Putnam, H. (1981) *Reason, Truth, and History*. New York: Cambridge University Press.

Rabkin, E. S. (1976) *The Fantastic in Literature*. Princeton: Princeton University Press.

Racault, J. -M. (2016) "Géographie". In Baczko, B., Porret, M. and Rosset, F. (eds.), *Dictionnaire critique de l'utopie au temps des Lumières*. Geneva: Georg, 488–511.

Resnais, A. and Sternberg, J. (1969) "*Je t'aime je t'aime*". *L'Avant-Scène cinéma*, 91.

Ricoeur, P. (2004 [1975]) *The Rule of Metaphor. The Creation of Meaning in Language*. Translated by Robert Czerny with Kathleen McLaughlin and John Costello, SJ. London/New York: Routledge.

Rittaud-Hutinet, J. and Rittaud-Hutinet, C. (1999) *Dictionnaire des cinématographes en France (1896–1897)*. Paris: Honoré Champion.

Robert, V. (2006) *Filmer peindre. La représentation filmique de l'acte pictural: miroir/faire-valoir de l'acte cinématographique*. (Unpublished Master's Dissertation) University of Lausanne, Switzerland.

Robert, V. (2010) "*Le Scaphandre et le papillon* et l'adaptation filmique du 'je' littéraire: l'œil qui écrit". *Décadrages*, 16–17: 104–117.

Roob, J.-D. (1986) *Alain Resnais, qui êtes-vous?* Lyon: La Manufacture.

Ruiz, R. (1995) "Théorie du conflit central". In *Poétique du cinéma*, t. 1, Paris: Dis Voir, 9–23.

Ryan, M. -L. (1980) "Fiction, Non-Factuals, and the Principle of Minimal Departure". *Poetics*, 8: 403–422.

Ryan, M.-L. (1991) *Possible Worlds, Artificial Intelligence and Narrative Theory*. Indiana: University of Bloomington & Indianapolis Press.

Ryan, M.-L. (2001) *Narrative as Virtual Reality: Immersion and Interactivity in Literature and Electronic Media*. Baltimore: J. Hopkins University Press.

Ryan, M.-L. (2006) *Avatars of Story*. Minneapolis/London: University of Minnesota Press.

Ryan, M.-L. (2010) "Cosmologie du récit des mondes possibles aux univers parallèles". In Lavocat, F. (ed.), *La Théorie littéraire des mondes possibles*. Paris: CNRS, 54–81.

Sadoul, G. (1952) "*La Fête à Henriette*, un film français de Julien Duvivier". *Les Lettres françaises*, 388: 445.

Saint-Gelais, R. (1999) *L'Empire du pseudo. Modernités de la science-fiction*. Québec: Nota bene.

Saint-Gelais, R. (2011) *Fictions transfuges. La transfictionnalité et ses enjeux*. Paris: Seuil.

Saito, S. (2015) "Beyond the Horizon of Possible Worlds: A Historical Overview of Japanese Media Franchises". *Mechademia: Second Arc*, 10: 143–161.

Salt, B. (1992) *Film Style and Technology: History and Analysis*. London: Starword.

Schaeffer, J.-M. (1987) *L'Image précaire*. Paris: Seuil.

Schaeffer, J.-M. (1999) *Pourquoi la fiction?* Paris: Seuil.

Schmerheim, P. (2013) "From *Psycho* to *Pleasantville*. The Role of Color and Black-and-White Imagery for Film Experience". In Brown, S., Street, S., and Watkins, L. (eds.), *Color and the Moving Image. History, Theory, Aesthetics, Archive*. New York/London: Routledge, 114–123.

Sconce, J. (2000) *Haunted Media. Electronic Presence from Telegraphy to Television*. Durham/London: Duke University Press.

Shelley, M. W. (2000 [1818]) *Frankenstein*. Boston: Belford/St. Martin's.

Simon, J.-P. (1983) "Énonciation et narration". *Communications*, 38: 155–191.

Slotkin, R. (1992) *Gunfighter Nation. The Myth of the Frontier in Twentieth-Century America*. Norman: University of Oklahoma Press.

Sontag, S. (1966 [1965]) *"The Imagination of Disaster"*. In *Against Interpretation, and Other Essays*. New York: Farrar, Straus and Giroux.

Soupault, P. (1979) *Écrits de cinéma*. Paris: Plon.

Souriau, E. (1950) *Les Deux cent mille situations dramatiques*. Paris: Flammarion.

Souriau, E. (1951) "La structure de l'univers filmique et le vocabulaire de la filmologie". *Revue internationale de filmologie*, 7–8: 231–240.

Souriau, E. (1953) "Préface". In Souriau, E. (ed.), *L'Univers filmique*. Paris: Flammarion, 5–10.

Steinberg, M. (2012) *Anime's Media Mix: Franchising Toys and Characters in Japan*. Minneapolis: University of Minnesota Press.

Sternberg, J. (2009 [1961]) *Un jour ouvrable* [*A Working Day*]. Strasbourg: La Dernière Goutte.

Sternberg, M. (1978) *Expositional modes and temporal ordering in fiction*. Baltimore/London: The John Hopkins University Press.

Stewart, G. (2015) *Closed Circuits. Screening Narrative Surveillance*. Chicago: University of Chicago Press.

Street, S. (2009) "'Colour Consciousness': Natalie Kalmus and Technicolor in Britain". *Screen*, 2009, 50(2): 191–215.

Strugatsky, A., and Strugatsky, B. (2012 [1972]) *Roadside Picnic*. Translated by Olena Bormashenko. Chicago: Chicago Review Press.

Swift, J. (2005 [1726]) *Gulliver's Travels*. Oxford: Oxford University Press.

Taylor, H. M. and Tröhler, M. (1998) "De quelques facettes du personnage humain dans le film de fiction". *Iris*, 24: 33–57.

Therrien, C. (2006) "Le cinéma sous l'emprise du jeu". In Audet, R. et al. (eds.), *Jeux et enjeux de la narrativité dans les pratiques contemporaines (arts visuels, cinéma, littérature)*. Paris: Dis Voir, 93–103.

Thiellement, P. (2011) *Les Mêmes yeux que Lost*. Paris: Léo Scheer.

Thirard, P. L. (2002) "Un film d'auteur". *Positif*, 98, 1968, in Goudet, S. (ed.), *Positif, revue de cinéma. Alain Resnais*. Paris: Gallimard, 208–214.

Thomas, F. (1990) "Entretien avec Alain Resnais: de la littérature de catacombes à la destruction de la planète". *CinémAction*, hors-série ("Cinéma et bande dessinée"), 237–241.

Thon, J.-N. (2016) *Transmedial Narratology and Contemporary Media Culture*. Lincoln/London: University of Nebraska Press.

Todorov, T. (1973 [1970]) *The Fantastic. A Structural Approach to a Literary Genre*. Translated by Richard Howard. Cleveland/London: The Press of Case Western Reserve University.

Tolkien, J.R.R. (2014 [1947]) *On Fairy-stories*. Edited by Verlyn Flieger and Douglas A. Anderson. New York: Harper Collins.

Towarnicki (de), F. (2007) *Les Aventures de Harry Dickson: scénario de Frédéric de Towarnicki pour un film (non réalisé) par Alain Resnais*. Nantes: Capricci.

Triclot, M. (2011) *Philosophie des jeux vidéo*. Paris: La Découverte.

Tröhler, M. and Kirsten, G. (2018) *Christian Metz and the Codes of Cinema. Film Semiology and Beyond*. Amsterdam: Amsterdam University Press.

Truby, J. (2007) *The Anatomy of Story. 22 Steps to Becoming a Master Storyteller*. New York: Barnes & Noble.

Van Hise, D. (1985) *Killing Time*. New York: Pocket Books.

Venkatasawmy, R. (2013) *The Digitalization of Cinematic Visual Effects. Hollywood's Coming of Age.* Plymouth: Lexington Books.

Verne, J. (1900 [1892]) *The Castle of the Carpathians.* Akron: The Saalfield Publishing Company.

Verne, J. (2010 [1875]) *The Mysterious Island.* Ware: Wordsworth.

Vernet, M. (1988) *Figures de l'absence*, Paris: Cahiers du Cinéma/Editions de l'Etoile.

Villiers, de l'I.-A. (2001 [1886]) *Tomorrow's Eve.* Champaign: University of Illinois Press.

Von Neumann, J. (1951) "The General and Logical Theory of Automata?". In Jeffress, L.A. (ed.), *Cerebral Mechanisms in Behavior: The Hixon Symposium*, London: Chapman & Hall, 1–31.

Vu, R. (2017) "Fantasy After Representation: *D & D*, *Game of Thrones*, and Postmodern World-Building". *Extrapolation*, 58 (2/3): 273–301.

Walters, J. (2008) *Alternative Worlds in Hollywood Cinema: Resonance Between Realms.* London: Intellect Books.

Wells, H. G. (2017 [1896]) *The Island of Doctor Moreau.* New York: Oxford University Press.

Wendland, A. (1985) *Science, Myth, and Fictional Creation of Alien Worlds.* Michigan: UMI Research Press.

Weston, K. (2018/2020) "*BlackKlansman* review: Spike Lee Fails to Get to the Heart of Racist America". *Sight & Sound.* URL: https://www2.bfi.org.uk/news-opinion/sight-sound-magazine/reviews-recommendations/blackkklansman-review-spike-lee-john-david-washington-adam-driver

Whissel, K. (2014) *Spectacular Digital Effects: CGI and Contemporary Cinema.* Durham: Duke University Press.

Williams, W. J. (2009) "In What Universe?". In Harrigan, P. and Wardrip-Fruin, N. (eds.), *Third Person: Authoring and Exploring Vast Narratives.* Cambridge/London: MIT Press, 25–32.

Wittenberg, D. (2013) *Time Travel: the Popular Philosophy of Narrative.* New York: Fordham University Press.

Wolf, M. J. P. (2012) *Building Imaginary Worlds. The Theory and History of Subcreation.* London/New York: Routledge.

Wolfe, G. K. (1986) *Critical Terms of Science Fiction and Fantasy. A Glossary and Guide to Scholarship.* London: Greenwood Press.

Wood, R. (1986) *Hollywood From Vietnam to Reagan.* New York: Columbia University Press.

Yacavone, D. (2015) *Film Worlds. A Philosophical Aesthetics of Cinema.* New York: Columbia University Press.

Zarader, J.-P. (2003) "Éloge de la contingence". In Badiou, A. et al. (eds.), *Matrix, machine philosophique.* Paris: Ellipses, 43–53.

Index of films and TV series

C

L

M

N

R

S

X

Y

Z